The
Alphonso
Lingis
Reader

Also by Alphonso Lingis
Published by the University of Minnesota Press

Trust

The Alphonso Lingis Reader

Alphonso Lingis

Edited by
Tom Sparrow

UNIVERSITY OF MINNESOTA PRESS
MINNEAPOLIS
LONDON

Published by the University of Minnesota Press
111 Third Avenue South, Suite 290
Minneapolis, MN 55401-2520
http://www.upress.umn.edu

Printed in the United States of America on acid-free paper

The University of Minnesota is an equal-opportunity educator and employer.

24 23 22 21 20 19 18   10 9 8 7 6 5 4 3 2 1

LIBRARY OF CONGRESS CATALOGING-IN-PUBLICATION DATA

Lingis, Alphonso, author. Sparrow, Tom, editor.
The Alphonso Lingis reader / Alphonso Lingis ; edited by Tom Sparrow.
Minneapolis : University of Minnesota Press, [2018] |
Includes bibliographical references.
Identifiers: LCCN 2018024372 (print)
ISBN 978-1-5179-0510-1 (hc)
ISBN 978-1-5179-0511-8 (pb)
Subjects: LCSH: Philosophy, American–20th century.
Classification: LCC B945.L4581 S63 2018 (print) | DDC 191–dc23
LC record available at https://lccn.loc.gov/2018024372

Contents

Editor's Introduction
A Philosopher of Transience

As I sit across from Alphonso Lingis on the terrace of a nondescript franchise hotel in downtown Memphis, he listens intently as I offer him searching synoptic interpretations of his life's work, trying to demonstrate that I have made some headway in distilling his expansive thinking into a coherent narrative, a discernible path that he could recognize as his own. The irony of this is not lost on me, and neither is it lost on Lingis. As I speak, a faint smile appears at the corner of his mouth and I cannot help but feel that he delights in watching me struggle to translate his adventuresome personal and intellectual career into several boring academic theses. If I were not already so familiar with the generosity of his spirit—Lingis says yes to every invitation made to him—and aware that I was projecting my own insecurities onto him, I would have relented and just asked him to tell me a story about his voyages to more than a hundred countries. A brightness becomes visible at the corners of his eyes before he responds to my propositions in the way that only someone like Lingis would respond: "I've never really thought about my original contribution to philosophy. It never occurred to me to think about what I write as a coherent whole." He pauses for a bit before taking the bait.

As usual, Lingis replies with autobiography. He proceeds to tell me about how it was an undergraduate logic class that got him hooked on philosophy at Loyola University Chicago in the 1950s. He admits that it was less the content of the class than the personality of the professor, or rather the professor's fetishization of rationality, that attracted him. That someone could be so intensely committed to a particular idea of orderly thinking fascinated him. Learning this fact after spending more than a decade reading and reflecting on Lingis's work, I do not think it is too far-fetched to say that the majority of Lingis's published work enacts a kind of expressive interrogation of his logic professor's commitments in both their intellectual and affective aspects. Lingis goes on to tell me that later on, as a junior faculty member at Duquesne University in the early 1960s and then at the Pennsylvania State University, where he spent the majority of his career as a beloved teacher until his retirement in 2001, he only began submitting his work to conferences and trying to publish at the urgings of his senior colleagues. It never occurred to him that he might have something significant to add to the philosophical conversation. What he has added, and it's been this way for decades now, is an unmatched voice and a renowned approach to delivering his philosophical findings.

While Lingis and I chat on the hotel terrace in Memphis, inside the venue hundreds of philosophers have convened for the annual meeting of the Society for Phenomenology and Existential Philosophy (SPEP), an organization with which Lingis has been affiliated for decades and at which he has presented countless papers. But unlike the other philosophers in attendance, Lingis is now famous—or infamous, depending on whom you ask—for performing his talks instead of reading or presenting them to the audience. Even those who have never witnessed a Lingis performance will have heard that his spoken texts are frequently accompanied by ambient music or images projected behind him; how sometimes he shrouds the room in darkness; how occasionally he will have donned unusual costumes or adorned his face with makeup and masks. He has been known to illuminate his face with a flashlight like some academic ghost-story teller, transporting the audience from the conference room to the campfire. These performances are not elaborate or sophisticated. They are far from orchestrated, and the viewer cannot help but feel that they could devolve into awkwardness at any moment.[1] They are sincere and deliberate; they approach the ritualistic. They often come across as last-minute decisions or DIY improvisations. There is something punk about them.

Reports have surfaced that testify to the time that Lingis, speaking about death, gave his talk while lying supine in a coffin. Perhaps this is just one of the many apocryphal stories that have accumulated around someone who is arguably the most eccentric, captivating, and generous thinker in the field. It is impossible to know. Given his appreciation for outsider art, no one should be surprised by any of this.[2]

Unlike the vast majority of his counterparts on the American continental philosophy scene, Lingis has never aspired to make a name for himself as a traditional scholar. He has never been obsessed by the European master thinkers—Heidegger, Derrida, Foucault—and he actively refuses to romanticize the soil of Freiburg, the Paris arcades, or even the Athenian agora. In his contribution to the 1999 volume *Portraits of American*

Continental Philosophers, Lingis indirectly indicts his fellow contributors, all of whom make a point of swearing allegiance to one luminary of European thought or another, when he writes:

> A thinker gains nothing today by traveling to Paris, Berlin, Tokyo, Shanghai. Whether you go for a conference or on sabbatical leave, you will only encounter educated people who think what you think about democracy and market economy, about Christian or Islamic fundamentalism and the Sendero Luminoso, about highbrow conceptual art and middlebrow Madonna, about virtual reality and cellular phones.[3]

When I attended my first SPEP meeting in 2004, the year that Derrida died, I witnessed this intellectual fealty firsthand as memorial speaker after memorial speaker tried their best to prove that they were closer to Derrida than the next person, and therefore a legitimate heir to deconstruction's legacy. Lingis was never enthralled by deconstruction's founder or his troubling of language, and he has never given off the impression that he wishes to be remembered as one of the premiere expositors of this or that thinker from the Continent.

Those who have never witnessed a Lingis performance or read one of his countless authored books, chapters, or essays might still have found themselves engaged with his work. Some of his earliest publications from the 1960s are his English translations of two major French phenomenologists, Emmanuel Levinas and Maurice Merleau-Ponty. Readers of Merleau-Ponty's posthumously published *The Visible and the Invisible* and Levinas's two major works, *Totality and Infinity* and *Otherwise Than Being,* will be familiar with Lingis's renderings.[4] Having completed his graduate studies at the University of Louvain in 1961, under the direction of Alphonse de Waehlens, before embarking on informal study in Paris, where he heard lectures by Sartre, Merleau-Ponty, and Lacan, Lingis returned to the United States to take up his first teaching position at Duquesne University in Pittsburgh, Pennsylvania. While in Pittsburgh Lingis met Paul Ricoeur, himself on a visit from France, and inquired about the latest developments in France. Riceour informed him about Levinas's remarkable *Totalité et Infini* and, at the request of the publisher, began work on the translation, which was published in 1969. His translation of *The Visible and the Invisible* appeared the year prior, and later he would publish two other translations of Levinas as well as Pierre Klossowski's study of the Marquis de Sade, *Sade My Neighbor.*

Many of Lingis's earliest published essays are standard critical engagements with major figures in phenomenology: Heidegger, Sartre, Merleau-Ponty. Remarkably, the signature voice of his later texts is already audible in these essays, while some of his writing from the 1960s and 1970s are already preoccupied with themes that he will eventually treat at great length—symbolism, ritual, sexuality. But it is important to see that nearly all of Lingis's work is touched by his early engagements with phenomenology. For Lingis, philosophy fundamentally should be a "revealing discourse" about reality, not a commentary on philosophical texts or problems.[5] Once again, Lingis signals his defection from much of the mainstream American-Continental philosophy of the late twentieth century. Philosophy should aim at better and better descriptions of reality, and phenomenology is particularly well-equipped to do this, he thinks.[6] Even when he is speaking historically, anthropologically, sociologically, or psychoanalytically, Lingis's mode of operation is rooted in phenomenology. But his phenomenology has always been an embodied phenomenology, and one for which the body is always an object of interrogation and fixation.

In the introductory texts that accompany his translations readers can detect Lingis's idiosyncratic interpretive concerns with phenomenological description. In these texts the entire world of Levinas or Merleau-Ponty, for instance, is refracted through a cluster of concepts that recurs throughout Lingis's oeuvre and defines his perspective: sensation, sensibility, affect, corporeality. It could be argued that Lingis's idiosyncratic concerns distort his readings of the phenomenologists, but this would be at best a misplaced objection. He never aims for a systematic or complete interpretation; he regards each thinker as a unique portal to the world, as a specific means of refining our description of reality. Lingis has said that, when he teaches, he prefers to have students focus on small chunks of text, fragments of a book instead of the book as a whole. Intensive study and discussion of these fragments, when done properly, can act as a lens on the world that will reveal things that no principles, systems, abstractions, or generalizations can.[7] This is the pedagogical method that Lingis applies in his early textual scholarship, and which he adapts into a singular brand of anthropological travel writing in his later work.

From the beginning Lingis has been uneasy about the way that Husserlian phenomenology tends to divide reality according to the structure of human consciousness. Despite its best efforts to keep consciousness tethered to the world with the concept of intentionality, phenomenology harbors a problematic dualism that lends undue privilege to human subjects by regarding them as the only entities capable of transcending the material world through free conscious acts. Which is not to say that other entities are capable of transcendence, but that the phenomenological account of the transcendence of the human ego may be overblown. Whether or not this characterization gets phenomenology "right" is beside the point. What Lingis is alert to in his early essays on Husserl, Heidegger, Sartre, Merleau-Ponty, and others is the fact that consciousness is always embodied, that the body is always immersed in a material reality, and that it is necessary to focus on the immanence of human beings in nature, as natural organisms capable at times of exceeding (which is not to say transcending) their natural environment. Following insights originally gleaned from Whitehead and Nietzsche, then later Deleuze, Foucault, and Bataille, Lingis has always strived to naturalize phenomenology so that it is maximally attentive to the material variations of the human body and their impact on thought, knowledge, and action.

All of Lingis's work is puzzled by the body, by what individuates and disindividuates it, what holds it together and what pulls it apart. Where Husserl asks about the unity-in-separation of consciousness and world, Lingis inquires about the ecstatic undoing of this unity by the body's sensitivity and eroticism. Or, better, Lingis is perpetually wondering about the stability of the conscious body's relation to the world and, more puzzling still, the body's relation to itself, its identity. His early work grapples as much with apparently minor or secondary issues—sensation, sentiment, sensibility—as it does with the primary phenomenological themes of intentionality, freedom, world, anxiety, death, and perception. Lingis's investigations reveal the need to shift sensibility and sensation to the center of phenomenological analysis, even and especially since these tend to resist such analysis, and to think the radical immanence of these terms. Sensibility marks the interface of body and world, while sensation is responsible, at least in part, for the body's motility. Intentionality is kinesthetic. Husserl knew this and Merleau-Ponty made this insight his life's work. Lingis reminds us, however, that rendering the body fully immanent to the world may very well acknowledge its materiality, but it also raises all of the problems of immanence engaged by poststructuralism, feminist theory, and neo-Spinozism. Phenomenology, by contrast, seems unequipped to answer these problems.

Perhaps the most significant conclusion drawn by Lingis's early work in phenomenology is that sensation cuts in two directions. It is not merely the means by which the world impresses itself upon the mind, as empiricism might have it. It is not simply the passive reception of sense data. On the one hand, sensation involves an intelligibility, a form or structure that discerns the shape of things, and, on the other, it involves an affectivity that enables the body to feel itself gripped by reality, constituted by things. Sensing beings like ourselves find themselves always already caught up in the sensuous environment, constituted and reconstituted by the material forces that generate and eventually extinguish consciousness. This truth cuts through the entirety of Lingis's corpus.

Lingis's contribution to academic philosophy, particularly phenomenology, cannot and should not be diminished. But it must be
acknowledged that it is not this corner of his oeuvre that accounts for his
attraction to readers from a broad array of disciplines, from psychology
and anthropology to religious studies and geography, which is to say nothing about his appeal for readers outside of the academy. Were he to have
pursued publishing through trade publishers rather than university presses, like Diane Ackerman or Lynn Margulis or David Abram, no doubt his
books would have found their way into the libraries of even more members of the reading class.

With his first book, *Excesses: Eros and Culture*, published in 1983 after
a series of articles on Nietzsche and the will to power, Lingis had already
heralded the philosophical and literary territory that would define his life's
work, and which has established an academic genre all its own. The genre
could be described as phenomenological travel writing, although surely
there is a more poetic label for it. To date he has published seventeen books,
not including his translations or photographic works, nearly all of which
explore the affective life of the body and the myriad forces—social, cultural, aesthetic, libidinal, physical, mythological, and so on—that shape and
animate it as it moves through the world, among people and places both
foreign and domestic, familiar and unknown. If his early writings take up
the themes of perception, sensation, and affect in order to interrogate the
integrity of the phenomenological subject, then Lingis becomes progressively more beguiled by the countless ways that subjectivity is constituted,
reconstituted, and compromised by its aleatory encounters with others.

Lingis is a philosopher of transience. As a transient himself—as someone who has visited and revisited more than one hundred countries, who
has woven this itinerary into his writing and allowed it to give form to
his thinking—Lingis has made travel, becoming, change, the fleeting, the
impermanent, the transitory, and death his themes. They populate nearly all
of his writings and tend to coalesce under the rubrics of passion and desire,
each of which threatens to destabilize the subject's control over its thought,
knowledge, and action while at the same time operating as individuating
forces that intensify the sense that one is here in this specific place, at this
specific time, feeling this specific way. Lingis writes in his essay "Aconcagua,"
whose name is borrowed from the tallest mountain in the Americas,

> Vehement wonder, lust, rage, courage, or terror, jealousy, grief fill one's mind
> and body, swollen with surging energy and heightened sensitivity. All our
> senses are enflamed. Impassioned states give us the experience of being self-
> identical and undivided. Mind and body are one. Rage saturates the mind

and is felt throughout the body, in the postural axis, in the clenched fists and beating heart, the trembling limbs.

Impassioned states are not experienced as events occurring to the self, which would be experienced beneath or above them. Instead, the self arises in the passion, takes form in it. In wonder or in rage the sense of self surges, the self surges, and it is an awestruck or enraged self. In impassioned states the self arises, a force that confronts, makes claims on others and on the world.[8]

Lingis does not speak about what happens *in* the body or *to* the self, as if the self were an already existing thing to which passions accidentally attach. He insists instead on how the self and its world, the body and its environment, conspire to generate subjectivity and identity as the excessive by-product, the excrement, as Lingis would have it, of bodies in contact with one another.[9] Lingis calls these "passionate outbreaks" and this phrase gives a clue to how his work compels us to rethink the very nature of subjectivity. It also poses the problem of how to speak of this original vision of subjectivity. Subjectivity is not a constant, unchanging, or sedimented substance. Just the opposite: it is episodic, shifting, contingent upon spatial and temporal location as well as the specific material conditions that "carve out" a subject capable, if only momentarily, of saying *Here I am.*[10]

Most of Lingis's books are collections of essays rather than academic monographs. These collections are made up of chapters loosely related by a common theme or two, such as trust, death, emotion, or eros. Likewise, most chapters are anchored in a specific geographic locale that gives rise to the reflection that ensues. The place might be Rio de Janeiro, Papua New Guinea, Bangkok, the Great Rift Valley, Machu Picchu, Calcutta, Mount Kilimanjaro, or Mount Washington in Pittsburgh, Pennsylvania. The reader of Lingis's books is immediately transported to these places by the photographs that inaugurate his chapters, almost all of which are taken by the author himself and serve to introduce the reader to the subject under consideration by setting a visual tone. These photographs, which are sometimes of buildings or mountains but often of the faces and bodies of other human beings, are not merely aesthetic adornment or used to illustrate some textual point.[11] They are integral to Lingis's phenomenological explorations and instrumental in his attempts at articulating the universal in the particular, which is arguably the greatest advantage of the phenomenological method. As he has said,

Photography was a kind of transfiguration of perception that was very precious to me. And I think it was made more dramatic when I started photographing people. I think natural perception tends to take in the person as a whole; when you start photographing it is rare that you would do that. For close-ups you might crop the face or the hands or something like that, and so one begins to see people this way. I also really discovered beauty in physical types and ethnic types that I don't think I would have discovered otherwise. I felt it was a very dramatic development in perception.[12]

In addition to the photos published in his authored collections, Lingis has published a book of photos, *Contact* (2010), which spans more than four decades of photographic work. If part of his problem as a philosophical traveler is to figure out how to represent the elusive qualities of his subject matter, to render them temporarily present, then photography has been a partial answer. "This transfiguration of the environment into scintillating moments of pure presence, and these moments of ecstatic participation, are the reason to walk with a camera," Lingis confesses.[13]

Correlatively, Lingis has tackled the problem of representing the transient and the elusive with one of the most captivating prose styles developed by any philosopher living or dead. He writes and speaks with a cadence and rhythm that draw the reader or listener in, pulling them along with repetitions—of words, phrases, refrains—that accumulate into a constellation of ideas, gradually revealing like incantations the truth he has uncovered in whatever geographic locale has inspired him. In this way Lingis's texts reproduce formally the experiences and events recorded by his itinerant body. His texts often switch between the first-, second-, and third-person perspectives, so that readers cannot help but find themselves at once addressed by and implicated in his narratives, which are at once rich with detail and constantly threatening to dissipate their meaning. He will suddenly succeed at making perfect sense in one sentence after faltering for several paragraphs. But these hesitations and false starts should not be seen as superfluous. They are the textual equivalent of our perpetual failures to communicate as we struggle to make contact with others, to make sense of the alterity we inevitably face while traversing the world.

The failure to make sense, however, does not only pertain to our attempts to connect with others, either linguistically, intimately, intellectually, or otherwise. Indeed, Lingis is just as fascinated by our inability to make sense of ourselves and the strange forces that trouble us from the inside, as it were. The preamble to his 2005 book *Body Transformations* characterizes this fascination in its synopsis, which doubles as a précis of the content of many Lingis texts:

These studies ... alternate with analyses of the content of our experience. To have been born structures all our subsequent experiences, and we experience not only others being born but also others who have long existed being born into our lives. We have a whole gamut of feelings of our bodies, and these give rise to images of our bodies and ideal images of ourselves. We experience a longing for integrity and wholeness, but drives to dismember our bodies as well as orgasmic and artistic compulsions are in us.[14]

The deep influence of Lingis's psychoanalytic and postpsychoanalytic forbearers, including Nietzsche, Freud, Lacan, Bataille, and Deleuze and Guattari, is evident here.

If in our everyday lives we seek to make sense of our environment and the others with whom we share it, our attempts are frequently thwarted by forces that indiscriminately operate to disrupt our sense-making capacity. Sense, for Lingis, is a polyvalent thing: it partakes of intelligibility as much as it does affectivity. And it is the affective modality of sense, which ultimately defines our sensuous life, that works to undo us from within, against our will. "One loses oneself in [strong emotions], divests oneself of one's role, function, character, conviction, identity. There is an inner momentum to this dispossession."[15] Our failure to know the other is always matched by a failure to master our own affective life or to comprehend the forces that surge within us. The alterity at the center of our lives, paradoxically chaotic and individuating at the same time, is a hallmark theme in Lingis's texts and one that bears the indelible stamp of Nietzsche.

As a writer who seamlessly fuses philosophy, ethnography, anthropology, art criticism, cultural geography, psychoanalysis, linguistics, and other disciplines into deceptively unassuming travel narratives, it is almost impossible to identify the primary focus of Lingis's work. And it is almost as pointless as citing exemplary passages from his essays, as if these exemplars were the gems among a collection of rocks, when in actuality Lingis only deals in gems. The difficulty with applying ordinary scholarly tactics to Lingis's oeuvre is that the scholar cannot help but feel like a fraud while paraphrasing, summarizing, and outlining what cannot be captured with the usual academic strategies. All the better for this editor, who is only responsible for curating a selection of Lingis's writings so that they may speak for themselves. Not that this is as inconsequential as it sounds, of course.

At the risk of unjustly mitigating the diversity and nuance of his writings, the reader will no doubt find that a Lingis essay is usually fixated on some aspect of the embodied nature of human existence. Whether writing about love, lust, trust, religion, ritual, sacrifice, violence, eroticism, or knowledge, he is obsessed by the many ways the body is constituted by and susceptible to the forces that cross it. But just as much, he is adamant about our capacity to make direct contact with material reality, the other in its many guises, and our receptivity to the other's attempts at contact. There is a fundamental volatility at work in the material vicissitudes of embodied life, and it is never certain how long one has to endure or enjoy the events that one finds oneself caught up in. If it is the body's sensibility that opens it up to the pleasures and pains of existence, and this sensibility is beyond one's control, then sensibility is marked by a basic ambivalence: it is what enables the body's movement and enjoyment of the world, but it is at the same time what allows disabling sensations and forces to infiltrate, and ultimately destroy, the body's capacity to act and exist.

There is never a point at which we find ourselves truly alone, completely independent of the presence of others or free from bearing the weight of reality. There is, as Lingis will say time and again, an imperative built into the nature of existence: we *must* sense, we *must* feel, we *must* respond to the contours of things.[16] To exist is to respond to a constant flow of material directives communicated to our bodies from within and without. Lingis maintains an uncompromising commitment to the reality of things and a generalized suspicion toward our efforts to control our lives and master the so-called outside world. Whatever degree of control we achieve over ourselves, others, or our environment is, like the emotions and thoughts that circulate in our bodies, always fleeting. A desire to arrest the fleeting and share it with others is what drives Lingis to write and perform. It is what impels him to traverse the developing world in search of the unexpected, the exhilarating, and the potentially deadly.

This is all very exciting and potentially quite terrifying. It announces the riskiness of travel, understood as a metonym for sentient life in general, as well as the necessity of trust, even and especially trust in those we do not know and with whom we have no relation. Such is the price of genuine profundity, not what passes for profundity in many academic circles. "The most profound thing I know," writes Lingis,

> is to find oneself on the other side of the planet, in a country with which one's own is at war, with someone as uneducated as one is educated, whose culture and religion one does not share or even know, with whom one shares no common tongue—and to find oneself utterly dependent upon that other for one's very life. Three times such a person put his own life at risk to save mine. What it means to find oneself in humanity then gaped open vertiginously before me.[17]

Here we find the appeal of Lingis's texts. It is not in his minute exegesis of some master European thinker or his sophisticated appropriation of fashionable theory. It is not in his clever English/French/German/Greek wordplay or his airtight arguments. Lingis promises none of these familiar scholarly devices. What he promises is a lyrical, sophisticated, and intimate report from the field. And that report will refract some human truth without fail.

Book titles like *Libido* (1985), *Abuses* (1994), *Dangerous Emotions* (1999), and *Body Transformations* (2005) all betray Lingis's preoccupation, which is almost to say fetish, for the dark shadow that transience casts over the life of the body. This transience is sometimes framed in terms of disindividuation, dispossession, loss of control. But it also signifies for Lingis the temporary stability and integrity achieved by living organisms like ourselves. What else is a human life but transience understood in this double sense? What else is a particular human being but a transient in the world, necessarily responsive and inherently vulnerable to all its material vicissitudes?

If a fetish is, as Lingis understands it, "where humans are subjects constituted by the action of objects on them,"[18] then his life's work acts as an extended reflection on the inescapability of the fetish, for fetishism seems an apt name for the embodied human condition as Lingis conceives it, not to mention for the relationship that his readers almost inevitably form with his texts.

This book is divided into five parts. Part I, "Sense," includes essays that showcase how Lingis has displaced perception as the body's dominant mode of engagement with the world, and established in its place the primacy of sensing and sensation. This innovative move places him in contrast with many of his phenomenological predecessors and induces him to reconsider the subject's relation to things and to what he calls, following Levinas, "the elemental." There is a refocusing of the phenomenological lens onto the body and its passions, as well as an emphasis on immanence that aligns Lingis with figures such as Foucault, Nietzsche, Deleuze, and Bataille. Part I is foundational to Lingis's thinking as a whole and is complementary to the essays in Part II, "Body," which demonstrate the body's centrality in Lingis's thinking. Here we find his preoccupation with the body's role in producing and undoing subjectivity, and we see Lingis urging us to see how the body enables us to gain a sense of self and to make contact with others, but also how the body is what eventually disintegrates and delivers us to death.

Part III, "Travel," begins with a general meditation on the significance of travel for philosophy, then presents several philosophical travelogues that capture the essence of Lingis's signature style. They display his deft ability to turn a significant travel experience into a philosophical exploration of universal human themes, which is to say, they display his gift for extracting an unexpected web of meaning from his encounters with unfamiliar bodies in foreign locales. Building on the previous section, "Excess"

(Part IV) presents a series of travel-inspired reflections on otherness. It paints a cohesive picture of Lingis's fascination with the unfamiliar forms of knowledge, communication, and meaning-making that emanate from other persons, cultures, and the inanimate world. Each selection in Part IV indicates an excess or difference that cannot be recuperated. It becomes clear that excess is a central problem for Lingis.

The final part of the book, "Together," complements Part IV and includes essays that exhibit Lingis's insistence on our common humanity, the sameness that we share with others no matter how familiar or unfamiliar they may be. In compassion, dignity, mourning, loss, trust, violence, lust, ecstasy, and death Lingis finds a universal human experience. These experiences, among others, have a way of transgressing social, cultural, and linguistic boundaries in order to unite us together. Here we find Lingis at his most hopeful, even at times humanistic, but in the most original and compelling ways, without sentimentality or superstition.

PART I

Sense

Sensation and Sentiment: On the Meaning of Immanence

The notion of "sensation" is one of those confused, equivocal notions. It contains the term "sense," and this is by no accident: the sense organs are organs for sense, for meaning. There is no doubt that what we see with our eyes, hear with our ears, touch with the exploratory touch is a form, and not pure matter, and the form, the *Gestalt*, is not a natural unit, but an intentional unit. (For example, when we see a chair, this multiplicity of sticks, boards, and screws holds together within our field of vision by virtue of the sense of "seat" it sustains.)

But sensation, sense perception is also *sensuous*. It is not only grasp of sense, it is also affectivity—contact, immersion of the form in a medium of pleasure and displeasure. It is also sentiment.

It would seem that inasmuch as sensation is grasp of form, structure, relation, and nuclei of relationships, it is intelligible. But that inasmuch as it is sentiment, feeling, sensuous, it is unintelligible. Feeling would be confusion, contact, immediacy without the gradient of relation.

This paper will endeavor to study the meaning of this implication of sentiment and sense, which is named in the confused notion of sensation. We shall attend to the way of being of this implication, as an implication of being as transcendence and being as immanence. Across this problem it is from an ontic to an ontological concept of immanence that we shall be led.

Empiricism and the Immanence of Sensation

The notion of sensation has fallen into a kind of disrepute among phenomenologists—who would rather speak of "sensibility," so as to implicate into that concept also the note of "sense." For what was proper to the empiricist analysis of sense perception was to make of sense a second instance, built upon a first instance of pure sensation: sense would be the sensations associated, in the pure classical form of empiricism; or it would be the sensations synthesized according to the forms of the understanding, according to the doctrine of an intellectualist analysis of perception, itself built upon empiricism, as its correction.

But what then is a sensation, without sense? It is pure impression, pure impact. Or it is sheer quality, pure subjective sense-data. Or it is the psychic correspondent of the way the body is affected by outside stimuli. It would be a moment of stimulus internalized, appropriated.

The sensation is immanence itself: it is an impressional moment of the psychic, a way the psychic is affected, a tone of the psychic. Divested of its sense, it can no longer even refer intentionally to the physiological impulse whose psychic equivalent it is. This no doubt generates the obscurity, in the account of sensations, as to how we are to discern, for example, the sense-data of the tangible, as pure qualities, from the sensations of feeling, without bringing in mention of their diverse origins—exteroceptive or proprioceptive.

And the immanence of the sensation to the psychic maintains within immanence the total percept, built on the sensations, by composition or by intentional synthesis.

It would seem, then, that the empiricist analysis can disentangle the factor of sense from sensation only by conceiving the residue in the mode of being of a tone of feeling. As though the sensation were an amalgam of sentiment and sense; or as though the percept were an association, or intentional synthesis of feeling. As though the intelligible were an association, or an intentional synthesis of the unintelligible.

Phenomenology and Transcendence and Two Kinds of Immanence

The concept of intentionality, elaborated by Husserl to name the very essence of consciousness, explodes all this immanence: the consciousness is transcendence. The novelty of this conception consists in affirming not simply that every consciousness is consciousness of something, but that this tension toward something, this direction of attention turned beyond, constitutes the very essence of consciousness; that the consciousness is not to be represented as something that is first, and then transcends itself, but that for the consciousness to be is to escape itself. Henceforth even sentiment aims at something; the very warmth of the sentiment opens upon something, upon a grain or flesh of being to which, by virtue of an essential necessity, there is access only by way of this affective warmth, as vision is the sole access to color. To think intentionality through, we would have to conceive self-surpassing as the very being of the self. Transcendence is the very being of immanence.

The consciousness is thereby radically de-substantialized: it itself is not a container with contents nor a substrate of predicates, but pure movement of intention, and its term is not a content, but a configuration of sense. "It was all we needed to put an end to the soft philosophy of immanence, where everything takes place by compromise, protoplasmic exchanges, by a tepid cellular chemistry," wrote Sartre in 1939.[1] "The philosophy of transcendence casts us forth upon the open road, in the midst of menaces, under a blinding light."

It would seem that such a de-substantialized consciousness could no longer have *any* contents—and such indeed was the conclusion of Sartre: the consciousness would be nothing but the opening-up of the primordial Clearing about which the world could turn a system of faces; it would be the work of the light that effaces itself, emptying space, in order to exhibit the surfaces of the world in their phosphorescence.

Yet that is not the way of Husserl. First of all, there are transcendent intuitions, turned upon the world, but there are also immanent intuitions, in which the objects of acts of consciousness belong to the same sphere of reality as those acts themselves. This is the case in acts of reflection.

But in fact this immanence turns out to be a double transcendence. On the one hand, the immanent objects themselves are nothing but instances of consciousness, that is, moments of intentionality which transcended themselves to aim at something beyond themselves. And, on the other hand, the immanent intuition itself, while it does not leave the system of acts constituting one and the same ego, nonetheless does transcend *itself,* to go direct itself upon another moment or act of that flux.

But there is yet another immanence. Husserl does not conceive the intentionality as the pure event of a Clearing, a distance both opened and traversed, which makes the presence of an object to a subject possible: rather the intentionality operates through a something—a passivity, a sensuous matter, named *hyle*—that is immanent to the sphere of consciousness. One has to distinguish: on the one hand, the aspects, qualities, moments of the thing, transcendent to the consciousness, and, on the other hand, the sensuous matter which figures, or reverberates, or adumbrates those aspects within the sphere of consciousness itself. The intentionality *animates* this "hyletic data," making them figure or announce to the consciousness the faces of the things.

And Husserl deliberately chooses the new term *hyle* so as to name the sensuous matter of the external senses as well as of volition and affectivity, indifferently. And indeed it is by thinking of affective experience that we can most readily conceive this sensuous factor, this *hyle*. Certainly it is far easier to conceive what the sensuous moment of feeling could be than to conceive what could be the sensuous matter for a color, or a spatial form, which, since the hyletic data are of the sphere of consciousness, can absolutely not be extended or spatial in any way. We think, then, that we recognize the sense-data of the empiricists, those shadows of the things cast upon the substance of the mind. There is, to be sure, an essential difference: empiricism wished to compose the objects of consciousness out of the contents of the mind, whereas the Husserlian intentionality does not coagulate or synthesize in any way the hyletic diversity through which it passes to intend its object, an ideal pole intended in identity across a diversity of hyletic moments. The hyletic data are *Abschattungen,* and the ray of attention passes through them as through shadows.

The incidence of the hyletic data makes of the moments of consciousness not simple openness upon the world beyond, simple windows, but contents filling a duration. The hyletic data are of the consciousness, are "psychic," but are not activity, intentionality, spontaneity; they are passivity and matter. A passivity of the consciousness with regard to itself: a consciousness encumbered, affected with itself.

To say the consciousness is consciousness of something is to say that it is not consciousness of these sense-data; they are neither creations nor objects of consciousness. It is rather encumbered with them: it lives them. The Husserlian consciousness is not just representation, or an epistemological function: it is life, *Erlebnis,* experience lived-through. To live oneself: it is not to objectify oneself; it is to be encumbered with oneself. To be affected with oneself.

But Heidegger will undertake to show that this second immanence is also a tissue of transcendence.

Heidegger and the Transcendence of Affectivity

For Heidegger, the affectivity is not blindness and confusion, the confused idea par excellence, nor is it confusion in immanence accompanying an act representative in transcendence; it is itself precisely revelation. And revelation in a preeminent sense: the affectivity is not only the power to reveal something, some depth or tone or grain of the things; it is more fundamentally the power to reveal to us what reveals all things, the horizon of op-position or of objectivity, the horizon of all horizons, the world itself and as such. Anguish is the advent of the uncanny, which spreads through all the configurations of the world, like a contagion, infecting them with the stupor of insignificance, discharging the force of presence of what is present within the world, casting all routes and urgencies and tasks into affective equivalence. The configurations of the world vascillate, sink away, and from this generalized evanescence arises the world in its worldhood, all naked and without relief.

In delivering Dasein over to the world as world, anguish delivers Dasein over to itself, as abiding in nothingness, delivered over unto the world. Anguish thus, secondly, reveals Dasein in its essential belongingness to the world, its disclosive submission to the world. Anguish discloses Dasein as the power that unfolds and receives, is affected by, that is, discloses the horizon of the world as such; anguish discloses Dasein to itself as transcendence.

Finally, anguish is an affective *disposition*: it is "to feel oneself disposed in such or such a manner."[2] This is the third essential revelation of affectivity: it reveals the *Geworfenheit,* the thrownness of Dasein, the facticity of being-there, and being delivered over into presence.

There is thus in affectivity a transcendent disclosure: anguish reveals the world as such, the transcendental horizon of being. The specifically ontological function of disclosing the world itself in its worldhood is not proper to anguish, but to affectivity as such, and consequently is to be discerned in every affective disposition—if only as the ground of the evasive turning-away characteristic of moods in the inauthentic mode. But in addition there should be a revelation in immanence: in the disclosive retreat of the world anguish delivers Dasein over unto itself, as a finite existence abandoned and delivered over unto the world as unto the horizon of its own death.

But what is the internal structure of this immanent revelation, this revelation of Dasein to itself, accomplished in affectivity? It is a disclosure of Dasein to itself in its facticity, its being already accorded and submitted to the world. Time is the form of this disclosure. In the measure that the affective disposition is a disclosure to Dasein of its *Geworfenheit,* its thrownness, it is an ek-static relationship with the past. "Having a mood brings Dasein face to face with its thrownness in such a manner that this thrownness is not known as such, but disclosed far more primordially in 'how one is.'... One's affective disposition is therefore based on thrownness.... Understanding is grounded primarily in the future; one's affective disposition, however, temporalizes itself *primarily* in *having been*."[3]

Consequently, the immanent relationship characteristic of affectivity turns out, for Heidegger, to be a specific type of disclosure of Dasein's past, its thrownness, in face of the world as such, horizon of its future and its death. But this is to say that the disclosure of Dasein to itself is here being construed as a mode of transcendence—in the very same sense that, for Husserl, reflection is immanence conceived as transcendence. In both cases, the act that discloses is separated, by its very being, from that which it discloses, even though that which it discloses is a moment of the same temporal flux.

This brings us up against what seems, to us, to be the unreduced mystery that subsists in the Heideggerian teaching on affectivity. The Heideggerian analysis exhibits to us very clearly that affectivity is revelation of a specific kind. In addition, the Heideggerian analysis exhibits to us very clearly what it is that affectivity discloses—the world as such, the thrownness of Dasein, and Dasein's deliverance unto the world, its transcendence. Consequently, the Heideggerian teaching shows us how it is in the very depth of sentiment, in the very way of being of sentiment, that the origin of sense is articulated.

But because the disclosure of Dasein to itself that occurs in affectivity is a disclosure across time, this disclosure is itself a mode of separation and a transcendence across a separation. Heidegger tells us how it is that anguish is the grasp of the solitary existence cast, committed to the world horizon defined by death; but Heidegger does not say how this is affectivity and not comprehension, why this is a tone and not a view. Heidegger does not tell us what is the *suffering* of anguish.

Dasein is, in anguish, cast open upon its own being-there, upon its thrownness, its dereliction in the world. But because this revelation is a temporal ek-stasis, a specific type of openness upon Dasein's past, Dasein is brought into proximity with itself across a distance—the distance of time.

There is, to be sure, a suffering of separation. Heidegger tells us "the pain that the proximity of the distant causes us is nostalgia."[4] The transcendent being, which can be present only across separation, Clearing, distance, awakens our suffering, to be sure. But Heidegger does not tell us in what the *suffering* of the pain of nostalgia precisely consists.

Immanence as Suffering

Guided by the work of Michel Henry, *L'Essence de la manifestation*,[5] we shall argue that the ontological conception of immanence must name not a relationship between a being and its contents, or a being and its properties, but between a being and its being—or, better, between a being and its existence.

Ex-istence is ek-stasis and transcendence, because it is the accomplishment of presence across distance. It is the reception of the presence of the other which abides, nonetheless, in the otherness of its own being. Transcendence is the accomplishment of presence across this kind of ontological distance.

The ontological concept of immanence would have to be constructed as a relation of revelation, of receptivity, with regard to one's own ex-istence. It would be the concept of an ex-istence that is passive with regard to its own being, that suffers its own being, is affected with itself. A being that is given to itself, receives itself, is revealed to itself in this relationship without distance. It is with such a concept of immanence that we propose to think the affective essence of affectivity.

Heidegger says that the things of the world can *touch* us only because Dasein is submitted beforehand in its being to the world. We want to say that the essence of affectivity is to be sought in Dasein's being submitted originally to its own being.

What then would it mean to suffer pain? Pain, we know since Sartre, is the tone, or contexture of the consciousness itself.[6] (Pain is nothing but consciousness, an unconscious pain is not a pain at all.) But what does it mean to suffer that pain?

It was Emmanuel Levinas who suggested that in pain I am abandoned to deal with my own being.[7] Suffering is to be encumbered, burdened with one's own being, with the existing one has contracted.

The suffering of pain is nonsignifying, it reveals nothing of the transcendental horizon of being; it is precisely the impossibility to escape oneself unto the other, unto the world. Suffering is the impossibility of wrenching oneself free of oneself, the impossibility of fleeing and of retreating, backed up against life and being. It is the impossibility of withdrawal, of sleep, it is a vigilance occupied with itself, the spasm of a consciousness that invokes an impossible night, an impossible nothingness, that cannot be relieved of itself. Suffering is to find oneself immediately there, without interval from oneself, meaningless vibration in the Inner Darkness on the hither side of the world.

Suffering is a solitude caught up, enclosed in the captivity of its own identity. Suffering is to be mired in oneself, it is the inmost exposition of the definitive, where the involvement, the engagement in existing is without equivocation and without respite. Is not then this very definitiveness, this impossibility of detaching oneself from the instance of existence, this impossibility of opening up, between oneself and one's existence, the least interval in which any sense could play, to relieve it of its brute contingency, is not this the revelation, or the production, or the very event of suffering? The very irremissibility of one's being, the impossibility of detaching oneself from the suffering makes up the very content of the suffering.

Heidegger says the things of the world cannot touch us unless we are submitted beforehand to the world. To be submitted beforehand to the world is the essence of transcendence, which is receptivity for the world, that is, finite intuition, that is—sensibility.[8] We argue that the world received cannot touch us, move us, unless we are submitted beforehand to, are receptive of our own being. To be receptive with regard to one's own being is to be affected with oneself, to suffer oneself, which is the essence of affectivity.

It is in the immanence of sentiment that the transcendence of sensibility is given to itself.

We think Heidegger has seen this. Even the pallor of indifference, he says, is an affective disposition, "it is in it that Dasein becomes satiated with itself. Being has become manifest as a burden."[9] But because Heidegger then goes on to understand every vector of manifestation in terms of the ek-stasis of time, that is, in the mode of transcendence, the affective essence of affectivity is not understood. To think the affective essence of affectivity, we would have to think through to the ontological concept of immanence: being as encumbered with itself, affected with itself, receptive with regard to its own being, submitted beforehand to itself, passion, suffering itself. Life is not just vision and light, *lumen naturale*; the living of life is to be encumbered with oneself, to be affected with oneself, it is the essence of suffering. Michel Henry says: "suffering forms the tissue of existence, it is the locus where life becomes living...."[10]

But it is only a being which, assembled with itself, affected with itself, encumbered with the brute contingency of itself, that could know the Parousia of the gratuitous fulguration of being, that is, that could know joy.

1967

The Sensuality and the Sensitivity

To sense something is to catch on to the sense of something, its direction, orientation, or meaning. Sensibility is sense-perception, apprehension of sense. But to sense something is also to be sensitive to something, to be concerned by it, affected by it. It is to be pleased, gratified, contented, and exhilarated, or to be pained, afflicted, and wounded, by something. A sentient subject does not innocently array object-forms about itself; it is not only oriented in free space by their sense, it is subject to them, to their brutality and their sustentation.

The sensibility that is in our nervous circuitry was implausibly conceived as a passivity of the mind upon which the physical action of the material world taps out impressions, which a free and spontaneous understanding can then take as signs, forming, relating, and positing referents for them. Is receptivity passivity? Is there in it a synoptic assembling of the multiplicity of sense data? Is there in it an intentional orientation? But is the sensuous element really a multiplicity of discrete impressions? Is the affective sensitivity but a side effect of sensibility, a factor of confusion and indistinctness in sense perception? Is there opposition between sensibility and responsibility—between the sensibility for sensible things and the sentiment of respect, which Kant called the receptivity of the spontaneity of the mind, the sensibility of the faculty of understanding? Were the metaphysical correlates of matter and form, activity and passivity, really imposed on the classical philosophy of mind by analysis of the phenomenon of sensibility?

There is a movement in sensibility. In the receptivity for sense, the capacity to catch on to the orientation and potentialities of things, Martin Heidegger has seen the propulsion that makes our being exist, that is, cast itself out toward entities exterior to itself, and cast itself beyond them to take in the context in which they could move. Our existence is sensitive; our sensibility moves with the movement of existence, ex-ists. The given beings make an impression on us because the active, self-propelling thrust of our being makes contact with them, and beyond where and how they are actually to their possible positions and employment, their futures. What we sense when we sense the solidity of the seat is neither a coagulation of chromatic and tactile impressions nor an idea, an ideal object, associated with them; it is a possibility. Sense-perception is in fact an apprehension of the forces of things, the possibilities things are, an anticipation of the future of the environment, a clairvoyance.

Our eyes focus, follow the light, circumnavigate the contours, sweep across the colored and shadowed expanses; our hands stroke the grain and the textures; our tongues circulate the brandy in our mouths; our postures center our sensory surfaces on things; our legs and torsos bear our movements. The existential movement in perception animates our bodies.

But the propulsive force by which our existence casts itself perceptively into the environment is oriented by the layout of things. There is subjection to the outlying environment in the sensibility.[1] Our emotions disclose to us, in us, how the things we envisage matter to us; our affective disposition, our moods, reveal how the layout as a whole besets us. It is not with their "primary properties," their contours, but also not with their forces, their instrumental potentialities, that the things first affect us; they trouble us by being there. Affectivity, far from being just a subjective factor of confusion and immanence in the mind, is a revelation of the environment, a revelation of its being. The environment is not only a layout of contours whose orientation, sense, and future we envision; in our affectivity the fact of their being there of themselves is imposed on us. We find ourselves exposed not merely to the phosphorescent appearances of things that are closed in themselves but to the incontrovertible plenum of their being, to all the infinity of the condensation with which their being has replaced and excluded nothingness. It is in itself that our being knows the being of the most remote things, of the whole environment. Heidegger says that while our existence distances itself from, and posits apart (entfernt), the forms and appearances of things through sensibility, our being is afflicted from the start with the pressure, the gravity, of the being of those exterior things (174). Our own being is exposed to the being of the most alien and remote things from the start, exposed to the dimensions of remoteness in which beings can be exterior; the weight of the being of the environment presses down on us. In fact the ecstatic thrust of our existence by which we cast ourselves beyond their actual forms and positions to their possibilities is not really a free-floating domination over them; it is a continual effort to escape the burden of their being which oppresses our being from the start (175).

These two sides to our original contact with the environment—projection into it and subjection to it, delineating a line of sense in it and being beset with the fact of its being—Heidegger sought to make intelligible, in their juxtaposition in our sensibility, by understanding them as dimensions of the movement of time, the inner time of our existence (235–37, 383ff.). Our presence is realized as an ecstatic transport from the state of being disposed by the environment to the synthetic grasp of its possibilities, a transport conjoining projective comprehension with affective subjection, sensibility with susceptibility, a transport of what has come to pass in us to what is to come to us, an existential transport of the being we have been given to our potentiality for being otherwise.

But this transport itself, Heidegger will show, is nothing else than the active realization of the subjection of one's being to nothingness, which is our vulnerability or our mortality (304–11, 348). The propulsion of the sensibility beyond the given to the possible, beyond the present to the imminent, beyond the entity into the space of the world, is in fact a projection into nothingness. The possibility that the sensibility grasps in the exterior is not simply a representation, an advance presentation of another format of the sensible surfaces drawn by the power of the mind to vary their actual appearances. It is also not simply the arrangement of them that is not yet there and which the mind perceives in advance. Neither the calculative skills of the mind nor its recombinatory imagination produces the real possible. The possibilities are the future of things, but a future which is not ineluctable, which is possibly impossible. The sensibility that reaches for the sense of things makes contact with impossibility in them.

When the perception that reached for the possible falls into the impossible, it reaches for adjacent possibilities in the environment. But the impossibility that lurks in any of them lurks in all; the being of the whole environment which besets our being is but a possible being, and possibly impossible. The weight and force of the world's being that presses down on our being is also the imminence and ineluctability of nothingness in which the contingent world is suspended, and which we sense in the mortal lucidity of our anxiety. The world that solicits us with its possibilities and promises, and that incites our existence to continually project itself out toward it, draws by withdrawing into its own being and into the imminent nothingness that does not cease to threaten its irremediable contingency.

It is this mortal lucidity of our anxiety that makes our existence perceptive, our sensibility clairvoyant. At the bottom of our concern for the possible beings there is a sense of being singled out by the nothingness that approaches of itself, that closes in, that touches us already. It is because we are first stricken with the void, haunted by the death everywhere lurking in the interstices of the world, affected by its nothingness, that we are touched, affected by, stabilized and steered by things, that the things have sense for us. They have sense and affect us not as material nor as forms, but as means, supporting gear or obstacles and snares in the way of our movements into the environment. It is with one and the same movement that our being projects itself into the open clearing of a world and into the emptiness of impossibility, the void of the definitive and irreversible abyss of death. Being-in-the-world and Being-unto-death are one and the same.

For Heidegger it is thus because we are exposed to nothingness that is exterior to all being that we are exposed to exterior beings. For Emmanuel Levinas sensibility is exposure not to nothingness but to alterity. And for him otherness is not decomposable into being and nothingness; possibility is not decomposable into actuality and the impossibility that threatens it.

Levinas's phenomenological exposition shows that prior to the anxious taking hold on things which for Heidegger makes our sensibility practical from the first, there is the contact with the sensuous medium, there is sensuality.[2] We find things, we find ourselves, in the light, in air, on terra firma, in color, in a resonant zone. Through sensuality we find ourselves steeped in a depth before we confront surfaces and envision the profiles of objects. Sensibility opens us not upon empty space, but upon an extension without determinate frontiers, a plenum of free-floating qualities without substrates or enclosures, upon luminosity, elasticity, vibrancy, savor. The sensuous element—light, chromatic condensation and rarefaction, tonality, solidity, redolence—is not given as a multiplicity that has to be collected or as data that have to be identified, but as a medium without profiles, without surfaces, without contours, a depth, an *apeiron*. We find ourselves in it, in light, in the elemental, buoyed up, sustained by it. Life lives on sensation; the sensuous elemental is sustenance, end, goodness of being we enjoy before any practical intention arises to locate means for our pursuits.

Sensuality is not intentionality, is not a movement aiming at something exterior, transcendent, that objectifies; it is not identification of a diversity with an eidos, an ideal identity term; is not imposition of form or attribution of meaning. Steeped in the elemental, contented with the plenum, its movement is that of enjoyment.[3] The enjoyment is the vibrancy and excess of our openness upon the elements, which delineates the movement of involution and ipseity: being sensual, one enjoys the light, the color, the solidity, the spring, the monsoon, and one enjoys one's enjoyment. The most elementary egoism in sensitive flesh is this eddy of enjoyment reiterated; the first ego is a pleasure.

Sensuality is vulnerable and mortal from the start. But this susceptibility inseverable from sensibility is not the vertiginous sense of the contingency of all being, the imminence of nothingness threatening one in all beings one touches. The sense of the contingency of the sensible medium, a flux or chaos without law or necessity, supported by nothing behind its appearing—for the things will be formed in it, out of it—is not to be identified with an intuition into the nothingness in which all being would be perilously adrift, and which could be foreseen as a real possibility just beyond the thin screen of the actual being. The contingency of the sensuous element is in the very fullness and abundance of the present, which plugs up the horizons, the future. Coming from nowhere, going nowhere, it is there by incessant oncoming. It is not there as though grudgingly parceled out by the malevolence of nothingness, but as gratuity and grace. Fortuity and goodness of the light, the vibrant colors, the radiance of tones, the liquidity of the swelling forces! Yet there is in sensuality a sense of vulnerability, not made of anxiety over the imminence of nothingness but of the liability of being wounded and rent and pained by the force and substantiality of the sensuous element. In pain one is backed up into oneself, mired in oneself, in-oneself, materialized; pain announces the end of sensibility not through a conversion into nothingness, annihilation, but at the limit of prostration, conversion into passivity, materialization. In savoring the materiality of things sensibility has the taste of its own mortality. It is in the materiality of being and not in its inconsistency, its being already undermined by the imminence of nothingness, that our death already touches us.

If Heidegger finds, subtending the capacity to be affected by the impact of beings, an exposure to or a projection into nothingness, it is because he conceives of sensibility as an outbreak of freedom from the start, an intentionality or transcendence. There is sensibility for beings and presence to being when our existence finds itself exposed to nothingness, or finds itself in a clearing or free space. He conceives of our existence being open as being an openness. Its first model is the hand that has leeway to move; he conceives of sensibility as handling things. The hand that reaches out for possibilities in things risks impotence. It is by being a possible menace that a means is an implement. It is by being a possible impasse and snare that the direction or orientation of a thing makes sense.

Levinas takes instead finding oneself in the light, in vibrancy and plenitude, as a primary model of what happens when life becomes a lucidity. He finds in the tremor of sensation not an exhilaration and ecstasy out of being, but an enjoyment, an intensity and an involution. For Heidegger things are implements grasped by their forms—not shapes outlined by a contemplative eye, but interlocking contours relaying and orienting a body force on the move. For Levinas, things are first substances, contained within their contours which lend themselves to being detached, moved, and destined for enjoyment. Things are drawn from the sustaining medium, and things grasped instrumentally revert to an elemental presence. One grasps the hammer to pound in the nail, but in the hammering the hammer becomes a substance sustaining the rhythm of the hand that enjoys hammering. The contours of things are not limits beset by nothingness, but delineations of alterity, reliefs in the elemental plenum.

Levinas's extended analysis of sensibility contains the bold and strange thesis that the exposure and subjection to beings is itself subtended by an exposedness and subjection to alterity.[4] He reverses the Kantian position; for him responsibility, sensitivity to others, does not conflict with and mortify sensibility for mundane beings, but makes it possible.

Heidegger already had located responsibility not in one suprasensorial faculty, the rational faculty, but in the sensible structure of our existence. Responsibility is not a receptivity for an ideal order, an order of the ought over and beyond what is. For Heidegger being is the law; it is being that orders and ordains. His *Introduction to Metaphysics*[5] initiated a diagnosis of the period when metaphysics extended its sway over all Western culture, determining the meaning of being by separating being from, and opposing it to becoming, appearing, thought, and the ought. For us being is the given, the actual, the facts, over against what ought to be. Heidegger repudiates this opposition; for him it is being that binds us, obligates us, is the law and the destiny. He will show this by showing that being in us is not just what is coextensive with us as the matter of our movements or the actuality of our acts. Between us and our being, there is not coinciding but relationship: in us our own being is a matter of concern. For us to exist is to relate to our being; we consider our being here, question it, are troubled, afflicted by it, wearied with our own being. But our being is not an object we envision; it affects us, weighs on us, afflicts us. Our affectivity is a sense of our responsibility for our own being. We do not engender our being; it is given to us, laid upon us; we are burdened with it, and have to bear it. We do not exist, simply; we have to be. Being in us is an imperative: we are bound to be. Socrates too felt that, when he castigated suicide as recreancy and desertion. The imperative is first an imperative to exist—in order to answer for existence.

This way we have to be related to our own being such that it affects us, weighs on us, is at the origin of the existential option being made between existing inauthentically, that is, anonymously, or authentically, that is, on our own. The primary awareness of our being is an effort to take a distance from it, to evade the burden of having our being as our own, of having to be on our own. Feelings contracted from others, passed on to others, perceptions equivalent to and interchangeable with those of any other, thoughts which conceive but the general format of the layout about one, sentences formulated such that they can be passed on to anyone—make up the rigorous and consistent enterprise of evasiveness in the face of the being that is one's own to be. Evasiveness in the face of one's own being is an evasiveness in the face of one's own time. It makes us live each day as it comes, making it a reinstatement of the day that passed, expecting always another day to take the place of the one that is passing; it makes us live out time as an indefinite succession of nows, of manageable units, workaday workdays. What makes us so continuously and consistently evasive with regard to the being that is our own to be is the fear of the anxiety that has never ceased to be felt over the nonbeing that is our own to become.

Responsible being originates at the far end of anxiety. The anxiety that rehearses dying, that anticipates the limits of what is possible for me, casts itself over and takes over the full range of what is possible for me, unto the last limits of impossibility. The anxiety that anticipates the nothingness that is to come for me delivers over to me the full range of all that is mine to become. One becomes responsible in anxiety.

It is one's own being that is imperative; the being that is given to me is a destination to a potentiality for being which my actual being engenders, and a destination to the nonbeing that is to come for me.[6] The imperative is an imperative not for the universal and the necessary, but for the singular; it is the imperative that my singular potentiality for being come to be. At the same time, however—and this is the central hinge forged in Heidegger's existential ontology—the being in me that I appropriate is being, being generally. In my own being the being of the world, universal being, presses upon me. I cannot answer for my own being without undertaking to answer for the being of all that is. That is why I am a pulse of care in the universe, not only anxious for my own exposed, vulnerable, mortal existence, but concerned for the world, for all that is. For Heidegger it is this being afflicted with, being concerned for, the contingent being of a world, and not merely anxiety over my own subsistence, that makes my existence practical. Responsibility is finding in the forces of my own existence the wherewith with which to come to the assistance of universal being, threatened throughout with nothingness. Responsibility is, he says in his late writings, to shelter the most remote things, earth, heavens, harbingers of the immortal, in my own mortal existence.

Responsibility is then not measured by authorship; it is not just the will or the project to answer for what originated in one's own existence. It takes over and answers for a situation one did not initiate; it is answering for what one did bring about, for what came to pass before one was born, for the deeds and failings of others. And responsibility answers already for the sequence of occurrences that extend beyond the force of one's own that steered them, answers already for what will come to pass when one will no longer be there.

Responsibility is coextensive with our sensibility; in our sensibility we are exposed to the outside, to the world's being, in such a way that we are bound to answer for it. A world is not just a spectacle spread before us but a burden we are entrusted with. What opens us to the exterior, what makes us exist, be a sensibility, is exteriority, which approaches of itself, and touches us, affects us, afflicts us. For Heidegger this exteriority is what is exterior to our being and to all being: nothingness or death. The approach of this exteriority is also what casts us back upon our own being and upon all being, and makes existing for us a response to the nothingness and a responsibility for being.

For Levinas, it is not the encounter with nothingness that could make us take on our own being and answer for all being; it is alterity. Alterity is not nothingness, which could only be as the nihilation of being. It is not ideality, self-sufficient and absolute in its immobile present. Alterity is what is positive enough to appeal to being, and separate enough from it to imperatively order it. This kind of alterity Levinas locates neither in the death that summons all that lives, nor in the ideality of law, without executive force, but in the face of another. For the face is not the surface of another being. In his face, by facing, the other takes a stand; otherness itself appeals to us and contests us.

In *Totality and Infinity* Levinas has worked out the phenomenological analysis of facing in such a way as to show that the perception of the face of another is a responsibility.[7] In turning to face me, the other signals me; his face, his expression, his word, is not only indicative, informative, but also vocative and imperative. She faces me with her eyes, unmasked, exposed, turns the primary nakedness of the eyes to me; she faces me with a gesture of her hand, taking nothing, empty-handed; she faces me with a word, which is not an instrument, an arm, which is the way to come disarmed and disarming. To recognize his or her move in facing is to recognize an appeal addressed to me, that calls upon my resources, and first calls upon me, calls upon me to stand forth as I. And he or she appeals imperatively. To recognize his or her voice is to recognize his or her rights over me, his or her right to make demands on me and to contest me, his or her right to demand that I answer for my existence.

There are then two kinds of sensibility: a sensibility for the elements and things of a world, sensuality, which is appropriation and self-appropriation, and a sensibility for the face of another, which is expropriation and responsibility. But in *Otherwise Than Being*, Levinas sets out to show that the space in which the sensuous material is laid out is already extended by the sense of alterity which takes form and becomes a phenomenon in the face of another.[8] This thesis involves the idea, already found in Heidegger, that before the beings of the outside world are set forth for me, they are possessed by others; that the material world is "human" even before it is a nourishing medium. That its elements are "objective" or "intersubjective," elements in themselves or open to others, before they are goods for me.

It is true that already in Husserl and in Heidegger the lateral relationship with others, as other points of view, or as other sites where being is exhibited, entered into the constitution of universal space. But Levinas advances two innovations. First, he thinks that the relationship with the other does not only enter at the point where my perceptual field, already extended by my own intentional perception or by the reach of my utilitarian operations, is fitted into impersonal universal extension; for him spatial distance is not extended by a sense of nothingness but by a sense of alterity. Secondly, the relationship with alterity can have this role because the relationship with the other is not, as in Husserl, perceptual, or, as in Heidegger, pragmatic, but ethical. There is then a difference of levels; the argument is not that the other is the first object of perception, or the first instrument with which one could get one's bearings in a field of things. It is that what institutes the first *here*, what constitutes my existence as here, is not the power to keep objects at a distance, but is the pain of being afflicted with the demands of the other.

For Heidegger what subtends the sense of space is the sense of nothingness; the space of the world is the very abyss of death. This is because Heidegger takes being to be presence, *ens* to be *prae-ens*, and presence to be dis-stancing distance. The *Entfernung* which realizes presence is situating at a distance, and Heidegger took the sense of distance and exposure to contain a sense of nothingness in general and in itself. In boredom and in anxiety nothingness nihilates; in antagonism, rebuke, failure, prohibition, privation nothingness nihilates—in all distance, including all separateness by which things take their stand about us, nothingness nihilates.

For Levinas what extends space is not the nothingness that separates and frees the entities of a world to be as they are where they are; it is contact, contact with what is other and withdraws in the midst of the contact. He first worked out the notion on the example of the neighbor whose proximity, whose nearness, consists in his touching us, affecting us, while remaining uncomprehended, unassimilable by us. In this move, a neighbor is other, shows himself as other. This occurs when the other faces us, that is, appeals to us, contests us.

The contact does not only reveal the proximity of the other; it determines the *here*, determines the one contacted as here. Being here, being a here in being, supposes in our substance not only a capacity to be oriented or disposed by the exterior but a susceptibility to being affected, altered—sustained and wounded. To be here is to be exposed to the other, exposed to pain.

Quite early Levinas studied the immanence of pain. To be pained is to feel one's own substance, as a passive affliction, in the torment of wanting to escape oneself. For to escape pain would be to be able to transcend it toward the world, or to be able to retreat behind it and objectify it. The inability to flee or retreat, the being mired in oneself, is the suffering of pain.

Later Levinas was to find this inner diagram of pain in the contact with the other. The approach of the other who faces, afflicting one with his exigencies and exactions, throws one back upon oneself. One is unable to establish distance by rendering present to oneself, representing to oneself, what afflicts one so pressingly. One is unable to retreat from the demand by apprehending or comprehending it, setting it before oneself by one's own initiative as though it emanated out of oneself. One finds oneself forced back into the resources of one's own being by the exaction put on oneself. This being backed up into oneself, this having to bear the burden and affliction of the other's wants and failings without being able to find anyone to take one's place, this being held to one's post, repeats, in the structure of the one being approached by alterity, the inner diagram of pain. Thus the *here* is fixed. To find oneself somewhere is to be exposed, not to emptiness and nothingness, but to suffer appeals made on one's substance and contestations made of one's stand.

The recognition of the imperative in the face of another is not an abstract and intellectual respect for the pure form of the law which the other would instantiate on the diagram of his moves; it is the recognition of a claim put on my substance and my life, the injunction to answer for the destitution of others with one's own bread and, a hostage, to give one's life in sacrifice. The other's wants are first material; they make claims on my own sustenance, made wholly of the substance of the sensuous element. It is not only some surplus of my possessions that is contested by his imperative need, but my appropriative life by which I appropriate myself. Responsibility is serious when it is not only my surplus that is affected but all that sustains my life and my very occupancy of this post.

To have to answer to the other is to have to answer for what I did not initiate and for his or her wants and failings and even for his or her approach that puts me in question. It is this position that is constitutive of my being here, and of my being vulnerable to being wounded by entities. The exactions put on me by others make me liable to death—not by taking away the ground under my feet and casting me into the void but by exposing me to the obduracies and lacks of material things. It is not in being delivered over to nothingness, it is first in being delivered over to beings, having to count only on their sustenance, that I am mortal. To this mortality I am delivered by the exactions of alterity; from the first a claim is put on my life, on my life living on the enjoyment of life.

Thus we find Levinas's texts taking on some of the pathos of the Kantian moral philosophy, for which the inclination to obey the moral imperative is always received as a humiliation and a pain by the sensuous nature of man. But in Levinas this pain is not only the intellectual pain of feeling negated and frustrated, even when the moral order is carried out by the executive forces of life; it is the pain of substantial wounding and of sacrifice demanded of life. For it is in depriving oneself to answer for the hunger of those who have no claim on one but their hunger, and in sacrificing oneself to answer to others for what one did not do, that responsibility is serious.

1986

A Phenomenology of Substances

The Production of Substances

A thing is a subsistent substance, consisting of formed matter. It consists of raw material to which a certain shape has been given by an agent. A thing is identifiable by its utility or end, which is responsible for its having come into existence. It is recognizable by its position in a practicable field. Someone who breaks with the sensory flux, the continuity of the ground, the heat, the air, and the damp and envisions things isolates things for use.

This Aristotelian account properly applies to implements, man-made things, made by craftsmen. A shoemaker envisions a shoe as a quantity of material—leather—upon which he imposes a certain form; he cuts the leather to certain shapes and sews the pieces together. The form he imposes detaches the sides of the shoe from the hide and closes the shoe in itself. The sewing makes the form from the hide and closes the shoe in itself. The sewing makes the form inhere in the subsistent material as its property. The shoemaker is the agent that produces the shoe. The protection of feet is the end he has in view. Before this protection exists on the wearer of the shoe, it preexisted in the image formed in the shoemaker's mind. The end, the final cause, once conceived, works to determine the action of the shoemaker.

The substantive conception of things, composed of matter and form, efficient agency and finality, was not drawn up from an analysis of natural things, like clouds, plants, or animals, all of which form and grow of themselves. Nor is it drawn up from an analysis of works of fine art like musical compositions, poems, or temples. A work of fine art closes in upon itself and separates itself from the practicable field of means and ends. The shaping of sonorous material in view of an end is a craftsman's conception of singing and drumming, which pick up the song of birds and the humming and drumming of insects and frogs. The arrangement of words in grammatical forms in view of—what? arousing emotions? conveying messages?—produces rhymes but not poetry. The materials, blueprints, techniques, and utility which construct buildings do not make them temples.

But does not the primary apprehension of things occur in the practicable field, by humans who identify themselves in their activities? And does not the understanding of things come about in the making of them?

The making of implements has been taken to be distinctive of human action, by thinkers who pass over the leaf-mold gardening of ants, the breaking of mollusks with rocks by gulls, the nest building of birds and beavers, the fishing implements of raccoons. Making has been conceived as an imposition of form upon matter by the agency of human force and skill. True production of implements was taken to be distinctively human because it was said to presuppose the conception of a purpose, the end for which the product was the means: the maker who makes an implement first makes an image of the use of that tool in his mind. The image of the end would determine the form to be imposed, and make a product a means.

The social history of production has determined essential changes in the nature of products. The division of labor already brings about the separation of making from using. The maker who has to market his products must form a representation of the ends they serve and communicate it to others. The importance of the representation of ends in the organization of exchange and in production privileges the point of view of the maker over the user. If you want to understand shoes, ask the shoemaker; if you want to understand motorcycles, ask the manufacturer. In our scientific work we feel we have really understood something when we can take it apart and put it back together again in the laboratory. We will have understood life really the day we will have put together a cell that lives.

The theoretical privilege of the point of view of the maker has been established for the whole of the natural universe by the theological conception of God as creator. In Genesis, God is first presented as Creator of the universe; the creative work of God is depicted, as is natural in this old tale coming from a people at the earliest stage of technology, as a potter fashioning pottery. He takes clay and fashions a figure and then breathes life into it; thus God made man.[1] *Homo faber* is man seen in the image and likeness of his creator.

The finalities found in things with which action deals are absent from the scientific representation of the universe. Empirical research observes all things in and through transformations, and verifies its observations by reproducing those transformations. Scientific thought, which is essentially calculative, conceives of all things known and knowable as a pure fund of energy-units subject to transformations in determinate ways, it is the human mind that would bring purpose into a material world where things form by mindless collision, and organisms by mutation.

Scientific thought, which arises out of empirical observations of reproduced transformations, gives rise to technological transformations of raw material, and forms given in nature. Our technological age finds all things subject to measurement, and all transformations subject to calculation; it advances across the planet and into outer space, technologically transforming nature into a fund of resources subject to transformations into the equivalent without end. It is the human mind that, by assigning values to some of the conceivable transformations, launches the technological production of things.

More and more, the environment that surrounds us is man-made. Our research laboratories do not study natural entities, but pure water, sulfur, pure uranium, all of which are found nowhere in nature, but rather are produced in the laboratory. The table of elements itself is no longer an inventory of irreducible physical nature; atomic fission and fusion makes them all subject to transformation. It is not its own nature, its properties linking it with its natural setting, that makes a thing useful to us, but rather the properties it reveals when inserted into the instrumental system we have laid out. Timber is first cut into rectangular boards before it can be useful; the trees themselves are first hybridized, thinned out and pruned, before they can become useful as timber. It is not willow bark in its nature as willow bark that we find useful for our headaches, but the extracted and purified essence synthesized into aspirin tablets. There are whole plantations now where biologically engineered species of plants grow not on the earth but in water, anchored on floats of plastic foam fed by chemical blends. There are reserves now where genetic engineering is producing new species of patented plants and animals. As a biological species we are ourselves man-made; our specific biological traits, our enormously enlarged neocortex, the complexity of our bodies' neural organization, the expanded representation of the thumb on our cortex, our upright posture, our hairlessness—none of this evolved to differentiate us from the other primates naturally, but rather, it evolved as a result of our invention of symbolic systems, evolved from feedback from the culture—the perfecting of tools, the organization of hunting and gathering, of the family, the control of fire, and especially the reliance upon systems of significant symbols—language, ritual, and art—for orientation, communication, and self-control. As a bionic species we find these systems of communication subject to the imperative form of calculative reason.

Heidegger's Relational Ontology

In *Being and Time*, Heidegger takes the environment about us in which we distinguish things to be, for the Greeks and for us, from the first and for the most part a practicable field. But Heidegger argued for the primacy of the point of view of the user over that of the maker. The things we identify practically are fabricated by others or just found in nature. It is by using them that we acquire insight into their natures and characteristics.

It is the user who apprehends the nature of things made to be useful. If you want to understand shoes, ask a dancer, a runner, a mountaineer, a construction worker. The shoemaker himself must be asked, if you want to understand a motorcycle, ask a biker. Who could fly hang gliders designed and manufactured by the earthbound?

The Aristotelian distinction between the substance and the properties of things was contested by modern epistemology. Berkeley and Hume argued that what is given is given sensibly, and that what is given of a thing is its shape and size, and its color, savor, resistance to touch, its resonance. The notion of the underlying substance or substrate that would support these properties is in fact a metaphysical notion, not given but projected behind those properties by the mind. Locke even argued that it is only the quantitative properties that are given. He argued that the qualitative features are in fact relational: color and savor are not in the thing itself, but in the relationship between the eye and mouth and that thing.

Heidegger's analysis is resolutely anti-substantive, anti-Aristotelian. He analyzes a thing into a set of relations. Its properties are in reality modes of appropriateness: what we grasp of a hammer when we use it is its weight inasmuch as it is heavy enough to drive in a nail or a spike, its balance inasmuch as it holds the orientation of the driving blow. Heidegger also thinks that the qualitative features of things are secondary: to see something as a hammer is not to contemplate the colors of its head and its handle. The primary qualities of a hammer are relational and functional: a hammer is an implement for some task, and is grasped as a hammer in grasping how appropriate or inappropriate it is for a job, for nails which in their turn are spikes, roofing nails, finishing nails, or picture-frame nails. In ascribing to things, as objective properties, their size and shape, modern epistemology had taken them as they are given to a geometrical contemplation. But we have to see that the geometrical observation is produced by the use of measuring instruments, and is only a particular case of things known in the handling and use.

The forms of things, their material, the agents for whom they are useful, and their finalities all have to be reconceived relationally. When a hiker reaches for her shoes, the shape of the shoes is not for her that geometrical diagram which guided the shears of the shoemaker, but rather a form appropriate to the mud and rocks of the mountain. She reaches for substantial footwear; the substance of her shoes is not for her raw material that sustains the shape the cutter has put on it, but a substantial support sustaining the forms of her own advance over the sharpness of the rocks and against the penetration of the muck. Her action reveals the functional form and substantiality of the shoes by heading for the mountain. Their shoes' consistency, their durability, their reliability, their flexibility, the affinity of their leather for the warmth and the damp of the earth are felt in the hike; their firm shape, their lines of tension which are lines of support, exist and are known in the rocks and the cliffs. The shoes belong to the mountains, and make her belong in mountains.

It is for his neighbor, the spectator, that the biker's motorcycle is so much metal of a certain shape, cluttering the view into the backyard or obstructing the driveway; for the biker, his bike is power, speed, roar, phallic thrust that he feels in the confidence and assurance of his body weaving through traffic, plunging by the semis on interstate highways, in a landscape dissolving in hot sunlight and roaring winds. The solidity of the motorcycle is revealed on the dirt trails; its streamlined form is revealed in the gale winds bringing the Pacific Coast down interstate highways.

For Heidegger in *Being and Time,* the final and efficient cause which Aristotle had identified are the same. The shoes are means for the hike, but the hike in turn is for the sake of the shining eyes and vigorous pleasure of the hiker. She will make forest shadows and mountain vistas exist for her.

Making is for the sake of using, and is itself a form of using. The hiker will make her shoes impermeable with a silicone spray. She will make a makeshift lace for one that broke by unraveling the strands of the cord on her backpack, and a makeshift hammer out of a rock in order to pound back the nails of a sole that came off. Shoemakers design hiking shoes by asking hikers what is unsuitable about the shoes made for woodsmen or construction workers. The shoemaker puts the hides of animals and the gum of trees to new uses. Making is not imposing a form on pure formless matter, but a re-adapting of existing things to new functions. Stucco and plastic are not a demiurgic work on a substance that will hold an infinite number of forms,[2] but substances formed in functional relations with geological strata, refashioned to serve functionally in machines and systems of implements.

The utility of things is not produced by an image of an end absent from the field of practicable reality, being formed in the mind of the maker who then shapes raw material. Raw material has internal properties and structure which interact with other substances. The serviceability of their natural forms and the reliability of their material natures are discovered in usage. A farmer does not build up the fertility of his land and build up his herds by assembling raw material and imposing a willful form on them, but by protecting the topsoil and caring for the cattle that are born and grow of themselves. The builder in the tropics discovers which woods crack and warp or come to harbor boring insects, and which palm leaves or grasses will serve effectively as thatching. The shaping of a form delimits, focuses, and stabilizes the reliability and serviceability of their natures, which sustain vectors of force with further things.

An implement is manufactured for an agent who envisions in advance an end, a work to be produced. The work to be produced is in turn for the sake of the agent. The home craftsman is using a hammer and a saw to make a bed—for himself. The hiker is using her knife to dig out roots or peel fruit to make a meal—for herself. The environment in which we identify things is a practicable field where things are useful, are means for ends, which in turn are means for that end-in-himself, that dignity, which is the agent himself. The agent himself has to be conceived relationally: someone who identifies himself as a hiker, as a homeowner, as a manufacturer.

In *Being and Time,* the force that extended these relations was the force of usage itself. It is the user who envisions ends—the hike, the house to be built—and then discovers the functional forms and the consistency and reliability of things that can serve as implements. The ends are the user himself or herself, projected into possible positions in the environment: the woman who conceives herself as a hiker and heads into the mountains; the man who envisions himself by the time winter comes as living in a house of his own. A human envisions ends for himself because he envisions his forces as ending—he does not hurl his arms and legs forth into inert, never-ending trajectories. All his movements are his own because he envisions all of them as ending. His forces as a whole are his own inasmuch as he envisions all of them as coming to a definitive and irrevocable end. The sense of his life as casting itself forth with all of its own forces to its end—the sense of dying—underlies and makes possible the sense of each of his movements being cast forth to an end. The absolute exterior—the nothingness exterior to his existence and to the being of the world—underlies and makes possible all the ends, and all the movements cast to an end, of his life.

The principal change that Heidegger (in his later writings on things) has made in this analysis is to conceive differently the correlation of user and ends. Already in *Being and Time,* the final end, death, nothingness, was not only that to which each of our forces, which is active only in discharging itself, casts itself toward, but was the *vis vacui* that attracts us as well. Death, or nothingness, is not something that our existence conceives and projects before itself; it is what our existence foresees in ineluctable anxiety. The general form of the end of the possible or the future—death or nothingness—is not extended simply by the force of ex-istence itself.

Instead, our being becomes ec-static, comes to ex-ist, to ceaselessly conceive a possible position for itself and cast itself with all its forces into that position, because it is drawn by the force of what withdraws, withdraws absolutely and draws us into the non-position of death. Nothingness, in gaping open before us, makes possible a range of specific ends of our intermediary movements, without making them ends subsistent in the world. As ends, they are possible and future, combinations of nothingness with mundane positions and figures. The envisioning of ends for actions in the world on this side of death is the work of our positive, still living, forces.

In his later writings, Heidegger envisions the general realm of ends as the sphere of goodness, or the divine. An end is not simply a possible future position of our actual position in the actual world. The power of a woman to displace herself freely through the rooms of an apartment building and to see, outside, a road up the mountain, is not enough to make the hike a goal. An end is not simply a possible and future; it is a good.

This goodness has to be itself conceived relationally and not substantively. When the woman reaches for her hiking shoes, she turns to the mountains, the crisp air and pellucid light, the rocks that rise over her as challenges and as sovereign panoramas over those that circulate in the plains. When the peasant welcoming neighbors and friends reaches for the wine jug, she and they turn to the goodness of days, to the sustenance of the ripe grapes in the fertile hills, to the sparkle of light in the outpoured wine and to the sun and rain and seasons, to the solidarity and festive friendship ahead.

The goodness draws as it withdraws. The divine is not located somewhere in the world, but opens up height and sublime distances as the axes in which the world takes form.

The ends which make us perceive our environment as so many routes and pathways and dynamic interconnections are exterior and command us—the dwelling to be built where fertile fields are exposed under benevolent skies and which beckons to him who lives in caring for the land, for living things, and for the open skies; the open road that insistently summoned Walt Whitman and Maxim Gorki and Jack Kerouac. It is the India in the Jain temples of Rajasthan and the ancient port of Mahabalipuram under the sea and in the faces and the pain of Harijans that looked at Gandhi seated behind the windows of third-class carriages of trains for a year of his returning that delineated salt and spinning wheels into instruments of liberation. In building a home of the flank of the mountain exposed to benevolent skies, in crafting a boat built for the open seas, in making from empty milk cartons candles to float on the festive river, in forging the bullets of revolution, we come to inhabit the mountain range, we come to dwell in a world of open seas, we enter the immemorial antiquity of feasts, we move on the intercontinental theater of a future advancing upon the world oppressed in the present. Our action brings us to the ends of the world.

In using things found or crafted, we do not simply invent these ends which bring to flush a practicable order in the things about us; we represent, without our minds, the ends that are outside, on the hillside under the skies, down the open roads, in the remoteness of medieval wonders and immemorial feasts, in the pain of others programmed in chanceries beyond the seas. It is not the maker that makes the final cause; it is the final cause that makes the maker. It is the dance that makes the dancer and the shoemaker.

The ends are not terms, subsisting in themselves, closed terminations, where some movement comes to an end. The finality that produces the dance shoes and the dancer is the open vortices of the universe, where sunlight plays, where birds circle in the open skies, where butterflies draw staccato rhythms across the meadows, where all things are at play in the fields of the lord Shiva Nataraj. "'O Zarathustra,' the animals said, 'to those who think as we do, all things themselves are dancing; they come and offer their hands and laugh and flee—and come back. Everything goes, everything comes back; eternally rolls the wheel of being. Everything dies, everything blossoms again; eternally runs the year of being. Everything breaks, everything is joined anew; eternally the same house of being is built. Everything parts, everything greets every other thing again; eternally the ring of being remains faithful to itself. In every Now, being beings, round every Here rolls the sphere There. The center is everywhere. Bent is the path of eternity."[3] It is this epiphany of the world the animals know, the horizons where sunlight dances over the forest floor, waves dance across the meadow, spiders dance across their webs, and octopuses dance across the reef that summons forth that movement in us that is not going anywhere, that movement is not directed to a stop but driven by melody, rhythm, periodicity, which is dance. We do not simply invent these finalities which extend an instrumental order in the things about us; we represent, within our minds, the ends that are outside, on the hillside under the skies, beyond the open roads, in the dance floors of nature.

The ends, exterior to us with the exteriority of an imperative, are exterior to one another. The consistency and coherence of the world is that of circular paths about resting places which laterally issue to other fields of circular paths about resting places.

The means hold the movement as ends that exclude other ends; around the meal of the Guatemalan campesino the door is closed to the trafficking and urgencies of the roads and the laborious body comes to rest; the motorcycle absorbs all the sensibility, skills, and intelligence of the biker;

the pigeons and the canary, which started as means to distract the adolescent boy shut up in his slum house, end up making that house their home and that slum boy their caretaker, their kin, himself Birdy; the currency of exchange for the capitalist metamorphoses into an end in itself for which the rain forests, the birds of paradise, the ozone shield of the planet, and his own life are sacrificed. The vistas of the practicable terrain are not stages of one linear itinerary of a single life-enterprise; the world does not extend as a highway into which all roads issue, conducting us to our cremation pyres at Varanasi. The unending paths themselves become ends, for the nomads who depart from every oasis in the Sahara, for the hobos of industrial America, and for the motorcyclist.

The Substantiality of Things

The phenomenology of Emmanuel Levinas contests all the theses of the Heideggerian analysis of things. Levinas contests the primacy of the practical world and the primacy of usage. He restores a substantive conception of things against the Heideggerian relational analysis. He contests the primacy of form over matter, and the functional analysis of form. He contests the implemental character of things. He contests the projective and comprehensive character of action. He argues for a primacy of possession over use.

Heidegger conceived of our existence with the concept of *Geworfenheit* being-cast into the world or, better, finding ourselves, at each moment, already launched into the practicable world. But our bodies do not simply maintain themselves as a "here" relative to which they locate things "there" in a reflexive sense of themselves. Heidegger says the body locates where it is in function of things "there" which are the termini of its actions and future positions of itself. At any moment I am on the way to the restaurant, building a house, amassing a fortune. Through all these end points, I am on the way to my death.

This analysis is phenomenologically incomplete because it leaves out the movement of return and rest which every initiative contains. It is finally not intelligible because the end which is death is not in the environment, but rather is the abyss upon which the environment breaks, and cannot by itself implant a succession of ends that are relays to further ends.

What would be the experience of a body that does not fix any point of rest in the environment, continually envisions positions "there," or, in Heideggerian terms, projects only relay points ahead of a movement, casting itself with all its forces unto its end? It could certainly have a feeling of itself, like that of a swimmer whose enjoyment marks a spiral in the uncharted expanses of the night sea. This haecceity of enjoyment is not enough to stabilize here–there axes in the environment where things could stabilize.

Action presupposes a prior constitution of a point of departure fixed in the environment. A runner need only relate the goal to his own body at each moment, yet the race requires a starting point fixed in the field. The perceiver or agent who envisions things "there" does not only do so in function of the constant "here" marked by his own body. A nomadic life excludes action. If things are perceived as such in action, the perception of things requires a point of view fixed in the field of the perceptible.

Levinas establishes a segregation of the environment into home, or sphere of intimacy on the one hand, and outlying stretches of the alien on the other; this segregation precedes and makes possible the perception of things. The home is a zone in the depths of elemental reality which is established and maintained as point of departure and point of return, a zone where reality is at rest.

A home is a zone of warmth and tranquillity, a condensation in the elemental. We enjoy our home. Enjoyment is a movement of sensuous involution in this warmth and tranquillity. The enjoyment rests in this zone. It is also a movement of retreat and recollection, a taking of a distance or establishing a distance, a collecting of ourselves, our thoughts, our feelings, our forces. From a home base we view the environment as a field of things. Recollection makes representation possible.

The mind is not a modular unit that has the innate power to take a distance from the whole environment, retreat into itself, and then form a representation of that environment. There are physical, bodily, conditions for recollection and for observing the things of the environment. While we are running, or on a roller coaster in a fairgrounds, we cannot take a distance from the environment, survey it, and form a representation of it. Philosophers never mention it, but nobody can work out an epistemological theory while sprinting through the Stock Exchange Building. There are material, environmental conditions for representational thought; philosophers require a place of recollection, even if they do not withdraw into an ivory tower, but instead, like Michel Foucault, into a carrel in the Bibliothèque Nationale, or, like Jean-Paul Sartre, to the upper floor of the Café Flore.

When we are just passing through a town, we experience a stream of images, patterns, and spectacles along a line of time, the time of the walk or the ride. Then one day we make ourselves at home there. We establish a geography where we can find things, do things. We trace out a Main Street—the path from our home base to our place of work. We establish lateral routes, to the grocery, the laundry, the post office, to the place where our heart yearns after someone. Beyond, there extend the alien region of the unexplored, marked on the horizon by the next towns and the cities to which we have been, and from which we have returned. When we represent the town for ourselves, we represent it as it extends from our door. To locate things marked in any other geography—that of the city street or state road map, or the geological map—we have to transpose to those maps a virtual home base. To actually locate sites marked on those maps we have to transpose them onto the coordinates of the geography we inhabit.

Recollection makes initiative possible. Action presupposes a prior constitution of a point of departure fixed in the environment. A runner need only relate the goal to this own body at each moment, yet the race requires a starting point fixed in the field. Our home is the commencement of activities which are forays outside in view of appropriation.

Things are not just patterns projected in space before us or streaming by; they take form in the space we inhabit. They await us in our home and along the paths extended from our door.

In modern philosophy the contours of a thing were seen primarily as the way the thing is closed upon itself. A thing was what occupies its space to the exclusion of other things. For Heidegger in *Being and Time*, the contours were seen relationally: they are ways implements fit in with other things, and convey the force of the hand that manipulates them. For Levinas the clearly delimited contours that constitute a sector of reality as a thing mark out the way it is detached from, separate from, or detachable from other things.[4]

Things are durable substances. They hold together of themselves and maintain themselves over time. Things are solids.

They are forms. The substance of a thing is graspable. Its form is the way a substance is closed upon itself, and holds the hand and eyes that reach out for it. A substance is what lends itself to be detached and removed. What is not graspable, what offers no surfaces that hold our apprehension—air, heat, warmth, light, ground—are not things, but elements. What offers a form but is not detachable—the mountain range, the clouds, the moon— are not things, but, as Henri Wallon said, "ultra-things."[5] Wallon discovered that children who draw houses, people, cars, and trees in relative proportion to one another do not know how big to draw the moon in relation to these things. The moon, the sun, the clouds, and the mountain range on the horizon belong to another dimension, that of the empyrean of ultrathings. The moon and the clouds follow us as we walk; they are movables, but not removables.

Things are attractions; they draw our perceptual movements to themselves and hold them. Things are not simply relays toward other things. They are not paving stones in a field of paths, or implements geared into one another. They are terms, that rest in themselves, termini.[6] The hand reaches out toward substances, relating them to the finality of needs. But it is not the hand just transporting the nourishment to the hungry mouth, but the hand depositing something in the home, keeping it in reserve for tomorrow, or marking its position on a path that leads back to the home, that grasps it as a thing, a substance.

Things condense the tranquillity of the home. We no longer reach for them as hungers and thirsts, insubstantial; contented and at rest in our home, we enjoy their substantiality. We rest within the solidity of the four walls and sink into the rest of the easy chair. From our window we view the garden gate, the tree-lined road, and the bridge over the river.

Things are things in being used, in being *zuhanden*—within reach, as Heidegger said. In breaking down, in wearing out, in remaining unused and encumbering the practicable field, they become just *vorhanden*—on hand. But this subsistence on hand Heidegger judged to be derivative of their original materialization as gear. When an implement being used breaks down, obstructs, or encumbers the practical movement, the inter-rupted lines of function of the practical layout cease to flow under the line of movement of the user, and rise in relief before the agent who stops in his work to survey the work that has come to a halt.

The things in-themselves appear, as their availability for-us recedes.

Things, however, do not momentarily take form in the indeterminate element, in the flow of light and shadow, heat and damp, along the ground, with the specific function the manipulating hand simultaneously outlines and makes use of. It is because they are already there, detachable substanc-es, in themselves and at our disposal, that we can envision uses for them. The use or value that a thing can have is separable and comes after. A thing can have several uses, and wear out, becomes useless, or remain unused, encumbering the home. A tool is not a transitory relay of a body that extends its force in an instrumental field. It is by being in our possession, kept in reserve, available, that a detached substance can function as a tool. Use presupposes possession.[7] Before things become implements (*Zeuge*), they are furnishings (*meubles*)[8]—movable goods, detachable substances which are not simply tools annexed to the body of the user, prostheses, but brought into the zone of the home, tranquillized, and kept in reserve. Attending to a dealing with things is not making a workshop of the outly-ing environment; it is furnishing our home.

The furnishings of our home are not known through utilitarian manip-ulations only. Once we have attended to their mechanisms enough to have acquired the proper use of them, they revert to a substantial presence in contact with our sensuality. The living-room furniture, the drapes, and the lighting all acquire the density of a sensuous harmony. The invigorating smells, air, and rigor of a gymnastics court or ski slope envelop the room of the student athlete. The vibrant disorder of the rocks, driftwood, and debris of urban construction fills the room of the sculptor.

A house is equipped with means—with kitchen equipment, tools for cleaning and repairing. It becomes a home by filling up with goods, with easy chairs, books and records, a fish tank, rocks gathered on walks, and pieces of driftwood. The town that becomes our hometown is not just the area where the grocery, the laundry, and the hardware store are within reach. It is the zone with the tree-lined streets for strolling, the park, the central square and café where we meet friends and acquaintances. Even the shops are not just displays of equipment and implements offered to our needs; the store windows are *tableaux* in themselves. We do not really do window-shopping on Saturday afternoons; we look at the window displays.

The sensuous properties of things do not only provide data for identifying them conceptually. The gaze is focused and supported by the dense brown of the wood and sinks into it, the touch is centered and condensed, the posture is stabilized. Our body comes alive and becomes sentient, and diagrams of movement form in it. The things support us, sustain us, exalt us. They buoy up our gaze, fill our hearing, nourish our energies, restore our movement. The delight that illuminates our sight, the tact and tenderness that refine our touch, and the refinement that makes high-spirited our hearing comes from them.

The notion of means misses their reality. The taste for things, the appetite for reality, is not an agitation to compensate for inner lacks. Water is not a means to lubricate our inner organs; the thirsty mouth drinks too much or too little, savoring the body and the bouquet of the wine, tasting the luminous mirth of the spring pouring out of the rocks. The foodstuffs obtained to refurbish depleted body protein and evaporated body liquids dissolve, for the taste that savors them, into terrestrial and celestial bounty. The berries we gather, that melt in our mouth as we walk through the meadow, do not catch our eye as refurbishments for our cells and muscles and means for our projects; we taste them to relish the savor of the summer superabundant in juices and saps. The substances that nourish the living organism are not means for action that will seek for more means which are each time means for something further. After a good dinner, we turn to squander our energies on flowers planted in the garden in the glowing sunset, in kisses and caresses lost on an affectionate cockatoo, on the somnolent body of our lover. The colors and the shadows that contour the visible and lead the restless gaze in aimless circumnavigations through the environment do not simply serve to locate what we need or want. Sight is not an intentionality made of distress or desire. It is not an apparatus life uses. Life extends as high-spirited sight vitalized, illuminated, nourished by the substance of colored and translucent things. Its contact caresses the colors, forms, contours, and shadows, making them glow for themselves with their own light.

The form does not so much expose and make accessible the inner nature of things as clothe them and conceal them. Under his or her clothing, someone's nakedness is intact, apart from the world, and abstract. Under his or her clothing, someone's nakedness does not belong to the world; it exists elsewhere, and to make contact with the nakedness of another is to make contact with the otherness of that other.

Under their forms which have made things graspable and domesticated, their inner natures are clothed and concealed. Their natures remain decent and abstract. The functional forms of things which make them implements or furnishings cover over their substantial natures. The fiberglass, metal alloy, or plastic substance of the automobile remain abstract and unknown under the molded forms; the form of the stone axe, which detaches it for our eye, leaves the substance which is uncovered by the broken and decayed form in all the abstract generality of "stone" or "fossil substance." Roquentin in the public garden senses how completely ungrasped, ungraspable is the substance of the bench under the forms and functions it exposes to the light.

The identity a thing acquires by virtues of its detachable form is not the identity of its constituent essence. The identity it acquires by virtue of its form makes it susceptible to being compared, exchanged, and quantified. It can enter a system of exchanges as currency, and be exchanged for currency. The anonymity of money, for which things are exchanged, reflects the anonymity into which their substances recede under their graspable forms.

In the sensuous density of these things, however, there are imperatives. The armchair offers repose and calls for composure in the midst of agitation and contention. The worktable calls for devotion to craft. The dining room silently calls for respect for the shared sustenance of the earth. The hi-fi set imposes respect for the lofty aspirations of music. The paintings on the walls, the photographs in the albums lift our eyes from egoist gratifications unto grave and noble temples, landscapes, and persons loved and admired who trace out the paths of destiny. The plants and the aquarium are not implements that serve us; to live with them is to care for them, to sacrifice our time for them, our projects. The farm woman knows that the aluminum kitchen utensils, which she will not replace with ostentatious and fashionable utensils, with which capitalist propaganda makes people into consumers, have the goodness of frugal dignity in them. The slum dweller finds in the squat-legged bathtub with cracked enamel in which water flows and reposes a lesson in the endurance of modest things and lives too.

Having a home is not simply being at rest somewhere, in the midst of things. It is to actively care for the things appropriated. We have to shelter things from the inclemencies of the weather and from our own and another's careless or reckless collisions with them. We have to be attentive to the needs of things that grow of themselves. We have to be attentive to, and supply for the needs of the land, the plants and the trees, the herds and the flocks.

Heidegger conceives of action on things, labor, with the notion of "project." The term designates both a projection, propulsive movement of hand, also a program, a design, the aim fixed in advance. It is within the layout of an instrumental field that the hand reaches for an implement.

For Levinas, work draws things from the elements. It grasps matter as prime matter. The working hand does not envision "matter" as a concept (of physics or even of technology), but as fundamentally indefinite and incomprehensible. It is the tranquillization and domestication of this prime matter.

The hand grasps and gropes in the elements of its own movement prior to any plan to be executed, any projection of a project, any finality fixed outside of itself. The movement of the hand does not have the technical efficiency of a movement lined up to a preexisting instrumental layout. There is not first a project, a plan, a finality before the hand activates; it reaches out, grasps, tears up, kneads, crushes. In the most skilled manipulations, there is an element of groping, Levinas says.[9] As we work at our workbench in the cellar, building a cabinet, the layout fades back continually into the indeterminate; one fumbles for the hammer, the screwdriver, the screw we just put down which has already sunk into the sensuous density of the environment.

In the handling of implements Heidegger sees the implements' basic comprehensive movement, which understands identities and their functions. The hand moves as a sense organ, gathering information; but it moves also as a sensuous organ, fondling substances and textures, fondling the silk and the velvet and the moss and the downy hands of a lover, rubbing out the shapes of things to reduce them to buoyant or fluid or vaporous depth or solidity that extends indefinitely into the depths of the earth. It enjoys the random play of its movements, enjoys being surprised.

The hand that reaches out for things does not make the outside more and more determinate. As we work, as the cabinet takes form under our hands, the working space fills up with wood shavings, tools left here and there in disarray, spilled nails. We make our way down the paths of the garden to look for the onions for our meal or to gather flowers for a bouquet, and we leave, and leave the rest to rest or to drift in the indeterminate. As we make a meal, the kitchen space fills up with knives and mixing bowls, husks and scrapings, and pots and pans in disorder. Action then does not lay out the axes and determinations and instrumental connections of the world. It stakes out a zone of the practicable, and in inhabiting it, this zone transforms or unforms into an unpracticable density in which we rest and dream.

This grasp operated on the elemental is labor. Levinas takes possession and labor to be equivalent. In the absence of a reflection on appropriation, *Being and Time* had presented an image of a laborer whose implements are means for further labor. Was this not an image projected back from the modern, capitalist organization of labor, where capital itself is conceived of as destined for investment in the productive enterprise? We argue not only that the appropriation of material makes possible its usage as implements, but that labor itself is appropriation and its implements become the furnishings of life. Appropriation takes effort and skill; and labor is not, as in Hegel, a stamping of the spirit on nature, but appropriation of furnishings, liquid assets *(biens meubles)*. Our automobile is not only an implement to get to one's workplace; it is an extension of our home. Our workplace itself becomes the zone in which our life is centered and from which we survey the outlying world.

For Levinas a thing is not so much for me, serviceable or recalcitrant, as mine. This mineness is neither the Hegelian existence of things as exteriorization of my intentions and will, nor as Heideggerian prostheses, extending my forces. Mineness consists in existing as furnishings of my needs, and subsisting as *nature morte*, exuding tranquillity, furnishing the zone of rest and enjoyment.

The paths leading from our door to the things of our environment also lead to the outlying regions of the alien. Our departures from the home are not all predatory sallies to acquire implements and possessions. J. M. G. Le Clézio speaks, in his book *L'Exstase matérielle*,[10] of walking the arid and sun-flooded mountains of the Côte d'Azur, and feeling his life all pouring out through his eyes. He is walking, nothing but walking, with no aim or goal, walking in the sun of high noon. The hands are forgotten, they are no longer groping and grasping. The understanding, the agitation of mental activities, has been so flooded with light, his mind is so flooded with the radiant epiphany of the sun, that all its thin crystal constructions are no longer visible in the inner darkness, which is now streaming with intense light. All he is doing is looking. His gaze departs, buoyed up by the beams of light, swept down the beams of light, and, like them, absorbed and lost in remote distances where they pick out no patterns or messages to him.

The things we come upon in the outlying regions of the alien are themselves alien forms. The carved rock in the clearing in the Guatemalan mountains forest, the bleached twisted log on the sands are not correlates of our hands that impose their uses on them; they are forms made by the growth of a long-dead tree and polished by the sea, made by geological upheavals and carved by a priest of a vanished people and softened by the rain and the moss. The albatross is a form varying itself rhythmically and drawing vanishing arabesques in the Antarctic sky. In the summer meadows the patches of grasses in seed, the thick green spiny leaves coiling around the stalk of a thistle form snares for our eyes, into which each time a wave of our life sinks and is lost. In the foreign city the cathedral, the parks, the colors and designs of the shantytown crystalize into ensembles which present us with unknown shapes and substances dense with imperatives of oblivion-seekers. When people first discover the coral seas, they often buy underwater cameras to take from the ocean depths its enchanted colors and forms, motivated primarily by the desire to share them with the surface-bound. But one quickly learns that the forms and colors fixed on photographic paper stabilized what existed in shimmering movement. In the depths of the ocean one is only a visitor.

In the vicinity of the home, the separateness of things comes from their detachability, graspability, transportability, but the separateness of things also comes from their taking form in the region of the alien. In the alien, a thing takes form as an attraction or a repellant. Here a thing is not a form lending itself to apprehension and appropriation, but a form that draws our bodies' powers, which adjust to it, are commanded by it. In its substantiality it draws our mobility. In its form it refracts our gaze to its surroundings, its own inhuman setting. Alien things present the reality not as implements but as imperatives—or as graces. Alien things function as matrices of expropriation. Indeed, the clothing and the forms of people are not so much how the other is exposed and accessible to my understanding, as how he/she commands my behavior.

Our look stops on a bleached gnarled log on the sands by the sea. We come upon a face carved in a rock set upright in the midst of the forest in the Guatemalan mountains. The visible surfaces contoured by shadow recede into depth where they close in upon themselves. In the density and grain of the surfaces, the substance of the log or the rock looks palpable and its position stabilized by its weight. We sense the muffled resonance contained within it. Our look is refracted from the log or the rock to the layout about it as to a multiplicity of sites to which it turns other faces. About its stability, the sands cease to be glitter and the forest undercover ceases to be shadow flowing under our feet to acquire the stability of sites—become a hollow on the beach where driftwood from the sea comes to rest, a clearing in the forest where an immemorial shrine broods and waits.

Such things crystallize as snares in which our look, our touch, our life flowing outward is channeled and sent further into the alien. They are entries into the inhuman. We find ourselves drifting far from our home toward the time of ancient gods of lost peoples, toward the geological epochs of the oceans and the continents.

1998

The Elements

We awaken immersed in a plenum. Feeling spreads into a tangible medium and into warmth or cold. Smell drifts in a dank or scented space. Hearing stirs in the bustle of the day or the rustling of the night. The eyes open and are flooded by the light or find themselves adrift in darkness. The look that springs forth is sustained by the radiance or the dark. The sensuous elements are not there as a multiplicity that has to be collected or as data that have to be identified, but as depths without surfaces or boundaries.[1]

Visual space is not pure transparency; it is filled with light, intense or somber, crystalline or mellow, serene or lugubrious. If the light seems neutral when we look at things, that is because its color is without surfaces and our eyes do not go to encounter it like an object. Our gaze is immersed in it and sees with its cast, sees the colors of things that surface as contrasts with the tone of the light. The directions in which the light, advancing across the planes and probing the hollows, conducts our gaze, lead to things and to open vistas and to horizons, seas, and skies. Each time we look for illuminated things, our gaze refracts off their surfaces into the luminous openness. The light is sometimes so dazzling that we can see nothing through it. Its radiance fills and thickens the space such that the surfaces of gleaming or shadowy things at a distance are dissolved in it.

Our hearing is not just a recording of sounds, noises, and words, with silences between them. For hearing to awaken is to listen in to the rumble of the city or the murmur of nature, from which sounds emerge and back into which they sink. At the concert hall our listening lets go of the static of whispered conversation and coughs to settle into the undifferentiated vibrancy of the symphonic field where the melody will begin to move.

A voice takes up the vibrant currents of the air and sends its intonations into them.

To awaken to the heat, damp, or cold is not to feel these as surfaces laid on the contours of our body. Sultriness or aridity extends space about us. The cold is an unbounded zone open about our mobile body; the torrid expanse spreads amorphous directions for languid movement.

Our awakening is terrestrial; we feel the stability of the ground, even when we try to imagine ourselves trying to get on our feet on a sphere whirling through empty space at twelve thousand miles an hour. The ground is not—save for astronauts and for the imagination of astronomers—the planet, an object which viewed from the distance is spherical. We do not feel ourselves on a platform supported by nothing but feel a reservoir of support extending indefinitely in depth. The ground is not there as the sum total of particles of dirt and rocks we have seen. Once we have made contact with terra firma the force of the ground extends indefinitely before our steps. The ground is there when we assume a posture and support ourselves upright to move and when we no longer position ourselves and abandon our limbs and organs to its repose.

To go to sleep is to entrust oneself to the immemorial repose of the terrestrial.[2] It is to let go of the layout of tasks and urgencies, to turn in one's bed and hold on to the pillow as the condensation of repose and support. Because our sensibility maintains contact with the ground in and by sleep, the great black bird that rises and falls and turns into a handful of ashes does not soar in directions that are only those of our respiration and sexual stirrings, and our dreams do not circulate in the paths of practicable fields but hover over the ground and are terrestrial.

When we lose contact with the ground, we find ourselves not in empty space but in wind and open sea. At the concert we find ourselves moving in a sonorous expanse whose density surges and rolls. The mountains that loom over the mists, the moon that draws us up from the darkened landscape, and the shadows into which fleeting visions beckon draw us into zones of mercurial elements. There are also apparitions in dreams that do not safeguard our sleep but, like omens caught sight of in ruined sanctuaries, summon us into spaces dense with nonterrestrial forces.

The elements are sensuous realities; they are not perceptible frameworks, dimensions, or intelligible structures. The elemental qualities are not properties of underlying substrates. Not contained within surfaces or boundaries, the cold, the dark, the gloom, the savage, the sustaining, the luminous, and the exultant extend in depth indefinitely. They are not terms, not nouns, but free-floating adjectives.

The elements are there by incessant oncoming. Their presence does not indicate a source from which they come. The illumination about us dissolves all traces of its own past tones. The light which opens the horizons obturates with its radiance the horizons of its future. Beyond its presence, its future is not a framework of consistency and coherence that assures the present but is the realm of chance and fortune. The light is there as by grace. The ground rises in incessant presence without evincing the universality and necessity of laws that would found it nor the abyss in which it would be contingently suspended. It extends its support before us without retaining upon itself, like an object becoming more consistent as we turn about it, the accumulating force of its past support, and it is there without guarantees for the future. Sonority floats in waves of presence which rise to shut out the distant rumble of waves to come and the echoes of its past. The ardor into which the voluptuous sensuality advances is there without its oncoming tide having been seen from a distance and without its endurance being measurable; it is there as the element of adventure where nothing was anticipated nor is promised.

Sensuality

The elements are not a multiplicity of discrete things successively perceived in their places from vantage points and collated; they are not sensed by a perception which identifies surface patterns. The elements are not given as a medley of information-bits, sensations that have sense and are signs given for us to organize and interpret. The sensibility for the elements is not the passive recording of a multiplicity of elementary sense data. It is not apprehension which makes contact with the contours of a substance, nor comprehension which takes hold of something consistent and coherent. It is not a movement that casts our synergic forces toward some object-objective present across a distance. Sensuality is not intentionality, is not a movement aiming at something exterior, transcendent, a movement that objectifies; it is not identification of a diversity with an ideal identity term; it is not imposition of form nor attribution of meaning.

Sensuality is a movement of involution in a medium. One finds the light by immersion, one is in atmosphere, in sonority, in redolence or in stench, in warmth or in cold. One feels the supporting element of the ground rising up within one's posture and within one's orgasmic prostration and in one's sleep where dreams hover. The elements manifest themselves adverbially, qualifying our movements and our composure. Liquidity is there by giving play to the hand that is immersed in it, by yielding before and sustaining the thrust of the swimmer. The light manifests its radiance by buoying up the gaze that is set free in it. The terrestrial manifests its sustaining force to the mobility of the one who stands upright and advances, and manifests its repose to the one who abandons his postural tension to it.

The element is not a means, not an intermediary. Sensing is a movement which ends with the given, which envisions no future and no possibility, ends in light, warmth, ardor, resonance, earth. Its involution, not an initiative but a conformity with what supports and sustains, a conformity with the sensuous medium, was identified by Emmanuel Levinas as enjoyment.[3]

Life has been understood negatively, when it is needs and lacks suffered in a material system that were taken to agitate it and move it toward outside resources. The force of life has been taken to be the force of these negativities. Life was taken to posit a constellation of entities in the void as its objectives, to be consumed. The movement in the self, by which an organism is for-itself, was taken to be an anxiety that recoils to negate the nothingness of needs and lacks. (This concept is verified in modern society, where overpopulation and the political management of appropriation makes life in the deprived labor for the needs of life, and where the human engineering of marketing implants ever more needs and ever more wants in the appropriators.)

Natural and nascent life finds itself immersed from the first in the superabundance of the elements, in boundless light, in terrestrial warmth, in resonating depths. Vitality is reborn in pleasure, contented with the ephemeral and gratuitous splendor of the twilight over the industrial zones of the city, with the repose of the warm flank of a hillside among the lazy buzzing of iridescent flies, with a drink of spring water come upon by chance in the shade, contented with its contentment that forgets the cares that brought one here and the death to come.

Needs and wants are not the essence of life; they are partial and superficial, accidents that befall the plenitude of an organism which is alive for itself in its sensuality. The ego that arises as an awareness of needs and wants, the self that forms as the cramp knotted over this negativity, is intermittent and shallow. Sentient life is not a succession of initiatives driven by need and want and aiming at objectives. Life is not the recurrence of need and satisfaction, eating and getting hungry again and drinking and getting thirsty again, in an enterprise that is gradually losing its reserve, in an anxiety repeatedly postponing death.

The care for reality is not at bottom an anxiety, which makes our life an apprehension of things and beings because it is apprehensive of nothingness. To be born is not to be cast into the imminence of nothingness but to find oneself in a sustaining medium. The perception of things does not arise out of a universal methodic doubt and its contact with the terrestrial is not a quest for certainty that is a quest for assurance.

The movement that senses the elements is not the movement of need or want, the movement of an emptiness that seeks, in the distance, a content;

sensuality finds itself in a gratuitous abundance. To be alive is to enjoy; the light, enjoy the support of the ground, the open paths and the buoyancy of the air.

There is enjoyment even in the repugnance that shrinks back from the lugubrious light and the rank and fetid zones. There is a complacency in the melancholy and moroseness that feel the gloom of the skies and the misery of barren time. Nausea does not succeed in preventing the rancid spell of decomposition from invading one; revulsion is already caught in the mire; horror is a fascination. These excremental feelings draw their momentum from their involution in the medium of decomposition. Filled with it as with a content, there is indulgence and contentment in them. Abhorrence and loathing with gulping breath and flared nostrils savor the taste and smell of evil until it sweats from all one's pores. One enjoys one's abhorrence and one's loathing, and enjoys with them.

Life lives on sensation; the elements are a nourishing medium. Enjoyment is savoring what one assimilates and that in which one is assimilated. There are intermittent and superficial hungers that are sated in the eating, and there is an appetite that comes in the eating, savoring without consuming. Prior to the practical perception that draws out a practicable layout and pursues objectives, there is the appetite for the elements. The light is not just transparency which the gaze slips through on its way to distant surfaces; our gaze delights in the vivacity of the light itself. It assimilates in its languor the soft depths of the dark. The sonority is not just a succession of sense data which the hearing identifies as signals and information-bits; the ears are contented with the resonance of realm beyond realm as with a content. The touch lets go of things to relish the terrestrial and solar warmth. The earth extends its indefinite expanses before the steps of the nomad who is not scouting for any retreat, moved by his appetite for open roads and uncharted deserts. Erotic sensuality is not a hunger, a lack that pines for some absent organ, some object-"a" from which it was castrated (Lacan). It surges in a vitality that lacks nothing, is fed and sheltered and contented, a vitality that greets the earth, the skies, the day, and the night with the ardor of kisses and caresses.

The Sensual Ego

We enjoy the desert air and the monsoon, and we enjoy our enjoyment. The movement of immersion in the elements turns upon itself. The eyes that are delighted with the light enjoy seeing, the lungs enjoy savoring the good air, the vitality caressed by the warmth of the day revels in its contentment, the gait sustained by the ground enjoys walking buoyantly. A home is not only a locked building full of implements and stocked to satisfy needs; it is a zone of tranquillity and warmth and a precinct of intimacy recessed from the uncharted expanses of the alien. We are contented with enjoying our home.

Life savors its appetites, which are not negativities, agitations arising out of lacks and suffering; they are contents, they fill up life. Life is nourished by its own tastes. The widow fills her life by enjoying the day, the sunlight, taking a walk, enjoying the smell and damp of the springtime earth, enjoying the air, enjoying the appetite for life that the plenitude of the day sustains.

Existing is not just being-there, in the contingency known by anxiety, finding oneself here by extending a field of objectives out there. A living being, immersed in the elements, arises in the discontinuity of a new pleasure. Immersed in the superabundant plenitude of the elements, a sensual life is itself an excess and a superabundance, a life that is good to live.

The inner movement in enjoyment, by which the sensuality affected with the elements is affected with its own savoring of the elements, is the first eddy of ipseity. The movement that diagrams a self, the as-for-me, is not an intuition but an intensification. The ego is a pleasure. A life that finds itself in the elements does not differentiate itself by consuming what it lacks and closing in upon itself. Its contentment overflows the content and is broadcast back to the elements. In the warm radiance of the day, in the serenity of the fields and hills and silver abysses of the skies, how good to be alive! How fresh it feels! How refreshing is this silence! How calm the evening is! The ego ex-ists not in the affirmative mode, a self-positing position, but in the exclamatory mode.

The ego is not an incorporeal entity that forms in the emptiness of needs, wants, and intentions. It is not suspended on the recognition of others, a signifier in discourse and in the grammar of kinship, economic, and political codes. It does not take form on the shape of recognizable skills, body armor, and uniforms. It also does not first arise with the postural schema that maintains itself in a field of objectives and emanates a "body image" about itself—that first form of reflection, Maurice Merleau-Ponty said.[4] The primary ego is not that of a body positing and positioning itself; it is the exclamation of a body in abandon exposing itself. The eddies of egoism form in the taste for enjoyment by which our skillful and armed body becomes sensual flesh. The ego is the nakedness of our body. This nakedness is not lived as vulnerability and in timidity and precautions, but, beneath its garb and its armor, as sensuality of life exposing itself to the elements, enjoying its exposure.

Things, that is, substances that have contours that contain their properties, can be apprehended, detached, and possessed. We identify ourselves and maintain our identity in the midst of things. The elements which extend no horizons of objectives, which pass into no stock that can be recalled, do not lend themselves to appropriation. One cannot make oneself something separate and consolidate oneself by appropriating the light, by making private property and depriving others of the atmosphere, by monopolizing the warmth, by expropriating the things distributed over the ground of their support. The light that invades the eyes depersonalizes and the anonymity of light illuminates in one's eyes; one sees as eyes of flesh see. The forest murmurs and the rumble of the city invade one's ears that hear as hearing hears. The ground that rises up into one's posture depersonalizes; one stands as trees stand, one walks as terrestrial life walks, and one rests as terrestrial life rests and as rocks and sands rest.

The primary sense of the self is not a movement that reflects itself and maintains itself by containing and consolidating or synopsizing a multiplicity of elementary sense data. Essentially exclamatory, it is a movement of involution that intensifies and releases its energies into the elements in which the sensual body is immersed. How calm the dawn is! How fresh it feels! How pungent it smells!—the zest and the savor vitalizing one's spiraling sensuality are cast forth again indefinitely into the depths of the dawn. Pleasure forms in multiple and ephemeral eddies of enjoyment. Sensual pleasures which throw forth the exclamations of their superabundance to the elements cast forth their eddies of involution elsewhere on the naked substance of the body. The elements are unfragmented and fathomless; in the sensual body immersed in them eddies of egoism differentiate, diversify, discharge, and dissipate. The sensual body is not one through a postural axis that maintains itself but through the labyrinth of pleasures that intersect and lose themselves in one another.

Sensuality is vulnerable and mortal from the start. But this susceptibility is not the vertiginous sense of the contingency of all being, an intuition into the nothingness in which all being would be perilously adrift, and which could be foreseen as a real possibility just beyond the thin screen of the actual being. The contingency of the sensuous element is in the very fullness and abundance of the present, which plugs up the horizons, the future. Coming from nowhere, going nowhere, it is here in incessant oncoming. It is not here as though grudgingly parceled out by the malevolence of nothingness, but as gratuity and grace. Fortuity and goodness of the light, the play of iridescent color, the resplendence of tones, the liquidity of the swelling forces!

Pleasure is exposed not only to the withdrawal of the element it enjoys but to the excesses of its torrential oncoming. The naked flesh is susceptible to being wounded and rent and pained by the force of the sensuous element. In pain one is backed up into oneself, mired in oneself, in-oneself; pain announces the end of sensibility not through a conversion into nothingness, annihilation, but at the limit of prostration, conversion into passivity, materialization. It is in the force of the elements and not in their inconsistency that our death already touches us and the sensual body knows its mortality.

Common Enjoyment

Modern epistemology contrasted the public existence of words with the private and ineffable existence of sensations. Another's mind would be composed of states and intentions accessible to itself alone; another's body will be exhaustively explored by the outside initiatives of observation and autopsy without finding any evidence of mental states other than those of the outside observer himself. Yet the surges of sensibility and sensuality in its movements are the very evidence of a body. What is more unmistakable than the radiant vision in the eyes of a child awakened in the car and shown the sea dancing in the sun? What is more evident than the warmth of feeling that awakens to the hands that draw off the covers and to the kiss with which we touch his face? In the darkness of the crowded bus, we feel the warmth of the body of the passenger next to us and the shiftings that stir from within. We do not make contact with his sensibility through some visible surfaces we see, some sounds we hear, and for which we find evidence that the other sees and hears them too. With no quasi-determinate sense of what it is the other sees and hears, we are awake with the sense of another sensibility in the dark parallel to our own. The albatrosses soaring around the planet, the minnows weaving through the seaweed are rays of vision that materialize momentarily for our eyes; the caterpillars bobbing along the tomato leaves, the octopods advancing across the coral reefs are probings of feeling palpating the tangible which we ourselves are fingering.

Imperative Pleasure

When modern philosophy depicted the whole of the outside environment as decomposable into elementary data possessing only the "primary properties" of extension and duration, each existing in exclusive occupancy of a point p and an instant t—determining them by negation—it found itself constrained to conceive of life as a spontaneous, self-activating force. But enjoyment is not just a spontaneous initiative of a life which nourishes itself from the outside and turns upon itself as upon an end in itself. Sensuality is awakened from the outside. The luminosity more vast than any panorama that the light outlines in it, the vibrancy that prolongs itself outside the city and beyond the murmur of nature, the darkness more abysmal than the night from which the day dawns and into which it confides itself—summons the sensuality. There is not mastery but obedience in pleasure.

Do we not find offensive the one who, when the landscapes fade out before the epiphany of the cosmic light, puts shades over his eyes so that he can read his texts or decipher the alleged text of the spectacle of a world; do we not turn away from the hubris of the one who persists in that hour to myopically engineer his layout of implements and gear? We turn away, as from a disordered and distempered organism, from the one who pulls the blinds of his windows against the glory of high noon to crawl into his bed and cover his head with blankets, only to then offend the night with his fidgety agitations under the glare of incandescent wires. We avert our eyes, as from someone leprous, from the one who is rigid and cold in the midst of the languorous immensity of the summer. We quickly move out of earshot from the one who prattles shallowness under the vaults of the Hagia Sophia in whose stones the gravity of Byzantine glory has come to rest. Do we not avert our steps from the one whose ears are scabbed with a Walkman when the winter arrives tinkling in on snowflakes, when the petals of the cherry trees of the Silver Pavilion of Kyoto fall in frail music, when the down of white birds intones the skies over Irian Jaya? We shudder before the temerity of the one who stalks resolutely after his prey through the day when the light and the green waves of springtime themselves are dancing. We flee from the contumacy of the one who looks with dry eyes and arid soul over his affairs when the spring rains return all things to their oceanic origins. Do we not smell violence and violation in the desiccating sarcasms of the one who holds on to his mast when the whole landscape streams, undulates, rushes into the dawns beyond dawn, the aurora borealis beyond every north or south pole?

Beyond the practicable and impracticable vistas through which the nomadism of life charts its own vital space, is it not summoned to the terrestrial, the oceanic, the ardent, the lambent, the night beyond night that no life charts or lays claim to?

Our sensibility is drawn into these depths beyond the profiles of things, summoned by them. Do not our visionary eyes, which are not stopped on the lustrous things which the light of day illuminates, obey another imperative in the light—the imperative to be a *lumen naturale,* a solar incandescence which squanders almost all of its light in the darkness without bringing any things within its reach? Is not our stand which enjoys the support of the earth also subjected to its order, to support itself and to repose? Does not the vertigo over the abyss that descends and descends without end obey not the imperative of the depth to maintain surfaces, but another imperative that depth promotes and is: to deepen? Does not the hearing that hears not the particular songs, cries, and noises of the landscape but the vibrancy beyond the corridors of a world, obey the imperative addressed to hearing that it become vibrant? Is there not in the ground, dampness, atmosphere, and light in which we are immersed the imperative that life live in becoming support, becoming oceanic, becoming aerial, spiritual, lambent?

To withdraw from the illuminated surfaces and contours is to give ourselves over to the night, to be drawn not by the insistence of the body but by an elemental imperative. Sleep is not an extinction of consciousness produced by the nothingness of the night which engulfs all things, but a summons come from the repose of the earth, reservoir of confidence, and from the night beyond night.

The sensuous involution in the elements makes our eyes luminous, our hands warm, our posture supportive, our voice voluble and spiritual, and our face ardent. In the involution of enjoyment is generated the gratuitous and excess energies that seek release in exultation. Enjoyment is freedom; in the enjoyment of the radiance of the spring day and the warmth of the ground, we forget our cares, our cravings, and our objectives; we forget our losses and our compensations and we let go of what holds us. Every enjoyment is a death: a dying we know, not as the Heideggerian anxiety knows it—being hurled from being into nothingness—and not as pain knows it—a being mired in oneself and backed up into oneself by the passage into passivity—but as dissolution into the beginningless, endless, and fathomless plenum of the elements.

1998

The Levels

As we approach an outdoor café in the night, we see a volume of amber-hued glow. When we enter it, our gaze is filled with the light. We begin to make out forms discolored with an amber wash, like fish seen through troubled waters. After some moments, the luminous haze neutralizes and the faces of people emerge in the hues of their own complexions. The tone of the light has become a level about which the colors of things and faces surface according to the intensity and density of their contrast with this level. The light ceases to function as a radiance in which we are immersed; we begin to look not at it but with it and according to it. Our gaze follows the light as it penetrates open spaces, outlines contours, stops on surfaces, and comes upon things it finds and does not make visible.

We enter a concert hall and find ourselves enveloped by the confused hubbub of the crowd and the rumble of the orchestra tuning. The conductor lowers his baton, the opening notes of the music begin, and our hearing finds the key and the volume level of the music. The shuffling and coughing of the audience recede; we hear the pitch, volume, and density of the notes as they rise and fall from the level. The level is given by sounding the dominant at the start. The hearing that remains anchored to it is not a sensory memory which reproduces this sound at each moment of the composition (which would make of each note heard a chord). It is a listening-according-to which orients the listening to the successive notes and chords. The musical characteristics particularize and individuate the succession of sounds as emergences and divergences from the dominant.

We enter a room where a reception is in progress and the babel that fills our ears makes us think it would be impossible to carry on a conversation there. But then we find ourselves facing someone, and our hearing adjusts to the noise level and we find ourselves picking out effortlessly what she is saying. We hear the call of the night owl rising in the whir of the wind. We listen to the droning of a bee and the murmur of the meadow ceases to throb gently on all sides and within us to become a plane along which the buzzing stops and starts again.

When we set out to feel something, our extending hand locates the level of the tangible, which it makes contact with not as an objective but as a directive, imposing the pressure, sweep, and periodicity of the movement that will distinguish the grain of the wood, the fur of an animal, or the Braille letters on the surface of the page.

The light shows itself in its hue and shimmering intensity; it begins to function as illumination and to lead us to things when we enter it. The level of the music is audible and extends the melody before us when we tune into it. The level of the tangible has to be found by the hand. The levels are sensory data that do not occupy a here and a now to the exclusion of other data. They do not simply extend into the space and time of a sensorial field; they extend that field. The odorous and the olfactory are not so many discrete events that make an impact on our sensory surfaces; the smell and taste open upon an odorous medium and a savorous medium and adjust to the level in which in the pungent night our sense of smell can find the perfume of a woman and our taste discern the tang of spring water.

The levels extend directions of support for a movement of vision, hearing, and touch that does not simply get displaced in spasms provoked by the impact of successive stimuli. The light extends an expanse in which things can be seen, extends a wave of duration in which distant things are things we have seen receding into a past and are objectives we shall see. The dominant extends the musical space and duration in which the melody will rise and descend, approach and drift off, expand and contract, in which a melodic initiative will be concluded. In the field of the tangible nothing materializes in the now; each tangible thing forms on a level along which its pattern and grain and resistance can be extended—a level which is also a wave of duration, and a tangible thing is as much a temporal formation as is a melody. In the perceived environment waves of duration are not segments marked out on an empty linear dimension of time prior to the intuition of any content; duration extends as levels of passing and approaching visibility, resonance, and substance along which movements of our look, our listening, and our touch are directed.

The environment does not extend in an empty geometrical space whose infinite dimensions are conceived by a formula or intuited a priori. Its levels are not the Euclidean dimensions of space and the linear dimension of time on which Kant and Hegel locate the here-and-now given *this*. The levels which open a sensible field before our perception are not a framework or the organization according to which things are distributed. By conceiving the perceptual held as the background behind a figure, Edmund Husserl's phenomenology conceives it as a multiplicity of possible figures and misses the functioning of levels. For him inner and outer horizons are ordered sequences of potential figures. The levels are not the system of connections or relationships, such as the spatiotemporal or causal or conditioning relationships specified within the scientific representation of objectivity. The levels are not the network of instrumental couplings Martin Heidegger took to constitute the primary layout of the environment as a practicable held.

The layout of levels is not a network of vectors of signification, where from the first each sensation-complex signifies or refers to other sensation-complexes for a sensibility that is intentional or comprehending. It is not a set of universal and necessary laws of which the things perception locates would be the instantiations.

A level is neither a purely intelligible order nor a positive form given to a pure a priori intuition; it is a sensory phenomenon. A level is neither a content grasped in a perception nor a form imposed on an amorphous matter of sensation; it is that with which or according to which we perceive. It is not an object formed nor an organization elaborated among objects but an ordinance taken up and followed through.

The levels of our practicable field, but also those of the unpracticable domains, the landscapes, the visions, the spheres of musicality, the oneiric and the erotic fields, the vistas through which our nomadic vitality wanders, are not suspended in void nor in the empty immanence in which our representational faculty a priori would extend the pure form of exteriority. They take form in a vital medium, in light, in the air, in warmth, in the tangible density of exteriority, on the ground, in the night, and in the night beyond night.

The Reliefs

The particulars we see, hear, touch, smell, and taste are salients, contours, contrasts, inceptions, and terminations that take form on the levels. The musical functions of a sound do not inhere in it as properties; a C-flat of itself is neither high nor low, thick nor thin, near nor far, lilting nor emphatic. A sound gets its particularizing characteristics—pitch, volume, closeness or remoteness, intensity, attack or terminating force—from the sonorous level from which it diverges, that of the party noise or of the key of the sonata. A color acquires its compactness, vibrancy, localization or diffusion, and inviting or obstructing function from the level of the light and from the general tone of the field which it punctuates. A roughness, sleekness, or tackiness is not a multiplicity of pressure points with tactile void between them; it is a rhythmic pattern which rises in relief from the level of the tangible at which the touching hand maintains its pressure and across which it moves.

The music can resound on the surfaces of the drums and in the throats of the trumpets and saxophones; it can pervade the space before us; it can reverberate in our ears; or it can rumble in our bodies not as something specifically acoustic but as visceral stridency, a harmonious quiescence, or a vital throbbing. The eyes are drawn to the red of the roses in the hospital room where it figures as a specific accent in the diffused chromatic atmosphere of the room. As the gaze settles on it, the red condenses a spiraled volume. As the eyes narrow their focus on it, the red intensifies and outlines flakes of surface, the contours of the petals. But even as it surfaces as a property inherent in a thing, the red also plays across the room; the red of the roses intensifies the green of the leaves, bleaches the whiteness of the sheets of the bed, and rouges the cheeks of the sick friend. The whole room became more vibrant when the roses were brought in. As our gaze, seduced, now travels around the coils of the petals, it is drawn inward, into the inner substance of the petals and into the brooding crimson darkness of the core. The red proves translucent, the surface-red makes surface the smoothness and elasticity of the petals and their fleshy thickness. If we remain with it long enough, the red no longer keeps its distance, invades our eyes, and is felt as a sultry ardor that spreads throughout our sensibility.

The red would not be the red it is were it not for the light which it invades and with which it contrasts, were it not for the leaves it greens and the sheets it whitens. In condensing and intensifying on the petals, it becomes tangible, and this red would not be the red it is did it not mold surfaces with a certain grain and elasticity and quilt depth with a particular spongy density. A color that would be just in a now, that would not have made itself felt a moment before as a solicitation in the tonal atmosphere, and that would not hold the gaze along a certain duration, would not be visible at all.

Painters know that colors are not given as opaque points or patches inertly held in their contours; they have an experimental knowledge of what a touch of color does—it bulges out or hollows out space, thins it or makes it dense, intensifies or fades a constellation of other colors, stabilizes or sends movement across planes and distances. A color is not an instantaneous impact in a dimension of empty time already extended; it presents a present, swells out or contracts a pulse of time, makes it diaphanous or dense; it emerges out of an atmosphere or separates progressively from another color, sends forth a wave which brings other colors into relief and solicits their approach, lays open a field of possibility, and thus materializes a wave of duration.[1] A tone is not an event localized in a line of time already extended. It extends a specific kind of duration in a space it opens; its attack and its aftereffects materialize a pulse of duration in a musical space whose scope and volume show through the visual shape of the concert hall which it interferes with and which does not define it. The sensory flux does not present itself as so many space-time points successively filled and emptied and filled again, but as a sphere in which points pivot, edges extend levels, spaces open paths, colors intensify themselves by playing across a field, tones thicken and approach and thin out and recede and send their overtones into one another.

The sensible is not there as the affirmed, the posited, as so many univocal and exclusionary occupancies of positions on the axes of space and time, so many terminations of the interrogation that is in our vacant and volatile looks. The sensible itself exists, Maurice Merleau-Ponty says, in the interrogative mode.[2] The sensible that we encounter when we look, listen, smell, and touch is not an answer to a questioning that is only in us, is not a plenum that fills in a blank opened by us, a positum that is the affirmative answer to our inquiries. The sensible is there as the surfacing of a depth, a crest on a wave that pursues its way. Our eyes touch lightly over the things, just enough to recognize on them the functions the program of our everyday concerns have put on them, but when we look beneath this human function to their sensible natures our eyes discover in the color, our ears in the resonance, not something that is just what it is here and now, without mystery, but something like a quest they join, a tone on its way calling forth echoes and responses—a red come from its own past, responding not to our question but to its own, seeking its redness beyond the moment and elsewhere, water seeking its liquidity in the sunlight rippling across the cypresses in the back of the garden. If, after so many years of looking at colors and listening to tones, they still continue to stir ever anew our curiosity, it is because we do not stand before them as well-appointed judges who demand yes-or-no answers to questions we have an indefatigable capacity to formulate; it is because we find ourselves, despite our own interests and our own answers, incessantly intrigued by the wanderings and mute wonderings, the intimations and divagations of which colors and tones are the materializations.

A sensory entity is a particular that can veer into a level. In some of Anton Webern's dodecaphonic compositions the twelve tones are first played in an order which constitutes a melody; as they are repeated, additional notes rise and fall about each of them. The tones which figured as particulars with which a melody rose and fell, advanced and returned, begin to figure simultaneously as keys about which micromelodies circulate. When the vase of red roses is brought into the hospital room, at first the uniform whiteness of the walls and sheets intensifies the redness of the roses which glows in the coils of the petals. But after a while the redness of the roses functions as the color level against which our arms appear pallid and the faces of visitors vibrant. The sensorial is a medium in which any point turns into a pivot, any edge into a level, any surface into a plane, any space between things into a path.

We should not say that, with time, a point does not maintain itself as something toward which the movement of sight advances and upon which it stops, but rather that it turns into a pivot with which the movement of sight orients itself. For there is not first a line of time, as there is not first a layout of empty space, in which sensory patches appear. The endurance of a tone or a color is not a reproduction of a particular in the succession of particular instants of time, and the perception that follows it is not a recall that superimposes upon the particular appearance in the now its particular appearances in a succession of past nows. It is the tone, by extending itself into a level along which other tones rise and fall, that extends duration in a musical space. It is the red of the roses, by inaugurating a new level in visibility along which the crisp whiteness of the sheets, the pallor of the hands, the bright complexions of visitors occur as events soliciting the vision to advance, that extends a wave of duration in the field of the visible. A level is the sensory content of a figure that does not cease to hold the movement of perception when that movement lets go of the contours of that figure; it is a visible that extends unobserved, a sonority that is no longer listened to but that prolongs itself along with the sounds and the silences, a substantiality no longer palpated but that subtends the reliefs and the contours felt—an objective before us that becomes a directive weighing on us.

Sensing is not a passive recording of impressions which would then be mentally organized; the sensibility in our organism is inseparable from its motility. If paper, silk, and balsa wood are just laid on our belly or hand, we feel only vague and indecisive pressures. In order to feel sizes, shapes, weights, and textures, we have to mobilize our fingers as one prehensile organ, support our hand movements with a positioning of our posture, and move across the surface and contours of the solid or through the air or water. To feel the sharpness of a blade, we have to move our finger across it, with the appropriate pressure and rate of movement which we pick up from the blade. The movements that feel the grain of the wood or the nap of the fur are neither desultory and spasmodic nor preprogrammed and willful; they organize as they proceed, with a pacing that is induced in them from the level of the tangible.

To see the water, our eyes do not fix on where it is, do not fix on the pool; our look is led by the light which precedes it and guides it and is led by the movement of the water which makes visible the zigzags of the tiles and the sheets of light within it and sends flashing ripples across the screen of cypresses at the back of the garden.[3] It is each time with a specific focusing and movement of the eyes rubbing across it and with a sustaining postural schema of the body that we see red, yellow, or green. We see yellow with a tightening up, green with a sliding up-and-down movement in the muscle tonus. Red is rending, yellow is stinging, blue and green induce rest and concentration. Green accelerates and red slows down movements outward. The body opens to see blue and green, contracts to view red and yellow.[4] When our body movements are concentrated on putting back together a typewriter we are repairing, the music subsides into an agitation that pulls on us without exhibiting a musical development; when though we keep silent our larynx muscles shape the surging music, when we dance to it, then the phrases, timbre, and cadences sound out. Touching, seeing, hearing, savoring, and feeling are not reactions and not spontaneous initiatives, but are conducted moves.

The Upright Field

The field of perception is not extended like the geometrical space in which science locates its objects. It extends upward and downward, from close to far, to the right and to the left.

Up and down mean nothing in geometrical space, nor in the universe considered objectively—unless we imagine an observer standing on a fixed platform in space. They are also not determined by the position of the images of things on our retinas; when we tilt our heads, the door frame, whose retinal image is now oblique, remains upright.

When we look into an inclined mirror in the shoe store, at first we see the walls and floor and us ourselves leaning at an angle; but after a few moments the scene acquires the normal up–down level and we see ourselves standing upright again. Clinical psychologist G. M. Stratton contrived eyeglasses that reverse the retinal images. He then at first saw a visual field upside down; then fragmented with some patches right-side up, and finally after a week of wearing them he saw things right-side up again in their normal upward or downward positions in the visual field.[5]

Is then the up–down axis a relationship which the mind inserts among mental images adrift in psychic space? But the judgment the subject wearing the eyeglasses makes that the floor is really below and the ceiling above is not enough to make him see the things arrayed in their normal orientation. Knowing, as we do, that our body has not tilted does not make us see upright the image of ourselves in that shoe-store mirror inclined at an angle. In Stratton's experiment, as in our experience with the shoe-store mirror, what realigns the visual layout about us is the effective engagement of our practical powers with the things they handle.

Certain cardinal visual things—the sink, the floor, the walls, and the door—extend not only surfaces across which the eyes can circulate but a level along which multiple practical operations are possible. They solicit our movements and govern our postures. In the measure that we handle these things, the up–down orientation of their manipulatable forms extends into their visual appearances that the mirror had tilted or Stratton's eyeglasses had reversed and reorients them. When we cease to view the image of ourselves in the mirror against the background of the room outside the mirror and look at our shoes in the mirror as we pace back and forth, this space the mirror shows in which we find we can function, can walk without tipping over, appears visually upright. In the course of the week as Stratton wore the eyeglasses, first the doors, the floor, the tables, and sink he locates as he moves and acts begin to appear visually upright again, and then constellations of objects about these things line up with them. The visual appearances of the things to which he turns line up again along the upward and footward directions of his practical movements.

The dominant up–down axis that emerges in the field is parallel to the axis of our upright posture. What aligns visual appearances along this up–down axis is not the statistical frequency of this parallelism. The vertical position of our heads is not the most frequent one with which we view things. Things remain upright when we lean over. The up–down axis which orients the visual appearances of things persists as our body parts bow and when our bodies, letting go of their tasks, lie prone.[6] But the up–down axis is the level of our most effective action. The upright posture is the posture with which our multiple body powers are most available for the principal things our body deals with and upon which it anchors itself.[7] In the freestanding position our two arms and legs are equally available to approach and handle things; our sensibility is symmetrically turned to the things before us. Movements in any direction are possible and ready.

The level along which multiple practical operations on accessible things are possible solicits a corresponding axis in our posture, which then aligns the visual appearances according to up and down. We enter an airplane, seat ourselves, adjust our position and movements to the practicable area about us, arrange the things we will occupy ourselves with during the flight—correspondence, a half-finished novel. The plane takes off; we look out the window, relating ourselves to the city below, putting ourselves down there with our car and our friends, trying to see our lover stretching out to us; we feel ourselves being tilted back as the floor of the plane lifts. Then the surface of earth slips back from our prehension, we can no longer make out its posts and occupations, its equipment; it becomes vague and inconsistent. We turn back to our papers, get occupied with our lunch, the cabin floor and ceiling become horizontal and the things align according to the vertical; when we glance at the window it is earth's surface that sways across it.

The level of orientation is also the level of reality; the landscape seen the first day through Stratton's eyeglasses appears not only overturned but strange and inconsistent. The aspect a person, and the room, show in a tilted mirror in the shoe store is not only disconnected from the upright things seen outside the mirror; the tilted forms in the mirror also appear less real. After an accident, the gathered crowd the victim lying prone on the ground sees does not only appear unrecognizable—caricatural faces perched over poles covered with fabric, hands flailing like tentacles—but appears as aberrations of reality. A face in a photograph turned upside down turns into patterns of color on a surface. It is when our position is lined up along the level of our most effective sensory-motor interaction with the things and the landscape that they settle into the consistency and subsistence of reality.

Even before the apparition and placing of any object, the perceptual field opens in depth as soon as our eyes open, as soon as our sensibility awakens and stirs. Even lying inertly on the bed with eyes closed, our perception is not reduced to pressures felt on our own surfaces; when no movement extends our sensibility outward to reach for things, the surfaces of our bodies cease to form a frontier between an inner space and an outer environment, leaving an undifferentiated voluminosity extending indefinitely in depth. When we sit on a bench on the edge of a lookout point over the valleys and stop locating landmarks or envisioning objectives, the planes lose their differentiation, the colors cease to congeal surfaces and become atmospheric, and we see distance extending about us. When we cease locating the sounds on the surfaces of the drums and in the throats of saxophones and trumpets, the music advances and recedes from us within a depth of musical space. When we feel, the tangible is not just what pressures our surfaces are in contact with; from the first we sense a depth of the tangible and extend our hands into it.

We do not perceive forms that overlap in the frontal plane, and then calculate the distances between them on the flat projection an eye located overhead would see. We see in a depth of reality which recedes from us. The close–far axis is not a dimension in the metric sense, extending discrete locations that are occupied by a succession of images of different sizes. It is a level our sensory-motor bodies find when they extend themselves, a range of the visible our gaze finds itself conducted across, a gradient of reality upon which our postures, gestures, and initiatives apply themselves. Down the close–far axis reliefs exposed to the adequate exploration of our powers harbor each a thickness of content and crowd back other content, and thus appear as real things.

The field extended by the up–down and close–far levels functions as a level of rest, across which movements pull at or break free from our prehensions.

The particular movements we make toward things that move or stabilize are made possible by the movement our sensory-motor powers make to maintain themselves on the levels that extend and maintain a hold. If, seated in the compartment of a train and waiting for the departure, we get absorbed in what someone is doing over in the adjacent train, then when one of the trains starts to pull out, it will be ours we experience as pulling us away from the scene or person we are holding on to with multiple interests. But if, when we entered our compartment, we settled into our seat, are now arranging our papers or starting a conversation with our fellow-passengers, then it is the adjacent train we see backing out across the side window. Later, engrossed in our reading or in conversation, it is the trees that lean over and file across the window of the train and not the car that pitches as the train mounts the hills.

As we move our movement is not an augmentation or diminution of the distance between perceived things and our bodies as perceived figures on the map on the landscape, a displacement indifferently attributable to either. When we stop before a stable thing, the rest is not the constancy of the positions of the perceived figure of our body and of that thing relative to one another on the map of the landscape, a constancy indifferently attributable to either of our relative positions or to the landscape. The levels are not seen like the lines of a diagram, and we do not look at our bodies moving across a field. The levels address our posture and are sensed in its stability and orientation. We sense the movement of our bodies become functional by advancing toward things which stabilize on or slip across those levels. The levels hold things upright and in place. Things at rest share the stability of the field. Things in movement—a leaf falling, a cart rolling down a hill—break from the levels and their movement is internal to them; they strain or break away from our hold on them.

The Coherence and Consistency of the Field

When we see we join a level of the visible, and monocular imaged, visual memories, and ideas represented by diagrams float disconnected from it. "If," Merleau-Ponty writes, "during the process of reflection, I cease to hear sounds, then suddenly become receptive to them again, they appear to me to be already there, and I pick up a thread which I had dropped but which is unbroken."[8] Once we hear something, we are henceforth open to a level of resounding reality; every subsequent sound and silence will be a crest or a trough along this level. The silence on the auditory plane is not that of the purely negative silence of the thought so absorbed in its tasks that it is closed to sensory receptivity.

The consistency and coherence of a level is not that of a continuity of real sounds succeeding real sounds and real visual patterns continually given. It is not that what is really visible maintains its visibility and becomes more clear and distinct as we look; memories and obsessive ideas can well be more consistent and sharply outlined than indecisive colors and fleeting patterns that form on the level of the visible. The consistency and coherence of a level is also not that of certain traits perceived in every audible or visual pattern. The visual is not constituted ex post facto, by an understanding that judges certain images incompatible with the rest, and therefore illusions, memories, or figments of the imagination.

A perceivable *style* is a distinctive kind of coherence. To recognize someone's gait in his successive steps that adjust to the terrain is not to identify some factor that remains the same in a series where other factors are different; it is to perceive each step displacing and departing from the form of the prior one and open to variation in turn. As we recognize a page of an author by the style, we recognize a friend by the style of his conversation, his gesturing, his way of entering into a group, of taking decisions or procrastinating. The style maintains a coherence we catch on to, which varies within a certain range without our being able to predict exactly what turn it will take. We recognize at once what does not belong to this style— sentences, postures, initiatives, and emotions that we perceive as not really his but imported from elsewhere.

Similarly, we recognize the visible, the audible, and the tangible by the way with which they diversely unfold the field. The purely negative silence of a thought closed to sensory receptivity does not have the bearing with which silences insert themselves in a conversation, a sonata, or a thunderstorm. Monocular images, mirages, and diagrams of ideas do not move with the style of the visible. The style of the tangible we recognize even in light and fleeting touches.

This coherence of the visible, this consistency of the audible level is not comprehended in a representation; it is given, we encounter it, we catch on to it. There is not a logic in the levels we perceive which our minds have the capacity to possess in advance in their formulas, but there is a style to the diverse levels which our bodies are competent to catch on to.

For our sentient and mobile bodies are fields in which each phase and each part catches on to the style of the others. In our bodies a particular movement forms neither as a simple reaction to a present stimulation nor as a pure invention; it forms as a variation of a prior movement, and it subsists as a schema that will be varied in turn. Every step inaugurates a gait; every displacement a gesture.

A posture, a gesture, and an operation form as each position and displacement of one limb of our bodies is picked up by and transposed upon the others. The buoyant style of the step initiated by the legs gets picked up by the swinging arms, by the scanning glance of the eyes. Through a transverse propagation of kinetic styles across its limbs and members our body holds together in movement. And its sensibility integrates as it advances, by not the visual qualia but something of the style of filling space that got picked on the eyes getting transferred and transposed onto the other senses.[9] Our sensitive-motile bodies are substances in which every particular position and initiative gets generalized, stylized, and engenders variants of itself.

Our bodies perceive and move in a field. In stylizing, their positions and initiatives pick up the style of the field, catch on to its levels, and follow its directives.

Levels of Coexistence

Our awakening to a field is not a succession of discrete acts that are so many spontaneous initiatives. We do not open our eyes, capture a flake of the visible, and then start again to capture another. With the first step a gait is launched; upon opening our eyes our look slides onto the misty or crisp level of the visible morning. Our awakening stylizes itself at once. The level of the visible is a directive that advances by unfolding its gradations and variations. Each move of the look varies the prior one and launches further variations. The look slides back and forth, seeing the visible from reversed and displaced directions. Each look takes form as one of a certain range of ways of looking, equivalent and interchangeable.

Our look is not a singular initiative that catches hold of a flake of the visible materializing uniquely from it, vanishing when the look shifts. It awakens in a variant of a looking that finds itself launched on an indefinite prolongation. We awaken to the level of the visible that sleep had not lost sight of; we awaken to see what we had been looking at the night before, picking up a thread that had been dropped but is unbroken. In awakening we rejoin an immemorial seeing.

When we come upon another carnal being moving along the levels of the visible and the tangible where we are moving, we sense that sentient body seeing and touching as we see and touch. We do not find ourselves in a private universe. The environment, open to indefinite variants of the seeing, touching, hearing with which we are moving in it, is from the first open to a seeing, touching, and hearing that went on before we awakened, can go on on the levels beyond what we see, touch, and hear, and will go on after we return to sleep. The ground supports and the skies are open to movements other than our own.

When our right hand touches our left, it makes contact with the level which directs the pressure and the pace of its movement that makes the pulp and rough texture thinly strewn with hairs of that left hand palpable.

But at the same time the right hand feels rising up in our left hand a movement of feeling to meet it, and feels that movement of feeling as a variant
of its own movement. When our hand takes hold of the hand of a child or
a feeble person to guide it to the handrail of the listing ship, the movement
of feeling and the diagram of force of our hand merges into that of the
child or feeble person. We feel our sensibility displace itself into the other
and to be a variant of that of the other. The other's body is not first a material mass stationed before us and exposed to our inspection and its sentient
life not a hypothesis we form in our mind to explain its movements. From
the first we find ourselves accompanied, in our movements down the levels
of the held, by other sensibilities, other sentient bodies.

We awaken to the rays of light, the expanses of the ground, the clouds
and the skies alive with a multiple, anonymous, and moving sensibility. We
can never make into a real possibility the notion that as soon as we turn
away from the tree it lapses into the inaccessible metaphysical apeiron of
the Kantian in-itself. The tree falling in the depths of the rain-forest night
is heard by innumerable animal ears of which our own are an ephemeral
variant. The deep-sea coral reefs and the Antarctic icescapes are not visions
our own eyes create; they are reliefs on levels of visibility visible in general.

Imperative Levels
The levels are not a framework of a field we find already there as soon as
we awaken. They emerge from the sensory elements, as directives that
summon. By following them, a field unfolds.

It is not with a conceptual apprehension of the system and the laws, nor
through an active collating of a discrete multiplicity of data, but with our
postural agility and tractability that we know the way the visible, the sonorous, the tangible, and the olfactory unfold and develop. This knowledge
is not a program we format moment by moment for our nervous circuitry
and musculature; it is a style of synergic mobilization of our sensibility that
is induced from the styles of the visible, the tangible, and the sonorous. For
a style is not something that we conceive but something we catch on to
and that captivates us. The continuation onward of the level summons and
guides us from beyond. The layout of a field is not a system of directions,
but of directives.

Our gaze sweeps across the environs but the views that form are not desultory; our eyes are led by the light down the paths that lead to things.
Vision is, Merleau-Ponty says, an inspired exegesis.[10] The visible reliefs and
contours separate of themselves from the perspectival deformations, the
appearances made unstable by the distances, dimmed by the intervening
medium, the reflections off other things or splashed over them by the light,
the monocular images and the mirages. The purely negative silence of a

thought closed to sensory receptivity separates from the silences inserted in a conversation, a sonata, or a thunderstorm.

The intersensorial field is not a system given ready-made and a priori intuited as the spatiotemporal framework and the system of laws which engenders its instantiations, nor is it constructed like a hypothesis out of the particularities of our own visual field and those of others. The correspondence of levels, their coherence and consistency, summon us as a directive. This directive is received not on our conceptual understanding and reason, is not first an imperative to conceive for each sensible pattern a universal and necessary category, is not first an imperative for our reason to connect up the objects we conceptually recognize with universal and necessary laws. It is received on our sensory-motor bodies, as bodies we have to anchor on the levels down which our vision, our touch, our listening move. This directive weighs on us, finalizing our perception toward perceiving a field and not a chaos of drifting and bobbling patterns. Obedience to the levels precedes and makes possible any initiative, any freedom, of sensibility and movement.

1998

The Pageantry of Things

Everything that is resounds. A voice conveys the warmth or coldness and vigor or timidity of someone speaking. The tolling parades the substance of the cathedral bell, the creaking materializes the dry wood of the stairs in the amorphous night, the crackling delineates the hard grains of the hail. But sounds also dematerialize the substance of the things they resounded and extend their own patterns, their pulse, rumble, melody, or din over the space vacated. They drift off things and link up with one another, and we hear a Morse code or jazz of sounds ricocheting in the free space.

Things do not only show their obstinate occupancy of their own places and their contours to our surveying look and manipulating hands. They project halos over themselves and cast shadows on other things. They scatter reflections in mirrors and in eyes and in water. The water of the garden pool projects shimmering waves on the screen of cypresses behind it. The dome of the Taj Mahal refracts its light upon the faces of the crowds in the dusty streets. From millions of light-years away, stars cast their dancing lights on mountain lakes.

The things that are really stabilized as things in our environment, the things possessed, brought into the realm of the home, he at rest there, substances kept in reserve. But the furnishings of our home also spread about themselves auras and patinas, shadows and densities. When we sink back into our wicker chair as it whispers again marshland murmurs, the patterns of the room vibrate off the layout and shapes of appliances, cabinets, and lamps.

The colors of a face do not only outline the surfaces and carpentry of that face, but interact with one another in a swarthy, lustrous, ethereal, or ardent complexion. At high noon the colors of the forest below disengage from the contours of the leaves and the trees into a billowing of dense green fog.

The professor is occupied in reading the explanations he has prepared to communicate to the students in the room. But the way he holds his lecture papers, his gestures, his complexion, the shape of his skull and the fall of his hair separate from this professorial presence, and form a foppish, buffoonish, or loutish physiognomy. The instructor disappears, as though he had left the room, leaving there only his trappings and paraphernalia.

A rabbit nibbling its way across the garden doubles up in the image of a child or a dwarf. People who are pursuing their tasks look like fidgety woodchucks scurrying about. The walls of a house double up into a facade whose windows are eyes and whose door is a mouth. The trees extending their bare branches against the wintry sky metamorphose into hands scratching and gesticulating fretfully. The hills rise out of the plain in the voluptuous twilight as breasts of a landscape prone in a swoon or in sleep.

These appearances are not transitional appearances that lead to the real properties of the things and vanish when they appear. They are not true and are not false appearances either. They do not function as signs relaying the gaze to the things themselves. They do not have that transparency; they thicken, materialize for themselves. The rhythm and musicality of their facades, shadows, reflections, and auras obscure our view into the position and composition of things which are uncovered, discovered, and grasped in action.

It is not that things barely show themselves, behind illusory appearances fabricated by our subjectivity; it is that things are exorbitantly exhibitionist. The landscape resounds; facades, caricatures, halos, shadows dance across it. Under the sunlight extends the pageantry of things. The twilight does not put an end to their histrionics. In the heart of the night the pulse of the night summons still their ghosts.

These apparitions are pushed aside when we grasp the appearances of things in concepts. To grasp hold of a hammer is already to comprehend it; it is to close our hand around its essence as an implement that can direct and concentrate force, and it is already to comprehensively hold in view a field encompassing nails, shingles, and boards. It is through action that we comprehend.

When we grasp things and fix their natures in concepts, these concepts offer the succession of things to our powers and connect up with other concepts in a dialectic. Yet when we set out to grasp things in rigorous and lucid concepts, we find those very concepts engendering images that are not images of their referents. Allusions, equivocations, evocations, evasions, insinuations refract off their crystal shapes and bewitch the very mind that cut those shapes.[1]

When we approach a lawn mower, the visible profile we see in the corner of the garage leads us to the handle side, the blade side, and the underside; it unfolds a time of progressive development and exposure. When we see its brown wood handle, we see how the wood was brown and will be brown. The facades, caricatures, projections, and reflections of things double up the linear and progressive time of action with a time of fate. The shadow or reflection of the chair we see in the window endures in a present without possibilities, not pregnant with another, future side or force. When we look at the face speaking and see the professor teaching, we see the expression and form of that face evolving in the elaboration of sentences and paragraphs. But when we see instead the double, the caricatural form, the foppish or buffoonish or loutish physiognomy, it appears immobilized in its fate.

These apparitions exist in a rhythm or a tempo rather than in a time with past, present, and future. A tempo keeps reproducing the Morse code of the dripping faucet. A pulse of the forest links up the splotches of light and shadows. They do not evolve or continue of themselves nor cause one another; their rhythm or their tempo commands them like a predestination.

The rabbit nibbling its way through the garden doubles up into an image of a child or dwarfish human not because our mind actively selects images and links them up, but because our mind is captivated by, caught up in a pulse that collects and reproduces sounds and apparitions. We are not grasping the carpentry of things in their appearances nor subjectively fabricating images of them, but find ourselves caught up in their images, their shadows, their reflections, halos, the harmonics of their colors, the rhythms of their forms. The facades, caricatures, projections, and reflections of things are interesting; they do not outline something of practical interest, but involve us in themselves. We find ourselves among them and carried on by them into a time of fate.

This is a distinct state of anonymous consciousness, different from habits, reflexes, and instinct. When we walk or dance to music, the movement is not automatic and unconscious; consciousness is acute, but without intentions or initiatives. We no longer direct our attention. We follow the music anonymously, like and with anyone who listens to it.

Seated in a train, we look out of the window, actively seeking to identify things, landmarks, towns, but soon the color and forms of the mountains disengage from the map of the landscape and distract us and our hearing gets enmeshed in the beat of the train wheels turning on the rails. Our gaze no longer probes and surveys on its own initiative, but follows the rhythm of trees and hills. Walking through the forest, the shadows link up in a fibrillation which lifts our eyes from the substance of the trees and underbrush and from the diagram of our gait and the shape of our body image. We become the splotches of sunlit flesh among the flakes of sunlit leaves. We become our shadow moving among the moving shadows of the forest. The flight of our gaze takes its place in the promenade of the clouds in a space without limits and without tasks.

The density and tempo of noninstrumental apparitions brings us the irresponsibility that charms as nonchalance and grace. It frees us from initiative. We do not continually push our way through implements and obstacles; we take refuge in the beat and melody of apparitions. We drop out of the progressive time of initiatives, summoned to the time of fate.

1998

The Weight of Reality

Having arrived on a night flight, I slept late and did not get to Giza until almost noon. Tourists were climbing into air-conditioned buses to be taken to air-conditioned restaurants for the next couple of hours. The local guides were gathering in the shade of the pyramids to siesta. I headed for the Great Pyramid of Khufu. Looming massive in the cloudless white sky, thousands, millions of huge stone blocks. All the pictures had not conveyed, indeed had excluded, the sense of mass and weight that now stopped me. Several guides saw me and came after me; I gave them thirty pounds each—some five U.S. dollars—to not guide me. I crawled up the tunnel to the tomb room. There was a fluorescent bulb on either side spreading a cold light across walls and ceiling. In the middle the now empty sarcophagus of the pharaoh. I paced the room and found it is some thirty-five feet long, seventeen feet wide; the ceiling was about twenty feet high, consisting of nine flat stone slabs. I intoned a mantra that the stone walls resounded. There was nothing for the eyes to scrutinize; they drifted in the stillness. The sense of the enormous weight of stone above this room pressed down on me. Moving from one side to the other, I felt it everywhere in the tomb room. I forced myself to think of the five thousand years that this hollow had endured, think that the nine stone slabs of the ceiling had held back the weight of the thousands of stones above them. But the weight of the stones continued to fill my mind and crushed any movements of thought about what this tomb room was, who this pharaoh was, how the pyramid was built. I was in a space without past or future, in a present that did not pass, a dead time. I lay on the floor next to the empty sarcophagus of the pharaoh.

I heard a sound in the tunnel; someone was coming. I got up and left the room. On the way down I crossed a bearded foreigner on the way, a lone backpacker. Outside I thought to look at my watch: I had been inside two hours. The guides were still dozing in the shadow of the pyramid. My eyes were dazzled by the sun and saw only the shadows and the sands rolling in dunes unto the horizon. Shadows cast by the pyramids but that did not weigh upon the ground, sands made of stone but drifting in the weak but steady wind.

Astronauts in a state of weightlessness observe the stars in outer space and planet Earth rotating in the void. When we read about the universe as physics and chemistry, electromagnetism and astronomy represent it, it gives us a strange sense of weightlessness; it is a representation where all things, and our bodies, are clouds of infinitesimal energy units in frantic motion.

Things in our environment that we pick up, throw, or shove have weight. This weight is not the same as the force of a mass pressing upon another mass that science measures and conceptualizes as gravity. The weight of a crystal bowl is not simply pressure on the elasticity of our muscles and limbs; it is felt in our sensibility. The feeling is a qualitative sensation not localized in the muscles and tendons actually being stretched. The whole body feels the weight of things; a gallon of cider is felt to have the same weight when lifted with one hand or with both, with a foot, and when laid on one's back. A rock is felt to have the same weight when lifted under water in a pond and when held in the air. The weight is felt to be not in the body that feels it but in the crystal bowl, the armchair.

Weight is felt in the sensibility and even in the mind. The weight of a backpack encumbers our mind that is working out a plan for the rest of the day or rehearsing what we will say to our lover with whom we have had a serious quarrel.

The weight of a book or an armchair lifted is not measured in units, pounds, or kilograms; "too heavy" is beyond what the body can hold, "very light" is a weight that the body barely registers. Yet what is beyond what the body can hold is perceived as having weight, roughly gauged and compared—the weight of the rocks in the Ryōan-ji Garden in Kyoto, of the pillars of Stonehenge, of a fallen sequoia.

In looking at things we see successive surfaces of things; in touching things we feel only stretches of them across moments of time. But the weight of a chainsaw, of a bag full of books is everywhere, unsegmented, in them. The sense of weight is a sense of the whole thing, which holds itself together and separate, disconnected from other things. Unarticulated, without internal structure, cohesive without coherence, the weight of things is not grasped and appropriated in concepts, is opaque and alien. The hands that hold the weight of a statue or a big dictionary are sense organs that do not apprehend the sense—meaning and direction—of things; they are receptive of, affected by the opacity of the substance of things. They are sense organs that are not considering but pondering.

We deal with the weight of things. Hands drop and toss, arms heave and hurl. They make things projectiles and are projectiles.

Things weigh in their settings. A truck abandoned in the weeds sinks into the ground. We have to go down steps to enter the Santísima Church in Mexico City; it has sunk more than nine feet since it was built. During the last Ice Age, beginning a hundred and ten thousand years ago, Scandinavia was covered with ice up to three kilometers deep; its weight pushed the landmass down into earth's fluid mantle. Since the end of the glacial period ten thousand years ago, the Scandinavian landmass has risen 275 meters—900 feet. The postglacial isostatic rebound, the geologists call it.

The weight of things, the import of things. We have a primary sense of importance; in everything we do to perceive is to perceive the important and the accessory or irrelevant. We distinguish between what is important for us and also what is important for an industry, an institution, a culture, or an ecosystem and what is simply *important,* that whose importance is perceived in it, whose importance is intrinsic. Importance of the Pyramids of the Sun and of the Moon at Teotihuacán, whose forms repeat that of the mountains all about them, linking the continental plate and the luminaries of outer space. Importance of the great ruby-red rock Uluru that commands the vast deserts of central Australia as the heart of the continent. Importance of a wilderness, of a herd of elk. Nonsignifying, density in itself, there is importance in weight, weight is in importance.

Reality extends from the weighty unto the weightless. Trompe l'oeil domes, walls, and pillars of baroque churches, mosaics, gilding, paint—they hide or deny the substance of things and have little weight themselves. A house where the walls are covered with paisley wallpaper, the floors and furniture veneered, the flowers artificial and the dishware plastic appears insubstantial and the inhabitants insubstantial.

Leaves fluttering in the air, feathers, dandelion fluff—we see forms designed in the emptiness, weight diminished to almost imperceptible in them.

Things whose weight appears only as an evanescent allusion—spray, vapors, mists, haze.

Reflections, halos, shadows, glows, glimmers, sparkles exist in the free spaces of the world of weighty things. They delineate the contours of things for us and lead us down paths and to horizons. Reflections, shadows, halos, will-o'-the-wisps captivate the eyes and keep us absorbed in the environment beyond the paths, implements and obstacles, and objectives to which our needs and practical interests attach us. They are glories and menaces that emanate off things.

"Ultra-things" Henri Wallon called beings we cannot reach, whose weight we cannot gauge: the moon that follows us wherever we go on the paths of the world, the clouds, the sun, the stars.[1] The aurora borealis, neither hovering over Earth as the clouds do not in the outer spaces of the stars, rippling in some fourth dimension. The Milky Way seen in the night sky, within which all the weighty things on Earth, the other planets, the sun, and the planets about other suns are assembled.

Looking, Martin Heidegger says, is on the move, traveling down paths, surveying implements and obstacles, envisioning objectives, taking them as resources that serve for further objectives, without end. Viewing each thing in its practical context, perception is comprehensive, already understanding. Conceptual understanding envisions things in series and in classes, in spatiotemporal coordinates and in causal relations. Understanding not standing under things is, Heidegger says, in ecstatic movement, advancing, searching, circumnavigating, detouring, manipulating, assembling. Restlessness of spirit.

There is also the understanding that comes with dwelling long with things. A villager in Bali carving wood sculptures. A hiker who camps and ponders the cliff above him as evening falls. An anthropologist participant-observer lives six months, two years in a rural village. A marine biologist over twenty years has recorded the songs of whales in the five oceans. The identifying, calculating, reasoning knowledge exists to serve our experience with things, dwelling with them, pondering them.

Words are not only units of a code, designating concepts; they have pitch, attack, timbre, volume, and duration. They are ponderous, conveying the weight of things, heavy, weighing down things, or light, lightening, trivializing.

The Weight of the World

For objects to take form about us, Immanuel Kant argued, we must first have an intuition of space and time—unlimited space, as conceptualized in the first science, geometry; infinite time. Martin Heidegger argued instead that the space in which we uncover and discover paths, implements, obstacles, and objectives is opened and extended with them. It is a practicable layout, a perceived clearing with depths and horizons of closure. In late writings he says that this clearing opens as skies with sun and night, wind and rain, winter and summer over the closure of earth; opens with movements both directed by the harbingers of goodness, of the divinities, and destined to the abyss of death.[2]

But if our practical movements blaze paths into the clearing, we do not constitute, project, or call up the presence of the world. We find ourselves destined for the world, cast into it. In its undifferentiated expanse the world from the first affects us, weighs on us. Emotions are affected by the lures and menaces of particular things and situations, but moods, Heidegger explains, are ways we are affected by the subsistence of the world as an undifferentiated whole. Sparkling with possibilities it energizes us and liberates us; a layout of undifferentiated equivalence it affects us with boredom; its density and opaqueness oppress us. For Heidegger the clearing of space opens before our practical movements in a world that from the first weighs on us in moods.

But the clearing in which we perceive things is not just, as Heidegger says, a spread of possibility and impossibility, and it is not empty; it is filled with light, heat or cold, humidity or aridity. They are elements, not things, Emmanuel Levinas wrote; they are without surfaces, are qualities without substances, fathomless depths. They are not perceived but given in a sensuous sensibility that finds itself immersed in them, moves in involution into them, and that vibrates upon itself in enjoyment.[3] There is also involution in gloom, which prolongs itself in resignation and finally in morose enjoyment.

Although the elements are formless, they have weight. Air, heat and cold, humidity and aridity lighten or weigh down things. Light may have a light touch that illuminates the weight of things and may also lift the weight of things, such that they float in the radiance of light. Darkness lifts the demands and resistance off things. Things dissolve in the density of darkness that oppresses and immobilizes us.

The ground upon which light, darkness, air, heat, cold, humidity, and aridity extend is not observed as things are observed. It is there as a surface over an unarticulated depth, a density supporting the weight of all things in their places. Its supporting weight rises in our postures and positions; we feel it and rely on it in our advances and manipulations.

When in fatigue the weight of our bodies inclines us to rest and sleep, we rest on the repose of the ground. We break our intentional and practical bonds with things, we abandon diagrams of movement and posture, we give ourselves over to the support of the ground that will support the practical layout without us. We confide our restless body to the bed and the pillow. We give over the weight of our cares and of our body to the depth of the ground.

The Weight of Life

We see the mass of our palms, stomach, thighs; we feel our tongue, cheeks, earlobe, eyes, buttocks. We feel the bulk of our bodies constricted on a narrow bed, an airplane seat, trapped in a tiny studio apartment. We stroke the firmness and give of our muscles, we feel the bones of our fingers, our elbows, knees, ribs, back. We feel the weight of our bodies in running and in high jumping and in sitting and resting.

The things we lift and hold are as substantial as we are and we feel we have weight as they do. We feel the give of the boards, the sand, or the forest leaves as we walk. We hold things down, crush them. Our initiatives leave their weight on things, on the world.

As we use our body parts as sense organs, we feel their weight. To perceive the elasticity or rigidity of things we have to push against them. To feel the contours and grain of things we have to not weigh hard on them but press lightly across them.

Clumsiness is the movements of the body encumbered by its weight. Energy and skill counter the weight of the body, switch it into drive and force. Graceful positions and movements maintain the weight of the body in balance and dynamic equilibrium. Dance movements reach for and grasp nothing, are movements that are going nowhere, absolute movements.

Fatigue is the sense of inner resistance to our initiatives and movements. We feel our bodies lagging behind the trajectories of movement we throw forth. Movements are no longer activated by a rhythm that once launched prolongs itself; each step, each manipulation has to be initiated anew.

We feel the weight of an arm lying across our belly, of legs lying one on the other. The dead weight of a swollen leg, of an arm whose nerves have been cut. Weight of the bored, depressed, catatonic body.

We support our bodies on guardrails, against walls, on the bodies of friends. Immersion in water lifts the weight of the body. To sit or lie down is to let the weight of our body be received in the weight of the ground.

Our bodies whose weight smashes cardboard boxes and small ecosystems in the prairie can be crushed by the press of crowds, by buildings shaken in earthquakes or bombed.

An initiative connects with, responds to a goal still in the future. It also retains, responds to its starting point and past phases. They supply and maintain the direction and the momentum of the movement. Focusing the impulses and energies of our body, narrowing them down, the past phases weigh on the free leap of the initiative.

Our past initiatives attained or aborted are definitively inscribed in the past, weighing on the world, materialized. They also weigh on the direction and moment of an initiative we take. As we advance in time we are weighed down by our very commencements, initiatives, freedom. We feel the increasing effort required to break and commence anew, the increasing fatigue. This sense of being encumbered with the weight of all our initiatives is the inner experience of aging. It is visible in wrinkles and scars, materialization. In aging we sense our body turning into the immobility and weight of a corpse.

We are moved by the surprise, elation, hope, pride, anxieties, grief of others. Our bodies explore others, touching them lightly. Others are not only opaque in that they can conceal their thoughts and mask their intentions; they are also opaque in their weight.

A handshake in greeting is not simply a gesture signifying recognition, and the handshake after a decision not simply a gesture that marks agreement and commitment. The handshake grasps the force of another's body, supports its weight and is supported by it.

The repetitive, aimless movements of caresses disconnect the instrumental intentions of the beloved's body from their objectives and awaken sensitivity in the substance of that body, such that that body is absorbed in itself. While affecting the beloved's body with one's pressure, warmth, and movement, the lover is affected by them, exciting pleasure within. The lover's hands roll the beloved's body and lift the head. The lover's body loses its posture and diagrams of movement; its arms and legs settle into their weight. Love-making, which is nonsignifying, movements without objective, vocalizations turning into nonsense, laughter, signs, and moans, nonetheless weighs on the lovers and in their world as the most serious practical initiatives do not.

Before the disconsolate grief of someone, we embrace him or her, hold tight, supporting a body whose initiatives are helpless, sinking. Unable to restore a loss, we offer the support of our body to the weight of grief.

When we can do nothing for and promise nothing to an injured or dying person, we lay our hand in his or her hand in a touch of consolation. The injured or dying person feels the weight of that hand but receives no message. With that touch we join the injured or dying person sinking into the weight of his body, in threatened or advancing materialization.

The weight of sleeping children we carry, of bodies wounded, fainted, in a coma, dead.

Bodies push against one another, push off one another, destabilize one another. Fights, violence, torture violate the space and integrity of the other and are strivings to know the other, his or her intentions, sense of self and of honor, powers. The dispute settles on the bodies of the combatants, on their fatigue and wounds, on the world. Verbal disputes and combat also leave wounds. Words shock, strike, jab, bite, pick on, harass, lacerate our bodies.

Bodies set in factories, their force converted into profit. Bodies massed in workshops, in the street, in firing lines. Bodies thrown onto trucks, into mass graves.

Our bodies are weighted down with raiment and adornments. Men and women are covered with furs and jewelry. In Myanmar Kayan Padaung women wind up to twenty kilos of bronze coils about their necks.

Bodies of the dead and also of the living are cast in bronze and stone. In public places heroic and erotic statues holding positions, indicating directions are set up as witnesses of decisive events and guides to hold and direct our lives. Statues of bodies gesticulate, leap, and soar, overcoming weight and held in the weight of bronze and marble. Powerful forces and spirits are materialized in idols and totems. The aspiring and the ecstatic, the beautiful and the ideal are given weight.

2012

Metaphysical Habitats

A Sea Change in Modern Culture

In 1922 Dr. Hans Prinzhorn published *Bildnerei der Geisteskranken*—translated into English as *Artistry of the Mentally Ill*[1]—in which he reproduced and analyzed 187 from the more than five thousand paintings, drawings, and carvings he had collected from insane asylums in and around Heidelberg and farther afield, mostly from patients diagnosed as schizophrenic. While psychiatrists before him had occasionally published paintings and drawings of their patients, analyzing them for purposes of psychiatric diagnosis, Prinzhorn found that he could not identify the mental disorders of inmates from the types of images they made. Prinzhorn had earned a doctorate in art history before becoming a psychiatrist; in his study of the works that he had collected he identified six basic drives that give rise to image making: an expressive urge, the urge to play, an ornamental urge, an ordering tendency, a tendency to imitate, and the need for symbols. These, he noted, are the very drives at work in professional artists. Prinzhorn gave predominant place in his book to ten masters, whose works, in expressive power and draftsmanship, he judged to be on the same rank as those whom society recognizes as master artists.

Artists such as expressionists Paul Klee and Alfred Kubin and surrealists André Breton and Max Ernst looked upon the works reproduced in Prinzhorn's book with awe and admiration; Paul Éluard called it "the most beautiful book of images there is." They began at once to incorporate elements of this asylum art into their work. Jean Dubuffet collected a large number of works of the insane and of children, and deliberately set out to paint as the insane do. Wassily Kandinsky, Enrico Baj, and Karel Appel set out to paint like children; Pierre Alechinsky, Keith Haring, and

Jean-Michel Basquiat even set out to paint with children. Subsequent contemporary professional art, from the Blue Rider group in Germany to Jackson Pollock, derives more from asylum art than from the Academy.

The discovery of asylum art empowered the search for art among uneducated or naive painters and carvers in Europe, among spiritualists, seers, and mediums, then in prisons (several of Prinzhorn's insane masters had committed crimes),[2] in children's drawings, in primitive or tribal works, African and Oceanic artifacts and ritual objects hitherto exhibited only in ethnographic museums, and in prehistoric and aboriginal rock and cave paintings. Art was recognized in all this "cultural production."

With the discovery of artwork among all these marginal peoples, there arose a new claim to their dignity and a demand for their social recognition. Schizophrenics are not simply deranged individuals who have to be treated by experts or cared for if incurable; they possess positive powers, even creative powers of value to society, perhaps as a result of their disturbed mental condition. "Primitive" or tribal peoples are not simply backward and retarded; their mental and craft productions may well be important and valuable for modern society. Children are not merely potential adults; the child's world has its own structures and its own visions and values that adults may well seek to recover.

The Original Authenticity

The discovery of art in insane asylums in Europe then had a quite different effect from the earlier discovery of art in China and Japan or among the Maya of Central America. What was recognized as art in those far-off lands was, like earlier European art, in the service of religious ideals and had long been crafted according to aesthetic canons. It was produced by trained specialists, on noble materials, and with perfection of finish. Those works could then enter the museums of modern Europe as works of high culture.

The works discovered in insane asylums sparked a radical contestation of high culture. The champions of this art denounced the fine-arts academies and the professional artists for producing works that, though they no longer illustrated religious stories and ideals, nonetheless promoted the reigning values and pretensions of the Western ruling elite. Artists, who had lost the patronage of the courts, had become cunning flatterers of the moneyed bourgeoisie. How much flattery went into portraits, into landscapes—how much falseness! In the Academy aspiring artists studied the forms and compositions with which society and nature had been depicted in fine art. But the very recipes derived from the old masters render the works of fine art lifeless. Dubuffet called the works he collected and championed *art brut*—"raw art," contrasted with the cooked, overcooked, cooked-up art of galleries, museums, and intellectuals. His word "brut" also evokes "champagne brut"—Dubuffet had managed a wine business—unsweetened, unsugared art. Authentic art is art not constrained by the canons of the Academy and dictated by the ideas and taste of the cultivated public. Authentic art issues from individuals who are authentic—who are one with their own fundamental and original forces and drives.

If high culture, instead of elevating human life to sublime possibilities, in fact functions to elevate pretense, status, egoism, and greed, the question was whether the primitive state of humankind did not contain resources and energies that high culture weakened and repressed. Energy, feeling, life, creativity would issue from a return to the origins—to primitives, to children, and to the insane, who were seen as still or permanently divested of reason.

Sigmund Freud had compared neurotics with children, and primitives with both, and set out to systematically exhibit repressed infantile drives in neurotic behavior patterns and identify the mental traits of children and neurotics in the mythical omnipotence of thought and belief in magic that are characteristic of primitives. Prinzhorn and the professional artists who acclaimed his book found, however, the fundamental urges that produce art strong in the insane, children, and "primitives," and they declared that these urges produced works of exceptional force because the insane, children, and "primitives" are not constrained by the canons and constraints of high culture and by adult reason.

The artists and critics who championed this work promoted an exalted conception of the artist: artists are creators of new visions, prophets and seers. Their opposites are not the untrained and uncultured, but professionals who work according to received canons of taste and enshrine in their works the received values of society: they are the real philistines. Artists are outsiders, heretics, iconoclasts, revolutionaries. Whereas artists in India, China, and Europe had worked on traditional themes with compositions and styles recognized and transmitted by aesthetic canons, now originality became everything: without originality there is no art. It was to be expected that the more original the work, the more readily it would shock the sensibilities of the general public. Shock value alone—depicting normal values in scatological or perverse guise—does not mean that a work reveals a new vision, but works that are shocking enjoy a favorable first reception among the true artists.

Note that art brut was separated from European folk art, which had also its admirers, historians, and collectors, because folk art is, even more than academic art, governed as to its subject matter, methods of presentation, materials, and styles by tradition. The original wellsprings of creativity would not be found there.

The insane artist, in his or her isolation from culture, is authentic; his or her vision comes from within. The suspension of the constraints of society and reason in him delivers him over to his instincts and visions. The more intense the feelings, the stronger the work. Dubuffet declared: "Madness lightens the man, gives him wings, and promotes clairvoyance."[3] "Insanity is the great art."[4] It was to be expected that originality in the work of these solitary visionaries would be reflected in their behavior—the more original their talent the more original or eccentric their behavior—and it was to be expected that they would be pariahs in society. The champions of their work were disdainful of the psychiatric classifications and stigmatizations of people who exhibit unsocialized forms of behavior; they tended to put psychiatrists and insane asylums in the same camp as the Spanish Inquisition. "We who love them," Paul Éluard wrote, "understand that the insane refuse to be cured.... We know well that it is we who are locked up when the asylum door is shut: the prison is outside the asylum, liberty is to be found inside."[5]

What the champions of the art of the insane, children, and "primitives" did retain from Freud was the notion of the unconscious. The creative source of art was now no longer the Muses, sublime or spiritual forces to which the artist ecstatically opens in inspiration; it is instead the unconscious stock of drives and energies with which humans are originally endowed. Art is expressive, expressive of what the artist finds within himself. Or rather, the artist does not "find"—discover and use—these unconscious forces and urges, but releases them with neither constraint nor judgment. But whereas Freud and also Jung conceived the unconscious as impersonal, here the unconscious was seen to be radically individual. It was culture that imposed common traits on individuals—common language, habitual forms of behavior conformed to the standardized tasks that society imposes, and sentiments and emotional reactions conformed to those tasks.

The attention to the art of children was motivated by, and confirmed, the conviction that the fundamental urges identified by Prinzhorn were part of human nature and found in everyone. Ananda Coomeraswamy said, "The artist is not a special kind of man; every man is a special kind of artist."[6]

Prinzhorn, in identifying the six urges in human nature that are at work in image making, had suggested that the image making of the insane gives access to understanding art in general; their work illuminates with exceptional clarity the conditions governing the genesis of artistic activity in humans. The professional artists who incorporated features of art brut into their work or, like Dubuffet, deliberately sought to paint like the insane, sought to put themselves into the mental and environmental conditions in which the insane, prisoners, children, or mediums worked, without becoming insane or being incarcerated. Salvador Dalí declared: "The sole difference between myself and a madman is the fact that I am not mad."[7] The surrealists took from mediums the practice of automatic writing and painted their dreams and nightmares. Paul Klee's work was especially close to the art of children, but he recognized that he worked with dexterity, skills, and experience with media that children do not have. It was through a savant procedure of identifying and eliminating features canonized by cultured taste that he worked.

Distinguishing Characteristics of Art Brut

What was so striking about the works Prinzhorn reproduced in his book that led professional artists to proclaim it "the most beautiful book of images there is"? How did Prinzhorn, who had first been trained as an art historian, identify ten masters from among all the images he had collected? What stood out was the originality and the powerful expressivity of the works. Although they had no art education, these individuals had through long and obsessive application come upon techniques and styles that gave their works both economy and maximum expressiveness. Some of them became extraordinary draftsmen, drawing out complex fractal geometries and gothic architectural constructions with surety.

Although it was the news that art, real art, pure art was to be found in insane asylums that was responsible for the far-reaching effect of his book, Prinzhorn did not title his book *Artistry,* but *Bildnerei—Image Making—of the Mentally Ill.* These insane image makers, for the most part schizophrenics, were oblivious of the whole system of academies, galleries, museums, collectors, critics, and intellectuals that separates art from mere craft or simple making. The staff of the asylums in which they were incarcerated viewed the drawings they made, often on paper bags or toilet paper, and the figures they shaped out of chewed bread as of no interest and cleared them out and destroyed them at the end of the day. Most of the works of those Prinzhorn identified as his ten master image makers had been destroyed. And indeed the makers of these images did not make them as art. Nor do prisoners, spiritualists, children—nor indeed do tribal peoples, whose productions were classified in ethnological museums as ritual objects, ceremonial paraphernalia, magical implements. John M. MacGregor explains:

> It is of crucial importance to understand that the motivation underlying the production of these powerful objects or images almost invariably has *nothing* to do with "art." These "things" are the product of an obsessional involvement with images in the service of extremely unusual preoccupations and ideas. Let me give some examples:

- Maps, of planets or worlds they have visited, and which they now wish to present in diagrams or images;
- Religious icons, but of private religions having little to do with any religion we may be familiar with;
- Embodiments of repressed but explosive sexuality, made for sexual reasons, not as art;
- Cosmological diagrams, illustrations of theories of the origin of this, or another alternate universe;
- Medical illustrations of bizarre biological and anatomical concerns;
- Influencing machines, or perpetual motion machines, depicted as plans (or actually built), or magical weapons for defense against imagined enemies;
- Spirit depictions of the "other side," inspired visions sent by the departed, or by God....

Commonly, there is no desire to share these things with anyone, and the images are kept secret, or are hidden. This is an art called into being in a desperate attempt to map or to depict unexplored, and occasionally frighteningly unfamiliar, aspects of human reality. Frequently, examination of the entire body of work of a single artist reveals an ongoing involvement with the creation of an alternate reality, another universe, conceived in encyclopedic detail.[8]

When, in 1995, a museum of art brut was opened in Baltimore, it was consequently named American Visionary Art Museum.

Although critics have not been able to identify distinctive features—of subject matter, materials, forms, colors, techniques, or style—of art brut as opposed to the art of the art world, several traits are quite common. There is a predominance of figures in two dimensions, and an absence of the representation of depth through the use of perspective—figures are not graded in scale to represent their positions in depth. There is also a tendency to completely fill up all the space. The image is saturated; however terrifying the figures, the terror and the anxiety are all there, completely laid out. Frequently an inmate spends years on the same theme, filling it out more and more completely. The aim is not "art," is not perfecting the depiction of an object, but materializing a personal environment, where the prosaic common environment of ordinary people is blocked out.

Critics have also noted that most often faces are presented in frontal view, their sides symmetrical, features inexpressive, stark and stereotyped, and eyes open wide as though staring at the viewer. This is also common in the carved figures, statues, and masks of African or Oceanic tribal art. In everyday life, facial expressions give us clues about the thoughts or mood of the one we encounter. In these works the face is staring directly into our eyes, revealing nothing of what he or she sees, yet holding us from surveying our environment and him or her on our own, making us aware of another environment that is holding these eyes transfixed. Roger Cardinal suggests that we think of the everyday experience of bumping into someone in a doorway. Abruptly halted, we gaze a little longer than decorum permits into the eyes of a stranger. At this moment the environment in which we were making our way is suspended, and we become aware that the other sees something different, which we become aware of only through an emotional shock.[9] The frontal staring faces that these works so often depict ensnare our gaze and turn us to a habitat unknown by us and alien to us.

Georges Bataille opposed forces in us concerned with survival and socialization, utilitarian drives issuing out of our needs and wants, with excess forces produced by the strong and healthy organism that have to be discharged, discharged without recompense. Artists were seen as devoting themselves to discharging their creative forces in works without utilitarian function, gratuitous, ends in themselves. This would be true only in the measure that art quite recently was disengaged from religious, political, social, and ethnic causes and enterprises. The champions of art brut exposed as hypocritical the professionals who produce high art: they channel the fundamental urges that give rise to making images into making images for others; they put these urges at the service of profit, prestige, celebrity. The insane, prisoners, and mediums and spiritualists who make art brut have, out of desperation, put those six fundamental urges that produce images at the service of visualizing, materializing a metaphysical habitat for themselves.

Recognizing, and Endangering, Authenticity

Prinzhorn wished to protect the image making of the asylum from being dismissed as the delirium of the mad by demonstrating that the fundamental urges that give rise to their image making are identical to those that drive professional artists. The urgency of this was evident from the start; as soon as the works of the insane were published and declared to be artworks by avant-garde professional artists, the defenders of the Academy mocked those works as delirious expressions of deranged individuals. The time was advancing rapidly when their work will be put in Nazi exhibitions of degenerate art and publicly burnt. Most of the asylum masters Prinzhorn had identified disappeared during this time and were presumably included in the Nazi program to liquidate the incurably insane.

What the champions of art brut discovered in asylums was authenticity, not only conceived negatively as works free from the pretense, greed, and ambition that falsify the professional art of high culture but also conceived positively as powerfully expressive of individual obsessions and visions, surging up from the positive forces of a distinctively individual unconscious.

It was at once realized that recognizing these works as art put this authenticity in danger. They would enter exhibitions, galleries, museums; amateurs would collect them; they would acquire monetary value and their makers fame; their makers would enter into the social stratum of cultural producers. All this could only put their authenticity in danger. Prinzhorn, who identified ten master image makers in the asylums in and around Heidelberg, did not reveal their names and attached pseudonyms of his contrivance to their works. Dubuffet set out to acquire thousands of works from authentics and eventually housed them in an institution in Lausanne, Switzerland, set up as an antimuseum. They would be thus kept outside of commerce. And outside of the art world; they would not be lent for exhibitions in art museums elsewhere. Alain Bourbonnais purchased hundreds of art brut sculptures from galleries and exhibitions and put them in farm buildings he had acquired far from any cultural centers.

Prinzhorn had concealed the names and biographies of the master image makers. But if these works were seen to emerge from the individual forces of the unconscious and owe their exceptionally strong expressive quality to the force of those compulsions, separating them from the whole of the maker's biography could only be artificial; these same forces must have also shaped the maker's conceptions, emotions, and actions, releasing them without the constraints of social conformisms. Works that were done for or in sexual excitement surely could not be separated from the maker's biography, since so much of society's mental and physical energies have gone into regulating the drives of sexuality. Adolf Wölfli, a schizophrenic semiliterate peasant who has been recognized as among the greatest of the asylum artists, had been incarcerated as criminally insane after repeated sexual assaults on very young children.

Dubuffet recognized the urgency of protecting the works of art brut from the art market. But declaring them to be artworks, as did professional artists who incorporated features of asylum art into their work, was to bring the art world to them. Professional artists like Max Ernst and Arnulf Rainer set out to acquire their personal collections of these works, as Picasso and Matisse had collected African and Oceanic masks and fetishes. If the works of Klee and Kandinsky were to acquire ever-higher prices in the art market, should not the works that inspired them also acquire such monetary value?

Before long the names of the masters in the asylum were revealed. Before long it was acknowledged that the recognition awarded to them outside should not be hidden from them, and that they should receive their just share of the big money publishers, collectors, and galleries were garnering from their works. As this happened, the makers began to react to the appreciation of their works, to the selections of collectors, and began to draw, paint, and carve in response to them. Dubuffet began to separate the genuinely authentic works from these subsequent works adulterated by the tastes of the cultured.

It is an obvious task, not yet undertaken, to systematically itemize the nature of these adulterations—to identify what conscious calculation does to the unconscious drives seeking to materialize metaphysical habitats, identify just what culture does to the six basic drives that give rise to image making. It is indeed surprising that professors of aesthetics, which from its beginning separated fine art from craft, decoration, mere illustration, and the designing of commercial lures, have not been busy at this task.

Disintegration of the Ideology Involved in the Recognition of Art Brut

The classical Freudian equation of neurotics with children and with primitives came into disrepute. Primitive art had been seen as primitive in that it had not gone through the European Renaissance discovery and incorporation of perspective and the succession of materials and technologies—fresco, ceramic glazing, oil painting on canvas—and the codification of the canons of taste that had evolved European high art, as tribal people themselves were primitive in that they had not gone through a history of sedentary and urban culture, nation building, and industrialization. But field anthropologists came to recognize that every culture dubbed "primitive" has in fact undergone a history of technological and cultural adaptation to its environment, and could have survived as it did in often inhospitable conditions only if it had made such successive adaptations. Hunter-gatherer tribes in the Amazon were found to be survivors of sedentary and urban centers destroyed by the Spanish conquistadors. Instead of sharing with asylum art the character of being the direct expression of the unconscious drives of individuals, the masks and ritual objects prized and collected by artists in Europe such as Picasso, Braque, and Breton embody the taste, ideals, and cosmology of a particular society. Field anthropologists found that these are works of skilled and recognized specialists in those cultures; they could not be taken as representative of the sort of creative impulse that Dubuffet held was a universal human endowment. They were anonymous only because the collectors had deigned acquaintance with the cultures. Once it was recognized that the art brut of the insane, the imprisoned, and spiritualists and mediums are in fact maps of planets or worlds, cosmological diagrams, icons of private religions, medical illustrations, influencing machines, magical weapons, or depictions of visions and of visitations of the dead, these works cannot be put together with the drawings and paintings of children.

The champions of art brut had hailed the source of art in the unconscious, a wellspring of creative energies found in everyone, even in children and the insane—found especially unadulterated in children and the insane. But already Prinzhorn recognized that asylum art is rare. He had selected to locate ten masters out of the five thousand works he had collected. Already these had been the result of a selection; he and his associate Dr. Karl Wilmanns had written psychiatrists and asylum directors that he was interested only in works that "are not simply copies of existing images or memories of their days of health, but intended as expressions of their personal experience," and are "outstanding individual achievements."[10] He recognized that many, even most, inmates simply show no urge to draw or paint.

What is more, the sources of asylum art seem to have dried up. With all the interest concentrated on art brut, master image makers are no longer discovered in asylums. It is therapy that is blamed. For the delirious forces that had expressed themselves in the intensity of powerful works are nowise relieved or cathected by these works; to the contrary, these works visualize and materialize for the maker the alien and abysmal elements that he had divined in his environment and intensify their fearfulness and enigma. They prolong and deepen his delirium. Now the generalized use of antipsychotic and mood-altering drugs reduces the intensity of emotions and drives. The widespread introduction of art therapy does not produce art brut; to the contrary. True art brut was a self-taught and in most cases secret activity, where the use of materials and the strokes were stabilized and perfected through obsessive repetition. Enjoining art activity from the outside, even though the art therapist shows no models and encourages the patient to draw or paint however he or she wants, inevitably results in works without inner compulsion or skill. It is enjoined in order to aid the patient to recognize his disordered perceptions and feelings; the recognition will issue in judgments and constraints. What this produces, John M. MacGregor reports, "is simply amateur art; mediocre, cliché-ridden, and dull."[11]

Something similar has been found for children's art: works of young children that are strong and expressive are in fact rare. And no sooner do children acquire dexterity and some experience with the materials, the mass of public images crowds in on them to guide their drawing and they too produce works that are mediocre, cliché-ridden, and dull.

Dubuffet had found art brut also outside the asylums—among the uneducated, in rural areas, among people who had no real contact with the canons and commerce of the art world and who had not been apprenticed in folk-art traditions. There the individuals who devote themselves to image making have for the most part begun to make images late in life, sometimes after some trauma, or simply after retirement. But today when television and advertising have invaded the most remote or backward corners of the land, it is less and less likely that individuals, even isolated in rural areas, can be found who sketch out drawings that are not guided by public and commercial models.

Outsider Art and the Eclipse of Authenticity

The great exhibition that opened in London in 1979 was titled "Outsiders," no doubt because there is no English translation that carries the connotations of the French "art brut." It did restrict itself to the works of people isolated from the professional art world either through incarceration or socioeconomic marginalization and untrained in the methods and canons of high art. Prinzhorn had originally separated the works from the biographies of the makers, to the point of concealing their names, but because art brut could not, like Impressionism or Cubism, be identified by common internal characteristics, it was biography that alone identified a maker as an outsider and therefore the work as outsider art. In fact, the term "outsiders" was becoming a broader and also more questionable category. Indeed, the great London exhibition brought these works inside and to the very center of the art world.

Resorting to the criterion of works produced outside the institutions and commerce of the art world—academies, museums, galleries, auctions, art historians and art critics—inevitably deflected attention to different regions of lowbrow or popular culture: postcard photographs, New Age images, videos, computer draftsmanship, jazz and tango, pop music and its album-cover and poster imagery. This production had been disdained as popular art and commercial art, and grudgingly still called art only by virtue of the quality of craft that went into it. It was taken to respond, not to the refined taste of the cultured but to crude emotions and tastes. But once the irrational drives and emotions of the insane had been recognized as the source of creativity in art brut, the crude, raw emotions and elementary notions with which the masses appreciate popular and commercial art could be seen to have kinship with them.

Avant-garde professional artists such as Andy Warhol and Roy Lichtenstein turned to this production with an appreciative eye. As earlier artists of the avant-garde incorporated features of art brut into their works, and even set out to paint like the insane, now the avant-garde selects images, colors, media, and techniques out of popular and commercial image production to renew and expand the domain of art beyond sculpture and painting in fresco, on canvas, and on paper. Popular art is fashioned to provoke a response from large numbers of people; commercial art uses colors, movements, and sounds to fix logos and advertising slogans obsessively in memory. Professional artists manipulate popular and commercial images to neutralize their commercial effects and provoke simple amusement, produce ironic or sarcastic effects, or convey images and messages of social or political revolt. Thus the avant-garde artist, however celebrated, however rich, maintains his status as an outsider—heretic, revolutionary.

British artists Jake and Dinos Chapman do not see any essential distinction between popular and commercial art and the art of today's avant-garde. Commercial art functions less to exhibit the real use-value of commodities than to cast glamour or prestige over commodities of banal, dubious, or bogus utility. It is less the real shampoo or vacation package we buy than the image created by that art. "Modern art is the absolute elaboration of capital," the Chapmans say, "because it's an object that can be bought for a huge amount of money without any intrinsic value.... So someone like Jay can say, 'Right, this is £1 million or £10m,' whatever, and once someone writes the cheque it has acquired that worth. If people are gripped by a romantic discourse about the meaning of a work of art, then all we can say is that the sublime is very expensive. You should pay well for it."[12]

Another Obvious Task for Professors of Aesthetics

One day in a shopping mall I noticed that a big discount store was going out of business; everything was on sale for half price. Thinking there are always things one could use in the house—towels, new kitchen chairs, dishes—I strolled about for an hour. I left without buying anything—driven off by the idea of bringing into my home any of these towels covered with pastel flowers, these pink plastic kitchen chairs, these dishes overdecorated in gaudy or insipid colors. I left thinking if, as aesthetics now tells us, art is all around us, in pop and commercial image and spectacle production, why is the greatest part of what is made mediocre, cliché-ridden, and dull? On the way back to my home, the question stuck: why do they make all these suburban houses looking mediocre, cliché-ridden, and dull? Why have the rich bought these oversize barnlike mansions with their fake-Tudor details, set in manicured lawns with neat foundation plantings?

One obvious answer is that the mass marketing of consumer goods requires designing them for the lowest common denominator. But that only raises the question: why do the masses, and the rich, want consumer goods that are mediocre, cliché-ridden, and dull?

The evident direction to turn is to sociology: since the masses acquire a sense of their identity and belonging by acquiring collections of consumer goods recognizable by others who appreciate such collections, conformity to the fashion and taste of a group is paramount. The rich seek out rare and one-of-a-kind things, Ferraris and yachts, designer clothing, original works by celebrated artists. They even acquire revolutionary, contestatory works that reveal new visions and consequently new ways of life. They triumph over them by appropriating them, by exhibiting with a smile a piece of graffiti art in their elegant drawing rooms.

But the sociological explanation only raises the question that we could call psychological, or the question about human nature. The champions of art brut were convinced that innate to every human is a creative urge, seated in the unconscious wellsprings of life. These are the innate strengths that make each human an individual. But there are also deep-seated weaknesses: are not people who fill their home environments with overstuffed, overdecorated furniture, Disneyland ceramics, and racks of golden oldies CDs driven by nostalgia for more familiar, more comfortable times past? The idle rich surround themselves with antique furniture and artworks that appropriate the exceptional labor and talent of rare individuals. Bad taste is produced by character weaknesses.

Then the artistic impotence of "normal" people is unhealthy, betrays deep-seated dysfunction, and reveals the institutions and procedures that make them normal, adult, rational as pathological.

Persistence of the Longing for Authenticity

"Authenticity" is a term that has disappeared from the vocabulary of our postmodern philosophers and from our cultural studies, occupied in explaining the cultural constitution of race, gender, person, Western individualism, and art brut.

Do we not have the everyday experience that others looking at us, talking about us or to us, are addressing the identity and worth that we have acquired with our accoutrements: they see and address the American, the professor, the inner-city street kid, the suburban SUV owner, the fashionable socialite. When we go to far-off places inhabited by members of our biological species, are not what our eyes see of them but tourist images—facial contours, complexions, and garb that look exotic only to us? And when someone there is standing before us, speaking directly to us, we have been cautioned that he is not speaking with his own voice but speaking the language of his gender, his family, his class, his education, his culture, his economic and political interests, his unconscious drives, indeed his state of physical health and alertness. The effort to know him gets detoured into efforts, ever more evidently fragmentary and superficial, to know all these layers. Today the professionals who study these things write books exposing how superficial and deluded have been the efforts of the experts: exposing the imperialist, Christian, Victorian, Romantic, or Orientalist fables written by those people who left their homelands and fell in love in some remote place, married, and never returned; the positivist, Freudian, or Marxist fables of the last generation of cultural anthropologists; the rationalist, structuralist, or postmodern fables of the current generation.

But when we confront the works of art brut, we feel, we see something else: we see stark stereotyped faces with eyes staring at us making the environment we survey fade away and indicating another world; we see the visualization, the materialization of a world unlike anything we have ever seen; we feel the vehemence of anxieties, terrors, explosive sexuality; we read words, the overfamiliar words of advertising slogans or biblical injunctions, here meaning something strange. However much these works have been museumified, interpreted by academics skilled in explaining the cultural constitution of individuality and authenticity, these works are disturbing. Inwardly we feel the mysterious forces of suffering, of yearning, of desperation. They are not the solutions invented in desperate situations; they are expressions, visualizations, intensifications, materializations of desperation.

And the concept of authenticity returns to haunt us.

The images made by the insane, obsessives, and mediums are not artworks, made for the public, for us. They are works so often made in secret. These works force us to understand the radical difference between what they, or any artwork, can mean for the maker and what they can mean for the public, for us. Already Jean Dubuffet realized that to call them art brut—art—is to resituate them among us, where for us they acquire a different function, significance, and value. Yet can we not join in what these works really mean for their makers? Do we not to some measure always project ourselves into the strange and alien habitat that the maker has visualized and materialized? Do they not draw us into the dark cauldron of his desperation?

Permanently on display in the Baltimore American Visionary Art Museum is a gigantic canvas eight feet high by seventeen feet wide in seven panels depicting two Michaelangelesque lovers themselves made of thousands of human figures painted with intricate and ever-varying detail and confident skill. The label tells that this is the only work of James Franklin Snodgrass who created it over decades and left it to his cousin when he died. It was by chance that a researcher came upon it and eventually acquired it for the museum. Each time I go there I sit to contemplate its radiant colors and fractal composition, then block off another square foot or so of it to examine close up, as the painting extends indefinitely beyond me and ahead of me. I see that I am caught in it and that this will go on for years.

One year the museum exhibited a room of pictures all 2.25 by 2.75 inches, enclosed in thick frames, pictures so small that one had to view them with the magnifying glass provided. Their maker, Ray Materson, as a youth had been arrested for cocaine and sentenced to twenty-five years in prison.

Doing time—it means doing nothing, enduring time. His mind had no future with which to occupy itself; it returned to the life he had lived, his childhood. Having to periodically repair the prison garb he was forced to wear, he found himself repairing also the garb of other inmates. He remembered his grandmother, who sewed. Who occupied herself the long winters indoors with embroidery. He began embroidering pictures of prison life, using for colors the unraveled fine threads from discarded nylon socks; the minuscule pictures he embroidered occupied very long stretches of time.

Peering with magnifying glass in hand, we rejoin him with the inmates behind the prison walls. How can we not, contemplating these scenes walled in with thick frames, made of millions of painstaking needle strokes, rejoin him, the future and the outside world so wiped off his life, in his desperate endurance of time, his finally transfigured suffering?

Encountering these works we do not simply appreciate them formally, aesthetically, but experience them as excitants to infantile, criminal, sexually explosive, and visionary compulsions in us. They materialize the zones outside of the common world that excite such compulsions, the abodes that harbor them.

2011

PART II

Body

Intentionality and Corporeity

The soul's reality is based upon corporeal matter, not the latter upon the soul.
—Edmund Husserl, *Ideen*, vol. 3

By absolute consciousness Husserl did not mean to designate simply an epistemological function; absolute consciousness is a region of reality (albeit the proto-region), an ontic existent, individualizing itself across its internal temporality as a singular ego. In addition, it inheres in a body.[1] This means that psychism is apperceived in the heart of Nature. But it also means that corporeity is apperceived within intentionality itself.

Consciousness Naturalized in a Body

Bodies are discovered in the course of our survey of transcendent Nature. They occupy sites in Nature's space and time—the time which is physically measured.[2] They are empirical unities of Nature, given primordially across sensory perspectives, and elaborated across the empirical-objective investigation pursued in the natural sciences. It is these things (*Körper*) that are animated by the reification or naturalization of consciousness. (Thus Husserl does not first seek the operation of consciousness in bodies by seeking to unravel the experience I have of *my own* consciousness at work in *my own* body (the *corps propre* of Sartre and Merleau-Ponty.)

The fully transcendent, empirical naturality of bodies makes them able to function as support for an emergence of psychism in Nature. Bodies appear perspectively as "sensible schemata" connected circumstantially-causally to concomitantly varying natural things of their environments, and eventually to the whole of Nature. Along the course of these sensible apparitions, and systematically connected to them, there is apperceived the non-perspectival stream of psychic states open to empirical observation according to the methods of psychology. Husserl admits two sorts of connections between corporeal states and psychic properties: psychic properties such as sensations, affects, impulses can be functionally linked to corporeal states as to their conditions,[3] or corporeal movements may be functionally linked to psychic sequences as their expression.[4] These psychic "properties"—functions, aptitudes, character traits, dispositions— inhere in an ego-substrate which, if not given perspectively,[5] is nonetheless manifested progressively across the course of apparition of psychic prop- erties[6] in a unity which is not that of a sensible schema, but of a stream—a temporal rather than a spatial *Gestalt.* The psyche is thus a real (realized) ego-subject, a self-identical empirical unity manifested in individual real properties, "interwoven" *(verflochten)* with Nature in that the course of psychic properties are systematically linked to bodily "circumstances" *(Umstände)* by a "functionality regulated by laws."

Thus natural, objectal corporeity, by a sort of overdetermina- tion of properties, supports upon itself a certain manifestation—an appresentation—of psychism in the sphere of transcendence. But the psychism "interwoven" with bodies, "functionally linked" to bodily cir- cumstances, is not presented simply to the perceptual intention that primally opens upon Nature. The transgression of bodily appearances toward their "appresented" psychic properties requires, in addition, the lat- eral operation of empathy *(Einfühlung).*[7] This means that the intentionality that discerns, apperceives, consciousness in Nature interwoven with bodies does so on the basis of the resemblance of those bodies *with the body with which it is itself interwoven.* There was thus first an intimate experience of a union of the corporeal with the intentional within, which was then, across the phenomenon of spontaneous corporeal association *(Paarung)* trans- ferred *(überträgt sich)* to all analogous bodies in Nature.

The animation of bodies in Nature, observed across natural perception, thus answers to a corporeity of consciousness, to be discovered within by transcendental reflection.

No doubt it sounds strange to speak of an incarnation of consciousness in this philosophy, whose unremitting intention is to free the theory of knowledge from every kind of naturalism by regressing to the sphere of pure or absolute consciousness, where the essence of mentality is inten- tionality, and where intentionality is not any kind of movement of or from one real being to another (for example, from the subject to the object), but is the purely ideal "movement" ascribing flux to identity, givenness to ideality—movement from the sensible to the intelligible. And yet corporei- ty appears impossible to conjure, and reappears—in a totally denaturalized and deobjectified incidence—after all the reductions, within the abso- lute sphere itself, as the incarnation of absolute consciousness. It is this "absolute" corporeity that seems to us the most extraordinary of Husserl's findings regarding the role of the body. For a philosophy of incarnate consciousness is not genuinely formulated by asserting that the conscious-ness moves a body (living and operating on the outside, in the spectacle of Nature), or that a body is the vehicle of consciousness, but by showing—or discovering—by internal examination of reduced consciousness a cor-poreity *within,* by showing how corporeity is implicated in the internal structure of what is meant by consciousness.

What then is the intimate experience of corporeity known within itself?

The Emergence of Corporeity in the Sphere of Absolute Consciousness

In three ways Husserl uncovers a certain corporeity—nowise objectified, nowise naturalized, nowise transcendent—implicated within the absolute sphere itself, implicated in the very operation of intentional constitution.

1   A certain corporeity of the subject is discovered in the object-structure of objects—not as a component or ingredient of objects, but as a factor of the objectivity-structure *with which* or according to which conscious-ness constitutes objects. Husserl uncovers in two ways such a corporeity of the subject implicated in the object-structure of objects: (a) the things are relative to a body in the polarity of their orientation, and (b) "real" and "unreal" properties of things are relative to a set of normal or abnormal "states" of the subject which are an inevitable part of the total context of "circumstances" within which sensorial appearances vary and things take form as invariants.

(a) The object-unity of things is intended across the series of perspectival sensible apparitions. The disparate succession of sensible apparitions can motivate and legitimize their coalescence into an object-unity because the intrinsic structure and grain of each is compatible with and conforms with that of the others. But in addition, disparate sensible apparitions caught across different moments of time can be apparitions of different sides of one and the same thing because each is an appari-tion of that thing from a different point of view. Each has an index of orientation. Each aspect refers to other aspects by referring to a center of orientation that refers to a system of other centers of orientation. Thus the constitution of objects requires an intentionality that is situated somewhere—within the very space it constitutes. And the ascription of a multiplicity of sensible apparitions oriented differently to one object-identity requires the variability of the situatedness of intentionality.[8]

The situatedness and free mobility of consciousness is felt within consciousness itself in the form of kinesthetic sensations. But Husserl does not treat kinesthetic sensations as discrete representations or

motor images of body movements recorded or reflected in the immobility of subjectivity. The field of kinesthetic sensations is taken as
part of the total system of moving "circumstances" in the midst of
which poles of object-identity take form; they supply the orientation index which motivates the coalescence of a series of sensible
appearances into one object.[9] Thus they function not as representations of objects (such as the body-object), but as motivations for the
objectification of objects. Kinesthetic sensations make felt, within the
sphere of consciousness, the relativity of each perceptual profile to
a certain orientation. They reveal that the intentionality that means
or intends an object is also a movement of orientation with regard
to that object.

If I move my eyes, my hand, my stance, I acquire other views of the
things: each profile is oriented in a context of possible movements
and possible positions. The awareness of this motivation is not the
performance of a reasoning; it is the kinesthetic awareness of a free
variability of orientation, the free mobility of the subject, motivating
the coalescence of a series of views into one object.[10] The "if ... then ..."
conditionality is the very mode by which kinesthetic sensations are
"kinesthetic" and not representational.[11]

Thus the crystallization of object-units out of a dispersion of differently oriented sensorial apparitions cannot fail to reveal a kinesthetic
field, functioning in the constitution of every object. The field of kinesthetic sensations is not a representation, within the subject, of a
materiality; it is the auto-disclosure of the materiality of the subject. It
reveals subjectivity itself as oriented, already turning in the very space
it will constitute by constituting objects.[12]

(b) The corporeity of the subject is also revealed in the difference between
the constitution of real objects, objects really perceived, and simulacra
or phantasms. For this difference involves a difference between normal
and anomalous "states" of the perceiver.

The invariant structure of a sensible thing is discerned across the
course of sensorial apparitions varying in function of the context of
"circumstances" (Umstände). But certain variations cannot be ascribed
to circumstances given in the phenomenal field, and thus, not integrated into the field of determinable phenomenal links, do not acquire
solid reality, remain phantasmal.[13] When they are affected, compen-
sated for or eliminated, by changes of position or attitude, they are
rejected from the system of sensorial properties of a thing and ascribed
to the material state of the subject. "With each flutter of my eyelashes
a curtain lowers and rises, though I do not think for an instant of

imputing this eclipse to the things themselves; with each movement of my eyes that sweep the space before me the things suffer a brief torsion, which I also ascribe to myself; and when I walk in the street with eyes fixed on the horizon of the houses, the whole of the setting near at hand quivers with each footfall on the asphalt, then settles down in its place."[14] Thus the underbrush of sensorial phantasms is denounced as such by the "true" apparition of the things, and discloses the set of subjective adjustments that will conjure them from the world. These adjustments are not adjustments of a hypothetic *Sinngebung* being repudiated by the noncompatibility of a series of sensible appearances; they are rather material adjustments—adjustments, of position, stance, or state. In these adjustments, and in the necessity for them, there arises the evidence of a state of normal corporeity of the subjectivity ("psychophysical conditionality"),[15] subject to anomalous states.

Thus the possibility of intending objects across the flux of sensorial apparitions involves the disclosure of corporeity in the form of a "position" and "state" of the subject. Consciousness is localized in this position and in this "state." The localization of consciousness, *implicated* by the panorama of the things, is revealed *within* by the states Husserl names *Empfindnisse.*[16] *Empfindnisse* are states of contact (touch, pressure, heat, cold, etc.) and of "being moved" (in both the kinesthetic and the affective sense: states of tension and relaxation, pleasure, pain, agreeableness, disagreeableness, etc.). They are states in which the distinction between subject and object, between the Feeling "act" and the felt "content," is not yet discernible; in them an ambivalent sensoriality reflects both the sensible qualities that announce the presence of a transcendent thing and the sensitivity of the perceiver localized in an "extensivity." *Empfindnisse* "spread out" from within in an extensivity *(Ausbreitung)* of sensorial content which contrasts with the extension *(Ausdehnung)* of the transcendent objects intended across them.[17] They reveal consciousness in a voluminosity, in hands that feel the heat, feet that feel the cold, fingers that feel the relief and grain of things;[18] they reveal consciousness as a sensitivity that inhabits organs that move.

This first analysis of the meaning of corporeity in consciousness has been exterior and retrogressive; it consists in surveying the field of objectivity in which objects take form, and in discovering the subjectivity as part of the "circumstances" which form the context of every object. Corporeity here means that every consciousness of a space of objects has itself a position within that space, and every consciousness of real things and of phantasms has a normal, and an anomalous, "state." The analysis of the ambivalence of *Empfindnisse* reveals an internal experience of the consciousness localized in that position and state.

2   If we turn now to the Husserlian explanation of intentionality we shall discover an incidence of corporeity revealed through direct reflection on the essence of consciousness.

Objects are the telos of consciousness; they are attained in intuition, wherein their "carnal" (*leibhaft*) presence is immediately *given*. But for them to be given is not for objects to be received into some receptacle; consciousness orients itself toward objects, and is synthetically receptive of them, inasmuch as it posits or presumes (*meinen*) the ideal identity regulating the indefinite differentiation of their sensorial aspects. The givenness of the object is in the ideal identity that is maintained and affirmed across the flux of conscious attitudes and states in its regard.

But objects are (perhaps always)[19] intended across the materiality of hyletic data. Hyletic data are "sensations." They are intrapsychic, they belong to the sphere of reduced consciousness, and can be discerned by a kind of reflection.[20]

The Husserlian doctrine on sensations is expressed through a conjuncture of a hylomorphic conception of the mind—undermined—with a hermeneutic conception of the mind—undermined. On the one hand, the "sensations," the hyletic data, are mental "material"; they are to intentionality as matter is to form, and intentionality constitutes objects by "animating" (*beseelen, durchgeistigen*) this matter. Intentionality is the formative animation of psychic matter. And yet the patterns of hyletic matter (they do form "patterns")[21] animated by the intentional operation of the mind, forming "representatives" of things in the mind, in no way form "mental representations" of things; it is not these patterns that the mind knows, consciousness is not consciousness of these hyletic patterns. The objects of consciousness are not representations "formed" out of this matter. (This is the fundamental difference between the phenomenological and the empiricist conceptions of sensations.)

On the other hand, Husserl uses a hermeneutic schema of the mind-undermined. He says that intentionality is an "interpretation" (*Deutung*) of sensations in the mind, "taking them to mean" the presence of transcendent objects. The "movement" of intentionality which goes forth unto the things themselves is the purely ideal movement of interpretation of intrapsychic data. It is the purely ideal movement which presumes or posits (*meinen*) poles of ideal identity across the flux of sense data, taking the sensorial *as* adumbrations *of* something intelligible. And yet this "interpretation" is peculiar in that the data "interpreted" are not first given in themselves. It is because they are not themselves given that hyletic data can be "taken as" the immediate evidence of the presence of transcendent objects. (This is what keeps the phenomenological explanation from being an intellectualist conception of perception.)

The hyletic materiality is *required* both by the Husserlian conception of the things and by the Husserlian conception of consciousness. In casting these *Abschattungen*, these shadows, on the substance of the mind, things announce their carnal *(leibhaft)* presence—as "bodies" present to somebody. And the nature of their identity—presumed, meant, but presumed on the basis of data—requires the duality of a transcendent ideality and an intrapsychic impact.

And while both the hylomorphic and the hermeneutic conceptions of the mind are maintained, conjoined, and undermined in Husserl's conception of the operation of intentionality, neither can be conceived without the intervention of sensations, of hyletic matter. The Husserlian intentionality animates/interprets this mental materiality without making of it any kind of tableau; materiality affects, encumbers the Husserlian consciousness and makes of it not just an epistemological function, but life, *Erlebnis*, experience lived through. The hyletic substance is the *corps de l'esprit* (Valéry), a corporeity *of* intentionality.

3 Starting with the object-body perceived in the sphere of transcendence, moving to the corporeity that appears as "position" and as "state" within the sphere of objective "circumstances" surrounding each object as its functional context (and felt within in the form of *Empfindnisse*), moving inward to the hyletic data that subsist in the reduced sphere of absolute consciousness, we have been finding an incidence of corporeity in each stage of the regression unto absolute consciousness. For Husserl the ultimate stage of phenomenological elucidation, in which the essence of the absolute will be scrutinized for itself, is the reflection on internal temporality.

Consciousness, as a synthetic operation that can intend ideality, identity, across a passing sensorial diversity, becomes possible because it is the auto-generation of a time field, primally produced by a time phase that retains past time phases and anticipates coming time phases. The retention and protention of time phases is the tension within the present of the "living now" which primally makes possible the intention toward identity that synthesizes the sensorial dispersion.[22]

Husserl conceives the phase of the "living now" as an impression, and thus the field of temporality as a mutual implication of intention and impression.[23] The "life" or "animation" of the primary sensory contents is their continual survival in retentions of the phase of the "living now." The "living now" is the *Ur-impression*: the primal impression, the originative impression. The substance of the mind is ultimately *impressional* in nature.

What is meant by such an impression? Assuredly, to think the essence of the absolute sphere in the term "impression" is to think the substance of the mind as materiality and passivity; it is to think the absolute as Fact and not as Concept.[24] But it is no longer to think that the elementary mental event can be causally linked, as impression to impressor, as effect to cause, with physical events; Husserl thinks the primal mental event as impression *after the whole of the transcendent physical universe has been reduced.* The "living now" which he calls an impression is not an effect of a physical process; it is that in which the totality of physical processes are constituted. It is an impression that is not impressed on any prior mental substance; it is, as it were, an impression that is its own substrate.[25] It "is the absolute beginning ... the primal source, that from which all others are continuously generated. In itself, however, it is not generated; it does not come into existence as that which is generated, but through spontaneous generation. It does not grow up (it has no seed): it is primal creation."[26] It is with itself that the impressional phase is linked, in the continuous differentiation of itself by which it originates its survival in retentions and its renewal in protentions. Thus the "living now" is originative: *Urimpression.* But it is impression: givenness, a "passive reception, which gathers in the novel, strange, and originary."[27]

Corporeal Intentionality

We have seen an inevitable corporeity emerge within the reduced sphere of "pure" consciousness itself. But corporeity here no longer means "extension" or "sensoriality"; it is an utterly denaturalized and de-objectified corporeity, whose essence is conceived as "kinesthetic sensations," "psychophysical state," "*Empfindnisse,*" "hyletic materiality," and "impressionality." The concept of corporeity can no longer be treated as a subspecies of the concept "thing."[28]

Merleau-Ponty founded his theory of the essence of corporeity in his early work upon a transposition into corporeity of the very format of intentionality itself. He sought to show, in *The Structure of Behavior* and *Phenomenology of Perception,*[29] that intentionality, Heideggerianized as "existence," is enacted by body movement. Intentionality will be the Concept that would bring intelligibility both to bodily behavior observed physiologically and psychologically, and perception explored transcendentally. It was this, and not the elaboration of a descriptive account of a dimension of corporeity lived in the first person singular, the "lived body" or "*corps propre,*" contrasted with corporeity in the third person, the "objective body," that was radical in his work. It is true that already for Husserl the ultimate substance of the mind is impressional in nature, and, since the whole hyletic layer involved in the constitution of objects is localized in *Empfindnisse,*[30] every intention aiming at objects is also a movement of orientation in regard to them. But in abandoning the conjugated hylomorphic-hermeneutic schemata of mental activity and in transposing the format of intentionality into the essence of corporeity, the intentional analytic no longer operates within a metaphysics where consciousness is to Nature in the relation of absolute and relative, origin and derived, but now operates in a philosophy of Nature where consciousness itself is produced by an "overlapping" of Nature upon itself. Intentionality, which for Husserl was a transcending of the sensible, becomes a power of the sensible.

Merleau-Ponty has not fallen upon this theoretical program as a result of a simple naturalization of the transcendental. The pivot of this transposition is a new analysis of the ontological structure of the sensible thing.[31]

Repudiating the analysis of a thing in terms of facts and essence, sense-data and intelligible essence, qualia and eidos,[32] Merleau-Ponty subjects the sensuous aspect of things itself to renewed scrutiny. Contrast with ideal being had led to relegating to the sensuous an existence in the here and the now, the ineffable opacity of a presence that is total or null. But the properly sensuous aspect of things is reducible neither to atomic sensations (*Phenomenology of Perception* was to show the inconsistency and, finally, the incomprehensibility, of the very notion) nor to qualia.[33] What kind of being then do the sensuous moments have? Merleau-Ponty argued that the sensuous aspects themselves—the color, the tone, the odor—are *dimensional*; they exist in trajectories of time and space and in depth.[34] In addition, each has a kind of internal microstructure; red is not a blank opacity of a certain degree of density; it articulates a certain style or way of filling out, of occupying, its field—explosive, implosive, recessive, tightening, homogeneous or periodic, vibrant or absorptive, etc. Each is "a certain style, a certain manner of managing the domain of space and time over which it has competency, of pronouncing, of articulating that domain, of radiating about a wholly virtual center—in short a certain manner of being, in the active sense, a certain *Wesen*, in the sense that, says Heidegger, this word has when it is used as a verb."[35]

This concept of the inner being of the sensuous aspect permits Merleau-Ponty to conceive in a new way the *Gestaltung* that produces a thing. A thing can now be conceived as a set of sensuous aspects which each, in its own register of sensoriality, reflects the microstructure and style of all the others. One "manner of occupying space and time"—thinly, symmetrically, periodically, tautly, etc.—reverberates across all registers of sensoriality, answers to each kind of sensorial sampling. Thus the essence of the thing is itself sensorial.

Merleau-Ponty was strongly influenced by Saussurean linguistics, and in his late work sought to express the relations between things and the relations between things and their meanings according to the model of the linguistic field analyzed structurally. The phenomenal field must then be conceived as a "diacritical, relational, oppositional system,"[36] which is "phrased" into things by systematic internal processes of articulation. Thus things do not take form about ideal poles of identity posited by the intentionality of consciousness, around which sensorial profiles would be assembled; rather, things are engendered by a relief of the divergence each marks from the others—they take form by systematic lateral differentiation rather than by vertical identification. It is the lateral and oppositional relationship of one term to another that makes each of them significant, such that meaning appears at the intersection of and as it were in the interval between them.[37] And thus, just as one does not learn the significance of language by learning the meaning of words one by one, additively, so one cannot apprehend the phrasing of the phenomenal field into things by "acts" which posit the identity of each.

How then are such beings perceived? The sensuous datum can no longer be conceived as ineffable moments of opacity reflected against the mind, or as matter formed by the mind. Each sensuous phenomenon is rather a specific articulation of a field of space and a trajectory of time, and the sensibility receives its presence within itself by actively taking up its vibrancy and internal microstructure, by actively conforming with it as upon "rays of the world,"[38] by eye movements, by exploratory movements of touch, by shiftings of postural schema.[39] To see it is to see according to it, to see with it. The sensuous is both what we see and the dimension into which we see. If the sensuous aspect itself is conceived as dimensional, its reception must be enacted in a *movement* across space and time, by a being whose own substance is able to conform to the style and grain of the things, and thus receive within itself the echo of their structures.[40] Such a being must then not be defined as the metaphysical opposite of the beings it knows (as subjectivity is defined by its op-position to ob-jectivity); it must be of the same sort as the being it knows, sensible like it.[41] "My body is to the greatest extent what every thing is: a *dimensional this*. It is the universal thing—but, while the things become dimensions only insofar as they are received in a *field*, my body is this field itself, i.e., a sensible that is dimensional of *itself*, universal measurant—"[42]

But if the sensible knower then is able to conform itself to one of the aspects of the thing, one of these "rays of the world," it already is in the presence of the thing itself. The thing *is* nothing but a configuration in which all the sensorial aspects implicate and mutually express one another. Transcendence is displaced, in the thought of Merleau-Ponty, from being the defining characteristic of consciousness, intentionality, to the "flesh" of the sensible as such, whose being is to be "always further on."[43] The sensible "is nothing else than a brief, peremptory manner of giving in one sole something, in one sole tone of being, visions past, visions to come, by whole clusters."[44] We *see*, we *touch* the thing itself; the unity of a thing is not a presumption *(Meinung)* of consciousness, but is exhibited in the fabric of the sensible itself: the structural complex which is a thing, intersensorially observable, is not reached by an "interpretation" of sense data which would "adumbrate" it; it is not an ideal unity of aspects which would be reached by an intentional act transcending the sensible toward the ideal. For Merleau-Ponty the passage from one sensuous aspect to the thing itself is effected by the convergence of all the receptive powers of the body upon it, a convergence effected by the synthetic, or synergic, unity of the body schema. "The whole Husserlian analysis is blocked by the framework of *acts* which imposes upon it the philosophy of *consciousness.* It is necessary to take up again and develop the *fungierende* or *latent* intentionality which is the intentionality within being. That is not compatible with 'phenomenology,' that is, with an ontology that obliges whatever is not nothing to *present* itself to the *consciousness* across *Abschattungen* and as deriving from an originating donation which is an act, i.e., one *Erlebnis* among others.... It is necessary to take as primary, not the consciousness and its *Ablaufsphänomen* with its distinct intentional threads, but the vortex which this *Ablaufsphänomen* schematizes, the spatializing-temporalizing vortex (which is flesh and not consciousness facing a noema."[45] As the telos of the convergence of corporeal sensitivity, and not an ideal essence comprehended in its coherence, the thing-structure remains the term of progressive exploration, retains its transcendence and its opacity.[46]

The concept of intentionality one has is commanded by the conception one has of the internal structure of the object, telos of intentionality. Merleau-Ponty exhibits the operation of intentionality as a receptive movement of a being whose metaphysical constitution is like that of the being received—sensible like the world; intentionality (he rather says "existence") is enacted by body motility, it will be the very essence of corporeity. Merleau-Ponty's first two works endeavored to show that this is not only true of the corporeity discovered within, by transcendental reflection on the reduced sphere of absolute consciousness, but also true of the corporeity observed without, in the form of behavior opening upon a "world."

The "Mind's Body" and Nature

We have seen that the concept of intentionality, as exposed by Husserl and by Merleau-Ponty, requires a denaturalized, de-objectified conception of an "absolute" corporeity—the "mind's body" *(corps de l'esprit)*. In both cases the "mind's body" is essential to the conception of the essence of mentality; the concept of intentionality is then not a "spiritual" or "mental" concept, and in conceiving the essence of consciousness in the notion of intentionality we do not conceive a mental activity which would then have to be linked to a body, by compound or by composition.

It is true that this corporeity is conceived differently by the two philoso-phies, and this difference is commanded by their divergent understandings of what is to be meant by intentionality.

Husserl conceives the operation of intentionality, across a hylomorphic-hermeneutic schema, as a receptive intuition which synthetically posits objects by transgressing systems of data toward their ideal identity. The motility of the subject is involved in every coalescence of differently oriented *Abschattungen*. This exposition involves corporeity under the con-cepts of the "position" and "state" of the subject, "kinesthetic sensations," "*Empfindnisse*," "hyletic data," and "impressions."

For Merleau-Ponty the apprehension of things (which assuredly cannot be a process of passive reduplication of them in a mental substance) is no longer an apprehension of their ideal meanings for a mind; it is a captiva-tion, in oneself, of their "manner of filling space and time," their sensible essence. For Merleau-Ponty, already the apprehension of any sensible phe-nomenon (and not only the apprehension of a sequence of differently oriented sensorial aspects) must already be a movement across time and space, because all sensible phenomena exist in spatiotemporal "rays," are dimensional, and because to apprehend them is to capture in oneself the internal microstructure that governs the deployment of each.

And to Merleau-Ponty it is unintelligible to attribute this power to a being of a different metaphysical constitution than the sensible things: only a being *like* the sensible can capture in itself their essence and micro-structure ("a mind could not be captured by its own representations; it would rebel against this insertion into the visible which is essential to the seer").[47] But then what we have called the transcendental or "absolute" corporeity of the mind is not to be metaphysically opposed to the corpo-reity (*Leibhaftigkeit*) of the things themselves; the "mind's body" is the very inscription of Nature within.[48]

This brings Merleau-Ponty to the view that consciousness is not enact-ed by acts and positings, but by intentional transgressions, *Überschreiten*, which are not the initiatives of an ego, but overlappings of "Nature"—"Being"—upon itself. The ultimate elucidation takes the form of a reflection on the primal unity of the "Natura naturans" or "Being" anteced-ent to the segregation into mind and into phenomenal Nature, and on the internal radiation or "overlapping" upon itself upon which "acts" and "atti-tudes," including the "act" of intentionality, are founded.

But for Husserl's ultimate intentions, the "corporeity of the mind" itself is to be suspended upon "acts," hyletic data are to be shown to be constituted by the "longitudinal" system of acts by which consciousness is primally constituted as a time-field.[49] Thus the "absolute" corporeity dis-covered inevitably within the mind after all the reductions of Nature does not have the sense of an inscription of Nature within the mind: Husserl will maintain to the end the conception according to which the mind is to Nature in the relation of absolute and relative, origin and derived, unity and difference.

1970

I Am a . . .

When we speak about things, they become clearer; they break apart or connect up differently; words may well make things and situations first appear. Words also present the speaker. "Here I am!" "I saw, I heard, I did . . ." "I say, I tell you . . ." The "I" presents the speaker and maintains him or her present.

Linguistics has labeled the word *I* an empty "shifter"; it designates the one who is now uttering this phrase and in the course of a conversation it designates first this person, then that person, then that other person. Literary critics have pointed out that the word *I* in a text can designate the author of that text, or the narrator in a novel who puts himself forth as having seen these events or lived through them, or a fictitious speaker to whom the author has ascribed certain states of mind and actions.

What I ascribe to the word *I* when I use it can be the same as what anyone else ascribes to it: "She is the thirteenth on the wait list for that flight." "I am the thirteenth in line for that flight."

But there are instances where the word *I* has a special force. "I am on my own now." "I am a mother." When, alone or in the presence of others, she says "I," she impresses it upon herself, and her substance retains it. With these words, she takes a stand and faces ahead. The next time she says "I," this subsequent "I" corresponds to and answers for the prior one.

"I got mad when my petition was just ignored . . ." "I am so happy I quit my job." With these words, the present I puts the past I in the present I. The I that quit or that got mad is the I that is now speaking.

The power to fix my own word on myself is a power that leaps over the succession of hours and days to determine the future now. One day, deep in the secrecy of my heart, I said, "I am a dancer," and it is because and only because I uttered those words that I am now on the way to becoming a dancer. Already to say "I am a man" is to commit myself to manly behavior; to say "I am a woman" is to commit myself to womanly deeds. To say "I am young still" is to put my forces outside the roles and role models set up about me.

The remembering of these words that we implant in ourselves is made possible by brushing off the thousands of impressions that crowd on our sensory surfaces as we move through the thick of the world. The I arises in an awakening, out of the drowsy murmur of sensations. It especially requires an active forgetting of lapses, failures, and chagrins—which persist as cloying sensations that mire our view, occluding the past and the path ahead. There is a fundamental innocence in the I, which stands in the now and from this clearing turns to the time ahead and the time passed. To say "I" is to commence. "Now I see!" "I will go!" There is youth and adventure in the voice that says "I."

"Now I see!" These words, once I fixed them in myself, leave me free to observe the passing scene without tentatively arranging it around one center and then around another. "I will go" leaves me free for whatever interruptions, distractions, and momentary amusements the day brings. Through innumerable interruptions, contraventions, invitations, and lures to do other things, I feel the uncanny power of these words that is the sole evidence that they will prevail.

"Now I see!" "I am still young." To utter "I" is to pledge to honor those words. Nobility characterizes, in someone of high station or of low, the man who is as good as his word, the woman whose word is a guarantee. Servile is he whose words are not his own, she who is not in her actions.

Our word I, "I say …," "I am going to …," "I am a …" is the first and fundamental way we honor ourselves. Saying "I am a dancer," I will seek out dance classes, I will train every day with exclusive resolve, I will endure being left out of company selections, dancing in troupes that get miserable reviews by the critics; I will never act on the basis of failure. It is myself, and not dance, I dishonor if I do not do these things.

The word of honor we have fixed in ourselves is the real voice of conscience. Already "Now I see!" or "I have no idea what to do with my life" are words that remain in me, that orient and direct my words and deeds.

Our dancer conscience is not at all a critical function, a restraining force, like the daemon of Socrates, which speaks only to say no to the instincts. Our artist conscience does not torment us with guilt feelings. In the words "I am a dancer!" "I am a mother!" "I am young still!" we feel surging power. Our pride in ourselves is a trust in the power of these words. There is a trembling pulse of joy in those words and a foretaste of joy to come. We trust our joy, for joy is expansive, opening wide upon what is, what happens, and it illuminates most broadly and most deeply.

The word we have put on ourselves is fixed in our sensibility, our nervous circuitry, our circadian rhythms, and our momentum and its tempo. It vanishes from the conscious mind, which can fill itself with new words and scenarios. I no longer have to recall, in the midst of morning concerns that require my attention, that word *dancer* uttered in myself; I instinctually head for the dance studio and feel restless and tied down if I am prevented from going.

The chance revelation of the importance of dance, the grandeur of the wilderness, the majesty of the oceans first called forth the words—"I am a dancer!" "I am a forester!" "I am an oceanographer!"—with which I passionately endorsed and committed myself to these experiences. The enchanting force of the word *dancer* resonates with the mesmerizing force of dance that has impassioned me. There is gratitude in being able to affirm these words.

To be struck by the importance of dance, of mothering a child, or of freeing the rivers of pollution is to see the urgency of what has to be brought about, protected, rescued, or repaired. Seeing that I am the one who is there and who has the resources, the I arises and takes a stand.

To say "I am a dancer" is to commit my body to travail, injury, and pain. To say "I am a mother" is to commit my body to set free the child, and the adolescent and adult it bore, or to care for the genetically defective child it gave birth to until its death. To say "I am a doctor" is to commit my body to total mobilization for hours and at any hour and to the daily proximity to deadly diseases.

And how much more strength is required to say "I am an explorer of myself by being an explorer of a hundred towns and lands!" How rigorous is the conscience of him who affirms, "I am someone who risks all that I am in every new land and adventure!" But to be really a dancer is to be a runaway youth on an unknown road, to be, like Martha Graham, a beginner at the age of eighty. To be a mother can be, like Celia de la Serna, to be dragged out of the cancer ward and thrown in prison in Buenos Aires for being the mother of her son, the mother of Ernesto "Che" Guevara.

This power to fix our word in ourselves generates the power, Nietzsche said, "to see distant eventualities as if they belonged to the present, to decide with certainty what is the goal and what the means to it, to distinguish necessary events from chance ones, to think causally, and in general to be able to calculate and compute."[1] How many are those who do not distinguish what is essential from what is incidental, who do not see what possibilities are within reach and do not even see goals! How many are those who do not think, whose minds are but substances that record what baits and lures the communications industry broadcasts at large! They do not commit themselves to the systems of thought that track down the causes of injustice and sociopathic behavior, the causes of environmental deterioration, the causes of literary and artistic achievement.

Compelling insights, foresight, purposive thought, causal thought, calculative thought—thought in general—these do not arise from the regularities of nature passively recorded by the mind. The rows of trees and the daily movement of clouds overhead, the birds that chatter in the backyard, the landmarks and the paths we take every day, the tasks that are laid out for us every day, the patterns of conversation with acquaintances, the concepts that exist to classify these things and the connections between them—these lull the mind, which glows feebly in their continuities and recurrences; they do not make it thoughtful. Thought results from language, thought arises out of the word we put on ourselves—a word of honor. This word interrupts the continuities of nature and silences the babble of others in us. The power that we feel in ourselves when we fix ourselves with a word, that stands and advances in that word, the feeling that we are making our nature determinable, steadfast, trustworthy, makes us look for regularities, necessities, calculable forms in the flux of external nature. Once I have said, "I will be a dancer," I begin to really determine what the things about me are; I begin to understand anatomy, the effects of exercise, of diet, the effects of great teachers and grand models, the workings of a whole cross section of urban society. It is the man of his word, the woman whose word is a guarantee, who is thoughtful.

To say "I" is to disconnect myself from the others, the crowd, the company, the system. It is to disconnect myself from their past and their future. "For my part, I think . . ." "Here is what I am going to do . . ." I disconnect from the view another may have of me and the image I have constructed of him, and from the interpretation he may have elaborated of what I said. "Yes, I did say I would clear up the place before the social worker got here. So what? I am no longer the suburban housewife you knew."

Because the utterance "I" is a commitment, it is also the power to disconnect myself from a past experience, undertaking, or commitment. "I didn't see what was going on." "I was drunk." "Oh I was so much older then. I'm younger than that now." And it is also the power to disconnect myself from the future that was mine. "The troops are already shelling the village and you say they are going to level it? Well, I am a doctor and I am staying right here to tend to the dying."

To say "I" is to disconnect myself from the others and from discourse with others. "Now I see," I say in the middle of a discussion, and I may stay in the discussion to argue for what I see and try to affect the subsequent movement of their thoughts and their decisions. More likely, the main effect of my insight will be to determine the line of my thoughts and decisions after I leave the others. My word of honor does not get its meaning from a dialectic, and its use is not primarily in a language game with others. He who goes around saying to everyone "I'm going to be a dancer" is seeking their permission and support, and there is cause to suspect that he has not really or not yet fixed these words in his heart. There are those who have never told anyone and who are driven by their secret intoxication with this word. Secrecy sets this word apart from the profane common talk; it sacralizes it. Secrecy also maintains for us a space for giving free play to doubts, second thoughts about what we have said to ourselves, as well as giving free play to fantasy about it.

The walls of secrecy fragment our social identity. He who has said in his heart "I am a dancer" will not be the same person among his fellow prelaw students in the university, before his parents, when seeking private lessons from a renowned teacher, when playing football with cousins at the family reunion. The secrecy of our words can function to preserve affable and nonconfrontational relations with others who have different commitments and those who have different plans for us.

To say "I am a dancer" is not to impose upon myself an overall coherence and cohesion. In the heart of myself I am a dancer; but the whole of what I am is a singular compound of fragmentary systems of knowledge, incomplete stocks of information and discontinuous paradigms, disjoint fantasy fields, personal repetition cycles, and intermittent rituals. Inner walls of secrecy maintain a space where quite discontinuous, noncoordinated, noncommunicating psychic systems can coexist.

How do I understand that I came to believe that I am destined to be a dancer? How do I explain it out of the segments of information I acquired about the social and cultural structures about me, the successive role models that I fixed in memory, the fantasies of my childhood, the resentments and rebellions I accumulated against my parents, the ways I came to disdain pragmatic judgments and occupations? But I may not want to penetrate behind those walls about my dancer destiny: let this word *dancer!* be separated and secret—sacred. Saying yes to the enigmas and accepting the discomfiture within myself, I remain astonished at the Dionysian demon that has come to possess me.

One will not become a dancer unless one says, "I am a dancer"; one will not become an adventurer unless one says, "I am a adventurer." But I will not become a dancer or an adventurer unless I believe what I say in my heart. By an act of will I may want to be a dancer, but I do not by an act of will make myself believe that I am a dancer.

Is not belief in oneself one of those states that cannot be brought about intentionally or willfully? I can make myself eat with an act of will, but I cannot with an act of will make myself hungry; I can make myself go to bed but cannot make myself sleepy, can willfully bring about self-assertion or bravado but not courage, meekness but not humility, envy but not lust, commiseration but not sympathy, congratulations but not admiration, reading but not understanding, knowledge but not wisdom.[2] I cannot by an act of will make myself be amused; I cannot make myself laugh by tickling myself.

The word of honor that we fix on ourselves that makes us thoughtful also makes us insightful. In uttering "I," I make myself present—present to things and events where and as they are. To say "I," to say "Here I am," is to commence to see lucidly where and what here is; to say "Now I see" is to put myself in the clear light that illuminates what is ahead; to say "I am a dancer" is to know what dance is, is to know dance taking possession of myself and activating my nervous circuitry and musculature with its rigorous dynamics.

What is revealed in an impassioned experience is sudden and unexpected, revealed to us gratuitously. The revelation of dance reveals in us the capacity and the latent talent to dance; the revelation of the healing powers of medicine reveals in us skills, perceptiveness, focus that we consecrate in saying "I am a doctor!" They reveal what we are, by nature and by chance, by luck. All the good things in life are free.

To believe something is to be compelled to hold that belief because there is evidence that it is true. A patient is told she has cancer. Believing that there is no hope will certainly depress the immune system. She has to believe that there is hope. But how to make herself believe there is hope? Is there any other way than to find reasons to believe that chemotherapy and radiation treatments or the treatments used in Chinese hospitals are effective?

Paul Gauguin abandoned his family in order to pursue his art. "I am moving next month to Fatu-iva, a still almost cannibalistic island in the Marquesas. There, I feel, completely uncivilized surroundings and total solitude will revive in me, before I die, a last spark of enthusiasm which will rekindle my imagination and bring my talent to its conclusion."[3] He did have reason to believe that he had talent. He did not know if he could bring that talent to its conclusion. If the ship, on its long voyage through stormy seas, would not arrive, if he had succumbed to disease on the way, no one would ever have known.

Here is this man who has fallen ill with a strange sickness or into a deep depression. He suffers and seeks to be healed. But strange illness, depressions, hallucinations are part of the initiation of every shaman. What might happen is that he becomes a healer. How to know that this is his destiny? I. M. Lewis and Georges Devereux reclassified shamans as neurotics. But neurotics are dysfunctional in our culture and shamans do heal dysfunctional individuals in their cultures. Field researchers have long observed shamans performing tricks—pulling out of the sick person's body the cause of the sickness, a bloody object that he had furtively put there. Does the shaman who makes others believe in his healing powers believe in them himself or make himself believe in them? Shamans recognize that there are charlatans, all of whose healing is a sham. They also see people they treat getting well.

This pastor in Northern Ireland or Rwanda—does he really believe that all things are in the hands of an omnipotent and benevolent Divine Providence? Does this man passing as normal really believe he is normal? Is it not by passing as heterosexual that we quit our bisexual preadolescence or indeed nature? Nietzsche observed that the noble always go masked, masked as noble.[4]

David Abram is a young American who was working his way through college putting on magic shows. When he finished, he applied for and received a number of small grants to study magic in old cultures. He went to Sri Lanka, Bali, and Nepal. In fact, there are no magicians in those places; there are shamans and healers. In Bali he formed a relationship with a healer. She revealed to him some of the power objects and rituals of Bali. She intimated that he should share some of his powers with her. He tried to explain to her that he had no power; all he had were prestidigitation and tricks. But the concept of a magician in the Western sense was alien to her and her culture. Finally he realized that if he did not share something, she would shut him out and he would lose the person from whom he was learning most. This woman had some time back broken her thumb, which had set badly so that it had lost mobility. For her it was a serious debility, because she earned her income by the practice of massage—the healing was, in the culture, done without charge. One night things came to a head; David had to do something. He improvised a ritual over her hand, using some of the power objects of the culture. To his consternation, the next day she showed him how her thumb was beginning to regain mobility, and insisted he repeat the ritual. To his horror, in the days that followed, the thumb recovered completely.[5]

The hang glider who on his first leap off the cliff crashed on the rocks below knows he must immediately, the same day, leap off that cliff again until he soars in the winds. The day will come when soaring will have shown him pretty much all it can, and he will cease and go on to other explorations. But if he stops before he has overcome the cliff, he will have definitively reduced belief in his powers.

Cowardice, which husbands our forces, holds back, intensifying the sense of our needs and wants, produces an inward sense of impotence and misery. Every misery we feel over ourselves is the result of some cowardice.

Because she said I am a dancer and believed it, she could become a dancer. Can she be deluded? Can she even be lying to herself?

In the dance studio she found she really belonged there, her body belonged. If doubt arises, it is because she finds reasons and evidence for those reasons to think that she cannot be a dancer. Out of fear of the truth, she can hold back from looking for those reasons and that evidence. She can selectively scan the evidence, selectively weigh it, evaluate new pieces of evidence separately rather than cumulatively, or fail to take in negative evidence.[6] Later, she says, "I was deluding myself."

We do not really knowingly mislead ourselves. What is possible is that we may lack evidence or lack the ability to evaluate the evidence. What could count as decisive evidence that I will never be a dancer?

Yet do we not honor those who are true to the word they have given, although they are deluded about their talent or resources or about the importance or validity of the cause? It is not only historians who work to recuperate the honor of all the losers of history—Brutus and Montezuma, Gandhi and Che Guevara. The victors do not desecrate but bury in cemeteries their fallen enemies and receive with military honors the officers who, their cause lost, come to surrender.

In reality there is no honor in delusion. I will not be able to continue, having one day recognized that I have no talent, that I am not a dancer. I can recognize no honor in representing the party, once I learn that it has become corrupt and its program is now only propaganda.

If we continue to fight for a cause we know is lost, we do so to demonstrate to ourselves and our comrades and to those as yet unborn that the cause that is winning is ignoble.

2007

Orchids and Muscles

The Bodybuilders

Bodybuilding is a cult, certainly, not an enterprise—that of *mens sana in corpore sano*—that culture can know and integrate. It has its clandestine repairs, its passwords, its initiations, its legends, its rituals, its undeciphered codes. The alerted eye can spot the body builders in the crowds, not, like punks, by the tribal garb and arcane jewelry, but by the way neither work nor leisure garb fit their bodies, by the strained fabrics, the pulled seams. Sportswear and beachwear, designer conceived for voyeurist eroticism, are pulled tight over their loins like chastity belts. If they wear jewelry, they most often wear it not as embellishments or citations but as amulets. In the bus stations and sidewalks, in the midst of the streams of the busy and the preoccupied, space warps and strains about them as though lacking the gravity these sprung arms and plowshare thighs are made to furrow. The civilized head that looks at them is deviated; it wonders not where they are going but where you can get with them. The erotic eye, that which scouts the erotogenic terrain in the body of another—not the rolling surfaces of taut cutaneous membrane, but the spongy zone of susceptibility just beneath and the mucous membrane of the orifices—is disconcerted to run into packed thongs of drawn muscle. Not muscle that answers to the ungendered resistance of tools and implements, but specifically male and specifically female muscle alignments. One cannot resist feeling the very hardness of these muscles to be the badgering of the glands of lust—whole anatomies pumped like priapic erections, contracting poses and shifting with held violence from one pose to the next with the vaginal contractions of labor pains. They flaunt in the nose of an antiseptic consumer public leathery rutting odors; they gleam with oils that deviate the hold the inspecting eye fixes on these bodies into the sliding suctions of octopus eros.

Their codes are undeciphered; one does not understand the programming or the decision process that assigns them their hours in cellars full of iron millstones and rudimentary machines. The process that elaborates, selects, and distributes the programming is not in the control rooms of culture nor even in the science of coaches and trainers; it is rigged up in their own taciturn and superstitious skulls. The unguarded, unwary eyes with which they walk in the frenetic halls of stock exchanges or in the night of urban jungles do not seem practiced in the predatory uses of the sense organs perfected by the millennia of hunters whose genes we inherit and, unlike the surveillance a miller maintains on the ox or the waterwheel that turns the millstone, their eyes unfocused on their unrotating wheels of iron seem instead to watch the inward spread of monotonous fatigue and seeping pain. Their arms that handle but poles without fulcrum and wheels that grind nothing are uneconomic, detaching or transforming nothing from the raw or recycled materials of nature and industry. In their handshake we feel no understanding; we feel an indexterous hand that is not held to the equipment of our culture. Like kundalini yogis forcing the semen flow back upstream and upward, they detach the few implements they use from the instrumental complex of civilization, detaching themselves from these very implements even as they fit themselves into them, forcing the power and the mass back upstream, from clenched fist toward drummed vortex of the solar plexus.

The Civilizing of the Body

Natural evolution elaborated the neurological and physiological potentials in the human primate that made culture—implements, language, social institutions—possible. But Homo sapiens is a domesticated species; his nature is civilized. What has civilization done to the biological nature of this primate? Paleoanthropologist André Leroi-Gourhan distinguishes four stages in the technological history of our species that have decisively evolved our biological nature.[1]

The first stage is that of the use of tools—cutters, choppers, and grinders. The baboons, as all earthbound mammals, advance into the world snout first; it is with their teeth that they maneuver their way. The human primate puts chipped stones in his front legs to cut, to chop, and to grind. He exteriorizes the functions of his teeth and powers them with what have now become hands. He transforms himself biologically into an upright animal feeling his way with his hands, lifting his eyes to survey the distances. At the same time the senses of his nose and the power of his teeth begin their atrophy. The exteriorized teeth, the chipped stones, still have to be maneuvered with muscle power.

The next species-decisive stage is the harnessing of exterior motor power—that of animals, water, and wind—to drive his implements for him. The primacy of the sense of the vision that surveys is definitively enhanced—even in his sexuality, which now, Freud hypothesized, becomes unseasonal, for primarily excited not by menstrual odors but by the visually exposed genitals of the upright ape. At the same time his hide thins into skin and his muscles begin their atrophy.

But the wind, water, and draft animals that operate his implements in place of his own hands still require his surveillance. The next species-decisive stage is the invention of machines—contrivances that start and stop, control, and, more and more, correct their operations. This stage begins with the invention of the mechanical clock. Its new virtue, by comparison with the sundial and the clepsydra, is that it recycles itself and can trigger other movements. The first clockmakers of Europe immediately set out to construct clocks which filled towers and, as they struck the hour, opened doors from which the three kings and the four horsemen of the apocalypse advanced and gesticulated, while the cathedral clarion tolled above without a bell ringer. Mechanisms now liberate humans from their surveillance—and the attention span of machine-age humans begins its atrophy. Television-viewers, their fingers on channel-change knobs, today look with incomprehension at Guatemalan Indians whose attention may be held on the patterns of a loom for hours on end.

Still, the surveillance mechanisms have to be programmed by the neurological circuitry of the human brain. Today our technological civilization has entered into an information-processing revolution—which is also a new state of our biological evolution. Computers henceforth assemble and evaluate the data, and make the decisions. The faculties of memory, reason, and decision—evolved in our nature through the history of our civilization—now begin their atrophy. The film *The Terminator* is set a generation from now, when the master-computers deciding the racing of the military-industrial complex determine the use of all resources and of the human species. A band of guerrilla resisters, led by John O'Connor, is waging operations of sabotage against the cybernetic police. The master-computers select the Terminator (Arnold Schwarzenegger) to be time-projected back into the twentieth century with a mission to terminate the life of Sarah O'Connor, John O'Connor's mother, and thus ensure that the guerrilla leader will never be born. The human species has, with the next evolution of its technological civilization, undergone regression back into manpower, and the film plots its retrogressive abortion as a biological species endowed with initiative. This film is in fact no science-fiction fantasy; today the stockpiling of weapons of extinction is the most important sector of our industry, and its exponential advance is already programmed by internal feedback circuitry. This forty-year-old industry has already stockpiled nuclear weapons enough to detonate a Hiroshima-size thermonuclear bomb over a city of our civilization every day for the next 3,500 years. The equivalent of the annual production of the poorest fifth of toiling humankind is now devoted to weapons—the total productive energy of one human being employed to fabricate weapons to exterminate the other four. Certainly it is not our fellow citizens, and not their political leaders either, who are in control of the military industry. Our secretary of defense awaits the data, electronically satellite-espionaged from the other military powers, to be processed by the Pentagon computers, and they will make the decisions as to what new weapons our technology must manufacture. The executive offices of the other powers are only relaying the decisions of their computers.

We have already evolved into pure spectators, the Mouse Folk Kafka imagined,[2] with huge eyes feeding into massive brains, floating in the air, with minuscule atrophied limbs dangling. Or, Leroi-Gourhan says, into orchids. Orchids are plants with atrophied trunks and limbs, parasitically clinging to the rising trunks that shut out the sun, flowering their huge showy sex organs, awaiting the bees for their orgasmic unions. With our sight disconnected from any decision or motor functions, its content determined by the image-industry programming, our bulbous and succulent organisms, hoisted into the space of visibility on the massive trunks of cybernetic forests, are biologically evolving into mammalian orchids.

Is not the glorification of our primary and secondary sexual splendors— the orchid-woman flowering against the hood of the Mercedes, the orchid-man flowering under the skydiver parachute—also destined to lose its biological relevance and to atrophy, in the measure that it will be the flickering computer chips of biological engineering, and not our physiological ostentations, that decide which genes will be reproduced?

Every great epoch of culture, Nietzsche wrote, is not only an epoch in humankind's cultivating of nature—transforming of nature's resources in accordance with its own idea—it is also an epoch in the history of humankind's cultivation of its own nature—transforming its own nature in accordance with its ideal. Every great culture, marked by distinctive intellectual, artistic, and moral productions, has also set up a distinctive icon of bodily perfection. The physical ideal of the yogi, of the lion-maned moran of the African savannah, of the serpent-plumed Mayas, of the Olympians of the age of Pericles, of the samurai, of the baris knights of Bali—each great center of culture has set up the corrals, perfected the breeding and training methods, ordered the subjugations and testings for its own body-ideal. In the new institutions specific to modern Western society—barracks, factories, public schools, prisons, hospitals, asylums—Foucault identified the specifically modern ideal of the *disciplined body*.[3]

All these ideal bodies have now become obsolete. Yukio Mishima remarked on the anomaly of the cult of bodybuilding; it appeared in Japan only after the defeat of the Second World War, that last samurai fantasy—that is, in a Japan where massive musculature is without employ in high-tech industry and pointless in a nation whose constitution forbids remilitarization.[4] It is, indeed, irrelevant across our planet without such constitutions, where the next war will be won or lost (will be conjointly lost) by fingers pushing buttons, and where in the hour it will last there will be no occasion for ingenious strategic plans, skillful tactics, heroic feats of endurance, or nonparticipation.

The Cause, the Adventure, the Corrida

There is a pervasive resentment of the exhibitionism of bodybuilders. It is not a resentment of physical exhibitionism; human nature in our epoch is cultivated especially by means of the glorification of athletes, female nudity, and feats of physical bravado.

A cause wins with the athlete—the school, the French nationalized automotive industry, the nation-state, the free-market world. In the team instincts of football players, the tailgaters read the name of a brand of beer that is on their own gregarious chests too; in the personal engineering of mountain climbers, the telespectators read the name of a multinational corporation in which they are programmed stockholders; in the single-mindedness of boxers they read the ruling finality of one of those multi-corporation consortiums with a world market in view that are called nations. The bodies of athletes are causes. They are also feedback loops in the marketing industry. Achievement comes from the computer-revealed genetic potential, individually computerized diet and training, drugs, and publicity and marketing. The purely abstract, formal, numerical causes of their competitions feed into the causes of the rising and falling stocks of multinational corporations.

At Penn State, which I found myself honored to belong to by readers of newspapers in London, Tokyo, Singapore, and Managua for its number one football team, a bodybuilding meet is held at the local high school. Not even the high-school kids were there, only the bodybuilders, their siblings, and their spouses. The amateurs have no patrons and train and go to exhibitions at their own expense, which the trophy the top one of the class will receive will not reimburse; even the world-class professionals can earn extra dividends as ad layout models only for barbell companies and vitamin-supplement products bought by other bodybuilders. One encounters the amateurs pumping and oiling themselves in the dilapidated movie theaters of small towns, in locker rooms covered with graffiti, and in class-rooms whose blackboards are covered with musical scales and high-school geometry formulas. Indeed, the public imagination depicts them as fixated adolescents in high-school locker rooms after hours. In the absence of a public cause before them and before us, the public mind can only rum-mage around for psychological causes producing these cases—distorted father-figure, antisocial underworld instincts sublimated by fear of the police, fixated libidinal compulsions. One sees them narcissistically pump-ing themselves into ostentatious sex symbols—but symbols the sexually liberated public recognizes as the obsolete figure of virile protector, who was also a phallocrat and wife beater. When the mind finds itself seduced to look where there is no cause written, it turns away in resentment.

What is she trying to prove, that woman who has gotten herself hung up on a centimeter here a centimeter there on her calves and neck? The image-industry of our time instead glorifies the exhibitionism of the unathletic female—but not male—body. The nudity of the male athlete is a locker-room nudity before or after the competition, just the time to buy or sell a Marlboro. The nudity of the male non-athlete is that justi-fied baring of the arms to operate machinery, baring of the legs for speed, stripping for underwater welding. The precision-tooling gives the male body seriousness and seemliness; the axis of bravery can give it nobility. Without the gearing-in to the tool—or without a vision of bravery at grips with death—the unathletic male nudity is ridiculous. The female anatomy verges on the ridiculous too, as our advertising, our high art, and our por-nography know; it has to be relayed with stage props—be they reduced to the minimum, as in Noh theater, to high-heeled shoes, a garter, atmosphere spread with Vaseline on the camera lens, or, as Marilyn Monroe said, per-fume. With the props, the female anatomy is exhibited in a theater—where acts, even that of lying there indolent and fatuous, have consequences and weave a plot. The theater of adventure is a space maintained alongside the politico-economic fields of our enterprises. Maleness is exhibited in an enterprise, where the causes that produce results are also the causes of our industrious and mercantile zones; femaleness is denuded in a theater, where the causes are aleatory and the chain of consequences an adventure. Secretively, clouded with gauzy sunlight, or brazenly, in front of a cast-off nurse's uniform, the female nudity is a cause in the plot of an adventure that justifies it. The voyeur, crouched behind his telescope lined up with the windows of the building opposite, or sprawled before his video screen, thinks not of blueprints, data, and willpower, but dreams of luck and white magic, believes the chemistry of alchemical legends, the chance encounters by which an ineluctable destiny in the time of horoscopes is deciphered. He fiercely resents those women who, rebuilding their bodies out of muscle, are ruining the anatomy of the central character required for the theater of adventure.

What about the corrida? No woman spread-eagled in a strip show is as brazenly exhibited as the matador in the corrida. His body and his blood are exalted in a monstrance of scarlet velvets, spun-silver lace, and jewels over against the black fury of the bull. Insolence flaunts his torso, contempt splays his thighs, flash fires of foolhardy intelligence crackle across his tensed and derisive posturings, his testicles and penis jeweled in the cod-piece and provocatively exposed to the lust of the crowds.

It is, Hemingway says, not gladiatorial spectacle, but tragic theater.[5] It also became this only in our time. Only a century ago did the corrida change from being an activity of aristocrats for the sake of killing bulls into a theater for the glorification of the torero, whose splendor blazes not in the ecstatic love of killing (the love of, and consequently the gift for, killing is, Hemingway reports, all but obsolete in the legendary matadors of our time), but in the sovereign power to lead the raging horns of the doomed bull to his own brandished torso and to a torrent of blood and death at his feet.

Hemingway misleads us to think of it not as Roman gladiatorial spec-tacle, but as Greek tragic theater. Greek tragic theater is a theater not for the exhibition of deeds, but for the ineluctable revelation of a concealed truth. The death of the hero is decided by a destiny that the spectators are induced to grasp with a higher intelligence, which the insertion of the indi-vidual into a cosmic order or providence or political cause makes possible. In the corrida it is not the death of the torero but that of the bull that is plotted, in the third act, within fifteen minutes of the opening of the gates. The facts are that all the toreros do get gored, but most die of syphilis or tuberculosis. The death present in this Black Mass is not a sacrificial death; it is not the Orphic death of a god by which his power will pass into the cosmic order; it is not the intelligible exposition of death in nature where the dying of an organism is its redistribution into others; it is not a cultural death where a dynasty, an age, a revolution triumphs through or perishes with the death of the tragic hero. Here there is not a solitary life that con-fronts its place in a kingdom of God, the cosmic order, or a revolution; there is an animality in which nothing is visible but a condensation of the ferocity of nature, a single-minded and brave, unretreating rage that drives the bull to his death, but which has made of the organization of life in him the most powerful in nature. The corrida then is not a theater with a plot of interactions to be intelligibly grasped, nor a truth to be deduced from events, nor a confused spectacle to be understood in narrative order, with beginning, middle, and end; it is a ritual of atavistic nature, in the time of repetition, the time of "in the beginning." What is true is that the inner force that calls forth death is here revealed as what the male body is made of. This force is the dark blood of nobility that swells the phallic anatomy. All the minor arts of costume and jewelry, of choreographed mannerisms and manicuring, all the flattering cultivation of patronage and the priming of critics with gifts, which would make an athlete fall to the ridiculous, do not tarnish but set off the dark light of nobility in his exposed carnality. The ritual of the torero is made of precise and complex and instantaneously discharged intelligence, to be sure, and neurological precision, and the impeccable taste breeding and not training can produce, and the unwavering force of valor. All this visibly is inscribed on, is sustained by or produces an epiphany of arrogant and fateful phallic sexuality. It is virility erected in splendor at the brink of raging death.

What our culture's mind can understand is a *virile body*, a body where virility is virtu, the primary virtue of courage. Socrates at his trial, where the virtue or aberrancy of his pedagogical enterprise was to be defended, instead spoke of his courage in battle, which all his fellow citizens knew. Aristotle was to explain further, when in the *Nicomachean Ethics* he put courage first in the list of virtues, that courage is the transcendental virtue, the condition for the possibility of all the others; without courage neither honesty nor magnanimity nor service nor even wit in conversation are possible. All courage, the courage to endure physical pain as well as the courage required to make decisions, is but the ramification of courage in the face of death. It is from the power to hold one's own posture as the ground gives way beneath one that every other power to take a stand is derived. Is it not the dim sense that all the causes and works of civilization are so many ideals or idols set up to defy death—that the virtues of laborers and of athletes, inasmuch as they are ways of holding firm when pain assaults and when the support of others gives way, are derivative of the power to withstand the confrontation with death—that saves us from seeing a ridiculous anatomy under the glory we flood on their bodies? Is not the corrida a ritual in which this dim intuition is maintained in the midst of our laborious culture which only produces comfort and security?

There is then perhaps in our resentment of them a dim sense that the cult of the bodybuilders desecrates the ritual structure with which we maintain dignity in and conjure ridicule from our physical nature. The public does not see in bodybuilders ferocious and destructive brutes which offend its sacralization of civilization—they are known to use their massive power as guardians of bourgeois property, taking jobs, typically, as night watchmen and bouncers in nightclubs where the rich idle, and are suspected of being steroid-pumped eunuchs from whom the debutantes have nothing to fear. The resentment senses in them a virility insulated from death. Years of training that led to no corrida, only to the footlights of a high-school stage. Not a brave contest with death, but a sentimental fantasy of immortality on glossy photographs, fetishized into the metal figures of trophies. The dueling scars obligatory on German university students of the last century confirmed the nobility of their caste; the steel of the bodybuilders' equipment is nothing but inertia, exorcised of the death that forged the saber. There is a feeling at large that the musculature gained in work and in rule-governed contests, the bodies of construction workers, deep-sea divers, and boxers, is virile and virtuous; the musculature built in the rituals of the bodybuilder's cult, grotesque.

The hands of the bodybuilders do not contend with the inertia of implements or weapons, but rise to unfold in the sunlight or fold to frame their great swollen bosoms; beneath their wasp waists their legs pirouette; Arnold Schwarzenegger studied in a ballet studio how to walk with the grace of a prima donna. The discomfort so voiced today before the new breed of women bodybuilders makes rise to the surface the vision of the hermaphrodite that one meant when one called the excessive anatomy of the male bodybuilders grotesque. Psychoanalyst Julia Kristeva, after viewing the film *Commando*, spoke of how explicit this has now become: Arnold Schwarzenegger in happy domesticity, tender, caring, feeding his child—no mention of a woman that would have given birth to this child or of what had become of her. The bodybuilder does not only stand in phallic hardness; he or she also moves rhythmically with the tensed violence of labor pains.

Is it not true that this body is not ennobled with the contention of power with death within it because it is oriented in the other direction— toward the fatality of genetic potential it is grappling with, toward birth? Bringing the dead weight of the steel within hermaphrodite muscles, the bodybuilder brings him-herself ever closer to that limit determined by birth. Our genes harbor another death, an inner death; as soon as we are born we are old enough to die, says an ancient wisdom. In pushing back to the genetic coding of the genus, one pushes one's way to the death sentence written in the individual by the immortality of the genetic formula. The living organism, Freud taught, discharges its forces to ward off the death exterior to it only in order to seek its own death, its own advance to the death that is its own. The courage that forces us into this internal death, this death that is for each his or her own, is the very courage with which we are born. Freud was only thinking that every living organism has a life span that is indistinguishable from its definition as a species, even though its life forces are so many resistances to the death-dealing blows that fall upon it from without. The sequoias are not killed by the lightning that strikes them every year and burns out their cores; the seed was programmed to live for two thousand years, and then to die. But the bodybuilder tears down, muscle system by muscle system, all the strength in his-her fibers and cells against the death of the steel, and he-she knows that the hard will that takes him-her all the way to the limits of his-her exhaustion is the very movement by which power, and new, greater, power is born. His-her work, his-her feats, are nothing but labor pains; and he-she knows what is genetically coded to be born in him-her only in knowing the time and the effort it takes to leave all his-her force on the dead inertia of the steel. There is then in the force with which the bodybuilder assumes all that is and could have been born in him-her also a courage and a splendor. Even if, viewed from the outside, it appears as the monstrous excrescence of maternity in the virile figure of power.

Triton Conch, Swallow-Tailed Moth, Quetzal Bird

This monstrous, that is, anomalous, gigantic, and ostentatious, figure would be the way the cult overcomes the ridiculous view of the human anatomy reduced to nature. Is not the conviction that our anatomy, ridiculous by nature, has to serve as the material for art coextensive with all civilization?

The civilization our species has launched and pursued to relay its evolution appears in nature as the exteriorization not only of the powers but also of the splendors in our organs. Leroi-Gourhan demonstrates that the first art is the most inward—an artistry done on one's visceral core in the yoga of Mohenjo-daro and Harappa four thousand years ago, an artistry that condensed song into a mantra that is sounded only inwardly, that interiorized the dancing motility of the body into the scanned rhythms of the circulations of air and blood and semen.[6] The compulsion for ordering the circulation of men and goods in outer, public space—which Freud found contemporary with the first beginnings of technological civilization, and which he attributed to the compulsion of the principle of economy—we would see to be an exteriorization of the sense of inner rhythm and circulation which were the materials for the first artistry our species worked on its own nature. The first artists worked, Nietzsche wrote, with the noblest clay and oil, the artist's own flesh and blood.

The epochs of the splendors of civilization appear to Leroi-Gourhan to be epochs of the progressive exteriorization of this inwardly working artist compulsion. Thus the art of body movement and vocalization, dance and song, would issue from the older visceral artistry of the yogis. Glorification of the body surfaces exposed to view comes out of the distant epochs where dance and song were the media for our species's self-glorification; making of the body surfaces a collage of bird-of-paradise plumes and boar's tusks, or a cuneiform tablet of tattooings and scarifications is an artistry that arises in a culture of festivity and chant. A subsequent stage of exteriorization is that of the architectonic splendors of Babylonian, Athenian, Mayan, Ottoman, and Gothic culture, which honored as major artists those who framed the construction and urban layout that houses human movements. The art exteriorized on surface effects—in the age when those who are preeminently called artists are painters—the "humanist" art of the European Renaissance and subsequent modern period of painting was an artistry worked on the exterior spectacle as blocked off and framed into a perspective by the human eye. Now the buildings that man's earlier artistry had surrounded him with serve as the points of departure for an artistic eye that orders into splendor the views from the balconies and the towers. Our contemporary art now extends itself beyond the perspective spread out before the human sense organs to the spaces reached for by the mind and by its electronic relays—to microcosmic and macrocosmic exteriority. Contemporary art is conceptual, framing the designs of microchemistry and astronomy; contemporary music captures the songs of the whales and those of the earth's magnetic field.

The meaning and the origin of the drive productive of splendor seemed to Freud as enigmatic as it seemed certainly coextensive with the defensive and utilitarian drives that transform nature and transform our nature. Living things are not only equipped with organs to perceive what is exterior; they are also equipped with organs destined to be perceived. Splendor—if created by the chance coincidence of random events in a canyon in a desert, in a sunset over equatorial waters—is also an organic production of living things. This was the thesis of Adolph Portman, who argued that the patterns of animal body surfaces have their own intelligibility.[7] The morphology of the inner, functional body, the form and the arrangement of the skeleton, of the respiratory, circulatory, digestive, and reproductive organs, and of the prehensile and locomotive organs, does not make intelligible the always regular and often intricate and ostentatious patterns of the body surfaces and extremities. These have to be understood, he argues, as organs-to-be-seen, whose designs and colors become intelligible only when we correlate them with the specific powers of the witness-organs for which they are contrived. The inwardly coiling horns of the mountain sheep and the hairless, protuberant buttocks of the baboons are, he says, organs as closely fitted to the eyes and lips of the spectator as the jaws and hoofs are fitted to the terrain and the specific foods of the species.

In the human primate, a distinctive reflexive circuit was set up with the evolution of the hand. The human species began by putting the cutter, chopper, and grinder functions of the jaws into its hands. The front legs no longer serve to drive the jaws to make contact with the world; they rise from the ground and conduct samplings of the world to the head. The human animal now acquires a face. Its muscular configurations no longer react immediately to the front line of contact with external nature, but turn to its own hands. A smile and an apprehensive grimace now become possible—movements that are *expressive,* that is, that address a sample, a representative of the independent exterior held in the hand and, soon, held with a mental grasp before an inner eye. An animal that faces considers representations it has apprehended. Its manual musculature becomes not prehensile only but also expressive; the hands position their take for an appraising eye. They address themselves also to the eyes of another animal that has acquired a face; they speak. Little by little our whole musculature has learned to speak. The throat muscles designed for devouring and for expelling substances and the body's own biles and rages now learn from the hands how to shape the samples and representatives of the outside, how to exteriorize the comprehensive expressions the hands first learned to make. The whole torso becomes organs-to-be-seen, the abdomen struts and cowers, the legs and thighs acquire humility and pride, the shoulders and back, turned from the face-to-face circuit, sway with resentment and defiance.

Unlike the birds of paradise and the mountain sheep and the baboons, the human species did not develop distinctive organs-to-be-apprehended in addition to its organs-for-apprehending. Its hair, become functionally obsolete, is in an advanced state of disappearance; it has not deviated into a patterned pelt. Its teeth, whose functions were exteriorized onto tools, are in an advanced state of atrophy, and have not deviated into coiling tusks to make impressive the face. With the upright posture, the primate genitals are permanently exhibited to the frontal view of another, and, Freud assumed, this has led to the primacy of the eyes over the smell as the chief organs for sexual stimulation, and to the end of a rutting season, the unseasonableness of human libido. But the human genitals remain organs fitted for contact, and have not become expressive organs. To be sure, the human species has contrived snares for the eye—penis sheaths, cache-sexes, pendants hung over the breasts—but these are exterior to its own genitalia, which remain glandular, orifices of the inner, functional body.

But the human muscular system has taken on the second, expressive, role for which the other animals have evolved distinctive organs-to-be-seen. The human muscular system is not only the scaffolding that positions and turns the sense organs, the organs-for-apprehending; the vectors and surges of motor energy illuminate the muscular network itself and make its mesh and mounds snares for the eye. On human bodies muscle frettings are their peacock tails, curls worked on the lips their crests, biceps and pectorals their coiled horns, finger waverings their lustrous pelt.

Civilization—in that epoch when the hunter-gatherers mutated into self-domesticated animals—altered the human muscular system. As it exteriorized motor efficacy from the human muscles to the animal, wind, water, and steam power that relayed them, it exteriorized the ostensive functioning of muscles into masks, talismans, and costumes.

To be sure, this exteriorization is not yet complete and definitive; there still floats in civilization an imagination that feeds on muscles. Indeed, the imagination, that unpenetrating, superficial vision, vision of surfaces without depth, is a faculty of the muscles. Mishima spoke of the displacement of his sense of himself when, an intellectual, he committed himself to bodybuilding;[8] there is a specific sense of one's identity that rises out of the visceral or cerebral depths to find itself henceforth in the contours one's substance spreads out to the sun. This self, spread in the tensions of the musculature, doubles them up with an imagination fascinated with forms, patterns, and surfaces, which dwells on one's own surfaces. And muscles are not exposed without doubling up their surfaces before the imagination of another. It is the first effect of their reality; their contours excite the imagination before they displace resistances. That the visceral system does not have such an effect can seem puzzling. The awareness of the contents of fluids in us of the saline and mineral composition of ocean water, the inner gulf streams, currents, and tides, the coral reefs, the channels lined with tentacled anemones, and the floating plankton within does not double up our sense of ourselves with a vision of the oceans from which—tide pools now enclosed in a porous sack of skin—our muscles have carried us. In fact, the imagination is not divinatory and does not penetrate the deep; it is a surface sense, its mirages mirroring superficial mappings of the terrain, excited by the contours of muscles. And our muscles, becoming more and more obsolete in mechanized industry and automated war, become the more designed for the faculty of imagination.

In the obsolescence of an epic imagination does there not spread now only a tropical erotic imagination? The Marlboro man, a torso hardened, according to the legend, by riding the range, is perhaps a torso riding the range in order to be hardened into a Marlboro model. The editorial writers of *Playboy* and *Playgirl* declare that the anatomies they exhibit have been fashioned by Olympic nautical training and ocean sailing, but swimming, sailing, bicycling (on stationary machines before mirrors), and workouts on universal gyms are perhaps designed to produce the play musculature. Is the human muscle sheath, strapped to machines, monitored by cardiovascular and fat-ratio dials, turning into the showy carnal corollas and petals of human orchids?

This evolutionary destiny is unclear; the future is complicated by the existence of the cults. In them the body-substance is turned into muscle everywhere, the glands of the abdomen and its coiled membranes into muscles that can parry the blows of a fist, the atrophied mammary glands of males into matrices of trust and power, the cords of the neck are not neglected, nor the bands aligning the finger joints. They use the most elementary bars and weights; to this day no world-class bodybuilder has trained on the Nautilus machinery scientific intelligence has designed for them. These are atavistic bodies, halted before the age of the self-domestication of the hunter-gatherers. We found no real difference between the scene in Gold's Gym and on the banks of the Ganges, where the origins of every method to divinize the mind with every possible cosmological system, but also where every method to divinize the body with sublunary power can be traced back to, and where we saw, in 1980, young men making the prostrations before the idols of the Aryan ape-god Hanuman which we term push-ups and calisthenics, and, while intoning mantras, lifting before him rocks and pairs of millstones fixed on poles. Cults where we see not body-mechanisms made on machines, but primogenitor bodies made of *the elemental*—the weight of the terrestrial, and rivers, and sun.

The bodybuilder's implements do not relay the passage of the body's force outward. The bodybuilder confronts the steel, the opaque, inert mineralization of death, with all the body's animate power in what is no contest but a process of symbiosis or synthanatosis. He-she tears down the hermaphrodite muscles on steel, exhausting all their force on it, and when muscle failure has been reached, receives from the metal its properties. His-her biceps become tempered flails, his pectorals, that is, his mammaries, his femaleness, become gearing, the membrane of his-her abdomen a sheet of corrugated steel, his-her knuckles themselves brass. The luster of the muscle-contours acquires for the eye the opaque impenetrability of metal. At the same time in the repetitions, the contractions and flexions, the bodybuilder internalizes into channels of surging power the fluidity of the sweat and the oils, the vaporous currents of steam, showers, surf, and sunlight. The power that holds the bodybuilder upright is no longer that of a post before equipment civilization has erected. Tide pools of the maternal ocean enclosed in a porous sack of skin carried up to dry land by developing muscles, the muscled body stands erect now with the form that a fountain maintains by the incessant upsurge and fall of streams of power.

The bodybuilder senses his-her identity on the bronzed, metalized luster of the beams of musculature exposed to the sun; it is on the sweat-sheets across this hard skin and the surface gleam of the sun, and on the surfaces of mirrors displaying the oiled definition, that he-she now seeks him-herself. Existence, for the self, no longer means inwardness, visceral or cerebral involution, but exposure. This self is a movement to extend itself across contours and forms, and not to maintain a point of view, a repair in space. As the ego surfaces, distends, and exposes itself, it depersonalizes. The steel does not only transfer its properties into the living tissue that has exhausted its own force on the steel; the homogeneity of the steel drives out the principle of individuality in the bodies that devote themselves to it. It does away with the eccentricities—the dry and irritable skin, the concave fainthearted chest, the indolent stomach, the furtive hand, the shifting eye—by which movements of retreat set up the as-for-me of individuality and leave their marks on the body. On his-her contours the bodybuilder watches emerging not the eccentricities his or her tastes and vices leave in his or her carnal substance, but the lines of force of the generic *human animal.*

How little the rest of us see of our bodies! Our genitals we conceal, even from ourselves, judging them, with Leonardo da Vinci, of an irremediable unsightliness; our visceral and glandular depths, the inner coral reefs and pulsating channels of antennas and gyrating polyps, our very imagination blinds itself to. Our musculature we attend to with a clinician's or mechanic's inspection. The drive to visibility, to high-noon exposure, is so alien to us that it has to be driven into our substance by the steel. The bodybuilders have watchmaker eyes for the individual components. They do not, like the rest of us, see a charm or a brutality; their eye is specialized for details, trained in instant measurings, intolerant of dissymmetries. As they wait in the wings for the decisions of the judges, the contestants line up in almost exactly the order the judges will have placed them. As though it is not the individual eye permanently fixed in a point of view and a perspective that sees, but the impersonal eye of a species in evolution appraising its organs and limbs for an advance whose duration and direction are unknown. Bodybuilders look at one another, and each at him-herself, also with an alchemist's eye full of chemical formulas, protein supplements, quack remedies inspired by analogies, and drugs made in biochemical laboratories. They know their muscle substance with a cellular and not general and conceptually formulated knowledge, with a knowledge that thinks in the pain of cells being stretched and elongated, being torn down, a knowledge that does not preside over, but yet somehow accompanies the invisible movements of the millions of antibodies within that are the real cause of and reality of the separateness of our bodies.

One does not know what role evolution will find for these prodigies of musculature—or what evolution their artistry is contriving for the species. No one, Nietzsche wrote, is more readily corrupted than artists. Their souls, their taste, can be bought by venal priests of pagan religions, by the big investors in the image-industry, by the master-computers of the racing military-industrial complex, and by their own followers and flatterers. Today the names of the bodybuilders whose names are known are the names of so many industries, auxiliary epicycles in the wheels of the planetary machinery.

The imagination that feeds on muscles imagines something else— imagines that the deviation their cult makes from the path of civilization might be carried further. Civilization destined the self-driving power of human bodies to be transferred into tools, and then to be transferred out of human muscles into draft animals, wind, water, steam, atomic fission. The bodybuilders at this late date reverse the movement, disconnect from the tools, having interiorized their elemental properties, and make of musculature a splendor. Civilization destined the powers of surveillance in human sense organs to be directed toward the motor force now exteriorized in draft animals, windmills and waterwheels, electric and atomic-fission generators, and then to be transferred out of human sense organs into automatic and feedback mechanisms. Can we imagine at some future date the eyes, the touch, the heart disconnecting from the machinery that feeds in the images and the information, and glowing with their own resplendence? Civilization evolved the faculty of memory, reason, and decision, and destined it to program the electronic sensors and feedback mechanisms that make the human sense organs obsolete. Can we imagine at some future date the faculty of memory, reason, and decision disconnecting from the computers which it now serves, ceasing to be but an organ-for-apprehending, and, swollen with its own wonders, becoming an organ-to-be-apprehended, an orchid rising from the visceral and cerebral depths of the cybernetic forest with its own power, rising into the sun?

1986

Cause, Choice, Chance

It had started to rain lightly in the Deer Park in Sarnath, where the Buddha gave his first sermon. I took shelter under the huge arms of the bodhi tree, which was grown from a cutting taken from a tree grown from a cutting taken from the bodhi tree in Bodh Gaya, under which the Buddha attained enlightenment. Someone else had taken shelter there, a man of around forty, dressed in white dhoti and kurta with cream-colored scarf. His presence was very beautiful, composed and gracious, his voice resonant, and he was physically beautiful too. He said he was an astrologist. I said I would like to hear about his work. He is consulted by people who are troubled, who find that they are unable to cope with their situation. He helps them get in touch with material reality and their bodies. He explains that our bodies are composed of oxygen, carbon, hydrogen, nitrogen, calcium, phosphorous, sulfur, potassium, sodium, chlorine, magnesium, silicon, iron, fluorine, zinc, rubidium, strontium, bromine, lead, copper, aluminum, cadmium, boron, barium, tin, iodine, manganese, nickel, gold, molybdenum, chromium, cesium, cobalt, uranium, beryllium, and radium. He recommends meals of varied and wholesome foods, dusted with ground precious stones, rubies and sapphires. He then prepares their chart, putting their birth and the cardinal events of their lives in the cosmic map of the most remote heavenly bodies.

There are, he said, necessity, choice, and chance. There is today a rigorous discourse on determinism—the natural sciences, including anatomy, physiology, neurology. He said there is today a rational discourse on decision—ethics and politics. But in the West there is no longer a reputable discourse on chance; it only survives in the marginalized talk of gamblers and fortune-tellers. Each day we attend to the causalities that determine the physical well-being of our bodies and their safety, the causalities that determine the layout of possibilities and obstacles in our environment. We make decisions about the goals we want to pursue and the responsibilities we undertake for the welfare of our children and our community. But all the major events in our lives are due to chance—our birth; a teacher who captivated us and engaged us in mathematics or nursing, music or football; the person we happened to meet and fell in love with; the job opportunity that abruptly opened; our child who was born or who was autistic or who died; the car crash that crippled us; the tumor that grew silently in our inner organs. There is, he said, an element of chance and risk in every relation with another human being. We never really know what someone might think or might do. We can only trust him or her. Chance is the unpredictable, the incalculable, the incomprehensible, surprise, shock, good or bad luck.

In any experiment the formalism of quantum mechanics can predict the possible outcomes and the probability of each of those possible outcomes but cannot predict a definite outcome for a particular experiment that might have more than one outcome. Statistical mechanics calculates probabilities in large systems. In the world scrutinized down to the level of atoms, subatomic particles, and radiations, microphysicists accept the Heisenberg uncertainty principle. In the universe viewed back to the Big Bang and the subsequent dispersion of clouds of gases that collected into stars and novae and galaxies, astronomers recognize that the determinisms established for observable and measurable events on this planet do not apply. Random mutations occur in species, most of which stunt the off-spring or make them maladapted to their environment, some of which are beneficial and make the offspring more adaptable, and some of these eventually issue in new strains and new species.

When I think of the chance encounter of this woman with this man—out of the seven billion humans on the planet—of the chance that she pleased him and he her, and of the chance that they disrobed and made love, and then of the infinitesimal chance that out of 200 million spermatozoa repeatedly ejected into her vagina this one met with and got absorbed into this ovum, I can only think that my existence was extremely improbable.

Each gamete contributes twenty-three chromosomes. They could combine in more than seventy trillion different combinations. This particular combination that I am had but one chance out of seventy trillion to take place. Had any of these other combinations taken place, the child who would have been born would not have been me but someone as different from me as a brother or a sister.

Then I think that in my grandmother's womb the chance that my father was who he is and not someone different was also one in seventy trillion. Likewise. my mother is a staggeringly improbable chance combination, and likewise each of my ancestors.

The more, now, that I study the world, with all the books and laboratories of physicists, chemists, biologists at my disposal, determining, for each event in the world, the conjuncture of disparate causes that brought it about, the less I see that my existence was anywhere decided by the course of the natural world. Beneath me, behind me, there is nothing that programmed me, required me.

Our enterprising understanding finds itself blocked by unforeseeable chance, struggles against chance. But my primal recognition of chance is to celebrate the chance of my existence. And thus there is excitement, exhilaration in the recognition of chance events and encounters.

That my facial features are refined or commonplace, that my hair is brown or blond are effects of chance. I find I have beauty, vivacity, flair, style, dash not through character management but by good luck. As I have the bad luck to be ugly, dull, lumbering, low vitality, and low libido.

As some people have the good fortune to have quick and penetrating minds, there are also people who have a talent for happiness. In the workplace, in everyday situations, in the rain and the snow, they are not dulled and darkened by despondency and laugh a lot. Whereas others, equally endowed with health, self-confidence, intelligence, physical skills always seem to be in neutral or even dull; they have to force themselves to feel happiness.

By a stroke of bad luck some people have genetic and biochemical predisposition to sociopathology. As there is physical bad luck, there is also moral bad luck. And there is moral good luck, as philosopher Bernard Williams argued.[1] There are people who are spontaneously generous, people who impulsively leap to help a person in distress at risk to themselves, being brave by nature. People who easily resist peer pressure to go along with shabby and venal behavior. People who do not get overwhelmed with anxiety when a moral decision involves risk to themselves.

Passions are distributed to humans by chance. The passion for truth, which drives great scientists—they say they found it in themselves; it was not really put in them by education. Likewise, the passion for justice—in Mohandas Gandhi, Martin Luther King, and Che Guevara. Passion for adventure, for love.

Morality exists to counteract Fortuna, the good or bad luck that befalls individuals. It aims at an order where goods are distributed according to merit. It excludes chance, caprice, folly. By postponing the recompense of merit to another world, the rational autonomy Kant celebrated is achieved independently of the accidents of nature and of history.

The compulsively thinking mind, confronting bad and good luck, seeks to find causes and reasons for strokes of luck. People find inanimate objects, charms, amulets, talismans, tattoos, found or kept on one's person, that bring good luck, and malefic objects and events that are encountered that bring bad. They find willful agents, spirits, gods, or demons. The Roman god Fortuna and the Hindu god Lakshmi were acknowledged to be distributors of luck. The Christian theological concept of Providence attributes all strokes of luck to Divine Plan. Thornton Wilder, in *The Bridge of San Luis Rey,* recounts that on July 20, 1714, an Inca suspension bridge over a canyon in Peru broke and precipitated five travelers into the gulf below. Franciscan Brother Juniper witnessed the horror and could not help asking, "Why did this happen to these five?" He spent the next six years interviewing hundreds of people in an attempt to prove, empirically, scientifically, that Providence had determined that what appeared to common mortals a blow of catastrophic bad luck was exactly the right moment for these people to die. But after six years of interviews he realized that there was much that was uncertain and much that was not disclosed in all his research. The authorities of the church recognized that and pronounced the work heretical. They ordered his book to be burned and its author with it.

We know only by raising questions, and everything we discover gives rise to further questions. We pursue knowledge knowing that death will cut short our interrogation before the answers are supplied. We have no idea what significance being a jazz musician, a Southern novelist, a physicist, a nuclear engineer, an American, a Westerner will have at the end of the century. We will die of AIDS without knowing if a cure will be found a year after our death; we will die of cancer without knowing if the ozone shield hole will be closed or opened ever wider by the advance of industrialization and fossil fuel usage.

Our understanding, in recognizing causalities, and also in recognizing choice and its consequences, locates causes and choice in the linear time of the before and after. Chance events occur without being foreseen in our survey of the causalities of the environment. They occur in a field of time without progression, the time of fate. This time is not given in a separate intuition; it is caught sight of in an event—a birth in all its unforeseeable newness, a death, the annihilation of something irreplaceable.

It happens that a chance event changes not only our circumstances but also our identity. The economic downturn and three successive years of drought, and he was forced to sell the farm, which had been in the family for three generations. A fall, an injury, and she is no longer a dancer; she has to become someone else.

On the second day of the Fifteenth Conference of the Association for Medical Humanities held in Dartington, Cornwall, we gather in a small theater. Emily greets each of us as we entered. She is perhaps forty, wears a big bouffant silver-blond wig, scarlet lipstick, deep eyeshadow and very long false eyelashes like a cabaret performer, no, drag queen. She sashays vamp provocatively before us. She is wearing a pale blue hospital gown. When we are all seated on the banked rows of seats, she tells of how she became a woman. "I learned that if you are young and beautiful and you offer tired, thirsty travelers ripe, juicy grapes they will do whatever you want, so long as you are dressed in green." She dances and says she had a big poster of Patrick Swayze over her bed when she was fourteen. "I am dangerous. I am inside you. A little kiss, a little bite, creeping through you. My fingers will spread through your body. My tongue will lick from the inside out." She tells us these things in raucous slang and with the wanton gestures of a cabaret performer. She is making the turns in her story goofy. She takes off the hospital gown; under it she is wearing another hospital gown, decorated with ribbons and red net petticoats, French cancan knickers. She undoes the top ribbons and slowly lowers the gown to reveal her flat chest with no nipples. "I got the first of my scars and lost my hair. I lost my left breast. The right one went as well. My ovaries are next on the list. This is how I forgot how to be a woman." She does a provocative dance in the red net petticoats, wig, cosmetics with Patrick Swayze portraying Johnny Castle in *Dirty Dancing*, possessed with the force to hold him in life.[2]

She leaves, then returns, now no longer in costume, sits with us to listen to us. To a question, she explains that when she was pregnant with her first child they discovered a lump in her left breast. She did not have a full mastectomy, as the anesthetic would have been too strong for the baby, but a year later she had a recurrence and so had the mastectomy. A further year later they found she had a BRCA 1 gene variant that necessitated the second mastectomy and oophorectomy in order to prevent ovarian cancer or another breast cancer. "Who, what am I?" she said. "My body is no longer that of a female," she said. "I am no longer female." She says she never considered a breast reconstruction as she doesn't want to make her cancer invisible or endure further surgery. She says she finds her scars very beautiful.

The recognition of necessity, the recognition of causality or law, is an act of understanding and reason. The recognition of choice is the recognition of possibilities. The recognition of chance is the recognition of something unforeseeable and unpredictable. The recognition of chance is anxiety and exhilaration. Anxiety and fear are the visceral sense of risk, of bad luck, that fills our minds and saturates our nervous sensibility and our musculature, our bodies. Confrontation with chance, with the unpredictable, provokes intense activity in the mind that seeks to understand but thwarts resolution and decision.

I knew that Owen and Alexa, married when in graduate school, had wanted a child born of their love but had delayed until both had secured teaching positions. The pregnancy now went well, Alexa noting that in comparison with some of her friends she suffered little from morning sickness, heartburn, constipation, or back pain, and even fatigue was minimal. But one night she was rushed to the hospital and delivered a baby girl. At twenty-four weeks. They named her Claudia.

The doctor asked Owen and Alexa if they wished Claudia to be on palliative care or put in a neonatal intensive care incubator. Owen found on the Internet statistics for very premature infants, those born after twenty-three to twenty-five weeks of gestation.

> If they are given palliative care, they will die.
> Of those who are given neonatal intensive care 62 percent survive; 38 percent die.
> 27 percent will survive without moderate to severe neurodevelopmental impairment.
> 38 percent will survive with moderate to severe neurodevelopmental impairment, such as cognitive impairment, cerebral palsy, autism, deafness or blindness, psychosis, bipolar disorder, and/or depression.
> 18 percent will survive with profound neurodevelopmental impairment.

The Netherlands has a national policy not to put infants born at less than twenty-five weeks' gestation in intensive care.

The doctor explained that they could choose palliative care for their very premature infant, a care aimed at making her short life as painless and peaceful as possible. He gently but honestly told them there is some risk that even with the most conscientious palliative care the infant might suffer. Owen and Alexa thought with anxiety of day after day visiting their infant doomed to die. They forced themselves to think of how afterward they would deal with their decision. To resolve the doubts, misgivings, and desolate memories that may trouble them, they would not have those consoling words (perhaps the only honest consoling words in face of tragedy) "You have done everything you could."

Owen and Alexa recognize that if they choose intensive care Claudia could be among the 38 percent who die in the neonatal intensive care unit. They hope that she will be among the 27 percent who survive without moderate to severe neurodevelopmental impairment. How does one weigh a 27 percent chance of a healthy life against a 56 percent chance of death or profound impairment?

They had to assess whether they would be able to bear the financial costs of the lifelong care of Claudia if she turns out to survive with severe neurodevelopmental impairment.

Owen and Alexa could not keep from thinking of their mental and emotional strengths and the professional and social activities that made their lives meaningful to them, which would have to give room to care for a possibly severely impaired child. They wondered if they could want to have another child. They thought of the impact a severely impaired child will have on the time and resources they would devote to another child.

They consulted the doctor who delivered Claudia and who had had experience with very premature infants. But they wondered: Was he saying what he thought they would do if they understood all factors involved? Was he taking account how he thought they would or could handle the decision and its consequences? Was he saying what he would do if he were the parent?

In this situation with so many factors unknown, they wanted to hear the experiences and thoughts of other parents who had put a very premature infant in neonatal intensive care. They found that they had to envision the circumstances and character of those other parents and also assess the reasoning that led to their decision.

They met parents who resolved the uncertainties by deciding on the basis of principles that they had decided were certain and that they appealed to and reaffirmed to make their decision. Religious principles, for example. They thus delivered themselves from uncertainties and the risks of a decision that they would perhaps later regret. But finding themselves now in a situation where the risks in so important a decision were undecidable made Owen and Alexa see that to take those principles as certain was a decision those parents made in the past. Owen and Alexa had not made such a decision.

The will to open our eyes and our life to the length, breadth, and depth of what comes to pass drives us in extreme pleasure and extreme pain.

Without anxiety—without extreme anxiety—chance would not even be perceived. Experience, that inner rending by which we open to the unforeseeable, unpredictable, and unmanipulable, is painful. Pain undermines our firm stand on familiar ground; every pain is a chance to catch sight of an unknown happiness.

We were taking a drive in the countryside outside of Melbourne. Paul was telling me about one of his patients, a young woman of twenty-two, who had an aggressive breast cancer and underwent a double mastectomy and now aggressive radiation and chemotherapy. Her family was comfortable enough, but she had not gone on to college and recently had been working as a salesperson in a women's clothing boutique.

"One can skim over the world, skim over life," Paul said after a while. "Have a job, just doing each day what there is to be done. Evenings, weekends, talking on the phone with whoever is there. Watching whatever is on television."

I thought of days, weekends like that. "Like it's one distraction after another," I said. "Like not a distraction from what you chose to do or what is important. Every distraction is a distraction from another distraction."

"Sometimes a serious illness," Paul said hesitantly, "might be the best thing that happens to a person. The occasion to work to see what is important and what frivolous. What people are important to you, what activities, what pleasures. The occasion to get a sense of oneself as someone distinct who will one day disappear."

The intellect, the reasoning, reckoning intellect tracks down regularities, bases predications on past regularities. This kind of calculative intellect belongs with action, for our initiatives, our projects count on regular patterns in the environment being repeated.

But chance quickens the will. There is excitement, exhilaration in taking chances. Gamblers know this exhilaration, but we also know it in climbing high ladders to paint window frames on the second floor of our house, in speeding on the highway.

Chance is caught sight of in events that befall us and cast before us superabundant gifts. Chance suddenly supplies resources for an undertaking I had not dreamed of; a chance discovery in a laboratory brings me a cure for a malignant condition that had kept me an invalid for twenty years. Chance offers a radiant midwinter day. A chance encounter brings me a lover.

Cameron is the veterinarian whose clinic is closest to my place; I have gone to him with ailing animals and birds. Over the years I have occasionally met Melissa. When you see Cameron and Melissa together you see they are in love. The way they look at one another. The way each attentively follows whatever the other is saying. The way their hands easily touch one another. Love, that attachment to him out of dozens, hundreds of men she met over the years, that attachment to her out of all the women he has met.

I discovered that some of the paintings, austere minimalist abstractions, in the veterinary clinic were done by Melissa. Her day job was in a women's shoe store. Cameron was thirty-one when they met. A dating agency would not have matched them up.

Melissa had brought in a blue-gray-barred pigeon that she had rescued from a neighbor's cat. The pigeon had flopped about without being able to take off and fly; what was she to do? The receptionist said, "We do not treat street pigeons." Cameron stepped into the waiting room. He said, "We do not treat street pigeons." Melissa said, "I think he—or she—has a broken wing." Cameron took an X-ray of the wings. Melissa watched him clean the wound and set the little broken bones. "What do I owe you?" Melissa asked. "Nothing," Cameron said. "We do not treat street pigeons." Melissa returned a few days later with the bird for Cameron to clean the wound and change the dressings. Three weeks later Cameron removed the dressings and waved his hands up and down with the pigeon who lifted off and fluttered around the room. He opened the window and they watched the pigeon fly off to a nearby tree. They went outside to look at the pigeon; it was well. And Cameron and Melissa looked at one another with tenderness. Nothing is more contrary to love than to interrogate, to seek to explain that magnetism, that sorcery, to imagine everything in her or his behavior predictable. Nothing is more contrary to love than to exclude strokes of luck, of good luck and therefore to exclude strokes of bad luck too.

Immanuel Kant defined happiness as the abiding state of satisfaction of all our needs and wants. But the English word *happiness* derived from Old English *hap* (chance, fortune), and meant lucky, favored by fortune. From Greek to Irish, most of the European words for "happy" at first meant "lucky."[3] Surprise is essential to happiness. See "happen," "happenstance," "perhaps." Happiness is not an enduring good, is not acquired by character management and merit, is not ruled by the morality of good and evil. It is the state of someone lucky to have found this man or woman to love as no one else can love him or her. It is the state of someone who finds the earth lucky that it has glaciers, sequoias, hummingbirds, chameleons. Who finds himself lucky to be able to help, to give directions to a stranger on the street, to protect the rain forests, to safeguard the Ozark big-eared bats.

Moments of supreme happiness—after a laborious trek through forest reaching a cliff over the ocean where radiant colors vibrate the skies like driftings of euphoria, watching comets flicker across the desert sky, seeing a wild turkey parade across the lawn with ten downy chicks, greeting one's grandmother recovered from surgery after a car crash, receiving one's newborn infant in one's arms. The supreme happiness surges like a gift of chance; no satisfaction achieved through planning and labor is akin.

The sense that the given is given, is a gift of chance, is gratitude. Gratitude is active: it consists in receiving with embracing hands what is given, holding it together, and showing it to, sharing it with others. Happiness is radiant; it gives freely to passersby, to fields and forests, to mountaintops, to the coral reefs, to the depth of the earth, not asking anything in return, not even thanks.

"West Penwith is at the toe of the foot of Cornwall, perched on a massive upwelling of granite. At the rugged north-west edge igneous rock bursts through the hills, exposing high cliffs hovering over windswept beaches."[4] Everything looks random, the shape of the rocks, the foaming crests of the waves, the gusts of wind, the drifting clouds. Sam Bleakley was born in Penzance. When he was five his father took him with him on surfboards into the waves of the ocean. Sam grew up in love with the ocean. "The wave rises, heavy and thick at the base, light and crisp at the lip as it peaks and throws, breaking free from the anchor that is the deep swell, the incessant tidal motion, the undercurrent, the pulse, the bass-line. As the wave throws bright foam heads, it plays an improvised run against the background *mordros*, round blue notes against a big beat. Waves are a delicate presence weaved into the sea's force."[5]

"Nature makes no noise," Thoreau wrote. "The howling storm, the rustling leaf, the pattering rain are no disturbance, there is an essential and unexplored harmony in them."[6] Sam grew in love with the sound of the waves. The sound of the sea and the movement of the waves are unpredictable, improvisational, but harmonious melody, like free jazz.

Surfing, along with kiteboarding, snowboarding, parachuting, rock climbing, parkour, is considered an adventure or extreme sport, one that has a high level of inherent danger. In the eyes of the public participants are taken to be thrill seekers, enjoying a brush with death. Surfing is indeed dangerous. "One slip and your skin is sloughed, your bones ready to show. Even the smallest contact with those electric coral heads will cut, and without quick treatment an infected wound follows."[7] Burst eardrums cannot be restored. But surfers and other adventure sports enthusiasts find their pleasure in attaining a high level of knowledge of their unpredictable terrains and great skill acquired in situations of extreme difficulty.[8]

"Speed is essential to surfing. It is about confidence and rapid decision, positioning, getting in the pocket, but also using the body as a motor making your way into the sweet spot rather than waiting for it to happen." [9] "For me, control through style became the goal of surfing. I modeled this on a supposed conversation between bird and fish (or, strictly, mammal)—the equipoise of the hovering kestrel and the grace and playfulness of the dolphin, with its sudden bursts of power, and the balance between keeping the beat and improvising a solo that is central to jazz.... Control is poise and presence, not force or arrogance; poetics, not persuasion." [10]

"The top end of ecstasy in the perfect moment—the tube ride, long hang ten or big weave drop—is a small part of surfing's endless grind and challenge in paddling, duck diving, wipeouts, shark anxieties, bodily wear and tear (because the joints and ligaments give way long before the will).... This is not masochism, but living the blues, improvising life, making meaning." [11]

The causal determinisms that we track down in our physics and chemistry explain why when we view the sun at the horizon the layers of atmosphere reflect light to us of varying wavelengths but do not explain why one sunset is more beautiful than another or why a sunset is beautiful. Our botany and biology do not make predictable that the flowers of trilliums are beautiful, that the plumage of pheasants is more beautiful than that of geese, that one Chinese woman but not her sister is beautiful. It is by chance that there is beauty in the world.

See this. See the intricate designs of tiny Alpine and huge tropical flowers, the powdery wings of butterflies and moths, the colors of the 319 species of hummingbirds that are not due to pigment but to the way the crystalline cells of their minuscule feathers reflect the light. See the streaming colors of the coral fish and the tiny rainbows flashing briefly on bubbles in the surf. See how the setting sun emblazons the skies with unnamable colors different every evening, different every minute of the evening.

2018

Return of the First Person Singular

The Science of Subjectivity and the Sciences

At the beginning of the twentieth century, Edmund Husserl launched phenomenology as a rigorous and positivist science of subjectivity. It was set up to deal with specific problems in other scientific disciplines. The discovery of paradoxes in mathematics had put in question the ultimate rationality of mathematics and of the mathematized empirical sciences. Husserl's phenomenology worked to trace mathematics and logic back to their fundamental units and operations and to exhibit the mental acts in which they are constituted. Subsequently he judged that every scientific discipline was in need of a phenomenological investigation of the subjective acts in which the distinctive objects studied by that discipline are constituted, given to intuition and their meanings ascribed.

Empirical and ideal objects—the essences with which objects are identified and classified—are given in intuition; intuition constitutes them as objects. Intuition occurs in acts in the first person singular—"I see." These acts can be brought to light by a specific kind of reflection, also an act in the first person singular. The successive intuitive and meaning-ascribing acts, and the second-order intuition that is reflection, retain and anticipate one another, forming a distinctive individual stream of consciousness that is the first person singular. The science of subjectivity is based on the reality of the first person singular.

By midcentury, developments in other sciences led to discrediting the phenomenological conception of subjectivity. Structural linguistics had exhibited system in the phonetics and syntaxes of languages and demonstrated that languages change in systematic ways. The meanings of words and expressions form within language and are determined by the existing vocabulary, grammar, and paradigms of a language; they are not the products of individual subjective acts.

Anthropology discarded, as post-Enlightenment Western, the concept of individual subjectivity as an abiding identity and source productive of meanings, judgments, decisions, and initiatives.[1] It is cultural symbols that, Clifford Geertz affirms, first articulate, generate, and regenerate thought. To think is to identify things and relate them with words and other cultural symbols. Symbols are external to the thinker; they are words and also images, markings, gestures, rituals, graven idols, water holes, tools.[2] Their meanings are in their uses, and the ways they are used are accessible to observation without divining the minds of the users. "The meanings that symbols, the material vehicles of thought, embody are often elusive, vague, fluctuating, and convoluted, but," Geertz affirms, "they are, in principle, as capable of being discovered through systematic empirical investigation ... as the atomic weight of hydrogen or the function of the adrenal glands."[3] Thus anthropology can dispense with the dubious methods to access other minds and become a natural science like any other.[4] Claude Lévi-Strauss set out to show the underlying structures, not explicitly conscious, in kinship systems, myths, garb and adornment, cuisine. He set out to show that fundamental generative structures are universal across cultures.

Emotions surge focused by words and symbols. Indignation, a feeling of injustice, of frustration of our expectations and plans, envy, jealousy, triumph—words and cultural symbols, not produced by the individual mind, make them possible. "Not only ideas, but emotions too, are cultural artifacts in man," Geertz declares.[5]

For the postmodern philosophy of mind meanings are articulated in the taxonomic contrasts, semantic systems, grammatical forms, and rhetorical paradigms of languages, which are social and institutional productions. The meanings of speech acts produced by individuals are determined from the specific tongue, milieu, profession, and social and practical situation in which they are uttered and from the distribution, condensations, and displacements of signifiers in the unconscious. Perceived things and events are not only identified with language; the vocabulary, grammar, and rhetoric of a specific language determines what we perceive and how. Action is ordered by the material imperatives of things and the cues, watchwords, and orders of social institutions.

For postmodernism, Ellen Fox Keller explains, "subjects are ... constructed by culturally specific discursive regimes (marked by race, gender, sexual orientation, and so on), and subjectivity itself is more properly viewed as the consequence of actions, behavior, or 'performativity' than as their source.... Selves are multiple and fractured rather than unitary, mobile rather than stable, porous rather than enclosed, externally constituted rather than internal or 'inner' natural essences."[6] The agency in me that says "I" is not a substantive identity; it is intermittent, fragmented, transitory.

Art is now no longer seen as a discontinuous succession of individual creations; its themes and styles are engendered by the history of art. Postmodern theorists have abandoned the notion of creative force in the depth of the individual, indeed the notion of creativity: a society produces innumerable materials, mediums, forms, colors, meanings; artists select and combine from this existing fund. Their productions are constituted as art by being accepted into the history of art by the institutions and commerce of the art world.

The postmodern philosophy of mind is seen to be realized in the practice and usage of electronic media. Media broadcasts diffuse representations of events and products; information about everything is instantly available on the Internet. Knowledge is stored as neutral units of information, detached, as in Wikipedia, from the experience and perspective of a thinker. Cyberspace engineers and theorists see themselves producing a global brain in which potentially all things and events are represented, all data stored in memory, and linked in all possible ways, connected, combined, synthesized. Individuals connected on the Internet constitute the noosphere, the collective consciousness that emerges from all the users of the Internet and that is greater than any one of them and greater than all of them. It would be analogous to the hive mind of ant, termite, or bee colonies studied by biologists. Its axioms, paradigms, technologies of image and message production, and distribution technologies studied by cyberspace theorists and culture studies.

Surveying the field of scientific research today, we see three sectors of research that break with the postmodern conception of subjectivity.

Anthropology and the Problem of the Informant

Classical ethnographers observed the habitats, implements, economic activity, institutions, and beliefs of a community in view of producing an account of a particular "culture," conceived as a functionally interrelated structure of economic, political, and ideological systems. Their work was scientific not only in the rigor of its observations but also in that the representation of a culture is translated into the vocabulary, paradigms, and explanations of scientific economics, sociology, political theory, psychology, biology, and physics.

How are these productions of an anthropology that aims to be scientific verified? In most cases, another ethnographer does not go back to that community to verify what the first has written. In most cases, the members of that community cannot or do not read the account of them the ethnographer has published. In practice a monograph is accepted by the anthropological community for internal characteristics—the appearance of detailed and exhaustive data and the apparent rigor of the reasoning and conclusions drawn from them.[7]

Agricultural practices, housing construction, tools and equipment, economic exchanges, and kinship systems are recorded and translated into the objective terminology of modern sciences. But all these are found to be determined by the natives' understanding of causality and the symbolic meanings ascribed to them. In practice the ethnographer sets out to learn the language, the categories, the imagery of the users of symbols and learns them by speaking to the natives and being understood by them. The anthropologist conceives the "culture" as an overarching and integrated system of symbols and representations, distinctive to a society, that provides individuals with a meaningful framework for orienting themselves in the world around them and to one another.

But field researchers have come to recognize that the ideology or mythical or religious elaborations of a community are very unevenly present in the understanding of any informant. Pieces of the ideology and myth combine but also conflict with the practical knowledge each individual acquires of his or her particular natural environment and workplace. The discourse of the informant is also shaped by the sensibility, energies, and skills of his or her body. Consciousness waxes and wanes as sensory thresholds, states of wakefulness, fatigue, and also instincts, cravings, appetite, agitations, drives surge and recede. Two women working alongside of one another planting and harvesting crops, the one with superabundant energy, the other with slow metabolism, the one young, the other aged after multiple childbearings, do not experience the same articulation of that field, and though they use common words to describe it, the words do not have identical force and meaning for each of them. The singularity of a person's body also figures as a force of resistance to the identities attributed to him or her by others and by the ideology. Individuals with somewhat different pieces of ideology and myth and practical knowledge interact and engender changes in practical enterprises and social institutions and also in ideology and myth.

The entry of the field researcher into a community alters the network of social relations in that community. The researcher does not go unnoticed into every field and room, a fly on the wall. What an informant tells the ethnographer is selected and oriented by the political and psychological relations the informant has with other members of the community and with the researcher. The informant, commonly paid by the ethnographer, has a political and psychological relationship with that researcher. The informant is motivated by ambition, pride, cupidity, suspicion, affection, a longing to be recognized and admired.

There may be much dishonesty in the relationship the researcher has with her informants; the researcher often conceals what she knows in order to increase the likelihood of acceptance and does not reveal her research goals. Her relationship with her informant is shaped by her curiosity, fascination, protectiveness, lust, frustration, anger, vindictiveness, disdain, craving for privacy, homesickness. The publication, twenty-five years after his death, of Bronislaw Malinowski's diaries—where he writes often of how he was just sick of all these truculent and fickle savages—has made ethnographers aware that they are not simply recording what an informant says but are in an obscure agon with an individual.

Anthropologists write for readers in their own culture, primarily the academic community, but have to first understand and represent the native's point of view, more exactly, represent the individual informants' point of view. This has led to the search in recent decades for new forms of writing.[8] There is need for theory to conceptualize the forces that make the discourse of the informant his or her own voice.

The mind of the informant is not simply a locus where the ideological system of his culture is inscribed; it is a force of commitment—commitment to some pieces of this system but also to his work and his maneuvers in the network of his political and psychological relations with others.

Medical Practice

Anthropologists have come to see that every community has contact with other communities and imports some of the representations of other communities, modified, renamed, reversed and assimilated, some sections badly integrated, coexisting or overlapping with sections of its own representations. In zones where a people has been invaded or conquered by another and have to contrive their lives between different economic and institutional systems with different cultural and mythical systems of interpretation, there arise cargo cult messiahs, Vodou serviteurs, ialorixás, mediums, curanderos. They deal with individuals in individual predicaments and work with parts of the Christian and parts of the Aztec or Yoruba mythology to make sense of what is happening in this individual. They have to invent, to fill in the gaps, to work by inspiration. They improvise rituals and sacraments.

Today anthropological field researchers everywhere encounter such encroachment of an alien system of understanding on communities in the entry of modern scientific medicine. With the intense and highly profitable penetration of pharmaceutical marketing across the planet, many people, especially the poor, are treated by local health workers and by their families with a mix of modern therapeutic methods and pharmaceuticals, traditional healing resources, and religious and ritual practices. Medical anthropologists set out to assess and understand the impact of healers and rituals. They come to recognize that individuals are forced to take responsibility for their illness and healing with whatever resources and understanding they can assemble.[9] Medical practitioners have come to recognize the difference between a patient assenting to and obeying the doctor or the faith healer and a patient taking responsibility for his disease and its cure on the basis of his daily sufferings, observations, and judgments. Their practice will be different if the doctor has to take account of the patient himself or herself taking responsibility for his or her disease and its treatment. We need a theoretical understanding of the first person singular in this force to take responsibility for one's illness.

In our Western societies folk medicine and faith healing are vanishing alternatives to scientific medical research, institutions, and practice. Medical science has constructed a highly technical vocabulary and grammar to formulate the results of its laboratory and clinical research into pathologies and their treatments. When a sufferer goes to the doctor, the doctor translates the patient's account of his ailments into this language, and the patient is induced to learn this language to understand his ailments, communicate them, and assent to treatment. Increasingly patients download explanations and treatments from the Internet before and after their consultations with the doctor. The extraordinary advance in pharmacology and hi-tech surgical interventions has made this language more necessary and more difficult for the patient to master.

Medical practice finds that it must also deal with economic, political, and juridical institutions. The patient must learn and understand the medical discourse and to some measure also the economic, political, and juridical discourses.

But the patient has also to endure the suffering and to assess its impact on his family, his work, his sense of the life he henceforth has to lead and the death that he has to face. For all this, the medical discourse is of no avail. Indeed, the real and promised advances of medical biotechnology, organ transplants and prostheses, and life-support systems work to defer death, rendering suffering and death intolerable and unintelligible. The sufferer has to elaborate a narrative of her aspirations and her fate, her destiny, her lifetime. The patient's narrative of that alien event in her life that is her illness will determine what treatments she will accept and may even have an effect on the efficacy of those treatments. This narrative is composed not out of concepts but out of bewilderment, anxieties, fears, attachments, dereliction, and pain. The sufferer gets sight of the indifference of the material world, the impenetrability of brute reality, gets sight of the aleatory, improbable reality of his or her existence. Suffering and anxiety are not simply cultural artifacts; they are not made possible by the words of a culture but seek words for a private language, the narrative the sufferer composes by and for himself or herself.

Creative Image Making

Anthropologists who have studied mentally disturbed very poor people in Java, Brazil, and India find that the family of the psychotic may accept whatever therapy and psychopharmaceuticals are available while also invoking images and conceptions and rituals from the prevailing religion.[10] These images and conceptions function to fix, to bind, the rampant strangeness of the sufferer's experience and behavior for them. Medical anthropologists have investigated these phenomena in view of explaining the social and cultural context in which modern psychiatric practice in these places must be pursued.

The psychotic himself may identify himself and his states with concepts and images from the prevailing religion. However, the psychotic works an individual transformation of them, giving them new and distinctive structures and force, often viewed as heterodox and fanatical by the family and by religious leaders. They may often be mixed with practices of black magic and sorcery. Anthropological researchers have come to recognize positive and productive forces in these heterodox beliefs and practices: they function to isolate the sufferer from his or her family and the community in a protective withdrawal that enables the psychotic to recognize the distinctiveness of his or her sufferings and anxieties, establish some kind of distance from them, and produce images and discourse of strong coherence and emotional intensity.

In 1921, Dr. Walter Morgenthaler published *Ein Geisteskranker als Künstler (Madness and Art)* about Adolf Wölfli, interned as psychotic in the Waldau Psychiatric Clinic in Bern, Switzerland. Wölfli had spontaneously taken up drawing, and eventually produced his imaginary biography in an epic forty-five volumes of twenty-five thousand pages with 1,600 illustrations and 1,500 collages. In 1922 Dr. Hans Prinzhorn published *Bildnerei der Geisteskranken (Artistry of the Mentally Ill)* in which he reproduced and analyzed 187 of the more than five thousad paintings, drawings, and carvings he had collected from asylums in Heidelberg and farther afield, mostly from patients diagnosed as schizophrenic. Professional artists such as expressionists Paul Klee and Alfred Kubin and surrealists André Breton and Max Ernst hailed them as great art, a creativity freed from concern with competition, acclaim, and social promotion. Jean Dubuffet collected thousands of works of the insane, prisoners, and also spiritualists, mediums, and children, people ignorant of the canons and taste of the art world, calling them "art brut." English writers refer to them as "outsider art."

Charles Dellschau, who had been a butcher, after retirement over twenty-one years filled notebooks with drawings, watercolor paintings, and collages. After his death, the house where they were burned and everything in it was thrown into a landfill. An unknown person salvaged thirteen notebooks that then remained under a pile of old rugs in the warehouse of a used furniture dealer. They were shown in a gallery seventy-five years after his death.

Henry Darger worked as a hospital orderly in Chicago. In the room where he lived he wrote, over forty-three years, the 15,145-page, single-spaced manuscript of a novel entitled *The Story of the Vivian Girls, in What Is Known as the Realms of the Unreal,* illustrated with more than three hundred drawings and watercolor paintings; a novel entitled *Crazy House: Further Adventures in Chicago,* in fifteen volumes; and *The History of My Life,* 4,672 pages in eight volumes. These were discovered by the landlord when Darger was removed to a nursing home shortly before his death.

James Hampton, an African American, worked as a janitor. Over fourteen years in a garage that he had rented he secretly built an elaborate religious throne surrounded by 180 sacred objects and composed a text in a script that remains undeciphered. They were discovered by the owner of the garage after his death.

In 1982 some twelve hundred wire sculptures were found by a passerby in bags and cardboard boxes on trash pickup day in an alley outside a transient home in Philadelphia. Based on objects contained in the sculptures they were dated to around 1970. Despite extensive research, no one was found who knew the maker, who is now called the Philadelphia Wireman.

Dubuffet realized that to understand the phenomenon of art brut a new conception of the first person singular is required. He invoked the unconscious, not, as in Freud, constituted by what is foreclosed from and by consciousness but instead a wellspring of positive, creative energies, and not as impersonal but as radically individual.

This image making goes beyond the working out of rational perplexities and of traumas. The sense of terrifying, mesmerizing, lascivious realms of the world and of alien and violent feelings and forces within drives the image makers of the asylum and of marginals untrained in art. These images often acquire exceptional coherence, intensity, and expressiveness through techniques and styles that result from the long and obsessive application to the same themes. Not made as art, in the ignorance of the canons and history of the art world, these images are made for oneself and often in secret. They constitute a metaphysical habitat in which the image maker dwells more and more exclusively.

The postmodern philosophy of subjectivity increasingly provides theory for cultural studies, literary theory, aesthetics, and art practice, and for cyberspace visionaries. Will these areas of contemporary research trouble and displace this philosophy of subjectivity? To the extent that anthropology becomes a compendium of reports of individual voices, its relevance to sociologists and policy makers becomes the more negligible. The sophisticated biochemical, genetic, and surgical treatments being developed induce patients to yield decisions about their suffering to experts. The theorists of art brut early recognized that acknowledging these images made by the marginalized and the confined as art resulted in their techniques and styles being assimilated by professional artists and their works integrated into the history of art, and in the image makers responding to the recognition and marketing of their work and producing images in response to the taste of critics and collectors.

Yet these loci of subjectivity may well become more acute in the decades to come. To the extent that biotechnology extends its sway over individual lives and combats death with juridically imposed life-support systems, suffering and death become the more incomprehensible and unendurable. In the measure that anthropology reduces "culture" to a multiplicity of individual experiences, collages of representations and judgments, and individual voices, sociological generalizations become the more questionable. And perhaps the ubiquity of images may continue to induce people outside the art world to elaborate their individual visions.

2018

Contact

Every day I realize that others looking at me and talking about me or to me are only addressing some role I occupy in a society, some work I am performing, the white collar, overalls, or tank top I am wearing: they see and address the office worker, the farmer, the beach bum. While I—this individual me—think for myself and act on my own, behind that image they see. Doesn't it work the other way too? The agent or agency inside my head listening and interpreting is decoding according to its own code. So we are insistently told that we have to be made to recognize this and examine that code, its ethnic, class, race, and gender categories and paradigms. When someone there is standing before us, speaking directly to us, don't we have to take into account how this is the male or the female point of view, the urban or nomadic perspective, the way corporate officials or black prisoners see things, the way our cronies, out of so many shared interests and amusements, or the way Jamaicans or Thais in the tourist or the sex industry talk to people like us?

Yet it happens every day that someone exterior to me approaches and makes contact with *me*. "Hey you!" "Hey Al!" In the diffuse hubbub of the environment, how I feel these words coming straight at me! They have penetrated right through the garb, the pantomime, the role, and found me. The appeal they make singles out the real me, whatever I can take to be me; the demand they make is put on me. Each time I do answer on my own, I have found it undeniable that that is what has happened. I may well sense immediately that he who stands before me and addresses me has a mistaken idea of what I am and what I have done, but how his word *you* touches the real me to arise behind that mistaken idea!

When someone with whom I have been in touch only by telephone for a long time greets me, "Hey Al! Come in! How happy I am to see you!" I feel, I know that I—the real me, this individual—am welcomed. When I am insulted, the words and the gestures touch me inwardly: I can brush them off, ignore them, dismiss them with contempt, act as though my status and my composure are utterly unaffected, but inwardly I am humiliated, wounded, diminished, mortified. When someone apologizes to me for some tactless or slighting words, for some hurt or outrage, the words penetrate right to the core of my life, which is vindicated, reinstated, restored. When someone is speechless at the sight of me, visibly constrained, paralyzed, I know that he or she does feel my pain, is afflicted with my suffering. When someone, exasperated by the officious personage, the decent and public identity with which I persist in confronting him or her, seeks deviously or directly, viciously, to hurt me, torment me, it is not that personage or my corporeal shell but me with which he or she makes contact.

2007

Mortality

Socrates made learning how to die the subject matter of philosophy and made philosophy the daily practice of dying. He speaks of the relief he will feel when the opacity of his body will be broken. His last words, "Crito, we owe a cock to Asclepius"[1] say that life is the sickness for which death is the cure. Did not Socrates here claim to know things that he did not know: what death is—that death is a relief—and what life is—that life is sickness? Socrates died the way he did in order to demonstrate his belief that the soul is of its nature immortal.

Socrates had seen men die; he had committed himself to defend Athens in war, and he had killed men in battle. He does not speak of how they died or of the relief he felt when they died.

Death and Nothingness

Martin Heidegger, proclaiming the end of the metaphysics launched by Plato's Socrates, makes death—one's own death—again the central topic it had been for Socrates. Heidegger disclaims the conception that death is an accident that befalls a life that of its nature would endure unendingly. He sets out to show that we die of our own nature, that our life casts itself with all its forces unto its end.

Heidegger finds the experience of one's mortality in anxiety.[2] He distinguishes anxiety from fear. Fear is the grasp of something dangerous. It gives me the sense of my vulnerability. Fear gives rise to a mobilization of my powers to center on the threatening object or event and overcome it or flee from it. Anxiety has no identifiable object; it is a sense of danger lurking everywhere. It is the sense of one's whole existence being threatened. Anxiety, Heidegger says, anticipates my experience of dying. He interprets anxiety to reveal that my dying is passage from existence to nothingness, annihilation, and annihilation, for me, of the world about me. Anxiety, that sense of being cast adrift, the environment no longer supporting me, sustaining me, is a premonition of being cast into nothingness. Heidegger means to force me to see that my death is pure nothingness, that I am destined to be nothing.

Heidegger thus also claims to know what death is. He identifies it—it is this one thing, nothingness.[3] The death I know is my death; the nothingness I know is the imminent nothingness of my existence and of my field of experience. From the opening pages of Leo Tolstoy's *The Death of Ivan Ilych,* Heidegger finds that witnessing the death of others is not the source of my sense of my mortality. At the wake, I have only seen the body of another immobilized, tranquilized, but still fully, completely there. I have not seen annihilation. But annihilation is what my death will be for me.

Nothingness, Futurity, Possibility, Finalities

Heidegger brings together the future, the possible, goals, death, and nothingness. The sense of mortality that is anxiety is a premonition of being cast into nothingness. It anticipates a moment ahead when nothing further is possible. The anticipation brings into relief a field on this side of the brink of nothingness, where things are still possible. This field is the future.[4]

For my sense of the real future is not simply the logically possible— what I represent now by varying the layout of the actual. This representation exists only as a representation and exists in the present. My sense of the real future is also not simply produced by drawing out the implications and possibilities that I see in the present; this likewise produces but a representation in the now. What is really future is actually possible, and the actually possible is possibly impossible. The sense of the actually possible and future is produced by the anticipation of the really impossible.

Finally, the anticipation of ending makes possible the fixing of ends (289–90). The sense of my death is the sense of ending definitively and irrevocably. It gives me an inward understanding of termination in the continuity of the world, which makes possible every sense of goal and every sense of destination. The sense of one's life as a trajectory that casts itself with all its forces unto its end makes action possible, where life casts some or all of its forces toward some term.

The sense of the future, the sense of the possible, the consciousness of goals and the sense of mortality are thus equivalent. Heidegger also brings together the most thoroughgoing freedom with the utter inevitability of death. To exist in view of death is to live in the future and the possible, is to set goals and advance toward them.

But has Heidegger seen correctly the relationship between death, the last moment, and the future? For Heidegger, anxiety, by which I cast myself ahead over the whole range of the possible unto the brink of definitive and irrevocable impotence, is what brings out into relief the extent of a future that is my future. My death is the last moment in my time. But it is not a not-yet-present moment in the line of future moments, moments coming toward presence. It is a moment without duration, an instant, an instantaneous cut in the line of time extending before me. And the last moment does not really lie at the end of a line of moments to come; it is imminent in any moment. The next moment may be the last moment. The possibility of my death lies with each step of my advance into the outlying environment; a falling roof tile may strike me; my heart may fail. Anticipating my death in anxiety does not open before me the field of the moments of time to come; it divines the abyss lurking in any moment.

Then the undercurrent of anxiety can freeze initiative at the start instead of engaging the anxious one in the possibilities ahead and the resources at hand.

Death and Singularity

Heidegger separates utterly the death of others, observed outside, from my death, sensed inwardly in anxiety (281–85). It is this sense of my death that isolates me and posits me for myself as a singular existent. To look at the environment about me is to look ahead; to see things is to see possibilities: paths, implements, obstacles, tasks, opportunities. They extend indefinitely, possibilities open for anyone. My death advances toward me as the brink of the abyss, of utter impossibility. It outlines, in the outlying field of all that is possible in general, for anyone, an expanse of what is yet possible for me. It also reveals, under my feet, resources available to me. The acute sense of my mortality thus illuminates for me an expanse of possibilities possible for me. At the same time the anxiety that throws me back upon myself makes me feel what is unrealized in me, the potentialities and powers that are in me and have remained in suspense. Hence the sense of my vulnerability, contingency, mortality is also the sense of my being, my powers, my singularity.

Heidegger thus traces how the sense of the negative, pushed all the way, converts into the most positive, positing experience. It posits my existence in all its singularity. Death, the last limit of impotence, is turned into power, my power. Feeling myself adrift in the void, nothing supporting me, nothing to hold on to, I am thrown back upon the powers that still subsist in me, the powers that are my own. No longer counting on the support of the world or of others, taking up the powers that are my own, I now resolutely act on my own, exist on my own. To live one's life is to live out one's life, to discharge one's forces in the tasks and resources that the environment presents one. And that is the active enactment of dying.

Heidegger sees the anxious one resolutely driving his life with all his forces toward his death as toward its closure. But death comes, of itself. Death is stalking me and strikes when it wills. Death is not like a future, the brink where the field of possibles ends in the abyss, that we can envision and advance toward. The death that is coming for me remains exterior to the death I anticipate. This exteriority of death undermines the Heideggerian project to appropriate the power of death, to make of it my ecstasy and power.

Knowing Nothingness, Longing for Nothingness

Does anxiety really identify death to be nothingness? What is distinctive of anxiety, as contrasted with fear, is that anxiety has no identifiable object. It is a foreboding concerning what is indeterminate. What I am anxious about is the unknown—not something that I know to be nothingness.

We could compare the situation that arouses anxiety with our edginess in the night. What makes the night disquieting is not a perception of something dangerous but the fact that possible dangers are not localizable in things. We no longer perceive things; their contours are dissolved by the night. But this no-thingness is not nothingness; there is left the darkness of night, which fills space and invades us, is within as much as without. The dissolution of contours and boundaries renders whatever dangers the night harbors possible anywhere, everywhere.

The deep uneasiness before the unknown that afflicts me does not turn into a recognition that I exist on my own and can, must, act on my own. I would instead overcome, or at least endure, anxiety by seeking support in what is known, though it is now out of reach.

Death is ungraspable, unconfrontable; it has no front lines. We do not know that death is nothingness—nothingness is not some thing one knows.

But nothingness is what we can long for, out of all the density and suffocating opacity of pain and suffering.

Dying in Nature

Anxiety, Heidegger observes, can be fled or covered over, and it is thus concealed in everyday preoccupations (299–304). But when we see that death is unmistakably imminent, our existence would be nothing but the dull pounding of anxiety, driving the resolute plunge into nothingness. Yet anthropological research has shown that many people sink calmly and peaceably into death, and many cultures have elaborated practices that help people to die without anxiety. See the Tibetan *Book of the Dead*.

We have had a premonition of this calm. When we go to the forests and the meadows, to mountains and glaciers, when we descend into the coral reefs of the oceans, when we contemplate the movements of the clouds, we find ourselves not in the Heideggerian world of implements and objectives, pathways and obstacles, but in nature. A nature that we are not surveying with a circumspection governed by our interests; our look drifts among beings seeing them as they are, as they exist on their own. There is a dissolution of any governing and integrating force in our consciousness, and the systole and diastole of our consciousness disconnect to exist as pulses of luminous energy picking up the movements of light, patches of shadow, restless leaves, bird calls, sparkles in the water. We lie back in the meadow or in the depth of the coral seas, our postural axis fades out, we give over the support of our trunk and limbs to the ground or to the water, and in our bodies small surges of blood and nutrients and biles go on, in sync with the drafts of breeze, the pulse of sunbeams, the rhythms of the sea. We no longer stand upright to exist and act on our own; we lose our will to make our organisms into self-moving, self-motivating, self-programmed agents; we sink into nature.

This experience is a premonition of dying. Of dying in nature, into nature. A dying that seems to us to be the natural destination of our organisms. This destination no longer appears to us to be an inexorable fearful iron fate or a supreme duty we owe to authenticity or to our freedom but the calm movement with which nature flows through time.

We have spent days or weeks or months in other cultures sharing with them their experience of going to nature. We have accompanied on camel the Tuareg of the Sahara whose instrumental complex is reduced to a tent and a few utensils packed in a bag, and spent days in rhythmic movement over ever-drifting sand dunes seeing the footprints of the camels being erased by the winds. We have spent days on small boats with Moken people, the sea gypsies of the Andaman Sea, our bodies and our consciousness filled with nothing but the waves of the sea. We have spent long evenings with the never-Christianized Lacandon of the Chiapas rain forest, watching the embers of the fire glow and listening to the basso continuo of frogs and night insects. We have understood how dying for them would not be fraught with Heideggerian anxiety or resoluteness.

See the Corpse

Heidegger separates radically my experience of my mortality, the anxiety that reveals my dying as annihilation, from my observation of the death of others. Anxiety reveals to me that my death will be a being cast into nothingness. For me the death of others that I observe (and my death that they observe) is transition from active ex-istence, incessantly projecting a future state of itself and of its field of experience, to the state of a corpse. The corpse is unreservedly present, no longer generating intentions or possibilities. It is utterly present in a world as full as before. Thus holding wakes, going to wakes, is tranquilizing—an insight Heidegger finds in the opening pages of Leo Tolstoy's story *The Death of Ivan Ilych* (254nxii).

Anthropologists have instead reported in so many communities the outbreak of wild grieving and outrage not only of the loved ones but also of the whole community in the presence of a corpse. In societies subsisting in harsh environments, the Kalahari Desert, the Amazon, the Arctic tundra, the swamps of West Papua, where death is common, a corpse of a fallen warrior or of a child is excruciating for the community.

Heidegger defines the corpse as an existence that has turned into simply and utterly present being. But a corpse is a locus of violence. It is an organism where violence has struck, from without or from within, and where violence continues, bacteria, viruses, or tumors having assaulted the homeostasis of the body, releasing toxins that will break out of the organs and cells, contaminating the ground with blood, biles, infectious seepage, and excrement, polluting the air with foul gases.

Max Weber argued that the sense of the strange powers at work in a corpse, a fear of the corpse manifested, he says, by other species of animals, is at the origin of the ancient practices of burying or burning corpses and of the later practices of mummifying corpses, providing them with a tolerable existence, giving them offerings of food and drink, preventing them from becoming envious of the possessions enjoyed by the living.[5]

A corpse arouses horror in us, but we are also drawn to it. The first effect of bloodshed is hatred and the compulsion to shed blood in turn. The sight of the victory of violence in the corpse provokes the will to take on that violence, to wield it as one's own power. Anthropologists find many societies where every death in one's community produces an active initiative to kill someone practicing sorcery in a hostile community, or just to kill someone, anyone, in that community. Today, without belief in sorcery, the sight of a corpse continues to provoke the violence that requires another corpse—see crimes of passion, gang battles, wars, torture, capital punishment.

The Corpse I Am Becoming

Aging, the growing inertia that weighs on my initiatives, wounds, scars, infections, debilitating diseases give me a sense of my mortality. A corpse befouls and pollutes. The intense experience of shed blood, in wounds but also in menstruation, as well as body effluvia, vaginal fluids, semen, mucus discharges, and excrement show me my becoming a corpse.

It is striking that from Tolstoy's *The Death of Ivan Ilych* Heidegger only attends to the opening scene—the corpse cleaned, dressed in fine clothing, appearing, at the wake, to have achieved perfect rest, which gives the visitors an increased sense of their own buoyant vitality. But the body of the story is all about the small bruise that Ivan Ilych suffers when he is back at home and that does not heal and the growing pain that finally fills all of his days and nights and that gives him first an inkling, then the appalled recognition of death inexorably coming, already at work in him.

Pain is an experience of being riveted to oneself, unable to escape oneself by turning to the outside environment, unable to retreat behind the pain to observe it and deal with it. To suffer the pain is to be unable to turn away from oneself, to look outward, to forget oneself. Suffering is to be mired in pain, mired in one's own substance. The pain fills one's substance and smothers the force of the I. It weighs down and chokes one's initiatives; it depersonalizes. In the unstaunchable progression of the pain, Ivan Ilych experiences the progressive reduction of all his powers toward total prostration. Suffering contains a premonition of one's death in the guise of the last limit of prostration, materialization, becoming a corpse.

There is insight in suffering. What I had heard talk of, what I had conceived, imagined, feared, I now understand. Until I suffered, I did not really know what suffering was. And in suffering I first realize what the suffering of others is; I find myself suffering as all that lives suffers. And suffering and aging give me a premonition of the unrelenting reduction of my powers, prostration, materialization, becoming a corpse. Seeing others struck dead does give me a vision of what pain and aging inwardly announce in me. In suffering and aging I find I am dying as anyone, everyone dies, as everything that lives has to die.

Voices of the Dead

Burial of the dead, which archaeology now dates back at least eighty thousand years, and mummification, which among the Chinchorro peoples of present-day Chile began seven thousand years ago, do not by themselves prove that peoples that did these things with the dead did not regard the dead as *vorhanden* to be gotten rid of or as mementos of what no longer exists. But when the dead are found to have been buried or mummified along with utensils, weapons, and foodstuffs, anthropologists recognize these as evidence that for those peoples some of the life forces and powers of those now dead persist in some sort of existence. Ancestors endure in some form and affect the living beneficently. Widespread also is the sense that the dead are resentful of the living and pains must be taken to protect the living from them, to drive them out of the habitat of the living.

Heidegger, however, affirms that the death of others that we witness is their transformation to the state of a being utterly present, on hand, *vorhanden*, from which their lucid or oblivious future and possibility-ordered ex-istence has utterly vanished.

Today theories of communication induce us to depict the others about us as agencies with which we exchange information. But when we actually communicate with people about us, the exchange of information is a small part of our conversation; most of the time we utter words of welcome and camaraderie, give and receive clues and watchwords as how to behave among them and among others, gossip, talk to amuse one another. The other is evidently there, a person, for us not as an agency that issues meaningful propositions, information, but as an agency that orders us and appeals to us.

This fundamental presence and reality of the other as an agency that appeals to me and orders me can be separated from the perceptible presence of him or her. A voice uttered at a distance can penetrate to the core of our identity and appeal to us and put demands on us. A child may be ordered by the voice of a parent when that parent is no longer there; an adult may hear that voice when the parent is no longer alive, may hear too the parents of that parent. What in an earlier, evolutionist anthropology was dubbed "animism" recognizes that voices addressing us and ordering us may be the voices of other species and voices of the absent and the dead. Indeed, is there any society where the voice of ancestors is utterly silenced?

For us the voices of the dead order us and appeal to us often more forcefully than the voices of the living about us. The voice of our father invalidates the lecherous suggestions of our gang, our cronies, and the opportunist maxims of our boss. The voice of our grandfather makes us listen still to the cries of the peregrine, the drumming of the ruffed grouse, the voices of the pines and of the aspens in the evening breeze. The voices of Socrates and Hume strip authority from the sententious affirmations of our teacher. The dead also torment us. The voice of a parent who in words or without words said to us from childhood "I do not love you" curses us still today, twenty years after he or she died. When our mother or our child dies, we are tormented by all the things that we failed to say.

2018

PART III

Travel

The Unlived Life Is Not Worth Examining

How strange that a human, a living organism, is conceived as a material system in which needs and wants agitate it to open its eyes to the outside and seize the contents that satisfy its appetites and leave it to close back upon itself in contentment. How strange that life is conceived negatively, that the spirit is conceived as negativity.

A guppy, a cockatoo, a monkey, a human are organisms that continually generate excess energies that are discharged without thought or need of recompense. These superabundant energies are not simply dissipated; emotions that isolate, frame, crop, color, and shade events of the environment give them direction. Emotions, which dramatize, are the strength of vital movements; the primary emotions are active and thrust an organism into the thick of things.

How strange that emotions are conceived as reactions to things perceived, identified, and evaluated. Emotions break through the packaging and labeling of things that make our environment something only scanned and skimmed over. They are the forces that seek out and engage reality. Emotions are the forces with which we discover nature that summons in what we perused as the text of the universe.

Only those subjugated to the implacable discipline of common sense conceive of laughter and tears reactively—laughter as a relieved, tears as a panicky, reaction to a failure, a local breakdown, in the network of reason and order. An effervescent vitality generates the hilarity that seeks out what is incomprehensible, dysfunctional, preposterous, or absurd in any system where everything works. A brave vitality steadied by pain extends the gaze and the hand in compassion to all that suffers. When hilarity and compassion no longer drive a man or woman, he or she is moribund.

Blessing is the force poured upon the fragments, riddles, and dreadful accidents by a laughter that knows its own power to make them flourish and shine. A father is a blessing for his son not in the providential care that has set aside savings for education, life insurance, and a trust fund, but in the hearty laughter that sends the youth off on his motorcycle to roar the western highways all summer, a laughter that will invigorate the youth's own when he laughs at all the thunderstorms, tight-assed waitresses, and nights in jail in the months to come.

There is no strong grief that does not act by casting curses. Curses are not impotent reactions to the mindless blows of adversity; they are outbursts of torment that know their power to pursue the malevolent into its own lairs. Face to face, you see the force of your curses shatter the composure of the one you curse. Our curses drive the juggernauts of determinism that crush the innocent back into the no-man's-land of the unacceptable. Life knows that, like stars generating energies that produce effects across millions of light-years of empty space, it is a power to produce its effects across distance and time.

How strange is that kind of comprehension that aims to encompass the whole. How strange that kind of understanding that aims to identify everything. Mental life producing only grids and the et cetera. Resentful of disturbances, resentment of the passage of time that washes every content assimilated, it ends in contentment, the torpid satisfaction over content assimilated. Vitality drives another kind of understanding—one that opens up more, goes further. Such understanding is hilarious and grieving, blessing and cursing.

There is an inner momentum in the appetite for reality; emotions are not dissipated when released, but escalate. When one goes off to live in the mountains, one will long to hike all their trails, sleep in their rainy spring nights and winter snow, and climb all their cliffs. Once one gets a feeling for the sea, one longs to sail and dive the oceans. Lust is not content with respectful and considerate caresses and tension release; it wants another, yet wilder, orgasm, it wants orgasms on jet airplanes and in tropical swamps, it wants bondage and whips. One gets sick of the glut of cities, cultures, and nature converted into edited and framed and narrated images on the cathode ray tube; one wants to climb Machu Picchu, get lost in the favelas of Rio and the slums of Calcutta, get dysentery in Kabul and body lice in the bordellos of Marrakesh, sleep weeks in the Amazonian rain forest and ski Antarctica.

Over the forests and skies, continents and oceans satellite-mapped and computer-programmed for the satisfaction of human wants and needs, laughter and tears, blessing and cursing have gone out of a world become silent and desolate. But blessing is the beginning and end of all environmental or ecological ethics. A curse put on the suffering of all things is the source of all religion.

Perhaps there is nothing more other, remote, foreign to us than someone of our own kind. How strange that philosophy today mainly concerns itself with the relationship between objectivity and intersubjectivity and philosophy yesterday concerned itself with the citizen in the republic of ends or the polis. As though the other concerned us as the agency that promotes our beliefs into truths—another mind, an alter ego—and as our collaborator in the collective work that is called civilization. The strong, active emotions force through to the reality of the other, the reality of otherness. They drive on to someone to laugh at, weep over, bless and curse. And to laugh and weep with, bless and curse—the world, oneself—with.

The most profound thing I know is to find oneself on the other side of the planet, in a country with which one's own is at war, with someone as uneducated as one is educated, whose culture and religion one does not share or even know, with whom one shares no common tongue—and to find oneself utterly dependent upon that other for one's very life. Three times such a person put his own life at risk to save mine. What it means to find oneself in humanity then gaped open vertiginously before me.

A thinker gains nothing today by traveling to Paris, Berlin, Tokyo, Shanghai. Whether you go for a conference or on sabbatical leave, you will only encounter educated people who think what you think about democracy and market economy, about Christian or Islamic fundamentalism and the Sendero Luminoso, about highbrow conceptual art and middlebrow Madonna, about virtual reality and cellular phones.

The only places worth traveling to, and living in for as many months as one can, are Irian Jaya, Calcutta, Bangladesh, Laos, Honduras, Nigeria, Bhutan. Oh, many more: four-fifths of humanity are outside the archipelago of the technopoles. How supremely important to know the joyous cremation potlatches of Bali and *carnaval* in Salvador de Bahia, on our planet today where interminable butchery goes on in central Africa and central Europe and the only cause that can unite the industrialized and democratic nations is the control of cheap Middle Eastern petroleum.

It started the night I arrived in Bogotá, when I stepped out of the hotel to get a newspaper, and the woman greeted me not with a smile but with laughter to share. The next morning I bought one hundred sheets of typing paper and twenty-five envelopes the day after, and the shopkeeper had to count them over and over again, losing count because doubled up with some joke she remembered or was inventing. Waitresses in greasy spoons tell you a joke they have just heard before they hand you the menu. There is a ragged man who has a tiny newspaper stand around the corner. Every morning I go there at 6:00 a.m. He is singing. He spots me, reaches under the box for the most subversive paper, and dances up to me. I pay him ten centavos and turn back. He calls; I turn around. He asks me if I have heard this joke. I laugh but he knows I didn't get it. While I am laughing, with great skill he tosses a piece of candy into my mouth. Late afternoon, strolling crowds. Every few steps another outburst of laughter in the people I was passing by. You can't imagine what ten days of this does to you. It's worth crossing the seas for. It's more important than any political, economic, or institutional phenomenon in society today on the planet. It's as important as *carnaval* in Brazil.

The strong, active emotions are excremental, expenditures without return, ever-escalating devotions to the unfeasible, the impossible. One loses oneself in them, divests oneself of one's role, function, character, convictions, identity. There is an inner momentum to this dispossession. No one doubts this when he or she turns to eroticism, the most intense pleasure a human being can know, Freud said, and the force of every exultation. The supreme risk: one is never more vulnerable than when in love, when seized with erotic passion. It is through erotic passion that the other is other—goddess and tigress, god and wolf. Eroticism is the antipode of possessiveness—addiction to expropriation.

The understanding of humanity—the end of that preposterous condition known as self-respect and the joining of humanity—takes place outside the archipelago of the technopoles, in exile, in nomadism, and it commences when finally one night, driven by one's own carnal craving, one abandons oneself to a stranger, destitute in every way as one is destitute spiritually, upon whom one pours all one has of kisses and caresses. It is then that one can begin to join the sensibility, the sensuality, the alien ways of touching and shaping out of which what outside observers and experts call another culture becomes not a booty one brings back in one's souvenirs and snapshots but a force, a hilarity and a despair, a blessing and a curse.

Deep is the world, deeper than day had been aware, and deep its woe, said Zarathustra. But deeper still is joy. Joy is the most comprehensive state, he said; it alone is antimetaphysical, alone able to affirm love and hatred, woe, hell, disgrace, the cripple, world—this world, oh, you know it! Modern philosophy, which called itself antimetaphysical, undercut any possibility of believing what joy reveals of the world; joy is subjective, immanent, an intrapsychic event with but one witness. How rare today are people who are able to believe their joy; they wait for the surge of exultation to pass and make their decisions in prudence. Philosophy today needs the deep thinker who can deconstruct the epistemology of dispassionate objectivity and show that joy is the most comprehensive mind, the most penetrating mind, and that it is in the summits of joy alone that each one will see the path to take. Each important decision must be taken in joy alone.

How strange that there is a "must" in the realm of the rational activity of the mind, and in all the other realms only the prudent calculations of a human life with no other aim than its contentments. No one doubts that an imperative weighs on the rational intellect; as soon as one thinks, one finds oneself bound to conceive things with consistent concepts and to connect them coherently. The epistemology of science admits many forms of rationality, but never doubts the force of the imperative for reason, for consistency and coherence, that weighs upon every thought that arises to think.

This epistemology inherits from Kant the schema that although the force of the imperative for consistency and coherence is laid on the mind, the forms are the mind's own, and outside there is the amorphous content that thought conceptualizes and organizes. Kant was able to conceive the content of thought as without order or ordinance of its own only because of the dogmatic drowsiness of his phenomenology of perception. In this century the phenomenology of perception has been able to construct terminology and identify the patterns of consistency and coherence in the perceived world which command the forms of rationality that prevail in the diverse sectors of the natural sciences. There is a teleology in perceptual life, the phenomenology of perception demonstrated; perception is oriented toward the perception of unequivocal and scrutable things and a layout of compossible things. Perceived things are not given; they are imperatives. They do not appear in coordinates of empty geometrical space but in an ordered layout, a substantial and sequential field, which for its part is not given in perception but is imperative.

But a perceived layout of things along paths is itself suspended not in the void but in the depth of the light, in warmth, in liquid flows, upon the supporting depth of the ground. Light, warmth, flow, the ground are not objects or multiplicities of minute things; they are sensuous elements without boundaries or profiles, elemental depths which support and sustain the perceived and the perceiver. Our relationship with them is conceived only as enjoyment—an involution by which sensuous subjectivity takes form: we enjoy the light and begin to see on our own, we enjoy the support of the earth and move on our own. But the light is not only a means to see, the earth not only a means to support our self-movement to seize hold of, things. The elemental itself summons us imperatively to become luminous, warm, ardent, carnal, terrestrial.

If the phenomenology of perception has shown that things which perception perceives are not givens, but imperatives for perception, that nothingness which is the oncoming of the night is also imperative. A sentient life is not destined for things only, but for the nocturnal. The

Enlightenment philosophy that set up human life as destined to know things also invested that life with mastery over things, and divested it of any destiny in the world. But the night that invades and depersonalizes summons every life, summons imperatively.

The Socratic courage, first virtue and transcendental virtue that makes the other virtues—truthfulness, magnanimity, and even wit in conversation—possible, first erected human life as a force that maintains itself of its own forces at the brink of death. The modern philosophy that divested human life of any destiny and made its freedom its supreme value made freedom in the face of death the highest stake. Dostoyevsky's Kirilov and Heidegger are two projects to interiorize all the force of death itself. But death comes, of itself, summons us: one day we will have to—every day we have to—obey the summons of death.

Vital tasks for philosophy: to recognize the multiple imperatives in the perceived landscape, in the elemental, in the night, in the abysses of death. To set forth the clairvoyance and decisiveness of joy as obedience to an imperative.

1999

Lust

The Calypso. It's the biggest theater on Thanon Sukumvit, Bangkok's Fifth Avenue. It has seats for two thousand; expensive seats for the well-heeled and upwardly mobile: Germans and Japanese and Americans and French and Saudis and Kuwaitis and Chinese from Hong Kong and Singapore. There is a cast of a hundred, a different show each night. Palaces, skyscrapers, desert oases drop upon the huge stage in outbursts of electric lightning. The Empress of China appears, seated on the uplifted hands of muscular men whose naked bodies have been metallized in gold greasepaint. Gongs and the *shakuhashi* propel the advance of the traditionally transvestite dancer of Japanese Kabuki theater. Now the stage fills with ballerinas spinning out adagios and minuets from *Swan Lake.* Mahalia Jackson with rapturous voice sees the sweet chariot comin' to take me home. Mae West comes sashaying in with a chorus line of nuns. Marilyn Monroe resurrects with puckered lips to coo for diamonds; your incredulous fingers want to feel for the wound to be sure. Divas, grande dames, vamps, pop superstars, they are all, of course, men in their early twenties. Now there is the stripper. With rose-blushed complexion, under a sunny cascade of Farrah Fawcett hair, clad in a silver-sequined gown, she uncoils in the cone of a spotlight. She slinks toward you on spike heels, her lips tremble and part, her sultry eyes fix you, her silvered fingernails clutch at her sides, grip her breasts, slide down between her thighs. She unbuckles her waist-sheath with convulsive movements, flings off her skirt. You slide into the movement: props and plumage being shed to reveal flesh and nature. But at each stage of the strip the more is exposed of her body the more female she gets! Your mind is getting twisted behind your eyes by the contradiction between the ample thighs, soft belly, full breasts your prurient eyes see and what you know. Her eyes are pulling at you with torrid magnetism. Finally she snaps off the *cache-sexe*: you see pubic hair, mons veneris. How the hell could she gyrate like that with her cock somehow pulled between her thighs? Then abruptly, for just a second, the cock flips out and the spotlight goes off and she is gone.

This now must be the last number. A big iron cage is wheeled out by a stout matron in safari garb and wielding a whip. Inside the cage, a dozen extravagantly beautiful women. There is a Thai in Siamese courtesan costume, an Indian in a sari, an Indonesian in a sarong, a Filipina in a *terno*, a Vietnamese in an *ao dai*, a Cambodian in a *sampot*. They are clinging to the bars of the cage, shivering with fear and weeping. On the right side of the stage there is a gathering of men, German and Japanese and American and French and Saudi and Kuwaiti and Chinese from Hong Kong and Singapore. The matron in the safari drag unlocks the cage and brings out the women one by one for inspection. One by one, each man makes his selection and leaves, until the cage and the stage are empty.

After some moments the audience applauds briefly. Then they file out, looking at the floor, past the performers who are lined up in the lobby, their hands folded in the traditional *wai* greeting.

Antifeminist theater: transvestites are more sensual, more charming, more tantalizing, more seductive than one has ever seen debutantes, fashion models, starlets, or British princesses. They are the ones who have cut through all the inhibitions to realize the consummate feminine look, that—Baudelaire said—blasé look, that bored look, that vaporous look, that impudent look, that cold look, that look of looking inward, that dominating look, that voluptuous look, that wicked look, that sick look, that catlike look, infantilism, nonchalance, and malice compounded.[1]

They always let you know. Something shows through—the lean flanks, the curves only drawn in by posturing, the unmuscled but overset shoulders: the body underneath not female though not masculine, virile, either. They lip-synch to perfection songs of a dozen languages they do not know, but you do see that it is not these Adam's-appled throats that are trilling these soprano songs. If the performer has finally had so much plastic surgery done and is so artfully costumed that you no longer see the squarish shoulders or the pelvis too narrow for maternity, then the magic is gone and there is just an ordinary female singer imitating an act another woman created. These are not males pathetically trying to look and act like women; they try harder than women, dare more, outdo women. These twenty-year-old guys emanating, delighting in, flaunting one-night-stand sexual identities which we in the audience have known as destinies and obligations.

You, who came dressed up or dressed down for the show, feel your femaleness being discredited in this gala of divas and superstars. You, her husband or her date, or just there with the guys, feel something aggressive against you in all this glamour and gaiety, which you, after showering and shaving, would never try to concoct.

One hardly ever notices transvestism in the streets in Bangkok; the cabaret is its space. Space not for the discontent of nature, but for the specific pleasure of theater. We foreigners, gaping at the female voluptuousness affected by these male performers, don't get a lot of what is going on, especially when the numbers are Indochinese female impersonations with Indochinese songs. The cabarets of Bangkok compete in sumptuous costuming and dazzling stage effects; the performers, superlative dancers and poseurs, virtuosos of an enormous range of moods and expressions, queens in realms of colored floodlights and canned music, affect more glorious and hilarious female wiles than one had realized Thai culture had created and foreign cultures exported. When I left Bangkok for Paris, I went to see the shows in the Alcazar and the Madame Arthur and found them really uninventive by comparison.

There is the specific pleasure of transvestite theater. There is no script for which a director seeks actors who are naturals for the part. They don't do plays, stories; they just do the femme fatale, the czarina, the college cheerleader, the Brooklyn Jewish mother, each the matrix of an indefinite number of plots and intrigues. They have no director, no one is a natural for a role, each one inverts and transposes his nature entirely into a representation. Each is a parthenogenesis in his own laser-beam placenta.

Primal theater that recommences today in Harlem discos and rock concerts rediscovers transvestism. It is only bourgeois theater, which the Balinese think is not theater and Artaud dismissed as recited novels and pop psychagogy, that is not transvestite. The female roles of Elizabethan theater were played by boys. In this theater of the greatest and most single-minded age of English imperialism, these boys were parodies of imperial males. The Queen found much of Shakespeare to her distaste. In Japanese Nô theater, the high theater of the samurai caste which glorifies their Zen ideals, all the roles are played by mature men. Kabuki, the low theater of the merchant class, originated in the red-light district of Kyoto and its plots parody the plots of Nô theater. Female prostitutes played all the roles; Kabuki was performed as an entertainment for male merchants. But it happened that Kabuki was so rich in theatrical innovations that it attracted clandestine visits from the samurai, who soon appropriated it, upgraded it, composed music and text for it, and it too came to be performed entirely by male actors. The T'ai people are profoundly matriarchal, and rural Thailand, Laos, and parts of Myanmar are to this day. Patriarchal culture entered Siam late, through the royal family, which, though to this day Buddhist, in the late Sukhothai period—as Angkor long before it—imported brahminical priests and, with them, Vedic patriarchal culture. Under King Chulalongkorn's program of modernization, large numbers of Chinese coolies were imported to build the land transportation system across this river kingdom; these were to stay on and settle into the traditional commercial activities of Chinese everywhere in the cities of South Asia; today a third of Bangkok is Chinese. They are the second entry of patriarchal culture into Siam. Since the Sukhothai period, in the now patriarchal court of the king, all the roles in the high court theater of Siam have been performed by women; it was conceived as an entertainment for the king. Village culture centered in the temple compounds, the *wats*, which are regularly the scene of religious feasts and fairs. There popular theater developed—entertainment featuring rogues and outlaws, burlesquing, as low theater everywhere, the manners and heroic legends of the court. And working in, under cover of comedy, ridicule of state policy and even of the monks. Low theater inverts and parodies high theater. The popular theater of matriarchal plebeian Siam put males in and out of all the roles.

In the cabarets of Bangkok today this theater has been reoriented for an international audience. Even in the cheap cabarets full of Thais, the *farang* tourist has the impression that the show is being performed for him. Although every show contains some acts from Siamese popular theater, in the sound systems, the disco music, the media superstars being impersonated, the cabaret is very Western and Hong Kong–Singapore–Tokyo. This occurred recently, when the military junta put in by the Americans during the Vietnam War realized that the planeloads of dollars that came into the country with the tens of thousands of GIs on R'n'R in Bangkok and Pattaya could be kept coming by maintaining Thailand as the R'n'R place for businessmen and professionals; today 82 percent of the tourists are unaccompanied males. After the Vietcong victory, the junta in Thailand liquidated the socialist and separatist guerrillas in its territory by itself, by decreeing economic enticements to foreign industrial investors, de-emphasizing agriculture, and guaranteeing a cheap labor pool (the bases for the Asian Tiger economy that Thailand became in one generation), but also by conscripting the young men in its own army and the young women from the undeveloped provinces into the Bangkok and Pattaya sex resorts.

Those who go to the performances of Siamese classical dance the Ministry of Tourism puts on at the National Theater don't want to be tourists on the make, more ugly Americans in post–Vietnam War Southeast Asia. You're on R'n'R, but you're not a GI. What you want, here in Bangkok, is not some meat to get off on; you want Miss Thailand. In the sex resorts, they do not just line the street with naked young women and men; they put on the beauty contests, in which Miss Thailand wins the international one year. To tell the truth, the lay will not be very good; the bodies are too mismatched, and in the end you will do a kind of pathetic reciprocal masturbation in the dark. So they provide the cabarets with the real women, the Onassis and Donald Trump kind of gal, performing for the credit-card troops, who frankly can't relate too well to those little Siamese dolls swarming around the barstools. Mae West, Tina Turner, Margaux Hemingway, or Margaret Thatcher come join you at your table between acts.

You are sitting there, digging the show they are putting on for you, a little abashed at how far they are willing to go to be sex objects for you, to the point of changing their sex, to the point of themselves glorying in being the latest kind of corporate-produced media siren. Yet the cheaper places full of Thais who have paid to get in have the same kind of shows. They all seem to be honored to stand in the dark and watch the high theater created for the entertainment of the white kings. A high theater they have inverted: the voluptuous entertainers are men. Might it not be for the Thais around you low theater, travesty of the manners and intrigues and even of the state policy of the white court? In old Siam the kings used to go in disguise to the fairs in the village *wats*; the players had to learn to cover well their ridicule with entertainment. In Bangkok the white kings are welcomed by the ruling junta—they pay. The ambiguity of low theater has to be yet more elusive.

You do feel uneasy in those places. They make it look so easy, to be a white superstar, these twenty-year-old farm boys from the rocky Himalayan foothills of the Isaan who just got to Bangkok last year. The added gender confusion they put into the creations that Michael Jackson, Madonna, and Grace Jones have made of themselves. And that number where a Thai man turns into a very female, pansy, body, to do a Thai woman doing impersonations, for your AC/DC excitement, of Rock Hudson, Tom Cruise, or John Travolta.

"You there, from Cincinnati, you from Frankfurt, you haven't seen half these your women back home; here in Bangkok you can see them all in a single night. Oh come on, we're all bisexual; you really would dig a blow job from a Thai boy wouldn't you, only five hundred baht? What's that? You say, frankly you would from a Greek sailor, but Thai men, well, are just not your type? Okay, just give me a half hour.... Now how do I look to you? Madonna! We're men, of course, but you did not come here to watch the conscripts on parade, did you?"

"Oh love, how beautiful you are, how I wish I could trade noses with you, is your handbag a real Gucci? Sister love is the real thing—are you staying at the Oriental?"

They do try to put you at your ease, these charmers chatting with you so ingratiatingly at intermission, greeting you by name, like your friends already, in the lobby after the show. Yet you leave without one of them. They have made you feel inferior, sexually inferior, not as daring, not as attractive. The next night you and your sisters head for a singles bar, advertised in the Tourism Ministry brochure, featuring a go-go show of men. Thailand is a matriarchal Garden of Eden. The owner, welcoming you at the door, is an aged queen. The show consists of youths dancing desultorily to Western pop music who occasionally strip of their G-strings. They, you discover, hardly speak any English—selected for their looks from among laborers trucked in from the provinces to work in construction gangs in Bangkok. Men without the apparatus of virility. You notice that most of the other clients are gay men.

The next night you go to one of the massage parlors, where there are a hundred straightforward country girls, seated in banked rows behind a one-way plate-glass window with numbers on their bosoms; you can pick one and she will massage, blow, and spread for you. But they have spoiled it for you, on the stage at the Calypso, with their last number with the cage and the matron with the safari suit. The one you picked stroking the baby oil now on your thighs is just a farm girl from the Isaan in Bangkok to put her kid brothers and sisters through school. You think of the glamorous ones, of the Calypso stage; you toy with the idea of going back and taking one of them to your room, taking up the challenge. Taking one of these guys that dares everything back to your room, and seeing what would happen, between two more or less bisexual guys stripping for one another.

Back in the company lounge, when you are asked about your trip to the notorious Bangkok, what you will tell is not about the clumsy peasant girls lined up by the hundreds waiting for somebody to fuck them for a few bucks. You will tell about having Miss Thailand in your room for a night; you will tell about the Calypso—in the classicalized genre of the narrative: "There she was, at the bar, the most gorgeous thing you ever saw, huge boobs, et cetera ... and then when we got back to the room at the Oriental and I got her dress off, I couldn't believe my eyes, imagine my disgust!"

It's the show in the world's biggest sex resort, but you are not sitting there with a newspaper over your lap. The libido in this libertine theater is not a matter of nerves going soft, postures caving in, lungs heaving, sweat pouring, vaginal and penile discharges. The theater of sex is a theater of representation. A woman in Port Arthur, Texas, with her voice, her movements, her own concupiscence, had the spunk to create a number; it is transported whole to the other side of the planet; she factors out; her very physical nature of being a female factors out. It is the representation of the self that carries the erotic charge. But the performer—this male Thai—is there, and shows through, and is now blended into the act to heighten its brazen glamour. What makes the number the more wanton and suggestive is that he is there as a representative male (his own masculine personality all covered over, his specific maleness factored out), and also as a Thai doing an American woman. It is not just the physiognomy, the swagger, the enfant terrible of the Vietnam War–torn sixties Janis Joplin that is being represented; it is a Thai representing her that is being represented, representing inevitably with himself the position of low theater with respect to the ruling icons and effigies, representing economic and cultural subordination, representing a certain moment of geopolitical history— smelted into an erotic trope. You went for the charge, but to those who hold themselves to be serious cultural travelers and not gross tourists and who go to the performances of Siamese classical dance you now say: if you really want to know about Thailand go to the cabarets!

It is the specifically erotic figure, and not the classical dancers, that has this representational power, because it implicates you. Not only because the cabaret show is also the presentation of the charms of the escorts all of whom are available to you to take back to your hotel, but because even while you are sitting there just watching the show you feel yourself being challenged to an intercontinental sexual duel. The decent theater is spectator theater; on the stage of the National Theater or in the restaurant of the Oriental Hotel, jeweled and masked courtesans pursue their dangerous liaisons, from which the decorous hands of time have disentangled the foreign voyeurs—as well as the ushers, the maître d', the waitresses, and the performers themselves.

When you splash cologne over the greasy pores of your carnivorous body, take out the more rakish of your shirts from the suitcase, go and pay for the ticket, speaking English to the teller, your credit card, your shirt and your boutique-bought dress, and your suave and unflappable manners are so many props in the theater of libido. All your words are phallic or lambda symbols; if you mention the plane to Hong Kong you have to catch tomorrow, speak of the comfort of the Oriental Hotel, if you answer, when they ask, what company you work for, or what university, all this is so many tropes in the rhetoric of seduction.

The farm boys from the Isaan whose libido can be contained within the confines of village possibilities and constraints are in Bangkok for a few years working on construction gangs or in the sweatshops; it is those with excess sensuality who are working out in gyms, in dance classes, grooming themselves, cultivating suggestive gestures, learning English, learning the rhetoric of seduction. This cabaret superstar is a representative of a backward Isaan economy whose only productive resources are bodies, the unreproductive bodies of the Bangkok sex theater; you are a representative of a productive economy that produces professionally qualified bodies, assets with which you acquire productive wealth. It could be that you are challenged by his provocations and feel a lascivious urge to take him up on it: after the show, in my hotel room Mr. Cincinnati and Miss Bangcock! Frau Frankfurt und Kuhn Butterfly!

The libido makes the self a representative. Libido is not nostalgia for, and pleasure in, carnal contact. One was a part of another body, one got born, weaned, castrated. The libido does not adhere to the present, but bounds toward the absent, the future; it extends an indefinite dimension of time. What makes this craving insatiable is the way back blocked: the way back to symbiotic immediate gratification. Libidinal impulses are not wants and hungers but insatiable compulsions, sallies of desire, which is desire for infinity, for Jacques Lacan's *l'objet a.* It is libidinous desire that stations the self in the Oedipal theater, in the polis, on the field of objectives which is the objective universe and which is the universe of objectives of desire, in the world market, in *le symbolique.*

If our libido is a part of ourselves, the libidinous gesture or move, reaching for the universe of desire, represents the whole self. Psychoanalytic pansexualism turns into a science of the subject.[2] And the self is a representative of *le nom-du-père,* the Oedipal theater, the reason and the law, the corporate state, the cybernetic digital communication chains, the West. The libidinous gesture or move transacts with another, not for discharge into a set of carnal orifices, but for another libidinous gesture which is a representative of another self, a representative of another reason and law, transnational corporation, corporate state, continent. The love one knows is the gift from the other of what the other does not have.

One would have to read the libido, see it in its context, interpret it. Our phenomenology of sex is an interpretation of intentionalities, representatives, a decoding of barred objectives of desire, a transcription of dyadic oppositions, an inscription of *différance.* Tracking it down we end up, like Plato, finding the whole of culture—including its technology and its relationship with the material, the electromagnetic universe. Lately we have also been doing a machinics of libidinal bodies, a mechanic's analysis of what the parts are, the couplings, how they work, what they produce.[3] We find, with Ballard in *Crash,*[4] our landscape of automobiles, high-rises, MIRV missiles, and computer banks very sexy, representative of our own libidinal machinery. We have also been doing, with Lyotard,[5] a microanalysis of freely mobile excitations, inductions and irradiations, and bound excitations, representing our erotogenic surface as an electromagnetic field. The I or the *Ça* (the Id) that is aroused in the Calypso is a representative of *le nom-du-père,* of the phallus, of the text of culture, the technological industry, the electromagnetic universe. Intelligent talk about sexual transactions among us is talk about transactions with representatives of the self.

But on stage at the Calypso you caught sight of something else—the body underneath not female and not virile either, the pelvis too narrow to harbor a fetus, the lean and unmuscled thighs, the still adolescent shoulders: the indeterminate carnality. You remember passing by this young guy in jeans and sneakers heading for the backstage entrance. That body, now slippery with greasepaint and sweat, belly cicatrized from the tight plastic belt, feet raw in the spike heels, troubles you. He came from a rice paddy in the Isaan, you came from a farm in Illinois, a working-class apartment in Cincinnati. If one could somehow join, immerse oneself in the physical substance of that body, one would have a feel for the weight and the buoyancy, the swish and the streaming, the smell and the incandescence of the costumes, masks, castes, classes, cultures, nations, economies, continents that would be very different from understanding the signs, emblems, allusions, references, implications. Something in you would like to know how it feels to be that bare mass of indeterminate carnality being stuck in spike heels, sheathed in metallized dress, strapped to a crackling fiberglass wig, become phosphorescent in a pool of blazing light. Something which is the stirrings of lust.

Lust does not know what it is. The mouth lets go of the chain of its sentences, rambles, giggles, the tongue spreads its wet out over the lips. The hands that caress move in random detours with no idea of what they are looking for, grasping and probing without wanting an end. The body tenses up, hardens, heaves and grapples, pistons and rods of a machine that has no idea of what it is trying to produce. Then it collapses, leaks, melts. There is left the coursing of the trapped blood, the flush of heat, the spirit vaporizing in exhalations.

There is the horrible in lust, and lust in the fascination with the domain of horror. The landscape of horror is strewn with Hieronymus Bosch and Salvador Dalí bodies with faces softening and oozing out of their shapes, limbs going limp and shriveling like detumescent penises, their extremities melting and evaporating, flesh draining off the bones, bones crumbling in the sands. This horror, which does not trouble our minds which compulsively fix substances in their boundaries and in their material states, troubles us in our loins. Lust is the dissolute ecstasy by which the body's glands, entrails, and sluices ossify and fossilize, by which its ligneous, ferric, coral state gelatinizes, curdles, dissolves, and vaporizes.

Muslims say they have to veil their women in public, because when lust stirs it takes over the whole of a woman's body. Arnold Schwarzenegger,

to those who objected that most women really don't find these Conan the
Barbarian bodies sexy, and anyhow how could anyone get it up spending
as much time in the gym hoisting barbells as you do, answered, "Pumping
iron is better than humping a woman; I am coming in my whole body!"
The orgasm continues in the jacuzzi where the hard wires of the motor
nerves dissolve into sweat and the pumped muscles float like masses of jelly.

Lust is flesh becoming bread and wine and bread and wine becoming
flesh. It is the posture that no longer holds, the bones turning into gum. It
is the sinews and muscles becoming gland—lips blotting out their muscular enervations and becoming loose and wet as labia, chest becoming
breast, thighs lying there like more penises, stroked like penises, knees
fingered like montes veneris. It is glands stiffening and hardening, becoming bones and rods and then turning into ooze and vapors and heat. Eyes
clouding and becoming wet and spongy, hair turning into webs and gleam,
fingers becoming tongues, wet glands in orifices.

The supreme pleasure we can know, Freud said, and the model for all
pleasure, orgasmic pleasure, comes when an excess tension confined,
swollen, compacted is abruptly released; the pleasure consists in a passage into the contentment and quiescence of death. Is not orgasm instead
the passage into the uncontainment and unrest of mire, fluid, and fog—
pleasure in exudations, secretions, exhalations? Voluptuous pleasure is not
the Aristotelian pleasure that accompanies a teleological movement that
triumphantly reaches its objective. Voluptuous pleasure engulfs and oblit-
erates purposes and directions and any sense of where it itself is going; it
surges and rushes and vaporizes and returns.

To be sure, blond hair represents for Thais as for Nietzsche the master
race, candlelight and wine represent grand-bourgeois distinction and
raffinement, leather represents hunters and outlaws, diamonds represent
security forever. But lust cleaves to them differently. Encrusting one's body
with stones and silver or steel, polishing one's skin like alabaster, sinking into marble bathtubs full of champagne or into the soft mud of rice
paddies, feeling the ostrich plumes or the algae tingling one's flesh like
nerves, dissolving into perfumed air and into flickering twilight, lust surges
through a body in transubstantiation.

Libidinous eyes are quick, agile, penetrating, catching onto the undertones, allusions, suggestiveness of the act—responding to the provocation
in the Janis Joplin number being done by a male Thai, the looks are par-
ries in the intercontinental sex duel. The eyes of lust idolize and fetishize
the representation, metallize the crepe the performer has covered himself
with, marbleize the powdered poses of the face and arms, enflame the body
strapped in those incandescent belts and boots. About the materialization
of these idols and fetishes, there is radioactive leakage; the castes, classes,

cultures, nations, economies collapse in intercontinental meltdown. Wanton hands liquefy the dyadic oppositions, vaporize all the markers of *différance* into a sodden and electric atmosphere.

Lust does not represent the self to another representative; it makes contact with organic and inorganic substances that function as catalysts for its transubstantiations. Lust does not transact with the other as representative of the male or female gender, a representative of the human species; it seeks contact with the hardness of bones and rods collapsing into glands and secretions, with the belly giggling into jelly, with the smegmic and vaginal swamps, with the musks and the sighs. We fondle animal fur and feathers and both they and we get aroused, we root our penis in the dank humus flaking off into dandelion fluff, we caress fabrics, cum on silk and leather, we hump the seesaw and the horses and a Harley-Davidson. Lust stirs as far as does Heidegger's *care* which extends to earth and the skies and all mortal and immortal beings in thinking, building, dwelling—muddying the light of thought, vaporizing its constructions, petrifying its ideas into obsessions and idols, sinking all that is erect and erected back into primal slime, de-creating all dwelling into the Deluge that rises. It is lust that, in Tournier's novel *Friday*, embraces Robinson Crusoe in the araucaria tree:

> He continued to climb, doing so without difficulty and with a growing sense of being the prisoner, and in some sort a part, of a vast and infinitely ramified structure flowing upward through the trunk with its reddish bark and spreading in countless large and lesser branches, twigs, and shoots to reach the nerve ends of leaves, triangular, pointed, scaly, and rolled in spirals around the twigs. He was taking part in the tree's most unique accomplishment, which is to embrace the air with its thousand branches, to caress it with its million fingers.... "The leaf is the lung of the tree which is itself a lung, and the wind is its breathing," Robinson thought. He pictured his own lungs growing outside himself like a blossoming of purple-tinted flesh, living polyparies of coral with pink membranes, sponges of human tissue.... He would flaunt that intricate efflorescence, that bouquet of fleshy flowers in the wide air, while a tide of purple ecstasy flowed into his body on a stream of crimson blood.[6]

Lust is not a movement issuing from us and terminating in the other. It is the tree that draws Robinson, holds him, caresses his breath with its million fingers. "The sea that rises with my tears"—obsessive line of a love song in Gabriel García Márquez's novel *In Evil Hour*.[7] Lust of the sea, of the polyps liquefying the coral cliffs, of the rain dissolving the temples of Khajuraho, of the powdery gypsy moths disintegrating the oak forests, of the winter winds crystallizing the air across the windowpanes.

There is a specific tempo of the surges and relapses of lust, there is a specific duration to transubstantiations. For the sugar to melt, *il faut la durée*. But the turgid time of the wanton contact is not the time extended by society. The associations that form society first establish an extended time in which the carnal pleasure of contact with another can be interrupted and resumed. This time is a line of dashes in which compensations for what is spent in catalyzing another become possible, an extended time in which the water that is turned into wine and consumed can be turned back into water once again.

In society one associates with another—for portions of the other, for the semen, vaginal fluids, milk of the other.[8] The association first extends an interval of time in which one portion can be poured after the other. Transubstantiations become transactions, become coded, become claims, to be redeemed across time, claims maintained in representations.

One associates with another—for parts of the other, for the tusks set in his nostrils, the fangs implanted in his ears, the plumes arrayed in the hair of this lord of the jungle who has incorporated the organs of the most powerful beasts of prey into his body. The association extends a stretch of time in which the transfer of these detachable body parts of his bionic body into yours can be delayed, a time in which the representation of self and the representation of the other forms.

One associates with another—for prestige objects, for productive commodities; one transacts with representatives of oneself and of the other. The association extends the infinite time of the libido, of desire which is desire for the infinite. A time to transact with the phallic objectives, the transnational corporation, the corporate state, the continent of which one is a representative.

When, in the midst of social transactions, there is contact with the substance of the other, and lust breaks through, it breaks up the extended time of association with its clamorous urgency. But sometimes the extended time of society of itself disintegrates.

Lust throws one convulsively to the other; its surges and relapses break through the time of transactions to extend the time of transubstantiations. Shall we conceive of the transaction with representatives of self to function to postpone, control, exclude, suppress the surgings of lust?

Theater, which represents transactions with representatives of self, represents society to itself, but also opens up a space of its own outside society. In its absolute form, transvestite theater, does it travesty, parody, undermine, consume all our representatives of self, in an implosion of all our simulacra, leaving, as Baudrillard says,[9] the absolute of death alone on the stage? Or darkening a space for the naked surgings and relapses of lust?

There is something not said in the absolute, transvestite theater, where one dares everything. Is it transposing or releasing, subverting or trumpeting lust? That is its secret. The power to keep its secrets is the secret of its power.

Secrecy can be a force that exalts and sanctifies ritual knowledge. It can function to maintain the identity and solidarity of a group. The secrecy of individuals can determine the division of labor. The power to deny access to knowledge can constitute certain individuals or groups into subordinates. Secrecy can be a force to maintain a friendship on a certain level and in a certain style; I may choose not to reveal what I did last night, not because I did anything that you should or would object to were I to explain the whole context, but because I choose to avoid a confrontational relationship with you, I value the affable and ingenuous tone of our interaction, where each of us spontaneously connects with what the other says. The one who can say and also not say can make intentions and instincts that circulate at large his or her own. The established practice of reserve makes it hard to confront liars, and thus maintains a social space for different compounds of knowledge, fantasy, and ritual behavior. To lose face for a Thai is not simply to feel embarrassment; it is to feel loss of one's defining membership in overlapping groups and loss of the social attributes of position. The importance of keeping up appearances, and of the presentation of respectfulness, unobtrusiveness, calmness, of avoiding saying things in opposition to what is expected not only organizes social interaction but penetrates even into the psychological attitudes of Thais toward themselves. "This attitude may go so far as his not wanting to engage in a private self-analysis whose result might be inimical to his own self-image."[10]

The walls of secrecy fragment our social identity. One is not the same person in sacred and in profane places, in crowds and behind closed doors, in the day and in the night; one is not the same person before different interlocutors. There are politico-economic motives that enjoin us each to be individuals, enduring integral subjects of attribution and responsibility. The immense field of ephemeral insights, fantasies, impulses, and intentions that link up in disjointed systems are forced to somehow form an individual whole in our bodies.

Our theories continue to conceive this whole either as an isomorphism between strata, a distributive organization of different behaviors for different contexts, or a dialectical sublation of each partial structure and phase in the succeeding one. But these paradigms do not succeed in making intelligible our *personal identity*. The intrapsychic organization, whether isomorphic, distributive, or dialectical, would be something general. It would give us the identity of a minor, a father, a person, subject of rights and obligations, a citizen, a chicano or a Wasp. But for each of us, our personal identity is not simply a molecular formula of continual knowledge and skills; it is a singular compound of fragmentary systems of knowledge, incomplete stocks of information and discontinuous paradigms, disjointed fantasy fields, personal repetition cycles, and intermittent rituals.

In what psychoanalysis cataloged as multiple personality disorder, two or more persons inhabit the same body. But when Freud identified the unconscious, an infantile and nocturnal self that does not communicate with the public and avowed self, he generalized the phenomenon of multiple personality disorder, no longer a rare and aberrant case, but the case of each of us. Then one can drop the notion of "disorder"; a division of one's psychic forces, each system dealing with its own preoccupations, noncommunicating with the others, may work quite well. Rather than deal with all her problems with the integral array of her methods and skills, the self-assured office manager closes off the rape victim she also is and will be exclusively when she walks out of the office at night. The wall of sleep falls over our responsibilities of the day, and our infantile self is free to explore again the tunnels on the other side of the mirror.

Freud first explained the split in each of us by the concept of repression; the content of the unconscious would be produced by a censorship that represses representations from consciousness. But repression proves to be a shifty concept. In order to repress a representation, the censorship would have to represent that representation; repression is a contradiction in terms or an infinite regress. The censorship the child installs within himself is an interiorization of the decrees of the father. But why does the father repress? Because he was repressed as a child. Another infinite regress. Freud saw that he was left with the fact that there is repression in the human species and the enigma of that fact. If we recognize the vacuous nature of the explanation by repression, we are left with these multiple psychic systems in our body, and walls of noncommunication between them. These walls of secrecy function in multiple ways.

It is one of the functions of walls of secrecy to maintain a space where quite discontinuous, noncommunicating, nonreciprocally sublating, noncoordinated systems can coexist. A space where episodic systems can exist, where phases of one's past and of one's future can be still there, untransformed and unsublated. Behind multiple generic identities, each of us builds his or her personal identity with inner walls of secrecy.

It is too simplistic to suppose that the libidinous desire in us—which represents the self and makes the self a representative which transacts with representatives of others who are representatives—functions to suppress, control, or mask the lustful body surging and relapsing in its transubstantiations. The noncommunication between libidinous desire and lustful transubstantiations can function to maintain the identity and solidarity of one's libidinal representation of self, to exalt and consecrate it. It can function to establish a division of labor between libidinous desire and lust, each in its own sphere and time. It can function to maintain an intrapsychic space for different compounds of knowledge, fantasy, and repetition compulsions.

Desire is desire for the absent, for infinity; libidinous eyes are quick, agile, penetrating, catching onto the undertones, allusions, suggestivenesses, cross-indexing. They are also superficial; they see the representation of a self and the self that is a representative. If they do not penetrate the wall without graffiti behind which lust pursues its transubstantiations, this wall may not at all function to exclude and to repress. It may function to maintain a nonconfrontational coexistence of different sectors of oneself. One may value an affable relationship with the beast within oneself. One may not want to penetrate behind that wall, not out of horror and fear of what lies behind, but because one may choose to be astonished at the strange lusts contained within oneself. One may want the enigmas and want the discomfiture within oneself.

1994

Lust was written in Bangkok in 1990.

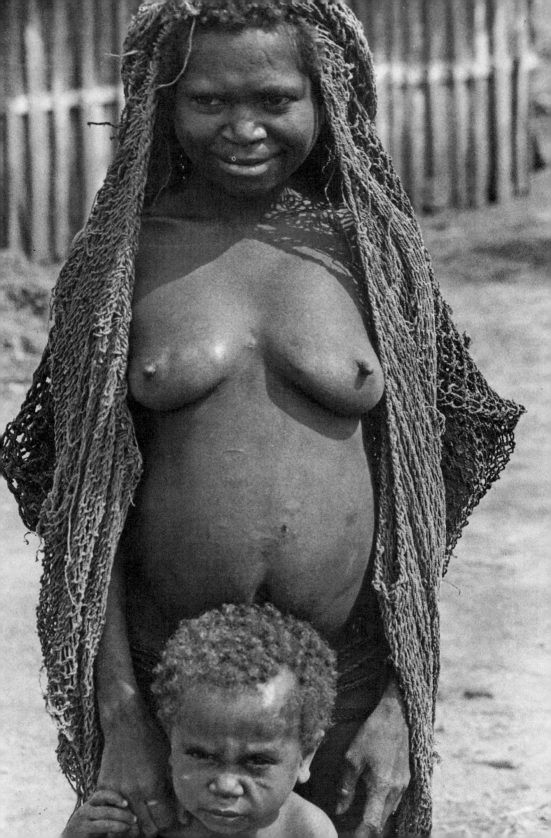

Fluid Economy

Metaphoric Economy, Metonymic Economy

Out of the basic elements of life in common, the various possible consistent configurations into which they can be composed determine an array of possible forms of society. Shirley Lindenbaum distinguishes, in the Melanesian cultural arena, three forms of society.[1] In these societies where the division of labor and the organization of authority are gender based, the primary social act is that of the man who goes to another compound to transact for a woman. The transaction is with her father and brothers. For the woman given, a woman must be returned.

In a first configuration, the paradigm would be men who exchange their sisters. This configuration is found in the egalitarian communities of the Malekula and the Small Islands, the Southwest Papuan Gulf, and the Great Papuan Plateau. The system in force among the Sambia (who emigrated from the Great Papuan Plateau), where typically the brother receives for his sister his niece for his son, would be a variant of the sister-exchange paradigm.

Nature unfortunately does not dispose of the distribution of differently sexed children in a correspondingly systematic way. Human engineering, in the form practiced by the Banaro, where infanticide of children of undesirable sex is the rule, would compensate for the nonsystematicity of nature.[2] Delayed exchange plays on time to correct inequalities. At the time the bridegroom will give to the men from whom he receives a woman the equivalent of himself, his male essence; in the next generation his daughter will be returned for his brother-in-law's son.

The immediate exchange is metonymic; for his bride, the bridegroom will give her brothers a part, more exactly, a portion, of his own male fluid

in which his productive power is materialized. He will give them, in fellatio, a portion of his male essence; he will be the man in their compound
that produces men.

These are societies with a dual economy: agriculture, the domain of
female labor, and hunting and fishing, the reserve of male prowess. Married
men eat male food, drink the milk sap of the pandanus trees they culti-
vate and tend, and eat the game they hunt. They cook and eat together in
the men's house. Relations among men are fiercely egalitarian. Women
garden and eat their own food. The productive existence of men and that
of women are, like their bodies, more parallel than complementary. A wife
remains bound to her own family, and in time of conflict she may lend her
force to theirs. The infant is their coproduction. The parents do not educate their sons into the skills of men and of women; they will be initiated
by the whole clan into the skills and tasks of each stage of their development. In the basic social transaction, the man who goes to the adjacent
hamlet does not receive the whole woman, an assistant in his productive or
political existence, nor someone who will produce children and give them
to him, or educate them. What he receives is essentially a supplier of female
milk for their coproduced children, and in return he contracts to give his
male milk to her younger brothers. The fundamental act of association
which organizes society is a transaction with portions of the self, fluid portions of a fluid self.

A second form of society, which we find in the Eastern Highlands of
Papua New Guinea, is characterized by bride-price. For his bride, the husband gives to her brothers, not his male milk, but a bride-price consisting
of the products of male power, that is, of the hunt: tusks, fangs, fur, plumes,
shells. Among the Sambia, a people of Lowland origin who immigrated
to the Eastern Highlands, the milk sap ingested from trees becomes male
fluid; there is then in the forest an equivalent for male fluid, and it figures
in conjugal commerce. But the conversion to the prime substance of male
power takes place within the body.

The form of society characterized by this kind of bride-price is found
where the distinction between the female sphere, agriculture, and the male
sphere is strongly felt. Men devote themselves exclusively to the hunt and
war—more exactly, headhunting, since the combats are not for territory,
booty, or women. The headhunter is not protecting the women, who are
nowise being threatened; the men are pursuing combats of prestige and
cannibalism among themselves. There are no war chiefs or concerted battle
strategies; each male arrayed in tusks, fangs, and spectacular headdresses
of the shimmering plumes of the bird of paradise is seeking out the most
powerful, spectacular, and brave male in order to cannibalize his body and
thus incorporate his spirit.

The bride-price the bridegroom gives the bride's father and brothers is economically unproductive; it is not wealth that they will use to increase wealth. The tusks, fangs, and plumes offered by the husband will be *incorporated* into the nostrils, ears, arms, heads of the father and the brothers, enhancing their male power as hunters, incorporating in them the weapons and power of the most lordly animals of the jungle. It is not a boy but a man who comes to transact for a woman; the tusks he bears in his nostrils, the fangs in his face and ears, the plumes in his hair are not symbols of male power, but parts of his hunter and warrior body. They are the detachable parts he can pass over to be incorporated in the bodies of the father and brothers. The fundamental social transaction is with parts of the self.

A third type of society, found in the Western Highlands of New Guinea, is characterized by bride-price that is a true price, objects obtained by male power and which remain external to the body, objects useful, ceremonial, or decorative. The bridegroom will offer the bride's father and brothers quantities of rare shells, ritual objects or insignia of status, or else large quantities of foodstuffs, pigs, beverages, which cannot be kept but will be consumed in potlatch feasts in which the connections of and obligations to the father-in-law's family will be increased. Here the exchange has become metaphorical: for the possession of a wife, the husband gives not a part of himself but a representative of himself.

These are societies in which the herding of pigs and extensive cultivation of crops make female labor not complementary to male hunting but in disequilibrium with it. The sphere of male power is that of status in the political organization, control of ritual and of the ideological superstructure. With their political organization, the men control the surplus agricultural production and engage in financial transactions that issue in the concentration of wealth. The male economy is organized such that men can traffic with other men for the acquisition of many women. The dominant discourse concerns, not women's generative role in social reproduction, but women as producers of external wealth.

In these societies, the male culture produces not men, but "big men." The idea that men create men gives way to the notion that men "give birth to" key wealth.[3] Homosexual transactions disappear in these societies. Male lactation, male breeding of men, is here no longer a sociosexual concern. The tolerance for gender ambiguity diminishes as erotic attention is directed to the trappings and blazons of the self, rather than to treasured internal substance.

In this century such Melanesian societies have entered into relationship with Western societies. Food production in the village is supplied by the women; with game scarce and headhunting suppressed, the young men are drawn off to the plantations and the mines of the white men. But there they do not enter into a productive economy themselves; they work for wages while the white men control the productive resources and the tools. They really cannot use their wages to acquire productive wealth, plantations, or mines; the profitable plants cannot be grown in their Highland homes. They use their wages to acquire male regalia: metal-buckled belts, wrist-watches, gaudy and macho clothing, eventually motorcycles, which they will take back to their villages to offer as bride-price in exchange for women, the local wealth producers. The fathers-in-law then hoard these things as prestige objects, representatives of their status within male society. Filling his compound with the sumptuary objects of white male prestige, the father extends his prestige to white male society also. For the greatest male power a father can have is to be the headman of the village with which the white labor recruiter will have to deal.

The white men themselves have a society in the region. In their associations they do not transact with body portions or body parts that produce girls out of infants and men out of boys; they transact with money and productive property. They transact not with other white men for wealth-producing women, but with the black "big men" for black laborers for their plantations and their mines. Among themselves, they transact for the raw materials they manufacture, the commodities they market for a profit, the wages they invest for a profit. The fundamental social transaction is not for the reproductive body of a woman but for things that produce more things; the transactions among white men produce not men, but "big men." For these things that produce more things are also prestige objects. As resources they supply one's needs; as property that produces more property they materialize one's independence, freedom of initiative, and status. They are representatives of the self. But the self in question is in turn a representative. The prestige objects are representatives not of one's body but of one's training, education, business acumen, and connections. By entering into social commerce, one builds up a business, one builds a home that represents success. With these one has credit, can get loans, one can transact for more productive wealth. The business, the home, represent one—not oneself as a body, but as a name that means something in the real world.

The Sambia

I receive, from the other settlement, which we had long viewed with suspicion, a young wife. When she comes to dwell in my house, I enter into a pact with her family. Her younger brothers will daily kneel before me, and will open their mouths for my penis, and will drink my male fluids.

I stand before my wife kneeling before me, before her brothers kneeling before me, as they harden and suckle my penis. I lower myself over my wife, laid over the forest mosses and ferns, and pump my fluids into her. I withdraw glistening with pleasure and power in the sun.

I see my fluids drunk by my wife bringing her to menarche and fertility; poured into her vagina, day after day, they coagulate into the bones, organs, and flesh of our child. My fluids drunk by her brothers make them strong: I see their boyish frames harden with muscles, their faces grow beards, their penises grow and harden. With my fluids I pour a protective spirit into the fetus forming in the hollows of my wife's body; with my fluids I pour a virile soul into the hollows in her brothers' tender bodies.

Day after day I pour forth fluids. As my fluids drain from me my own strength flows out with them. My body, now hard as the trunk of a tree, grows no more; I see it destined to shrivel and bend like the bodies of old men given over to death. I go in secret to the pandanus tree and drink from the aerial roots hanging from its trunk the breast milk of the land my fathers five generations ago took possession of before it took possession of their bones and fluids. I find the milk of the trees flowing again from my penis. I breast-feed my wife with the milk of my penis. I breast-feed my wife's brothers with the milk of my penis. My wife breast-feeds the child whose bones, organs, and muscles formed in the male milk I poured into her womb.

Who am I? Call me a Sambia. Where we live few outsiders have ever ventured. We call it the nest of the high-ranging eagle. From the heights of our terrible isolation we see the cliffs lifting the voracious jungle over the roaring cascades below to the oceans vaulting above. For nine months of the year the rains descend upon the mountains, the jungle, our small thatched shelters, our bodies. Our settlements perch on mountain spurs rising steeply from the valley floor; the sides of the ridges deteriorate rapidly into small streams draining from the mountains, making our steps treacherous, but also fortifying our hamlets with deep gullies and watercourses against the approach of our enemies. Often we feel the earth below tremble and the mountains shift. The jungle surges with oak, pine, beech, and broad-leafed trees; bright orchids float in the rain pools caught in the crotches of their limbs, their branches streaming with vines and creepers. Above our settlements the forest thins out to a single layer of gnarled and crooked trees whose branches are hoary with liverworts and ferns drifting in the cold fog. The trails from our homes and our gardens into the green summits above weave around aerial roots, limestone outcrops, banks of vines and lianas, often passing over slick tree bridges suspended over streams and rivers hurtling down ever-deeper gorges. Over them we circulate, conduits of blood, breast milk, penis milk.

Who are the Sambia? Gilbert Herdt, the Stanford anthropologist who lived among them in 1974–1976, and again in 1979 and 1981, does not reveal to us their real name, and has taken pains to conceal their exact location, somewhere in the Eastern Highlands of Papua New Guinea, in order to protect them and their secret institutionalized homosexuality. He tells of them in his book *Guardians of the Flutes: Idioms of Masculinity*, and in the books he edited, *Rituals of Manhood* and *Ritualized Homosexuality in Melanesia*, books that have made this minuscule and isolated population and its culture the key to unlocking the meaning of gender identity forged in diverse but related male rituals among perhaps up to 20 percent of the known cultures of Melanesia.[4]

The Sambia number about 2,300; they live in small hamlets in six population clusters. Gardening, mainly sweet potatoes and taro, and hunting are the main economic pursuits. Women do most of the garden work. Men do all the hunting, primarily for possum, tree kangaroos, cassowaries, other birds, and eels. A strict division of labor and ritual taboos forbid men and women from doing one another's tasks; a hamlet, and each house, is divided into male and female spaces; the spaces between houses and the gardens about them, the valleys below and the forests above are traversed on paths reserved for each sex and taboo to the other. Late arrivals in the Eastern Highlands from the Great Papuan Plateau, the Sambia lived subject to raids and ambushes; with only his hand weapons between each individual and his and his family's death, each man could count only on his bare physical strength and personal valor to survive and protect his home. Men are even now seen as destined to be warriors, and the qualities of a warrior—strength, endurance, a fund of violent emotions, bravery, and individual cunning—are perceived to constitute maleness.

Females are perceived to mature "naturally," without external aids, for their bodies contain a menstrual-blood organ *(tingu)*, whose flowing pool of blood feeds their physical and mental development. Their bodies are hot with their superabundant blood, and survive infancy better, acquire motor and linguistic skills earlier, mature earlier, are stronger, and live longer than those of males. Boys possess *kereku-kerekus*, or semen-organs. This organ is not functional at birth; it contains no semen naturally, and can only store semen, never produce it. Only oral insemination, Sambia declare, can activate the boy's semen organ and develop the musculature, hirsute face, voice, and genitals of virility.

The girls progressively associate with and master the skills of women as they grow. Boys, however, are allowed to roam freely with their age-mates, acquiring their own skills and amusements. They are not educated into male gender identity, the masculine social persona, nor the skills of virile professions; they are initiated.[5]

The first three initiations, at ages seven to ten, at eleven to thirteen, and at fourteen to sixteen, function to forcibly break the boys from their long association with their mothers, and their milk. At the first initiation, the seven-to ten-year-old boys are weaned from their mothers' milk and foods to male foods and the penis milk of youths of their brothers-in-law's clan. After the third initiation, they will serve as fellateds to feed semen into first- and second-stage boy initiates. The fourth initiation purifies the youth and issues in cohabitation with his wife; he will henceforth have to inseminate his wife orally to bring her to menarche. The fifth-stage initiation comes at the wife's menarche; the husband will have to henceforth inseminate her vaginally, and is given the highly secret practices, especially his breast-feeding from the white milk sap of thirteen species of trees, to compensate for the semen depletion vaginal intercourse will entail. Sixth-stage initiation comes upon the birth of the first child; it endows the father with the social personhood of one responsible for the production and the reproduction of the clan. But he will have achieved not only masculine personhood but male gender identity, indeed physical maleness, and these attainments, which semen depletion in the years ahead will undermine, are maintained only in the giving. He must, with his semen, give masculine personhood, male gender identity, indeed physical maleness to his wife's real or classificatory younger brothers.

Sambia do not conceive semen as so many little seeds but one of which is required to germinate in order for the fetus to form. They conceive the womb as a receptacle, into which blood flows from the *tingu*, the menstrual-blood organ. When it is kept full of male fluids, the fetus can form, coagulating in the mix of maternal blood and male fluid. Consequently, to form a fetus a male must inject his fluids into his wife constantly, up to the last stage of pregnancy. (It is then misleading for us to speak of semen or sperm.) The womb is a container and transformer of fluids; there male fluids change into the bones, internal organs, muscles, and skin of a fetus. Only the circulatory blood in the fetus comes from the mother. Some of the mother's menstrual blood is transmitted to the female fetus's *tingu*; this blood will be the innate or "natural" source of her psycho-biological feminization.

To give male fluids in fellatio is *pinu pungooglumonjapi*—pushing to grow. Male fluid, ingested orally by the mother, is conducted to her breasts and there transformed into mother's milk, which grows the infant's soft body. Growth is aided by eating pandanus nuts, and it is part of the work of procreation for the father to tend pandanus trees and scale them to obtain the nuts.

After weaning, girls continue to grow without further external human fluids, whereas boys falter, staying puny, soft, and weak. Male growth after weaning comes from fellatio, which is male breast-feeding (*monjapi'u*). A portion of the ingested male fluid is stored in the boy's *kereku-kereku*, and drawn on after puberty to produce the new growth of musculature, body hair, and genitals. The strength—size, valor, and force of speech—of men comes from the male fluids they have received from other men.

The male fluid taken from other males and stored in the boy's *kereku-kereku* will also provide the youth with male fluid for his own later sexual couplings. The first sign of surplus male fluid in the body comes in emissions in wet dreams.

How utterly anomalous seems a society that could make of the whole period of the boy's development from childhood to adulthood a period of exclusive, positively valued and erotically exciting homosexuality, could make of this homosexuality the royal road to heterosexuality! For us such a society could only risk its reproduction and such a culture its coherence.

The Liquid Currency of Social Transactions

In our conception, body fluids flow, quite outside of, and beneath, our political economy—fluids enter our bodies naturally, unnoticed by our conscious surveillance and uncoded by our social codes, and evaporate or are discharged in the extreme privacy of our closed-door bathrooms and our dark bedsheets as we retire alone, an emission outside of social laws, unmentionable in our socially significant discourse. We would inquire into how and why they are produced, or where and when they are consumed and discarded, or by whom, only in the biological or medical discourse in which our organisms figure only as entities of anonymous and silent nature.

For the Sambia, the vital fluids transubstantiate as they pass from one conduit to another.[6] They are the scarce resources of the life, growth, strength, and spirituality of the clan. Among the Sambia, body fluids do not flow; they are transmitted from socius to socius, metered out in social transactions. Sambia society is fundamentally constituted by these transactions.

Trees are regarded as of female sex; the white milk sap of pandanus trees is obtained from the thick hanging aerial roots, which are the breasts of the trees. The strength of trees, of female nature, is transubstantiated into male fluid in the bodies of the men who suckled them. The pandanus trees are carefully planted and tended by the clan on patrilinear territory, and the fathers regulate the distribution of this milk to the fifth-stage initiates in secret ritual practices.

The abundance of male fluid produced in the men is transmitted to the mouths of boys, where it masculinizes them by being stored in their innately empty *kereku-kerekus*. It is marriages contracted for that determine which boys have access to the male fluid of which men. A man who contracts for a wife contracts an obligation to give his male fluid to the mouths of her real or classificatory younger brothers. Boys who have received enough male fluid so that the abundance begins to flow from them in ejaculations enter into the obligation, marked by the third-stage initiation, to give their excess to a regulated set of younger boys.

The fourth-stage initiation puts youths under the obligation to give their penises to their wives to suck. Transmitted into the mouths of women, their male fluid transubstantiates into female milk. When the breasts of the young bride swell with its abundance and she reaches menarche, the fifth-stage initiation orders his male fluid to be transmitted into her vagina where it transubsantiates into the bones, internal organs, muscles, and skin of a fetus. Sambia do not recognize unproductive orgasm with her as the end of vaginal intercourse, and they show no concern with bringing their wives to orgasm.[7]

While men sometimes masturbate in preparation for being fellated, solitary or reciprocal masturbation to orgasm is, as far as Herdt has been able to determine, quite unknown among them.[8] Male-fluid emissions in wet dreams are regarded as fellatio with spirits, and come under the category of play since they are not productive—spirits are not engendered through them. Nocturnal emissions are regarded with some anxiety, for the spirits drain and deplete the male-fluid storers they suck, and probably wish to harm them (143).

The discharge of blood is also completely socialized. The female *tingu* is a fountain of blood; women's bodies give forth blood in a superabundance that is disquieting to the men:

> Blood keeps the body cool; sickness goes into a hot body. Women have cold skins *from too much blood.* Men are hot-skinned *from too little blood....* Women hold the source [*kablu*: tree base] of blood. They have a blood pool [*boongu*].... Sickness avoids women, their coldness chases it away. Women don't die quickly, they are never ill. We men have small buttocks, we go up trees. Women have big buttocks, like tree trunks, they live a long time. (Tali, a Sambia informant.) (191)

All menstrual flows are regulated with detailed ritual anxiety. Bloodstains left on the ground are highly taboo. The menstrual blood of the mother belongs to the fetus that will form in it; the surplus blood production is required by the female fetus, for from the blood infused and stored in her *tingu* all her biological and social growth and maturation will depend. Men spit immediately after vaginal intercourse, to expel any bloodstains left on them. The excess blood that pours from a vagina, rather than being absorbed in a fetus, breaks the chain from socius to socius; the shamed woman must withdraw to a menstrual hut outside the confines of the settlement and undergo ritual reintegration to return (182, 190–94).

After battles, shamanist ceremonies expurgate the blood of slain enemies from the weapons and bodies of warriors, delivering it back to the ghosts of the slain. This purge, when completely successful, would disconnect the circuit of reprisal attacks by the exsanguine ghosts of the victims (46).

Finally, the transmission of breast milk is always a social transaction. Lactation in a woman is not an anonymous biological process; it is marriage and the husband who pours male fluid into her mouth that instigates and maintains the milk flow destined for the mouth of the child.

Fluid Value

Male fluid, blood, and breast milk are resources given and received; we must differentiate, then, between their use-value and their exchange-value. When commodities are transferred to be of utility to the other party who offers another kind of commodity or service in exchange, or who transfers them in turn to a third party, or when a delay intervenes before the exchange, they may acquire a value supplemental to their perceived utility. Male fluid, blood, and breast milk are values in an economy.

Marriages are arranged, preferably among infants, betrothed by their fathers, normatively between clans, preferably of different hamlets, which are potential enemies. Homosexual contacts are prohibited between all clansmen, matrilateral kin, age-mates, and with ritual sponsors. The clan that donates the wife also confers the husband's homosexual partners, her real or classificatory younger brothers. The male-fluid transaction ties the unrelated groups; one does not give or receive male fluid from true, intertribal enemies, only from potential enemies. Male-fluid transactions *distinguish* kin from non-kin, and friendly from hostile persons. Thus, to the male-fluid transaction the value of political and economic alliance is added.

For his male fluid his work makes available to her—work of multiple, regular male-fluid prestations, and work of tending the pandanus trees and procuring their milk-white nuts to supplement breast milk for her growing children—the donor receives in exchange the work of his wife, producer of garden products and producer of his children. The potential for male-fluid donation is the basis for ownership of persons; wives are inalienably owned by their husbands and their clans; in case of warfare, all ties of the wife with her clan are abolished. Adultery is seen as "stealing another woman's male fluid," and is called *kweikoonmulu*, "male-fluid fight."[9] Thus, while a wife becomes her husband's exclusive sexual property and her labor— complementary to, rather than cooperative with, his—belongs to him, she acquires exclusive property rights over that scarce resource, his male fluid.

Not only the capacity to give male fluid, but also the way of giving invests the donor with power. Sexual contacts are effected privately in the forest in the evening. Sambia use only one position, the standing one, for fellatio with boys or women, and husbands use only the "missionary position" with their wives for vaginal intercourse. "Foreplay," caresses, body contact, is minimal; the male-fluid donor withdraws quickly after ejaculation. Orgasmic pleasure, then, comes with male-fluid donation, in body positions that materialize instant freedom to withdraw at will. Boys rarely experience erection or orgasm while serving as fellators; women rarely, or never, experience orgasm in intercourse—their orgasmic pleasure comes in breast-feeding their children. Direct male-fluid transactions are asymmetrical; the donor materializes as power, the recipient absorbs growth, strength, spirituality. (And yet—men view sexually experienced women as consumed by insatiable erotic appetites, and do know that boys relish the savor and texture of abundant male fluid in the youths the boys court) (210n7).

There is a collective male-fluid pool, contained in the bodies of all men living within neighboring hamlets. As a boy draws strength from numerous men, who deposit their male fluid in his reserve for his future use, so men are kept strong by having their male fluid safely contained in many boys. This explains why, for the Sambia, homosexual contacts are less depleting than heterosexual—and why there is no ritual concern with replenishing one's male-fluid supply by ingesting the white milk sap of the breasts of trees until the fifth and sixth stages of initiation, which initiate a male into heterosexual intercourse (184–85). Since recipients harbor portions of one's male fluid (strength and spirituality) inside them, one is kept healthy in them—through sympathetic-contagious magic. A woman lacks this protection; she is not a cult initiate, and her male fluid comes from only one man, her husband. Nor is a man protected by depositing his male fluid in women or creating children. This is a conception quite the opposite of ours; our sympathetic-contagious magic thought finds the prolongation and maintenance of our virile life, strength, and spirit in our children.

In mediated transactions, male fluid is transmitted to someone whose body transforms it into something else useful to a third party. Thus the male transmits male fluid to the woman vaginally, whose body stores and transforms it into the bones, organs, muscles, and skin of the fetus. His male fluid also infuses a soul and conveys the spirit familiars to her male fetus. He transmits male fluid to the woman orally, whose body transforms it into breast milk, used by the infant for its sustenance.

A boy ingests male fluid from his real or classificatory brothers-in-law, who relay his father as male-fluid—growth, strength, and spirituality—donors. When this son becomes a male-fluid donor in turn, he will trade his sister for a wife, and his male-fluid-fed strength and spirituality will be transmitted to her and her offspring, as well as to her immature real and classificatory brothers.

Finally, the milk sap of thirteen species of trees is received by the male, who transforms this breast milk into male fluid, in order to give it in turn to his brothers-in-law, his wife, and, through her, to his child.

In these transactions which benefit a third party, the breast milk of trees and male fluid acquire the supplemental value of fetal tissue, spirit familiars, breast milk.

Interest Accrued over Time

A man from one clan obtains from another clan in an adjacent, potentially hostile, settlement, a woman, a garden producer and coproducer of babies, who will perpetuate his clan. His real and classificatory brothers-in-law receive male fluid from him. The husband may give one of them his sister for marriage. Or he will give one of their sons his daughter for betrothal in infancy; they will trade her for a wife from a third, related group. Thus the male-fluid transactions acquire the supplemental exchange-value of a promissory note to be redeemed in the next generation (203–4).

The exchangist politico-economic structure of the transmissions of body fluids coded and metered in Sambia culture fashions time cyclically. Resources that flow out of one group are destined to find their way back, if not in this generation, then in the next.

The establishment of a ritualized social economy of closed exchanges of the equivalent has the paradoxical effect of giving time a value-producing force. The time a return can be delayed will add or subtract a supplement of value to what is exchanged. For example, in a society whose codes of honor determine that offenses each require a specific revenge, the one on whom a certain vengeance is obligatory can maximize the force of the vengeance by determining that it fall at once or perhaps that it be long delayed. Among the Sambia, where every transmission of male fluid, blood, and milk is regulated and its direct and indirect exchange-values coded, the individual's own initiatives consist in being able to maximize his or her resources by delaying or accelerating the obligatory return in transactions in which they have value (207–8).

An individual is not a producer of his or her own resources that have value in social transactions, nor the seat of initiative that determines their use and exchange-value. The individuality of the individual consists in the possession of strategies that manipulate the productive force of time, in the initiatives at his or her disposal to create a supplement of value by manipulating the delay of the obligatory return. The Sambia have a fluid individuality, forming and dissolving in the force of the flow of time.

The Mystification Value of Fluid Commodities

In transactions with male fluids—as with detachable parts of male bodies and with representatives of self—the exchange-value of these commodities doubles up with a symbolic—a rationalizing and mystifying—function. The economics of fluid exchange is also a political system. Every exercise of political power, Foucault wrote, depends on masking a substantial part of itself.[10]

The dumbfounding and perhaps overdetermined secrecy of the Sambia homosexual years is not easily interpreted. How extraordinary that it was only in 1974, among the minuscule population of the Sambia, that a practice was discovered that has since been found to be pervasive throughout Melanesia—an enormous geographical area which covers tens of thousands of square miles, from Fiji in the east to the offshore islands of Irian Jaya far to the west![11] Up to 20 percent of known Melanesian cultures have at this very late date been found to enjoin homosexual practices on all males. Herdt himself lived five months among the Sambia, slept for weeks in the men's house, without suspecting that all males from ages seven to ten practiced homosexual fellatio virtually daily for the next ten to fifteen years, and some continue throughout life.

The practice is not only kept secret from outsiders, from anthropologists, whom the local people quickly sense would use it immediately as a rationalization of their white contempt. Among Sambia themselves, at the first initiation, when fellatio is enjoined, the boys are threatened with immediate death if they reveal it to uninitiated boys or to any female. What is the reason for this secrecy, and what is the secret the reason rationalizes?

Sambia men are warriors. The defense of the community, by hand-to-hand combat with rudimentary weapons, where treachery, ambushes, and raids have to be met with bare physical prowess, audacity, and the ability to take pain, is the obligation of every male. Women, drawn from potentially hostile neighboring communities, retain contact with and share the political interests of their brothers and their clans; they remain potential spies in the households of their husbands. Groups are small enough to be highly vulnerable internally.

By the coding of male fluid as a valued resource, men are placed firmly in control of their part of the means of sociobiological reproduction. The metering of male fluids keeps women and also boys in their socioeconomic place. If male fluid were free or easily at hand, its value would deflate. The coding that makes of body fluids commodities and regulates body-fluid transactions keeps in place political networks through which senior men make peace, negotiate marriages, and carry on exchanges.

The Sambia coding, cast in physical-cosmological terms, says that what men produce is men, who are not engendered and matured by natural processes, but produced through isolation and ordeal, initiation, revelation of male secrets, and male breast-feeding. But the coded procedures of the production of men also produce a cultural order. Women's sexuality and reproductive powers are natural, uncontrolled, and threatening to this order. The women's physical control over reproductive processes and emotional control over their sons must be overcome by secrecy, taboo legislation, and dramatized male power. For us, the Sambia coding dissimulates a politico-economic project which employs ordeal, fear, and cruelty and produces domination; legislation, and religion function as ideology. The coding "naturalizes" and "celestializes," as Marx would put it, an order that is cultural and historical. The male ideology and initiations function to ensure male power over female resources—periodicity, fertility, child care, and labor.

The initiation system requires that those who submitted to psychologically traumatic and physically painful initiations as boys cruelly inflict these ordeals upon the succeeding generation in the service of a cult ideology whose cruel motivations and partly fraudulent ritual trappings have been discovered by them in the male initiations procedures. Is not bad faith constitutive of their codings?[12]

Such systems, Roger Keesing writes sternly, are fraught with contradiction from within.[13] These men depend for their physical survival on the labor of the women they exclude and demean. By separating the men's realm from the women's to create male solidarity, their system leaves beyond male control the everyday lives—and minds—of women. Do they not know this?

It seems hard to believe that in cultures so restricted—one closely studied Papuan culture, the Baktaman, comprises but a few hundred people[14]—the women really could know nothing whatever about the daily practices of their men and their sons. That there is deception built into their codings, and self-deception also, seems evident.

Herdt, as most male anthropologists, had no access to the female ideology, culture, experience, and judgments. Terence and Patricia Hays did, in their research among the Ndumba, an Eastern Highlands people who show some influences from the Sambia. They ask, "Why do Ndumba women thus actively cooperate in the performance of ceremonies whose central meanings consign them to subservient positions in society and whose main theme appears to be misogynistic?" Their research concludes that "Ndumba women believe in their mystical powers and the dangers they pose to males as fully as do the men and ... they also see the need to control these powers if men and society are to survive. For the common good, women must educate girls and remind each other that they possess forces that are so powerful that men cannot, working alone, safeguard themselves.... To possess such awesome forces is a heavy responsibility and, perhaps, one that carries its own satisfactions."[15]

The Experience and Use of Male Bodies

To denounce the cognitive content of a culture as an ideology is to interpret its positive ideal negatively. The reverse reading employs concepts that come from the cognitive content of another culture. One interprets the maleness Sambia initiation procedures produce and male culture celebrates as envy of female powers and as death drive. The validity of the interpretation depends on showing that these concepts fit better the Sambia inner experience of their bodies and the warrior use of their male bodies.

Bruno Bettleheim could see in the subincision practiced on their penises by Australian aborigines a procedure to give to male bodies by culture the missing organs of female fertility.[16] Is the institutional secrecy of Sambia male society and culture the institutional projection of an unconscious censorship which both dissimulates and reveals envy of women? Does it betray male envy of female bodies, of their superabundant blood, their superior health, their superior work capacity, their greater longevity; male envy of their reproductive and nutritive resources; male envy of the cosmic periodicity of their vitality—which men compensate for with the construction of an exchangist politico-social economy which engenders a cyclical time of the cultural order; male envy of that biopsychic and conflict-free pre-Oedipal stage which characterizes, according to psychoanalyst Robert Stoller,[17] the first months of the infant's symbiotic life in the bosom of its mother—for which men compensate with the construction of male warrior solidarity?

For us, male and female bodies are morphologically complementary, and we use the dyad active/passive to conceive them as functionally complementary (male musculature/female glands and curves; male erection/female orifice). The inner states of individuals—sexual attraction, revulsion, fear, envy—must differ where the inner and outer perceptions of male and female bodies differ. The terms "sexual antagonism" and "death drive" used to characterize the inner states of men in Melanesia in their relations with women and with other men cannot mean what these terms mean for us, who do not have the same perceptions of our bodies and have not had the kinds of sexual couplings and combats they engage in.

For the Sambia, male and female bodies are parallel, analogous conduits of vital fluids; the individual body is but a local conduit of their flow across nature and the human community. This fundamental concept of their system of thought must express the distinctive focus of their inner experience of themselves, which precedes and makes possible their system of thought. The female body is not privileged with organs for conception; there is in fact no real notion of conception, the fetus coagulates in the receptacle of the womb when it is filled with a mix of maternal blood and male fluid. In fact, our notion of conception, which makes the male action transitive, though minimal and brief, is a recent notion, and it is not an experiential notion but one derived from empirical induction.

In morphologically parallel conduits for fluids, the fluids must flow. The female body contains a pool of superabundant blood, stored in the *tingu* of the female fetus prenatally and released over time; the bodies of boys have an empty and inactive *kereku-kereku* which has to be filled from the outside. For fluid to flow in their conduit bodies, boys must draw upon the male fluid of mature males, and upon the white milk sap of pandanus trees. They are not trying to annex to themselves the specific organ of females, but making their own organ functional. For Sambia, fellatio among men does not transfer female nutritive powers to males; it forges male identity in a body lacking it innately. The experience of maturity in being a male fluid donor must be fundamental, and give its specific sense to what boys are perceived to lack.

The initiation through sexual practices that are psychologically traumatizing and physically painful is, positively, a promotion to the pride and solidarity of warriors. Herdt, however, conceives war psychoanalytically as an exteriorization of the death drive:

> Twentieth-century intellectualized researchers have not emphasized how catastrophic war can be, socially, economically, and psychologically, especially that primitive form of warfare that depends on stone-age weaponry—through man-to-man combat—which we have never known. Such facts relentlessly condition the very meaning of male existence.
>
> War had been, after all, chronic, pervasive, and destructive. How is it really possible, now, even to attempt to recapture the sense in which a Sambia man lived life in the face of the day-to-day possibility that he could be snipered in his gardens, be cut down in battle and axed to death, or have his wife stolen by another man, physical strength and stamina his only steady insurance against such threats? How is it possible to forget past battles and brushes with death? And nothing can erase the memory of brutally massacred comrades and kinsmen and friends.... On the raid, no less than in the battle, a man had to demonstrate his masculine "strength" or face destruction. This demonstration might mean a show of aggressive bravado, seeking thrills and quick-witted demonstrations of virility through physical action.... In what follows, we must remember that man's myths and idiom belong to that stark reality.[18]

But the term "warfare" is in the end ethnocentric and inappropriate in our discourse about them; their raids and battles do not result in economic conquest or political domination. What Kenneth Read observes of the Gehuku-Gama is also true of the Sambia:

> The constantly recurring (and tedious) chronicles of intertribal warfare epitomized one aspect of the dominating ethos; for unbridled warfare (*rova*), as distinct from feuding (*hind*), required no precipitating event (though often some were cited). Warfare did not lead to conquest (in the sense of extending boundaries or imposing sovereignty over others), though one of its aims was to destroy the villages of enemy groups and force their inhabitants to seek temporary sanctuary elsewhere. But in the course of time, the defeated (who always intended to return) were commonly invited back to serve once more as a foil for testing and demonstrating the ultimate expression of strength and masculinity.[19]

Male ontogeny in Sambia tends, Herdt observes, to the implantation of overweening, vain, male susceptibility, given to acerbity and brute and fiery violence.[20] This is perhaps too impressionistic an appraisal. Sambia warriors apply to the shaman after the battle that he purge them of the blood shed and return it to the ghosts of those fallen in battle. Must not the fact that each boy has spent his formative years drinking of the male fluid of his potential enemies determine the deep structure of his warrior character?

Combat among Sambia is not only eroticized as hatred and a death drive directed outward and given full sanction by the culture; it is also a relation between males whose first bond was that of a reciprocal donation of male substance, a donation intensely eroticized, the sole voluptuousness of the formative ten to fifteen years of their lives. The contests in which these males will spend their adult lives as professional warriors must also be an eroticized form of male-fluid circulation. What is at stake, erotically, in the return of the defeated in an interminable and self-perpetuating cycle of bloodletting must have the same circulatory diagram as their domestic vital-fluid transactions.

Fluid Erotics

In the mountain fastness of the jungle drenched by rain nine months of the year, the Sambia live in intense awareness of their own fluids, blood, male fluid, milk—these inconstant resources of life, society, and culture. To speak of the specific force of the erotic exploration of the self and of others among the Sambia, the erotic quality of their lives, the inner erotic states, we have to divine them as they must be lived in the perceptions they have of their bodies, or rather "fetishized" body parts, and in their erotic transactions, with portions of the self rather than with representations of the self.

The release of a surplus tension was for Freud the diagram of orgasm, the greatest pleasure our kind can know, and also the model for every pleasure. The release of the superabundant semen produced in the male body, spermatozoa in incalculable numbers when but a half dozen are needed for the reproductive capacities of a woman's lifetime, is the material substance of this pleasure; Bataille built on this superfluity his erotics and ethics of excess, of expenditure at a loss, of gratuitous discharge.[21] For us, the excesses of semen in the male give him the inward sense of maleness, male power and male passion, as a gratuitous excess to be discharged in transgression and in glory. A woman is, on the contrary, to be protected; a woman is the materialization of limited resources and vigor which have to be economized, and which are depleted in the reproduction for which the woman sacrifices herself for the life of the species.

For the Sambia, it is the woman's body that is the locus of excess, of excess blood that streams from her menstrual-blood organ, materialization of great health, unbridled sensuality, reproductive powers that are natural, uncontrolled, and threatening to the social order men create. Sambia men do not experience in the nocturnal emissions the insignificant or glorious discharge of an excess. For them male fluid is a scarce resource that they will not squander in masturbation. It is donation, and not gratuitous discharge, that focuses their surveillance and intensifies their voluptuousness.

When a child is born, there is no male presence. Genital copulation—polluting contact with the bloody womb from which the child came—is taboo for up to three years after the birth of a child, and a father will very often not so much as see his son for the first six months of his life. The boy lives entirely with his mother, her breasts always accessible to him, and the father has no role in the disciplining or education of his son until initiation. Physical contact with him is scrupulously avoided, since the child bears too much the smell and stains of vaginal blood. Fathers avoid sleeping near their sons, for since they share the same male fluid the spirit familiars that dwell therein may wish to migrate from the fathers' bodies into the more handsome bodies of the sons.

Psychoanalyst Robert Stoller speaks of the first months of an infant's life as a conflict-free phase, in which nonmental learning, conditioning or imprinting, biologic and biopsychic patterns are merged with behavior patterns imprinted by the mother. This complex forms a matrix of habitual, automatized core character, free of intrapsychic conflict, whose gratifying affective nature confirms it and implants it as a set of repetition compulsions. The primary fantasy-field is generated at this stage, "to modulate the impact of the outer world and inner stimuli, protecting us from—*giving us explanations for*—otherwise unmanageable forces that impinge from outside and from within."[22] The long duration of this primary maternal symbiosis among the Sambia—well beyond the year and a half or two years in which, according to Stoller[23] and Money and Ehrhardt,[24] core gender identity is formed, beyond the five or six years at which, according to these authors, it is almost irreversible—must mean that this maternal symbiosis remains an exceptionally cohesive stratum of the erotic subjectivity of Sambia throughout life. The dominant theme of breast-feeding in all their adult eroticism—orgasm *(chemonyi)* in males coming with fellatio with boys or wives, orgasm in women associated with breast-feeding their children rather than with vaginal intercourse—figures as the index of this primary eroticism.

At the first initiation, at the ages of seven to ten, boys, hitherto maintained in the most stern sexual ignorance, are forcibly separated from their mother's sphere, and initiated into homosexual fellatio. The boy will have to not only sleep in the communal men's house, but hide his face from all women, and avoid so much as walking on the women's paths in the hamlet, garden, and forest. The weaning of the boy from mother's breast to brother-in-law's penis is then a break of the most radical, and emotionally traumatic, sort, for both mothers and sons. These "late procedures of ritualized gender surgery must rattle the very gates of life and death."[25]

The extreme emotional tension and violence of this forced initiation is coded in secret male collective rituals, in which the most secret myths, culminating in the great myth of male parthenogenesis, are revealed. Nothing in Sambia culture is more invested with mystery and sacred awe than the wailing songs attributed to spirits and which are now revealed to issue from flutes offered to the boys for their first fellatio, sucking these songs into their bodies and male-fluid organs.

It is true that the initiation involves castration threats—if the boys will be found seeking sexual commerce with senior men's wives. But, unlike the Freudian Oedipal scenario, the severance from the mother is not here an initiative of paternal jealousy intended to create sexual anxiety and make the incest taboo sure, and inaugurate the long sexual latency period that will endure until puberty. Here the boys, far from being forced into self-castration and self-excoriation of the primary-process erotogenic surface of their sensuality, are weaned upon a relay of the paternal penis, and are offered a more powerful, virilizing breast milk. The initiates are indeed subjected to psychologically traumatic and physically painful ordeals, stretching, egestive, and ingestive rites, such that the homosexual fellatio is forced upon them in the midst of fear, worry, and anger. But the fear, worry, and anger are not contrived to implant a permanent castration anxiety before adolescent sexuality; they are intended to open the heart, to produce a heightened awareness of seeing, hearing, tasting, touching, and smelling, in which sexual excitement flares.[26]

A Sambia's homosexual partner is typically the husband of his sister. Layard argued psychoanalytically that the junior partner realizes his repressed sexual desire for his sister through a homosexual relationship with a man eligible to be her husband.[27] The symbiosis in which the daughter continues to live with her mother would motivate this erotic transference of the boy upon his sister, which in turn would motivate the transference upon her future husband. Then, in the kind of severance Sambia initiation effects, incest is not so much prohibited, as in the Oedipus scenario of Freudians, as it is displaced and then positively valued. It is the mother's brother who acts as ritual sponsor for the boy, conferring upon him his sister's future husband as the boy's maternally sanctioned sexual partner.

The initiates now enter years of avid craving for male fluid and dreamy romanticism over males, nowise drenched with shame but annealed with honor, with both their own sense of virile, self-virilizing pride and their sense of the nobility of the males they seek out as sexual partners. The magic flutes, detachable penises, fetishized in both the psychoanalytic and the anthropological sense, script their public eroticism. Among boys the fellated's penis size is not accorded much importance, whereas the amount of flow, consistency, and savor is. Fellators are fascinated with the quantities, densities, textures, and tastes of male fluid, which they discuss interminably, Herdt reports, like wine tasters.[28] For boys become literally addicted to the drinking of male fluid, mystical participation in the primal myth of male parthenogenesis will script the erotic imagination of the homosexual infatuations.[29]

At the third initiation, youths must reverse positions in homosexual inter-course; an older male must never again serve as fellator for a younger. The youth experiences the male identity of being male fluid donor and the pleasure of that identity.

At the fourth initiation, the youths are given access, in addition to boy fellators, to the fellating mouths of the wives with which they have been betrothed since infancy. The social and erotic access to sexual contacts with both males and females must determine the individual's sense of erotic impulses in himself. "The social acceptance of same- and opposite-sex contacts introduces the experiential element of subjective comparison—the feelings and consequences of homosexual versus heterosexual contacts—in organizing sexuality, which is alien to most Westerners' experience," Herdt writes. "This dual sexual regime makes homosexual and heterosexual relationships far more open to self/other evaluations."[30] It makes gender identity relational and multiple. It must make the erotic feeling multiple and relational.

At the fifth initiation, the male becomes functional in heterosexual genital intercourse. For us, the extreme sexual polarity—of economic roles, political status, and social esteem—maintained by the secrecy of the Sambia male ideology, which has as its effect that the real lives, thoughts, and experiences of women are inaccessible to males, makes it astonishing that the same overwhelming majority of males in this society become preferentially heterosexual as in any other society, the percentage of adult males preferentially homosexual in their practices about the same—perhaps 10 percent—as in our societies. Anthropologists since Mead, Read, Burton, and Whiting have expatiated on the "sexual antagonism" characteristic of Papuan cultures. Herdt also speaks of the visible awkwardness of the bridegroom before his bride, delaying intercourse with her sometimes as long as a year or even beyond after they begin cohabitation. But in the end he appeals to Stoller's recent psychoanalytic theories of sexual excitement. "Homosexual experiences, distance, and dehumanization of woman are often needed to create *enough* hostility to allow the sexual excitement necessary for culturally appropriate heterosexuality and the 'reproduction' of society. Men need this sexual polarity and hostility to maintain their personal boundaries in love, marriage, and sex. . . . In place of dry typologies of ritual, we urgently need a theory of sexual excitement."[31]

With the sixth-stage initiation, upon the birth of the first child, the male acquires the social personhood of one responsible for the reproduction of the clan. He must give, with his male fluid, maleness to his wife's real or classificatory younger brothers. We are confounded over how a married man, enjoying exclusive conjugal rights over his wife and with licit and enjoined access to her mouth for fellatio, can be libidinally satisfied by being fellated by a seven-year-old boy. But his erection—the only part of a man that never lies, Cocteau said[32]—proves that he is.

Male-fluid flow that is orgasmic is categorized as play *(chemonyi)*. Orgasmic play is asymmetrical, episodic, and nonappropriative. In Sambia culture the husband/wife dyad is the most symmetrical relationship; two males considerably separated by age introduce asymmetry. Thus a male fluid recipient is perceived as having "more heat" and being more exciting the younger he is. Exclusive access to a fellating mouth is inversely related to play; a man's wife, as his sexual property, is less exciting than a boy or woman taken at first (as a virgin) or once only, on the sly.

Regular, constant, frequent seminal transmissions, such as those which are necessary to keep the womb full of a mix of female blood and male fluid in order that the infant can coagulate, are categorized as work (*wumdu*). The male's fluids are a limited resource; the donor male is being depleted. Work is expenditure at a loss.

Voluptuous symbiosis with the mother, incestuous relationship with the sister's husband, voluptuous fellatio, voluptuous male-fluid donation in homosexual and heterosexual fellatio, voluptuous vaginal male-fluid donation to a woman positioned at a distance of ritual antagonism and excitement, reciprocal bloodletting in battle—how do these radically disjunctive formations of eroticism fit together in the unity of one individual?

The codes of our culture have as their aim to make isomorphic primary core gender identity, determined by genetic psychobiochemical factors and by the character of the biopsychic imprinting of the first months of life, the gender identity attributed to us by others and that we attribute subjectively to ourselves, and the optative gender identity we desire or envy.[33] For the Sambia, there is no innate core gender identity, and attributed gender identity, subjective gender identity, and optative gender identity come together and come apart in different ways at different stages of life. Clifford Geertz instructs us that "the Western conception of the person as a bounded, unique, more or less integrated motivational and cognitive universe, a dynamic center of awareness, emotion, judgment, and action organized into a distinctive whole and set contrastively both against other such wholes and against a social and natural background is, however incorrigible it may seem to us, a rather peculiar idea in the context of the world's cultures."[34]

The unparalleled secrecy that rules in the sphere of male culture in Sambia does not only function to maintain male solidarity, to sanctify ritual knowledge, to support the economic division of labor, and to serve the perceived need for power and control over women. In addition, secrecy maintains the social space for one's own compound of fragments of knowledge, ritual behavior, and fantasy that is one's personal identity. The Sambia sensuality is an erotic field of episodic, asymmetrical, nonreciprocally appropriating foci of erotic subjectivity. Intrapsychic walls of secrecy maintain the psychic space for them.

A Fluid Self

We conceive of our person as a subsistent constant, perceivable in the stable shapes and contours of our bodies, the recurrent verbal and behavioral patterns of our initiatives, and the recurrent diagrams of our emotions, attitudes, and posturings. It would be perceivable too in the consistent ways in which we clothe and adorn our bodies and in the stable social roles and functions in which we insert ourselves. We were not especially confounded by the psychoanalytic thesis that our identities are phallic, that they find in the hard erection of the concealed organ of our gender difference their corporeal materialization. We relegate the body fluids to the status of transitory properties of this subsistence, their passing does not undermine it as it does not enter into its specific identity. The fluids in our substance but transport refurbishments to this substance, and lubricate its morphologically fixed operations. Their seeping into and evaporation or discharge from it does not enter into the discourse in which our identities are coded. Our biology differentiates sexes by their distinctively functioning organs, and differentiates and relates species—dinosaurs and birds—by skeletal morphology; fossils reveal species and gender differences. We have fossil identities.

For the Sambia, gender identity determines economic and political tasks and roles, social attitudes, behaviors, emotions, and the very sense of selfhood. To be incomplete or immature sexually is to be not yet a person and not yet a self. But gender identity is not determined by the innate morphology of the substantive body. The bodies of men as of women, and their distinctive organs, *tingu* and *kereku-kereku,* are receptacles, depositories, and conduits for fluids. Power, strength, growth, and spirituality are possessed only in giving or receiving their material, fluid, substance. The specificity of fluids, and of their courses, determine gender; male and female gender identity, and identity *tout court,* are predicates of fluids that pass through these conduits. Agnatic blood, male fluid, menstrual blood, and milk form the basic elements from which the essential nature of the self is formed. It is the flow of blood that defines femaleness, the donation of male fluid that defines maleness. One's sense of selfhood is an essentially erotic, an orgasmic adhesion to this donation, this outpouring into another.

While female nature is in potency innate, and unfolds into girlhood naturally as the blood stored prenatally is released, it matures into womanhood only upon being coupled orally and vaginally upon the penis from which it draws the male fluids that make it reproductive and nutritive. Sterile women are not complete persons; reproductive and nutritive functioning defines integral femaleness.

Hermaphroditism is known to the Sambia, is perhaps even more prevalent among them than the statistical average in the human species,[35] and Sambia acknowledge change from maleness to femaleness or from femaleness to maleness even at an adult age. They know a dozen such cases in their own small population.

Maleness and femaleness exist only within the transactional field, which circles across nature and society and spirals down generations. Maleness and femaleness are episodic, fluid, formations, perceived in an intensive sense of one's own inner fluid substance, identities forming and passing in the course of fluids through one's body. The individuality of an individual male or female is a fluid individuality, forming episodically as strategies become possible for manipulating the productive force of time, for creating a supplement of value for one's resources in the transactional circuits by manipulating the delay of the obligatory return.

Sambia identify very strongly with the spectacular birds of paradise whose glittering and phosphorescent plumes they incorporate into their headdresses. As among themselves, gender identity among the birds is volatile and episodic: chicks are recognized as all female; fully plumed adult birds with shimmering colors are recognized to be all male; the dull-colored birds that lay eggs are taken to be older birds, which become female again.[36]

Fluid History

The introduction of colonialism and neocolonialism has altered male power in Melanesia. Young men in ever greater numbers leave their hamlets for years to work on plantations, factories, and tourist resorts. When they return they see that their wives, betrothed to them in infancy, have matured to menarche without their male-fluid infusions. They return with European goods, which, unlike shells, feathers, and tusks, are not incorporated into their bodies to become parts of their bodies, but remain external representatives of their power. They have had access to women far from the adjacent villages with which their clan had long established political and economic reciprocity. Do not these new conditions—far more than the contemptuous moralities of missionaries and the Pax Australiana which puts an end to the traditional male destiny to be warriors—doom institutionalized homosexual male-fluid transactions? Will it not also put an end to the specific erotics which simmers over, intensifies, shapes their bodies as conduits of male fluid, blood, and milk, and makes their subjective identity a culturally shaped property of, rather than the subject of, these flows? In another decade or two will we not be describing their erotics, no longer with the hydraulic model we have here elaborated, but with the machinic model Deleuze and Guattari have elaborated[37] to describe the libidinal experience of sexually individuated couplings in the Western disciplinary archipelago? It is not only the informed transcultural observer, like Robert Keesing, who recognizes that "it is an unfortunate fact of contemporary Papua New Guinea that the alternatives to traditional cultures are marginal participation in world capitalist economy, with the frequent consequence of pauperization and exploitation, and an alien and anachronistic religious ideology of sin, fire, and brimstone";[38] the Papuans themselves know this with their own daily perceptions and in their bodies. In still another decade or two, will we not be describing their erotics with the electromagnetic model Freud and Lyotard have elaborated[39] to describe the fields of freely mobile and unbound excitations of our sensuality in a universe we know through our

physics and whose energy is controlled by our electronic and thermonuclear technology?

The answer, we think, is not yet decided. The demise of all "primitive"
cultures in the face of modern communication systems and postcolonial
systems of politico-economic exploitation, a common theme of the last fifty
years of anthropology, to be regretted or accepted with resignation, is not
as complete as has been predicted. Many zones have shown obstinate cultural conservatism and even resurgent traditionalism. It is not certain that
imposed obligatory schooling, the evidences of scientific anatomy, physiology, and biology, will convince them that the terms with which they code
their bodies as conduits for fluids, and their identities as transitory predicates of those fluids, are but those of a fraudulent ideology. Cultural history
today can no longer hold to the simple Durkheimian view that the ideology
of a culture expresses in an integral manner the ecological, economic, and
political structures that condition the survival and productivity of a people.

The Sambia coding of their own natures, bodies, identities, is an affirmation of their distinctness. "Different cultures within a region appear to be
commenting on one another," Lindenbaum wrote, "quiet chamber music
performances, with each group attuned to the sounds of their neighbors."[40]
Each improvisation elaborates its own difference, "statements of their own
distinctiveness, expressions of their identity," Keesing says.[41] One possible
response to the current European invasion, alien influences, and cultural
destruction and subversion is to use these symbols of ethnic distinctiveness
to express commitment to continuing survival as a people, to a culturally
expressed identity.

It is known that the Sambia, in particular, had immigrated between two
hundred and 150 years ago from the Great Papuan Plateau, and that their
culture is a collage of elements brought with them, elements answering
to their new ecological, demographic, political, and economic situation,
and elements borrowed from their neighbors. What they will now borrow
from the neocolonial implantation may also figure in the collage.

We must recognize a specific force to erotics. The perception of their
bodies as conduits for fluids, for those scarce resources which are male
fluid, blood, and milk, is not simply the by-product of a social organization
that structures its political economy in terms of a strict division between
women's gardening and men's hunting and warfare, sister and niece
exchange between potentially enemy hamlets, and the absence of material
wealth that would be equivalent to human bodies themselves. The eroticization of body-fluid hydraulics functions as a force fixing this perception.
As, in Freud, the primary-process sensuality of infancy persists, timeless
and compulsive, beneath the Oedipal, phallic, and genital stages that succeed it, so, among the Sambia, the intensive eroticization of their own body

fluids has a force that is not simply reducible to the structural force of a coded economy where people transact predominantly with portions of self rather than with representatives of self.

If, as the ecological, demographic, political, and economic conditions for the survival and productivity of a people change, their specific erotics, outlining their bodies as conduits of fluids, could persist, what about us? Will the machinic model of our erotics prevail among us as long as the ecological, demographic, political, and economic conditions of our existence are those of disciplinary biopolitics? Will an electromagnetic model of our erotics prevail in our advancing postindustrial revolution, driven with electrical and nuclear energy, under electronic, self-regulating surveillance, programmed cybernetically? Might our own erotics elaborate something like a perception of our orgasmic bodies as conduits of fluids? Might, as the Sambia borrowed their agriculture and their hunting from their new neighbors in the Eastern Highlands, some of us borrow our erotics from them, and thus formulate the distinctiveness of our identities and that of our pleasures?

1994

The Navel of the World

Te Pito O Te Henua, the Navel of the World, is the most isolated inhabited island there is, thirty-six hundred kilometers from the South American coast, two thousand kilometers from the nearest inhabited island—tiny Pitcairn, where the mutineers from the *Bounty* settled with their Tahitian women. It is thirteen miles long and at its widest point seven and eight tenths, a pebble in the vast Pacific. Its low rhythmic profile is the result of three volcanic rises from the ocean floor—three million, one million, and six hundred thousand years ago—connected by secondary volcanic cones. There are no rivers, no bays, and no coral reefs about the island. Three volcanic craters contain lakes of rainwater. Most of the surface is strewn with black chunks of jagged lava. Here and there are expanses of built-up topsoil a few feet thick. Once mantled with tropical forest, the island has long been treeless, and today only a few planted eucalyptus groves stand here and there to ripple the trade winds that constantly blow eastward. The entire population of the island—two thousand five hundred, half Chilean, half now mostly mestizo natives—have been settled in the one village, Hanga Roa. In this season, the rains are beginning with intermittent drizzle and so the island is green. Tourists come—only some four thousand a year—in the dry season and for the "Easter Island Week," when the locals put on a "native" show. There descended from our Tahiti-bound plane the inevitable group of Japanese tourists I would occasionally see in the days that followed, seated in their bus with their Japanese guide, and a few stragglers as solitary as I: when we happened to arrive at the same site, one turned away to contemplate the horizon until the other left. I stayed in a room in the house of a very old couple who spoke hardly any Spanish.

A living organism is a dense and self-maintaining plenum. Out of the energies it assimilates from its environment it generates forces in excess of what it needs to adjust to that environment and compensate for the intermittent and superficial lacks produced by evaporation and fuel consumption. The discharges of these superabundant forces are felt in passions. But the environment itself is full of free and nonteleological energies—trade winds and storms, oceans streaming over three-fourths of the planet, drifting continental plates, cordilleras of the deep that erupt in volcanic explosions, and miles-deep glaciers piled up on Antarctica that flow into the sea and break off in hobbling ice mountains. How can the passions of penguins, albatrosses, jaguars, and humans not lift their eyes beyond the nests and the lairs and the horizons? How can these passions not sink into volcanic rock and the oceanic deserts?

When you are there you have the impression you will stay indefinitely. The extinct volcanoes have settled into a placid harmony of low, grass-covered cones in the balmy mist. Along its edges the island drops in sharp lava shards whipped by the waves; beyond there is the shimmering blue. From the top of any of its rises, you see the ocean all around and the curvature of Earth. Above, the clouds thin out and the sun illuminates limitless depths of sky. There are two hundred forty long, low stone altars spaced all along the edges of the island, a thousand giant stone statues, and some fifteen thousand other archaeological sites—remains of dwellings, petroglyphs, caves.

But it is nothing like visiting a vast, open-air museum, inspecting the details and decoding the significance of a thousand works of art. All the giant statues have been hurled from their altars since that Easter Day in 1722. All the smaller statues and carvings have been removed by collectors and tourists; the tiny museum has only copies. Thor Heyerdahl's account of his plunder is in *Aku-Aku*, a sickening book. Only in four sites have the statues, mostly broken, been reerected in recent times. Called *moai*, the monolithic statues were carved over a fourteen-hundred-year period. They are remarkably uniform, all very stylized busts of legendary ancestors. Out of a thousand, three are vaguely female.

Mostly you walk, led on by the grassy harmony of the island, and at a site you rest and enter a kind of empty reverie over the crumbled altars and the broken *moai* fallen face forward over the rubble.

When you come upon one of the four restored sites, you find five or seven *moai*, cemented back together where possible, very worn by the wind and the elements and the centuries. The head of a *moai* is as big as its chest, and it has no feet; the thin arms and long fingers are traced in relief over the abdomen, always in the same position. The head, very flat, is really just a face, with low forehead, sharp, square jaw, thin, tight lips, a strong nose with wide-open nostrils carved in a spiral, and huge empty eyes. The face is turned upward somewhat; the eyes do not, like the eyes of the Buddha, look compassionately on the people below. They look inward to the island, and over the low grassy width of the island to the ocean beyond. They are the depersonalized faces of the legendary chiefs who fifteen hundred years ago sailed four thousand kilometers and disembarked on this volcanic crust. Stern, hieratic, rigid, uniform, these figures certainly impose a severe order on the inhabitants, and anthropologists indeed say that early Polynesian society was very structured. But surely their great size—twelve to thirty feet high—and their eyes fixed expressionless and unbenevolent on remoteness beyond the horizon, demanded and commanded their passions. To the wanderer among them today, these huge empty eyes fixed on horizons beyond this island, beyond any visible horizon, rule one's every, increasingly aimless, step. With their jaws designed by geometry, their thin, tight lips, the only animation on these faces is in their strong splayed nostrils, pulling in the forces of the winds.

The "mystery" of this island, kept up by anthropologists applying for funding, by travel writers and tourist brochures, was created by the Westerners who came upon the island, saw the statues, looked at the islanders, and concluded that the present inhabitants could not have created the statues, that they were the work of a lost civilization colonized from Egypt, Greece, India, the lost continent of Mu, or outer space. How were the statues transported on this island that had neither trees nor vines that could serve as ropes? There were no pack animals, indeed no mammals at all on the island, nor wheels. The islanders had no metallurgy, no pottery, no weaving. They lived on the edge of the sea and fished and cultivated gardens of sweet potato, taro, and bananas. They wore no clothing and instead covered their bodies with tattoos. Missionaries labeled the people cannibals. Thor Heyerdahl was struck by how the altars are made of separately carved and polished stones fitted together into jigsaw walls as perfect as those of Qosqo, and he sailed the *Kon-Tiki* to prove that the island was colonized by people from Inca Peru. By the islanders' own account, Hotu Matu'a had set sail with three hundred of his people fleeing volcanic eruptions in their homeland, the islands those who live there call Te Fenua Enata—"The Land of Men," which we today call the Marquesas. It has only been in the past thirty years that archaeologists got around to determining that the island had been settled around a.d. 300 by a people who began carving statues almost at once. When the Europeans first came upon them, there were hundreds of enormous statues being carved in the quarry, one sixty-five feet tall weighing three hundred tons. The language of the islanders has been found to be akin to that of the Marquesas, four thousand kilometers to the west, and blood and gene sampling has shown no evidence of migrations from other places. The islanders clearly had very advanced navigational science, steered by the stars, had knowledge of sea currents, observed the flight patterns of birds, and must subsequently have gone on to the South American continent, since their staple food, the sweet potato, has never been found growing wild anywhere outside South America. They alone, of all the peoples of the Pacific, invented writing, *rongo-rongo*, partly phonetic and partly ideographic, and inscribed it on wood tablets. Every house had such tablets, and each year there were two competitions in which learned scholars chanted the contents of their tablets before the king and the whole people. The history, cosmology, and science of the islanders became a mystery in the nineteenth century, when the population was enslaved and decimated, the few survivors were Christianized, and the surviving twenty-one pieces of this writing, taken by collectors to Rome, Venice, and Petrograd, became undecipherable.

The volcano Rano Raraku rises out of a flat landscape near the edge of the sea. Virtually all of the thousand giant *moai* of the island were quarried out of the yellow stone of its crater wall. In that crater wall today there are 394 statues in all stages of completion. First the face, then the abdomen were carved and polished, with stones of lapilli, until the statue was attached only by the rib of the spine. Recent experiments have shown it would take at least a year for a team of men to carve a small *moai*. When a *moai* was finished—save for the eyes—it was cut free, slid down the mountain, and set upright. Those carved inside the crater were moved out through a passage cut in one side of the crater wall. Some seventy-five *moai* lie fully completed at the base of the volcano; these have been covered up to the neck by the erosion from the mountain over the last two hundred years. A half-dozen lie facedown on the way to their final locations.

Recent experiments to move them with sledges or fulcrums only showed that the *moai* would have been ground down by the rubble on the way. It is possible that they were actually carried on the backs of hundreds of assembled people, then somehow set upright.

The red topknots were quarried inside the Puna Pau volcano, then somehow rolled out of the crater, and finally somehow hoisted up onto the statues; many weigh ten tons. When the statues were erected on their altars on the edge of the sea, the eyes were carved and their gaze directed into distances beyond all things to see or messages to capture.

Heyerdahl dug out the buildup of dirt from the completed statues at the base of the volcano to expose them; they have since been covered back up to preserve them. In Cairo ten years ago, in the museum, I saw all the mummies, torn out of their tombs, stripped of their flowers and gods, and laid out in plain wood cases under glass with their blackened faces exposed; on the walls an American scientist had put his X-ray photos of their skeletons, and the urn containing the entrails of Queen Hapshetshut was split open and brightly illuminated. Rano Raraku is a quarry of works in progress. Should we now dig out these *moai* and erect them on rebuilt altars? Philosophy too consists of works in progress, cut short by the death of innumerable philosophers. Should we, using Merleau-Ponty's working notes, write the rest of *The Visible and the Invisible* for him? Should we complete Mahler's Tenth Symphony?

The crater walls are very steep; from the top you see the blue ocean beyond extending to the sky, which you then find reflected on the lake within. Only one side of the crater was being carved, but there *moai* were emerging head up, head down—not a foot of rock that was not taking on form. The sea is eroding its way toward this side of the crater, but if the carving had continued the volcano would have been carved away before the waves of the ocean arrived. At the base of the volcano, only the heads of the completed *moai* are seen, bent over and blind, their bodies covered to the neck by the mountain that has eroded from above upon them. I spent two long afternoons among them, alone save for one hawk soaring above. It understood, perhaps, that I was waiting for my death.

After apparently living for fourteen hundred years on the Navel of the World unknown to the world, God, or themselves, the islanders were discovered by the Dutch captain Jacob Roggeveen on Easter Day in 1722. Captain Roggeveen named the island Easter Island, shot dead thirteen and wounded many more of the inhabitants who welcomed him, and left the next day stocked up with foodstuffs. In 1770 Captain Don Felipe González came upon the island, disembarked with two priests and a battalion of soldiers, who advanced in formation to the center of the island. He named it Isla de San Carlos, forced some natives to sign in their rongo-rongo script a Spanish document addressed to King Carlos III beseeching to be annexed by Spain, and left. In 1774 Captain Cook arrived, and stayed three days. He sent his men to search the whole island; they found only a hundred men and no women or children, shot one native for touching an officer's bag, forced the others to load up baskets with potatoes for the scurvy-infected ship, and set sail again. On the ship the sailors found the baskets filled with stones under a covering of potatoes. In 1786 a French warship under le Comte de la Pérouse stopped at the island for eleven hours; the cove where the warship anchored is "honored" today with his name. An unrecorded number of pirates, whalers, and sealers also came upon the island; one whose visit was recorded was the American sealer *Nancy,* whose captain set out in 1805 to capture the natives for slavery on his Juan Fernández island base. He was able to capture only twelve men and ten women. After three days at sea, he untied them; they all leapt overboard and drowned. He returned to the island to round up more. In 1822 the men of an American whaler, the *Pindos*, rounded up island women to take with them; they later threw them into the sea and shot at them. On the island syphilis and leprosy spread. Starting in 1859 slave traders regularly raided the island. In 1862 an armada of seven Peruvian ships commanded by Captain Aguirre was able to capture two hundred men for slavery in the guano mines of Peru. Eighteen more slave ships came in the following year. Under pressure from the French administrators of Tahiti and the English, the Peruvian authorities ultimately agreed to repatriate these slaves. Only a hundred were still alive; of these eighty-five died on the return voyage, and the fifteen who disembarked were infected with smallpox which decimated the island. All the giant statues of the island were hurled from their altars between 1722 and 1864. A Catholic missionary was brought in, the people were converted, the rongo-rongo tablets burned, and family collections of heirlooms, statues, and wood carvings, said now to be the work of demons, were destroyed. The missionary also brought in tuberculosis. In 1888 Chile annexed the island, rounded up the remaining population of 111, put them in a barbed-wire corral at Hanga Roa, and allotted the rest of the island to sheep ranchers. Few Chileans were interested; it was British who bought the ranching concessions and turned the island over to seventy thousand sheep, which denuded the island of its shrubbery and chewed the grass to the roots. Too distant for economically feasible transportation, the sheep were eliminated in recent years and replaced by horses and cattle owned by two Chilean corporations. In 1934 the French anthropologist Alfred Métraux made the first cultural exploration of the island; the Chilean government was persuaded of its tourist possibilities and in 1935 made most of the coastline a national park. In 1986, after the explosion of the *Challenger*, the American space program NASA built an airstrip on the island for the recovery of satellites falling into the Pacific.

About halfway through grade school I brought up a linguistic problem to the teacher. She—and the textbook—called the Roman civilization a great civilization. It was said to be at its greatest when its military dominated the greatest number of lands and peoples. When its empire shrank, it was said to be in decline. This terminology persisted in history class after history class throughout my schooling, and in museum after museum I have visited since. The great religions are the world religions. Civilization advances with military and economic expansionism. A euphemism is competition: without competition there is no artistic, literary, or religious advance. (Without grades, prizes, honors, there is no philosophical achievement.) My first trip was to Florence, where I was beset by the evidence that its grand artistic, literary, and musical achievements coincided with its richest and most rapacious century; as soon as that century was over, Florence could only sigh on in mannerism. Today Florence is rich through tourism, but without political expansionism its artistic and literary culture is comparable to that of Oklahoma City. Culture is the glory of a civilization that rises in the glint of advancing swords and cannon. The frantic theories of Thor Heyerdahl and the others striving to prove that the sculpture and the altar walls on Te Pito O Te Henua show cultural imports from Inca Peru, from Egypt, Greece, India, or China are based on the conviction that an isolated culture always declines.

I crisscrossed Te Pito O Te Henua many times, exploring this crust of volcanic cinders covered with grass, ending up inevitably at the featureless sea and the curvature of Earth beneath the unending flow of wind and sky. The small flowers in the grass you see everywhere: the island has but thirty species of indigenous plant life. There are no coral reefs swarming with fish to attract sea birds and sea mammals. The few sparrows and small hawks you see are recent imports. No rodents or lizards scurry through the chunks of lava. There are no cliff fortresses—only the harmonious low cones of volcanos extinct a million years ago. The population of the island stabilized at about fifteen thousand; for fourteen hundred years the rulers continued the hereditary line unbroken from the founder Hotu Matu'a. The statues had already reached gigantic size in the seventh century, and the evolution of their stylization was gradual over the next thousand years. Though the now mute rongo-rongo books can no longer tell the wanderer of the history, cosmology, and science of this civilization, the statues' great eyes and splayed nostrils tell him of its passion. An obsessive drive, nowise economic or rational, erected these depersonalized stone faces with eyes looking out into the featureless emptiness. The force of this passion was the force of volcanos and the wind and the ocean and the sky.

The southwest end of the island, called Rano Kau, is a four-mile walk up slow-rising, rolling grassland, with many pauses to contemplate the sea and the island. Only when you step over a grassy rim at the top do you suddenly realize that Rano Kau is an extinct volcano: below is a rocky bowl containing a circular lake a mile wide. You walk along the crater rim; the land is a high plateau to your right. When you reach the far side the plateau drops a thousand feet into the ocean; the outer wall of the crater here is a vertical cliff. Below, a few miles away you see three small islands, the first a stalagmite rising abruptly out of the ocean, then two rocky outcroppings. Near the volcano rim on the edge of the cliff, there are boulders covered with petroglyphs—images in high relief of men with bird heads, of vulvas, of faces of the god Makemake. This is the place called Orongo.

Down a short slope from the boulders, along the very edge of the cliff there are fifty-three small buildings. Seen from above they form clusters of grass-covered ovals. When you descend among them, you see that their walls are made of uncemented sheets of slate laid flat and corbeled. The entrances, all facing the ocean, are at ground level, two feet high and so narrow you have to lift one side of your torso to crawl inside. It is the sacred precinct of Mata Ngarau. These are the residences of the priests of the birds. The islands below were the nesting places of the migratory terns, the manu-tara.

Each year when the manu-tara returned, the tangatamanu, the birdmen chosen in dreams by the priests in the sacred precinct, descended the cliff. They swam across the straits to the island called Motu Nui among sharks racing through the wild currents. All the birdmen were strong and brave; chance determined which of them would find the first egg laid. The bird-man who was able to return to Mata Ngarau with that first egg had his hair, brows, and eyelashes shaven, carved his birdman image into a boulder, and, as the new king, descended to cross the island to the crater of Rano Raraku, where he would live in complete seclusion among the silent and eyeless *moai* for the year of his reign. Under his crown of plumage his hair grew, and he did not cut his nails. His food was brought by a servant who took pains not to be seen. On the islands thousands of terns jostled and hatched their eggs; on the cliff above, the people performed entranced orgiastic rites. The reign of the birdman kings was recent, beginning in 1780. During the year, the other birdmen and the priests at Mata Ngarau were paramount throughout the island, not so much ruling as descending upon its settlements in orgiastic raids. It was they Western historians were describing when they wrote that the last period of Easter Island civilization was a time of decadence and anarchy.

The bird culture is the late dominance of an aboriginal stream of this civilization. The founding king Hotu Matu'a who had set sail with the orig-inal colonizers in the third century was surely led to this minuscule island by birds. The colonists brought with them poultry, which remained their only domestic animal. They also brought their Marquesas deities, among whom Makemake, the god of the bird culture, gradually became domi-nant. But for fourteen hundred years the culture was structured, hieratic, under hereditary rulers.

It was in the eighteenth century, when the island became prey to plunderers from the outside, when the thousand-year-old temples were overturned, when the people hid in closed volcanic caves at the first sight of any foreign ship on the horizon, that the period called anarchy by Western writers came about. The ancient hereditary kings, the last of whom died in slavery in Peru, were replaced by men whose prowess naked in the raging sea marked them to be temporary sovereigns. But their sover-eignty was not an administration of a structured society, which now existed no more; he who brought the first egg of the manu-tara was king, and his sovereignty was as pervasive as he was invisible, until the terns returned to the sea. What he presided over was not a panicky totalitarian culture bent on preserving its sedentary economy from the depredations of yet more rapacious agents of the mercantile societies of the Dutch, English, French, Russians, and Peruvians, but, in its ruins, the liberation of a totally different kind of culture—a culture of pride, daring and chance, violence and eroticism. A culture of birds.

The last birdman reigned in 1866; his name was Rokunga. By 1868 the last pagan on the island had been baptized by the Picpus missionary Eugène Eyraud.

The migratory terns called manu-tara, of the species *Sterna lunata,* no longer return to the island called Motu Nui.

Historians go back to the individual initiatives and collective enterprises that were undertaken by those now dead—more exactly, to the texts that recorded those things and to the monuments, artifacts, and ruins which are not only described in texts but can be read as texts. When historians write the text of history, their work is not so much to inscribe those initiatives and enterprises, triumphs and defeats themselves, as it is to reinscribe their meaning. When scholars take a text of Euclid or Herodotus and set out to determine what it meant, their first task is to recycle in their brains the thoughts of a man long dead. Writing exists to make that possible. A text has surely the meaning it had for the author as he composed its sentences, but the scholar also sets out to determine the meaning it had for the readers to whom the author addressed it, and for the readers whose conditions, concerns, and values the author could not envision with clarity or certainty, as well as for readers he did not envision at all. The historian's text inscribes not only the meaning the individual initiatives and collective enterprises had for those who launched them, but also the meaning they had for those who celebrated them or defeated them, and the meaning they had for the generations that came later and built and destroyed in the world which those initiatives and enterprises had shaped. And the historian formulates the meaning of the past for his own generation and their descendants. History presumes that we must learn from the deeds, triumphs, and defeats of the past.

From time immemorial people gathered about the fire and told tales of the great deeds, great triumphs, and great defeats of their heroes. In listening to the tales and in reading the chronicles of their people, men and women found their hearts pounding and their brains fevered with the audacities, hopes, loves, and hatreds of heroes and heroines who were dead. The historian may decipher those emotions on the texts, monuments, artifacts, and ruins he finds.

But the modern historian writes dispassionately, neither exulting in the victory of Cortés nor weeping over the defeat of Moctezuma. He is not writing in order to feel again and make his reader feel again the torrential emotions of men and women long dead. He is not writing to crowd his soul with all the loves and hatreds, despairs and exultations of those who wrought great deeds and those who suffered terrible defeats. He thinks that his contemporaries and their descendants should learn from the lessons of history before launching enterprises and unleashing the passions that will drive them; and he thinks that the lessons are not yet in, the data are fragmentary and so often ambiguous. He knows well that the Spanish and the Mexica drew contradictory conclusions from the fall of Tenochtitlán. And he thinks that if emotions focus the mind, they also limit it. There is an opacity to emotions; they cloud the mind such that it does not see things in their whole context.

Emotions color the line drawings with which cognition represents reality. The philosophical distinction between the cognitive senses and private feelings can be traced back to Aristotle; it continues to our day in the concept of objective scientific knowledge. We take emotions to be distinctively human phenomena. Outside the crystal ball of the human psyche, there are only grass that does not wince when we tread on it, trees that are impassive as the chain saw slashes them, water that does not shiver with pleasure when we stroke it, atoms drifting through the void without anxiety and colliding without pleasure or pain. If these things move us, it is because we are moved by the colors we project onto them. All colors, according to John Locke and seventeenth-century epistemology, including the "color" of emotion, are subjective effects within the psyche of the viewer.[1]

For Nietzsche, man's glory is to be not the contemplative mirror in which nature is represented but the Dionysian artist who in giving style to his movements makes an artwork out of the most precious clay and oil, his own flesh and blood—and the Apollonian dreamer who gives form to the waters above and the waters below, to the stars and the dry land, to the creeping and crawling things about him. Nietzsche praised as old masters the dancer and dreamer in us whose emotions are a pot of colors.

Emotions are also forces. The grand colors come from strong surges of prodigal energies within a life.

For Nietzsche emotions are excess energies the organism produces that overflow those operations with which the organism adjusts to its environment. Strong surges of energies in the environment itself, disintegrating the placid order of settled things, are not part of the explanation for emotional forces. After all, Nietzsche would point out, a weak, contented or resentful, human and one of exalted, frenzied vitality view the same spectacle—a thunderstorm over the mountains or the ocean waves breaking against the cliffs—differently, and a scientist can view a flood in Bangladesh or on the Mississippi plain with dispassionate composure.

The modern philosophy of mind took emotions to be inner states, experiences with only one witness. One infers, on the basis of perceived behaviors, that there are feeling states in others analogous to those one knows within oneself. No dentist feels his patient's toothache; everyone can agree on the size and shape of the Mona Lisa's smile but there is no agreement about whether that smile is mellifluous or irritatingly priggish.

Yet what is more evident than the pain of an accident victim, than the agony of the mother of that victim? At ten days, a newborn infant recognizes with a smile the smile of his mother. What is more visible than the glee of an infant playing with a kitten, and if that infant toddles off into the woods, can there be any doubt about the joy of the mother when he is found?

The hilarity, the fear, the rage, the relief, the agony, the desperation, the supplication are what are most visible about those we look at. At a glance we see that the cop or the office manager is incensed, even though we find we cannot say later what color his eyes are and had not noticed that she had dyed her hair.

Indeed, the mirth and the despondency, the irritability and the enthusiasm, the rapture and the rage are the very visibility of a body. A body's shape and contours are the way that it is held in a space that excludes other bodies and us; a body's colors are opaque expanses behind which the life processes are hidden. It is through its feelings, drawing our eyes into their fields of force, that a body emerges out of its self-contained closure and becomes visible. Through the windshield the hitchhiker sees the distrust of the driver of the car. As we walk by trees and figures in the park, it is the pleasure radiating out of the smiling face and the exposed arms and fingers of an old woman feeding pigeons that make us see her. Walking through crowds in the street, we see mortification or heartbreak outlining in relief a middle-aged woman clad in a sensible and ordinary coat.

People poke at mountain goats and reptiles in the zoo; they throw stones at lions. The irritation, the fear, or the anger of the animal are not behind its opaque skin or in its skull; the molester feels the irritation or the anger against his eyes, against the mean smirk on his face. The passerby who sees the irritation, fear, or anger that make the python, fox, or tiger visible— when that emotion is directed against the zookeeper or against another animal—at once feels himself caught up in the range of that passion.

The elations, gaieties, lusts, rancors, miseries, apathies, and despairs of living organisms catch the eyes and hold the attention of passersby. They intrude into the perceptual fields and practical concerns of others. Our emotions reorient others, disturb their trains of thought, seep into the blueprints of their projects, contest them, and afflict them with misgivings and self-doubt. Power among humans is not simply the physical force with which one material body may move another; it is the force to distract, detour, maneuver, and command. Every pleasure we indulge in and every pain we suffer exerts power over others.

We do feel that people who live in flat lands tend to have flat minds and flat feelings, that people who live in cubicles in public-housing developments tend to have narrow, constricted feelings. We feel that the objects and landscapes upon which emotions are released can limit the range of emotions that run up against them and eventually cause those feelings to aim at only nearby things.

Not only do emotions discharge their forces on the outside environment; they have their source in it. Was it not the mists and the driving sleet, the blossoming prairies, and the swallows rhapsodic in the tides of summer that opened our hearts to ever more vast expanses of reality, beyond all that is made to content and satisfy us? Rage does not come from nowhere, nor does it come only from the overheating of the organism itself. Love is not a passion felt in human beings alone, nor does it derive from inner needs and wants. Strength and superabundant energies are not generated simply by an inner psychic will that is a will to power. Emotions get their force from the outside, from the swirling winds over the rotating planet, the troubled ocean currents, the clouds hovering over depths of empty outer space, the continental plates shifting and creaking, the volcanos rising from the oceanic abyss, and the nonsensical compositions of mockingbirds, the whimsical fluttering of butterflies in the racket of a wallow of elephant seals. Their free mobility and energies surge through us; their disquietudes, torments, and outbursts channel through us as emotions.

People who shut themselves off from the universe shut themselves up not in themselves but within the walls of their private property. They do not feel volcanic, oceanic, hyperborean, and celestial feelings, but only the torpor closed behind the doors of their apartment or suburban ranch house, the hysteria of the traffic, and the agitations of the currency on the stretch of turf they find for themselves on the twentieth floor of some multinational corporation building.

If one person regards a thunderstorm over the mountains or the ocean waves breaking against the cliffs as dangerous and another as sublime, the reason is not, as Immanuel Kant wrote, that the first clings to feeling the vulnerability of his small body, while the second initially verifies that his vantage point is safe and then forms the intellectual concept of infinity, which concept exalts his mind. And it is not simply, as Nietzsche wrote, that the first cramps his weak emotional energies back upon himself, resenting what threatens his security, while the second has a vitality whose excessive energies have to be released outside. It is that the first draws his emotional energies from the forces that hold walls together and closed. A scientist, paid enough to have a mansion in the suburbs, views the storm from the confines of a laboratory in an earthquake-proof building where the fluorescent lights never go off during a thunderstorm. And the second sails the open seas and the winds, driven by some volcanic eruption in his Marquesas homeland.

Alone, wandering around Te Pito O Te Henua, I learned very little. For all its fame, there are not many books about "Easter Island"—those by Alfred Métraux, Thor Heyerdahl, Jo Anne Van Tilburg, and a few dozen monographs by archaeologists. The few remaining rongo-rongo books are indecipherable; the giant statues are nameless figures of unknown cults. What the islanders believed, what cosmology and myths were the framework within which they carved and transported the giant statues, what cosmogony and epics gave meaning to the recent bird cult, are almost completely lost to us.

Garrulous researchers, who get funded to come to the island to produce a text, set themselves tasks: how many statues are there, how big are they, how much do they weigh? They set out to carbon-date them, classify them according to style, and then try to correlate the statues with kings or gods mentioned in the sparse eighteenth-century sea captains' logs or with the demons mentioned in the journals of nineteenth-century missionaries.

Yet how one is struck by the depersonalization and repetitiveness of the *moai*! In Wat Pô, in Bangkok, there is a colonnade that contains a thousand statues, each of the Buddha larger than life size. In Sri Lanka, Myanmar, Thailand, Laos, and Tibet I had seen whole walls of caves carved into statues—all statues of the Buddha, in the same position, genderless, depersonalized. What to make of a whole cave lined with Buddha images all alike?

You do not view the Buddha image as an artwork; you meditate. Your body must be in equilibrium, without any tensions that would produce cramps or shifts. The mind must be empty, so that all thinking, imagining, remembering, speculating will have faded out, leaving you centered on the task of intoning a mantra across the length of a diaphragmic breath. The sacred mantra "OM" means "the Jewel in the Lotus." But the meditator does not think of the meaning or its referent, or if he does, he does so only for the effect it produces. He will intone it again and again, each time more inwardly. Finally the mantra does not resonate outwardly at all. With its simplicity, its sustained purity and endurance, the mantra has become the inner state of his vitality, the still surface of a summer lake so undisturbed that the remote clouds and the shadows of transparent insects can play on it without the least distortion.

The Buddha image is not intended to represent that particular man named Siddhartha Gautama who was born in the Nepalese Himalayas about five hundred years before the Christian era. It is the image of a soul in equilibrium, centered, available for a compassion that is cosmic. The Buddha image is not an icon but a means of meditation, of composing one's forces. Down the corridors of temples and on the walls of caves it is repeated like a mantra.

There is on the giant statues on the rim of the island of Te Pito O Te Henua no trace of the idealized anatomy of Greek anthropomorphized gods, of the haughty sovereignty of Roman emperors, of the sacrificial pathos of Jesus. The *moai* succeed one another along the edge of the sea and deep in our hearts like mantras. They do not direct us to be on the look-out for another island or for stray ships full of Peruvian gold. They lift our eyes from the surface of the island, and direct our gaze beyond the horizon. Their strong nostrils take in the wind.

I had read all the texts that recent researchers and scholars have written about the statues. But as I wandered from one statue to another, each so like the rest, all these texts faded away. The people who carved them also had put a subtext on them, long ago effaced. I was sure that what I felt, as our texts faded from consciousness, as had theirs long ago, was what, under their subtext, the people who carved the statues and lived among them felt. Walking the volcanic rises of this island and contemplating these broken statues, what these vanished people had felt was clear, palpable, as though I were walking among their very ghosts, as though those ghosts had come to inhabit my nervous circuitry and sensibility. The statues, the very earth, the ocean, the sky, the winds convey what they felt. It was inconceivable that this kind of work, these giant stone statues, could have been erected in the rain forests, or in the temperate latitudes in the middle of continents.

I felt in the vast restlessness of the ocean the profound resolve of these people as they left their Marquesas Islands homeland exploding in volcanic eruptions. I felt in the winds their terror, their bravado, their anxieties during the four thousand kilometers of steering in the uncharted Pacific. I felt in the sea birds' tacking in the trade winds their insomniac trust in the flight of the sea birds that led them here. I felt in the drumming and flash of the surf their exultation at setting foot on the crust of this island. In this navel to which all Earth was reduced, before this vacant ocean, under this empty sky, in the midst of these never-ending east winds, I felt their appetite for life and for reality. In the low grass-covered cones in the balmy mist, I felt the placid harmony of the fourteen hundred years of their work and repose. In the huge eyes of a thousand *moai* of volcanic stone turned to fathomless distances, I felt their taste for the impossible.

On Te Pito O Te Henua it was clear to me that the passions turned to fathomless distances that raised those stones into giant statues were drawn from the upsurge of the volcanos themselves, that those vacant eyes reflected the radiance of the skies, that the song of the winds and the seas was on those lips, and that those great stone faces and their raiment held the color of the ardent lava and of the restless oceanic depths.

2000

Araouane

It was two weeks by camel to get to Araouane and back to Tombouctou; Robin and Ken had to leave Africa before then. Azima, a Tuareg of twenty-five, arranged for a vehicle. Azima was born in Araouane; his family lives there. Unschooled, he speaks fluent French and very good English and, like most people in Mali, four native languages. The driver Izzah arrived with a Land Cruiser the next morning. Dressed also in a Tuareg blue *boubou* with a pale blue turban of fine fabric on his head, he was a stout middle-aged guy with perfect teeth and excellent French, energetic and jovial. Fie had a lad, Mohammed, with him identified as his mechanic; during the trip Mohammed also did the cooking. We picked up a middle-aged, lean, Arab-looking guy, Amadou, always serious and silent, who was to be the guide.

We drove through the sand roads of Tombouctou and into desert scattered with thorn trees and tufts of a grass inedible for camels and goats. The men covered their faces, save for their eyes, with the ends of their turbans to filter the sandy air. Under the vacant sky the vehicle growled across dunes and hollows sometimes white with salt. Now and again there were blackened depressions where water had stood. On a crest the vehicle got stuck; Mohammed got out and let some air out of the tires, to increase the area of their traction.

After a few hours, we stopped at a small tree, laid out blankets, and prepared lunch. We had mangoes and dates and dark flat breads. The men cooked lamb and rice over a fire of sticks. I strolled off into the distances. The sands were very fine, yellow beach sand, rippled like the patterns in watered silk. A white mist of salt swirled over the surfaces. Here and there were small fields of black basalt pebbles. The sands were drifting in sheets, eastward to Niger, Chad, Sudan, to eventually silt in the Red Sea.

Walking over the sand gave me a hitherto unknown sensation of walking on the very surface. In the waves of the Sahara that range over three and a half million square miles, I was a water bug gliding across the surface of a pond. Everywhere else I have walked on this earth, I have been shadowed and enveloped by buildings and trees higher than myself. The presence of a dark depth beneath, into which elsewhere the trees sank their taproots and in which the dead are buried, was missing here. One is on sand, and below there is sand. Here I could only be buried in sand and disinterred by the winds.

We reached whole stretches where not a blade of vegetation was visible. The time of human concerns, and that of our own journey, faded out before the presence of geological time, which extended across the crests and hollows drifting under the featureless sky. The horizons that opened unendingly upon flowing desert, the presence of deep water into which occasional desert wells descended, the blackened basins where water still stood during the rains took one back across centuries indistinguishable from one another. We stopped; the men got out, spread blankets across the sand, and once again prostrated themselves in homage to Allah. Over them the empty silences of the sky opened upon cosmic time.

Amadou is directing Izzah across a path that the *azalai*, the camel caravans of the Tuareg, have taken for a thousand years, each camel bearing four two-hundred-pound slabs of brown salt from the mines at Taoudenni. Yesterday, an hour ago, camels left their hoofprints somewhere in these spaces, but the winds have erased them already. The great dunes that loom up are as ephemeral as the crests of waves in the oceans. Everything is ephemeral in this immemorial time. The tufts of grass visible here and there will be gone in another hour when another camel caravan passes.

Amadou indicates the way with small turns of his hand. Azima and Izzah know the way, but not this well. Izzah says that Amadou has the map in his head, and the invisible paths to Mauritania and Libya and Niger too. The camel caravans travel by night guided by the stars: celestial navigators. When the sky is overcast a Tuareg verifies the way by tasting the sand!

In the late afternoon we have a flat tire. I see a man with a child coming across the emptiness. For his children, sick with fever, he asks for aspirin. Which I had.

At the end of the day we stop to gather some sticks; Izzah tells us there will be no more to be found from now on. He does not seem to care about the approaching dark. Indeed it is soon upon us. For hours I have watched Amadou signal the way across utterly trackless desert; now its dimensions are reduced to a band that the headlights extend into the night. He directs Izzah with precise movements of his hand, peering into the cone of light ahead. He has literally memorized the shapes and spacing of tufts of grass over hundreds of kilometers! I try to project what his mind is doing into my head—in vain. I think that no scholar reading the philosopher Hegel has so exacting an attentiveness to so vast a mental space. Perhaps Ravi Shankar improvising a six-hour raga on the sitar could give an idea of his mind.

About ten o'clock, we are suddenly in Araouane. I can barely make out a few walls in the dark. The people warmly welcome Izzah; they exchange the long litanies of greeting. They lay out blankets and pillows on the sand for us, and we are surrounded by some twenty young men and kids, noisily joking and laughing over us. Then suddenly they all rush off: the mullah is there. He seats himself on the blanket, lays out a small charcoal brazier and kettle, and at length offers us the ritual three glasses of mint tea: the first *bitter as death,* the second *mild like life,* the third *sweet as love.* There is no moon; the stars are dim in the sandy haze of the night. The heat is gone, but the sands envelop us with their balmy warmth and the wind moves clouds of light sand continually over us.

I woke as the black of the sky was thinning into a russet haze. Great dunes surged about us, and, in the hollows, the ten flat banco buildings of Araouane half buried in the sand. The sun rose a pewter disk in ochre mists. Azima brought a kettle of water for us to rinse our faces, crusted with sand. A little girl came to offer us necklaces, one with a piece of amber, the other with five small shells, formerly used as money in the desert. We had tea in the house of the mullah, whom the light showed to be an old man with pale skin—perhaps of Berber ancestry. The room was small; high in the corner there was a shelf with a few books. Sand was deep on the floor. Breakfast was balls of rice and millet—and sand. Outside a dozen small children were learning Koranic texts written on wood paddles.

Araouane is older than Tombouctou; many old banco buildings are buried deep under our feet. Now Araouane, halfway between Tombouctou and the salt mines of Taoudenni, is an overnight camp for the *azalaï.* But it is also a holy place; mullahs come to study with the resident holy man. The present mullah had done his studies here with the prior resident. Here is Islam as it first appeared in this place, Islam reduced to the Koran, the prayers, the fasts, in the simplicity, the emptiness, the eternity of the sands and the skies. The sacredness is tangible, in the complete absence of anything trivial.

Izzah proposed to take us to Dar-Taleg. This is a nearby ancient town that had been covered by the sands, then revealed by the winds, and, Izzah tells us, in 1962 explored by an archaeological team. They dated it from the third century CE, collected pottery and artifacts, and left. The sands had covered over their work, but left visible on the surface the white ridges of walls of a dozen rather big houses and a mosque, like the diagram for a future city. There is no vegetation; Dar-Taleg's water source had long ago been buried.

We headed back. I marveled to see now how rare was the salt grass and how featureless the hundred kilometers that Amadou had conducted us across last night.

We stopped twice to get water at wells, where herds of camels, goats, and sheep were being watered. The wells are very deep. A leather bag attached to a long rope is dropped into the well, a camel is led a distance the length of the rope to pull out the bag full of water, and a man swings the bag over to the trough and empties it. I admired the flocks of goats and sheep, who stick together in groups, waiting their turn like so many Catholic boarding-school classes.

At the second well we bought a sheep; Amadou cut its throat with the knife every Tuareg carries at his waist. I was sickened to see its body long thrash spasmodically the way a decapitated chicken does. When finally it was still, we tied it to the front of the car and set out.

Suddenly the back window shattered—the spare tire had banged against it. Izzah looked around, grinned broadly, and drove on.

In midafternoon we stopped, and Mohammed and Amadou skinned the sheep and cut up a potful of meat, boiling it over a fire of sticks.

We drove on. Then abruptly, crossing a dune indistinguishable from any other, there was Tombouctou, upon which a peaceful desert haze muses.

At Araouane the mullah had a tablet, like those purchased in towns for schoolchildren, in which a few dozen visitors had written their impressions. Soldiers and civil servants wrote florid lines of awe and gratitude for having been able to come here; some tourists had also written their impressions, less eloquent but equally intense. All said that Araouane is a holy place. The sacred is manifest in the decomposition of the arenas of work and reason. The sacred is manifest in the dunes that shift and engulf the houses of Araouane, the winds that spread into them granules of rocks and mountains from far away, carrying off the dust of the banco houses to the trackless distances. The sacred is manifest in the desolation of boundless surfaces spread out under the abysses of the sky.

In fact Araouane had already been a place of power in ancient times of "animism." The sacred is not only the outer spaces, where the world of work and reason dies away. The sacred is also in the past, definitively beyond the designs of work and reason. Before Tombouctou, Araouane was the capital of the Tuareg federation in this region. It is also its great antiquity that makes Araouane a place of pilgrimage today. Like Angkor in Cambodia and Ayutthaya in Thailand, this ancient capital, now reduced to a few houses, has become a holy place.

Great camel caravans from Taoudenni, Marrakesh, and Gao once paused here, rested, and traded. Until quite recently Araouane was a market especially for slaves. Even today the Tuareg keep slaves, *bella,* nominally emancipated in Mali. The market closed down two decades ago. Trucks are relentlessly replacing the camel caravans that Azima still joins, on thirty-two-day journeys each way to bring merchandise from Algeria and Libya to Tombouctou.

The Tuareg, the blue men of the desert, are the great warriors who for ten centuries have been masters of the length and breadth of the Sahara. They became legendary for Europeans, the last and most ferocious resistance to the French, Spanish, and Italian colonial encroachment. During the drought that devastated the Sahel in the eighties, international humanitarian aid was pillaged by the government officials and did not reach the Tuareg, who were most affected by the famine. They entered into rebellion in 1990, and the military government of Mali struck back, destroying nomad camps, poisoning the wells, shooting down camel herds. The people of Araouane fled, the women into tunnels dug in and stabilized under the sands, the men to fight with the rebels. The restless dunes covered their abandoned houses.

Around the fire while the sheep was being roasted, Izzah spoke to us of the depopulation of the region. The great drought of the eighties and the civil war that ended in 1996 destroyed enormous numbers of camels, sheep, and goats. Everybody can see that each year the Sahara is covering with its sands another band of the Sahel denuded of its grasses by the goats. "Our government does nothing!" he said. "But you Americans," he said to me, "you know what to do!" He said an American prospecting team had recently come and begun to search for oil. "Surely, with all the riches Libya derives from oil, there are great resources here!" His gaze turned to the vehicle, which had blown two tires and the rear window. I knew what he was thinking: his expenses would be greater than what he had agreed with us as the price of this trip. He turned back to me and ruefully smiled: "The first thing the Americans will do is lay down a paved road here!"

I was jolted out of my sacred reverie: Araouane would become an oil workers' town, with shacks where tires are vulcanized, stands where trucked-in food is cooked under the blare of television sets; there would be shops. Truck carcasses and garbage would accumulate along its roads; the dunes, like those all around Tombouctou, will be littered with plastic bags. The profane world of work and reason extends only by desecration.

Izzah had stopped five times that day to spread out his blanket over the sands and fervently make his prayer. He has no sense that inviting the American oilmen here is sacrilege. In fact the profane world extends its work and reason without acknowledging its violent compulsion to desecrate. But the compulsion to desecrate is in religion itself. Religion does not create but acknowledges the zone of the sacred, and religion desecrates. Already when Islam came here in the eighth century, the animist gods were driven out of Araouane and the desert was left empty for an Allah to dwell in a transcendent realm above. Is not sacrilege a religious act? It was men serving religion who massacred and burned the ancient gods of Araouane and those of Babylon, Egypt, Constantinople, Tenochtitlán, Qosqo. Temples are built on the ruins of and with the plunder of temples of other religions.

Work and reason are calculation, of benefit and loss. War enlists all the resources of work, reason, and life in a cause of unlimited destruction, where the conquerors are equally delivered over to death and destruction. For it is not only in contemporary war, it was also in the Crusades and the Hundred Years' War, it was in every war, that there are no victors. It is through their thirst for war and conquest that civilizations that perished were destroyed. Religion sends men off to war; every religion blesses and sacralizes war. Religion opens the dimension of the absolute; it absolutizes the always only relative wrongs a people have suffered from another people. Today the Tuareg rebellion continues in Mauritania, Algeria, and Niger.

There is a contemporary horror of desecration, that of postmodern minds in rich postindustrial and multicultural nations. We have come to understand that our future, our wealth, are not in blackened industrial centers but in high-tech miniaturized electronic and information industries. We seek to protect whatever our multiple cultures, and cultures wherever we encounter them, have set aside as sanctuaries. We turn them into information and cultural enrichment—a higher level of desacralization.

I did not hire Izzah to drive me in his Land Cruiser the four days over the sands to reach Mopti. There is an airstrip in Tombouctou. In four hours I was in Bamako, and in another five hours in Paris. Then six hours over the Atlantic to New York. Below there was the trackless ocean, a Sahara of water. I looked out the porthole of the plane into the transparent sky. Our eyes here are relayed by the eyes of astronauts in outer space. We see our own planet from beyond, a blue and green marble in the immensity of cosmic voids. The Hubble telescope shows us photographs of the swirling spirals of incandescent gases exploding billions of light-years ago. Astronomers measure the number of years yet ahead before the incineration of our planet, the extinction of our sun, the burning out of all the stars of the Milky Way galaxy. Our cosmological and astronomical science has extended the time of the universe beyond the time of our own tasks, of our civilization, of our species. It has reduced to infinitesimal proportions whatever significance we can assign to ourselves in the universe. It opens us upon a cosmic space and time where the end of our species, of our planet, of our sun are marked. To our pragmatic perception of the practicable field about us, our science superimposes a deanthropomorphized and apocalyptic cosmic vision.

Four and a half million years ago the sun hurled out of itself a molten rock, flaming in the dark spaces like a torch heralding destiny. As the surface of the rock cooled, bacteria, along with the fungi and algae entered into symbiotic lichens, proceeded to crumble that rock into sand. We humans continue to decompose the surface of the planet. In the voids of outer space, we can now see the end of the time of work and reason, the end of time. The sacred is manifest in the comets and meteors that crash into planets, in the solar storms, in the extinction of stars grown old and cold. The sacred is manifest in the emptiness of the desert surfaces spread out under an empty sky.

2000

Rings

There was then a time when nothing had meaning. The time when, as an infant, we reached out to kiss our mother or to suckle her breast, to make contact with what was being offered us or what we saw at a distance, or we covered our face, pushed our hand back from what touched us. From a few days old, when we started smiling, our body was animated with "expressions"—grins, grimaces, pouts, frowns, cries, hand-waving, and soon dances and an astonishing gamut of vocalizations. These do not express meanings conceived inwardly; they anticipate contacts our body will make, go back to embraces our body has already made and no longer makes, slow down the couplings our body is making with things and events or accelerate them, detach them or unite them, map them out or segment them. Our fights are in this sense "expressive." Today too; an argument gets *settled* with a fight. Especially an argument about our courage, our honor, our loyalty, or the sincerity and strength of our love.

Soon we used sounds to refer to things, first to joyously acknowledge, or to demand, their being given or taken away, then to acknowledge or demand details. Then we learned words; they designated meanings taken from things and we used words in the absence of those things. Each word refers laterally to a constellation of other words with whose meanings its meaning contrasts: a fork is not a spoon or a knife; each of those words refers to further constellations: don't play with that fork, you'll hurt yourself. It is the ring of words about this word that determines its meaning, and the rings of words about each of them that explain their meanings. This increasingly articulated system of words and their meanings extends a chain-link fence between us and the forces of things, plants, and animals.[1]

It was not all by ourselves that we started asking, What does it mean? and entered into these circles upon circles of interpretation. After all, we do not ask ourselves what it means that we have oatmeal with strawberries for breakfast, that we sink into a hot tub for a half hour when we get back from work; we do not ask ourselves what it means that humans eat breakfast, that humans eat, that humans immerse themselves in warm water—unless, of course, a psychoanalyst faces us to ask, What does that say about you? As little children we were allowed to suck on our thumbs, play for hours with a puppy, run again and again through piles of autumn leaves, without having to worry about what it all meant.

But then they started. Our parents, our teachers faced us and demanded that we give an account of what we did. Now the social worker turns up, and asks, What is the meaning of this new big-screen television in your house, since you are on welfare? Every time we turn on the television there are those faces: senators and pundits demanding what it means that we do not vote, experts demanding what it means that we parents are not disciplining our children, preachers demanding what it means that we don't seem to care that no real meaning can be assigned to our lives, to human life on Earth. Week after week newsmagazines ask what it means that high-school kids are shooting down their comrades in school, that people are buying more and more cellular phones, that the hit film of the year is *Fight Club*.

Whenever we wonder, What does this mean? we get caught up in these rings interlocked endlessly upon rings. In another land we have a conversation with someone and then a dinner together. In this place where no one knows us we abandon ourselves to the longings and pleasures of lovemaking. It happens again the next night and the night after that. Then questions start up in our head: Is she really drawn to me? Is she playing some sort of game with me? Is she faking orgasm? Does she expect presents, money, does she want to tie me to her so that I will bring her to America? Does she want to trap me by getting pregnant? Everything she does becomes a sign to be interpreted—every phrase, every sigh or gasp in lovemaking, whether she comes early or comes late, whether she dresses up or dresses down. Then we find ourselves shifting into another cycle of questions: Is she aiming for some kind of triumph in seducing a white man, one of the colonial race? Is it because the GIs were here during the Vietnam War that the local morality broke down and women started going to bed with foreign strangers? Then: What do her parents think of her and of me, what does her society think? Are they simply Buddhists free from Judeo-Christian hang-ups about sex? Or is it the breakdown of their society under the pressure of Western world-market consumerism that makes her willing to go to bed with me—something that women back home do not do? Another circle. And what about me? Is this a serious affair, which I will have to explain to my wife when I get back? Or is it a secret affair that means something only to me? Another circle. What does it mean in my life that I am having an affair, far from my wife? How does this affect my conception of myself, my status as a married man? Another circle. What will it mean when I go back to my post as a university professor, will I miss this detour into exoticism? What will it mean when I teach ethics to young people, I who am indulging in this secret double life? Another circle. The way we respond to the question, What does it mean? is to say: the fact that she is late means that I am not the center of her life; she has a double life. The fact that I am having an affair means that I am being unfaithful to my wife and children. The interpretation opens upon the question what a double life means, what infidelity means. We find ourselves in a realm where there are no facts, only interpretations of interpretations. Infidelity means violating my marriage vows to my wife. But what does marriage really mean? And what does having a wife, what does saying "my wife" mean?

These questions do not arise spontaneously, as though for us to live is to itemize the meaning of everything we see and touch. The question, Does she want to get something from me, does she expect presents, money; does she want to tie me to her? anticipates the time when we will be leaving and she will face us and ask us to take her to America. The question, Is it because the GIs were here during the Vietnam War that the local morality broke down and women started going to bed with foreign strangers? anticipates the time when someone back home with political and ethical convictions will call us to account for what we were doing with that woman in a backward country. The question, What does it mean in my life that I am having an affair, far from my wife? anticipates some friend back home, or some marriage counselor or pastor, some prosecutor who will demand an accounting of us.

Travel far enough and we find ourselves happily back in the infantile world. In Antarctica our gaze is captivated by contours and crevices in the ice sheets, forms and facets in the cliffs for which we can attach no concepts, not even identify by the names of geometrical forms. The sun streaks colors in the ice that we amuse ourselves trying to name: azure, mauve, sodium, cerulean, amethyst, jade, emerald, violet, lavender, lime, absinthe, quetzal—but all these names of blues and greens that we saw in liquid, mineral, plant, and animal substances do not match these gleams in the crystal cliffs. There is nothing here we can link as means to ends; The Ice is a continent we cannot inhabit. Wandering in the deserts of southern Ethiopia, our eyes pass through the encrusted layer of concepts, categories, and explanatory paradigms in our brain and we see again camels, people, dunes, and skies as we did before meanings got spread over everything.

Ken has been traveling since he finished college. Then he took stock of the fact that he would need a job to keep on traveling. He went to graduate school and got a post in academia because academics get more time off you can spend traveling than anybody else except press stringers and writers of airport potboilers. Ken has the kind of health and endurance that can go anywhere. He is big, broad-shouldered; he has built powerful, competition-class muscles. Muscles that are pointless in a university professor who needs only strength enough to turn the pages of a book, tap on a computer, and lift a glass of cheap wine at departmental socials. In Israel and in Syria people asked him if he was in the army. But Ken disdains musculature built to be put to use; he wants to be a freak. He never played football in high school. He has big, wide-set green eyes, candid, without guile or irony, like those of a child. They are incessantly warmed with pleasure, with appetite for all he sees. He is not stocking up on things. Wherever he goes he writes no essays or diaries, takes no pictures.

Ken was once engaged to be married, and bought rings, handmade silver rings he found in Mexico. He dropped out of the engagement, but kept his ring. He likes it, crafted by jewelers from the scraps still found in what were once the richest silver mines in the world. His parents were disappointed; they had liked her.

The other primates in Africa form bands bound together by a basic intraspecies attraction, affection, and sexual interest, as well as for defense. Human societies are formed inasmuch as humans are interdependent on one another in the regulated exchange of goods and services. The recognition of promises, obligations, and debts in the market is the basis for all subsequent development of societies governed by internal laws. We no longer pledge our commercial commitments with a handshake; we use our hands to write our signature on a contract. But we secure our commitment in marriage on our hand; a wedding ring shows that the marriage contract binds our bodies together as with metal loops that cannot be opened. An engagement or a wedding ring encircles our finger tightly, and the last of our taboos prevents it from being removed in the workplace, street, or bar in a convention hotel.

Just now three women are in love with Ken; he lives with one, travels with another, and visits the third. Every month or two he meets another woman and falls in love. His grandfather is ailing; his parents have let Ken know that the old man wants to see his grandchild, inevitable anyway one day, before he dies. Ken took off for Ethiopia.

I agreed to join him. He got there first and found a hotel in Addis Ababa. Waiting for me, he went down to the hotel's office to e-mail his girlfriends. When I got there I saw that the young woman in the office could not take her eyes off him. Ken would disappear in the e-mail room several hours a day.

What did we know of Ethiopia? The Semitic peoples of Ethiopia had occupied the high mountainous plateau, the greatest altitudes in Africa, preserving their ancient Coptic Christianity as Islam swept across North Africa. At the beginning of the last century King Menelik II conquered vast stretches of the savanna below, where the people speak languages of the Oromo and Somali families and are Muslims or "animists." Since the end of World War II, landlocked Ethiopia has been trying to extend its territory to the Red Sea by annexing Eritrea. Some fifty thousand people have died in the most recent phase of the war, hundreds of thousands have been displaced. We arrived during a cease-fire arranged by the Organization of African Unity. It was summer; drought ravaged the lowlands. The vast area called Ogaden that King Menelik II had seized, now occupied by Somalian nomads, was in a continuing state of insurrection against Addis Ababa. These things we knew from reading the press in our own countries. In Addis Ababa we learned nothing more from the couple of four-page newspapers in English, published essentially for the foreign delegations from English-speaking African countries, and carefully censored. We met ex-soldiers returned from or deserted from the front; they had no idea where the front extended and if they told us why the war was launched they did so offhandedly, as if to indicate that that anyway was what they were told. They could speak of the government that took power upon the overthrow of Haile Selassie in 1974, the expropriation of feudal landowners, the collectivization of the land, the civil war waged against it by the Tigrayans in the north, for Mengistu Haile Mariam had covered the country with billboards with slogans of the Marxism he had learned from the Albanians. But Mengistu was overthrown in 1991, and now the northerners are in power and Marxist directives have vanished, but nobody had an idea what, if any, policies the present government has for the country. We certainly were not making any sense of anything.

We met a middle-aged white man named Thomas married to a beautiful Amhara woman; his father had come here from Yugoslavia. During one long somnolent afternoon he explained in heavily accented and broken English his mechanic father's improbable life story in increasingly entangled detail. We only grasped that he somehow slipped between front lines during World War II in Yugoslavia and somehow ended up in Ethiopia, scene of an Allied invasion against Mussolini's occupation troops. In the yard out front there was a battered Land Cruiser, the 1967 model. We asked if we could rent it for a trip to the south. He agreed and told us he would supply an English-speaking driver and some tents.

That evening the driver looked for us at the hotel. He said his name was Belete, but as soon as he left we realized we had not committed it to memory. Balding, perhaps sixty, somewhat stout but sturdy, radiating a stabilized inner serenity, he spoke unceremoniously and offhandedly as though he had always known us. We liked him at once. He took us to a nearby night market where we bought provisions. We were skeptical of the piles of vegetables and dried meat and found instead packages of biscuits, tins of tuna, and some jars of chocolate sauce. He then told us that people we photographed will have to be paid, and took us to a black marketer where we got bundles of one-bir notes.

At six the next morning we picked up cartons of bottled water and set off. We were on the main highway across Ethiopia. The first hundred kilometers were being asphalted with, we saw, European Union heavy machinery and no doubt funds. Some forty kilometers out of Addis Ababa, Belete stopped the car on the bottom of a volcano and from the brim showed us the lake inside the crater on which the clouds of the sky rested untroubled. We watched the local women coming up from the lake with clay jugs of water. The first woman to notice us stopped, swung the jug from her head, and poured us clay cups of cool water.

At midday we stopped for lunch at a small dusty roadside place called the Bekele Mole Hotel. From then on whenever Belete found a roadside place to eat he judged suitable for fastidious foreigners, it was another Bekele Mole hotel. Out of some unconscious short-circuiting in our brains, we began addressing him as Bekele in the days that followed. We were taken aback and horribly embarrassed when, the last day of the trip, I found in my shirt pocket the name card that the Yugoslav had given us, with his real name Belete Gebre written on the back of it.

Soon we descended the Great Rift Valley, that gigantic crack in the continental plate that splits the mountain fortress of Ethiopia in two. At the bottom we were in the southern deserts. Bekele-Belete found us lodging at a Bekele Mole hotel, small rooms with mud brick walls. We were the only guests; this was a truck stop but the truckers on their way to and from Kenya slept in their trucks. Some of the trucks were loaded with bags of grain; these, Belete said, were being supplied by international aid for the famine-stricken deserts into which we were headed. Belete's English was simple but adequate, and in the days that followed we saw he also knew enough of the languages of the nomads to arrange things everywhere. At food stalls along the road he bought some of the dishwater-gray crêpes the Ethiopians call *injera* and some meat that he had the hotel woman cook for us. When we retired, a boy brought us buckets to urinate in during the night; the toilet was in back of the compound and dark.

It was the last of the Bekele Mole hotels, until our return back up this road. From now on we camped. Belete had found a stand of trees by a now parched and cracked riverbed the following night. No sooner had we set up our tents than we heard a crashing through the trees and four very large dark brown baboons circled us, looking indignant at our invasion. We gave them the supplies we had bought; they even seemed to like the chocolate sauce with tuna.

In the days that followed we drove through scrub desert where grasses were dead tussocks and bushes were leafless. From time to time we saw the skeletal remains of sheep and goats whose flesh had been consumed before they died of the drought. One day as we drove through a vast area that Belete identified as the Mago National Wildlife Reserve, we saw approaching us in a cloud of dust a Jeep and three stout men in safari khaki holding rifles; they did not hail us as they passed. "Hunters," Belete said. "Hunting is allowed?" Ken asked. Belete explained that foreigners pay the government big sums for permits—three thousand dollars for a kudu, five thousand for a lion, ten thousand for an elephant.

Belete's body, though not muscular, seemed possessed by the nerves and sinews of a warrior as he swung the Land Cruiser over potholes and ruts in the track, then found an unmarked fork to turn on and navigate down the desert. In fact he had a very precise itinerary in his mind; each day he drove us to a nomad market.

These were gatherings of a hundred, two, three hundred people, where about a well there were stands of ragged trees. This, Belete would say, is the Tsemay market. This is the Turmi market. This is the market of the Bena and Ari peoples. We strolled about among the people as Belete found *injera* and someone to roast some skewers of goat meat for us. Markets, he called them, but nobody seemed to be buying or selling. There were not sheep, goats, or camels tethered for sale; there were not, as wherever else I had been in impoverished Third World lands, piles of missionary-supplied clothing being sold. There were no craft items that might have interested us to buy. Everyone was clad in the most extravagant garb of his or her own making, women in colorfully beaded goatskin skirts, their faces tattooed, their arms and legs ringed in embossed copper coils. The men had astonishing coiffures, their kinky hair close-cut with shaved lines shaping diagrams, imbued with white and red and blue clays and decorated with carefully placed feathers. Their skin was painted, very often their legs in white with arabesque designs. Usually it was a cloth band they wore about their loins, as though their virility needed no animal-hide emphasis. They each carried a small stool of polished black wood, which they rested on to keep the ground from smearing their body paintings and which also served, Belete told us, as a pillow sparing their headdresses when they lay down to sleep. The men, young and old, carried well-oiled and polished rifles and belts of gleaming bullets about their waists. Eventually we noted that there was something for sale in the market: some women were seated before piles of powdered pigments. And women were serving from great clay pots a kind of beer. We also saw that a man had brought an antelope he had been lucky enough to kill, but he was not selling it, he was celebrating: joyously distributing pieces to children and old women and to his friends who joined the feast with jugs of beer.

Feasts then were what these "markets" were. These people had come long distances on foot in the most spectacularly impractical garb. There were no officiants and no rituals scheduled for this day, no troop of entertainers, no singers or dancers to see. It was their own beauty they were celebrating. Indeed, from halt to halt we began comparing their tall elegant stature, their perfect complexions, their noble features and radiant smiles. One day we gaped in astonishment at Karo people and decided that, men and women alike, they were the most beautiful of all.

For many years I traveled without a camera, thinking that it objectifies people with whom I wanted to interact, thinking too that there is something false and delusive in trying to fix and stock up images and situations from the past, thinking that it was the changes in my heart I brought back that were alone real. But one day a student friend took me to a camera shop where he was buying a new camera and gave me his old one. I left for India, and for days pointed the camera only at buildings and landscapes. Then one evening I was in a *shikara*, a gondola, on Dal Lake in Kashmir and I focused the camera on the willows that veiled the edge of the lake. As the boatman slowly rowed on I saw in the range finder that I had just snapped some men bathing in the lake. I looked up; they had seen me—and were shouting. They were grinning and shouting, "Thank you!" Pondering this, I realized that they were pleased that it was they and not the landscapes and monuments of India that I wanted to record. I was learning to take pictures by developing a roll at once—in any Indian town black-and-white film could be processed—and studying the results. I realized you can always find poor people again, they will be there the next day, or their acquaintances will be. And I soon realized that photographs of themselves, people who have no, and never will have, possessions, is the most innocent gift I could give them.

The people in the nomad feasts glanced away but did not turn their beauty from me. We would not come this way again, and these nomads have no addresses to which I could mail them their photographs. But I had become very greedy to take their beauty back with me. I ventured to take out my camera. It was impossible to be unnoticed; at once anyone I turned toward demanded one bir. I had arrived and turned the feast into a market.

In my country there are beautiful people who turn their pale emotionless faces and lissome bodies to cameras for millions. Here no doubt someone some years back had passed by, dazzled by the physical splendor and superb body decoration of the people, published his photographs, and then passed by again to show them to them. They had asked to keep the book, and were told it sells for fifty dollars. So they realized that if they were to be models they should be paid. One bir, I reflected, is U.S. twelve cents; the film roll works out to about that per frame. Any tourist who can afford twelve cents for a film frame can afford twelve cents for the model. On the other hand, for Ethiopians twelve cents is a great deal; wage earners in the capital get eight bir a day. The one bir I or other travelers pay them is the only source of money these nomads could have access to. I asked Belete what they do with the money. Buy bullets, he said, for the rifles they have traded camels for in Kenya.

Belete called us over; skewers of broiled meat were laid out on *injera* for us under a tree. The woman who had cooked them, a woman of about forty, was not especially attractive and her beaded goatskin skirt was worn. She had some tattoos on her weatherworn face, and but one piece of jewelry, a ring. Ken went over to her, asked to see her ring. One saw that it was a piece of thick aluminum wire coiled about her finger. "Trade?" he asked. She smiled shyly. Of course she did not understand the word. He gently removed it from her and replaced it with his.

2004

Typhoons

Charles Darwin discovered in the Galápagos flora and fauna that had evolved on those isolated Pacific islands; Madagascar is where biologists rush today. Not geologically a part of Africa, this "Great Red Island," the fourth-largest island on the planet, is a fragment that drifted off when Pangaea broke into continents 250 million years ago. Madagascar is known for its lemurs, protosimians found only there, but biologists have verified that virtually all the native plants, reptiles, and mammals on Madagascar are endemic species. Today the island's human population of 14 million is projected to double within twenty-five years, and its rain forests—only 10 percent of which remain—are being slashed, burned, and logged. The oceans are red with millions of tons of soil being eroded from its mountains, its savannas, and its deserts. Hundreds of endemic species are on the brink of extinction.

When one thinks of going there—as a scientist frantic to catalog the vanishing species or a tourist curious to see lemurs or unique lizards and frogs—one learns that Madagascar is among the ten poorest countries on the planet. Its agroexport business collapsed when, after gaining political independence from France, its military rulers sought out Soviet economic and political advisers and expropriated foreign holdings without compensation. The socialist vision turned into an ideology. Madagascar's current president, in power for twenty years, allegedly has millions in Swiss bank accounts while the country is bankrupt, under the tutelage now of the International Monetary Fund and the World Bank. Public funds go to maintain the bureaucracy and service the national debt; under World Bank–dictated public-service cuts, three hundred schools have been closed. One will expect that any assistance from government agencies or police comes at a price. The traveler feels anxiety about his personal safety. He has little confidence in a personal or institutional ethics to hold back the impulses of mass desperation. The trip there has something of the feel of an act of recklessness and bravado.

A friend invited me to join him on a walk into the jungle. He had chosen the zone of mountains and swamp most inaccessible to loggers. We left Antananarivo in a *taxi-brousse,* descended to the coast, and went to the end of the road, then by dugout canoe to the beginning of the river. We trudged through muck, then up and down rocky mountains in the rain. It was exhilarating, but I lagged behind my friend, he so full of vigor and determination. We crossed a young Malagasy of about twenty on the path; he looked at me and with a smile and a sign offered to carry my backpack. I accepted. After a couple of days I wimped out. As my friend continued into the jungle alone, I lingered at a hamlet we had come upon, dried my clothes, got fed. The next morning, the young man who had carried my backpack appeared again; I indicated I was going back. He reached again for my backpack and set out.

He spoke not a word of French; I could not, by nodding my head and appealing to him, even learn the Malagasy words for "yes" and "no." He wore secondhand running shorts distributed by some missionary; my coarse cotton pants, purchased to protect my legs from leeches, rasped against my thighs and left them raw. He strode barefoot up the rocks and through the rivers; my jungle boots blistered my feet and filled with muck. He was always well ahead of me, or behind me; he would put down the backpack and wait a half hour to let me get ahead or would catch up with me. When the path forked I could only wait for him to arrive, or come back, to indicate which branch of the path to take.

In my backpack I had an expensive camera and six hundred dollars in cash. Were I he, sitting somewhere ahead or behind with that backpack, I surely would not resist the temptation to look in it. He could do whatever he wanted with my backpack, and with me, with impunity. I knew his name was Javalson, but where he lived I had no idea.

But when night fell he found a hut for us to sleep in and produced some bananas found or purchased somewhere. The next day we reached the river, and he found a dugout canoe to take me back down the river. Among the people gathered at the river's edge I found someone who spoke some French and asked him how much I should pay my guide and savior. Fifteen thousand francs, he pronounced, and indeed Javalson seemed pleased when I handed that to him: three U.S. dollars. He was gazing at my backpack: I opened it and wondered miserably what gift I could give him: I had given away all my medicines on the way and the inadequate food I had brought was gone. He pointed to my extra socks, took them with a grin; we shook hands, he disappeared. Of course, without shoes, he would not wear those socks in the muck and on the rocks; I understood he would keep them as a bemused—and affectionate?—memory of my absurd outfitting.

A few weeks later I was in London. In a spring sunshine that had not welcomed me there before, I explored its gracious streets, flabbergasted as one always is after a prolonged stay in destitute countries by the material abundance. That night, a Saturday, before going to bed I turned on the television and learned that a bomb had exploded in a crowded street in a London district inhabited mostly by blacks. A week later, again on early Saturday evening, a bomb exploded in a crowded street in a district inhabited mostly by Bangladeshis. The police determined that the bombs were simple explosives packed with nails that tore into and maimed people across the street, and that the bombs had been brought to these locations and left in a gym bag. The television did specials on skinhead and neo-Nazi gangs, showed Internet sites of hate groups, reported police investigations of linkages with American militia organizations and Serbian agents. Newspapers received letters claiming responsibility for the bombings from an organization called Commando 18 (cipher for Adolf Hitler). But the police revealed that they had infiltrated that organization and instead suspected a break-off sect that called themselves White Wolves. The television showed repeatedly a video from a street camera that had recorded a young man circling the area of the bomb the hour before it exploded. Hundreds of undercover police were assigned to Jewish and Muslim areas, awaiting the following Saturday. But on Friday early evening, a bomb exploded instead inside a gay pub in a crowded street in Soho. The three nail bombs had killed seven people and injured more than three hundred, some now in critical condition, others with amputated limbs and destroyed eyes.

Whenever I went out I found my eyes scanning the curtained windows of brick apartment blocks, behind which people conduct their business shut from prying eyes. As evening fell it was not in the empty side streets but in the crowded streets that I began to feel the pervasive fear.

Two days later the police, tipped off by neighbors who had recognized the young man in the video, raided an apartment and found bombs made with materials that could be purchased in any hardware store, and packed with nails. They arrested the tenant, a young engineer of twenty-three, and the next day reported they were confident that he had acted alone.

For three weeks the media had run specials by criminologists, sociologists, and culture critics analyzing the skinhead, hooligan, and neo-Nazi subcultures in democratic and prosperous Britain, specials on immigrants and racism, on the culture of violence on television and in pop, punk, and rap music. Civic leaders, beginning with the prime minister, called for a national examination of conscience on the pervasive and unremarked racism of everyday life and attitudes and for a national commitment to the rule of law and to multiculturalism. Now the newspapers and television channels ran specials on the genetic, biochemical, and social causes of criminal psychopathology.

For days the image of this young engineer hovered in my brain, and the image also of that other young man on the trail in the Madagascar jungle.

A history of foreign invasion, colonial oppression, economic exploitation, then a violent struggle for independence followed by homebred dictatorship and bankruptcy reduced an island twice the size of the British Isles to increasing illiteracy and desperate poverty. Add to that the trauma of forced imposition of foreign culture, religion, and language, the local society corrupted, its religion discredited. And yet a rich foreign visitor, there to take a vacation trek in the jungle, finds he is secure alongside a local man encountered by chance on the path.

The motherland of modern democracy, a Britain confident in the new European community, prosperous, with five centuries of the rule of law behind it, a people identified for the value of fair play, a city priding itself in its cosmopolitanism and multiculturalism—there a young engineer, acting alone, makes the whole population, including this American visitor, afraid to walk the streets on a Saturday evening.

To be sure, social scientists, psychologists, and ethnobiologists elaborate explanations: in an overpopulated and ecologically devastated place like Madagascar, excluded from the multinational corporate global economy, where the imposed modern national and political systems work only for the profit of a military oligarchy, the destitute young man subsisting in the jungle returns to his ancestral tribal culture and cults, which place preeminent emphasis on mutual aid. In the high-performance, information-highway, retraining and recycling economy and culture of contemporary Britain, a young engineer who does not fit in, victim of some childhood or adolescent trauma, has no cultural backwater to retreat to and finds his only effective force is his indiscriminate hate.

All that can and must be said, if we are to understand. But as I listened to the political scientists, sociologists, cultural critics, religious leaders, psychologists, and ethnobiologists explain on television, I found myself going back to the very experience of trust, and of terror, that I had known. In that experience there glowed some inner understanding that I had to bring out.

Knowledge induces belief, belief in what one sees clearly or in a coherent and consistent account that supplies evidence or proof. Trust, which is as compelling as belief, is not produced by knowledge. In trust one adheres to something one sees only partially or unclearly or understands only vaguely or ambiguously. One attaches to someone whose words or whose movements one does not understand, whose reasons or motives one does not see.

Is it all the things that are known that encourage the leap, in this one instance, to adhere to something unknown as though it were known? Is it not because of a long past tried and true that someone becomes a trusted adviser? Is it all that one knows about the laws, the institutions, the policing, and all that one knows about the values, the education, the peer pressure of individuals in a society that induce one to trust this individual met at random on a jungle path? But the more one knows about a tried and true adviser, the more clearly one sees that every act of loyalty opened an opportunity for disloyalty. The more one understands about the laws and programming of a culture, the more clearly one understands how they are imposed upon, but do not eliminate, can even provoke, impulses contrary to them.

Trust is a break, a cut made in the extending map of certainties and probabilities. The force that breaks with the cohesion of doubts and deliberations is an upsurge, a birth, a commencement. It has its own momentum, and builds on itself. How one feels this force! Before these strangers in whom one's suspicious and anxious mind elaborates so many scheming motivations, abruptly one fixes on this one, at random, and one feels trust, like a river released from a lock, swelling one's mind and launching one on the way.

I determined, at a glance at this young man whose words I could not understand, to trust him to guide me out of the jungle. To have put trust in him is to have to put still further trust in him, each time he was a half hour ahead or a half hour behind me with my bag. Once trust takes hold, it compounds itself.

The one who finds himself trusted knows the path because he has trekked it regularly, come by this way just yesterday, but he knows that in this rain mountain paths collapse, rivers crossed yesterday may be untraversable today. He knows there is much he does not know; he trusts himself to be able to deal with the unknown when it shows itself. He then counts on his trust of himself more than on his knowledge. Once one puts one's trust in him, this trust can only generate yet more trust. The force of the trust one puts in him makes his trust in himself the dominant force in him, dissipating his anxieties and vacillations.

Trust binds one ever more deeply to another; it is an energy that becomes ever stronger and more intoxicated. Upon watching Javalson leaving me at the edge of the river, how I felt I had known him so much more deeply than if I had listened to someone who had, the length of an evening, recounted his life to me in a language I could understand!

The act of trust is a leap into the unknown. It is not an effect of ideological, cultural, historical, social, economic, or ethnobiological determinisms. But trust is everywhere—in the pacts and contracts, in institutions, in forms of discourse taken to be revealing or veridical, in the empirical sciences and in mathematical systems. Everywhere a human turns in the web of human activities, he touches upon solicitations to trust. The most electronically guarded, insured individual is constantly asked to trust.

"He was a good neighbor, didn't bother anybody, always polite," the neighbors said of the London bomber—neighbors say each time a monster is identified in their midst. Someone you trusted to rent that spare room to, you trusted to keep an eye on the baby while you went down a few blocks to get some groceries, turns out to have been making bombs to kill innocent strangers indiscriminately. Trust turns into terror. A cause, an ideology, a group marginalized in the dominant society, or a vendetta does not explain the solitary bomber. He was not a member of the White Wolves. Because the police suspected he was, because they saw racism in the first bomb in the black neighborhood and the second in the Bangladeshi, they did not foresee that the third would explode in a gay pub. Like trust, does not hate too arise beyond or even outside of knowledge, outside of reasons to hate, and feed on itself?

The psychologists and criminologists look for reasons for a hate that first flared in the infancy or adolescence of the young bomber. Was he abandoned or abused as a child? Traumatized as a pubescent adolescent? But we have to recognize that hatred is not the direct reaction to someone or something detestable. The young engineer, who still hated his father who had sought to socialize him, could have despised him instead or now consign him to insignificance. He who loathed his father who had sexually molested him could have instead used his father's libido as the excuse to liberate himself from parental authority and affirm his own virility. If hatred arises, it goes beyond reasons to despise or condemn. Before the father's order, hatred pushes aside the inclination to explain and justify oneself, to acquiesce or evade. Hatred is a force that breaks loose. It has its own momentum. It seeks out reasons or excuses to hate on. When the father is just chatting amicably with his friends or just dozing on the sofa, hatred feels the more free to intensify its force and indulge its virulence.

That is why the one whom one hates, even if he is one's father or she one's ex-lover, becomes someone generic and anonymous. I hate my spouse for her castrating words, but at the moment she is visibly someone just making our evening meal; to sustain my hatred is to dissolve this image of someone who enjoys cooking. Before hatred, she becomes more and more "a bitch," "*the* bitch." For this young engineer, those before whom his hatred first arose had inexorably become "the others." Thus it could seem to him that his hatred acted effectively in wiping out strangers in a black neighborhood. Once he heard the indignant television reports lament that the dead and injured were random strangers, his hatred could find in random strangers in any London district its target.

Opposition can be measured and counteracted, but hatred is feared. Fear is fear of what is unknown; it is not simply a reaction to the manifestly dangerous. Before a mountain path one knows will give way if one steps on it one either refuses to advance on it or else feels a resigned acceptance of death; it is before the mountain path whose stability is unsure that one feels fear. It is not the Commando 18 agent known and identified by the police who spread fear across all London's neighborhoods but someone possibly acting alone and without ideology who might explode a bomb anywhere, or who might stop his activities and live somewhere in London without those three bombs ever being attributed to him. Because the unknown is without mappable boundaries, there is also an inner spiral in fear, which suspects in the unknown yet ever further circles of the unknown.

The one who hates feels the force of his hatred in the waves of fear that spread about it. And those who become ever more fearful and irresolute intensify the hatred of the bomber, whose hatred extends to ever more indeterminate others.

Fear in turn flows into, becomes, hatred. The hatred of the solitary bomber ignites the hatred of millions against him and also against any polite young engineer who keeps to himself. Were it not for the fact that only the laboratory staff studying videos from the street cameras and the desk staff in the police stations studying their files could identify and locate the bomber, and that the police officers arrived by stealth in the neighborhood and sped him away in an armed vehicle, he would have been lynched by his neighbors. The specials the television featured with psychologists and criminal pathologists were not only broadcast in order to satisfy the public craving for understanding; they were also broadcast in an effort to smother the flames of public hatred. Human-rights organizations warned the public against antiterrorism legislation that would curtail their own liberties. They fear that the police equipped with forensic and detective science and rigorously controlled by parliamentary legislation are themselves instruments of terror. The citizens come to fear, and thus to hate, their own terror.

The individual one does not know and entrusts one's life to and the solitary individual one can only be terrified by each exist, then, in a social, economic, historical, ideological, cultural system that does not completely produce or explain them. Trust and fear-hatred, like typhoons launched by the fluttering of a butterfly, emerge and intensify with their own momentum. Since they seem to be opposites, the mind would like to think that they exist in a dialectic. Educators are sure that only acts of trust can put out the rage in delinquent children; parole officers extend measured trust to convicts whose bitterness has smoldered for years in jails. They are right to do so, for trust is as strong as fear and hatred.

Yet in the rice-terracing economies of Cambodia and Indonesia, economies that for hundreds of generations required the most intense social cooperation and evolved the most selfless ethics, the most barbaric and senseless massacres break out. In the center of prosperous, cosmopolitan London, a solitary bomber strikes.

2004

PART IV

Excess

Faces, Idols, Fetishes

Modern epistemology set out to rigorously distinguish the real appearance of a thing from its perspectival deformations; its appearances in positions set askew or upside down; obscured or confused appearances due to the poor lighting, the intervening medium, or the distance—to segregate the real appearances from illusory ones. Then it set out to demarcate the appearance given and perceived in a here-and-now presence from the traces of its appearance, retained by memory, of a moment before and from the anticipations of its appearance in a moment later. It set out to isolate the here-and-now given from the relationships between past, present, and surrounding appearances elaborated by the synthesizing operation of the sensibility that identifies something selfsame in a series of appearances extending across a span of time. This epistemology seeks to separate, in the multitude of appearances a thing extends in time and space, what is due to the reality of the thing from what is due to the intervening medium and what is due to the mind. It set out to inventory the pure data and to identify in the retinal imprints what is due to the thing itself.

The contemporary theory of perception declares this project infeasible. It is by converging our posture and sensory surfaces on something that it is perceivable. A thing reduced to its simple location in a here-now instant of presence is not visible or audible; an external thing is real by presenting itself in a wave of time and a field of extension, sending echoes and heralds of itself back into the past and into the future, and by projecting its form into us as an organizing diagram for our sensory-motor forces. Things are not reduced to their reality by being reduced to factual givens; the "pure facts" of empirical observation are abstracts of intersecting scientific theories, logics, and effects of technological engineering.

But things do not only project their appearances across different perspectives, in different media, and on the surfaces of our sensibility; they also cast shadows and form screens and phosphorescent veils; their surfaces double up into facades. They generate phantasmal reflections of themselves, refract off hints and lures, and leave traces.

The surface space of the purely visual, the range of harmonies and dissonances, the labyrinth of voluptuous contours and seductive hollows, the ether of obsessive presences and phantasms—these refractions off things are not private constructions built out of fragments of the core things or disconnected mirages that ill-focused eyes send to drift over the hull of the practicable world, made of substantial and graspable things. The practicable carpentry of things is itself suspended in their tectonic fault lines. These refractions off things are not private constructions in a space, which, like the invisible and impalpable space in which the community of scientists elaborates a representation of the world given in perception—a space we do not believe in and cannot inhabit, a space contained within us— exists only by hearsay.

It is because things turn phosphorescent facades on the levels and horizons of sensuous spaces that they also engender a graspable shape. What there is cannot be defined as a core appearance extracted by epistemological method, which can exist without its perspectival appearances, their doubles, masks, and mirages. The essences of things are not core appearances: it belongs to the essence of sensible things that they appear only in profiles and that their characteristics caricaturize themselves. A thing *is* by engendering images of itself, reflections, shadows, and halos. These cannot be separated from the core appearance which would make them possible, for they make what one takes to be the core appearance visible. The surfaces of things are not more real than their facades; the reality that engenders the phantasm is engendered by it. The monocular image, phantasms, lures, forms made of shadows, omens, halos, and reflections make the things visible and are the visibility the things engender. The echoes and the murmurs that wander off things, the odors that emanate from them, the voluptuous contours and hollows of things and of the waves and rain that caress, the mossy forests and nocturnal fragrances that fondle one's surfaces and penetrate one's orifices, and the night they cast about their luminous outcroppings belong to the reality of things and make the things visible and real.

The things are not only structures with closed contours that lend themselves to manipulation and whose consistency constrains us. They lure and threaten us, support and obstruct us, sustain and debilitate us, direct us and calm us. They enrapture us with their sensuous substances and also with their luminous surfaces and their phosphorescent facades, their halos, their radiance and their resonances.

It is by presenting ourselves, exposed visibly and palpably in the light, that we engender the monstrous shadow that precedes us and soaks into the ground under our feet. The professor who enters the classroom the first day has been preceded by the legend or myth of himself which the students now see materializing before their eyes. They adjust practically to the level of his voice and to the arena of his movements; he knows they are looking at the personage and fits his person into it as he enters the room. He will use this professorial mask as a fetish, to intimidate them.

They seek to penetrate beneath this mask, and their look finds the colors and contours of a caricature. If we recognize our acquaintances in the drawings made by the caricaturist, it is because our seeing was already not anatomical but caricaturizing. The perception that looks under the mask finds another, monstrous mask; the students see the pedant under the pedagogue. The look rebounds between layers of doubles that the face engenders. When the professor inspects his face in a mirror, his eyes are caught between the professorial mask and the pedantic caricature. When in the classroom he slouches over his papers and stifles a yawn, he is not simply shrinking back into a bare anatomy moved by fatigue, he is agitating his masks disdainfully or ironically.

When a face enters a room where people are gathered, borne exposed like an idol over a uniformed and coded body, marked with black and scarlet paint and adorned with flowers and the plumes of dead birds, the glances that turn to it lower or move obliquely across it. It would be hard to justify normalizing the practical imperative, hard to argue that the face whose clearly and distinctly exposed colors and whose firmly grasped carpentry is most palpably evident is the essence in which unpracticable forms of that face are absorbed, like monocular images in the real thing. A face is a face by not being a rubbery substance to be grasped and palpated or a skull to be handled gingerly like a costly china bowl; it is a face by commanding the downcast eyes that touch it with respect; it is a face by presenting the coded mask of a social drama. Mouth and cheeks, by idolizing themselves, are not jaws and jowls—or rather, jaws and jowls are the caricature that the mouth and cheeks double into. Is not the idolatrous look that reveres and profanes the face the norm, of which the anatomical and practicable scrutiny is a deviant? The face is the place of exposure and vulnerability of the organism; one does not look at feathery crystals in the moist membrane of the eye with the focus of a jeweler's eye which guides the precision movement of his adjusting hands; one look softens before the eyes of another, one's mobilization is disarmed; vulnerability and exposure order tenderness.

The face of the other is the surface of an organism, a surface upon which the anatomical inspection can follow the muscle contractions, nervous spasms, and blood circulation in the depths of that organism. The face of another is an expressive surface, a surface upon which the signs designating objects and objectives beyond can be read. The face of another is an indicative surface, upon which are spread indices of the moods and states of mind, the curiosity, doubt, skepticism, boredom of the other. The face of another is a surface upon which one senses directions and directives that order me; when another faces one, an imperative surfaces. The face of another is a landscape of contours which are inertly expressive: heavy, overhanging brow; aquiline or infantile nose; thick, carnal lips; weaseled or stolid chin; which the other, fixing his dark-eyed stare or fluttering her eyelashes wet with tears, learns to maneuver for effects.

The face of another also doubles up into an idol and a fetish. To raise his or her face before the world is to move among the others and the things as an idol spreading its light and warmth over them; to set his or her face over and against the others is to materialize as a fetish.

Sovereign and solitary, the idol glows with its own light and radiates strange light and warmth about itself. It does not signal and give messages; the idol gives force, gives not for asking, and gives without requiring anything in return.

The fetish is a caricature, not of the essential reality, but of the idol. With the force of its downcast and opaque coldness, it spreads black light and fevers about itself. A fetish is used to obtain something one needs or wants; it is put forth in the service of one's fears or one's cupidity. The idol is noble; the fetish is servile.

The terms idol and fetish are more often applied to things made of noble or base material, to which a face, derived from the human visage, is given. The face that advances as an idol, before which the eyes lower, turns into a mask and a caricature; the idol made of stone or gold metamorphoses into a face that keeps watch. But if the appearance of the human face can be cast on a thing, doubling it up into an idol and a fetish, that is because the human face first doubles itself up into idol and fetish.

The face, locus of expression and of valuation, is also locus of self-valorization—idolization. And, in a caricature of idolization, it also fetishizes itself.

The modern epistemology we have invoked has to say that the face of the other presents itself as a perceived datum—simple patches of color. The value the perceiver sees in it is a predicate he assigns to it. The relationship between a being and its value, including the relationship between a perceived carpentry of a face and the idol and the fetish it doubles into, is taken to be a predicative relationship and is studied in the grammar of axiological predication. Modern epistemology does not take this value as inherent in the face one perceives; instead, the value is a way of ranking it with regard to other faces and other things. The perceiver would possess a system of value-terms—good-bad, useful-useless, threatening-reassuring, etc.—with which he compares and opposes all things—and the face of another.

But does not the face of itself double into idol and fetish? The production of value-terms does not simply indicate or inform an idolization, but intensifies it. The ascription of predicate terms to itself to distinguish or oppose itself to others does not simply indicate or inform, but intensifies a fetishization. The value-terms with which it illuminates with marvelous light and ardor or spreads tenebrous fevers over the things and faces about itself, are terms first formed in this idolization, and fetishization, with which a face forms.

Let us look to the genesis of the value-terms that express idealization or, we shall say, idolization and fetishization.

Epistemology observes, given in culture, diverse sets of value-terms. It quickly says "value-systems," because when one looks at individuals applying these terms to the things and people about them, it seems that evaluation is ranking, and that it establishes gradation. It seems that value-systems are dyadic systems; for every value-term there is its opposite: good-bad, just-unjust, virtuous-vicious, beautiful-ugly, and useful-useless. These terms seem to be constructed as specifications of the most extreme kind of opposition, that of positive and negative. This absolute opposition would be what makes them intrinsically systematic; the meaning of the one can seem to be the simple negation of the other. The axes of kinship—male-female and parent-child—are not oppositional; the coexistence of a multiplicity of needy humans in a limited field of resources is, no more than the coexistence of a multiplicity of fish or baboons, not intrinsically oppositional. It seems to us that the value-terms in use are intrinsically oppositional systems and that they introduce oppositions into the goods and activities they evaluate. Among the other gregarious animals, even wolves and rats and the beasts of prey, their gregarious nature prevents competition for goods, territory, or prestige from becoming murderous. But in the human species, gregarious animals torture and wage war on their own kind in the name of values; value-oppositions make one see one's competitor as an opponent, to be annihilated.

But then value-terms do not simply discriminate and classify. Their specific operation is not that of informing by delineating (positing a representation by negating, defining it by opposing it to other representations). They are forces. Forces not reacting to boundaries, but acting on forces. An affirmative valuation is a confirmation. When we say to someone, "How beautiful you are!" this saying does not work on the one to whom it is said as a simple recognition of what he is already, a re-cognition of what he already knows; it summons forth and incites his forces. She will smile a gratuitous, radiating smile and a blush will color her face more beautifully; she will move and will speak still more beautifully in the space made luminous by the rainbow-colored word arching over it. When we say to someone, "How sicko you are!" he will outdo himself to grimace still more sickly and mutter some still more sick retort. There are people who never, or rarely, say "How beautiful you are!" not because they, unlike the rest of us, never see every waitress, every bus driver, every student, every passing stranger as attractive or unattractive; or because they take seriously Jesus' recommendation, "Judge not and you shall not be judged"; but because they are all too aware of what you do when you say that. All too aware that when you say that to your wife it's a ploy or a compensation thrown her way, that when you say that to a man you identify yourself as a closet pervert, that when you say that to a student you are laying yourself open to a sexual-harassment suit.

Hume introduced a new way of ranking ideas; he ranked sensory ideas and abstract ideas according to strength and weakness. But he then subordinated his new ranking to the old one by valuing the strong impressions from the senses as more veridical than the faint abstract images that are their aftereffects, just as Descartes ranked ideas according to their clarity and distinctness only to see in the clarity and distinctness of ideas the index of their truth. For Nietzsche, axiological discourse is completely separated from apophantic discourse. The beautiful words beautify, the noble words ennoble, the strong words strengthen, the healthy words vitalize; the ugly words sully, the servile words debase those who speak them but also those to whom they are spoken, the weak words emasculate and debilitate, and the sick words contaminate. They do not only illuminate forms in the mind of the one who understands them; they, like laughter heard that quickens and tears that trouble one, energize or unnerve the body in which they resound. It is because we see that our flattering or slandering words color and stiffen the corporeal substance of the one to whom we address them, even while his or her mind rejects them, that we believe our blessings and curses alter the course of things, even though our professed mechanism has long since isolated nature in itself from the enchantment of our voice.

Axiological discourse is not one language subordinated to or alongside of apophantic discourse; it is the primal one. The value-terms are not only the most important words of language, they are the stars about which the other constellations of language turn. Language is not fundamentally a means of identification, but a means of consecration. An infant is drawn into language, not because of the importance of saying, "It's the jam I want, not the butter," which he does not need words for, but because of the forces in the words *Love* and *Pretty Baby* and *Good* and *Yes*. It is through valuative words that the others intensify the world for him: good to eat, bad to put in your mouth, good warm bath, bad fire, pretty kitty, vicious dog, dangerous street. The most noble words in language are the most archaic; Homer only mentions three colors in all his epics—this is not explained by his blindness, because none of the epic literature of India, China, the Middle East, or the Yucatán mention any more. But we have hardly added much to the gamut of adjectives and epithets Homer used to exalt heroes.

With the malice that understands what had been set up as the highest form of life by what was taken as the lowest, Nietzsche understands the most noble form of language, the language of values, as an atavistic survival of insect cries. Of course the language of gregarious insects, ants and bees, is representational, is governed by correspondence with the layout of things, and is a kinesics of truth. But language begins with the evolution of organs for vocalization among insects not socialized into colonies, whose vocalizations consist entirely of a seductive chant. Their organs for vocalization: scaly feet, rubbed thoraxes, and vibrating wings, radiate out a periodic, endlessly repetitive, vibratory chant whose repetitive codings are not representing, producing representations and ideality, but reiterating and reaffirming the forces of beauty, health, and superabundant vitality. Their vocalization is a gratuitous discharge of excess energies and the solar chant of expenditure without return.

Valuations are gifts of force given to the forces of things. It is with forces, welling up in oneself, that life confronts and opposes, but thereby incites, other forces. The strong sensations, those with which the force of life confronts what comes to encounter it, are not passive affects of pleasure and pain left on life by the impact of things that pass. The strong sensations are those with which an active sensibility greets what comes with laughter and tears, blessing and cursing. The cursing and the tears are themselves forces. The laughter and the tears quicken and trouble the landscapes, the blessing and the curses ennoble and unhinge the course of the world. The laughter is independent of the tears and comes before the tears; the blessing comes before the cursing. In the hands made for blessing, there is more force than in hands that claw at things unrelentingly driven by need and want. The recoil with which life discovers its weakness, and can resentfully will to weaken and appropriate, comes second. Life's blessing extends over a universe made of fragments, riddles, and dreadful accidents; it extends over them, not a nova of light in which they could be comprehended as one whole, their riddles solved, their contingencies revealed as instantiations of universal and necessary law—but extends over the dawn and the mists a rainbow of blessing that a fragmentary universe flourish and divide yet more, a universe of riddles extend its enigmas yet further, an accidental universe turn eternally in impermanence and transience.

Those who give the forces of value are those who have them, who have first given them to themselves. The value-terms, these new forces, originate in those healthy with a superabundant health: the passionate, the sovereign, the eagles, the Aztecs. The primary, positive and active, value-terms do not acquire their meaning in the grammar of indicative or informative speech acts, but in speech acts of the exclamatory form. They do not function to identify, to hold as identical, but to intensify. One arises from sleep, charged with energies to squander, one greets the dawn dancing over the trees, one greets the visions and mirages of the dawn, and the aborigine in one exclaims: How good it is to be alive! The goodness one bespeaks is a goodness one feels, within, in the feeling of excess energy, energy to waste, that is affecting itself and intensifying itself with each dance step one makes in the pas de deux that the dawn is choreographing. One says it because one feels it. And in saying it, one is not simply reporting on it; one feels good and feels still better for the saying of it. The goodness surges within and transfigures one's surfaces of exposure. One steps into one's bathroom; one's glance plays in the infinite echoes of one's naked body shimmering in all the mirrors like a quetzal bird, and one murmurs, How beautiful I am! One could only understand what "How beautiful I am!" means in the artist feeling for one's sinews and contours and carnality; in the selective, framing, and glorifying artist eye that captures and holds, as worth contemplating for years, an ephemeral event of nature: the shimmering and gratuitous grace of the morning mirage of oneself in the mirrors. And in saying that, one feels still more beautiful. One sees the beauty one's murmur makes reverberant in the shimmering image of one's punk mug, one's dirt-farmer skin. After the morning workout pumping iron in the gym to muscle exhaustion, one bounds up the steps to the street outside babbling, How healthy I am! One could only understand what "How healthy I am!" means in the force that would produce that exclamation in oneself. This health is not a negative concept, defined by the negation of its negative, like the capitalist who learns from the doctor's report that so far no ulcer, no degenerative heart disease, no cholesterol-clogged arteries; therefore you are healthy. This health is the feeling of force to squander gratuitously on barbells, on shadow boxing, and on racing the deer through the forests and the zebras across the savanna.

These exclamatory speech acts, in which the value-terms arise, are dis-continuous vortices of force that redouble the spiraling vitality in which they arise. They are not arbitrary decrees of a legislative subjectivity impos-ing its own order and ranking on amorphous and neutral and indifferent material. The potbellied business-suited academic can lift up a glass in the end-of-term departmental luncheon and ejaculate, "I, one of the few, func-tionary of the celestial bureaucracy, how *kalos kagathos* I am!": it doesn't take; his voice rings hollow in the muffled coils of his sluggish intestines stuffed with dots of cheese and cheap departmental wine.

The positive value-terms do not acquire the definiteness of their mean-ing from their definitions in a dyadic system. The goodness there, the superabundance, the gratuity, the excess over and beyond being there, is not a distinctive category that gets its meaning from its opposition to the reverse category.

The primary positive value-terms are not comparative; they do not function to differentiate an observed datum from its opposite, nor do they function to report on a comparative degree of change from a prior state one is recalling. When one exclaims, How beautiful I am! one is not notic-ing the differences between what the mirrors shimmer and what a mental photograph of the acned adolescent one once was shows; one does not mean that while the angle of my virile jaw is not up to that of the Marlboro Man, my gut is not as flabby as 53 percent of the other real-estate agents and academics. When one exclaims, How healthy I am! the meaning one knows in it is not determined by comparative observation of the exhausted and the stunted one contemplates in the rat race of the wage slaves glancing at their watches with anxiety-filled eyes in the street below; and one is not simply recording that, unlike yesterday, there were no shooting pains in the rhomboids even after ten reps on the cable row. When one exclaims, How good it is to be alive! one is not comparing one's big solid body with some miserable image of a clot of gray jelly one was before the cheap condom burst that night on the old man. The value-terms are not discriminations of difference within a field maintained by memory. They are not effects that depend on the power of memory but productions that produce the power of forgetting. The woman from Puerto Rican Harlem who steps out from the gym and pushes her hard thighs down Fifth Avenue between the limp Long Island debutantes is not remembering childhood dysenter-ies and ringworms and dinners of boiled spaghetti; she knows she always was healthy, was conceived in health by her whore mother opening her loins one night to some dock worker. The Lao youth who catches sight of his dirt-skinned punk mug blazing like a comet in the mirrored walls of the Bangkok disco and maliciously parades before the ravenous and fevered eyes of the rich white tourists like a prince before slaves is not remembering the stunted boy nobody deigned to notice in the muck of the plantation; he knows now he always was as splendid as the panthers that descended by night to prowl the plantation manor.

The positive and active value-terms do not acquire their use within language games which are ways of socialized life, communication systems. Presenting themselves in an incantation, idols are mute to the others. These terms are not fixed in a system of opposition to their negations. For those of noble sensibility do not really have a sense of the bad, they do not really understand the morbid, the cringing, the rancorous, and the cynical. They look upon them with a look of pity that does not penetrate too deeply and that already feels contaminated by that pity. Bad for them means ill-favored, unfortunate. Their terms are not war cries and slogans in a combat against the others; their vitality, health, beauty, and joy is not threatened by the multitudes of the impotent, and they have not made themselves feel joyous by inventorying the whines and complaints of others. They avoid them, and are unjust to them, out of ignorance.

There is not one dyadic system, where the positive value-terms are defined and posited by their negations; the denigrating terms are reactive, come second, and consecrate not excessive but morbid forces of life.

The servile are those who understand evil, and their morality is built around the notion of evil. Their central concept is this reactive and malignant concept. For by evil, they understand nothing else than the very image of those with sovereign instincts, who are felt to be dangerous by their own impotence, an image refracted and degraded in the acid of their rancor. The evil one for them is the one who is strong, that is, violent; beautiful, that is, vain; healthy, that is, lascivious; noble, that is, domineering.

This belligerent concept is not a simple opposite produced by negating the noble concept of good. The specter of evil is a strong and obsessive image, not simply a vacuous negation; it is the powerful creation of powers of weakness that have recoiled from confrontation and accumulate in rancor. Their eyes are fixed on the others, on the sovereign ones, and they understand them more deeply than they know themselves; they are able to envision in advance the whole picture of the sumptuous and horrifying flower of what is germinating in them. Their visionary artistry sees the Jezebel in the four-year-old who paints his lips with his mother's lipstick, the snickerings of the world-dissolving Cartesian evil genius in a bunch of unruly kids in the ghetto school, the rapist-cum-axe-murderer in the strong arms of the Chicano trying to hitch a ride on the highway.

It is the idea of good that is for them a pale aftereffect of their sense of evil. They do not know it in their own instincts and their own joys but on their faces whose fearful and rapacious grimaces echo the words of the noble. In their lips, health means closure from the contagions of the world, beauty means enclosure in the uniforms of serviceability in the herd, goodness means productivity, and happiness means contentment with the content appropriated. It is we who live the good life, they say. But this goodness is itself a belligerent term, not an affirmation of gratuitous sovereignty, but a demand put on others.

Their forces, disengaged from the substances of things, recoil upon themselves and turn a surface of closure to the world. On this surface set against the others, the image of sovereignty is reflected and consecrated with rancorous and rapacious force as a demand put on the others. They face others representing values, face others with their fetishes, their faces doubled into fetishes.

We have been using words like *notion, concept, idea* of good, of health, strength, vitality, evil, and contentment. But the value-terms do not really designate concepts, forms which contain content or matrices which diagram essences. They are not terms which get their use and their definition from a structure of terms in systematic opposition, with which individuals determine and communicate their conceptually apprehended identities in opposition to one another. The servile sense of evil is not produced by simply using the grammatical operator of negation on the content of the noble and ennobling concept of good; the specter it invokes arises to consecrate and hallow a rancorous recoil of life that feeds on itself and intensifies itself. It is not an instrument in a system of communication; it is a war cry in an assault that advances by intelligence, that is, by cunning, deviousness, deceit, and entrapment. It does not communicate; it contaminates and spreads by complicity.

Every value-term is a consecration of an excess force by which a living organism disengages from its integration in the forces of its setting and from its subjection to the reproductive imperative that subordinates it to the genus. The health that is not simply determined and defined by the set of tests the doctor administers to detect the symptoms of disease and organic and psychic degeneration, the health that is invoked in an exultant feeling of power is an excess known in the squandering with which it is continually replenished. It is the health that does not characterize one's functional integrity, but is, essentially, many kinds of health, known and yet unknown: the health of satyrs and guerrillas. It is a pledge and not a report, it is the trajectory of a dancing star born of a churning chaos of excess forces. The life that values its beauty—the artist compulsion in its original form, which, according to Nietzsche, works with the noblest and rarest clay and oil, its own flesh and blood—jettisons its natural forms and the forms its artistry has made second nature, for the sake of unknown dreams and dances. Were it to fix its sense of beauty on forms now acquired or contract-ed, mummifying them, they would turn into the grimaces of a fetish. The life that values veracity opens each of its austerely won convictions to every contestation to come. The life that values responsibility sees every response made as a settlement not responsible enough, that has to be subjected to still further demands.

The exclamatory speech acts that posit value-terms are intrinsically dis-continuous and consecrate moments of expenditure at a loss. Values are terms in the name of which riches and capacities, assets and securities, edi-fices and institutions accumulated and conserved through months, years, centuries, are squandered. They arise not in compulsions to realistically adjust to reality, but in compulsions to discharge one's forces and resources, in the exultation of the solar consummation flaring up in the immensities of the cosmic voids.

Value-terms, then, are not designations of a fixed order of forms that transcend space and time. They do not introduce into the beginningless, endless, flux of empirical events a factor of abiding permanence and con-servation. They are not idealizing ideas; they do not function to idealize oneself, to fix one's presence in an abiding, selfsame form—an ideal pres-ence. That is why we use the term "idolizing": an idol exists in apparitions which do not fix the order of a common discourse, but glows with its own light that radiates light about itself and gives force, gives not for asking, gives without requiring anything in return.

Value-terms are not understood in mental acts which operate the sys-tems of information and which delineate the meaning of one term more and more decisively by delineating more exactly the meaning of the other terms; they spread by contagion and spread contagion. The war cry with which the healthy, the powerful, the proud, and the joyous are designat-ed as evil does not convey information; it infects the language and it is picked up like a virus. When President Ronald Reagan identified President Daniel Ortega Saavedra as a "two-bit dictator in designer glasses," he spread an old man's rancorous castrating hatred of a young revolutionary to mil-lions, confirming them in their belligerent ignorance. When a dive master ascending from the Java Sea reports to the waiting boat, "Narked!" the rap-ture of the deep spreads to them, already, as they don wet suits and buckle weight belts.

One describes, as descriptively as possible, even clinically, the scene in the Bangkok cabaret where the seventeen-year-old Lao waiter sudden-ly climbed on a table and dropped his livery uniform on the plates and the glasses, his body heaving with abandon, his gorged erection throb-bing at eye level of the white-haired sapphire wholesalers and silk-clad fashion designers—then, as your listener awaits your appraisal, the word

"Wonderful!" or "Wow!" breaks the narrative. This utterance does not classify the narrated event in a judgment according to the social and normative codes; it exclaims that what was just narrated—what had never before been done or seen—was outside all the codes and norms with which one judges what one sees. It communicates to your listener by its tone—communicates something more than, and something different from, what the description, photographic and clinical as you could make it, communicated. Something unavowable, unconfessable, infantile, and perverse—your involuntary, searing envy; your miserable pity that abruptly welled up—pity for your own seventeenth year, of child abuse; your seventeenth year in which your erections were shameful, guilty, hidden in the odors of urine and shit of locked toilets; your seventeenth year when your coming into biological, sexual maturity was sealed with castration. And in your listener, who listened to your description as the description of something he or she had never seen or heard of or imagined, whose somewhat frightened, scandalized mind was teeming with social, ethical, normative judgments and condemnations, suddenly blushed with the heat of the contagion of that feeling your word infected him or her with. Something was understood; something was understood between accomplices. Something was said that made the other your accomplice.

The surfaces of another, which can be scrutinized as an expanse of symptoms of the inner musculature, glands, and nervous circuitry of the functional organism, double into a face. The face of the other is the original locus of expression. The sensory-motor forces that turn its contours and shape its movements speak, are intentional, designate objects and objectives of the environment.

At the same time, the sensuous forces that open the eyes and the posture and expose the surfaces to the landscape and that well up in superabundant vitality and make the eyes radiant, the ears attuned to distant melodies, and the face ardent, speak. The face refracts a double of itself, made of warmth and light, which speaks, not messages addressed to order others, but vitalizing and ennobling, confirming and consecrating words intoned to itself—words uttered not for their representational form but for their condensing, intensifying force—mantras. The expressive face doubles into an idol.

The forces that double up the one who turns his face to the world into an idol are not the intentional—cognitive and communicative—forces; they are sensuous forces that animate the surfaces of the other. For the sensuality there is in our sensitivity is not simply the affective effects by which the impact of outside stimuli, which are recorded as information-bits, double up into irradiations of pleasure and pain on our sensory surfaces.

Pleasures and pains designate only the reactive affects of a passive sensibility. Sensuality in our organism is force and active; with the intensities of our sensuality, we turn to expose our bodies gratuitously to things our organism does not need to compensate for its needs and its wants; we open our eyes to distant vistas and mirages and to the most remote stars, and we open our ears to the hum of the city and the messageless murmur of forest insects and rustling leaves; we fondle the silk of robes and the powder of the butterflies still gaudy in death, and we expose our carnal substance to the grandeur of the oceans and the celestial terror of electrical storms. The strong and active forces of healthy sensuality are not pained by the absurd, but drive into it with the forces of laughter; they are not defeated by the mindless cruelties of the universe, but drive toward them with the forces of weeping and curses. The strong and active forces of healthy sensuality speak, speak words of consecration and imprecation.

The strong and active forces of sensuality on the surfaces of the expressive face double it with the laughter and tears of an idol. And speak their exultant and ennobling, consecrating, words. These words uttered by nonteleological, repetitive, insistent, intensifying forces chant and do not discourse. They do not designate what anyone sees, but make visible an apparition over the one that utters them. Words of joy and of lamentation which do not compare this apparition with others or address it to the demands or resources of others, they are sovereign words—mantras with which an idol crystallizes and sends forth flashes of light.

In the weak, passive sensuality there are also forces, rancorous and belligerent forces, and not only passive affects of pleasure and pain. The bitter and reactive sensuality rubs over its wounds and scars until they shine; it represents itself with the image of the good life in order to badger the others—fetishizes itself. It seeks to fix the ebbing forces of life with fixed forms, abiding and selfsame. Its idealizing words are fetishizing messages—demands addressed to others. The one who understands them understands their forces—that is, they spread not by their forms being comprehended by the discriminating and identifying intelligence of others, but by their cunning finding accomplices in the severe sensuality of others.

It is on the faces of others that we discover their values. It is not in the meaning of their expressions but on the figure they materialize, shaped not by the pressures of the world but by the joyous or rancorous inner force in them, that we see what their sensuality idolizes or fetishizes.

When someone coded in the common codes of civilization turns up and faces us, his or her face says, "Here I am!" He or she faces not simply as another particular upon which the social categories are instantiated. What faces is what the meaning one might give to this surface cannot contain, an excess over and above the forms and their coded significance. The facing is an exclamatory act that interrupts the exchange of messages picked up from others and passed on to others.

The I, the idol, that makes an apparition, saying, "Here I am," is not understood in an act of understanding that delineates the meaning of the term "I" by delineating how the he, she, and they who are around are coded. One abruptly finds oneself confronted by the apparition of the solitary animal: the eagle, the falcon, the satyr, the sphinx, the separated, the sacred one, the idol. To recognize what makes its appearance is not to re-cognize, to recode another instance of a category; it is to respond to the singular apparition. The "Wow, it's you!" with which one responds is an exclamation that breaks the commerce of messages and that responds with a surge of sensuality and with a greeting that is laughter or weeping, blessing or cursing. An exclamation that, by its tone, communicates.

Something passes between one sensuality accomplice to another. Something was understood; the *password among accomplices* was recognized. Something was said that made you the accomplice of the one that is one of his kind: quetzal bird, savage, aboriginal, guerrilla, nomad, Mongol, Aztec, sphinx.

1994

The Murmur of the World

We communicate information with spoken utterances, by telephone, with tape recordings, in writing, and with printing. With these methods we communicate in the linguistic code. We also communicate information with body kinesics—with gestures, postures, facial expressions, ways of breathing, sighing, and touching one another. The communication here too uses abbreviations, signs, and conventions.

To make drawn lines into writing, we have to conform with the convention that dictates that certain strokes correspond to a certain word and notion. Even those among us with excellent manual dexterity, good training, good health, and alertness make slips in our penmanship and our typing. There are always typos in the many-times copy-edited critical editions of classic authors. There is no speaking without stammerings, mispronunciations, regional accents, or dysphonias. Typing and printing are designed to eliminate the cacography, yet in every book we have seen some letters and words that are so faintly impressed that they are inferred rather than seen. Recording, and radio and television transmission, are designed to eliminate the cacophony, but there can be static, cutoffs, and jamming; there is always hysteresis, the lagging of transmission due to shifting in the electromagnetic field; and there is always background noise.

Entering into communication means extracting the message from its background noise and from the noise that is internal to the message. Communication is a struggle against interference and confusion. It is a struggle against the irrelevant and ambiguous signals which must be pushed back into the background and against the cacophony in the signals the interlocutors address to one another—the regional accents, mispronunciations, inaudible pronunciations, stammerings, coughs, ejaculations, words started and then canceled, and ungrammatical formulations—and the cacography in the graphics.

Communication and Contention

It is striking that the development of knowledge is conceived in military terms, such as *hunt, raid, strategy, battle,* and *conquest.* Yet is not knowledge developed in and for communication? When individuals shielded and armed encounter one another and make a move to communicate—extending bared hands and speaking—their violence comes to a stop. Discourse interrupts violence and words silence the clash of arms. Communication finds and establishes something in common beneath all contention.

But communication itself has been classically conceived as an agon, a contention between interlocutors. Communication takes place in discourse, that is, a dialectics of demand and response, statement and contestation, in which interlocutors oppose one another.

One sees communication as a continuation of violence, but with other means. One sees in the dialectical cadence of communication, proceeding by affirmation and contestation, an interval in which each makes himself other than the other, when one sees each one speaking in order to establish the rightness of what he says. To speak in order to establish one's own rightness is to speak in order to silence the other. Yet Socrates from the beginning excluded the possibility of establishing one's own rightness. Communication is an effort to silence, not the other, the interlocutor, but the outsider: the barbarian, the prosopopoeia of noise.

Michel Serres argues that there is indeed force being exercised to resist and silence another in all communication, but it is not in the dialectic of demand and response, statement and contestation, in which interlocutors position themselves and differ the one from the other.[1] What the one says may oppose—question, deny, or contradict—what the other says, but in formulating opposing statements that respond to one another, interlocutors do not entrench themselves in reciprocal exclusion. For speaker and auditor exchange their roles in dialogue with a certain rhythm; the source becomes reception and the reception, the source; the other becomes but a variant of the same (67). Discussion is not strife; it turns confrontation into interchange.

However, when two individuals renounce violence and set out to communicate, they enter into a relation of noncommunication and violence with outsiders. There could well be, and in fact always is, an outsider or outsiders who have an interest in preventing communication. Every conversation between individuals is subversive—subversive of some established order, some established set of values, or some vested interests. There is always an enemy, a big brother listening in on all our conversations, and that is why we talk quietly behind closed doors. There is nothing you or I say to one another in conversation that we would say if the television cameras were focused on us for direct broadcast.

There are outsiders who have an interest in preventing *this* rather than *that* from being communicated; they do so by arguing for that, by presenting it in seductive and captivating ways, or by filling the time and the space with it. There are outsiders who have an interest in preventing us from communicating at all. They do so by filling the time and the space with irrelevant and conflicting messages, with noise.

Formerly the street walls of buildings were blind, without windows; anyone who came to speak had to ring a bell and tell his name. Today the street walls of buildings are screens upon which messages are written in neon flashes—irrelevant and conflicting messages which are not received and responded to but which agitate and merge into images that dazzle, inveigle, and excite the consumer frenzy of contemporary life. The roads and the paths to the furthest retreats in the country are lined with wires tense with stock-exchange pandemonium; beams bounced off satellites in outer space penetrate all the walls.

The walls we have to erect about ourselves are immaterial walls, the walls of an idiolect whose terms and turns of phrase are not in the dictionary and the manuals of rhetoric. Not only the talk of lovers, but every conversation that is resumed again and again becomes, over time, incomprehensible to outsiders. There is secrecy in every conversation. In the measure that this wall of secrecy gets thinner, we more and more utter but current opinions, conventional formulas, and inconsequential judgments. Heidegger quite missed that; it is the big and little Hitlers lurking in every hallway, every classroom, and every bar where we went to relax and get our minds off things, that produce *das Gerede*—"talk."

There are also allies—outsiders who have an interest in promoting the communication between us. The company wants the section members to communicate with one another; in disputes the police want us to try to communicate with our neighbors before calling them. Even authoritarian governments want the citizens to communicate at least their fears and resignation to one another.

When we cannot communicate, we appeal to outsiders to help. We enroll in classes, to learn from professors mastery of the established forms of discourse and the state of the current debate, so as to be able to communicate our insights effectively. We appeal to the scientific community, its established vocabulary and rhetorical forms, in trying to communicate with fellow scientists from Japan or agricultural workers in Africa. Descartes, having established the existence of his own mind and his own thoughts, then appeals to the great outsider, God, before he moves on to consider the existence of other minds and the possibility of communicating with them.

In making philosophy not the imparting of a doctrine but the clarification of terms, Socrates, like analytic philosophers, like recent pragmatic philosophers, makes philosophy a facilitator of communication. Socrates, who evolved from soldier to philosopher in the service of the community, struggled against the babble and the barbarian who is the real enemy of truth.

But Michel Serres interprets the Socratic effort in such a way as to make the elimination of noise, in the rational community, a struggle against the rumble of the world and to make the struggle against the outsider a struggle against the empiricist.

The Signified, the Signifier, the Referent

To communicate is to take an emitted signal to mean the same to the speaker and to the auditor. And it is to take an emitted signal to mean the same as a signal emitted before. The meaning designated by conventional signifiers at different times and in different places is recognized to be the same; Husserl characterizes the meaning of expressions as ideal. Meanings exist, not intemporally and aspatially, but by the indefinite possibility of recurring and by the indefinite possibility of being designated by signifiers issued anywhere, anytime.

There is, in language, no first or last occurrence of a word. A word can have meaning only if it can be repeated. The words that have suffered obsolescence can still be referred to, by linguists and students of literature, and can be returned to the language; their demise is never definitive. The first time a word is constructed, if it is to be able to enter into the usages of language, it must appear as already latent in the structures and paradigms and rules of formulation of the language.

It is not only the signification but the signifier, too, that is ideal. What signals in a sound is not its particular sonorous quality as really heard, but the formed sound that is taken to be ideally the same as that of other sounds uttered before and yet to be uttered. To hear sounds as words, to hear signals in the noise, is to abstract from the soprano or bass, thinness or resonance, softness or loudness, or tempo of their particular realizations and to attend only to the distinctive feature that conventionally makes the sounds distinct phonemes in the phonetic system of a particular language. The word as a signifier is already an abstraction and the product of an idealization.

Recognizing what is written involves epigraphy, a skill in separating out the ill-written features of the letters and words. The geometry class abstracts from the fact that the drawing the teacher has put on the board is only approximately a right triangle or a circle. When she draws a circle with a compass, one ignores the fact that the pencil angle shifts as she draws and the line is thicker on one side than on another. The reader systematically neglects not only the erroneous lines but also the particularities with which the letters have to be materialized. He disregards the fact that they are written in blue or black ink, or set in a Courier 10 or Courier 12 typeface. Reading is a peculiar kind of seeing that vaporizes the substrate, the hue and grain of the paper or of the computer screen and sees the writing as will-o'-the-wisp patterns in a space disconnected from the material layout of things.

To communicate is to have practiced that dematerializing seeing that is seeing patterns as writing and that dematerializing hearing that is hearing streams of sounds as words and phrases. It is to push into the background, as noise, the particular timbre, pitch, volume, and tonal length of the words being uttered and to push into the background, as white noise, the particular color, penmanship, and typeface, of the visible patterns. Communication—by words and also by conventionalized kinesic signals—depends on the common development of these skills in eliminating the inner noise in signals and in dematerializing vision and audition.

To communicate with another, one first has to have terms with which one communicates with the successive moments of one's experience. Already to have a term which, when one pronounces it now, one takes to be the same as when one pronounced it a moment ago, is to have dematerialized the sound pattern, dematerialized a vocalization into a signifier, a word. Memory works this dematerialization. When one conveys something in words to another, how does one know that the communication is successful? Because one hears the other speaking about that experience, responding to it, and relating it to other experiences, in terms one would have used. To recognize the words of another as the words one used or would use, one de-particularizes those words of their empirical particularities: their pitch, timbre, rhythm, density, and volume—their resonance. One disengages the word from its background noise and from the inner noise of its utterance. The maximal elimination of noise would produce successful communication among interlocutors themselves maximally interchangeable.

The meanings we communicate—the ways we refer to objects and situations—are abstract entities: recurrent forms. The signifiers with which we communicate are abstract, universal: ideal. But the referents, too, are abstract and idealized entities.

If we speak to another of a mountain vista, it is because that mountain landscape spoke to us; if we speak of a red, not brown, door, it is because that door emitted signals in the vibrations that made contact with our eyes. If our words, signals addressed to one another, have referents, it is because things address signals to us—or at least broadcast signals at large.

The medium teems with signals continually being broadcast from all the configurations and all the surfaces of things. To see that color of red, to pick up the signals from that door or that vista, is to constitute an enormous quantity of irrelevant and conflicting signals as background noise.

But to refer to that color of red with a word that one has used to refer to red things before and that will be used by one's interlocutor who does not see it or who sees it from his own angle of vision, is to filter out a multiplicity of signals given out by this particular door in the sun and shadows of this late afternoon and received by one who happens to be standing just here. What we communicate with the word and concept "red" is what, in this red door, can recur in other things designated by this word. The reception of signals from referents in view of communicating them is not a palpation that discerns the grain and pulp and tension with which each thing fills out the spot it so stubbornly and so exclusively occupies. It is seeing the red of the door, and the gloom of the forest and the shapes of the leaves, as modular patterns stamped on the unpenetrated density of things. Only this kind of leveling and undiscerning perception, Serres argues, could be communicated. "The object perceived," he complains, "is indefinitely discernible: there would have to be a different word for every circle, for every symbol, for every tree, and for every pigeon; a different word for yesterday, today, and tomorrow; and a different word according to whether he who perceives it is you or I, according to whether one of the two of us is angry, is jaundiced, and so on *ad infinitum*" (70). To communicate is to consign to noise the teeming flood of signals emitted by what is particular, perspectival, and distinctive in each thing.

To abstract from the noise of the world is to be a rationalist. The first effort at communication already begins the dematerialization that thought will pursue. The effort to render a form independent of its empirical realizations issues in the constitution of the universal, the scientific, the mathematical.

The City Maximally Purged of Noise

We face one another to emit signals that can be received, recognized, and reiterated, while about us extends the humming, buzzing, murmuring, crackling, and roaring world. Our interlocutor receives the information by not harkening to the pitch, volume, accent, and buzz of our sounds, and attending only to the recognizable, repeatable form, consigning the singular sonority of our voice and sentence to noise internal to the message. And he turns to the thing, situation, or event referred to by our message as a recurrent and abstract entity, not as the singular vibrant density sunk in the morass of the world and emitting its particular signals, static, and noise. The practice of abstraction from the empirical implantation of things is what brings about communication. To eliminate the noise is to have successfully received the message. To communicate it is to reissue the abstract form. The abstract is maintained and subsists in the medium of communication.

The community that forms in communicating is an alliance of interlocutors who are on the same side, who are not each Other for each other but all variants of the Same, tied together by the mutual interest of forcing back the tide of noise pollution.

The Socratic effort to communicate with strangers is, in reality, the effort not to rationally certify the existing Athenian republic but to found an ideal republic of universal communication—a city maximally purged of noise (68). It is an effort to found a scientific and mathematical discourse and to silence the rumble of the world. In constructing an objective representation of nature out of abstract mathematical entities, one produces a community in quasi-perfect communication, a transparent Rousseauian community where what is formulated in the mind of each is what is also formulated in the minds of the others. That community would be imminent today, as all information becomes digitally coded and transmitted by satellite in the silences of outer space.

But is it really true that universal, abstract, objective, scientific discourse is de-particularized and is the discourse of anyone? It can't be just accidental that to do philosophy is to compose one's own philosophy, a philosophy that will decompose with one. "If philosophy is autobiographical, in a sense that science is not …," I was saying, when a philosopher of science interrupted me to refuse the distinction. "It is fatuous to say that if Einstein did not invent the special theory of relativity, someone else would have," she objected. "Everybody now understands that the data he was working with and the theories he was trying to integrate could be formulated and integrated in any number of different, imaginable, and so far unimaginable ways. If Einstein had not slipped out in time from Nazi Germany, there is every reason to think we would never have the special theory of relativity." The term "electricity" has a different sense for a television repairman than for an electrical engineer working on urban power generators or on CAT-scan equipment, but also for a meteorologist, a solid-state physicist, or an astronomer. Its meaning is different in each laboratory; the different models and paradigms with which any scientist works spread a different array of paths about the movement of his terms. It is not only the new hypotheses posited and new experiments devised that generate new conceptions; when a scientist reads the work of another scientist, the terms may generate a different movement in the paths of the conceptual operations of the reader than they had in those of the writer.

Is not, then, the ideal of the kind of maximally unequivocal transmission of messages in the industry of a social space maximally purged of noise that Serres invokes another idol of the marketplace—idol of the communication theory (devised for the service of our military-industrial complex)?

Serres's argument leads him to identify, as noise, the whole of the empirical as such. "To isolate an ideal form is to render it independent of the empirical domain and of noise. Noise is the empirical portion of the message just as the empirical domain is the noise of form" (70). "The 'third man' to exclude," Serres now concludes, "is the empiricist, along with his empirical domain.... [I]n order for dialogue to be possible, one must close one's eyes and cover one's ears to the song and the beauty of the sirens. In a single blow, we eliminate hearing and noise, vision and failed drawing; in a single blow, we conceive the form and we understand each other" (ibid.).

Rationalists—mathematicians, scientists, and the miraculous Greeks—eliminate the signals emitted by the particularities of empirical particulars and transmit only the abstract idealities; empiricists pick up all the static being emitted by the particularities of empirical realities and use different words for every circle and every pigeon, for the circles and pigeons others see from their perspectival points of view, and for circles and pigeons perceived with jaundiced eyes or the feline eyes of carnivorous interlocutors. They are Evil Geniuses of interference butting into every effort at communicating an unequivocal information-bit from one to the other. "The more [empiricists] are right, the less we can hear them; they end up only making noise" (70n11).

Empiricists are the demons that rule the world. But one cannot progressively assimilate more and more of these ephemeral proper names for the signals of the world; one has to struggle against them. The only solution is to say, with Leibniz against Locke, that "empiricism would always be correct if mathematics did not exist" (70n12). The community that establishes communication has to take its existence as proof of its validity. The only solution is to "not *want* to listen to Protagoras and Callicles—because they are right." This, Serres writes, "is not an *ad hominem* argument; it is the only logical defense possible" (ibid.). The community we must want must not want to hear the glossolalia of nonhuman things—the humming, buzzing, murmuring, crackling, and roaring of the world, must not want to hear the stammerings, quaverings, dronings of one another's voices, and must want its hearing perfectly adjusted to hear the mathematics relayed by satellites in outer space.

What an extraordinary outcome of the ancient Socratic philosophy of dialogue completed now in a contemporary theory of communication! The struggle for the establishment of transparent intersubjectivity is a battle against the relayers of the signals of the world. Communication depends on, is the other side of, noncommunication—a *wanting* to not communicate and an active battle to silence the empiricist demons. The only logical defense of rationality and logic is the active and combative will to not listen to Protagoras and Callicles—because they are right!

The Encounter with the Other

Serres conceives of communication as an exchange of expressions that have the same informative value for the receiver as for the emitter, expressions whose value reduces to exchange-value. Expressions that would discern what differentiates one circle from another; one symbol, tree, or pigeon from another; one yesterday, today, or tomorrow from another; or your angry or jaundiced perception from mine, have no communicative value. Serres then conceives of interlocutors as emitters and receptors which interchange their functions. In the measure that what was received was what was emitted and that what was communicated was the abstract, de-particularized message, each partner in conversation becomes the same for the other: the auditor becoming speaker of what he heard and the receptor source of what he received.

Serres argues that in a dialogue, the two interlocutors are "in no way opposed" (67), but are variants of each other, are variants of the Same, because the questioner and the respondent exchange their reciprocal roles, with the source becoming reception and the reception source, "according to a given rhythm." But does not this rhythm oppose them? Is it not the time gap between emission of the signal and its reception that opens up the space of hysteresis where the interferences and the misconstructions enter? In the ideal republic that Serres invokes—the city of communication maximally purged of noise—would not the emission and reception have to be simultaneous? The less time involved in the communication means the less thermodynamic energy involved and the less entropy. Two modems, transmitting and receiving information-bits simultaneously, would be the model.

But to affirm something is not simply to make oneself the momentary source of a formulation whose abstractness makes it equivalent of what any interlocutor does or can issue and receive; it is to present something to someone for his judgment, his confirmation or contestation. To set oneself forth as a subject of discourse is to expose oneself to being contested and discredited. To make oneself a subject in discourse is to subject oneself to another. Already, to greet someone is to recognize his or her right over one.

To question someone is not simply to make oneself a receptor for information which one will soon reissue; it is to appeal to another for what is not available to oneself. To address a query or even a greeting to another is to expose one's ignorance, one's lacks, and one's destitution and is to appeal for assistance to one nonsymmetrical with oneself.

To address someone is not simply to address a source of information; it is to address one who will answer and answer for his or her answer. The time delay, between statement and response, is the time in which the other, while fully present there before one, withdraws into the fourth dimension—reaffirming his or her otherness, rising up behind whatever he presents of himself, and rising up ever beyond whatever I represent of her and present to her—to contest it or to confirm it.

To enter into conversation with another is to lay down one's arms and one's defenses; to throw open the gates of one's own positions; to expose oneself to the other, the outsider; and to lay oneself open to surprises, contestation, and inculpation. It is to risk what one found or produced in common. To enter into conversation is to struggle against the noise, the interference, and the vested interests, the big brothers and the little Hitlers always listening in—in order to expose oneself to the alien, the Balinese and the Aztec, the victims and the excluded, the Palestinians and the Quechuas and the Crow Indians, the dreamers, the mystics, the mad, the tortured, and the birds and the frogs. One enters into conversation in order to become an other for the other.

The Noise in the Message

We are necessary as efficient causes of new sentences, producers of new information formulated with old words. But in our particularities, our perspectival points of view, and our distinctive capacities to issue and to receive meanings, we are part of the noise. The time it takes to formulate those sentences is a time filled with the opacity of our own voices. How transparent communication might be if there were not resistance in the channels that conduct it: no lilting, bombastic, stammering voice pronouncing it!

Yet is there not also a communication in the hearing of the noise in one another's voices—the noise of one another's life that accompanies the harkening to the message? What kind of communication would that be?

The particular, the material, the empirical, Serres says, is indefinitely discernible. It is a succession of signals, each with its own name, in a static that cannot be recorded or reproduced. Yet surely every day we do succeed in communicating to one another, not only the abstract formula of an insight, but the unique spell of the encounter with an early-winter afternoon, the charm of something someone said that was never before said, or the weirdness of a feeling never before felt. Language is the amazing power to say, with a limited number of words and grammatical structures, sentences never before said that formulate events that have never before occurred.

Every new sentence that succeeds in saying something does so, Merleau-Ponty said, by a coherent deformation of the sentence paradigms already in the language. Every new sentence also continues the bending, extending, and deforming of the code. "Let us agree," Serres writes, "that ... communication is only possible between two persons used to the same ... forms, trained to code and decode a meaning by using the same key" (65). But when an American, brought up on Indian legends, says to an Englishman, brought up on legends of imperial conquerors, "He's brave ...," they do not have the same key to this word. If, nonetheless, the one understands the other, it is by improvising the key as one goes along.

Is it not also false to suppose that only the meaning attached to words by a code, fixed or evolving, communicates? The rhythm, the tone, the periodicity, the stammerings, and the silences communicate. In the rush of the breathless voice, the tumult of events is conveyed; in the heavy silence that weighs on the voice, the oppressive tedium of a place is communicated. "'Prove it,' demands the logocentric system that the art historian worships. 'Prove that you still love me...?'" Joanna Frueh, performance art critic, is saying it in different intonations, volumes, and crescendos—sparring with the voice of the academic demand, and circling around the male: "Prove it.... *Prove* that you still love me...." "Prove that you still *love* me...."

The noise of our throats that fills the time it takes to convey the message communicates the noise of the things or makes the things discernible in their empirical plurality. By the utterance of every insight we have into an empirical particular—a particular circle, tree, or pigeon we contemplated yesterday when we were angry or jaundiced—breaking into the universal circulation of passwords, watchwords, and orders; by singling out a particular interlocutor; and by interrupting the narrative or the explanation with an intonation, an attack and cadence, or with the redundancies that blur and interjections that wail, bray, or strike speechless; we do succeed in communicating the differentiation, the plurality of facets and of perspectives and the indefinite discernibility of empirical particulars. Anyone who thinks we are only emitting noise is one who does not *want* to listen.

The one who understands is not extracting the abstract form out of the tone, the rhythm, and the cadences—the noise internal to the utterance, the cacophony internal to the emission of the message. He or she is also listening to that internal noise—the rasping or smoldering breath, the hyperventilating or somnolent lungs, the rumblings and internal echoes—in which the message is particularized and materialized and in which the empirical reality of something indefinitely discernible, encountered in the path of one's own life, is referred to and communicated.

With this internal noise it is the other, in his or her materiality, that stands forth and stands apart making appeals and demands. The other is not simply the recurrent function of appealing to and contesting me; he or she is an empirically discernible vulnerability and intrusion. In *Visage* Luciano Berio composed not with words but with the sonorous elements with which words are formed—the sighs, gasps, waverings, dronings, hissings, sobs, giggles, whimperings, snivelings, screams, snortings, purrings, mutterings, and moanings—out of which, sometimes, words are shaped. He plunged them into a vast space in which electronic sounds hum, pound, sing, scatter, dissipate and where, finally, the roar of machines drowns out the human voice. In them, Cathy Berberian exposes herself more than her intentions and judgments could have revealed—exposes her sensibility, her susceptibility, her mortality, and the flux and scope of her carnal existence.

As efficient causes of expressions that convey information, we are interchangeable. Our singularity and our indefinite discernibility is found in, and is heard in, our outcries and our murmurs, our laughter and our tears: the noise of life.

The Background Noise

If the neo-Socratic communication theory of Michel Serres has not understood—has not *wanted* to understand—the noise internal to communication: the pulse and the wobble, the opacity of the timbre and density of the voice, the noise of life, the noise each of us is in his or her particularity; it has also not understood—has not *wanted* to understand—the background noise in the midst of which we speak.

Advances in soundproofing technologies and digital recording promise the complete elimination of background noise. Sensory-deprivation tanks were first invented in the 1960s by John C. Lilly who was working with dolphins and, like every diver, loved the silence and the bliss of deep-sea diving and thought to duplicate it on land. But the technology that eliminates the noise also eliminates the communication. In the absence of auditory, visual, and tactual background signals, one no longer senses the boundaries between outside and inside, past and present, perception and images, and one soon hallucinates. If the reception of a determinate signal is impossible beyond a certain level of background noise, the intention to emit a determinate signal becomes unrealizable without a certain level of ambient drone to escalate, punctuate, and redirect. Recorded white noise—forest murmurs, the rumble of the city—was added to space capsules; the recordings are sold to terrestrials living in soundproofed apartments.

We understand that background noise is essential to communication when we understand that reception in the communication system of our bodies is not the passive exposing of a preprogrammed surface of sensibility to outside stimuli, but picking a signal out of the multiplicity of irrelevant and conflicting signals. Where the receptor organ can receive a wide variety of signals, perception is the active power to focus in on, isolate, segregate, shape a figure, and reduce the rest to indifferentiation. If, each time we look, we see a figure standing out against the adjacent objects, this is not due to the physical stimulation that is being spread across our retinas; it must be due to an active power in our gaze. Since communication is, for the receiver, actively separating a figure from the background, then in the absence of the background there can be no figure either. If one looks into a closed, elliptically shaped box painted black and uniformly illuminated with white light, one cannot see the black and cannot see the surfaces at all; all one sees is a luminous gray density. But if one then sticks a white strip of paper on the wall of that box, suddenly the light becomes transparent and the hue of the medium recedes and condenses into black on the walls of the box. When the psychologist seats a subject in a room such that he sees only the homogeneous surface of a broad wall uniformly illuminated, the subject cannot see how far it is from him, cannot see any surface at all, sees only a medium in depth about him, and cannot say what color it is. John Cage once emerged from a soundproof room to declare that there was no such state as silence. In that room he heard the rustling, throbbing, whooshing, buzzings, ringings, and squeakings with which the movements of his muscles and glands resounded with the ripples and rumbles of the never-ending movements of the atmosphere.

If the reception of a determinate signal is the segregation of a sonorous field into figure and background drone, the emission of a determinate signal forms in the hum of the field. Communication theory identifies the background hum as a multitude of irrelevant or conflicting signals. To designate it, thus, as noise is to conceive it from the point of view of the individual teleologically destined to citizenship in an ideal republic maximally purged of the noise of life and of the empirical domain—the miraculous Greece or the totally transparent Rousseauist society. We shall conceive a different understanding of the background noise if we put vocalization among us in the perspective of evolutionary biology.

One day, while trying to drive in the chaotic traffic of Tehran, with each move I tried to make provoking taps on the horns of cars beside, behind, and advancing toward me, I remarked to a hitchhiker I had picked up, that after five blocks of this I felt like a road lizard on bad amphetamines. Oh, they are not, like us Westerners, using the horn as a warning or a threat, he said. They are like quail clucking as they feed on a ripe wheat field. They are, he meant, creating a sound environment with which they symbiotically merge with one another. I understood at once, because my mind flashed back to the long nights I had driven across Turkey and Iran when the next town proved to take, not the hour I had calculated, but six hours due to the devastated condition of the road and the flooded rivers, and how I had thought that night driving in a car is the absolute form of hermitage that civilization had finally invented. When you are alone in the middle of the night in a hotel room in an alien country, you cannot moan out your loneliness and misery without someone hearing you on the other side of the wall, but if you are driving nights on the highway you can scream and none of the cars crossing you in the opposite lane will hear anything. When I drive distances at night, I, like Simon Styletes on his pillar in the Egyptian deserts, invariably fall into extremist spiritual exercises revolving around the theme *Memento mori,* reviewing the meaning or meaningless of my life in the cosmic voids ahead. With the tappings of the horns, the yearnings or outcries of solitude penetrate the hull of roar with which one's car encases its motion, and merge and become common.

When one lives with birds one sees how the noise level of the birds keeps up with the noise level of the house, with the wind that begins to whisper and whistle across the sidings, with each notch up you turn the volume dial on your record player. It is the rumble and rasping of the inert things that provokes the vocalization of the animals; fish hum with the streams and birds chatter in the crackling of the windy forest. To live is to echo the vibrancy of things. To be, for material things, is to resonate. There is sound in things like there is warmth and cold in things, and things resonate like they irradiate their warmth or their cold. The quail and the albatross, the crows and the hummingbirds, the coyotes and the seals, the schooling fish and the great whales, the crocodiles infrasonically and the praying mantises ultrasonically continue and reverberate the creaking of the branches, the fluttering of the leaves, the bubbling of the creeks, the hissing of the marsh gases, the whirring of the winds, the shifting of the rocks, the grinding of the earth's plates.

This noise is not analytically decomposable, as communication theory would have it, into a multiplicity of signals, information-bits, that are irrelevant or that conflict: that become, in Serres's word, *equivocal.* The noise figures as resonance and vocalization that, like the scraping wings of crickets we hear, contains no message.[2] Olivier Messaien, in his *Chronochromie,* did not compose into music, into rhythm and harmony and melody, the enormous quantity of signals being emitted by the birds of the jungle that he had in his vast collection of tapes of bird cries; we hear in *Chronochromie* the sounds of metals—cymbals, bells, blocks, pipes, and rasps; woods—mahoganies, oaks, and bamboos; hides—cords and drums; fibers—whisks; and strings, gums, and fluids transforming into the wild exultant racket of multitudes of feathered and flying things. And as we listen, it transforms again into our own sounds.

For we too communicate what we communicate with the background noise, and we communicate the background noise. The communication takes place when the vibrancy of the land, the oceans, and the skies is taken up, condensed, and unfurled in the hollows of one's body, then released, and when one hears its echo returning with the wind and the sea.

In the highlands of Irian Jaya it seemed that no matter how late it was at night, there was always someone who could not sleep and who spent his insomnia singing and drumming. "Are they preparing a ceremony or feast?" I asked a missionary with whom I had taken shelter and who was keeping me up for Christmas midnight Mass. "No," he answered. "It goes on every night. In fact they are afraid of the night. They are like children," he said, with the weariness of his years. But their vocalizations did not sound to me to be issuing out of breasts where fear trembled. It seemed to me that their chants and yodelings picked up and reverberated sounds their own throats made, sounds other throats made, sounds the marshes and the birds of the night and the winds were making. J. M. G. Le Clézio lived long among the Indians in the Chiapas in Mexico and in Panama; to live among them is to live in the days and nights of their music: music made with bamboo tubes, perforated pipes, drums, shells, rattles, and also with a taut falsetto use of the voice, the throat having become a flute or whistle. Le Clézio heard it in the midst of the din of the rain forest: in the barking of dogs, the cries of the spider monkeys, the agoutis, the hawks, the jaguars, and in the vocalization of the frogs which fills the whole length of every night in the rain forest. It seemed to him that any musicologist who just studied the tapes of Indian music in the laboratories, filled with synthesizers, in Paris or Frankfurt would inevitably connect the specific scales, pitches, rhythms, and phrasings of Indian music with cultural values and conventions and would try to connect it with their myths and tragic cultural history. But theirs is a music made of cries and chants without melody or harmony, a music not made for dancing or pleasing; it is a music with which they see, hear, and feel in the anesthesia of the night. "Melodious music is first the conviction that time is fluid, that events recur, and that there is what we call 'meaning.'" But "for the Indian, music has no meaning. It has no duration. It has no beginning, no end, no climax."[3] Words are prisons in which the breath of life is imprisoned in human form; in a music without melody and without meaning, the Indian hears the animal, vegetable, mineral, and demonic realms. One had to listen to it there, in the nights of the Lacandon rain forest, to understand that this "music" is not an aesthetic production, that is, a creation of human subjectivities attempting to communicate immanent states like moods, feelings, values, or messages to other human subjectivities. It is a prolongation of the forest murmurs, the whispering sands, and the hum of the heavenly bodies.

Separated from the vocalizations, rumblings, creakings, and whirrings of animate and inanimate nature, music becomes a means of communicating between humans only. Words can be added to it, speaking of the loneliness of individuals overcome through human love. But this communication in a city maximally purged of noise is a recent creation. A friend recently played for me, on his state-of-the-art equipment, a CD disk of the only complete recording of the Balinese Kechak. Listening to it, I was at once astonished and mesmerized by the purity, transparency, and beauty of the digitally recorded and cleansed sounds. But after a few moments, I began to think of how abstract it was; one was hearing only a tonal mapping of the Kechak, like reading the score of a concerto for harp without hearing the tinkling crescendos or seeing the elegant and aristocratic figure of the harpist seated there in the baroque concert hall of old Prague. I had never succeeded in doing anything but irritate anyone who was riding in my car while I had Balinese or Javanese music on the tape player, and I would apologetically explain that, in fact, I had myself come to be so captivated by this music because of the whole setting: drifting through the dark and wet jungle after the day's work is done; idling for an hour or two among the gossiping Balinese quite unconcerned that the players have not yet arrived two hours after they said they would; settling into the throbbing of the frogs and night insects; seating myself on the ground as the circle of seated men expanded and the priest lit the torches that awaken the monstrous figures of the demons that guard the temple compound while the incense stirs the spirits that slumber in the flowering trees and vines, and the glistening bare bodies of the men massed on the ground begin to sway as the trance, ancient as the sea, spreads among them, then abruptly their animal outcries greeting the apparition of the gods weaving among them: dancing gods, bound in exquisite silks and batiks, their heads crowned with delicate-stemmed flowers and smoldering sticks of incense and their jewels throwing off ruby and sapphire flash-fires. The digital recording, cleansed not only of the noise of the reproductive equipment but of the background noise of the performance, does not, I thought, reproduce perfectly the sounds of the Kechak dance; it creates music. Western civilization which created, in the eighteenth century, the market economy and, indeed, economic activity; which created the abstract universal essence of libido;

which created people as female and as male; which created the value-free objective representation of nature and history and culture; which created sculpture out of African fetishes and created paintings out of *tang'kas*, those cosmic diagrams and instruments for centering in meditation found in Tibetan *gompas*; which created art, art for art's sake, out of ritual and civic ceremonies; has now created music out of the Balinese Kechak. The Balinese, for their part, have no word in their language for art and do not listen to the music; at night in the temple compound, they rock their squalling children, nurse them, chat with neighbors, go out to get something to eat, admire and severely criticize the performance of the fellow villager who is dancing the Rama or the Sita, fall into trance, come out of it, are transubstantiated into gods, demons, rivers, storms, and night. In fact, when Bach composed, rehearsed, and directed a cantata, he was not simply creating music; he was praising God, earning merit and salvation, paying for the upkeep of his twelve children, competing with Telemann and Purcell, enhancing the status of his prince-patron and his own station, and contributing to a successful Christmas feast for all the town.

The creation, in our time, of music, like every cultural creation, is an inestimable contribution to the wealth of our heritage and makes, Nietzsche would say, this old earth a sweeter place to live on. The music was produced by the electronic elimination of all the marginal and subliminal signals coming from the nonmusical sonorous medium: the chatter of the village, the people, and the history; the remote murmurs and rumblings of the gods and demons; the barking dogs and the crowing roosters prematurely awakened from their somnolence by the dawn they see flickering from the torches; the night insects and the frogs; the rustling of leaves; the clatter of the rain; the restlessness of the air currents in the night skies; and the creaking of the rock strata—the background noise.

We too do not vocalize and mark surfaces only because we have some message to transmit. Significant speech, utterances where one can, like Serres, distinguish the calliphony from the cacophony, the message from the noise, is only an abstract part of speech. When grammarians and linguists analyze any text, they are astonished at how much redundancy there is in all speaking; how much of what we say to one another is repetition, chorus, murmur, and drawn-out resonance. We are no different from the celestial birds, who chime in with one another but know that it is only occasionally, in all this effervescent racket, that some information about a delectable kind of seed that got put in the dish today or some danger is being addressed to them.

You were dozing in your room and you woke, wondering what time it was. You thought, like that disheveled figure on a bed in the French cartoon that you had glued at eye view of your pillow, "Si je continue comme ça, je ne serai jamais maître du monde!" (If I keep on like this, I never will be the master of the world!). You tried to get the blood stirring and some movement started, you shuffled to the kitchen, shaking up some things on the way, making the door creak by opening it with a thrust, so as to get some movement in the dead silence of the house. You came upon your housemate sprawled torpidly on the couch, like a cold-blooded frog in midafternoon: "Hey, man, like, whatcha doing, huh?" Where is the information-bit? You said that to get some night sounds going, some rhythm going, some hopping about started.

It is out of and in the midst of the reverberation of ambient materiality that the utterances we make get shaped, and they get sent forth to return to it. The resonance of things animate and inanimate is in the redundancies, the drawn-out vowels and consonants, the hisses and groans and ejaculations, and the babble and mumbling and murmur that is the basso continuo of all our message-laden utterances.

Computer technology, driven by the pilot-industries of the military-industrial complex, places top priority on transmitting the message as effectively, efficiently, and effortlessly as possible. It is computer technology that shaped and forms contemporary communication theory.[4] But so little of what we say to one another makes any sense! So little of it makes any pretense to be taken seriously, so much of it is simple malarkey, in which we indulge ourselves with the same warm visceral pleasure that we indulge in belching and passing air. It really is, Nietzsche long ago pointed out, bad taste to make serious pronouncements and work out syllogistically valid arguments in civilized company. So much of language added to industry and enterprises that are programmed by the laws of nature or rational science and that operate all by themselves, so much of language added to fumblings and breakdowns and even disasters has no other function than to provoke laughter. Laughter mixing in moans, howls, screams into the racket of the world. As much of what we say when we embrace we say to release our sighs and our sobs into the rains and the seas.

All these stammerings, exclamations, slurrings, murmurs, rumblings, cooings, and laughter, all this noise we make when we are together makes it possible to view us as struggling, together, to jam the unequivocal voice of the outsider: the facilitator of communication, the prosopopoeia of maximal elimination of noise, so as to hear the distant rumble of the world and its demons in the midst of the ideal city of human communication.

1994

The Elemental That Faces

One is called to the deathbed of a parent, and one, facing her, does not know what to say. Yet one has to say something.

The other has arrived at the limit—the limit of her life—when she can do nothing more. But she has yet this to do: to die. It is something she has to do, alone, and without any experience to appeal to, any means or resources. It is something she, nevertheless, has to do and will do well or badly, bravely or in collapse, resolutely or cowering. She has always known she will have to do this, has often thought of it, has often willed to die the one way or the other. For every time she did something bravely, or coward-ly, it was an anticipation of this final confrontation. Aristotle, who wrote the first treatise in the West on rational ethics, listed courage first of all the virtues. It is not simply first on the list of equivalent virtues; it is the tran-scendental virtue, the condition for the possibility of all the virtues. For no one can be truthful, or magnanimous, or a friend, or even congenial in conversation, without courage. And every courage is an act done in risk: of one's reputation, of one's job, of one's possessions, of one's life.

And you, called upon to be there when the other is at the limit, and also at the origin, of the virtues, the powers, that a life can have, find yourself at the limit of the powers of language.

The nurses say, "I am so glad you have come!" They know you can do, must do, something they cannot do—say something to the dying one. What can one say? Anything one tries to say sounds vacuous and absurd in one's mouth. It seems to you that the problem is not simply that you do not have the skills in speaking or that you cannot come up with the right things to say because you have no experience in this kind of situation, but that language itself does not have the powers. There is not, in the words and the combinatory possibilities of language, the power to say what has to be said. Yet you have to be there, and you have to say something. You have never been more clear about anything. There are those who do not go, to the bedside of the dying one, demoralized by the terrible impotence of language to say anything. It seems to them that, in their speechlessness, they are carried away already into the region of death and silence with the other. But if you somehow find the courage to go, you are sure you have to be there and have to say something. What is imperative is that you be there and speak; what you say, in the end, hardly matters. You end up saying anything—"It'll be alright, Mom"—which you know is a stupid thing to say, even an insult to her intelligence; she knows she is dying and is more brave than you. She does not reproach you for what you said; in the end it doesn't matter, what was imperative was only that you say something, anything. That your hand and your voice extend to her in accompaniment to the nowhere she is drifting on to, that the warmth and the tone of your voice come to her as her own breath gives way, and that the light of your eyes meet hers that are turned to where there is nothing to see.

Everyone has known such a situation in which the rift between the saying and the said opens up. A situation in which the saying, essential and imperative, separates from the said, which somehow it no longer orders and hardly requires.

In the rational community the other situation is the normal one—that where what is said is the essential and the saying inessential, that where what is imperative is only that whoever speaks, he say *this*.

Such is the situation when there is not simply, as in every community, a common stock of observations, maxims for action, and beliefs that are picked up from others and passed on to others. The rational community produces, and is produced by, a common discourse in a much stronger sense. The insights of individuals are formulated in universal categories, such that they are detached from the here-now index of the one who first formulated them. Discourse sets out to supply a reason, that is, a more general formulation, an empirical law or a practical maxim, from which the observations and practices could be deduced. Establishing the empirical laws and practical principles distributes the insights of individuals to all. And then one sets out to supply a reason for the reason—the theory from which the laws and the principle from which the maxims could be deduced. These function to contest the validity of all statements that attest to simply individual observations and beliefs. The common discourse is not simply an accumulation of information and beliefs and maxims, but a rational system in which, ideally, everything that is said implicates the laws and theories of rational discourse. Then, when any rational agent speaks, he speaks as a representative of the common discourse. The law he formulates for his own understanding and practice legislates for the discourse of everyone, not because of any force or authority in his particular voice, but because the consistency and the coherence, the cogency, of the integrally one rational discourse imposes this statement.

When one goes to someone and asks him to speak, the imperative one lays on him is an imperative that he govern his speech with the imperative that regulates the common discourse and makes it rational. One goes to the doctor, the veterinarian, or the electrician, and one first assures oneself that he really speaks as a representative of the common discourse of rational culture. You ask, discreetly, a few questions: Doctor, what about this Japanese research I read about last week on pacemakers? Doctor, I just read this article about leukemia in cats and thought to come to ask you about my Persian, Simone, who seems to be ailing. Sir, I read about these new halogen lights; do you think they might be bad for the eyes, like the old fluorescent lights? What you are doing is checking out whether the person you are consulting might not be an eccentric—an electrician who does not keep up with knowledge in his field, a veterinarian who has his own theory about viruses that is incompatible with the general theories of today's biology. What there is to be said is in the literature available in the public libraries; one is only asking him to efficiently speak as the spokesman for what one could oneself discover in the literature.

There is something to be said. In principle, there is, in the common discourse of rational culture, something that has to be said, even if it is that the current state of science does not know the answer to the question you formulated—because the cancer is in the bile duct in the midst of a tangle of vital organs and cannot be removed by surgical incision with today's instruments, because testing for eye damage from halogen lamps will require a few years and they have just come into production last year.

When one speaks to the doctor, the veterinarian, or the electrician, one speaks as a representative of the common rational discourse. One does not speak to the oncologist about the obscure intuition of fate in the individual circumstances of one's life one has long felt through only inward premonitions. One does not speak to one's veterinarian as a sentimental person who needs this cat as a child substitute. One might, to be sure, when outside in the hall making out the check, say to him, with a foolish smile, Doctor see what you can do with this cat, I love him like my own baby. The doctor will smile indulgently, and assure you he will do whatever science can do.

Speaking as a representative of the common discourse of rational culture is what we call serious speech. The seriousness in it is the weight of the rational imperative that determines what is to be said. Students demand of their teachers that they formulate, without eccentricities, the state of the art of their particular disciplines; one expects that what one learns in the sciences, in the humanities, and in the technologies will implicate the universal principles of the rational integration of knowledge. The vocalization of what has to be said in this particular voice, by this particular speaker, is inessential; the very saying is inessential, since what has to be said exists in the literature in the public libraries, or if not, is implicated already in the governing categories, theories, and methods of rational discourse.

We also indulge in eccentricities of discourse—our doctor inquires after our golf game; our veterinarian smiles indulgently over our neurotic sentimentality. That is part, no doubt, of the pleasure of speaking in a community—the eccentric tropes we put in our professional rhetoric, the odd metaphors and far-fetched adjectives we attach to the operative nouns, the sexual metaphors we indulge in, with which we fabricate a public ego out of eccentricities. We do not take all that very seriously, nor do we take it to be imperative.

The limit-situation we invoked—when one of the community is departing from among us, when someone is at the end of his or her life—is also a situation in which we who go to their side, who *have* to go to their side, find ourselves at the limit of speech. This is not where the necessity of language ends in silence, but where it is no longer what has to be said that is the essential, and the saying and the one that says inessential: now you find you have to be there and have to speak. You have to say something—something that language cannot say, something that is not in the resources of common discourse to be able to say, and something that is, in the end, inessential. It is the saying that is imperative: your hand extended to the one who is departing, the light of your eyes meeting the eyes of the other that are turned to where there is nothing to see, and the warmth of your voice brought to her as her own breath gives way. This situation is not only the end of language—the last moment when all we have to say to one another ends in the silence and death of the one to whom it has to be said and in the speechlessness and sobs of the one who has come to say something. It is also the beginning, the beginning of communication.

When we form that closed community that is the community of lovers, we often have the impression that our love does not need words. When people fall in love, they seem to have so much to say to one another, occupying the telephone long into fatigue of the hand to hold it and exhaustion of the ears to listen. One feels a compulsion to formulate the most trivial details of one's day, both as a kind of test—if she really will listen to all this, which nobody at the office would, she really must care for me—and as a rhetoric of seduction, an enterprise of making every detail of one's day into an adventure or an entertainment. But once their love is assured and sealed, they listen to music, watch television, or giggle nonsense. The talk that does go on is serious—she speaks of her professional worries and ambitions and he speaks of household repair problems and of his progress toward becoming a successful scientist or businessman, a representative of science or commerce. This serious talk seems outside their love; nobody thinks you really have to talk to your lover about laboratory or office problems at all.

It is when their love is dying that they feel something else. "You have to say something! About us! I don't want to hear any more about your boss or about what siding to put on the house! We have to talk about us!" You really do have to say something. You. And you have no idea what you can say. Even if you went through this before, when a love you then knew died. You find yourself saying anything—saying stupid things. It doesn't matter—you have to say something.

And then you get the idea that this had happened before—when you started. In a class it did not matter if it was you, or another student, that spoke in the seminar. What was essential was that the matter got discussed. The function of the seminar was that the professor formulate the problem out of the current state of the debate in political philosophy on the question of rights. The students were to formulate objections, alternatives, to the theses now being advanced. Sometimes you knew what was to be said, but let another student say it, because a seminar is not a place for you to be on an ego trip or become the professor's favorite. Then, with the adjacent student, some other relationship began to form—you found you were beginning to be lovers. Then, whenever you were together, you had to say something. What it was hardly mattered; what was essential was that you spoke, that the warmth of your voice accompany her in the uncharted zone of passion outside the classroom in which she was drifting, that the tone of your voice resonate in her languorous throat, and that the light of your eyes meet hers, unfocused on the task and the objectives, gazing toward the erotic darkness.

There are then two entries into communication—the one by which one depersonalizes one's visions and insights, formulates them in the terms of the common rational discourse, and speaks as a representative, a spokesperson, equivalent and interchangeable with others, of what has to be said. The other entry into communication is that in which you find it is you, you saying something, that is essential.

It is the last warm day of the autumn; the mother has to go to the park with her child. She forgets all the letters she has to write and the conference she has to prepare for this weekend; she forgets all her friends. She is totally absorbed in her task. She is seated at the pool, and a rainbow gleams across the fountain in the late-autumn sun. She is pointing to the rainbow in the pool. Her eyes are open wide and gleaming, jubilation trembling the coaxing lines of her mouth. She has to lead his eyes to it. This day. His eyes are too young to be able to see the rainbow in the sky. Next year it will be too late; he will be in kindergarten, with eyes already jaded by the electronic rainbows on television screens; he will have to look at books with pictures associated with the letters of the alphabet. She has to fix the focus of his eyes and teach him to see it. She has to teach him the word: rainbow. Rainbow in the fountain. He has to the learn the word and the wonder. She is wholly concentrated with the difficulty and the urgency of the task. She watches with anxiety and jubilation as the wonder fills his eyes, his eyes becoming wet with laughter, until she sees the rainbow on them.

What is it that speaks in these terminal and inaugural situations? Not the ego as a rational mind, as a representative of universal reason that possesses the a priori categories and the a priori forms of the rational organization of sensory impressions. What speaks is someone in his or her materiality as an earthling; one that breathes, sighs, and vocalizes in the rumble of the city and the murmurs of nature; one whose blood is warm with the warmth of the sun and the ardors of the night. One whose flesh is made of earth—dust that shall return to dust—who stands facing another with the support of the earth rising up in him or her; one whose face is made of light and shadow and whose eyes are made of light and tears.

We speak of aliens in our country, understanding by that people who do not share our language, who do not know the names we use to designate things and resources, who do not understand our laws and our principles of behavior and etiquette, and who therefore do not participate with us in building the work that is our common civilization. We also speak of the aliens that this work can make of those who participate in it; the alienation diagnosed by Marx is the dispossession of the products of one's labor, in which one had invested one's own properties—one's intelligence, one's imagination, one's skills, and the forces of one's muscles.

But there is also another alienation—an alienation from the elements. We go to places not only for the discourse that circulates there—the scientific community assembled there or the writers' colony—but for the sun, for the wide-open skies, for the tropical monsoons or for the dry sparkling air, for the desert or for the ocean. Sometimes when we go, we find ourselves immediately at home and resolve to stay there, even if we have no work there, know no one, and even do not know their language. But in most cases, we have to appeal to others to make ourselves at home. We appeal to the others to help us be at home in the desert, in the rain forest, in the tropics, in the tundra, and in the ocean. And in childhood, and in the strange nocturnal regions of the erotic, and in the shadow of death that advances.

This communication is other than and prior to, and it doubles up our communication as representatives of the rational community. It remains imperative when the other, with whom we had or not did not have a language in common, is departing. This communication that we all know has not been disengaged by our philosophies of language.

While classical epistemology endeavored to inventory the mental operations that identify, distinguish. and relate objects, our philosophies of language have set out to show that these operations are performed in speech acts. The communication by which our own individual field of perception gets integrated with those of others is viewed as the means by which our minds get extended beyond the range of things that our own sense organs can reach, to the world of objects identifiable by all.

While classical epistemology took sensibility to record an unstructured flux of colors, lights, shadows, tones, and pressures, today the phenomenology of perception demonstrates that perception is, from the start, perception of things, structures, contours, paths, and landscapes. The phenomenology of perception isolates the structures and dynamics of perception, both from the physiology of neural conduction and from subsequent cognitive operations. Before we identify something with a word and a concept, it already takes form before our eyes and our exploring hands as a unit or a complex of units. You open a box someone has mailed you, and you see a thing but have no idea what it is or what it is called. You do not just experience retinal imprints on the separate rods and cones of your eyes and pressures in your own fingers. You perceive a thing with its own size and shape and observe its balance, symmetry, colors, solidity, and grain.

Each thing that rises in relief in a sensory field, named or not, has a feedback effect on the subsequent patterns that form in perception. Anthropologist Colin Turnbull tells of taking a pygmy friend to the open savanna, where he saw a distant elephant as the size of a mosquito. Eyes that had learned to see in the depth of the rain forest, where the gaze in every direction had always been blocked within twenty feet by another tree trunk and where the skies had always been splintered by the forest canopy, were not able to see the small figure as a huge elephant at a remote distance.

But the system of objects we identify with our speech acts and relate with rational discourse also has a feedback effect on our perception. Others have directed our vision—with words. We are told how to look and given the names of what to look for. Someone who learns the language of meteorology sees the skies differently than before; someone who learns the names for things of an Amazonian hunting-and-gathering tribe sees the rain forest differently from the Western botanist and biologist.

The phenomenology of perception in recent decades has been much occupied with this feedback phenomenon between perception and the speech acts that identify objects with the taxonomy and grammar of a certain language. Paul Feyerabend argues not only that the languages of the different sciences, and those of different epochs of the same science, are incommensurable, untranslatable into one another, but also that the perceptions of the men of the Middle Ages, India, and the Amazon rain forest are incommensurable. Thomas Kuhn says that every new scientific revolution is not a new conceptual grid with which to view the same layout of nature and of the heavens; it is a Gestalt shift in which a new earth and a new heaven become visible.

These investigations move between the objective language of the rational community and the perception that has things as its objectives. The current phenomenology of perception takes it that when we look, our gaze is always, as Heidegger said, interested and preoccupied; we are on the lookout for something—some objective, tool, trap, or obstacle. The philosophy of language takes it that our natural, prescientific language functions to identify objects, instruments, paths, directions, or procedures, for one another. It envisions only that entry into communication that integrates the range of those things our own sense organs can reach, into the world of objects identifiable by all.

But if it is true that we do not live and act in the objective representation of the universe but in a perceived landscape for which the objective representation of the universe is a map, this perceived landscape is not simply a multiplicity of discrete things distributed at eye's reach. The things we can distinguish and identify in perception are themselves laid out in a clearing full of light, in a region of warmth and an atmosphere in which we can move and therefore explore perceptually, and over a ground that does not extend as another object but as a dimension of support. These nonthings in which things form are what Emmanuel Levinas has thematized as *the elemental*. The phenomenology of perception requires a phenomenology of sensibility—not an understanding of the physiological organs and psychophysiological channels which capture sensations, information-bits, but a recognition of the sensuous element sensibility knows and in which perception establishes some directions and positions some things.

We do not relate to the light, the earth, the air, and the warmth only with our individual sensibility and sensuality. We communicate to one another the light our eyes know, the ground that sustains our postures, and the air and the warmth with which we speak. We face one another as condensations of earth, light, air, and warmth and orient one another in the elemental in a primary communication. We appeal to the others to help us be at home in the alien elements into which we stray: in the drifting and nameless light and warmth of infancy, in the nocturnal depths of the erotic, and in the domain of dying where rational discourse has no longer anything to say. The philosophy of language which determines how things perceived are said and how the saying communicates, requires a phenomenology of the saying that occurs when the one faces the other with the light and warmth and carnal substance of his or her face.

The Pythagorean world of numbers, the Platonic world of forms, and the modern scientific universe of formulas are laid out like maps over the implements and obstacles stationed along the roads of the city and the halls of the constructions of culture, and over the landscape of things at rest, animals roving, plants proliferating, and minerals shifting in the contours of the earth. But the space where the things are encountered is not suspended in the network of geometric dimensions or in the void. It extends in the light, in the warmth, in the atmosphere, and in a clearing stabilized on the supporting element of earth. Light is not, like a thing, explorable from different angles and perspectives; it offers no sides, and it is not approached like we approach the surfaces it illuminates. We find ourselves in the light. It is not a substance, supporting and known through its properties; it is luminosity, not a property of any thing, a free-floating adjective. Warmth is not something we perceive from a distance and apprehend; we find it by immersion. Ground is not, save for astronauts and for the imagination of astronomers, the planet, that is, a spherical substance that can be viewed from the distance once one no longer feels its support. For us earthlings, the ground is pure depth of support, supported by nothing, which supports all things in their places. We know it from within, in the stability of our own axis of posture. The night is not a black surface that stops our sight on the surfaces of our own retinas; our look goes out into the night, which is vast; the night invades, it is within as well as without. The elemental does not extend, like a landscape of things, in horizons which show perception the distant and the future; its presence is full, there by incessant oncoming and without a future we apprehend or project, in gratuitous abundance. The elemental is immemorial; the vibrancy of the light about us dissolves all traces of its own past forms, and the supporting sustenance of the ground is felt present within the stability and agility of our posture which does not retain residues of past support.

Things are found in the elemental. Substances that have contours that contain their properties, they can be apprehended, detached, possessed. One identifies oneself and maintains one's own identity in the midst of things. The elemental which extends no horizons of objectives, which passes into no stock that can be recalled, does not lend itself to appropriation. One cannot make oneself something separate and consolidate oneself by appropriating the light, by making private property and depriving others of the atmosphere, by monopolizing the warmth, by expropriating the things distributed over the ground of their support. The light that invades the eyes depersonalizes and the anonymity of light illuminates in one's eyes; one sees as eyes of flesh see. The forest murmurs and the rumble of the city invade one's ears that hear as hearing hears. The ground that rises up into one's posture depersonalizes; one stands as trees stand, one walks as terrestrial life walks, and one rests as terrestrial life rests, and as rocks and sands rest.

The elemental is not a multiplicity of discrete things successively perceived in their places from vantage points and collated; it is not sensed by a perception which identifies surface patterns. The elemental is sensed in a pure sense of depth, not by an intentional direction of the viewing eye and the grasping hand aiming at objectives, but by a movement of involution. The movement that senses the elemental is not the movement of need or want, the movement of an emptiness that seeks, in the distance, a content; it is a movement of immersion in a plenum. The sense of the elemental senses itself affected with, filled with, and nourished by the elemental in a sensuous accord which the word *enjoyment* designates. The light bathes the eyes as soon as they open and buoys up the movement of sight toward the surfaces and contours of things it illuminates. It does not spread a screen of color before the sight; its own color dissolves to leave the colors of the things it illuminates glow with their own phosphorescence. But it is not neutral or pure transparency; the enjoyment in seeing senses the hue and the sparkle and vibrancy of the light. The eyes that see with the light enjoy seeing; the vitality caressed and sustained by the warmth of the day enjoys being warmed; the gait sustained by the ground enjoys walking and enjoys wandering aimlessly in the sustaining region of the terrestrial. The lungs that breathe in the air enjoy savoring the good air. The ears do not only harken to the signals and the threats; they enjoy hearing the forest murmurs and the rumble of the city. The home is not only a closed vault full of implements and stocked to satisfy needs; it is a zone of tranquillity and warmth and a precinct of intimacy recessed from the uncharted expanses of the alien, recognized in enjoyment. And we enjoy enjoying our homes.

We do not live by labor alone or by bread alone. Life is not a succession of initiatives driven by need and want and aiming at objectives. Life is not the recurrence of need and satisfaction, eating and getting hungry again and drinking and getting thirsty again, in an enterprise that is gradually losing its reserve, in an anxiety repeatedly postponing death. Life is enjoyment. We live in light, in warmth, in liquidity, in radiance, in the rumble of sonority and the music of the spheres, in the intimacy of home and homeland and in the immensities of the exotic.

The sensuous involution in the elemental makes one's eyes luminous, one's hands warm, one's posture supportive, one's voice voluble and spiritual, and one's face ardent. In the involution of enjoyment is generated the gratuitous and excess energies that seek release in exultation. Enjoyment is freedom; in the enjoyment of the radiance of the spring day and the warmth of the ground, we forget our cares, our cravings, and our objectives; we forget our losses and our compensations and we let go of what holds us. Every enjoyment is a death: a dying we know, not as the Heideggerian anxiety knows it—being hurled from being into nothingness—and not as pain knows it—a being mired in oneself and backed up into oneself by the passage into passivity—but as dissolution into the beginningless, endless, and fathomless plenum of the elemental.

It is before the face of another that our enjoyment becomes our own. Our own to give.

To see the other as another sentient agent is to see his postures and movements directed to a range of implements and obstacles about him. To see the other is to see her place as a place I could occupy and the things about her as harboring possibilities that are open to my skills and initiatives. It is to see the other as another one like I am, equivalent to and interchangeable with me. It is the sense of the death awaiting me that circumscribes the range of possibilities ahead of me. To see the other as one who has his own tasks and potentialities is to sense another death circumscribing the field of possibilities ahead of him.

But the other turns to me, empty-handed, from across that wall of death. She appeals to the skills and resources of my hands. Heidegger calls inauthentic, inauthentifying, the solicitude with which I substitute my skills for his and take over his tasks for him. What the other asks is not for this disburdening, this displacement from her own tasks. She asks of my hands the diagram of the operations her hands seek to perform, and he asks the assistance of my forces, lest his be wanting. But he or she appeals first for terrestrial support, the support that my stand on the earth has to give. Robinson Crusoe, in Michel Tournier's novel *Friday*, writes, "I know now that the very earth beneath my feet needs to be trodden by feet other than mine if I am to be sure of its substance." Peter Mathiessen asks that men of the Himalayas ground him on this mountain where he has come to study the snow leopard; Gertrud Trun asks of the people of the Lacandon rain forest that they ground her in Chiapas where she has come to photograph the butterflies and the orchids of the forests; George Abramson asks of the men of Africa that they ground him in the savanna where he has come to return the lions to liberty; Che Guevara asks of the men of the Bolivian Andes that they ground him in the rain forests where he has come to combat the dictator. The fatigue, the vertigo, and the homelessness in his or her body appeals for the force of terrestrial support from those whose earthbound bodies have the sense of this earth and this terrain to give. The other turns to the terrestrial support in my stand; if, while extending my skills to her tasks, I do not offer this support to her, she will prefer to work out the ways and the operations on her own, by trial and error.

The hand of the other extended to mine seeks not only the skills in my hand, which is an instrument among others available for his or her own tasks; in the clasped handshake with which we greet one another and set out each to his or her own tasks, each one seeks the warmth of the hand of another—the elemental warmth in which vitality is immersed.

The other, whom I see as a focus of vision open to the surfaces and contours of the landscape open to me too—a different vision that surveys the range of a landscape of possibilities whose relief the black wall of his or her own death circumscribes about him or her—looks at me with the nakedness and vulnerability of his or her eyes. His or her look appeals to the vision in my eyes. But not only for the foresight and hindsight that can chart his or her way for him or her: he or she appeals first for light. In solitude, Robinson Crusoe learns the frightening nakedness of his eyes. He realizes that the eyes of others had extended beyond the narrow radius of things he sees, fields of things already seen or being seen by us; alien eyes extend the map of the visible. His solitude means that these other lights are gone and black night narrows the visible to what he himself actually sees. His eyes cease to function as a light source that circulates among objects that were visible before he came upon them and remain visible on the margin of what he now sees. The colors and the shadows invade his eyes, like opacities inhering in them which the eye can no longer situate outside. His sight becomes a tube where a fragment of the visible abruptly blazes, like a blow struck without warning. When other eyes were there, they kept the light luminous beyond the narrow radius of what is actually visible to him.

When someone's eyes turn to me, it is other light sources they seek, glowing in the light, to extend the depth of light in which he or she circulates. Sometimes, to be sure, the other looks to me to receive from me the image of what my eyes have seen; the other I meet on the Himalayan trek asks of me if I have seen the path to the grand visions that eyes are made to see. But the other's look does not look to my eyes to see there the surfaces and contours of the landscape upon which I hold my look. It first seeks the vivacity and radiance of the light in my eyes, and it seeks the shadows and the darkness my eyes harbor with care. If it does not find them, if it finds only the look of a surveyor recording the topography, it will prefer to look on its own for the radiance and the twilights of the world.

The other turns to me and speaks; he or she asks something of me. Her words, which I understand because they are the words of my own tongue, ask for information and indications. They ask for a response that will be responsible, will give reasons for its reasons and will be a commitment to answer for what it answers. But they first greet me with an appeal for responsiveness. His words seek out a voice voluble and spiritual, whose orders, coherence, and direction are interrupted, of itself, by hesitations, redundancies, and silences, questioning him by questioning itself. In the very explanation and instruction the other seeks, he or she seeks his or her own voice in my silences and my questions. If my voice is not responsive to this quest, he or she will seek in books the answers to his or her perplexities.

The face of the other is a surface upon which the axes and directions of his posture and the intentions of his movements are exposed to me. The face of the other is a surface upon which the forms of her comprehension are expressed to me. The face of the other is a surface of suffering, upon which her sensitivity and susceptibility and her vulnerability and mortality are exposed to me. This surface is made of light and shadows, of carbon compounds, earth; his eyes glisten and move with the liquidity of the elemental; her voice is made of air and warmth. The face of the other is a surface of the elemental—the place where the elemental addresses, appeals and requires, the involution in enjoyment which makes one's own eyes luminous, one's hands warm, one's posture supportive, one's voice voluble and spiritual, and one's face ardent. The face of the other is the place where the elemental surfaces to make demands on the elemental resources in which the enjoyment of my life is immersed.

What the face of the other asks for is not the inauthentic and inauthentifying solicitude with which I substitute my skills for his, take over her tasks for her, view the forms and the landscape for him, formulate the answers to the questions in her stead. He does not seek his or her contentment in the content that will satisfy his needs and wants, which I can supply from my place and my resources and with my skills—the contentment which, when he has been displaced by me and disburdened of his own tasks, will leave him only the weight and death of the inorganic. In seeking the support of my upright stand on the earth, the agile luminousness that shines in my eyes, the warmth in my hands, the ardor in my face, and the spirituality in my breath, the other seeks the pleasure that is enjoyment in, involution and the dying in, the elemental. The other seeks the contact and the accompaniment.

1994

Phantom Equator

The colors, the textures, the resonance, the scents and savors condense into things that induce our postures to center our sensory surfaces upon them and conduct our movements toward them. But the colors also disengage from the things to play off one another. The visible ceases then to be distinctively visual and forms a realm of events and epiphanies unto itself. The sounds depart from the things to link up with other sounds and lead our hearing away from things, and the resonant ceases to be something we listen to and for. The blue of the sky and the green of spring, the tones that announce the symphony, the mossy floor of the night are the entries into and summons to these other realms.

For our sensibility to be saturated by the chromatic, the sonorous, or the tangible is not to retreat from the field of real things and adhere to the surfaces of our own organism. To the contrary, the unattached colors, the rebounding tones, the tangible engulfing our touch draw our whole sensibility into impracticable spaces full and complete in themselves.

At the airport in Lima, our eyes scan the paths, identify the counters and the gates, find the charter line, search the runways for the Cessna, try to identify the pilot. Our eyes guide us as we follow him through a maze of paths in the construction site under the muddy drizzle called *garúa* that will hover over the city for the winter months. Our eyes locate the seat belt, study the instrument panel. The plane takes off across the wet runway, rises into the murky gray fog, and emerges into the sun above. The flight from Lima to Nazca will take two hours. The sunlight spreads out unlimited depths of azure sky. Below, the fog is a powdery blanket that extends unwrinkled on all sides. To the right, below it, there is the invisible featurelessness of the Pacific. Far to the left, the peaks of the Andes push irregularly through the mist to accompany us in the flight with a distant rhythm. The blue radiance above and the white softness below are not the visible features of a landscape but a luminous dream over a world that we have completely lost touch with.

We walk down the paths of the floodplain, the raised mud walls carpeted with the dusty green of the compacted grass. The rice paddies extend on all sides, mirrors of the sky. The ripening rice blur in the breeze into a clear yellow mist suspended over the blue that is not of the water and the drifting white that is no longer that of clouds. The yellow does not materialize the substance of the plant stalks; it spreads in an ether where green shadows flow about it.

We enter the concert hall, locate our seat; we look at the musicians picking up their bows and sticks and reverberating the violin strings and the taut skins of the drums. Our eyes move from one instrument to another in the orchestra pit. Then the music begins, and the tones now disengage from the surfaces upon which they were vibrating and weave into the space between us and the instruments. Our hearing begins another movement, from one tone to the next in a lyrical space that dilates and condenses, expands over a vast horizon, approaches from distances nowise limited by this renaissance salon whose ornate mirrors present on each of its walls only the other walls. This space is complete unto itself and the musical forces, more than tones, do not evoke or depict visible and tangible things, but materialize emergences, events, and destinies inexhaustible in themselves. At the end of the concerto, we look about as though awakening from the caverns of a trance and relocate ourselves in the hall with friends and with refreshments outside.

By day the pavilion in the old Balinese princely residence in which we have taken up lodging offers all its furnishings at once to the glance that surveys its narrow confines; from the covered patio before it, the walled garden exhibits a panorama of flowering trees and meandering brooks with small bamboo-arched bridges offering a path encompassed in one view. Returning by a moonless night, we climb the steps through the gate to make our way through a space reduced to the tangible. The high gate steps have to be measured one by one by the groping foot; they materialize very differently now from when the eyes measured their breadth and height. We have to locate the level of the path below; the indeterminate closes in. For the hand that gropes for the door and bed, these things do not have the simultaneity of all their surfaces and contours they had for vision; their extension and substance form along and adhere to the movement of the touching hand. The tangible does not form into objectives as does the panorama of things at a distance that vision encompasses; it rises in relief in close proximity and across movement. The duration that it takes to delineate their contours loosens the simultaneity through which they were the contours of things, as a melodic pattern of sounds, while it has a more substantial presence, does not have the thinglike unity of the pattern of the written score. We find ourselves in a space made of oppressive presences, petrifications, liquefactions, transubstantiations.

The cooking and sewerage smells of Venice or Chandigarh, in the measure that we get absorbed in them, enclose us in their own swirling and dense space that obscures the spectacle of extending avenues and architectural monuments. The perfumes of a Persian garden introduce us into a drifting and radiating space that dissolves the exiguous garden walls that had confined vision. The damp of the monsoon in the cities of the Ganges, the asphalt heat of the strip cities of the American Southwest in midsummer leave about us the perspectives and distances of the visible and tangible cities as unmoored mirages.

These colors, tones, odors, saturating our sensibility, extending their levels imperatively about us, require not a laborious and task-centered posture but a vitality drifting in a play of phosphorescence, dancing in the moving pathways of melodies, exposing its surfaces to the caresses of the moss, the tropical damp, wholly lungs in the midst of scents rising at high noon or sliding through the sultry night. They command us to reconstitute our bodies as ecstatic, melodic, carnal, and no longer competent bodies.

Painters, musicians, *haute-cuisiniers*, and perfumers will represent the visual, the sonorous, the gustatory, and the olfactory in layouts that do not simply represent, as signs, the things. Aesthetic theory will disengage the laws that govern the effects colors and lines, tones, savors, or odors have on one another. An artist does not admit that his representation was produced by a decomposition of his sensory integrity: artists do not believe that textures or tones are so much raw material upon which they depict simply a form they have a priori programmed in their own reason. The colors on a Tibetan *tang'ka*, the concertos of Bartók have a consistency and coherence that the artist came upon by following the ordination with which colors and tones are given. If an artist can disengage himself from the practicable fields to devote himself so exclusively to colors and tones, it is because he finds himself receptive to an imperative he finds in the colors, that their own ordinance be seen, or in the tones, that their own ordinance be heard.[1] If she can take her work seriously, it is because she is sure that not only for her but for the others also, to be a sensitive organism is not only to be a prehensile system wired to grasp the carpentry of a practicable field but an organ that follows the summons of colors into another domain, that follows music into a sovereign order.

We might hesitate to call science the theoretical elaborations with which aestheticians, musicologists, acoustics researchers, perfumers, and wine tasters represent their knowledge. It is true that their observations are not objectifying, the phenomena they observe they do not locate on the coordinates of empty geometric space and linear time, simultaneity is not for them defined by the general relativity theory of physics, the regions they circumscribe and organize by correlations are not translatable into the region of the physics of vibratory events. But their knowledge has its own rigor, its controls, and its concepts, and, by extending the isolating method of scientific observation of entities into an isolation of fields of observation, it advances toward the state of reliable empirical knowledge by fragmenting further the domain of science in our time.

Depths of the Night

Sleep is not coma; our sleeping sensibility retains enough contact with the levels of the ground, the warmth, the damp, the tangible to awaken to them and locate on them the paths strewn with things to which one awakens.[2] Like the shadows which set forth the contours of things, the terrestrial night maintains our tasks for us and lays them out under the light for us again when we will have recovered our competence.

But sleep is not only commanded by the imperative of the day, which requires our restored competence exhausted by its tasks. To go to sleep is to enter through the corridors of the terrestrial night into a night not mapped by the stars and where we see with closed eyes visions that beckon to our sleeping sensibility.

The great black bird which hovers, falls, and becomes a handful of ash in the dream does not hover and fall in physical space; it rises and falls in directions extended, Maurice Merleau-Ponty says, by the tide of our respiratory and vital rhythms, by the aspiration of our sexual desire.[3] Yet this unpracticable space is not an inner psychic space; it is the great black bird which exists in flight, and not the emptiness of our craving, that establishes the levels of the space of dreams.

The space of dreams is described negatively as a space where distance does not separate the identities nor the causality of forms, which can instantly metamorphose, a space where surrounding sites do not maintain a thickness of lateral sides to the bird or the facade of a temple.[4] The hold the dream image has on the dreamer is described subjectively as fascination rather than obedience. But the oneiric apparition positively extends its own connections and lines of depth and remoteness. It is not simply an afterimage or a fragment of things found in the practicable layout of the day; its shape and its traits are strange. They reveal an alien depth and an enigmatic significance.

The psychoanalytic interpretation of dreams willfully identifying each oneiric man, woman, or monster with ourselves only collapses this alien depth onto the banal map of our daytime affairs. A more sophisticated psychoanalysis projects it onto the space of cosmic or private myths. Those who have instead recorded these nonterrestrial apparitions and metamorphoses without the bullheaded intent to adjust some prosaic practical or social incompetency in themselves have discovered the interpretations all leave behind the essential, the uncanny sense of the apparition, the unexemplary plot of events. They have recorded epics which project only to further epics without resolution. The oneiric apparitions summon our sensibility to the night beyond the protective terrestrial night, a night of unlimited disquietude.

The imperative of the night reveals its force not only when one follows down the corridors of the night not horizontal to the day but in depth, but also in the night that looms in the high noon of the environment. These are moments when we do not see things as having insides which consist of more visible things, destined to take form in the light, such that eventually all the content of things extends as a succession of phenomenal profiles— moments when we sense the beginningless, endless presence of night in them that remains while all the phenomenal profiles our initiatives pull out of things file out and pass as an inconsistent phosphorescence. There are times when the panorama of paths and tasks that summon with their urgencies appears as a screen behind which an immensity without tasks summons us to an assignation to which we will arrive divested of our competence and our I.[5] Examining the fossil of a trilobite in full daylight, there comes a moment when it is this night we pass into. Beneath the well-lit room and garden, we sense the night in the floorboards, in the core of the earth.

The nocturnal passions, the compulsions of antiheroes and underground men, the materialists whose passion is not for the terrestrial or the subatomic, the *bhikkus* immobilized in a heightened sensibility tuned to nirvana, the Orphic initiations—are they not misunderstood as longings for another world in which civic roles are inverted, in which king is slave and slave is king, man is woman and woman is man, human is goat and goat is human? Are they not passions destined for the night itself, obedience to the force of an imperative that holds us more imperatively than the transitory imperative of the practicable fields? How faithfully Isabelle Eberhardt wrote of these oblivion seekers, was herself one of these seekers after the night that awaits no day to come![6]

Unpracticable Spaces

Phantasms, visions, erotic obsessions, and hallucinations link up in constellations. They open abyssal corridors where distant forces synchronize and induce transformations in one another, where nearby forms and events disintegrate or metamorphose on contact.

A schizophrenic patient, in the mountains, stops before a landscape. After a short time he feels a threat hanging over him. There arises within him a special interest in everything surrounding him, as if a question were being put to him from outside to which he could find no answer. Suddenly the landscape is snatched away from him by some alien force. It is as if a second sky, black and boundless, were penetrating the blue sky of evening. This new sky is empty, "subtle, invisible and terrifying." Sometimes it moves in the autumn landscape and at other times the landscape too moves. Meanwhile, says the patient, "a question is being constantly put to me; it is, as it were, an order either to rest or die, or else to push on further."[7]

The caricatures and masks that absorb the sensibility of the dreamer, like the color that saturates our eyes, inaugurate a level which disengages from the verticality of a world upright before the upright posture to delineate another direction and directive. The schizophrenic who looks out into the garden which the others see and sees there a stranger the others do not see, who hears voices where no one is seen speaking, enters another space which shows through the practicable space, undermines it, and summons him to push on further. There are multiple spaces extending their own latitudes, for which the practicable world of things fixes no equator. There are journeys from which we do not return enriched, with a booty of spices and gold, souvenirs and snapshots. There are voyages to which we are summoned from which we do not return.

The One-World Hypothesis

The phantasmal theaters of dreams, hallucinations, erotic and psychedelic visions do not give themselves out as private and fabricated spaces made of distortions and errors. This, Merleau-Ponty explains, is because the real and common world does not give true things in a system we understand. There is absolute certainty of the world in general, because it is only by invoking the coherence and consistency of the world that we revoke into doubt any particular appearance, and do so by replacing it with another appearance drawn from the reservoir of the world, and because any other realm of entities, whether that of the scientific representation of the universe or any metaphysical or theological representation of ultimate reality, derives the entities it admits from observations and verifies them by soundings in the world of perception, and therefore could not be employed to relativize the belief in the reality of the world we perceive.[8] But there is no absolute certainty of anything in particular, because a thing is the termination of an indefinite exploration, a task, and exists in the interrogative mode. The world "takes in without discrimination real objects on the one hand and individual and momentary phantasms on the other—because it is an individual which embraces everything and not a collection of objects linked by causal relations. To have hallucinations and more generally to imagine is to exploit this tolerance on the part of the antepredicative world, and our bewildering proximity to the whole of being in syncretic experience."[9]

For Merleau-Ponty, the multiplicity of realms each with its own ordinance does not impugn the primacy of praktognostic perception or confound the normative force of the practicable world. "I never wholly live in varieties of human space, but am always ultimately rooted in a natural and non-human space" (293). The images, doubles, masks, caricatures, phantasms that populate multiple unpracticable fields owe their presence to the grain of the sensible made contact with in perceptual prehension. "Even if there is perception of what is desired through desire, loved through love, hated through hate, it always forms round a sensible nucleus, however small, and it is in the sensible that its verification and its fullness are found" (ibid.). "As I walk across the Place de la Concorde, and think of myself as totally caught up in the city of Paris, I can rest my eyes on one stone of the Tuileries wall, the Square disappears and there is then nothing but the stone entirely without history; I can, furthermore, allow my gaze to be absorbed by this yellowish, gritty surface, and then there is no longer even a stone there, but merely the play of light upon an indefinite substance" (ibid.). The perceptible things show through their dream-doubles, hallucinatory caricatures, and erotic mists, as the canvas shows through the painted landscape, the crumbling cement under the building, or the tiring actor under the dramatic character. And "human spaces present themselves as built on the basis of natural space" (294); this is true of spaces explored in dreams or hallucinations or erotic obsessions, as it is true of the all-encompassing metric space in which the scientist elaborates his representation of reality. "The sun 'rises' for the scientist in the same way as it does for the uneducated person, and our scientific representations of the solar system remain matters of hearsay, like lunar landscapes, and we never believe in them in the sense in which we believe in the sunrise" (344).

Not only does our dreaming consciousness have no access to entities save the awakened perception (or the peripheral sensibility that never fully sleeps and continues to be sensitive to the levels and sensorial regions of the world), and has nothing but drifting fragments of perceived things to materialize in the vital and erotic dimensions in whose tides they rise and fall, but, Merleau-Ponty writes, the dream-field itself owes its existence to the waking state that recalls it. "During the dream itself, we do not leave the world behind: the dream-space is segregated from the space of clear thinking, but it uses all the latter's articulations; the world obsesses us even during sleep, and it is about the world that we dream." "Though it is indeed from the dreamer that I was last night that I require an account of the dream, the dreamer himself offers no account, and the person who does so is awake. Bereft of the waking state, dreams would be no more than instantaneous modulations, and so would not even exist for us" (293).[10]

The carnal physiognomy to which the eroticized perception is directed is indeed different from the physical shape of another as envisioned in a practical perception and coded by pragmatic and polite forms of social interaction. The voluptuous tones that give it its sultry density are different from the colors that make its texture and pliancy visible to a perception that synergistically focuses in on it. But it is the perceptible anatomy of the other that anchors the voluptuous phantasm for concupiscent longing.

Dreams, hallucinations, erotic obsessions, and psychedelic intuitions "endeavour to build a private domain out of fragments of the macrocosm, . . . the most advanced states of melancholia, in which the patient settles in the realm of death, and so to speak, takes up his abode there, still make use of the structures of being in the world, and borrow from it an element of being indispensable to its own denial" (ibid.).

The field of real things then admits monocular images, reflections, mirages, noises, and fleeting tactile impressions, which the deviant consciousness elaborates into another space.

The practicable field of perception is for Merleau-Ponty the one world and it contains the corridors that dreams, hallucinations, erotic and psychedelic phantasms open in it, as the dimensions of the canvas contain the dimensions of the scene painted on it, even though there is not one universal set of geometrical dimensions upon which the spaces opened in dreams and in erotic obsessions can be measured. These spaces are absorbed into the geography of the practicable world, "as the double images merge into one thing, when my finger stops pressing upon my eyeball" (329).

> I perceive everything that is part of my environment, and my environment includes "everything of which the existence or non-existence, the nature or modification counts in practice for me": the storm which has not yet broken, whose signs I could not even list and which I cannot even forecast, but for which I am "worked up" and prepared—the periphery of the visual field which the hysterical subject does not expressly grasp, but which nevertheless co-determines his movement and orientation—the respect of other men, or that loyal friendship which I take for granted, but which are none the less there for me, since they leave me morally speaking in mid-air when I am deprived of them. (321)
>
> The world remains the same world throughout my life, because it is that permanent being within which I make all corrections to my knowledge, a world which in its unity remains unaffected by these corrections, and

the self-evidence of which attracts my activity toward the truth through appearance and error. . . . I may be mistaken, and need to rearrange my certainties, and reject the being to which my illusions give rise, but I do not for a moment doubt that in themselves things have been compatible and compossible, because from the very start I am in communication with one being, and one only, a vast individual from which my own experiences are taken, and which persists on the horizon of my life as the distant roar of a great city provides the background to everything we do in it. (327–28)

And since the unity of the world is not that of an intelligible system, not grasped in synthetic concepts and principles, but that of a style (as we recognize the style of a city while all the things in it are rearranged and replaced), it is the style in our perception, the postural schema with which we integrate our sensory-motor exposure to it, that prehends it. The world which is one individual that encompasses everything is the practicable world, and if it is not there as a given but as an imperative, it is an imperative that our sensibility be a praktognosis, and that we maintain ourselves integrally as practical organisms.

Multiple Realms

But is it true that the unpracticable spaces are constructed with fragments of real things lifted off them and elaborated into a private space by the deviant consciousness? Is it not true that the things themselves engender, along with their graspable contours, images of their presence in multiple locations and in impracticable spaces? It is the thing that produces the monocular images of itself on our retinas, the pool that makes itself visible on the sun-streaked cypresses. But is it the graspable substance of things that engenders these apparitions?

Does natural perception believe it is getting closer to the shark in discerning the viscous matter of its flesh under its power, its ferocity, its grace, its dominion in the sea as old as and uncontested through three ice ages? What kind of primacy would the practical perception have that sees goals and the paths and means to reach them in the cobblestone lanes and moss-covered houses of the medieval town? Would not the vision that penetrates to the practicable layout of the things itself derive from the reverie that lets the tones and the rhythms of the tile roofs and amber street lamps lift off in another wave of duration, that of the immemorial toil and repose, legends and festivity that slumber in its trodden paths and shrines worn smooth by innumerable reverent hands?

The gilt door of the thatched-roofed Balinese princely house presents simultaneously its domesticity, as a wooden door, and its glory. The wood is humble and terrestrial by reason of the gilt it displays; the gilt is glorious because it is the splendor brought to wood. The home is princely because it is clay bricks, exposed bamboo rafters, from the terrestrial sources of the land, that are carved and gilded to enshrine the luster of the civilization that presides over the island of Bali risen out of the sea in volcanic eruptions and sacred favor.

Does the practical focus that envisions someone's anatomy as a prehendable substance really have ontological primacy over the erotogenic surface, the voluptuous mirages that refract our gaze turned to strangers? Is the reality in things that which takes hold of and is taken hold of by the synergistic mobilizations of our practical postures? Are their sensuous density and substance that resist the manipulative hand and invite the caress, their twilight colors that seduce and soften the focus of the gaze and communicate with the sensuality of our organism rather than with its postural axis, in some way derivative? Is not to exist as a sector of the geographic space laid out in perspective simultaneously to exist as a landscape of reverie? The nocturnal trees that rub their twiggy hands and gesticulate in monstrous gestures we so readily recognize in old lithographs—have we not always seen the trees with these caricatural versions of themselves?

A thing reduced to its simple location in a here-now instant of presence is not real and is not perceivable, Merleau-Ponty says; a thing is real by presenting itself in a wave of transcendence, sending echoes and simulacra of itself back into the past and into the future, projecting itself in us as a diagram of our own forces. A thing is, we argue, by engendering images of itself, reflections, shadows, masks, caricatures of itself. Things are not reduced to their reality by being reduced to facts; the "pure facts" of empirical observation are abstracts of intersecting scientific theories, logics, and effects of technological engineering. But things are also not reduced to their reality by being perceived in their practicable format. It is because they engender carnal, caricatural images of their characteristics, turn phosphorescent facades on the levels and horizons of reality, that they also engender a practicable format. Reality is in this parturition.

The things exist in a movement which does not only project their integral essences down the tracks of practicable reality; across a wave of duration they refract off masks, veils, simulacra, shadows, and omens. The monocular images, phantasms, lures, and forms made of shadows make the things visible and are the visibility the things engender. The surfaces of things are not more real than their facades; the reality that engenders the phantasm is engendered by it.

Merleau-Ponty puts the inclination to obey the night itself, to let go of the general framework of a practicable nature, on the side of the abnormal and the incompetence of neurotics: "The distress felt by neuropaths in the night is caused by the fact that it brings home to us our contingency, the uncaused and tireless impulses which drive us to seek an anchorage and to surmount ourselves in things, without any guarantee that we shall always find them" (283–84). But is not the neuropathic distress instead produced by the willful effort to bring back a practicable world when it is the night that summons?

No dream, hallucination, erotic obsession, or psychedelic trip knows itself as the personal construction the philosophical formula "private domain put together out of fragments of the macrocosm" explains it to be. The artist who paints a clustering of colors that has its own consistency and does not disintegrate before our eyes as so many patches of paint on the surface of the canvas, the composer who arranges sounds in a consonance or dissonance that holds together has no consciousness of being a demiurge who imposes form on amorphous material by an a priori decree of the will. The painter, the dreamer, and the libidinous organism find themselves pushed further on by the urgencies by which the dreams, the doubles, the shadows, and resonances materialize an ordinance that commands him or her. Does not everyone who follows his dream, his erotic obsession, his vision, the beat and cadences of his music find that he constructs representations of his dreams, his erotic field, and his artistic visions only by subjecting himself to the fields in which they unfold as to imperatives? No one makes himself a dreamer or a visionary; those we admire—perhaps everyone we admire—are men and women who came upon a field imperative for them, the field of a visionary imperative, a musical imperative, a nocturnal imperative, a passionate imperative.

As our steps advance, the visible domain laid out as a geographic projection in which things are distributed in lines of perspective turns into a landscape made of the voluptuous contours and hollows of things and of the waves and rain that caress, of mossy forests and nocturnal fragrances that fondle our surfaces and penetrate our orifices. The night beyond night summons the insomniac to an abyss that does not lead to the day and its tasks. The unpracticable spaces of visions, of murmurs and melodies in which no one signals another, of the palpable and the impalpable that caress and the night that engulfs, and the practicable held of objects-objectives are disjoint expanses come upon along the zigzag itinerary of our days and nights. The space of the purely chromatic, the range of harmonies and dissonances, the labyrinth of voluptuous contours and seductive hollows, the ether of obsessions and phantasms, and the vistas of the essentially nomadic vital space that shows through the grid of the common coordinates—these are not private constructions built out of fragments of the macrocosm, disconnected mirages that ill-focused eyes send to drift over the equator of the practicable field of substantial and graspable things. The practicable field of things is itself suspended within their latitudes. They are not private constructions, which like the invisible and impalpable space in which the community of scientists elaborates a representation of the field given in perception exist only by hearsay, spaces we do not believe in and cannot inhabit, spaces contained within us. Each is a realm of exteriority not reducible to our representations, an exteriority that exists with the exteriority of an imperative. The nomad is summoned not by distant things fixed on one equator, but by multiple spaces, multiple ordinances; the equator is itself phantomal.

1998

Violations

What proves to me that the figures I see in the street outside my window are not hats and coats covering robots driven by springs is the fact that, taking the sounds they make to be intended as words, I find a coherent meaning in them. I verify my impression by asking the speaker if this is what he meant. For me, whatever utters a coherent set of words, and further sets of words coherent with that set, is someone with a mind like my own.

But isn't a knowledge of other minds required before language can function at all? The words are only sounds in the air unless we take them as uttered meaningfully by someone, just as marks on paper cease to be stains, and marks on rocks cease to be the effects of erosion when we take them to have been intended by someone to designate something to someone else.

> Words deny and lie. Language is so essentially a power of contradiction that, instead of saying that language is the way we recognize mental beings, should we not rather say that language is the way what others have in their minds can always be falsified?

We recognize as another human someone with whom we can speak; those whose tongue we do not or cannot learn are babblers and barbarians. But conversation with someone whose tongue we understand comes to an end when that person makes truth claims based on his or her tribal ruler, ancestor, or deity.

Something new dawned in the history of the human species, Edmund Husserl wrote, when men in Athens, conversing with foreigners, began giving reasons for the ways of Athenians. Until then, to the questions of foreigners—Why do you think as you do, do as you do?—the answers had been: Because our fathers, who founded our clan, nation, city, have taught us to do thus. Because our gods have said this. The men called philosophers set out to give answers that those who did not share those ancestors, who did not have the totem gods of the Athenians, could accept, reasons that just anyone, anywhere, with insight could accept. The practice of giving, and demanding, reasons, reasons that anyone with insight would endorse, breaks through the particularities of languages, traditions, and customs that not only shape the way in which what we know is formulated but that shape our very perception of things. This new discourse gives reasons for each of its assertions and submits each of its reasons to judgment. It admits anyone endowed with insight as its judge. It invokes, Husserl said, the idea of humanity—universal humanity, rational humanity.

> But as scientific discourse extends ever further the range of things for which it supplies reasons, the reasons supporting assertions about microscopic and macroscopic entities become ever more complex, and a proportionally ever smaller part of it is accessible in the discourse of any scientist or man in the street. We call ourselves rational when we can justify a small part of our discourse with reasons, but those reasons are reasons only because they can be justified by verified observations, laws, and theories which we assume others could supply. Our rationality functions to castigate as backwardness, mythic, and fanciful the discourse of others we sense to be at variance with that small part of our discourse we can justify with reasons—reasons whose justification we take largely on faith. Our rationality invokes the notion of universal humanity only to exclude many of our interlocutors from it.

How eccentric of Hegel to have imagined that when we go to encounter others, it is recognition we demand, recognition of the freedom and self-consciousness of the ego, confirmation, attestation, certification of our identity!

Is it not instead the others who demand that we identify ourselves? "Last week you said you would…." "But you are now a mother…." "But you just said that…." "How is your dissertation coming along?" "You said you loved me…." Our interlocutors seek coherence, a line of intelligibility in the phases and states of our duration. They seek to link up our past with the present, to know the future as what we say now commits us to.

When we respond to these demands, our words are so many positions, postures, we take before this witness. "Yes, last week I said I would, but here is what happened that made me realize we should not do that." "Yes, I am now a mother, but that does not mean I am giving up my course work at the university." "I said that, but what I meant was…."

How burdensome, how tedious, how vacuous it is to have to maintain all this identity, all this coherence, all this deployment of reciprocal recognition! In fact we get facetious. "Did I say I would last week? I forgot." "Yeah, now I'm Doctor Sweeney. But doctors in English literature don't make house calls, and most of our patients are dead." "Sure I said I loved you; otherwise you would not have written my term paper for me."

Morality takes thought and action to be polarized by the notions of good and evil. It assumes that we act in order to maintain, secure, or acquire what we take to be a good. Goods, as the goals and results of actions, are durable goods; they must at least endure the time it takes us to reach or take possession of them. And they should contribute to the conservation and preservation of those who acquire them.

Morality enjoins us to subordinate our forces to that good; the one who acts makes his or her organs and faculties serve to acquire something. The action narrows down and focuses our forces.

The violation of the existence and natures of things, of oneself, or of others is evil. Disrespect encroaches upon the space of others, and alters or empties their nature. Respect is respect for the limits, the boundaries, the space of others, and thus for their natures. Morally good action designates the active respect for others, for things, and also for ourselves.

Sometimes people seem to have found the formula early in life and they apply it with equanimity until they die: they are genial, affable, helpful. Others find the method is good sense: before any problem, their own or that of another, they appraise the issue, survey the alternatives, select the best one, and do not worry over it if, as often happens, the best available decision does not work. Does not the majority of people with whom we converse fall into these categories—the kind ones and the sensible ones? Trivializing, leveling kindness. Shallow, self-justifying sensibleness.

Respect for the other, for the sincerity, honesty, and integrity of the other, is said to be essential in the practice of discourse. There is no conversation, it is alleged, unless we, first, take what the other says to express the integral application of her sensory and mental powers to what she has seen and experienced, and, second, try to see what is true in what she says. Without abandoning our liberal concern for the plight of unwed mothers and sick immigrants, we must try to see the valid point the conservative is making.

It would seem that respect which initiates conversation is real only at the far end of conversation, when we have come not only to understand the informative content of what our interlocutor has said but have also come to understand the speaker's background, priorities, and competence.

Extending this model of conversation, as moral and altruistic, one constructs a moral formula for sexual intercourse. Violence and pain must be excluded. A force hurled at us becomes violence when it violates our inner space, when it violates our integrity and what we call our person. We respect the physical integrity of another by respecting her or his person, and we do that by respecting what she or he says. Sexual intercourse must be conducted by lucid conversation, where the integrity of each is affirmed.

What is awkward in this morality is that we ourselves, in conversation, do not want to be treated in this moral way. We went to Tibet to be uplifted and were deeply troubled. After returning, our head is still spinning, and we meet some stranger who, we hope, was there longer and saw more deeply than we did. We tell him, I went to the Potala, to the gompas, and I walked through room after room crammed with huge gold- and jewel-encrusted statues almost all alike, down corridor after corridor frescoed with intricate paintings of religious scenes that duplicated one another endlessly; I saw stupas covered with two tons of gold; I saw thousands of scroll paintings. This is supposed to be Buddhism, which teaches that everything we can see and touch is illusory, teaches that desire for such things is suffering and that blessedness comes through a complete liberation from attachment not only to all things we can see and touch but to this world and this life itself! I felt like Jan Hus in the palaces of the Vatican. If our interlocutor takes it to be paramount to show respect for our honesty and sincerity, takes what we say to contain a truth, then the conversation is nothing to us. What we are on the lookout for is someone who can contest not only what we say but what we saw and felt and experienced. Who can show us a totally different way to look at the wealth, the superfluous, unproductive art treasures of the monasteries, and the life of those professed Buddhists. Who can show us the stupidity in our thinking, who can send us back to really look. If we do not find such a one in person, we search for him in the books about Tibet.

It happens that we come upon someone who does not simply expose to us our obtuseness and stupidity and send us back to the monastery to look again, but exposes also his own mortifications, humiliations, and wounds. Who shows us that after a year, after ten years in a monastery, the art treasures of the monastery leave him devastated, emptied. The divestment, deprivation, and abnegation of the monks, now that he has tried to join them, to measure his strengths and determination to theirs, have left him abashed, mystified. When we meet such a person, perhaps the conversation does not serve us, is not useful for communicating more intensely with Tibet and its monasteries. But the conversation, in which each does not recognize himself in what he is saying, is a summit, a vortex, and a black hole of intensity.

And what else is erotic craving but a craving to be violated? In voluptuous turmoil, we are left not simply wounded, but shattered. The violent emotions that are aroused, that sense the obscenity in anguish, that push on in a momentum that can no longer derail or control itself, sense also the exultation of risking oneself, of plunging into the danger zone, of expending our forces at a loss.

Is it not in nonsense and indecency—in laughter and in erotic excitement—that we, rather than recognize, re-cognize, one another, find ourselves transparent to one another? And is it not this transparency that precedes the assumption in language that I am addressing someone with a mind like my own?

We see whoever laughs as one like us—even if we do not see what he or she is laughing at, do not see what is funny. And we are drawn to anyone who laughs by a primary movement of sensibility. Human interattraction is not at bottom a fearful and cautious alliance for purposes of mutual defense and cooperation in work.

You have for hand baggage a double paper shopping bag with an old sweatshirt stuffed on top. You are in the airport in Sendai, in the worn and crumpled clothing Americans often wear for long trips, even in other countries. It is the day after sarin gas was released in the Tokyo subway. You notice some Japanese turning furtive, wary glances at you. There are no seats; you push to the back of the room and sit against the back wall, trying to be invisible. A Buddhist priest comes into the hall, his simple white and black robes and sandals emanating confident assurance, impeccably clean. His serene demeanor seems fixed on timeless things. He does not see your leg stretched out on the floor, trips, catches hold of a bystander, but as he does so two bottles of Chivas Regal fall from his robes and smash on the floor soaking you in an alcoholic splash. The crash, but even more the spreading smell, strange for a waiting hall in an airport, freeze the bystanders in a panic. Then laughter breaks out, spreading wider as people get up to see what is going on. Laughter rises and falls and rises again as eyes meet eyes. The priest himself and you are laughing when your eyes meet.

In each individual, the laughter is now no longer pleasure over the unexpected, the incongruous, but pleasure over the dissolution of boundaries, of clothing, of the body armor of strangers in an airport, pleasure over the evident pleasure of others. It makes the object or event that unleashed laughter slip from attention and sets into motion an intense communication.

If the priest had tripped and smashed his smuggled Chivas Regals in the toilet, he would not have laughed. Awkwardness is transformed, into clowning, distress into exuberance, in the transparency of each to the others. And the gratuitous release of energy in laughter gives even the priest a sense of adolescent insouciance beyond what the bottles of Chivas Regal had promised. The laughter is felt by all who are caught up in it as a surplus of energy that was in them despite the fatigue of the night, despite the new security constraints that will affect their lives and yours. How we feel and see all this surplus energy when, ten minutes later, the flight is announced and everybody grabs their bags and jumps up with adolescent gusto!

Erotic excitement arises by contact and spreads by contagion, making us transparent to one another. A bare-breasted woman is dancing voluptuously in the street in Salvador during *carnaval*; we fix our fevered eyes on her and feel a current of complicity with the men and women about us, white or black, adolescent or aged. We find ourselves aroused by feeling the warm thigh of the dozing passenger next to us on the bus, as we are not aroused by the warm vinyl of the bus seat. During rush hour when we are standing in a packed subway car, we feel a ripple of excitement when someone's fingers lightly brush the inside of our thigh. Whether we are male or female, we feel aroused when, leaning over a gable, we see in the neighboring yard a woman sprawled on a towel spread over the summer grass, pleasuring herself. Though we are straight, we feel our penis pulsing when we look over some rocks on the summer beach and see the lifeguard naked and writhing under a gleaming erection. In his *White Book,* Jean Cocteau drew a picture of an aroused penis and labeled it: The part of a man that never lies. Whatever the educated, disciplined, decent mind may say, the penis stiffening, the labia and clitoris throbbing with blood and excitement and pleasure affirm, "Yes I like that, yes he or she is my kind, yes I am attracted to him and her."

Language, where all the words are common words, is not a means for the ego to be recognized as a pole of unity and also uniqueness, is not a means for my peculiar identity to be confirmed, attested, and certified. It is in tears, and in passionate rejection, that I experience my separation from others. But tears and passionate rejection do not bring forth some positive traits that make me appear to myself to be distinctive and distinct.

When my home burns, when I lose my job, when I discover that the investment scheme in which I put all my savings is a swindle, my desolation, finding expression in tears, contains the sense of the extreme difficulty of replacing these things. How immediately others understand those tears and, with them, all the significance that my perhaps ordinary house had for me! When, at the limit of frustration over finding myself unable to get anyone else—my family, my friends, my therapist—to see my point of view, to feel the gloom of my depression or the edge of my exasperation, even though I am using common words which everybody understands, I break

down in tears, these tears affirm not the unique traits by which I am positively distinct from all others, but how incomprehensible it is to me that
what I feel is incomprehensible to others.

Is it in passion, rather than discourse, that we demand to be separated,
distinct, and distinctive? In love we find ourselves the object of an extreme
and exclusive attachment on the part of another. We bask in finding our
principles, our values, our troubles taken seriously by at least one person.
In denuding ourselves before one another, we take off the uniforms, the
categories, the endurance, the reasons, and the functions with which our
existence had been clothed. I denude myself before my lover, as she or
he before me, and expose to the other all the singularity of my frame, my
pitted, birthmarked, and scarred skin, as so many signs of my singularity
and irreplaceability.

Passion pursues the denuding inward. Our sense of ourselves, our
self-respect shaped in fulfilling a function in the mechanical and social
environment, our dignity maintained in multiple confrontations, col-
laborations, and demands, dissolves; the ego loses its focus as center of
evaluations, decisions, and initiatives. If I draw out of our mutual exposedness something to hold on to when we part—if, for example, I take from it
a sense of my reality and my worth—this reality and worth become laughable. How ridiculous is the man who would say: Well, she gave me proof
that I am the most important man in the world!

We realize that what was at stake is unidentifiable, ungraspable, when
the intimacy of our communication is broken—by death, separation,
or a misunderstanding. The break is identified not conceptually but in
sobbing: inarticulate cries of anguish hold on to the moment when the
communication broke and what it awaited never arrived. In sobbing I realize that what I have lost by this death, separation, or misunderstanding is
not something we had. In desolation I feel forever gone something that our
weeks, months, years together had not yet made real, something that foresight, planning, and projects did not outline and make clear—what passion
divined only as an abyss of chance and luck.

In fact, does not the temptation to see in someone's attachment to me
evidence of my exceptional reality and worth spring from the fact that I
had not been able to justify them to myself by positive traits I had seen in
myself? And do I not find myself consolidating and promoting my separate
existence at the expense of others? The very sense of having a separate existence can be malevolent and pernicious.

The sense of having a separate existence, throbbing in tears and
erotic rejection, cannot take being an improbable and irreplaceable I to
be a good. Still less, to be the fundamental good that I seek in discourse
and in passion. I am attached to my separate existence, improbable and

irreplaceable, but would I be if I were not certain that I could just as well laugh at it? In laughing tenderly over my awkward and bungling adolescent horniness, in guffawing over my melodramatic love affairs, I become attached to them and to myself.

We laugh at "Freudian slips," when someone utters something he had no intention of saying; we are sure that what came out is what he really thinks or feels. We laugh at a kitten falling over itself in playing with a ball; we feel that we have just gotten a glimpse into the real nature of a young animal, of this young animal. We laugh at people whose oafish or slobby bodies are ridiculous, whose lives one cannot take seriously, whose jobs or careers are a joke, and who died in some glitch of the machinery, of nature, or of their own program for surviving. However miserable I am when my lover has left me for someone else, feeling that there was something uniquely in me that deserved so extreme and exclusive an attachment was, I plaintively realize, laughable. On our honeymoon on the island of St. John in the Caribbean there was that sign on a rustic hangout: You're here with only the hurricanes and the hangovers, two thousand miles from self-importance. What else can we do, do we do, but laugh, when we face the improbability of our birth, the ludicrously squalid death we are heading for, the filthy corpse our vaunted and incomparable existence is going to turn into? This laughter at the I, at the demand the I makes, laughter over one's birth, over one's death, need not be ironic or bitter. It can be as light as the laughter with which we greet the fanciful anatomy of a praying mantis or dragon pipefish, the pompous assertiveness of a bumblebee, the birth of a baby crocodile.

Looking at oneself while laughing turns into an erotic vertigo. How we are lustfully drawn to our own mouth that, in the mirror, we see wide open, exposing the wet, lascivious tongue! We stand in front of the mirror looking at our legs shaking, our belly rolling in peals of laughter, and, unable to stop ourselves, we stroke that belly, run our hands up between our thighs, fall back upon the bed. They fix mirrors on the ceilings and on the walls around the bed in bordellos so that we will be able to see the awkward, unmanageable contortions and flailings of our body and not be able to avoid laughing, and it is this, and not the simple sight of our genitals, that will jiggle us into the abandon and anonymity of orgasm.

And is it not by not taking ourselves seriously that we enter into conversation? It is with horseplay or farcical comment about his looks or about our own activity that he has interrupted that we greet a friend or the plumber or our father-in-law. When we meet Jamaican reggae musicians, Brazilian capoeira fighters, Haitian practitioners of Voodoo, or specialists in some sector of our white mythology of reason, the first thing we do is use language to unleash a laugh.

We use words to get to laughter, and laughter generates words—words that set forth and share—consecrate—the things that left us abashed, disconcerted, disheveled, the events that did not enlighten but delighted us. Linguistics misses this use of words when it envisions words as discriminators, functioning to delimit and contrast. Language, like everything real, is based on positive entities, the positive, positing words that illuminate and consecrate. Words do not simply isolate entities by contrast and delimitation; the radiance of passing strangers, birds, trees, cars, and landscapes resonate in their tones and accent. Their inner pacing and resonance pick up that of the languidly sprawling summer landscape, the secretive and melancholy medieval town, the vast desert under sheltering evening skies.

There is never a perfect fit of words on the things they designate; they are GI uniforms pulled over the gawky bodies of adolescent recruits. And the words are never completely artless; their meanings seethe with allusions and equivocations, their inner pacing and resonance connect with one another in haphazard short-circuitings. And so they are prone to bring out the awkwardness and bungling in the things they designate—the pretenses and the prankishness of things.

How transparent we are in laughter, and how understandable are our tears! We share one another's sorrow. Mourning is not a way our psyche, unable to confront the loss of a lover or the death of a friend, closes in upon itself to conserve that lost one in our memories. Most of us first mourned in childhood for a squirrel or a bird which we came upon dead on a wooded path, a creature of which we had no memory. The grief and weeping open upon the void left by that loss or that death. How visible is that void to the compassionate eyes of others!

As we advance in life and adulthood, we weep over the loss of lovers and the death of friends. We also grieve over gifted young people we never met who are struck down in accidents or in crippling diseases; we grieve over young and old heroes in remote lands who arise from nowhere and are struck down in noble and lost causes. Indeed, it is in our grief over these heroes that we feel the loss and death of those we have known.

As laughter generates words, words that consecrate, words of blessing, weeping generates words, words of imprecation, words that curse the human and cosmic villainy.

It is not in a discourse that demands and gives reasons for what we saw and did, and reasons for those reasons, that we recognize our common humanity. If we open a conversation with someone, it is because first we see him or her as someone with whom we could laugh and grieve. Prior to the speech that informs and the speech that directs and orders, there is the speech that articulates for those who were not there, and articulates further for those who were, what we laugh and weep over, what we bless and curse.

Our speech is polarized by the grand things, the blessed events that come as surprises and accidents from the outside, and by the sinister things.

Laughter and tears, blessing and cursing, give birth to the primary operative words of language—the value-terms. *Great, beautiful, strong, healthy, delicious, wild*—all of our conversations weave about such words. The value-terms are not labels that record observations or gauge gradations and comparisons. They find their meaning not in comparative sentences but in exclamations: How healthy I am! How strong I am! How happy I am! How beautiful I am! How good it is to be alive! We say these things because we feel them, and by saying them we feel still better. There are people who have no positive notion of health, for whom health is only the absence of illness, who regard themselves as healthy only after the annual checkup when the doctor has reported that no foreign bodies have been detected proliferating and all the vital functions test within the statistically average range. There are people for whom health has a dense and radiant meaning, for whom it is the sovereign value—men sprinting up the steps from the gym after a workout to muscle exhaustion, women setting out on their vacation to trek the Andes, adolescent boys on Patagonian ranches breaking the young bulls for rodeo. The value-terms are not forms that inform and classify; they are forces: the beautiful words make radiant the one to whom they are said and make gracious the one who says them, the noble words ennoble, the healthy words vitalize, the strong words invigorate; the ugly words befoul, the servile words demean those who speak them, the weak words enervate and enfeeble, the sick words contaminate. The value-terms concentrate our superabundant energies within us; we channel those energies outward in our hands made for blessing and in the cursings that come from our heart. Saying "How happy I am!" we leave our happiness on passersby hailed, on the trees and the clouds, in flowers left on the formica desks of offices.

Is it not because we recognize someone as one with whom we could laugh and grieve, speaking of absurd and of heartrending things, that we believe the reasons we find or construct will be recognizable by all those with whom we speak?

To enter into contact with someone is not to conceptually grasp his or her identity and respect his or her boundaries and inner space. We greet someone with "Hey man!" The vibrant tone of those words hail in that individual a man, not a child, a student, or a waiter. We address and answer someone in the words and forms of speech that are his or hers. We catch up the tone of the one who addresses us, his or her voice resounds in our own. We catch the urgent, frantic, panicky, exultant, or astonished tone. To answer the frenetic tone of a young person with the stentorian tone of officious and sedentary life is, before we refuse to really understand what we are being told, to refuse his tone; it is to refuse him.

The tone of the one who addresses me does not respect but pervades my inner space. His sounds are in me now, my body has become his. Inhaling and exhaling the air, the drift of pheromone, catching hormonal rhythms, my breath and his commingle in the atmosphere about us.

When we attend to someone who greets us, it is not to require confirmation, attestation, certification of our identity. To respond to someone who greets us is to drop our concerns and thoughts, and expose ourselves to her. It is to expose ourselves to questioning and judgment. Simply responding to her greeting is to recognize her rights over us. Each time we enter into conversation we expose ourselves to being altered or emptied out, emptied of our convictions, our expectations, our memories.

When we get together we talk about individuals we have seen or heard, or heard tell of, who exhibit extravagant health, sumptuous beauty, smoldering eroticism, bravado. These are also the people we talk to when we get together. In speaking with the father about his foolhardy and impudent son, we call forth the brash youth in him; in speaking with our suburban neighbors of the vixen we saw performing in the night club on our women's night out, we call forth the glamorous and seductive women in them.

Truth begins in conversations, shared laughter, friendship, and eroticism. But other people are not just other perspectives, other points of view, bearers of other data. How reckless and violent is the will to open one's eyes and face what happens, what is, among them! It is this reckless and violent will we seek contact with in them. We would not know what happens among them, if, exposing ourselves to what happens, what is, we did not know extreme pleasure, if we did not know extreme pain!

That is why so often the most moving, the most unforgettable conversations we have are with strangers, people from another land, another age, whom we have never seen before and will never see again. We seek communication with those most unlike ourselves; our most important conversations are with prostitutes, criminals, gravediggers. We seek to be freed from the carapace of ourselves.

Only a street kid dared to go talk with Edson Cordeiro after his concert in São Paulo; only an old peasant woman dared to speak with Subcommandante Marcos. For us to speak with them, we would have to be impetuous as youth, insolent and shameless as the old woman who has decided that at her age she can do what she likes.

To communicate effectively with those who fascinate us is to break through their integrity, their natures, their independence, their autonomy—to wound them. Communication through these breaches in our psychophysical integrity turns in a vortex, heedless of the consequences. Communication is not itself a "good." It excludes any concern for the time to come. It excludes any concern for our interests. Thus we are drawn to all who face what happens, what is, and who suffer.

2000

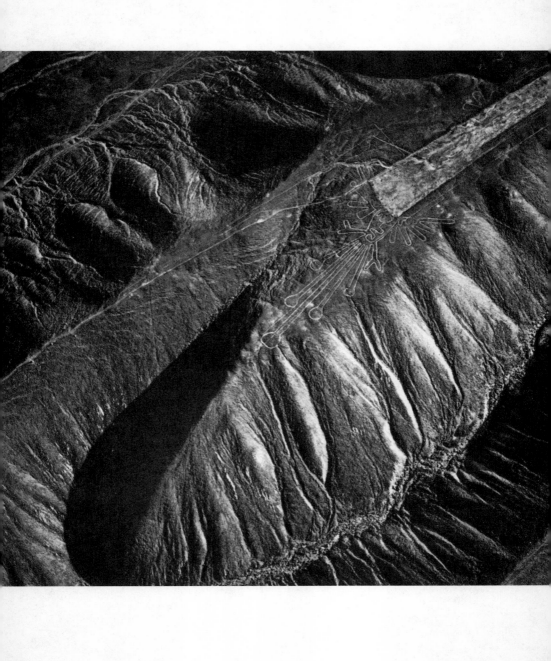

Unknowable Intelligence

The day I arrived in Lima the sun shone weakly for two hours. The next day there was sunshine for only an hour, the day after none at all. The *garúa* had set in, that strange cold ocean fog that covers the Peruvian coast for four months. As the weeks went by the fog became more dense, saturated with the city's traffic and industrial pollutants. In my room my clothes were damp and my papers limp; outside buildings were wet and the streets muddy, though there was no rain. Now for even short distances I took taxis, antiquated contraptions that stall at red lights and only keep on the streets by cannibalizing parts of those taxis that have expired. I had to escape; I decided to go to Nazca.

I took a taxi to the airport and waited at a pillar that had been designated for me. Soon the pilot appeared, Carlos, a mustached youth with dark glasses and a smart brown pilot's jacket. He led me out a back door and to the far end of the runway, to a Cessna. He seated and buckled me alongside him. The Cessna lifted and pitched into the *garúa* and then leveled above it. Here was the sun, glorious and sovereign, that I had not seen for months! Seen now from above, the *garúa* was an immaculate lamb's-wool blanket that extended uninterrupted and featureless over the ocean to our right; far to our left from time to time glacier-covered peaks of the Andes broke through it like a syncopation in that whiteness. It was impossible to situate myself any longer in relation to Lima and its dark wet streets, impossible to locate myself on any coordinates marked by roads, cities, continents; planet Earth had veered off and continued its way without us. For three hours the Cessna, untroubled by any turbulence, seemed not to move, poised in this solar space without markers.

Then Carlos turned the nose of the Cessna gently downward and the lamb's wool rose about it and then began to thin. And I began to see long pale lines in the white fog, elongated triangles, quadrangles, and trapezoids. A few minutes later as the fog lifted off them they stabilized on the gray plain below. Carlos now leveled the Cessna and circled back and forth over the coastal plain, where the lines spread in rays for, he said, 130 kilometers, heading off in all directions, hundreds of them, many intersecting one another. He pointed out here and there lines that spiraled and turned into a condor, a frigate bird, a hawk, a hummingbird, a parrot, a huge bird with a zigzag neck longer than its body. He said that there were eighteen birds. He turned the plane to show me a monkey, two llamas, a dog, a crocodile, an orca, a fish, an iguana, a spider, a flower, and then, on the flank of the first mountain of the Andes, the figure of a man with a circle for a head, which Carlos called the owl-man.

Finally we landed. Now I could see that the lines are very shallow, most only a few centimeters deep. The plain of fine pebbles, once under the ocean, has trace gypsum in it that holds the lines fixed. No sands have covered them nor has erosion smeared them. This region is the most arid place known on the planet; rain is rarer here than in the Sahara. The rare land traveler who since Pizarro's conquest passed by them assumed they were remains of ancient irrigation systems. The lines form diagrams so large— up to twelve hundred meters long—and the terrain is so flat that someone standing in the midst of them could not see the patterns. In the thirties they built the Pan-American Highway across them. Over this coastal plain the cold Humboldt Current coming from the Antarctic spreads a dense sea fog. Finally in 1932, Carlos told me, a pilot was flying a small plane under the fog and noticed that instead of forming the grid of an irrigation system, they formed strange geometrical diagrams.

We headed to the small cottage where Maria Reiche lives. On her veranda we had tea and some lunch. In 1932, as a young German mathematician working on her doctorate, she was spending her summer vacation in Qosqo. For a pastime she was looking into the astronomical mathematics of the Inca civilization. She met the pilot and then went to see the lines at Nazca. She started to map them, using surveying instruments and charting them on a scale of 1 centimeter = 10 meters. One day she was astonished to see that she was drawing a giant hummingbird. She never left Nazca. By carbon-dating some wood posts she has determined that the lines were drawn from 300 BCE to 900 CE, sometimes over previously drawn lines. Most of them are geometrical figures—zigzags, rays, oscillating lines, elongated triangles, quadrangles, bent trapezoids, spirals, double spirals, stars. They are found on vast plains, narrow plateaus between gorges, and on islands of even ground amid a maze of dry ancient riverbeds. They are drawn with astonishing precision—lines extending 2,600 feet deviate from the perfectly straight by but two inches. Those that depict the animals and the man that Carlos had shown me from the air are each made with one continuous line that never crosses over itself.

They were made by a people whose culture had disappeared long before the Inca extended their rule from Qosqo and Quito in the high Andes. The Nazca civilization had been one of great technological and artistic achievements, with splendid weaving—a piece of fabric was found with 750 threads per square centimeter, a world record—and some of the finest pottery of ancient Peru. But the lines themselves were their sole inscription. They, the greatest text or artwork ever created on our planet, lay in the fog of mystery.

One day, on the equinox, a friend of Maria Reiche's noticed that one of the major lines headed straight to the horizon where the sun was setting. It gave her her first clue. The lines form, she hypothesized, a gigantic cosmic map. The figures of condors, hummingbirds, and monkeys represent constellations. It is a hypothesis she is still working to verify. She has been able to coordinate only a small number of the lines with the night sky. All of her identifications are subject to question: since the earth wobbles on its axis over time, to determine that that line marked the setting sun on the day of the equinox one would have to know when it was drawn. But the lines were drawn over a twelve-hundred-year period. Others have tried other hypotheses. Anthropologists are convinced they must have religious significance: the exactness of the lines, drawn perfectly straight over many miles and over so many centuries, demonstrates that the lines had transcendent importance. Since the pictorial figures are made with one continuous line that never intersects with itself, may they not be paths for ritual processions? Yet major lines do not lead to any cave or spring that might have had sacred significance but instead just come to a stop in the empty plain. In places free of lines there are circles of ashes, but no trace of bones from possible sacrifices were found in them. Some of the lines continue to the foothills of the Andes and then go straight up, marking a supposed path no human could climb. The recent observation that almost all the lines drawn converge upon some sixty-two ray centers made anthropologists recall that forty-one lines radiated out from the Sun Temple of Qosqo, built five hundred years after the disappearance of the Nazca culture. On those lines there were marked 328 sacred points signifying elements from many levels of Inca thought—from cosmology, astronomy, natural phenomena, irrigation, kinship, social hierarchy, ancestors, and state ideology. Did so many levels of thought also enter into the drawings at Nazca?

The fact that the diagrams are so huge and the terrain so flat that the people who made them could never have seen them is deeply puzzling.

The Nazca people must have proceeded as Maria Reiche did when she drew her map of them, but in reverse, translating one centimeter into ten meters. The fact that they could not have seen the figures they drew gave rise to speculations that they were drawn for awaited or real alien visitors. The figure drawn ninety-eight feet high on the mountain, the one Carlos had called the owl-man, looks like a cartoon alien.

For more than fifty years Maria Reiche studied these hypotheses and others, and she continues her research into astronomical mathematics. Now suffering severe arthritis and in her nineties, Maria Reiche conceded to us that on her bad nights she thinks we may never decipher them.

Carlos and I went back to the Cessna and glided over the lines once more. Then the Cessna rose again into the somber fog and emerged from its radiant top surface. Carlos told me that recently he brought here a man who, it turned out, pilots a hot-air balloon in his country. When this man saw a piece of Nazca weaving, it occurred to him that fabric woven so fine would not allow air to pass through it—the fabric of hot-air balloons is not woven so fine. Perhaps the Nazca people observed their millennial artistry from hot-air balloons. That would explain those circles of ashes that were found in flat empty places on the plain and in which the anthropologists could identify no traces of human habitation or sacrifice.

Back in Lima, I picked up *Time* magazine in the airport and found that it contained a special report on the astonishing data supplied by the Hubble Space Telescope, including the first photographs of stars in the process of forming. I was staggered, thinking of how our small animal brains have been able to comprehend the inner processes of inert matter, even at the remote ends of the universe and back during the first milliseconds of the Big Bang. Yet at Nazca the thought behind these lines, not squiggles of disturbed minds sometimes seen in our mental hospitals, but a project executed with exacting precision and over twelve centuries by an advanced human civilization that came to an end not that long ago—fifteen hundred years after Greece, whose philosophers we quite understand—may remain definitively irrecoverable and lost to us.

2004

Breakout

Hilary had taken me with her to help her decide about purchasing a house in a small town on the edge of greater London. The house was also small and had the prim conventional shape of so many houses in so many English towns. The prior owners could say little to justify the asking price, and Hilary had to calculate and recalculate her finances to see if she could afford it. To persuade her, the owners kept us outside most of the time, in the quite large yard. They had planted the front with rare roses and flowering quinces; in the walled rear garden flagstone paths led between raised beds to two gazebos whose trellises were covered with clematis vines. The owners led us down the paths, identifying on either side of the paths azaleas, Asiatic boxwoods, oakleaf hydrangeas, buddleias, tree peonies, Japanese iris, lungworts, Carpathian bellflowers, foxgloves, Oriental lilies. The beds were also planted with thousands of tulips, daffodils, jonquils, Siberian squills, now dormant but which, the owners told us, spread blazes of color from earliest spring. We were dumbfounded by the botanical erudition and unremitting industriousness of the owners, which set them apart in this mediocre town where we had imagined only drab and conventional lives.

The following spring I was in England again, and on a warm late afternoon went to find Hilary. I had to check the house number to be sure I had found the right house: the roses and quinces were gone; the front yard was nothing but bare ground. No one answered the bell; I went around to the back and found Hilary, disheveled and joyous, driving her spade into the clumps of plants and overturning them. She embraced me with mucky arms and pulled me down on the soft lumps of overturned ground. We studied the whitish roots that twisted around one another in delirious masses and dug our fingers into the dirt to pull out rhizomes and bulbs, fat and white as tumors. We began tossing them at one another and, when darkness descended, pulled off our clothes and tossed them at one another and embraced on the warm earth. The next morning I asked Hilary what she was going to plant now, and she laughed: "Nothing!"

It was a year later that I went to spend a week with her again. The house was now surrounded with prairie. Wild grasses, clovers, and all kinds of plant stems branching into tiny flowers and furry seedpods were knee-high. "They came by themselves," she said, "flown in with the wind." The bare earth surface I had last seen was now everywhere throbbing with their frenetic compulsion to rise upward to the sun. Already here and there tree seedlings were pushing up and taking off. Hilary had restored the flagstone walls of the raised beds, and the paths were scrupulously swept clean. "I do that because," she said, "the neighbors complained that I had let the garden go to weeds and sent an official over from the Council. I told him I was a botanist and had planted each of the species individually for research purposes. He didn't look too convinced, but he wrote his report and hasn't come back." We lay in the warm late-afternoon sun and inspected at random the pale little flowers over our heads. I was back in my childhood on the farm, where I used to disappear for hours in the densely overgrown gullies and knew my first orgasms.

Once upon a time apes descended from the trees, advanced into the savanna, and stood upright. Though geographers refer to savannas, prairies, tundras, and steppes as grasslands, typically but 20 percent of the plants there are grasses; there is also a great variety of legumes and composites, algae, mosses, and orchids. Wood and tree leaves are mostly cellulose and lignin, but the grassland plants are high in pectin and protein, available in the whole tissue of the plants. Flowering plants produce seeds, embryos with concentrated stores of nutrients. Grasslands support a great diversity of animal life: insects that coevolved with flowering plants; birds that live on insects and on seeds, which they also scatter and plant; small and large mammals—hoofed herbivores and big carnivores and primates. The human apes did not give up contact with the trees, which they sought for shade and rest and which they climbed for safety and for the view.

When our moralists speak of living according to nature and respecting nature and our own nature, it is the spectacle of flourishing fields and forests, rising upright from the earth to the sun, that they invoke. It is fields and forests that the ancient Stoics, Emerson and Thoreau, Nietzsche and Hegel, the evolutionists with their tree or multistemmed bush of evolution and the ecologists of today see as the natural landscape of human rectitude and justice. Our subspecies of primate, standing erect, respects the upright, equivalent for us to dignity; esteems rectitude, for us equivalent to righteousness; values the elevated and praises eyes turned to the skies and the heavens, for us equivalent to the decent, the noble, the ideal, the sacred.

The sequoias, great upright poles rising 250 feet into the sky with only the sparsest of branches, are celebrated as the most noble of trees. The endurance of those trees that have seen so many peoples and societies and regimes come and go in the course of the twenty-five hundred years they've lived materializes fortitude and steadfastness for us. We tolerate, with bad conscience, the commercialization of our artists, our women, even our churches, but shrink back from cutting down the giant sequoias for timber. As long as they stand tall there is still something noble and just in America.

The branches and the twigs of the linden trees and great elms presiding over the main streets of our towns give us the vision of an architectural order, an ordered distribution of each part in its own place, post, and function—a compelling everyday vision of justice and harmony. Each in its place, the individual leafy stems exhibit purpose and dignity. When we come upon cities without trees we feel we have come upon zones of moral collapse.

But other emotions also emerge in fields and forests. Below the trunks and stems of fields and forests rising to the sun, roots descend and wind and knot and wallow like worms in the wet earth, lured by rank decomposition. They, however, must not be seen. Roots turned up in the air and sun die, and the whole plant dies with them; floods and storms that uproot the fields and the forests are disasters. The sequoias are not the oldest monuments in nature; in Africa and Australia there are baobab trees that are also twenty-five hundred years old. They have thick squat trunks, and then a brushy tangle of branches that look like the roots of trees uprooted by storms, and sparse leaves on those branches. They struck European traders and explorers as the very image of what is inverted, perverted, in darkest Africa. Our visceral sense of the base, the low, the mean, the vile in certain behaviors, attitudes, and inclinations designates their affinity with the dark and dank earth, with rot and decay.[1]

Some roots are particularly indecent. The mandrake root, short, thick, white, and bulbous, often branching into two at the bottom and often branching twice, presents an obscene image of a naked human body, headless and without muscle delineation. Carrots look too much like human penises, turnips like swollen testicles. These images give us the sense that there are base roots in our bodies—our clitorises, our penises, our naked fingers and toes pushing in disordered directions when our bodies have let go of their upright posture and uprightness in the night. To expose in the air and sunlight these dissolute bodies, these roots pushing into sweat and darkness, would be a moral disaster.[2] Yet intense emotions course tumultuously in these base organs of our bodies and into all subterranean nature.

Storms of orgasm overturn our bodies. Our posture, which holds our body upright and directed upon tasks, collapses, no longer integrating our limbs and sense organs, each in its own place, post, and function. Our eyes no longer scan the environment for the right path; our gaze drifts. Our hands and legs roll about without purpose or dignity. Our fingers fondle the mounds and orifices of another's body with aimless, repetitious movements, not exploring, not learning anything. The sighs and moans of another pulse through the nervous networks of our body; spasms of pleasure and torment in another's body shudder across our cheeks, belly, thighs. Our excitements expire in sweat and genital secretions and releases of hot moist breath over our beds damp as springtime earth. In the anxiety and exhilaration of orgasm, convulsion of what the ancients called our vegetative soul, we sink into the living depth of our nature and into the depths of vegetative nature.

In the south of Peru stands the white colonial city of Arequipa, its mansions, Mudejar churches, and monasteries made of carved blocks of white volcanic tufa. From there we took a four-and-a-half-hour truck ride on the dirt road around the volcanoes Misti, Chiacoan, and Pichi-Pichi. The terrain is all volcanic tufa, swirls of white crust as if poured out of a bowl, and so arid it is almost completely devoid of vegetation.

At length we reached the brink of a great fault in the continental tectonic plate: the Colca Canyon. Far below, a meandering river has dug it to depths deeper than any other canyon on the planet. A path descends the flank of the canyon. Here and there at the bottom of the canyon there are some Indian hamlets. These people were passed over by the Inca Empire and are too alien and too poor to be enlisted in the Peruvian state today. I was able to find lodging for the night. The full moon shone in crystal splendor; seeing it between the narrow walls of the canyon was like looking at it through a tube. On the upper edges of the canyon its light poured over the glaciers. I walked down the lanes, sensing the discreet but trusting proximity of the dark forms of strangers. I ended up in a room where four young men were playing a llama-hide drum, reed pipes, and two stringed gourds. The music had wild rhythms that pulled me up from my seat to dance and tragic melodies that tore at the heart. A young man knew just enough Spanish words to propose guiding me in the morning. He said his name was Santiago.

We set out at four o'clock. The natural terrain, from the glaciers down sheer bare rock and then to the slopes created by erosion and down into the deep gorge cut by the river, was a display of ever different cuts, different colors of cliffs, rocks, and clay. Over generations, the people had carved the canyon with the subtle eyes and patience of diamond cutters; the flanks of the canyon from the river up hundreds of feet were faceted with stone-walled terraces. The terraces were growing quinoa, potatoes, and many species of high-altitude corn that were irrigated by the melting glaciers and the springs and cascades that release the groundwater.

On the terraces and in the hamlets below, the women wore long multicolored bouffant skirts and broad-rimmed hats; as the canyon turned around mountains I noticed that the hat style differed in different settlements. Later back in Arequipa I read in a book on the native populations of Peru that two different populations settled the canyon, revering two different sacred *Apus,* mountains. They reflected the forms of their respective sacred mountains on their own heads, placing molds on their infants' skulls so that, in one people, their skulls would be cylindrical and in the other, flat on top. When the missionaries collected the people into fortified villages called *reducciones,* they forbade skull molding of children and imposed Spanish dress. The one group then devised high and cylindrical hats, the other high, flat-topped hats.

On both sides the mountains above were glacier-covered, but volcano Mount Sabancaya was gushing out dense clouds of smoke. At a place called Maca, Santiago indicated that earthquakes had shaken down a village two years ago and now the quakes were starting up again at the same spot. We went down to look at a big crack; the local people told Santiago, and he conveyed to me by pointing to hours back on my watch, that it had just opened up the prior night. Our slow and wearing ascent up the canyon, the grit crumbling under our shoes, measured the time of our effort and of our life against the geological epochs of the planet's crust and rock layers. The scale of geological time diminishes us and destines any footprints we leave here, indeed any works we build in our lifetime, to erosion and mineral decomposition.

We trekked to the top of the terracing and, chewing coca leaves, climbed ever higher; finally we reached Condor's Cross, where the canyon is deepest.[3] It is also very narrow, a knife-cut through twelve thousand feet of rock, at the bottom of which, like a crinkle of mercury, we saw the river. All around, the glaciers of the Andes began to blaze with the rising sun. Loftiest is the volcano Mount Mismi, whose melting glacier is the source of the Amazon. The sulfurous fumes of the Sabancaya volcano we passed hours ago in the dark are billowing in the sky. We settled on a boulder in this uninhabitable mountainscape. No human enterprise could take hold here; I could form no project here, not even an exploratory hike. Even if I had any shreds of vocabulary of his language or he of mine, I would not have anything to say to my Indian companion, not even any question to ask him. The discursive movements of the mind, staking out paths, laying out positions and counterpositions, were silenced. As soon as the sun emerged over the peaks of the Andes, it turned the cloudless sky magnesium-white. Its radiation spread over our faces and hands like warmth, although the thin air my heaving lungs were pumping in was cold.

After a long time spent motionless, I become aware that the sun is now high in the sky. And then, well before seeing it, we are aware of the condor, like a silent drumroll in the skies over the glaciers. Our eyes are pulled to a speck taking form in the empty radiance, imperceptibly becoming bigger, becoming a great bird never once flapping or even shifting its wings, gliding down from a great height and then into the canyon, descending to eye level in front of us before gradually descending deeper and becoming lost to sight. It is the first condor I have seen, with its fifteen-foot wingspan the largest flying bird on the planet; this one is brown, a young female. She is perhaps surveying the desolate cliffs and avalanches for carrion; perhaps she has already fed and is continuing her daylong life in the heights. And then—an hour, two hours later?—there are two: again we know they are there well before they are visible. They are close to one another, circling companionably in the airless heights. When they are overhead, I try to gauge their height, judging that they are above us halfway again the depth of the canyon—that is, some eighteen thousand feet. I, who could hardly climb much higher than our present thirteen thousand feet, feel my eyes, my craving, my fascination plunging to their almost immaterial realm, falling up into the region of death. We are nothing but a vision, a longing, a euphoric outflow of life hanging on to the flight of the condors. Their flight comes from a past without memory and soars into a future without anticipation. We are cut loose, unanchored, without guy wires, drifting in the void of the sky. We feel nothing but the thin icy air, see nothing but the summits and ice cliffs of the Andes and the granite walls of the canyon below. We are alive for nothing but for their bodies and their flight.

Climbing the rocky coves and promontories of Sydney Harbor hoping to catch sight of whales, mocked by the swift slippery seals, one gets tired. One hundred seventy pounds of mostly salty brine in an unshapely sack of skin—one's legs fold and strain to hoist this weight; the joints ache. How one can understand the dolphins and whales, mammals who evolved on land but long ago returned to the ocean! Still, movement on Earth's surface is not simply a blunder on the part of evolution, as the cases of serpents and cheetahs show. And after all, one can also return to the ocean with the whales and seals, strapping on an air tank and fins.

At closing time, I went back to the Manley Oceanarium. The staff had given me leave to enter the shark tank after hours with scuba gear. If walking across a continent's surface carrying my body weight on jointed legs was awkward enough, doddering across the basement of the Oceanarium with buoyancy compensator, air tank, regulator and gauges, face mask, weight belts, and flippered feet was ludicrous. But once inside the tank, having achieved buoyancy, I could slide through the water with my rubber fins. I gaped in wonder at how different the light and colors of the water looked compared with the view from the visitors' tunnel. Of course it is still diving in an artificial reef. But the Oceanarium is so big (the tank holds 4.6 million liters; the staff said they do not know how many animals are in there—thousands) that the behavior of the animals is not different from the behavior of creatures in the ocean. And in a lifetime of diving the oceans, how often could one get that close to great sharks! I was told to avoid letting them bump into me and not to touch them, for sharks, like all fish, have a slime coating on their skin that protects them from bacterial infections and that my touch could break. For an hour I watched huge sharks passing inches from my eyes and great rays folding their bodies over my head.

It is the cartilage, not bones, they have that gives them their extraordinary suppleness of movement. Their sleek bodies are as hydrodynamic as our bodies holding themselves up off the ground are un-aerodynamic. The rays are classified by science as belonging to the same family, but their movement is totally different from that of sharks; they are disks that shimmer and glide. Our bodies walk in a succession of falls stopped by a lurching of bones; their whole bodies ripple musically. Their movement is disinterested; movement is the nature of their life. Cold-blooded animals have to eat much less than do warm-blooded ones. Sharks go for weeks, even a whole winter, without eating at all. In the Oceanarium, it is a real job to get them to eat a fish to please the viewing tourists. They just keep cruising by. Liz has to stuff a fish into their jaws, and most of the time they refuse to bite down. The tank is full of thousands of other, smaller, slower fish, which do not panic as the sharks cruise by.

Each time a great shark slides by and pauses inches from my head, my eyes meet its small lemon-yellow eye fixed on me. His ever-open jaws display rows of teeth. My eyes are unable to circumscribe, survey, foresee what his eye sees. I feel my eyes and my soul and big bloated body utterly exposed to that pale unreflecting eye. It is by circumscribing, foreseeing, and manipulating that human apes have taken possession of every square meter of Earth's surface, subjugating and exterminating all the other species. Sharks, virtually unchanged through three Ice Ages, are lords of the deep by virtue of the incomparable perfection of their bodies. They are less tigers than vultures; not their eyes but their electrical sense detects the spasmodic movements of sick and dying fish, which they feed on, assimilating them into the perpetual movement of their lives. I have nothing to fear.[4]

Yet there is the absolute certainty that the shark and I are looking at one another, that our eyes communicate. The shark's eyes are immobile and inexpressive; our eyes in their liquid sockets are as restless as their bodies. We have had to work to make our eyes fearful and wary, to force them to circumscribe, survey, and foresee. In the gaze of the shark, my eyes lose their industriousness and return to their primal and infantile delight.

In Cairo I met Wael, a young refugee from Sudan. He took me to where he stays. It was in the middle of a vast wasteland that had been the city garbage dump for centuries, so polluted that not a weed was to be seen anywhere. Here the most destitute of Cairo's poor make bricks and pots out of the muck. The terrain was pitted to hold basins of water and adjacent basins of wet clay, and the brickmakers and potters themselves live in caves excavated in the muck or mud-wall huts covered with scavenged sheets of rusted metal. Their mud brick kilns are above and below these hovels, the black smoke that seeps from them hovering low overhead. It was like ground zero after the end of urban civilization. The substance of the muck is everywhere up against them, all their movements held in it, their glances and their touch ending in it, their thoughts inescapably terrestrial. I cast only oblique glances at them, apprehensive less of the aggressions against foreigners that had been so much in the press than of the resentment of the downtrodden everywhere when their homes and their destitution are stared at by well-to-do outsiders. But we went inside one of these hovels. Wael's mother, to welcome me, poured from a jug some water in a cup of clay. I suddenly thought I had been transported to ground zero where civilization began—for the first things humans made with their hands were pots fashioned of clay. Cupped hands lifting water to the mouth were the first pots, and the first pots of clay were made to hold that gesture.

Beyond this wasteland, I could see the dunes of Giza and the Pyramids. The next day I went there. Everyone has seen them so often, in pictures in books, in films, in news broadcasts, in cigarette ads; the images and impressions collected on the surfaces of my eyes, ears, and skin while wandering among them had already all been projected there many times already. Beyond these images and impressions, I tried to sense what the Pyramids are. In grade school and in the books I now read they were identified as tombs of kings who had divinized themselves—the colossal monuments of a monstrous excrescence of egoism. Which is to view them as did the barbarian grave robbers (not the last of these barbarian chieftains was Howard Carter, who sold half the plunder from Pharaoh Tutankhamen to the New York Metropolitan Museum for fourteen thousand pounds sterling). One could just as well describe a medieval cathedral as a mausoleum for a lord bishop or king on the argument that their tombs are found in them. These mammoth constructions are some kind of cosmic markers. Their essential function is to do something in the cosmos. But virtually all the coordinates of the cosmos in which they are set are incomprehensible.

When the midday heat drove the tourists to their buses and the air-conditioned restaurants, I headed for the entrance of the great pyramid of Khufu. The Egyptian guides had already retreated to the shade of palm trees, but some of them saw me and rushed toward me. I paid them for a guided tour if they let me enter alone; each only wanted a few dollars. I was able to spend two hours alone inside. The tomb room is astonishingly small, bare, and unsculptured and not at the real center of the pyramid. The now-empty sarcophagus is a plain stone box. I did not detect any hint of the pharaoh's ghost in that chamber; what confronted me was the enormous reality of the stone above and about and below.

Napoleon calculated that there was enough stone in the three great pyramids of Giza to build a wall ten feet high and a foot wide around France. The stones were not cut at the quarries in uniform blocks; they are of varying sizes and their sides of varying angles. They were cut to fit one another at the site and were there fitted together so exactly that one cannot slip a knife between them. They were fitted together that painstakingly not only on the outer face of the pyramid, but in all the tiers, all the way through. Something utterly transcendent, something of incalculable value, was sensed in stone, something to which all the energies and years of life of a laborer could be devoted.

I went up the Nile to Luxor and the Valley of the Kings, where later pharaohs were buried deep underground. I came upon the tomb of Meneptah IV, little visited because floods had pretty much destroyed the paintings, and once I entered I found myself alone. The tunnel is very long and steep, several hundred meters down. There is one landing halfway down, and then at the bottom a very large pillared room cut in the granite bedrock. In the center is the black sarcophagus in mint condition. On the stone cover the face and folded hands of the pharaoh are emerging from, or sinking into, the black stone. I am invaded by a sense of a human life coming to rest deep under millions of tons of rock. Here the surface agitations are so remote from him, and, the few hours I linger there with him, from me. I feel an imperative summons from the rock core of the planet to stay, and feel the serene immobility and majestic submission of the pharaoh to be an assignation.

2004

Wounds and Words

The process by which a wish, an insight, a feeling, even a negative thought or feeling, vocalized into song becomes a pleasure has, despite all its importance, thus far been beyond the reach of our neurology and psychology. The process by which a wound, a pain gives rise to vocalization is only apparently simple.

A wounded animal hisses, squeals, screams, or roars. The great energy of its vocalizations is threatening to an attacker. The outcries of a wounded young bird or mammal call for help from its parents; those of an adult call to the flock or herd for help. Birds and mammals (including humans) also mutter and whimper, moan and whine as the pain sets in and endures, though often their vulnerable situation counsels silence. Voltaire said that language has been given to humans so that they can dissimulate their thoughts, but in fact we have a natural impulse to say what we see and feel; we have to learn to lie. Wounds issue in vocalizations; we have to learn not to cry or moan when we hurt.

Pain is immanence; it is conscious, nothing but consciousness, a consciousness backed up to itself, mired in itself. To suffer pain is for consciousness to be unable to flee or retreat from itself, unable to project itself outside upon some outlying object or event. Suffering gives rise to whimperings, moanings, sobbings, and murmurings—typically rhythmic—with which the body mired in pain strives to reestablish internal kinetic melodies and with them make contact with the arpeggios and drumrolls of things passing outside.

The vocalizations of others can come to join this whimpering and moaning; their soothing murmurs and songs send their ripples into the turbid space of pain. For someone in pain, the sobbing and keening of onlookers amplifies the pain but amplifies also the vocalizations with which the sufferer's body seeks to reestablish its periodicities and kinetic melodies.

Wounds, pain, and suffering generate words. It is true that our vocabularies offer us but a limited list of words to describe our pain, as they offer us so few words to describe our pleasures. But wounds, pain, and suffering generate words to map out our reactions to them and the actions we have to undertake to foresee, avoid, repair, and heal them. We consult a doctor, and science takes over. The scientific discourse maps out genetic and biochemical deficiencies, bacteria or viruses that drifted in, or tumorous growths—events in a space without purpose and finality. The medical discourse draws up possible chemical or biochemical, genetic, or surgical interventions.

There is also among us an interpretative discourse, which aims to give meaning to our wounds and suffering and our mortality by evaluating their cause. It identifies incompetent doctors; uncomprehending, imprisoning, or castrating family members; irresponsible dieticians and medications; ignorant culinary traditions. It assigns culpability to the sick organism itself: counting on natural vigor, on the ability to recover from excesses, it has failed to care for itself properly. The suffering can then be interpreted as an admonition or a due punishment, in a social or cosmic space of finality and purpose.

How readily these words blaze into fulminations and accusations, intoxicated with their power! With them the sick body finds an authority it did not have when its youthful vitality made it curious and skeptical about all judgments. The requirements of convalescence, old age, and an ever-narrowing zone that we can manage hurl their needs as demands on the young and those with exuberant and far-ranging health. The sick incriminate their own organism inasmuch as it was moved by unbridled instincts and impulses—and is thus also an enemy to combat, to vanquish or control. This intelligence, ingenuity, craftiness, and cunning of interpretation have, from the age of Socrates and Euripides, proved powerful enough to assemble the bilious and morbid forces of the sick against the natural animal in us.

In the century and more since Nietzsche published *On the Genealogy of Morals*, the moral discourse bent on giving a meaning to suffering and death has undergone repeated assaults, not the last by Susan Sontag in her *Illness as Metaphor*.[1] The medical discourse, not only of physical but also of mental suffering, alone reinforces its validity.

A sufferer, seeking to face the stern truth, learns this discourse. She learns its vocabulary and grammar so as to understand her doctors and communicate her observations to them. In this discourse she ceases to be a suffering individual to become a patient, passive and receptive, a case in a universe where her word of honor, commitments, and anxieties have no significance.

Yet, in order to live out her ordeal and her life as her own, the sufferer must acknowledge her debilitated or surgically mutilated body. She must bring to light what the medical discourse passes over: her shock, her fears, her hopes and despairs, her obduracy and cowardice. She must map out her infirmities and her capabilities for work, for sex, for companionship, for thought. This discourse will link present with past and future; it will be a story she tells to herself. "An illness faced down, transcended, or even talked to death," Paul West notes, "becomes a prized possession, first draft of a novel you cannot bear to destroy but keep by you to hearten and remind."[2]

West, suffering a massive heart attack, implantation of a pacemaker, and then diabetes, masters the medical discourse and also elaborates his own story. He describes his body as an electrochemical contraption whose composition is as randomly material as that of the effusions out of which the stars form, and he describes his death as a fall of a material mass down the chute to the refrigerators of the morgue in the hospital basement. He masters every detail of the material and functioning of the pacemaker to be inserted into the left ventricle of his heart. He uses the medical discourse in mapping out how to reprogram his days and movements around microwave ovens, burglar alarms, arc welding units, power tools, induction furnaces, library checkout mechanisms. But to accept the pacemaker, he would have to tell a story of his own about it:

> [The surgeon] would slide the probe through a vein, and then the flanges would bend back along the lead, giving way easily as the probe passed from the vein into the right atrium, where much of my trouble was to begin with.... Once inside the ventricle, they were supposed to spring outward again to snag the soft pulp inside.... What set my teeth on edge was that slithering lead, when it went past the defenseless portals at my core, silver interloper where the sun had never shone and where there was never rest.... Round and round my mind went, repeating the abomination to exorcize it. Surely the lead would slip and then, like some zany butterfly, waft around, touching off twitches and convulsions wherever it landed, scraping and abrading, make me gasp.... My heart would be coddling a tiny propeller forever.... Then I realized that, instead of fending off all these images and tangents, I must allow them full play as my head's means of getting used to the idea; my imagination was translating for me, the barbaric into the tender, and I broke through to the palatable comparison that had been at the

back of my mind all along. Instead of that chimney-brush lead, I was going
to have the pink and velvet-gentle pistil of a hibiscus slid into my vein, with
five red-spotted stamens in the vanguard, behind them the shank of the pistil
and the tiny wire whisk of pliant golden commas that were the pollen.[3]

To reject the effort to make sense of our fate, to repudiate all moral
interpretation of our suffering takes strength, the strength to throw off the
authority the sick body gives to its recriminations. We find this strength in
telling the story of the enigmatic and awesome health the body knew and
still knows, which we did not create and do not comprehend:

> What all this "meant," I had no idea, and I still don't see why life, so long as
> we have it, should be "meaningful." We are here to bring our apparatus to
> bear, to pile up a mostly vanishing quota, say "thanks for the nice time," and
> go, which is why it seems to me worthwhile doing nothing more inventive
> than feeling my blood run, my eyes blink, my muscles twitch, all of these
> minima vaster than the nothing we go toward. We underestimate the deli-
> cious nullity of how things feel, in the body, when they're going right.[4]

The first draft of the novel the sufferer tells begins with the need to be
grateful for feeling his blood run, his eyes blink, his muscles twitch, for
having lived—a need to say "thanks for the nice time." Our life, which we
did not produce, which happened through our parents though they did
not fabricate it and is something the universe did not need, exists gratuitously. It was just given. Gratitude means recognizing the gift as a gift.
When someone gives us a gift, we receive it with embracing hands, retain
it, and provide space for it on the festive table or on the mantelpiece over
the hearth fire. Because words do embrace content, because they do hold
together and persist, the words "thanks for the nice time" do not simply
express gratitude, exteriorize a gratitude that is inward and mental; they
enact gratitude, they realize gratitude.

We can even say thanks for our ailments:

> He wants the body to be an affable host to its deadly diseases. He wants them
> to have a welcome, a space to move around in and show their stuff.... His ail-
> ments he regards as gifts given, trophies singled out to gift him with, and he
> takes a certain pride in owning them, in their ownership of him.[5]

"Thanks for the nice time" in the world—not because the world is such
a nice place, but the world does have so many beauties that arrive gratuitously. Though we do have to contrive to see them:

Do we embrace thoughtlessly, or do we somehow come to terms with the measured putrefaction we contain, and so develop a more open-minded sense of beauty? Severable beauty is a precarious thing, but that doesn't mean I'm duty-bound to kiss my sweetheart's feet because, properly reviewed, they're just as lovely as her lips. They're blessed, though. They help. They have structure. They call up certain Cézannes. Then why do I carry a snapshot of her face and not of them? Am I—are we—altogether too selective? If we relish life as such, shouldn't we admire it in the round? We cannot make a tree. We cannot make a liver either. And, if we could, would we take the same esthetic pride in the liver as in the tree?[6]

Could we come to admire the world in the round by just silent contemplation? Nietzsche asked:

How can we make things beautiful, attractive, and desirable for us when they are not? Here we could learn something … from artists who are really continually trying to bring off such inventions and feats. Moving away from things until there is a good deal that one no longer sees and there is much that our eye has to add if we are still to see them at all; or seeing things around a corner and as cut out and framed; or to place them so that they partially conceal each other and grant us only glimpses of architectural perspectives; or looking at them through tinted glass or in the light of the sunset; or giving them a surface and skin that is not fully transparent—all this we should learn from artists.[7]

Photographers show us beauty in the measured putrefaction that the world about us contains and that we contain; they photograph it from a distance where the eye has to add much, they frame it with other things or show it partially concealed or aflame with rare lighting, or they light up surface grain and glows. Words, just because they fragment things and grasp them with their outlines or skeletons only or focus our attention on some unnoticed detail or some relationship with remote things, can cast over things strange auras and spells. Perhaps indeed we can find our sweetheart's feet beautiful just by gazing upon them in the right setting and light. Yet is it not those words—"They're blessed, though. They help. They have structure. They call up certain Cézannes"—that give our contemplation that boost that makes us admire them in the round of things?

With words we move lightly over things. And words, with their streaming and their syncopation, their soft or hard, warm or cold tonalities, their beat and their micromelodies, their rumble and their hisses, their harmonies and their dissonances, pick up and amplify the sonorities loud and latent in the things. In doing so, they embrace and consecrate things and events. "Have not names and sounds been given to things that man might find things refreshing?" Zarathustra noted. "Speaking is a beautiful folly: with that man dances over all things. How lovely is all talking, and all the deception of sounds! With sounds our love dances on many-hued rainbows."[8]

And words, like the moaning with which the inner melodies of the body seek to come together again, can soothe and heal us. They can resonate through the body and help it reestablish its inner rhythms and melodies, its musicality.

The words that are bound to wounds also can break free of them; words can be an escape from illness, themselves become a life, a life of words. West discovers that the medical profession had fashioned a justifiable and concise taxonomy, which he learned not only for its utility for himself or for the old pleasures of scholarship but for the pleasure he finds in it: "I do get a sense of unique and ravishing complexity such as I get from a work of art, whether as maker or appreciator."[9] But he also escapes into writing fiction: "I keep managing to come to the end of another chapter, say, and I marvel at the plenary gratitude the human spirit can feel after the Furies have had it by the short hairs and it has managed to slink away, back into the operating theater of words."[10] So also with us: with our visitors in the hospital, how compulsively we talk of other things, leaving our illness behind. With words we connect with the words of others and with their lives. There is this ecstatic power in words.

2007

Sacrilege

A sanctuary, a sacred precinct, is a dark or radiant place marked out by prohibitions and taboos, separated from the profane sphere. To encounter there the sacred is to encounter the power of what is separated from, what marks the limit of the world of work and reason, of calculation and appropriation.

Sacred precincts are places of sacrifice. Modern world religions, which have striven to rationalize themselves, regard sacrifice—of goods, other animals, even of firstborn children—as traits of primitive and superseded religions. Yet, Henri Hubert and Marcel Mauss argued that sacrifice is the most universal, perhaps the most fundamental of religious acts.[1]

In a sacrifice something supremely precious—our finest harvest and livestock, our firstborn son—is set aside from all use, separated from the profane sphere. What is set apart from all profane use is separated absolutely, definitively, in being destroyed.

In a sacrifice the burning and killing reveals the separate, sacred, power that limits the space of all work and reason. In sacrifice of the food from the harvest the violent, indomitable power of the flames blazes over human works. The knife that tears open the body of the sacrificial victim tears apart the protective hide or skin exposing the writhing turmoil of spilt organs, reveals the violence of a stag or boar taken from the wilderness— the inner violence of its life—reveals anonymous untamed forces in the child. The knife of the shaman, the priest, Abraham reveals the unintelligible core of life and the inner impersonal violence in the composition of living things.

The sacrificial priest leaves the profane sphere to perform the sacrifice and acts in the name of the people. Bringing to him of their harvest and livestock, a beast of the wilderness, or their firstborn child, they participate in his deed. Those who perform sacrifice identify with the victim. The Aztec priests covered themselves with the blood of the sacrificial victims, excoriated them, and pulled the skin of the victims over their naked bodies. And we who consign to the sacred sphere our resources, the game from our hunt, our children, identify with them, identify with the victims. The stag or wild boar sacrificed would have sustained and nourished us. How could we not identify with our firstborn child, sacrificed to the mountain god Yahweh? At the moment of the blood sacrifice, the participants find their identity slashed with the knife. When the fire blazes on the sacred victim, it blazes too on us.

The communication continues in feasts where immense resources are consumed and in saturnalia where we abandon our sense of ourselves and controlling will and find ourselves possessed with the forces of pounding music and dance and with violent, erotic, excessive compulsions, and with the forces unleashed in the forests and rivers by night.

I had gone, one evening, to see an exhibition of photographs taken in rural Poland by a student in the fine-arts department. After a while I saw people passing to a room behind the photograph exhibit and joined them. There we saw a man, powerfully muscled and virile, naked, hanging upside down, his feet bound by a rope looped over a hook in the ceiling. Up against opposing walls of the small room there were stands with piles of knives on them—butcher knives, serrated knives, hunting knives. Against the other walls there were stands with guns and boxes of bullets. On the walls there were maps of the country with the numbers of people killed with such weapons in each of the states the prior year. For I think some forty-five minutes we stood around, viewing the man hung from the ceiling and looking at the stands in a kind of brutalized silence. This muscular young man naked and hung upside down exhibited human life at its strongest, now in a position of extreme vulnerability. The provocation, the temptation to cruelty surged in us. We glanced at the piles of knives and guns and the numbers of people cut down everywhere in the country and trembled before the abyss that we felt gaping open about us. Finally one of us took a knife and cut the rope; the man fell to the floor. I heard a student I knew, Andy, who was standing near me, muttering, "The show is not over like that," and saw him spring forward, seize a knife and bring it down with full force into the floor, grazing the arm of the fallen man. But he had thrust so violently that, without realizing it or feeling it, his hand had slipped off the handle and down the blade, which cut deeply into the palm of his hand and fingers. Seeing the blood pouring from his hand, he shook it violently over the fallen man, splattering him everywhere with his blood.

Andy is a musician, and several surgeries later the doctors had not been able to restore the tendons of his fingers enough for him ever to play again. He had a gathering of friends before the first surgery; he moved among us if anything more energized and ebullient than before.

We in the room felt vertiginously our bodies merging with, being absorbed in the man suspended and then fallen before us; his nakedness made us feel the nakedness of our bodies under our clothing, which protects them only from looks, and we felt his vulnerability with and in our flesh. The anxiety that infected us could be broken only by violence, and finally one of us had taken a knife to cut the rope and the man fell to the floor. But Andy felt most the intensity of violence that was not so easily spent and seized a knife to cut the arm of the man at our feet. When his knife slashed his own hand, it realized the identification with the man he struck, and we saw the fallen man everywhere bleeding with our blood.

We felt shock but also exhilaration in Andy's act; he acted in our stead, realizing the temptation to cruelty upon the fallen man we felt and enacting our impulse to release the tension with a cruel release of the blood from our bodies.

In Rio de Janeiro Avenida Atlântica extends along Copacabana beach, with a broad walkway on one side where restaurants and cafés extend their tables and tourists gather, facing the beach and the shimmering silvered ocean beyond. Around the tables about which people are dining, local people circulate selling paper cones of peanuts, small sausages, candies, cigarettes, and tourist souvenirs—straw hats, T-shirts, postcards. One day I was having a sandwich there, and I saw a man approaching and saw that he had both hands amputated, the one at the wrist, the other above the elbow; he was going from table to table badgering the people at their dinners.

As he approached, my eyes were drawn to him, as our eyes are before people with amputated limbs or crippled bodies; the sight of them arouses in us a wondering how they cope, especially if they do not look feeble and despondent but, instead, energetic and enterprising. There is something deeper: it is not in the nature of our bodies to tend always to a state of equilibrium like inert things; the excess energies our bodies generate prepare them for hard tasks and for dangers. But they also launch our bodies gratuitously into obstructed ways and on perilous paths. They drove our ancestors to cross the glaciers from Siberia to North America during the last Ice Age; they drive our contemporaries to descend into the ocean abysses and rocket into outer space. Subliminally our bodies see in amputees a premonition of wounds and mutilations and eventually incapacitation that lurk as possibilities in our most energetic drives.

When the man got closer, I saw that what he was selling, thrusting the stumps of his arms before the diners, were—knives. His performance was in the public space, but his audience had not come there or agreed to watch its demanding and grotesque plot. The diners at the tables were first repelled by another peddler offering them tourist souvenirs, then revolted by the sight of the stumps the man thrust under their eyes. Their revulsion was immobilized by surges of sympathy for not just another impoverished local but a mutilated human being. But then their horror before the sight of his fingerless and handless stumps returned before the sight of the knives he was offering them. Offering them, superficially, for sale, but also as a tourist souvenir of the knives that had cut off his hands, knives for them to use not simply to cut bread or meat but to cut into their bodies.

There are wounds cut open that do not heal. I have not been able to forget this man, his stumps, and his knives; each time I recall him I see him as vividly as the first time and the violent emotions his performance aroused surge again. No doubt some of those vacationers in Copacabana have been able to wipe out the sight of him from their memories. They would have had to stifle the passions, of empathy, of morbid fascination, of cruelty to him and to themselves that he had awakened in them. When he moved on, they would look at him from a distance and remind themselves that they indeed had sympathy for any unfortunate human being. They would recall the times, back home, in their gated communities, when they gave to charities, indeed, volunteered on Saturdays at the information desk of the hospital. They reassured themselves of the kindness of their hearts.

Sacrilege is akin to sacrifice; it is the converse of sacrifice. Sacrilege is a violence that breaks through the taboos and prohibitions that enclose the sacred precinct, to fiercely confront the sacred. Sacrilege encounters the power and violence of the sacred.

It is possible to view sacrilege as a violence directed against the culture and social structure of a people. The Frankish conquerors cut down the sacred trees of the Goths. As the Catholic monarchs conquered the Iberian Peninsula, in the thousand-pillared mosque of Córdoba they contrived a cathedral. Cortés destroyed the Aztec temple in Mexico City and built a cathedral on the site. Unable to dismantle the 4.45 million square meters of stones of the pyramid of Quetzalcoatl at Cholula, the greatest structure ever built on the planet, the Spanish built a church on top of it.

But J. C. Heesterman showed that in India the sacrifices of a society became individual sacrifices.[2] The seven-horse sacrifice performed by high civic officials in the name of the state was no longer performed by the beginning of the Common Era; instead individuals performed sacrifices. In

Haiti and in the Brooklyn home of Mama Lola sacrifices are rituals request-ed and performed by individuals under the guidance of a Vodou *serviteur*.[3]

Sacrilege, the violation of the places and rituals by which individuals perform sacrifices, would then be viewed as a violation of the conceptions with which an individual conceives his or her place in the cosmos and his or her significance and dignity.

Today secularists reduce the experience of sacrilege to the simple will to power of a conquering people. Michel Leiris, curator of the Musée de l'Homme in Paris, detailed in *L'Afrique fantôme* a two-year expedition in the Sahel to enrich the museum, tricking, bribing, and outright stealing ritual and sacred objects from the Kono and the Dogon.[4] Later, Thor Heyerdahl recounts, in *Aku-Aku,* how he acquired by fraud, espionage, and theft the family heirlooms and protective carvings from the hidden family tombs of the last of the Easter Islanders—a book that makes sickening reading today.[5] We see those who practice sacrilege—the curators of the museum in Cairo where the pharaohs are on display, taken from their tombs and stripped of their utensils, weapons, and finery destined for them in their afterlife, their heads stripped of their wrappings—we see the sacrilege as driven simply by rationalist and scientific hubris.

But there is more to it than that. Sacrilege is an intense experience, which involves a boldness to confront the sacred, to do violence with the violence of the sacred. The Frankish priests who cut down the sacred tree of the Goths, Cortés, and Pizarro did not think that the deities of the Goths, the Aztecs, and the Inca were nothing; they acted to show the power of the Christian god over the demons of the pagans. The researchers who pene-trated into the tombs of the pharaohs or set out to carbon-date the Shroud of Turin pit the power of rationalist civilization over the power of mythical and mystical cultures.

In the high Gothic chapel of the Holy Blood in Bruges in Belgium people kneel at the altar railing and the priest passes back and forth all day giving them to kiss the most sacred reliquary in Christendom—the Holy Grail, a rock crystal vial containing the blood of Jesus, blood of our redemption, brought there from Jerusalem in 1150 CE by Count of Flanders Diederik van den Elzas after the Second Crusade. The chapel is built over a much older Romanesque church, whose foundations can now be visited in the crypt. There, looking carefully at the upper backsides of the pillars, one can see hex signs carved deeply into the stone. There, beneath this most sacred shrine, people executed pacts with Satan. What terrifying boldness and loathing seized them as they did so?

Midafternoon. Twenty-eight years ago. It was my first sojourn in Islam. In the mosque of Süleyman the Lawgiver in Istanbul a hundred or so men had gathered to bow and pray; I seated myself in back on the rug and subsided in the cool of the great luminous domed building. Unlike the Catholic churches of Europe and of my youth, the prayer hall is not a sanctuary; Muslims today, as those of the first generation, perform their prayer equally in the desert. At the end of their prayer as the men stood and moved out of the mosque, a youth came up to me and asked where I came from. He was Omar, twelve years old, and he invited me to come see the mosque. A mosque is a place for the works of mercy; in this building complex designed in the sixteenth century by the architect Mimar Sinan, we visited the dispensary of food for the poor, for the distribution of clothing, the clinic for the sick, the school, the dormitory for the homeless. Omar said he would like to practice his English; we agreed to meet every other afternoon, and he would show me the city.

Before leaving to meet him, I would look through my guidebook. One day I suggested we go to the Phanar district where the guidebook had listed a few little-visited sights. This is the far end of the city, just this side of the land walls. It was two in the afternoon in midsummer; people were dozing in the shade of cafés and on divans behind the doors of their homes. We came upon the cathedral of Saint George. It is a brick and stucco church, smaller than any Orthodox church in Pittsburgh or Baltimore. But it is the seat of the Supreme Patriarch of Orthodoxy, cringing here far from the shadow of the Hagia Sophia that for a thousand years had been the largest building in the world. Omar signed that he would wait outside.

Inside, the dim light and walls grimy with the smoke of candles and incense contrasted with the vast luminous spaces of the great domed mosques of the city. Here the central nave would barely hold a hundred worshippers. In front, the iconostasis shut off the sanctuary behind which the Supreme Patriarch would perform the sacraments. It was impossible to appreciate the art of the icons stuck along the walls, for tin sheets covered all but their smoke-blackened faces. I turned to the right wall behind an arcade of brick pillars, where instead of a series of chapels I saw there were big marble catafalques. The covers had raised emblems with ornate crosses on them. These, I thought, must be the tombs of the Patriarchs of Orthodoxy. I walked the length of the series, to the front entrance, and looked back into the central nave, then up the left aisle; there was no one in the church. I thought of Omar waiting outside, and felt something of distaste for this place that he would feel. The last appurtenances of Orthodoxy had ended up here where the city ends.

I moved back to the first mausoleum I had come upon; it was also the most ornate. I looked down the aisle, turned back to the central nave: there really was no one in the church. Then, blood hot in my face, I leaned over and with both hands lifted the heavy lid to peer inside. But inside there was a bronze coffin. I lowered the lid, feeling jumpy and grimy. I looked back into the central nave, at the still closed entrance door. I moved back to the catafalque, lifted the lid again, set it back and lifted the lid of the bronze coffin. The space was filled with a chasuble of once-white silk now yellowed with heavy raised brocadings in black and purple and beaded everywhere with small jewels. Through the thick smell of dust I looked at the head, cushioned in embroidered silk, a dark brown skull showing under what looked liked shreds of dried beef, scabs in the eye sockets, and patches of skin shriveled from the crooked rows of the teeth. I quickly lowered the bronze lid and then the marble cover and slinked out of the building. I greeted Omar, who asked no questions about the cathedral. He suggested we go have some tea.

The enormity of what I had done tormented me for days, for weeks. Most people, if asked to imagine committing a mortal crime, could not really picture themselves doing so, and if they succeed in imagining committing murder, they can only think they would no longer be who they are. The sacrilege seemed to have undermined what I was.

In this forlorn brick and stucco church to which Orthodoxy had been reduced, sacrilegiously violating the mausoleum to find these sacred princes reduced to dusty skeletons, I violently broke with my own Christianity and went outside to rejoin Omar in the sun.

But I had not acted willfully, in an intellectual illumination of the impotence of a two-thousand-year-old politico-ideological institution; instead I had been mesmerized by a force that emanated from the church, the catafalques, like a temptation coming from them. The darkness of the church had invited me in as a place of secrets, the colonnaded ambulatories on the sides beckoned to me, the gilded lids of the catafalques lay there in the afternoon silence of the completely deserted church as there to be opened. As the minutes passed, the temptation emanating from these things intensified such that I could no longer muster the force of will to turn and leave the church. Jean Genet understood this power things have over us, power to captivate us, bewitch us, subjugate us—the jealous husband who one day bought a gun that from then on determined his days until inevitably, inexorably he became a murderer. The Church Fathers have written that there are incitements in things that are so strong that we can resist them only with the help of divine grace, only when the direct power of God intervenes.

What was revealed under the marble and the bronze covers of the catafalque was the unthinkable, unendurable power of death, the death of the Byzantine Empire, of its sacred rulers, of the most powerful intellects that had flourished, of the works and glories of millions of humans, death that defeats and mocks all human reason and all human works, my death too.

Revealed that in the imperialism and wealth of Byzantium, a two-thousand-year-old religious effort, intellectual and historical effort, had always been locked in combat with death. A combat that would continue in tomorrow's global mercantile world, where the rain forests, the glaciers, the polar ice caps, the unending stretches of outer space surrender to work and reason, are surveyed, invaded, and exploited by mercantile enterprises. Would continue in me, whose sacrilege has identified me with the sacred victim.

2012

PART V

Together

Our Uncertain Compassion

There are those, even our enemies, we want to live; there are those, even our friends, we want to die. We imagine death may be the end of pain, but we may well will our pain. We honor those who die with dignity, but dignity is not something we ascribe to ourselves or can be our objective.

We cannot understand why we have to die: all understanding stakes out and surveys a future. But death—our death, that of our friends—is the object of our most intense feelings. How unstable, how equivocal are those feelings!

To be a friend is to share the path with someone, to share the labor with him or her. To be a friend is to be there when pleasure can be shared and common. It is also to be there when one's friend falters and falls. To accompany someone on a part of the path of life is already to pledge to accompany him or her on the path that leads nowhere, the path of his or her dying. To be a friend is to be there and share the pain.

We can desperately want someone, suffering from a grave injury or disease, to live. Because she has not yet lived enough. We want time for her to flourish, knowing that her life is a radiance shed on others, on us. We can desperately want someone to live because we have not yet shown our love for her enough, not yet loved her enough.

One can doubt the straightforwardness of our wish that the other live: Is our wish that the other live a wish for her or for ourselves? Do we wish that she live so that we can show her we do love her, so that we can love her enough? Is there this guilt that we are seeking to circumvent?

In every hatred, there is wanting someone to die. Hatred is a powerful focus of our sensibility and drives: it is a will that is fixed on someone. The

wanting that someone die is a disclosure of uniqueness. Hatred singulariz-
es absolutely.

When individuals lose their singularity, they appear as belonging to
death. There is then a wanting to be rid of this carrion. When we think
of the six billion humans that now overrun the planet, there is no way
we can think of them as having singular lives. Then we cannot think of
the death that clears some space as an evil. Before individuals sunken into
comas from which they will not awaken, patients in advanced stages of
Alzheimer's disease who appear to no longer know who they were and
who they are, we cannot prevent ourselves from wanting death to come
claim its own.

But there is also love in wanting someone to die.

When someone we love who has been suffering dies, we feel a sense of
relief. We feel a loosening of tension, a repose. Death appears as a deliverance from dying—from the suffering of dying.

Suffering is finding existing itself to be a burden of which one cannot
relieve oneself and which one cannot lighten. One's existence is no longer
a dynamism generating excess energies, a momentum that pushes into
open roads and into the thick of things. Suffering is more than passivity; it
is having to deal with one's substance. One does not program the opening
of valves, the distribution of blood and the channeling of biles, the peristal-
sis and spasms, but in the dullness and weight of fatigue and in pain one
has to endure them. To suffer the pain is to be unable to turn away from
oneself, to look outward, to forget oneself. In pain one is mired in oneself. One has to deal with oneself; one's existence is an encumbrance for
oneself. One has to endure, one has to bear the pain, one is bound to one's
existence as to a responsibility one cannot escape. Suffering is an experience of identity, individuality, and solitude.

Pain and suffering deliver one over to dying. Dying in pain and suffering
is reduction to passivity and prostration. It is being cut adrift from one's
future, and from one's past. One knows that what is coming is death. This
death is not one of an array of possibilities one reaches out for and takes
hold of; it is for the dying one the end of all possibility, impossibility itself.
All the experience and skills one has acquired are powerless to deal with it.
As the imminence of death looms, it cuts one adrift from one's past. There
is nothing to do, but suffer and wait for death. One is held in the suffering, in the pain, in the present. The present stretches on, without passing,
without going anywhere. The last moment is not locatable in the array of a
future of stages and possibilities; it lurks in every moment, is imminent in
any moment. That death is coming is certain; when it is coming is indeterminate. What is coming is this unknown.

Is it just nothingness? One does not know it will be nothingness—nothingness is not some thing one knows.

But nothingness is what one can long for, out of all the density and suffocating opacity of pain and suffering.

Socrates had seen men die; he had committed himself to defend Athens in war, he had killed men in battle. He does not speak of how they died, nor of the relief he felt when they died. He speaks of the relief he will feel when the trouble and passivity and opacity of his body will be broken, when this long sickness which is life in a body will come to an end. His last words—Crito, we owe a cock to Asclepius—say that life is the sickness for which death is the cure. Did not Socrates here in fact claim to know two things that he did not know—what death is, that is, that death is a relief; and what life is, that is, that life is sickness?

The other's suffering is trouble for us—hours spent in hospital visits, in somber interviews with doctors, in looking after the sick one's affairs. The other so bound to his suffering seems to bind us: we feel a somber obligation that excludes insouciance.

We cannot view the sufferer's contorted hands, his grimaces, hear his sighs and moans, without these inducing contortions, grimaces, sighs, and moans in us, and with them, inducing a sense of the pain. His pain, that pain that rivets the suffering one to himself, to the limits of his own existence, reverberates in us.

To comfort someone, to comfort oneself—it is the most spontaneous of our initiatives. When we find ourselves helpless to comfort others in their distress, we comfort ourselves by believing that the death that comes to them as the last extremity of suffering and prostration is a deliverance.

We feel a sense of relief that this agony of another, which has been an ordeal for us, is over. Is the sense of relief a recognition that we are freed from the suffering and dying of another, that his death returns us to the lures and lightheartedness of life?

We want to think that the death that finally came to the sufferer is a relief to him too. Perhaps we can accept our own sense of relief only by thinking that the other feels relief too.

There is no doubt that the other can look forward to his own death as to the end of the pain and the suffering. But the death he awaits will not be the relief and renewal he knew when someone whose suffering he watched died. Death is not for him release, but the last limit of suffering and prostration. Our sense of release is his entombment. Our relief is burdened by a sense of our having escaped, having fled.

Pain does not only come from the outside, when a foreign object damages a limb or a foreign body invades an internal organ of our bodies. The concentration of our forces produces the pain of constriction, and their release produces exhaustion. This is possible because there is a passivity internal to life: life is passive with regard to itself. The pulse of life is in initiatives, in the surge and release of forces. One has to anticipate a future and endure the passing of time. And there is a substance and weight to the initiative that the force of life has to bear. To live is to find oneself having to exist, having to endure, having to bear the burden and weight of one's own initiatives.

Today modern medicine seems to promise the life relieved of all pain and suffering that Socrates sought in the hemlock poison. How much of the equipment of modern life is contrived to eliminate effort and discomfort! For long hours of the day we feel no discomfort; for long years no pain.

In Madagascar, people sleep on reed mats, turning often in the night to relieve the pressure on muscles and veins. They could, of course, make padded mattresses. They trudge through the muck. They do not complain: they do not imagine discomfort and pain could be anything but part of life.

All cowardice begins in the repulsion of suffering.

The suffering we see may well be a suffering that does not seek to be consoled: Nietzsche warned against imagining that we should alleviate a suffering which another needs and clings to as his or her destiny—the inner torments of Beethoven, the hardships and heartaches of the youth who has gone to join the guerrillas in the mountains, the grief of someone who has to grieve the loss of her child. To be afflicted with his or her suffering requires that we care about the things he or she cares for. The suffering of the one who faces me, a suffering visible in the bloodless white of her anguished face, may well be not the suffering of her own hunger and thirst, but a suffering for the animals in her care dying of the drought or the peregrines in the poisoned skies, a distress over the crumbling temple and for the nests of seabirds broken by the tidal wave, a grieving for the glaciers melting under skies whose carbon-dioxide layers are trapping the heat of the earth.

Do not the strong, even among us, seek to feel the pain, the pain that the maximum harnessing and release of their forces entails: it is a tonic for them, a fortifier. There is the materiality of the pain itself. It is like an acid in which one is immersed. It is dense, it has grain, substance.

There is also the fortifying effect of pushing on to what is behind the pain: death, the void. Thought is driven by an excessive compulsion, and is itself an excess over and beyond perception. Socrates practiced philosophy as a consolation: for him thought catches sight of order and harmony in all generating and corrupting things, and of its own momentum pushes beyond the pain of dying to the harmony and bliss that lies beyond. Our thought has instead pushed on, beyond our individual deaths, to the coming extinction of our sun, the extinction of all the stars, to the final Dark Era of the universe that will consist in a diffuse sea of electrons, positrons, neutrinos, and radiation spread tenuously across an infinitely larger region than exists today. Thought is seeing what exceeds the possibility of seeing, what is intolerable to see, what exceeds the possibility of thinking.

We do not simply see the pallid surfaces, the contorted hands and fingers; we feel a depth of pain. Our gaze is held to the limits of this prostrate life. There is contagion of misery. For one does not view the pain behind the surfaces of his skin; one feels it troubling one's look, one feels it up against oneself. The sense of sharing the pain of another, the sense of the barriers of identity, individuality, and solitude breaking down hold us. There is anonymity but also communion in suffering. One suffers as anyone suffers, as all that lives suffers. To look upon someone who is in pain is to have known pain, is to know what it is.

One is repelled, but one is also drawn to that pain. The other is suffering a pain involuntarily; it awakens a will in oneself to suffer that pain. The greater the suffering of the masses they saw, the more strongly Gandhi and Che Guevara willed to take on that pain. It drove from them all desire for comfort, for pleasure, for sweet oblivion.

Compassion is not simply the pitting of one's will against the suffering in another. To be compassionate is to long to suffer, to suffer with the other. One wants to be afflicted with this alien pain. One wants to hurt oneself, wound oneself. Among the Papuans of Irian Jaya a woman chops off a finger when she loses a lover or a child.

There is a complacency in compassion. There is an insidious temptation in the anguish with which one abides with the one who suffers—the temptation to know the ordeal, the inhuman abysses, the ultimate drama he is undergoing through him, without having to bear the prostration of his pain, without risking what he risks.

There is a force in suffering—the force to endure, to bear the pain. There is also the force to react to the pain, to turn against it. When this force is without effect, the force can turn against what is behind the pain, or who is behind the pain. The pain fuels vindictiveness, vengefulness. The sufferer can reproach himself, blame himself, torment himself with guilt feelings. In the violence of pain he strikes out against his own body, his own consciousness.

The healthy impulses of the active forces of life, of the doctor and the nurses, repel this contagion of misery, of passivity and prostration, this dispiriting and debilitating pity. Their compassion is active. Compassion acts in place of the suffering one, does what the prostrate one cannot do. Compassion becomes a knowing for another, knowing what is good for another, when, sunken into himself, mired in himself in the pain, the other no longer can see.

The force of the compassionate one can come to the assistance of the sufferer, to compound the force of the sufferer, to endure. The force of the compassionate one can use the reactive force of pain, the vindictiveness there is in the force of suffering. It can be directed outward—against the pollutants, the microbes, the market forces that released the pollutants and the microbes.

Active compassion can lead one into wanting someone—the one or ones responsible for the suffering of the one one loves, to die. It can lead one into willing to kill others.

It can also lead one to want the one who suffers, and whom one loves, to die. But between wanting someone to die and acting to put him to death there is always a segment of time, however minimal, in which the compassionate one's feelings are unstable and equivocal, in which that volition can hesitate.

Dignity is not a word we use much. We do talk about people who behave with dignity in certain situations, with the composure and assurance that formal and ceremonial occasions—state dinners, funerals—require. They know the codes. We also speak of people who behave with dignity in crises, when their competence is being impugned. The engineer behaves with dignity when he listens carefully and respectfully to all the criticisms being made of his work, knowing that he can answer them. The minister of the environment behaves with dignity when he resigns his cabinet post as the government grants the mining companies rights to national parklands. The nurse behaves with dignity when she listens attentively to the patient, or the doctor, telling her how she screwed up. It is especially during the ordeal of dying that we speak of dignity and honor it. Someone who suffers a long agony without illusions, with lucidity, without unrealistic demands on the medical staff, without rancorously searching for blame in the past, dies with dignity.

The dying one is dying, he is not reaching for dignity, dignity is not his goal. He does not have a goal: he is going nowhere. He is going without going on. Dying takes time; he is held in the endurance of time. It is not that he extends a field of time—like the person engaged in living, who foresees what is ahead, foresees objectives and foresees the paths and implements and obstacles on this side of those objectives. The dying one foresees nothing. The state of death, of the extinction of his life and of the environment his life lights up about him, is not something he confronts. It has no faces and no surfaces and no place. It cannot be located in the succession of moments of time. The last moment is ahead, not yet there, but it is imminent; the next moment may be the last moment. He is enduring a time without a future, a time from which the resources of the past are irrelevant and disconnected. His lucid recognition of that is lived as patience. Patience is a not just passivity, it is suffering, but it is suffering without grappling for release and without recrimination against the past which can no longer offer its forces and resources. Because he knows his time to die has come, because he knows he is dying and awaits what cannot be foreseen or confronted—because he somehow finds, in patience, the strength for this lucidity—he makes no unrealistic demands on the medical staff and does not rancorously search for blame in others or in his own past. And it is just that that strikes us as his dignity. But that was not an objective; it is a side effect.

Is it not the awesomeness of such an achievement, when all his resources are failing, in the midst of relentless pain, that makes us project the dignity we witness there back over the whole life of such a person? We are unable to witness such a dying without envy, without an intense longing to be able to die that way, when our time comes. It motivates us to wish to live with dignity.

But while we speak of dignity in others—it is even one of the things we are most impelled to call attention to and honor when we witness it—we are most reticent to speak of dignity in our own case. Is that not because to invoke dignity for oneself, to say "I have dignity" is to seek to designate a quality that will be in force in one's continuing life, whereas dignity is something we first observed in someone who was dying? What we designated there as dignity appeared to us to be the most improbable, inexplicable, awesome trait that emerged in the throes of physical collapse, pain, the impotence of mental skills, the process of definitive and irreversible defeat. The intense longing that arises in us to be able to die that way surges in us like a hope fraught with the sense of all the laxities, facilities, cowardices, escapisms, illusions, and fantasies with which our lives are interwoven. If the spectacle of someone dying with dignity is what motivates us to wish to live with dignity, whether we in fact do live with dignity will be known only when the time comes for us to die.

If to invoke dignity for oneself is to forfeit it, if dignity cannot be an objective, if it is essentially a side effect of that thing we have to do, to die, to lucidly see that we have fallen into a time which has no objectives, no future, then could it not be that dignity can only be a side effect of under-takings that we engage in that do have objectives? One cannot produce dignity intentionally or willfully; it can only appear as a side effect of doing other things well, aiming at outside objectives. Our dignity can appear as a side effect of caring for the suffering, accompanying the dying.

2006

Dignity

Dignity is not a word we use much. We do talk about people who behave with dignity in certain situations, with the composure and assurance that formal and ceremonial occasions—state dinners, funerals—require. They know the codes. We also speak of people who behave with dignity in crises, when their competence is being attacked. The engineer behaves with dignity when he listens respectfully to all the criticisms being made of his work, knowing that he can answer them. The minister of the environment behaves with dignity when he resigns his cabinet post after the government resolved to grant the mining companies rights to national parklands. The nurse behaves with dignity when she listens attentively to the patient or the doctor telling her how she bungled her job. It is especially during the ordeal of dying that we speak of dignity and honor it.

The dying one is dying; he or she is not reaching for dignity; dignity is not his or her goal. He does not have a goal: he is going nowhere. He is going without going on. Dying takes time; he is held in the endurance of time. It is not that he extends a field of time, like the person engaged in living who foresees what is ahead, foresees objectives, and foresees the paths and implements and obstacles on this side of those objectives. The dying one foresees nothing, has a premonition of the utterly unknown ahead. This state of death, of the extinction of his life and of the environment his life lights up about him, is not something he confronts. It has no faces and no surfaces and no place. It cannot be located in the succession of moments of time. The last moment is ahead, not yet there, but it is imminent; the next moment may be the last moment. She is enduring a time without a future, a time from which the resources of the past are irrelevant and disconnect. Her lucid recognition of that is lived as patience. Patience is a not just passivity; it is suffering—but it is suffering without grappling for release and without recrimination against the past that can no longer offer its forces and resources. Because she knows her time to die has come, because she knows she is dying and awaits what cannot be foreseen or confronted—because she somehow finds, in patience, the strength for this lucidity—she makes no unrealistic demands on the medical staff and does not search for blame in others or in her own past. And it is just that that strikes us as her dignity. But that was not an objective; it is a side effect.

Is it not such comportment in the midst of relentless pain, when all his resources are failing, that makes us project the dignity we witness there back over the whole life of such a person? We are unable to witness such a dying without envy, without longing to be able to die that way, when our time comes. It motivates us to wish to live with dignity.

We speak of dignity in others—it is even one of the things we are most impelled to point out and talk about when we witness it—but we are reticent to speak of dignity in our own case. Is that not because to invoke dignity for oneself, to say "I have dignity," is to seek to designate a quality that will be in force in one's subsequent life, whereas dignity is something we first observed in someone who was dying? What we designated there as dignity appeared to us to be something improbable, inexplicable, that emerged in the throes of physical collapse, pain, the impotence of mental skills, the process of definitive and irreversible defeat. The longing that arises in us to be able to die that way surges in us like a hope fraught with the sense of all the laxities, facilities, cowardices, escapisms, illusions, fantasies with which our lives are interwoven. If the spectacle of someone dying with dignity is what motivates us to wish to live with dignity, whether we, in fact, do live with dignity will be known only when the time comes for us to die.

If to invoke dignity for oneself is to forfeit it, if dignity cannot be an objective, if it is essentially a side effect of that thing we have to do, to die—to lucidly see that we have fallen into a time that has no objectives, no future—then dignity can only be a secondary effect of undertakings that we engage in that do have objectives. One cannot produce dignity intentionally or willfully; it can only appear as a side effect of aiming at outside objectives, doing other things well.

2010

Irrevocable Loss

Work is launched by envisioning an objective. Putting himself in the future with the objective, the agent segments the environment into hypothetical paths, resources, implements, and obstacles. Work takes time; it executes manipulations in a succession of phases of time. It applies force to subordinate materials and resources to and integrates them into the final objective. What has come to pass does not pass away, is not lost; it is possessed and integrated in the result that is gained.

Language may fix an objective for work, and the successive moves of a work may be represented in language. Georges Bataille saw that language has the intentional form of work. Language analyzes, chops up, a thing, situation, or event and lays out its components successively. The sense of the words successively put forth is not present in them; the words that follow one another await their meaning from the future, from the final words of the sentence. The final words retain the succession of words that have already passed and fulfill their meaning that had been in suspense. They reverse the passing of time, recuperate the loss.

The end does not close in upon itself, upon its presence; it opens upon more words to situate and fix its significance. "Language," Bataille says, "cannot isolate an end and say of it, positively, that it is of *no use*: it cannot keep from inserting that end into an endless circle of propositions where there is never any apogee, where nothing ever stops, where nothing is *lost*."[1]

A *performance* is an action that is turned to one or more witnesses. And the language that informed the action, that programmed and guided it, now acquires vocative direction and imperative force, addressed to the spectator. In addition, a performance can exhibit nonlinguistic, nonconceptual sense—acceleration, pause, silence, expansion, condensation, elation, blockage—now addressed to the spectator. An action is modified when it also functions as a performance; its stages are made more clear and distinct. The action may acquire formal perfection; it is performed with grace and style.

In *ritual* the action that is set forth is not tightly engaged with the material forces in the immediate environment. The pattern of the action can then be meticulously refined. "Ritual," Claude Lévi-Strauss explained, "makes constant use of two procedures: parceling out *(morcellement)* and repetition.... Ritual makes infinite distinctions and ascribes discriminatory values to the slightest shades of difference."[2] We turn to walk home, and when we set out our walk contracts a gait—a rhythmic and melodic pattern—that prolongs itself of itself. It can become ritualized, as when we attentively place every other step on a line in the sidewalk or step in three-quarter waltz time.

The close association of behavior and language that we see in work and in performance is broken in ritual. The ritualization of our walk may start with no intention formulated; it is not an acting out of a statement. Sigmund Freud noted that we repeat our personal or private rituals with extreme attentiveness to each step, while being unable to say what each step means. Rituals may well include words, words that are not descriptions but invocations and incantations, words of a language no one uses or understands, or vocalisms of no language, that function to accelerate or intensify movement or induce trance states.

Actions may become ritualized without language, but then in the gap between the ritual and the real environment is an open space where imagination or visionary states can insert the mythic languages that elaborate other scenes and narratives.

The ritual is not a segment of theater, is not an acting out of a preexisting myth; it is an action. Rituals are enacted, Victor Turner explained, to promote and increase fertility of men, crops, and animals, domestic and wild; to cure illness; to avert plague; to obtain success in raiding; to turn boys into men and girls into women; to make chiefs out of commoners; to transform ordinary people into shamans and shamanins; to "cool" those "hot" from the warpath; to ensure the proper succession of seasons and the hunting and agricultural responses of human beings to them.[3]

Victor Turner was studying collective rituals. His list does not cover all the rituals in our individual lives, does not spell out what our personal or private rituals do.

We devoted our whole life to a cause, it gave meaning to everything we did, and the cause has been lost. The words that proclaimed the cause and enlisted us in the cause have become impotent and empty. We are alive still; what can we do with the time that remains? We have lost our lover.

Everything that we did we did for and with our lover; every action was also a performance addressed to our lover; that love remains, grasping the immense void. What can it do? Before our grief, our friends discover the vacuousness of what they say, what anyone can say. And when someone who we did not love, who no one loved, is lost the abyss is yet more terrible, our anguish yet more desolate. Nowhere more than here is language impotent.

In the face of irrevocable loss, when work can have no effect, when performance has become absurd in the absence of lover or witness, we may find that our life continues in rituals, rituals that are not acting out of language, that do not give rise to language. What are the rituals doing?

In Gabriel García Márquez's *One Hundred Years of Solitude*, Colonel Aureliano Buendía had risen to become commander in chief of the revolutionary forces and the man most feared by the government.[4] He had launched thirty-two armed uprisings that each had been crushed. He had slaughtered uncounted enemy soldiers and noncombatants and led so many of his followers to defeat and death without heroism or legacy. By seventeen different women he had seventeen male children who because they were his sons were one after another hunted down and killed. As the years passed he saw the Conservatives but also the Liberals for whom he fought had abandoned all their principles, fighting only for power. After almost twenty years of war, he signed a treaty with the government putting an end to the insurrection.

He returns to the house in which he was born. He gives his military clothing to the orderlies, buries his weapons, and burns the poetry he had written since childhood. He destroys all traces of his passage through the world. He refuses to see anyone. Behind closed doors all day he works making gold figurines, little fish. He links their scales, laminates gills, puts on fins, and fits tiny rubies into their eye sockets. The fish are very small and frail but perfect. At first he sells the little fishes for gold coins, then melts down the coins to make little fish. But when he finds out that people are buying them not as pieces of jewelry but as historic relics, he stops selling them. He keeps on making two fishes a day and when he finishes twenty-five he melts them down and starts all over again. The attention, the concentration required by the delicacy of his artistry fills the persistence of time and also neutralizes his memories and disconnects his disillusionment with the war. Each little fish is perfect and each movement and moment of making it is perfect and dissolves as each fish is melted down. He is effacing the worth and worthlessness of all his deeds, effacing his very name, in these figurines.

He is also effacing the conquest that had founded Colombia. The conquistadors were searching for El Dorado, the Muisca chief who filled a raft with gold figurines and covered himself with gold dust and rowed to the center of Lake Guatavita, where he descended into the waters and scattered all the gold objects among the fish of the lake. The conquistadors tortured hundreds of natives to get them to reveal where the gold was mined and stored, and several times enslaved them to drain the lake, without recovering the treasure.[5] They decimated the Muisca, obliterated their culture and knowledge, such that today nothing remains but a small number of tiny gold figurines whose meaning is lost.

Death comes, comes when it will. As it approaches, in sickness or in old age, there is the time of waiting. It is a time when one's physical and mental powers progressively diminish, when the future that is imminent is the eventuality of total and irreversible impotence. The time of waiting is a stretch of time in which the anticipations, intentions, projects that envision the future lose their meaning and disconnect, a stretch of time in which the past, all the experience, knowledge, and skills of the past lose their meaning, fall away. In the time of waiting one finds oneself in a now that does not pass, that continues, without extending possibilities.

Baltimore, where I live, is the home of the American Visionary Art Museum, the first and most important venue for "outsider art" in the United States. Artworks made by people untrained in art, ignorant of the art world, sometimes by people unable to function in society, incarcerated in institutions for the insane. Over the years that I have visited the museum, I have often been struck by the extremely meticulous works made by people suffering from schizophrenia or severe neurological disorders, people with no hope of cure and release, enduring the unending now of their suffering. A whole room, pillows, quilts, bedcovers, curtains, even all the walls covered with sequins, each one sewn with precision in its place. Huge constructions made of toothpicks, 192,000 of them, each one glued with the precision of a jeweler. Filling each now of their unending and hopeless suffering with perfection.

About the time when Colonel Aureliano Buendía had returned to the house where he was born, his sister Amaranta began to weave a shroud for Rebeca. In her adolescence Amaranta had fallen in love with Pietro Crespi, who was betrothed to Rebeca. Amaranta had sworn to kill Rebeca before they could marry. But Pietro Crespi did not marry Rebeca and when he later proposed to Amaranta, she refused him. Unable to move her refusal, he put an end to his life. Years later Colonel Gerineldo Márquez declared his love to her, but Amaranta refused him. These two refusals had marked her life, which repeated and prolonged them.

Her mother Úrsula in her extreme old age and blindness came to see that Amaranta, "whose hardness of heart frightened her, whose concentrated bitterness made her bitter," was "the most tender woman who had ever existed, and she understood with pitying clarity that the unjust tortures to which she had submitted Pietro Crespi had not been dictated by a desire for vengeance, as everyone had thought, nor had the slow martyrdom with which she had frustrated the life of Colonel Gerineldo Márquez been determined by the gall of her bitterness, as everyone had thought, but that both actions had been a mortal struggle between a measureless love and an invincible cowardice, and that the irrational fear that Amaranta had always had of her own tormented heart had triumphed in the end."[6]

The hatred was a fear of the wild torments of love, and as love sometimes converts into hatred, hatred sometimes converts into love, both of them possible on the basis of a measureless understanding of solitude.

In old age Amaranta was now only waiting for Rebeca to die. "She had decided to restore Rebeca's corpse, to disguise with paraffin the damage to her face and make a wig for her from the hair of the saints. She would manufacture a beautiful corpse, with the linen shroud and a plush-lined coffin with purple trim, and she would put it at the disposition of the worms with splendid funeral ceremonies. She worked out the plan with such hatred that it made her tremble to think about the scheme, which she would have carried out in exactly the same way if it had been done out of love."[7]

As she worked, the attention and concentration spent on each stitch made each of her memories more scalding.

Then one day death appears to her in an apparition and orders her to begin sewing her own shroud. "She was authorized to make it as complicated and as fine as she wanted but just as honestly executed as Rebeca's, and she was told that she would die without pain, fear, or bitterness at dusk on the day that she finished it."[8] All her waking hours Amaranta works on her shroud; all her nights she dreams of the shroud. Sometimes after her dreams she unravels what she had woven to design it anew. It will be the most perfect, the most beautiful shroud ever woven. Over four years she works; each thread, each now absorbs her attention completely. The time span of the weaving is not like the time span of a work, making a shelter or a tool or utensil, which open upon a future time of possibility. The time span of the weaving is the dead time of the present whose past has fallen away, that prolongs itself into another thread, another now. A time of perfection, what is accomplished neither requiring anything further nor making possible anything different. "The world was reduced to the surface of her skin and her inner self was safe from all bitterness. It pained her not to have had that revelation many years before when it would have still been possible to purify memories and reconstruct the universe under a new light and evoke without trembling Pietro Crespi's smell of lavender at dusk and rescue Rebeca from her slough of misery, not out of hatred or out of love but because of the measureless understanding of solitude."[9]

The shroud is not a representation of her life but the meticulous and unremitting effacement of the bitterness of her life. Weaving the shroud is not a performance, addressed to witnesses. The shroud is not an artwork that will enshrine her in immortality; it will be buried with her.

Intensely present to us are those we love. Holding the beloved's hands, his or her substance supports us, the pulse of his or her life throbs in our body. Caressing the beloved we feel the beloved's pleasure in our pleasure.

But denuded, abandoned in our arms, the beloved remains distant. Our caresses pass repetitively and aimlessly over the beloved, having no idea what they are searching for. Love is symbiosis with someone who remains alien and exotic.

The beloved denuded, exposed, abandoned to us, is also exposed to the harsh edges of the world and wounding, exposed to deceits and disillusionments, offenses and insults. Love is wonder before the force of life in another, inseparable from anxiety over the frailty, the vulnerability of the beloved. Love is affection, passion, abandon, pulsing with readiness to act. Love dilates, swells, expands, can become the strongest of the intentions and drives in our life, its energies pouring into all our initiatives and undertakings.

When we love someone, there is somewhere deep inside us the terrible realization that one of us will one day be confronted with the death of the other. A death that we cannot understand. None of the world's reasons—the reasons in force in machinery that crushed him or her, the reasons in microbes—make rational the obliteration of the one we loved and who incessantly supplied reasons to live and to speak and to act. We cannot represent the reasons for his or her death and cannot represent the abyss left by his or her death.

Disconsolate, we mourn. Mourning seems to be concentration on the one we loved and who is no more. But Sigmund Freud saw in mourning a work that transfers our libido stage by stage upon other love objects. A painful work that has to be carried out over a long stretch of time. We have to mourn; this work is enjoined as the method to cease to love the one who is no more.

But we do not, and do not wish to, cease to love the one who has disappeared. From the beginning our love is attachment to all that is remote, inaccessible, absent in the one who is there. Now in mourning our love for the one who has disappeared continues. But action with and for the beloved and performance in view of the beloved are no longer possible. What can the force of this love do?

On that day Michael and Kelly had been married twenty-two months. On that day Michael was in Montreal. On that day, a hundred miles away, Kelly was the only one killed in a three-car collision. On that day Kelly was killed in a three-car collision.

Michael looked down at the coffin in the grave. Kelly was a black void. Michael's mind was a black void. His young life, sent forth to a radiant working and loving future was a black void. The funeral rite was accomplished, one after another the people touched Michael, sometimes tried to murmur something that did not register in Michael's mind, one after another they left. Nobody ventured to try to bring Michael away—for what? To do what? To say what?

Michael became aware that the gravedigger was there, with shovels. He timidly began his work. The shovels of earth fell upon Kelly's coffin, covering her forever with darkness. The gravedigger, a stranger. Michael without thinking took a shovel and together they filled the grave with earth, with darkness.

Michael lost his mind. Thoughts pick up the layout of the world, pick up possibilities, envision goals and reasons and paths and means. Thoughts formed in Michael's mind only to shudder and blur their lines and break against one another without being able to activate Michael. Feelings churned in a pit of darkness.

One day, a month later, Michael's mind was filled with hallucinations. Hallucinations of being there, with Kelly, seeing her stiffen, cry out, stomp her foot on the brake, seeing the car scream and buckle, seeing her body crushed, seeing her breath, her life escape her. Every day, all day, there was nothing in Michael's mind but the hallucinations. Michael did not seek counseling. He had never been afraid of the imagination. Then one day, three weeks later, the hallucinations were not there. They did not return.

One day Michael had gone on his bicycle to Kelly's grave. After, he did not return to his apartment. He headed east. Alone, on his bike. Two months later he reached the Atlantic Coast. Then he took a plane to Vancouver on the Pacific Coast and headed back east on his bike. Back to Kelly's grave. He biked for a year, alone, ten thousand kilometers.

To set out on a bicycle trip for weeks, for months, interrupting one's life, one's work, is not an initiative with a plan and a purpose. Young people sometimes do it, with a buddy; we fit it into our thinking in terms of purpose and goal; we say to ourselves they are building up their bodies, exploring their strengths, discovering the wider world. We hear of adults who are crossing the continent or the world on a bike for a cause, to promote international brotherhood or peace or to raise money for children with AIDS. The goal, the purpose always looks makeshift, added on. We who are committed to a job or a profession cannot really understand them; we can only imagine they are different, we cannot imagine ourselves doing that.

Michael had no cause, no goal or purpose. It was not something he was doing for Kelly; Kelly was lost forever in the black void. To pump the bike for ten thousand kilometers makes one completely physical. Consciousness exists now in the tensions and the relaxing of the muscles, in the feeling of strength and in the fatigue. Consciousness exists on the surfaces of the body all sensitive to the sun, the wind, the cold, the rain. A consciousness that excludes thinking, remembering, envisioning works and ambitions. The road without destination rising and descending, kilometer after kilometer. There is no planning the day ahead; who knows what the weather will be, what the road will be? The end of the day one sinks heavily into dark sleep.

Our place is a retreat or refuge that we have appropriated; where Michael stopped for the night was a place forthwith to leave. The open road drew movement into him. Stretches of the road rose in relief, throbbing with speed or tranquillity, with ardor and exhilaration. Sometimes the landscape opened upon vistas glistening with dew and birdsong. Sometimes physical fatigue blurred the eyes, the landscape dissolved into green dust.

Nature was surfacing with its assembled trees and wayward clouds, the dull rumble of thunder and the frenzied rage of lightning, the poised pause of deer and soft-furred scurrying animals, the birds sprinting and calling to him without him understanding their calls. Over ten thousand kilometers, nature was tunneling into him in his strong breathing, strong pushing, strong feeling, strong forcing, strong dancing, strong singing out. He felt nature guiding his body and felt an intensity of trust that he had never known before. The sun and the breeze fueled his body. He was a body in nature, like a hare in the prairie, a bird in the sky.

Michael carried a GPS that continually mapped the road with abstract intersections of longitude and latitude, but evenings when he looked through his book of maps he saw stretches of space pooling with the white of emptiness and desolation and the green of pounding energies, spread with the ochre of plenitude and the ashes of loneliness.

Then one day, in Saskatchewan, he stopped in a little gas and food station far from any town for breakfast.

Hear him tell it:

I had already been riding for about three hours that morning and managed to cover about seventy-five miles. As I was rummaging through my gear to find my wallet for my breakfast, a man about sixty-five years of age approached me and began asking me questions about my bicycle. He and his wife had just pulled into the Gas-Bar to have breakfast too. They were heading to Alberta from Ontario. I asked them where they were from in Ontario; they said they were from Perkinsfield. The man added that he'd doubted that I would have ever heard of Perkinsfield. I laughed and told him that my family's summer home was in Perkinsfield and that I was married in St. Patrick's Church, which is in the center of the community; naturally he knew the church.

We went inside and ate our breakfast together. The gentlemen asked me if my wife minded that I was away from home for so long while riding my bike across the country. I told them that Kelly had died a year ago in an automobile accident at the intersection of highway 12 and country road 6 (incidentally located in Perkinsfield as well).

Immediately the man said to me, "You're that poor woman's husband?!"

It all came as a shock that this gentleman had made such a knowing statement to me concerning Kelly's death. I held my breath waiting for what he was going to say to me next.

He told me that he was driving home from the grocery store in Perkinsfield when he came upon the accident in which Kelly had been killed, only moments after the collision. He got out of his car to see if he could be of any assistance, but he could tell that Kelly was badly injured. In a few moments the emergency vehicle arrived and Kelly was taken to the hospital.

We were all there in tears going through this short recollection of events that had had such an effect on us each. Jake had lived in Perkinsfield his entire life. I had been going there to our cottage for thirty-five years. His home was only one kilometer from where my parent's cottage was and we had never crossed paths before this moment.

There is the linear time of geology and astronomy and the linear time of history, and there is the time of each of us that is our lifetime. It is the time of our birth, infancy, growing up, education, engaging in a work or a profession, a family. It is the time of practical life, of work, and performance, where what has come to pass is possessed and integrated in results that are gained, where language reverses the passing of time, recuperates the loss. We measure the time of childhood, adolescence, and education in years; we measure the day in working hours and tasks in minutes. An automobile accident, a death throws Michael outside of this time, into the incalculable time of chance, of fate. A time that does not advance by measurable units, that is not progressive, that is a limitless stretch of duration in which events happen, themselves chance events, fateful events.

The time when Kelly was struck is not a time when what is detached is reassembled, where what is torn down is rebuilt; it is a time when loss is absolute, time of the irrevocable. The time of the bike ride is a stretch of duration without achievement or accomplishment. It is not a time of returning to action, to work, and language. It is not a time of the work of mourning, a work, according to Freud, of Michael detaching his libido from Kelly and attaching it to other objects. It is a time in which all the strength of Michael's love holds fast, without the possibility for action or performance, held before the void. It is a time in which, inconceivably, Michael finds Kelly again—finds the irrevocable loss of Kelly again. First, in the three weeks of hallucinations of being with her in the crash. And then in a chance encounter thousands of kilometers later with Jake who, in Michael's place, was there when Kelly died.

It happened that I was in Edmonton, where I gave some talks. At the end of my stay Michael came up to me with a thick volume of maps of regions across Canada painted in intense emotional colors. He called the book *The Atlas* and told me it was the map of his bike ride. I saw there were words written across the pages, words whose significance I did not grasp, words not addressed to others. Michael said that there was no time for me to read it now, that rather he wanted to read it to me one day. He asked me to write something on the Edmonton page. I trembled over the idea of my writing something on his great map and calendar of his journey in a time flowing into rivers and lakes and mountains of emotion but could not refuse. I sought for humble words to acknowledge and affirm the map of his journey determined and desperate, in the time of fate and irrevocable loss. How little did I then, and how little do I now understand the words I wrote.

We walk with others, we work with others. The words of others inform the objectives, paths, implements, and obstacles of our work and the inner diagram of our initiatives. When death claims our collaborator, we continue his or her walk, his or her work. We have taken up the projects, intentions, values, dreams of our parents. Our minds have taken up and made live again the intuitions and probings of thinkers dead centuries ago. Our eyes have shaped what we see with the exalted and anguished eyes of artists and seers. Our throats have sung chants of ancient bards and songs of vocalists our parents had loved and ballads of people in remote lands. We have continued the walks of Henry David Thoreau in Massachusetts and John Muir in the Sierra Nevada.

To walk with others, to work with someone is to be there to aid, support, protect him or her and to nurse his or her wounds. It is also to be there when he or she is dying, to accompany him or her who is going nowhere. It is to accompany him or her so that he or she not die alone.

It is not because someone has given us strength and skill and language and knowledge and collaborated with us that now we must accompany him when his strengths are failing, his experience and skill are falling away, when he is drifting to death where there is nothing to say. We must be there, accompany the one who was never our collaborator, who we did not love, who no one loved, now that he is going nowhere.

A society where we would no longer care for one another in our vulnerability undermines itself. A society in which we would leave the dying to die alone, in which we would no longer accompany those who are going nowhere, empties itself.

A port exists as a passage to elsewhere. I was reading about Trieste. I had never been there but it sounded not like a place one goes to but a place one goes from. Trieste was a free commune in the twelfth century, from 1327 the sole port of Austria and from 1867 of the Austro-Hungarian Empire. Annexed to Italy in 1920. Allied bombings during World War II destroyed the shipyards and the industrial section of the city. Trieste was chartered as an independent city-state under United Nations protection in 1947. But seven years later the city-state was divided and Italy and Yugoslavia each annexed a part. The city proper was predominantly Italian speaking, the suburbs and surrounding towns predominantly Slovenian; there were also smaller numbers of Germans, Croatians, Serbs, Czechs, Istro-Romanians, and Jews.

I had been to Australia. They say there are two hundred different ethnic groups in Australia, besides the aboriginal population, now but 2.5 percent of the total. After World War II, the Australian government launched a massive immigration program, believing that having narrowly avoided a Japanese invasion, Australia must "populate or perish." Since 1945 seven million people have immigrated to Australia. One out of four of Australia's today 22.6 million people were born elsewhere. Mary, who lives in Sydney, is the daughter of Greek immigrant parents.

She wrote to tell me that her friend Domenico de Clario would be in Baltimore and suggested we meet. Domenico, she said, is an artist. He makes paintings, drawings, assemblages, text performances, site-specific and installation art, and piano performances. Many of these visual and musical works are made with Domenico blindfolded.

Domenico came to my home. A man of average height, in his sixties, shaven head, a handsome and very mobile face, Ozzie accent. I asked him if he had been born in Australia. It's hard to find somebody born in Australia, he laughed. He told me he had been born in Trieste and asked what about me. I said my parents had emigrated from Lithuania. I grew up on a farm in Illinois. A small farm that my father worked with the tools and doggedness of a peasant.

Domenico said he was born in 1947 in Trieste. In a one-bedroom apartment that housed his parents, grandparents, and sister. In 1956 he and his family boarded a ship bound for Australia. When they arrived they were taken to a holding camp in a former military barracks. After six weeks a job was located for his father and they moved to the Italian quarter in Melbourne. Domenico said he studied architecture and town planning in Melbourne but left without completing a degree. When he was twenty he returned to Italy to study painting in Milan for a year. Over the years he was able to teach painting, drawing, sculpture, performance, and installation in Melbourne. And make his art. I asked him what work he was doing now. He said he had translated Calvino's *Invisible Cities* into English, Triestine, and music, and, in a lane behind his house each evening at dusk over fifty-six consecutive days, he improvised music for it and presented two stories, one recounting a journey he had made and the other describing a house somewhere in the world he wanted to live in. He presented the work for a PhD in art at Melbourne's Victoria University in 2001. "So I finally got a degree," he smiled.

We sat on the back deck, with glasses of the Italian wine he had brought, looking out upon my big backyard dense with bushes and trees. I said I planted all that; there had been nothing but grass when I moved here. Probably some urge to get out of the city, to go back to the country where I was a boy.

"I was nine years old when I left Trieste," he said. "The freighter that had somehow survived the war was very old. It was overcrowded to an extent that would not be allowed today. People were sleeping in the corridors, on the deck. They had brought sacks with all their possessions. They were leaving their homelands, their families and friends forever. Most of them had only a distant relative or friend from years ago waiting for them in Australia. We were forty-two days at sea. June and July; the summer heat, the small meals, bad food—people got in one another's way, quarreled, couldn't sleep, got sick."

Domenico was silent for a moment and frowned. "One guy was really losing it. Middle-aged, seemed to be alone, nobody knew who he was. He would lean over the deck moaning loudly and stomp back and forth for hours muttering. We finally arrived at Perth. Some people got off. This man pushed against the immigration officials that had come to meet the ship and shouted that he was going to Melbourne. They said the ship was going on to Melbourne. He mumbled miserably that he could not endure the ship any longer. Finally they took him to the immigration camp.

"Some months later we in the immigration camp in Melbourne learned that he had escaped and headed on foot for Melbourne. It is thirty-four hundred kilometers from Perth to Melbourne. We learned that he had made it about a third of the way then perished of exposure."

Domenico looked out over the backyard into the distance. After some moments he looked back at me. "Four years ago my parents had some people over who had been on that ship fifty years ago. They exchanged memories and at one point remembered that man. And I started to think of him again. A few weeks later I went to the library to search out the newspapers from that year. Finally I found a small notice in one newspaper. It mentioned the place where his body was found.

"A few weeks after that I packed a backpack and took the bus to that place. It's a flat empty stretch, desert all around. Then I started walking. I walked for ten days, then went back to my job. Anyhow, I was not trying to reach Melbourne for him. I was just walking with him.

"Then the next year I went back to the place where I had left off, to continue the walk. Another ten days. Last year I again went back, to continue his walk."

2017

Love Junkies

I hate lies, I would not tolerate lies from anybody. I've always been like that, you Wayne explain.

What passion finds is the child and the child in the old man, is the man in the woman and the woman in the man, is the leopard, serpent, mollusk in the man or woman and the man and woman in the bull, swan, crocodile, and octopus.

Billions of tons of salt water coursing around the vast Pacific brush against the south coast of New South Wales, detaching bits of rock and sod, spreading layers of sand sparkling below the town of Cronulla south of Sydney. Sand of vast coral cities built by multicolored polyps, demolished by ocean storms, sand that tufts of salt grass hold on to, that are swept back into the ocean by storms.

You Cheryl were born and abandoned in Cronulla. Somewhere a woman had met a man, they disrobed and embraced and parted, and silently you started to grow in that woman. The woman bore her pregnancy and then put you somewhere, and disappeared. You have no idea why you were not wanted.

A Swiss couple adopted you. They called you Paul. You have a brother whom you never see. He cannot understand your sex. Your foster parents always called you Paul, until a year ago—when, during what was to be their last visit, for they have moved to Queensland and are very old now, you made them call you Cheryl. They do, however, approve of Wayne. They love him.

You Wayne were born in Belmain, a working-class district of Sydney. You have a brother too but were separated from him when your parents divorced and your mother took him, your father took you. One day your father sent you to the shops to buy a newspaper, and when you came back there was five cents missing in the change. He flogged you with a feather duster for almost an hour and a half, trying to get you to admit that you had spent those five cents on lollies. But you hadn't and you wouldn't say you did to get him to stop. You hate lies. Your father started dating another woman and you were in the way. He charged you with being uncontrollable and put you in a boys' home. You were seven years old.

Junk velvets the hard edges of things. It's a silver fog rolling over all the cubicles, partitions, walls, and fences. How long is it that you have been shooting up, Wayne—thirty years? You Cheryl—thirty years in silver fog? There is plenty of junk around now, but you are on methadone. Wayne too. The maximum dose. You claim it is for the pain. It makes you spacey and hyper. You especially Cheryl are always fidgety and skittish. Medical researchers are now saying that methadone is more damaging to the organism than heroin. The idea is to progressively reduce the dosage. You Wayne and Cheryl are still on the max.

Your soul Cheryl is twitches and quiverings in the algae curtains of the stomach, the somber blue intestines, in the liver, the spleen, on the tips of your fingers under lacquered green fingernails. Your soul Wayne is turbulence and bluster and crystal calm in the blue veins, the slow heavy vermilion blood, the scurrying macrophages, the dense jelly of cells stirring the murmurs from years ago and far away.

You Cheryl are five foot nine, big-boned, very skinny, skeletal; right off you say your age: fifty-two. Your face is long, you have high cheekbones, your cheeks are sunken, your lips medium thin, your mouth small, delicate. You have very big brown eyes. You have shaved your eyebrows and you pencil in lines first thing when you get up. Your hair is thick and fine, brunette turning to blonde, cut short, combed to one side. Your very big hands are somewhat discolored with bleached pink, your fingernails clean and a little long. You have a gold watch with a very big face, a man's watch, loose on your wrist. You dress in moss green jail T-shirt and shorts, much faded, much patched, and on your feet, worn running shoes. About your neck you have a long string of small shells, the kind Filipino kids try to sell on the beaches. You keep two mirrors on the table; as you work you check your face, touch it up. You are a queen, if in green shorts. For nudibranchs creeping over the sands at the bottom of the surf, for naked frogs in the Sydney slums, for moths circling lights on the prison walls, beauty is imperative.

There is something giddy in our relationship with a mirror. Spaced away from ourselves, our gestures turn into grimaces, our manipulations into flailings, and our face screwed up by our scrutinizing gaze breaks into laughter. Looking at oneself while laughing releases lascivious impulses in our mouth, tongue, fingers, loins.

When you look in the mirror, you Wayne say, you either see your best friend or your worst enemy. You are a little shorter than Cheryl and maybe seven years younger. You have broad shoulders, strong arms, flat stomach. Your skin is very tanned. When you were outside, you several times ran the marathon. There are only migraines, nausea, insomnia in that body now. If your body does not shrivel and sink into itself, it is only because you are pumped with steroids. You are wearing a loose moss green long-sleeved light sweatshirt, light sweatpants—also much faded, much patched—and new good-quality runners. Your head is round, you have a thick black-brown walrus mustache, your mouth is small, your lips sensual. Your mouth is not sunken, though they have pulled out all your teeth. You have clear blue eyes. You look English, with your smooth pasty pale skin, your full head of bristly gray hair cut short in back. You are well groomed, very particular about your appearance. You wear two small silver rings in your left ear. You wear a silver chain with a Masonic cross. On your left hand you wear four rings, one on your right. You Wayne are handsome. Handsome and impish. You have a dry sense of humor. And a hellish hot glint in those clear blue eyes.

You are not at all sly. People know you would do anything for a friend. Just ask you. There is nothing you Wayne can't fix. You have earned twenty-eight certificates for computer courses. You type résumés for staff people; screws bring you their computers from home to fix some programming glitch. You are a sensitive bloke. You are very civilized. You are always very pleasant to the female staff. You are respectful of women, and respectful of Cheryl. Cheryl devotes herself to you, to entertaining you. You treat Cheryl very well.

Males, with their on average greater musculature and on average 20 percent greater size than females, do hard work in agriculture, industry, and construction. They tear up streets with air hammers, they weld oil derricks in the Timor Sea, they paint the bridge over Sydney Harbor, they man peacekeeping forces in East Timor, they are professional boxers. They are expected to maintain order and system. They are at least expected to do contracted work, even if something trivial or pointless has to be found, to pay their own expenses. Lazy chiseling parasitical louts are an affront to their own maleness. But nothing so fevers the mind as a man swanking his gamy good looks.

In fact you Wayne adore Cheryl. You say that if she dies you will die with her. You will certainly kill yourself to die with Cheryl.

The voluptuous embrace is necrophilic, bodies collapsing, decomposing, already soaking the sheets and themselves with body fluids releasing spasms, musks, microorganisms. The flames of pleasure ignite them in clothing, in swampy stains on the wood of the furniture, in the air whose

minute spheres of water vapor teem with protozoa, in the soil decomposing into unnameable fungi and bacteria.

You Wayne play computer games a lot. Your moves zap electronic
people, detonate cars and planes, pulverize whole populations. You're a
fighter. You have been in and out of institutions since the age of fifteen,
your existence the piece of bad luck that society found in itself. You never
had goals to give you a sense of yourself. Your sense of your individuality
comes from being isolated from society in institutions. Throughout your
street-kid childhood you were not, like the rest of us, continually told what
not to do and why not. They didn't tell you why not. One can just see how
you would react if some bloke came along and said, "Let's rob the bank."
"Okay, let's go," you would say.

You robbed, but it was petty shit. It was not to change things, to break
out and become somebody; it was only to keep up your habit. Again
and again you were caught and sentenced. This is your twenty-third year
in prison. Eventually they win, they get it their way. Now you are in the
middle of a fourteen-year sentence for armed robbery. Long Bay jail is a
maximum security prison; you are in the company of everything society gets in the way of real shit luck: switchblade stalkers, gangsters, child
molesters. Murderers radiant with the blood they have shed stalk the
prison with lewd authority.

Among them you met Cheryl, twenty-two years ago. She'd been in for
dealing, stealing, factory women have rough hands and dismissive eyes,
career women have manipulative fingers and skeptical eyes that repel the
cloying eyes of lust. What else did you Cheryl have to do but be beautiful?
Prostitution was the only source of wages you ever figured out. You Cheryl
and Wayne became lovers ten years ago.

It's you Wayne and Cheryl we engage in talk with when we visit the jail,
or want to hear about from those who do. You are delinquents and devi-
ants, and not just victims of society that we have to feel guilty about. Your
story is going to be funny—funny peculiar and funny ha-ha.

There is no end of things that one cannot prevent, ward off, overcome,
or repair. One got born looking like a dork. One had an abused childhood.
One got Oedipally triangulated. One discovered one had a queer gene. One
got caught up in a relationship that was hopelessly fucked up. There are
so many things that one can do nothing about. Could do nothing about
them at the time, can do nothing about them now. So many things that
all one can do with is laugh. But one can always laugh. One can laugh
at one's having been born with a ruined gene, looking like Olive Oyl or
Newt Gingrich, at one's microdick, about death itself. A neurotic is someone who is traumatized, that is, cannot get over these disasters. Cannot
laugh. Psychotherapists are hardly any help. How tight-assed they are, by

and large! They take everything the neurotic dreams over, broods over, so seriously. Every put-down from earliest childhood, every humiliation. They seal the neurotic in his neurosis.

You've had a lot of fights in your time Wayne, though you've never been stabbed. You got iron-barred once. The bloke that did that lived to regret it. You'll cop a lot of shit before you'll explode, but when you explode, you really explode. The first time is accidental, you say; the second time is coincidental; the third time is enemy action. You'll cop shit on yourself; you won't cop shit for Cheryl. If someone upsets Cheryl, then that's it; there's no second chances. No chances at all. There's people in this jail that don't necessarily like you; they got to respect you for the fact that you'll live and die for Cheryl. The truth is you have more friends than anybody.

There are long scars on your arms Wayne from fights, but most self-inflicted. Your hands and arms are covered with tattoos. On the base of the fingers of your left hand the letters L O V E. A tattoo you made, using a sewing needle stuck on the end of a toothbrush handle and activated by a motor you took out of a Walkman—you are very good at things mechanical!—keeps on your right arm your love for Diane Darling who had been a star performer at a transvestite cabaret on King's Cross and who died of AIDS in jail. You don't consider yourself a poofter, nobody else takes you for a poofter; they think: it's jail sex. Cheryl though fifty-two calls herself a girl, calls herself a queen. She has small plump breasts. She had, long ago, her testicles removed. You Wayne adore Cheryl. And in this, in your adoration of Cheryl, you are getting your own way in something at last!

Feeling the warm thigh of the somnolent passenger next to us on the bus, the hot breath of an excited woman bidding at an auction, the caress of a young monk in a Tibetan monastery amused by the down on our Caucasian arms, we are aroused. The penis stiffening, the labia and clitoris throbbing with blood and excitement and pleasure are the parts of our bodies that never lie.

On your right arm Wayne you have a large cross, with *In Memory.* Your uncle was a biker, finally crashed and smashed both his knees. When he died you were not allowed to go to the funeral. In jail, doing a tattoo on someone is cited as bodily assault, doing a tattoo on oneself as self-mutilation. You did this tattoo and then went to the warden and told him to cite you. This uncle had taken you when at the age of eleven you got out of the Boys' Home and put you to work in his carnival. You worked the cars, roller coasters, Ferris wheels. You traveled with the carnival all over Australia. Carnivals have a bad reputation: people think there'll be fights and they have to lock up their daughters. You do have to use force: when a couple of blokes come up for a ride, they are not inclined to put down their cigarettes and beer bottles. So you got into fights.

Hate can be cold, ingenious, devious. Love is lawless, volatile, and violent. The adoration that breaks out of us violates our integrity and breaks up our individuality. To be smitten by love is to be not simply wounded, but shattered. Your adoration Wayne is the inner experience of being violated in sexual embraces and of violating Cheryl. Your love Cheryl is a craving to be violated.

The ocean fog has settled in the stones of Long Bay jail a hundred years ago. The foul breath of caged men has settled in those stones. The toilets are ceramic bowls without partitions to separate the stink of one man's shit from another's. You Cheryl are fanatically housebound. You have amazing energy. You are high on washing and folding your and Wayne's laundry. Laundry is always happening.

You get up very early. You like to be maternal. You busy yourself darning socks, mending and altering the clothes of the men, skinny mother of brutes. You make small alterations that eliminate a bristly discomfort in a garment, that make the most threadbare garment fit and even flatter its wearer. You are ingenious. You vacuum all the floors of the education department. You take the vacuum to the apartment and vacuum it till there is not a wisp of dust lodged in any corner. You call the cell the apartment. It is only six feet wide, ten feet long. There is a bed bolted to the wall, a toilet, a sink, a jug, a Walkman. The cells are all open to the corridor, with only iron-bar gates.

Many people really dislike you. The staff, but also inmates. You are sneaky. You steal stuff people are using. You are a two-faced bitch. We have to be careful about what we say around you; you will blab about it. You trade in gossip. Whether we are a new inmate or just a visitor, you will have heard all about us before we get there.

To be incarcerated is to have no life outside. There is nothing to an inmate but his inner life. To be on top of all the gossip is the way to touch, probe, grip on to the inner lives of others, who have only inner lives. Gossip is the only way one has in jail to have an intense inner life, penetrating and sizzling with pleasure. Gossip is a pleasure. Pleasure of pursuing prey, of intervening in melodramas, intellectual pleasure of ingenuity and cunning.

The consummate feminine look is that blasé look, that vaporous look, that impudent look, that cold look, that look of looking inward, that dominating look, that voluptuous look, that wicked look, that sick look, that catlike look, infantilism, nonchalance, and malice compounded.

You Wayne insist that Cheryl be treated with respect, and you are violent enough to insist. Because Cheryl still has her penis, she can be housed in the men's section, and with you Wayne. The authorities like homosexual couples forming—it reduces the general aggression in the jail.

Harmoniously married couples outside spend at least eight hours a day apart, at their jobs. You Wayne and Cheryl are locked in a six-by-ten-foot cell together all but five hours a day. When you are working at your jobs you are also together. Because Cheryl's a woman in a men's maximum security jail, it's not safe for her wandering around by herself. If you hear a scream you know where the scream's coming from, you know where to go. Sometimes you Wayne are with Cheryl twenty-three hours one day; the other hour you are in some office working on a computer—and strange as it seems to people, you miss her for that hour! I hate it, you say. I hate it.

Why is it that it is the jeering or derisive remark about our sexual identity, appearance, behaviors, or words that smarts most? Why do we so easily turn being called peculiar into being distinctive, being called eccentric into being exceptional, but when abnormal means abnormal in our sex it is demeaning and mortifying? How transparent we are to one another in our lusts!

You Cheryl became a woman when you were fifteen. You trained to be a registered nurse. You were caught stealing drugs and dismissed. You drifted to King's Cross, where part of joining the scene was drugs. You did heroin, speed, cocaine, bennies, acid. You're not into pot. You performed as a female impersonator in the cabarets of King's Cross—Les Girls, Simone, Candy. Back then you had toured the jails. Carlotta now acts in the weekly show on TV called *Beauty and the Beast.* She still writes you twice a year, sends you the programs of shows.

The numbers drag queens do depend entirely on surprise, their effects momentary. Surprising the aggressor with a put-down so witty he finds himself unable not to laugh at himself. The master in oriental martial arts is one who catches the lunge of the adversary and throws him with the force of his own blow. Zen and the Art of Drag.

You Wayne and Cheryl are the top of the heap. You are very sharp on people. You see what is going on. You can make things happen. You do the clerical work for the education program. You earn twenty-four dollars a week. Money is clout; the ordinary prisoner can earn but eleven or thirteen dollars a week. You get real coffee or chocolate biscuits, sometimes, from the staff. You get conversation about the outside world. You even contribute to decisions—for example, about how the money is spent in the education program. Just now you Cheryl are in charge of some repairs and painting that are being done in the wing. You love organizing people. You would have been a very successful businesswoman. You and Wayne are chummy with the superintendent. You can put in a good word for a bloke if his parole is coming up.

You Wayne and Cheryl believe that a real relationship—not just a relationship like yours but even a relationship between two good friends—can't last if there's not total honesty at all times. It's something you never got from your families, so it's something you've always demanded from your friends and the people around you. In my time, you Wayne say, I've probably met ten to fifteen thousand people in jail these many years that I've been here. Out of those there's probably a hundred that would say that I'm their friend; out of that hundred, there's probably sixty that I would call my friends; out of that sixty, twenty that I would say that I know they're honest and up-front with me and I trust them implicitly, and out of that twenty there's five that I would die for or kill for.

A bloke name of Xavier had made his way from Brazil to Australia as a mule for some drug smugglers. They caught him. He was very mechanical. Out of bits of wire, discarded tin cans he would pick up, he made clocks. Big clocks, covered with glitter, with photos of cheesecake women, mug shots of criminals, car crashes from magazines. His whole cell, all the walls, were eventually covered with extravagant, hallucinating clocks. He was terrified of being transferred. One day, they did transfer him to another prison. The following day he was found murdered. He had not done his time. At the main entrance of Long Bay jail, there is a small shop where visitors can buy artifacts made by the prisoners. The prices are fixed by the prison staff. The most popular items are Aboriginal dot paintings; galleries in Sydney fix very high prices for Aboriginal dot paintings, and they are much sought after in the world art market. After Xavier's death, the shop put on an exhibition of his clocks.

You Wayne and Cheryl have used your clout with the staff to get in disinfectants strong enough to kill the HIV virus, for use with needles. There is heroin enough for all in the prison, supplied of course by the screws for those eleven or thirteen dollars the inmates can earn. You Wayne and Cheryl have also insisted that a condom dispenser get installed, but they then mounted it on the wall next to the officers' quarters. So blokes have to expose their intentions to the screws, and expose themselves to their shouts and jeers.

How foolish two people get when they become lovers—how infantile their speech, how naive their sentiments, how frivolous their behavior! How awkward, how ridiculous are the gropings and thrashings of people copulating, how empty the aimless repetitions of caresses, how mindless the compulsive buildup toward orgasm! We lock the door, pull the drapes. In sex theaters, all the movements are choreographed to be graceful and synchronized; nothing is left to the directness of lustful urges. When in the force of momentary grabbings and repulsions they do show through, we are repelled and embarrassed: suddenly we see what we do in our lovemaking. We free ourselves from our embarrassment by giggling, and outside the theater guffawing over what we saw.

But when we spy on others and cannot help laughing, this laughter spreads through our body and reverberates in dissolute and wanton impulses. Telling and hearing dirty jokes do not make us superior and aloof from lustful urges; they make us sink into our sensual nature. In laughter we are transparent to one another, the peals of laughter not expressions of an I or of a you, spreading like waves about a pebble dropped into a lake, with no more individuality than waves.

The lust that disconnects the body from its tasks and its seriousness and releases it on the languorous and agitated body of another is nothing but the laughter of that body. The throbs, the convulsive repetitions, the upheaval, the absurd pleasure of the bodies in lascivious excitement are the laughter not apart from, but in those bodies. They have locked the door and pulled the drapes so that their laughter may be uninhibited, one and undivided. Orgasm is the vortex of the generalized laughter of bodies.

The working-from-within-the-system seventies, the yuppie eighties, the neoliberal nineties passed you by. You Wayne and Cheryl are sixties counterculture freaks. You are survivors—more than survivors, you are fighters. You are real activists. You write letters to politicians. You are not just working in the education program for the money and the influence; you are both very firm in your dedication to education. You fight causes. You have a mission.

When in 1985 the prison services discovered that they had three HIV-positive inmates, they segregated them. When you Wayne heard that Diane Darling was in the AIDS unit, you went to the high ranker in the jail and asked if you could go in there and talk to her. They said No, that they wouldn't have people going back and forth. But you insisted. Finally they let you go in. You told her that if she ever needed to talk, or cry, or scream, you would be there. Six months later Head Office started what they called the AIDS Task Force—a group of civilians to enter the jail to educate inmates about HIV. They appointed you the first AIDS peer educator. You and Cheryl ran the HIV-AIDS and hepatitis C committee for almost six years. Every year you put on a different event for World AIDS Day.

Your old crony Ashleigh from the King's Cross cabarets got herself arrested and with you Cheryl organized the Long Bay Cowgirls. You sewed up an extravagant, theatrical frock for yourself.

It's with the other transsexuals that you Cheryl are having your own way in something. You give a lot of support to those who end up in the jail. One who was sinking rapidly had a great fear of dying alone. How envious she was of you and Wayne who will die together. You accompanied her all the way while she was going nowhere; you were there when she died, you were with her.

No police force could hope to prosecute and incarcerate all thieves, addicts, and perverts. Every convict is an expiatory sacrifice who suffers his or her life for all.

In heading off to the back alleys and wastelands where our heads are exposed to the blows of chance we know in exhilaration what we have received by chance, what we are by chance. Love is abruptly ignited in impasses and traps; it is the combustion of interpenetrating dreams of bodies collapsed and dysfunctional. It is the incandescence of luck in the most squalid, the most sordid circumstances, the worst luck.

Shit happens. You Wayne and Cheryl have been HIV-positive for ten years. You Wayne were stabbed with a needle by a patient while you were a sweeper in the clinic. A few weeks later you Cheryl were hospitalized with anorexia; in the middle of the night two men who were HIV-positive raped you. About the same time you both contracted hepatitis C. For the past eighteen months you Wayne have full-blown AIDS symptoms. You have bowel cancer. Shit happens. In 1993 you had come down with so many opportunistic infections Cheryl they gave you at best six months to live. Then they discovered that the virus was replicating not in your blood but in your bone marrow. There was only one other such case reported—in the United States. Shit happens.

You Wayne have a chest infection. Your skin is breaking out with Kaposi's sarcoma scabs. The ones that are on your backside, it's like sitting on boils. When you take off your underpants for the night, it rips the scabs stuck to them. You Wayne and you Cheryl take everything very methodically: We will have to deal with this, you say. And then, later, you say, We will have to deal with that. You each day defy the plague. You are very courageous. You savor each day you are alive. The level of energy you produce is a manifestation of your will. You keep each other alive. You Cheryl say, Whatever keeps us together even twenty-four hours. Even one hour. You are allowed to see a prison doctor every five weeks. You Wayne said to him, Listen, I will keep myself alive whilever Cheryl needs me. I will not allow myself to die whilever Cheryl needs me. I don't need your drugs to do that. I have the will in me, the love that I have for Cheryl in me, to keep myself alive whilever Cheryl needs me. But everybody knows the moment one of you dies, you'll both die.

When you get sick Wayne you see how it affects Cheryl: she hates to see you sick. That makes you feel guilty, because it really worries her. Quite often you'd be sick, and you'd try not to show it, for Cheryl's benefit. But then you chastise yourself, because the biggest and the best part of your relationship you think is the honesty. And you think, Well, if I try and hide it from Cheryl then I'm not being honest with her. But sometimes you think, Well, maybe she doesn't need to know. She just had a bad deal today. But then you think that if you knew that Cheryl was feeling this bad and didn't tell you, you'd be very upset with her. It's a big thing with you, honesty.

You Wayne protect Cheryl. A lot of people think that no one'll touch Cheryl, no one'll rape Cheryl because she's got AIDS. But there are blokes who think they can't get AIDS from Cheryl giving them head. Some think that unless they ejaculate inside her, they are at no risk. There are those who think there is no risk if they use a condom. But a number of people have approached you over the months and asked you for your blood! Some blokes want our blood, you say, because they believe if they get AIDS it can help them get out of jail a little bit earlier. Some believe that it can at least help them get some privileges. Some blokes want our blood because they want to commit suicide. Others want to square up on somebody they don't like. Most times you Wayne take him aside and say, Fuck off! Never ask me that again! But with a close friend, it's not that simple. One said, Come off, Wayne, you're playing God with my life.

Cancers, putrescent infections, blindness, madness, agonizing pain await people dying of AIDS. Those who care for them, those who love them leave their bedside, to go to the other room to get food, to answer the telephone, to receive visitors, they go out to buy groceries and do the laundry. They can, when they can no longer endure to keep watch, slip out of the room. They are not locked in a six-by-ten-foot cement cell all the weeks and hours, all the days and the nights of the infections, the despair, the agony, the delirium, the dying.

In taking our ambitions, our values, and our achievements seriously we turn ourselves into idols, which we cannot help fearing will soon be covered with graffiti and pigeon shit. What else can we do, do we do, but laugh when we think we got born though nobody wanted us, when we think they have to pay to keep us alive here because we robbed them, when we open our eyes to find our cell buzzing with the pompous assertiveness of a bumblebee, when a frolicsome mouse chooses to give birth to her babies in Long Bay jail?

The two men who raped you Cheryl are both dead now. May they rest in peace, you say. You went to the funeral service for them. Forgive and forget, you say. Just forget, you say. One would have to remember and forgive everything, from the day you were born and abandoned. Cheryl cannot change who she is, you Wayne say. It's one of the things you love so much about her.

Love attaches to the abyss. It is hate that circumscribes its own identity. Tell me whom you hate and I will tell you who you are. Tell me whom you love and I will know as little about you as before.

How lucky I am! you Cheryl think. How lucky I have been! How lucky to have met Wayne. How lucky not to die alone, like the other transvestites.

How lucky to have quality life. The level of energy you keep up is the energy of this defiance and exhilaration.

One day an old flame of yours, Cheryl, appeared in the prison. For weeks how anguished you were—there had now suddenly appeared to you one last chance to know a great passion before you die. Although you realized that leaving Wayne would kill him, Wayne said nothing whatever about what he quickly understood was going on. Then you understood that your great passion made of violence, adoration, and lust is Wayne.

And then one day the prison authorities summoned you Cheryl and presented you with your release. You were led back to the cell, you packed your green prison clothes in a state of pounding agitation. The gates of Long Bay jail closed behind you.

They gave you a small sum of money; it was not enough to buy a real gun. You took a perfume bottle, practiced holding it in your hand wrapped in a scarf. You went to the McDonald's a little after midday; you handed the cashier a piece of paper on which you had written: "This is a holdup. Give me $200." On the back of the paper you had written your name, your address, your phone number, your jail number. And "P.S. Don't call until 9:30; I won't be ready." By midnight you were back with Wayne. You tell him how, shrieking with drag queen laughter.

2003

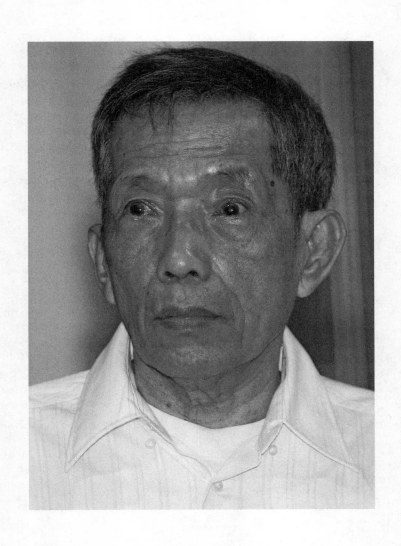

Truth in Reconciliation

I spent the month of August 2009 in Phnom Penh and attended sessions of the Extraordinary Chambers of the Courts of Cambodia, the joint UN–Cambodia Court that was trying five "Khmer Rouge" leaders of Democratic Kampuchea for crimes against humanity, genocide, and war crimes.

Let me summarily recall that epoch. Cambodia became a French colony in 1867 and acquired independence under Prince Norodom Sihanouk in 1953. Sihanouk maintained neutrality during the American war in Vietnam, as he was personally convinced that the Vietcong would ultimately triumph. But he ruthlessly suppressed leftist movements within Cambodia, whom he dubbed "Khmer Rouge." In 1970 Sihanouk was overthrown by General Lon Nol. Lon Nol entered into alliance with the United States and authorized the American secret bombing of suspected Vietcong bases in Cambodia, which soon became a carpet bombing of the eastern half of Cambodia. Several insurgent armies, joined as the Cambodian People's National Liberation Armed Forces, advanced under heavy U.S. bombardment, defeating the demoralized Lon Nol troops, and on April 17, 1975, they occupied Phnom Penh. A twelve-person "Standing Committee of the Communist Party of Cambodia" was set up as the highest governing body. In November 1978, a Vietnamese army of 180,000 troops invaded Cambodia, and on January 7, 1979, entered Phnom Penh and set up first Cambodian Heng Samrin and then Hun Sen as prime minister. But the "Khmer Rouge" continued to occupy large areas of the country, representing Cambodian resistance to the Vietnamese occupiers. Vietnam withdrew its occupying army in 1989, leaving Hun Sen in charge of the government. Four armed factions then fought for power until 1998, when their troops accepted amnesty and their leaders were integrated into the Hun Sen government.

The joint UN–Cambodia Court that is trying five top surviving "Khmer Rouge" leaders of "Democratic Kampuchea" aims to fix on these four men and one woman personal responsibility for the deaths of up to a million and a half people through executions, hardship, disease, and malnutrition during the three years and eight months, from 1975 to 1979, of Democratic Kampuchea. The court will execute retributive justice, inflicting punishment on these five for their deeds. The punishment meted out is to serve as deterrence against future ill-minded political and military leaders in the world. The trial is also to serve as a forum in which victims will be heard and their dignity restored. It intends to establish the truth about gross human-rights abuses. The Cambodia of the future where former enemies will have to be reconciled or at least live in nonviolent coexistence can, it is believed, only be built on the basis of knowledge of the truth, truth about the years from 1975 to 1979.

The first defendant put on trial, in February 2009, was Kaing Guek Eav. He had been the director of the S-21 interrogation center in Phnom Penh, where party officials and military officers suspected of subversion or treason were interrogated. In the three years of its existence, at least twelve thousand people were interrogated there, kept in harsh conditions and tortured. Almost all of them were then taken outside of the city and executed. Only seven are known to have survived.

Kaing Guek Eav was selected to be tried first because the S-21 interrogation center kept detailed documentation of the proceedings there and much of this documentation was recovered when the city fell to the Vietnamese army. In addition, when he was arrested, Kaing agreed to cooperate with the police and then the court. The prosecutors plan to use his testimony in the trial of the other four, who have not pleaded guilty.

Kaing Guek Eav was born in 1942 in a poor rural area in central Cambodia. Only when he was nine years old did he receive his first schooling, from a monk who taught him to read and write. But he proved to be exceptionally gifted and went on to secondary school and then to university, majoring in mathematics. In his baccalaureate examinations he placed second in the nation. He returned to his home region and became a teacher and then vice principal of a lycée. Suspected of leftist sympathies by the police of Prince Sihanouk, he was arrested in 1968, imprisoned, and tortured. Two years later, Sihanouk was deposed by General Lon Nol; to marshal support Lon Nol amnestied political prisoners, and Kaing was freed. During the U.S. carpet bombing of Cambodia, Kaing joined the resistance, taking the nom de guerre "Mit Duch"—"Comrade Duch." His unit captured a French anthropologist, François Bizot, whom they suspected of being a foreign agent. Mit Duch interrogated Bizot without harsh treatment for three months, gradually became convinced that he was in fact an anthropologist, and then argued his case with Pol Pot. Bizot was released.[1] After insurgent forces occupied Phnom Penh and the Communist Party of Cambodia organized the new government, Mit Duch was posted in the S-21 interrogation center and later was made its director. He had requested a transfer to the industrial sector, but his request had been denied.

On January 7, 1979, as the Vietnamese armies entered Phnom Penh, Mit Duch and his family and staff fled. In the "Khmer Rouge" strongholds that resisted the Vietnamese, over the next twenty years Kaing Guek Eav set up schools and wrote textbooks. He learned Thai and English and taught mathematics and English. In 1995 assailants attacked his home and murdered his wife; Kaing was injured but managed to escape. While grieving the death of his wife, he began to frequent an evangelical Khmer-American preacher named Christopher Lapel. He was baptized and practiced his new Christian faith fervently. In 1997 he was recruited by the American Refugee Committee to work as the community health supervisor in a refugee camp in Thailand. The next year he returned to Cambodia and worked with World Vision, a Christian relief agency. In 1999 he was identified as the former Mit Duch by Irish journalist Nic Dunlop, who made a media sensation of his discovery. Kaing was subsequently arrested and held without charge for nine years until the joint UN–Cambodia Court was constituted and he was put on trial.

He admitted his role as director of the S-21 interrogation center and all his recorded and unrecorded actions there.[2] He affirmed that he had not wanted this position but had been unable to refuse, that he reported all his actions and his meticulous records to the Interior Ministry and everything that he did was under specific orders, and that he was under constant surveillance; had he deviated he would have been liquidated and his family with him.

Each day Kaing Guek Eav watches and listens as survivors and relatives of those incarcerated in S-21 and subsequently executed tell of their lost ones; they are given unlimited time by the court to speak. Kaing never relaxes his focused attention. At the end of the testimony, he is asked to respond. If he has nothing to question about the testimony, he declares his excruciating grief and remorse for their suffering. Sometimes his voice breaks, he sobs. But sometimes he contests something; he says the witness could not have seen him where the witness had said and explains his job and procedures as evidence. Or he asks the court to bring up the relevant prison document; he has examined the thousands of pages so well that often he can ask for a document by its identification number. When the document has been projected on a screen for all to see, he will say: "You see, that is not my signature."

His trial concluded in November 2009. There is no death penalty now in Cambodia. In view of his cooperation, the UN-appointed prosecutor asked that he be sentenced not to life but forty years imprisonment. The defense lawyers argued that while many top policy makers of the "Khmer Rouge" are not on trial, Kaing Guek Eav had no room for maneuver in the position he held. In view of his remorse and his full cooperation with the investigations, and in view of his now ten-year imprisonment, the Cambodian defense lawyer argued that he be released.

The European press saw in this political pressure from the Hun Sen government. The "Khmer Rouge" had never been defeated militarily; it was by granting amnesty not only to soldiers but also to top leaders that the Hun Sen government was able to end the civil war that had raged from 1979 to 1998. In the former "Khmer Rouge"–held territories the same authorities are in power, now invested by the Hun Sen government. But the Western powers want the "Khmer Rouge" leaders being tried to be sentenced to maximum punishment for what they identify as the worst case of crimes against humanity since Nazi Germany.

I for my part could not keep my eyes off Kaing Guek Eav and wondered what it is like to be Kaing Guek Eav. And wondered what good it would do to now imprison this sixty-seven-year-old man, who for the last twenty years had been a schoolteacher teaching mathematics and working with relief agencies. What would be accomplished, for him and for us, and for twelve thousand people now dead, by imprisoning him for the rest of his life?

I was each day struck by the commitment he so assiduously maintained each day as he devoted his full attention to each witness: that what occurred and what he did be truthfully recorded. His memory and his mathematical intelligence were now wholly employed to record the exact truth. I wondered over this, this single-minded devotion to the truth.

The truth of the past conflict is incontestably essential for political leaders who have to reconstruct society and build political institutions with factions that have been in conflict. It is supremely important to people to know when and where their family members and comrades were disappeared, if and how they were tortured, if and when they were executed, and where buried or burned. The truth of the past conflict is vital for victims who have been dishonored and maligned. It is important for perpetrators who have to come to terms with their past and their futures. Establishing the truth is imperative for historians who have to help provide humanity with an understanding of its conflicts and disasters.

But in Phnom Penh I came to wonder about how effective a trial, such as the joint UN–Cambodia trial, is to produce truth about the past. What is adjudicated in criminal justice courts is limited to the accusation the prosecution has prepared and by the limits of the verifiable evidence available. Further, the courts are ill equipped to deal with the broader context of an aggression or injury, for example, a state of generalized hostility and disorder that may characterize two communities in conflict.

On trial with Kaing Guek Eav are the four surviving members, three men and one woman, now all in their eighties, of the former twelve-person Standing Committee of the Communist Party of Kampuchea.[3] The other seven members of that committee have died in the meantime. The Hun Sen government argued, and the UN reluctantly conceded, that prosecuting the "Khmer Rouge" leaders who had accepted amnesty and been integrated into the army and government would break up the fragile state and possibly relaunch the civil war that had ravaged Cambodia. Thus considerations of the political unity and stability of the state, or, more exactly, of the Hun Sen regime, functioned to restrict responsibility to these four men and one woman.[4] The inevitable veto from the UN Security Council prohibited the UN–Cambodia Court from indicting U.S. president Nixon and Henry Kissinger who ordered the carpet bombing of neutral Cambodia that killed, according to the CIA, two hundred thousand people, drove two million to seek refuge in the cities, and destroyed the dikes and irrigation systems upon which the food production of the country depended.

Criminal justice courts are also ill equipped to deal with the trauma the victim is suffering or the forgiveness that the victim may have achieved. Nor are they equipped to deal with the remorse and determination to amend and restore the harm inflicted that the perpetrator may have. Yet these issues are central to what has to be discussed and dealt with for reconciliation to occur. Would other kinds of commissions or meetings where these things can be set forth produce the kind of truth that is required for reconciliation?

More generally, I wondered how truth is determined among people whose different perceptions and judgments led them to war. What kind of truth can be established? How much of the truth about their violent past is necessary for communities to begin to coexist and build a common future?

A certain number of physical facts can be established, although normally by official agencies and experts, not by the parties meeting to speak. Mass or hidden graves can be exhumed, corpses identified, secret prisons and torture chambers located. Documents and records can be located and made available. But just having victim and perpetrator each tell of what he or she did and what he or she suffered and having each side respond to the other does not produce "objective truth." In the criminal justice courts, it is believed that that requires an outside, third party—the judge and jury—to assess each account.

We say, "History will judge," thinking that it is the historians who will later produce the objective account of what really happened, in South Africa, Chile, Kosovo, or Cambodia. But historians acknowledge that their accounts are written according to contemporary concepts of causation, contemporary concepts of how demographic, geographic, economic, political, and ideological factors intervene to produce historical events. Their account of the Cuban missile crisis, even their account of the wars of Genghis Khan are written for contemporary American or Mongolian readers, whose interests and concerns the historian to some measure shares.

Is it then instead "subjective truth" that is put forth when the parties in conflict agree to meet and listen to one another? That is, a sincere and honest account by each party of how each views the situation, what evaluations and judgments, what goals each holds, and what feelings of anger, humiliation, craving for revenge, or of empowerment, freedom, and impunity each finds in himself or herself?

Could there be produced "intersubjective truth"? After the confrontation both parties may recognize that they have found or produced agreement about a certain number of events and how they are to be described. But there may well remain areas of disagreement, because each side has incompatible legal claims to the same land or resources, or because the sides have irreconcilable conceptions of the economic and political order that they take to be just.

How does one know that the account one gives is sincere and honest? How good an account can one give of how one views the conflict? There may be factors in the political and social situation that induce one to see things in a certain light but that one does not recognize. How good an account can one give of the feelings, of anger, humiliation, craving for revenge, or of empowerment, freedom, and impunity one finds in oneself? There may be unconscious feelings, memories, and drives that one does not recognize. The way a militant views his actions during the conflict may not coincide with how he views them later when his side has been defeated. Will he be able to give a lucid account of that difference?

There is something distorting in a situation where an individual stands alone and recounts what he or she did; this situation tends to ascribe or attribute individual responsibility. But to really understand how individuals commit violent aggressions, we may have to take into account the training and conditioning those individuals were given and also a situation of generalized conflict and violence that may have obtained.

And how will others know that one's account is sincere and honest?

It is not enough that the victims know who perpetrated crimes against them and why; the perpetrators must acknowledge them. They must declare, confess, what they did, and do so before their victims who still survive. They have a moral duty to confess their crimes, to restore the dignity of those they humiliated, tortured, and killed. It is only in this acknowledgment that the victims are no longer denied recognition of their humanity.

What the perpetrator will say, can say, will be affected by the consequences he or she foresees. Will he or she be punished or amnestied? Accepted into the community or shunned as a pariah? Will he or she be tracked down by comrades who denounce him or her for betrayal or by victims who will seek vengeance?

Will the acknowledgment be accepted? Will it be perceived to be sincere?

Leigh Payne's book *Unsettling Accounts* studies cases where members of police, army, and intelligence units confessed to crimes in the civil wars and military repressions in South Africa, Argentina, Brazil, and Chile.[5] Some of these confessions were perceived by the public to issue from remorse. Some were seen to have been made to obtain amnesty. Others were declarations of the heroic nature of the cause in which the crimes were committed, the loyalty and dedication of the perpetrator, the depravity of the enemy. Others were seen to reveal a sadistic satisfaction in perpetrating crimes and also a sadistic satisfaction in imposing accounts of them on the public. Many involved silence about or denials of many abuses and silence about co-perpetrators. Some seemed to exhibit a sort of traumatized amnesia about horrors in which the confessing one participated. Some appeared to be motivated by the perpetrator judging himself to have been betrayed by his superiors or collaborators and wishing to betray them in turn, to implicate them in ignominy.

The public was largely skeptical of confessions where the author of the confession was perceived to be betraying his colleagues, seeking to distance himself from them, or seeking amnesty. When the one confessing appeared frequently on television or published a book, belief in him or her decreased. The rhetoric of the confession, the demeanor and body language of the one confessing also significantly determined whether the public believed him or her or did not. Even his or her dress was a factor, and the one confessing was aware of that, sometimes dressing in military dress uniform, or in the clothes of the common man.

The victim too has motives, conscious and unconscious, for distorting, exaggerating, even inventing abuses he or she suffered. Much of the force, even convincingness, of the account depends on how it is told. Rhetorical factors shape the victim's account.

In Cambodia today victims are recounting their sufferings to the joint UN–Cambodia Court trying crimes against humanity. How accurate is human memory of events from thirty years ago? How reliable is identifying a person you last saw thirty years ago?

Greatly traumatic events are not simply retained by memory; they are integrated in a course of mental life that continually opens upon a future of new events and actions. In some cases they block access to the future: the victim lives in his or her trauma and cannot live in a now that is different and envision a future that arrays new possibilities. In other cases the reverse happens: the trauma is closed off to consciousness, cannot be recalled, cannot be understood or interpreted. In every case, as the years pass what one has undertaken and lived through modifies what one remembers of a traumatic aggression and how one remembers it.

It is currently said that knowing the truth brings closure, or that truth heals. The notion that, through meeting with the other side of the conflict, through declaration and response between victim and perpetrator, when some measure of intersubjective truth is established, closure is accomplished—that notion is metaphorical and misleading. There may be the sense that the essential has been said and agreed upon. But the sincerity and completeness of what was said by victim and by perpetrator remain provisional; each side will always feel that there is more to be said. And agreeing that the essential has been established by no means brings an end to the suffering of the victim.[6] Nor does it bring an end to the career of the perpetrator, who is afflicted with the tormenting problem of how to live his or her life now that his or her cause has been acknowledged to be unjust, his or her militancy futile, and his or her status in the community dishonored.

The notion that "truth heals," that when the victim is given voice to speak and be heard and the perpetrator acknowledges the harm inflicted, the victim's reputation and dignity in the community is restored—this notion is also metaphorical and misleading. When one has been tortured or raped, one's loved ones disappeared, when one has lost years of life in imprisonment, there is no restoration or compensation. When people have suffered a grave physical, psychological, or moral injury or the loss of those closest to them, they have to harbor this loss, honor and cherish what was lost, and assemble whatever resources are possible to be able to live. To begin to live again, the victim will also have to find material and social resources. Vivid reexperiencing of the event, fear, nightmares, feelings of helplessness, depression, self-blame, relationship difficulties, feelings of social disconnectedness, anxiety, sometimes substance abuse are all sufferings that may take long-term community support, professional care, and time to diminish, and they may never diminish.

Communities and individuals will not seek reconciliation with their formerly armed enemies as long as they are convinced of the overriding justice of their cause and the real possibility of imposing it by violence. And it is illusory and indeed repugnant to seek to induce peoples to maintain tolerant and respectful relations with one another when they are being occupied, oppressed, humiliated, and killed by the political and military forces of another. Unless those peoples can envision and hope for a situation when they would coexist with their enemies without being degraded and oppressed by them, coexistence and reconciliation will not be possible.

Truth seeking also requires certain social conditions. All sides in conflict will have to be open to the possibility that crimes that they have committed will be disclosed. Their dignity and very identity may be at risk. For peoples and communities to take that risk, a certain level of social and cultural security will have to have been established.

Confrontation of victim and perpetrator to establish the truth of past crimes, oppression, and abuses is not the only and may not be the best way to work for restoration of the wounded and traumatized victims and reintegration into a community of coexistence. Methods to achieve integration on another plane, a symbolic plane, are widespread across cultures. The sufferer may make some kind of sense of his or her suffering and find resources to begin to live again by situating his or her suffering in the cosmic realm, identifying it with the suffering of spiritual beings or gods, and seeking help from beneficent deities. Since myths and religions are social structures, the sufferer is supported by the religious community and its ministers. Anthropologist Claude Lévi-Strauss, in his study "The Effectiveness of Symbols," has shown this process in his study of shamans and healers.[7]

Historical figures of victims, of perpetrators, of mediators, and of peacemakers also come to exist on the symbolic plane, and peoples and communities seeking a new coexistence will identify with them and understand their situation and their longings through these symbolic figures.

Since truth can harm people as well as benefit them, sometimes it may be better that some facts about the past remain unknown. The most effective methods for obtaining the truth may violate the rule of law, personal privacy, or the right not to incriminate oneself. Such methods might be too costly in relation to other goals. The joint UN–Cambodia Court to try the surviving five "Khmer Rouge" leaders of Democratic Kampuchea, scheduled to last five years, has in the first year of its operation cost $170 million, and one might wonder if such a sum would not be better spent to provide psychiatric services, health services, schools, and economic aid to the country.[8] Some truths about the past may be irrelevant to reckoning with the disasters and sufferings of people left by past conflicts and crimes.

There may be times when, for reconciliation, telling what happened and what one suffered may be less important than not repeating the inflammatory words of the past and the accusatory and fighting words of the present.

There is, finally, the troubling phenomenon that meetings where the sides in conflict recount the crimes they endured and inflicted may deepen hostility, arouse waves of revenge killings, increase the level of hostility and violence. When there is generalized violence in a society, that in itself conveys a sense that violence is intrinsic to human nature, promotes cynicism, and produces more violence. Did all the publicized crimes revealed in the South African Truth and Reconciliation Commission contribute to such a situation? The high levels of criminality in South Africa since the end of apartheid have been accompanied by gross human-rights violations by the police. Between April 2001 and March 2002, 585 people died in police custody or as a result of police action. The torture of criminal suspects by the police continues. A recent survey revealed that 70 percent of South African respondents of all races "agreed" or "strongly agreed" with the statement that "criminals have too many rights." Thirty-one percent of all South Africans feel that the police have the right to use force to extract information from criminal suspects.[9]

Still, facing one another and telling one's suffering and telling the deeds one has perpetrated does bring about an expansion of information and also understanding of motives and suffering. It limits the denial and also the dramatization of suffering, what has been called "triumphalism of pain." It complicates the process of rationalization both perpetrator and victim have undertaken, have had to undertake.

The community and political leaders in projecting future institutions and economic projects will have to take account of how each side saw the situation. But those views can change.

After the devastating civil war in Finland in 1918, the internecine conflict between collaborationist and resistant French after World War II, after the end of the Cultural Revolution in China, as after World War II in Japan, there were no institutions set up to establish the truth of crimes perpetrated on fellow citizens. Yet reconciliation between the parties in conflict did take place, as the political leadership concentrated on building the future. It is true: the past passes. And there is also the biological renewal: generations pass, and the new generation will not have all the causes for conflict and for recrimination of the older generation.

The Extraordinary Chambers of the Courts of Cambodia, where the joint UN–Cambodia trial is being conducted, are located in a building in a military base some thirty kilometers outside of Phnom Penh. Each day the NGOs, funded by outside countries, bus in people from the outlying countryside to watch the trial for a day. The NGOs want the Cambodian people, who have had little reason, for the past 150 years since their country became a French colony, to trust in courts, to see the exemplary case of a United Nations trial, thorough and fair. They want the Cambodian people to see that the terrible sufferings of thirty years ago will not pass with impunity. The commitment to justice of these NGOs is clear.

But I learned that they sometimes hear different words from the Cambodians they bus to the trial. Some of them are uncomfortable with the concept of punishment, retribution, revenge. They may invoke the teaching of the monks: that to wish evil on those who have done evil is to harbor evil in oneself. Thirty years have passed; more than half of the population of Cambodia was born after these events; to hear them recounted and to represent them to themselves do not arouse the intense passions they arouse in those who have lived through them. They feel that it is by an effort of imagination and will that they produce feelings of revenge in themselves. They may recognize a troubling kinship of what retribution they may will with the will of the evildoers on trial. Former deputy secretary of the Central Committee Nuon Chea had long retired to his home village, occupying himself raising ducks. When the UN-mandated police came to arrest him, some of his neighbors said to reporters: he is an old man now and no harm to anybody. Of Cambodians polled by the Documentation Center of Cambodia in 2002, 68.96 percent said that they would not get enraged and want to take revenge if they discovered that surviving villagers were those who killed their relatives.[10] Many were explicit that taking matters into their own hands would put them on the same level as those who committed the original crimes.[11]

As expressing one's emotions of anger, bitterness, and vengefulness or one's sorrow and suffering is not the norm in Cambodian culture, so apologizing is also not the norm.[12] Laura McGrew reports a discussion of the trial conducted by an NGO in which a participant said, "To say I'm sorry is a difficult thing to say. It is not a Cambodian habit to say this. We seldom find people who will say excuse me or pardon me."[13]

The Venerable Yos Hut Khamacaro explained:

Buddhism doesn't recommend repentance or regret. You must have a good spirit to accomplish good things here and now. If you live with remorse you cannot focus on the present actions. You shouldn't continue to suffer, if you commit a crime. You should just try to understand that if you have done this bad thing, you will have bad consequences. You should consider the past crime as a mistake or error, and you should try to learn and gain advice for your present actions. If you live in the past, it is not good. There is no need for remorse, just understand the cause and effect and try to learn from your mistakes.[14]

The NGOs heard some Cambodians invoke the concept of karma—what the evil men do will have its effects on the evildoers, if not in this life in another. Although this doctrine seems to confirm the principle of human retributive justice, it also acknowledges the limits of that justice.

Rationality is calculation of what is due to each, and from the beginning of philosophy Socrates affirmed that evildoers are punished and the wise and just are rewarded. But health, a sound body and mind, the resources of the world are not equitably distributed by nature; all too often we see the unjust prosper and the just struck down by disease or accident. Medicine strives to correct deformities and heal sickness; moral systems and judicial institutions seek to stop and punish the corruption and violence of the unjust. Yet chance and bad luck will not be eliminated, and our political and economic institutions have not been able to counteract the greed and cruelty of many. Will trials such as the joint UN–Cambodia trial succeed in putting an end to juridical impunity in Cambodia, in deterring tyrants and oppressors? The Nuremberg trials have not done so.

We must, in order to coexist, devise norms to govern our actions—the more urgently today when local conflicts affect much wider regions and peoples and when the weapons we have stockpiled are devastating. Yet we do find that those who govern their actions by those norms all too often are cut down while those who defy those norms succeed with power and cunning. This situation constitutes one of the major metaphysical dilemmas that confronts all ethical and political thought. In face of this situation there are perhaps three positions possible for us: We can wager that the evil men do will have evil consequences on the evildoer, if not in this life in another. We can wager that an omniscient and just God will undertake to punish evildoers in this life and in the next. We can accept a tragic view of human life in an indifferent natural world and of a history whose directions we have not understood how to master.

One day, having listened intently for seven hours as witnesses recounted the torture and execution of their families lost in mass graves, Kaing Guek Eav was shaking with tears and blurted out that the court must sentence him "to the most severe punishment they could devise. Like the torments of Jesus," he gasped.

My mind was reeling. Can the human mind make any kind of sense out of the irreparable? When someone has lost those he or she holds most dear, does any kind of restitution make sense? Is not our juridical practice of consigning huge sums of money—millions—to victims a mockery of reason? Does the torture of one man restore the thousands whose torture and execution he managed? If God had tortured his only son, how has that changed the world he created where millions continue to be oppressed and tortured and massacred? What can a man who acknowledges that he has perpetrated irreparable crimes do with his life henceforth?

In 1979 in Nicaragua the Sandinista guerrilla armies entered and occupied Managua. Dictator Anastasio Somoza Debayle fled by plane to the United States with his family and the funds of the national treasury. Tomás Borge was the only leader of the original Sandinista rebellion who had survived the war; he had been captured and tortured in Somoza's prisons and his wife had been raped and murdered in his presence. He was named minister of the interior of the new government. One day some from his staff came to him and told him that among the captured prisoners of Somoza's army they believed they had identified the men who had tortured him. Borge went to the prison and confronted the men. He confirmed that they were indeed his torturers. He ordered them freed.

But the main body of Somoza's army fled to Honduras and Costa Rica, was reorganized and armed by the United States, and continued the war.

2011

Catastrophic Time

How strange that the sequoias of California, which live two thousand five hundred years, die! Lightning has struck each of them innumerable times, burning the dead wood of their cores, without killing them. For nothing, until humans invented chain saws, can kill a sequoia. When they die, they die of a natural death. Their seeds were from the start programmed for them to live twenty-five hundred years and then die.

There is a specific duration, a lifetime, intrinsic to all living things. Whenever we see plants or animals we see infancy, youth, maturity, aging, and dying.

The perception that evolved in living things is not only a seeing and touching of other things. There is no perception without a perception of time. Plants have no recourse but to undergo whatever befalls them, rain and sunshine or scorching sun and tornados, but animals, which can move, are able to flee. They feel fear, they sense they are vulnerable, they sense the imminence of their death. Those that care for their progeny, as well as those that do not, have a sense of their own infancy and of the infancy of their offspring. They see, in their own species and in other species, infancy, youth, maturity, aging, and dying.

This biological time intrinsic to their natures can be transformed into a field of work in some organisms. Work circumscribes and structures time.

A human primate detaches something—a loose stone, a branch, a pipe wrench—from the continuity of the natural or fabricated environment. With his tool he detaches himself and shifts his view from the environment continuous with his body to goals or results beyond it. Between his tool and the goals or results he sees a relationship of means and end, cause and effect. The identification of distinct substances, and the understanding of a relationship between means and ends and between causes and effects, is the core of reason. Everyone who works is rational.

Knowledge is not given to us in a sudden illumination of the mind; to know is to strive, to work. We learn that this chipped stone can serve to cut and to chop; that stone, blunted, can serve to grind. We learn that this is iron and that is sulfur, by putting them successively in reactions with other substances. Once we see what we can do with a broken branch, a chipped stone, a bone or steel knife, we figure out what falling rocks, streaming water, the roots of trees do by themselves.

We work in order to maintain, secure, or acquire what we take to be a good. Goods contribute to the refurbishment and protection of those who acquire them. Something acquires value by being promised in the future, and by withstanding, and helping us withstand, the passing of time, by enduring.

The human primate makes of himself a tool; he inserts himself into the field of work and reason as an implement that can be used to reach ends, a cause that produces effects. The order of means and foreseen results, of causes and effects, enters into him. His mind turns into a place where his limbs and senses are subordinated to purposes, where his present consciousness is subordinated to an anticipated future. What has come to pass in his body—his strength, his skills—and in his mind—his memories—is subordinated to the future. His enterprise, all his efforts, require the future to make sense.

The one who works maintains a sense of individual identity, by envisioning himself in the future. I identify what I am doing by specifying what I shall be doing. It is tomorrow that gives sense to whatever I do today; it is tomorrow that gives sense to whatever I am today.

The one who works envisages others as collaborators or as obstructors. Our work space, however much it is our own, inevitably finds itself surrounded by the work spaces of others whom we have to count on, at least as unwitting accomplices. Like tools, they stand detached and destined for results and products, for a future. The results and products they are working for, their futures, give them individual identities.

In the shifty eyes of others, in their duplicitous movements, we sense a disaster that could befall us through their negligence, or a malevolence or madness that could single us out. We detach ourselves from them, and also detach weapons we could use against them. Words are among these weapons; each of us has in childhood learned the words that can hurt others, more deeply than sticks and stones. But with our work we build walls too to contain their violence.

Work extends, circumscribes, and delimits a zone of time. The future is articulated as a field of possibilities, the past as a field of resources retained in our know-how and skills.

Work is measurable as a half-day's job, a day's work. The movement of the sun across the sky or a pointer round a dial can be marked in hours, minutes, seconds, nanoseconds. Equivalences are virtually interchangeable: a day, as a day, is interchangeable with another day, an hour with another hour. This equivalence and interchangeability of measurable segments of time make the events that take place in those segments appear from the first as repeatable, reversible, and repairable. To survey the time of the world is to see to what extent the succession of things can be reproduced, varied, and reversed.

Death strikes. Death suddenly strikes down a collaborator. Death does not annihilate her; the body is there and takes up as much space as before. But death violently and at one blow destroys this worker's future and strips of their meaning, not only the undertaking she was engaged in when it struck, but retroactively all the work that led to it. Death strikes in the now, and immediately drives its shock wave into the future and down the past of that life. Death strikes, reducing to nothing the instrument she had made of herself in the world of work, reducing to nothing her individual identity. She died from an infection picked up while working in the emergency room. He fell from the scaffolding of his half-built house. Her half-completed medical education, his half-finished house, appear as intensive efforts that, had this outcome been foreseen, would never have been made.

When someone we know dies, we weep: it is impossible that she should be dead. We say over and over again, I can't believe it.

It is unthinkable that this companion, this associate, is dead; to think of him, of what he was, is to think of him as a being whom we identified from the function which the field of tasks before him and the future ahead of him gave him. Whenever we think of him now, we inevitably think of his image, his ghost, his soul still involved in his concerns. If we think of our dead parent or lover, we think of her watching us or speaking to us as she used to do. We think how proud our father would have been to see us at this law-school graduation; we see again in a spasm of perfidy and shame our dead lover as we sell his motorcycle to pay for computer programming lessons. But this sense of the ongoing existence of the dead is accompanied by the knowledge that death has annihilated the possibilities and tasks of their future. The ghost or soul we visualize when we think of the dead one is a trembling, vacillating vision that darkens the world of work and reason.

A catastrophic event destroys the time of work and reason, and opens upon the empty endurance of void. Duration, beneath or without any things that endure and that pass and without any processes, is not, as Immanuel Kant thought, given from the start in a separate intuition. It is caught sight of in an event—a catastrophic event which strikes down a companion, annihilating all his future and nullifying all his past.

The death that strikes this associate of ours and the death that strikes someone elsewhere are events separated by stretches of duration. The later death is not the effect or the result of the earlier one. The deaths that come to pass do not accumulate like resources. The expanse of duration between them is empty of them.

The death of a collaborator gives us an unnerving premonition that a like violence—a heavy or sharp tool that slips, an automobile collision, a microbe—could abruptly befall us in our time and space of work and reason, and could annihilate, along with our future, the significance of our past. A violent blow can also destroy our future and past without destroying the present, as when an automobile accident or disease paralyzes the hand of a music student or a surgical intern.

Violence may erupt in a fellow worker, who strikes out amok and abruptly destroys our future. A war breaks out, and we find ourselves drafted into the front lines, or a foreign power begins shelling and bombing the towns and homes about us. A revolution breaks out and, in the fever of revolt, we throw our investments, our homes, our families, our lives into the chaos and violence of the insurrection.

We cannot imagine our dead companion and imagine him annihilated, but we cannot imagine our own death without imagining ourselves cast into the empty endurance of the void. Yet in dying we are not liberated into the abyss of empty time; we sink into the dead weight of a corpse. Fatigue and aging, which make us feel encumbered, held back in the spring of our initiatives, by the weight of our bodies, make us feel already the corpse that death will turn us into. An infected wound makes us see, smell, and feel the decomposition and corruption already at work in our bodies. We die like dogs, befouling the ground and poisoning the air.

It is not only our own death that destroys all the structure of intelligible time in our lives. Our life can be so intertwined with that of our child, everything we do motivated by the future of that child, that when she is killed in a hit-and-run accident, not only her future, but our own and our past, are devastated. Our life can be so spliced onto that of our lover that when a stray bullet in a street leaves him paralyzed and in an iron lung, not only our plans for a future together, but our strength to pursue any plans, are obliterated. Sometimes it is some nameless and unidentifiable anxiety that cuts an untraversable abyss between us and any promises or lures that extend a future, and makes of our life an empty desolation.

The time that orders the future, present, and past in which we work appears to us to be linear. It also appears to us to exist on the surface of things and on the surface of Earth. It appears superficial when a catastrophe reveals the time of the empty endurance of the void. This empty endurance appears to us to be deep, the void an abyss. It lurks in the depths of Earth.

Work detaches things from the surface of Earth—plants, animals, branches, and loose stones used as tools. We detach ourselves by standing back, supported by the expanse of the surface of Earth. The first fires to be used appeared on the surface of Earth, but they came from the storm clouds, and seemed to bring to concentration the inner heat of the ground. At length workers began to disembowel the earth to pull forth ores to be smelted with fire into iron and bronze. Fire and iron made more effective tools; they especially made devastating weapons. Previously, people had turned their tools as weapons on one another; now a torch thrown burns down a whole hamlet and its field crops; a raid with metal weapons disembowels everybody who fights as well as all who flee. In raids, pillages, and massacres with fire and iron, catastrophe erupts in settlements.

We work on Earth's crust; we see movements of Earth's substance—shifting continental plates, earthquakes, volcanic eruptions—that are calamitous for us and for innumerable other living organisms. In the lightning that sinks into it and in earthquakes, geysers, and volcanic eruptions, we sense all the inner incandescence of our planet. We sense that only on the surface is Earth a crust that can be turned into enduring goods, that beneath the deepest mines there is the inner core of fire. We sense that Earth is a particle of the sun, separated from the sun in a cosmic explosion. We see that it is in the midst of a cosmic cataclysmic time that our work extends its transitory and vulnerable intelligible time.

The corpse is there, it has to be washed, the casket has to be selected and paid for, a hall has to be reserved and a meal arranged for those who will come to the funeral. A preacher will be hired to tell of some real or imagined achievements, which some of the family and friends recall from the life that was snuffed out before it got anywhere, and deck them with the names of exemplary virtues. Willy-nilly, we bridge the calamity, as though it were but a temporary setback in the open road of intelligible time.

Back from the funeral, we think we felt the grim reaper swing close; we feel him stalking us. We ward off anxiety before the imminent and inescapable annihilation awaiting us by establishing control over our life and field of operations, by projecting an advance representation of what each day brings, and by measuring our enterprises to our forces. We arrange our home and our situation and our workday in such a way that we retain, behind the forms of our performances, a reserve of force for the tasks that will recur the next day. We settle into an occupation that requires only those mental tasks for which we have already contracted the mental skills. We frame our pleasures and our angers, our affections and our vexations, in the patterns and confines of feelings we can repeat indefinitely. We avoid going to places utterly unlike any other, which would leave us wholly astonished, with an astonishment that could never recur. We seek out partners others might also fall in love with, and we love our partner as others love like partners, with a love that we could recycle for another partner should we lose this one. For we sense that were we to expend all our forces on an adventure, discharge all our mental powers on a problem, empty out all the love in our heart on a woman or a man unlike any other, we would be dying in that adventure, that problem, that love.

Alternatively, sensing the imminence and inevitability of the disaster that will annihilate all our forces, we resolve to activate all of them in the present. We commit all our forces formed and shaped by past events and give their skill, sensitivity, and momentum to our present work. We make the work before us the condensation of all the works we ever wanted or shall ever want to accomplish. A jazz musician sets aside all the concerns of others to improvise his own song now, with the sense that he does not have time for business investments, does not have time to get a job teaching the music of others to others, that he has to make his music now. He improvises with all the resonance of his birth in a certain family, a certain ethnic group, a certain neighborhood, and puts into his composition all the yearnings, hopes, and heartbreaks that have shaped his sensibility. A gymnast goes to the bars and rings each day with the sense that she was born with this exceptional body, in this place on the planet where the gym and the trainer are available, and does not have time to take a full liberal-arts course, does not have time this afternoon to go to the picnic with her housemates, because the gymnast in her will be dead by the age of twenty-one. The guerrilla sees all that is possible for his country in this revolutionary moment, and all that is possible for himself, and takes all that he has lived through and suffered and learned from childhood as preparation for his decisive and dangerous mission.

The citizen-activist, statesman, or guerrilla fits the day or years before him or her into the broad time of history. The possibilities for which she marshals her resources may not be possibilities that will become actual for her; they may belong to her comrades, to the next generation, after the victory has been won, a victory for which she may well have given her life.

The sense of the imminence of disaster transforms the intelligible time of work, and of history, and gives us the sense of the time of our own life. I see the trajectory of time from my birth to my death and I situate on it all the initiatives I now undertake. My sense of coming to an end, of ending, is what gives my life the sense of ends, of goals, and makes me determine initiatives that are determinate. I act resolutely to bring the momentum of all that has come to pass in me into my acts, and I extend my acts unto their ends. For me living becomes the living out now of all my powers, discharging all my forces in my present work. Living is dying on my own and with my own forces.

Witnessing a fatal accident on the highway when coming back from the office, we pull our minds back to where we have to go tonight and back to driving the car. We awaken after the heart attack and find ourselves paralyzed on one side and half blind; as the shock levels out, we begin to think of how we will manage. Awakening on a stretcher after a battle, come to the realization that we will most likely not leave the field hospital alive, we think of disposing of our savings for the use of those who will survive us. We lay out works that will consume our life, and count on there being others for whom maintaining the fertility of this farm, managing this business, reading books will be significant. Ecologists today speak urgently of the steps that will have to be taken lest pollution, destruction of the ozone shield, and the greenhouse effect put an end to human life, even all life, on this planet. Astrophysicists who speak of the inevitable extinction of our sun hold open the possibility that before that happens we may well be able to colonize other planetary systems around other stars. They count on thought, scientific-technological thought, which arose and arises out of work and operates in the service of work.

Though the sense of imminent—and inevitable—disaster may drive us totally and resolutely into the intelligible time of work, the time of work cannot be shielded from the fall of a heavy or sharp tool, an automobile collision, a microbe, or the violence that seizes a collaborator or a passerby, those occurrences that drop us into the time of the empty endurance of void. Yet the catastrophic time that devastates us can also strangely hold us, and even draw us into it. There are drives in us that let us be drawn into catastrophe, that live in catastrophic events.

We had long planned this trip to New Orleans, California, Paris, or India. There, our education would flower, we would find the exciting people, we would find a real life, we would find love or enlightenment. But once there, we found the streets, the buildings, the roads, the landscapes alien and indifferent to us. No opportunities opened up before us. We did not connect with people, find friends or a lover. We saw that the streets, buildings, and landscapes looked bleak and harsh to those who lived there. The men and women looked preoccupied and weary; their routine lives without urgency or glamour seemed empty and sad. We who had left our job and our place in a mediocre community found our life diminished just by observing the barrenness of people's lives in these narrow confines, the pedestrian neighborhoods and landscapes that had been so mythologized. We found ourselves in a state of detachment and anxiety, disconnected from any initiative or adventure, and feeling the emptiness of our days.

One rainy evening, we were seated in a bus. We were not on a trip heading for some opportunity—only returning to our rented room again for the night. We looked out the bus window into the rain and the fog. And then our eyes got absorbed in the trees emerging from the fog, their branches almost bare of leaves now with the oncoming of the winter. The splay of their branches was different for each tree, not foreseeable, and as they emerged into view they were already passing out of view forever. Memory retained no hold on them. Along with the patterns of the trees emerging and passing back into the fog without meaning or function, we felt the empty endurance of the void. The bare branches emerging and fading away filled all our consciousness, so that we no longer felt a separation between them and ourselves. We felt desolate, barren, alone, but the strangeness of these barely substantial trees in the fog brought a sense of gentle melancholy and a wistful serenity.

Along the Pacific Coast of Peru is a narrow strip of land, walled in on one side by the Andes, and exposed on the other to the ocean, kept cold all year by the Humboldt Current coming up from Antarctica. The air over this coastal strip, heated by the sun, expands out over the cold ocean, so that moisture from the ocean does not drift back over the land. It never rains; most of this coastal plain is drier than the Sahara. To the south the land is geologically very unstable; you cross the desert utterly devoid of vegetation, even of cactus, stretches of white volcanic tuff poured out by some eighty-five volcanoes. You reach the brink of Colca Canyon; it is the deepest canyon on planet Earth. At the bottom winds a river, fed both by melting snows from the Andes and by deep groundwater. How wrong David Hume was to declare that causality is a mental diagram we construct and project over material reality, which is merely present and nothing but present! In Colca Canyon we cannot see without seeing causality. You cannot look without seeing the successive layering of rock and lava, the cross sections cut in them and the scalloping of the exposed edges by the shifting of the continental plates and by wind and water erosion across millennia. Your slow and wearing descent into the canyon, the grit crumbling under your shoes, measures the time of your effort and of your life against the geological epochs of the planet's crust and rock layers. The scale of the Andes and of the canyon diminish you. The scale of geological time diminishes you and destines any footprints you leave here, indeed any works you build in your lifetime, to erosion and mineral decomposition.

There are some Indian hamlets at the bottom of the canyon. These people were passed over by the Inca empire and are too alien and too poor to be enlisted in the Peruvian state today. You are able to find lodging for the night. You are awakened several hours before sunrise and led by your Indian guide up the river and then up the canyon wall. By the time the sun has risen you have reached the point where the canyon is deepest. Your guidebook says that the Grand Canyon of the Colorado is 1,638 meters at its deepest; here Colca Canyon is 4,174 meters deep. It is also very narrow, a knife cut through sixteen thousand feet of granite, at the bottom of which like a crinkle of mercury you see the river. All around, the glaciers of the Andes begin to blaze with the rising sun. Loftiest is the volcano Mount Mismi, whose melting glacier is the source of the Amazon. Billowing in the sky are the sulfurous fumes of the Sabancaya volcano you passed hours ago in the dark. You are seated a very long time on a boulder in this uninhabitable mountainscape. No human enterprise could take hold here; you could form no project here, not even an exploratory hike. Even if you had any shreds of vocabulary of his language or he of yours, you would not have anything to say to your Indian companion, not even any question to ask him. The discursive movements of the mind, staking out paths, laying out positions and counterpositions, are silenced, deadened. As soon as the sun has emerged over the peaks of the Andes, it turns the whole cloudless sky magnesium-white. Its radiation spreads over your face and hands like warmth, although the thin air your heaving lungs are pumping in is cold. After a long time spent motionless, you are aware the sun is now high in the sky.

And then, well before seeing it, you are aware of the condor, like a silent drumroll in the skies over the glaciers. Your eyes are pulled to a speck taking form in the empty radiance, imperceptibly becoming bigger, becoming a great bird never once flapping or even shifting its wings, soaring down from a great height and then into the canyon, descending to eye level in front of you before gradually descending deeper and becoming lost to sight. It is the first condor you have seen, with its fifteen-foot wingspan the largest flying bird on the planet; this one is brown, a young female surveying the desolate cliffs and avalanches for carrion. And then—an hour, two hours later?—there are two: again you know they are there well before they are visible. They are soaring close to one another, circling companionably in the airless heights. When they are overhead, you try to gauge their height, judging they are above you halfway again the depth of the canyon—that is, some twenty-four thousand feet. You, who could hardly climb much higher than your present thirteen thousand feet, feel your eyes, your craving, your fascination plunging to their almost immaterial realm, falling up into the region of death.

You are nothing but a vision, a longing, a euphoric outflow of life hanging on to the flight of the condors. Their flight comes from a past without memory and slides into a future without anticipation. You are cut loose, unanchored, without guy wires, drifting in the void of the sky. You know nothing but the flight of the condors, feel nothing but the thin icy air, see nothing but the summits and ice cliffs of the Andes and the granite walls of the canyon below your flight. You are alive to nothing but their bodies and their soaring, you are alive for nothing but for them.

The abrupt denuding of someone in our presence thrusts a small hiatus into the time of our everyday work. Yet the dense armor of taboos forged over human nudity in our society and in most societies bears witness to the catastrophic effect denuding has been felt to have, has been found to have, on the world of work and reason and on the sane identity of functional citizens.

When we go out in the street, or open our door to someone who knocks, we have first washed the traces of the night, the anonymity and abandon of the night, from our face and rearranged the turmoil of our hair. He dresses up in a business suit or dresses down in jeans; she puts on a pearl necklace or a neck chain of Hopi beads. We also dress today as we did yesterday and last year; she maintains the two-piece crisp look of a career woman with responsibilities; he wears a plaid shirt and sneakers even when coming to our dinner party in the city. In the uniform we see the uniformity of a series of actions, undertakings, thoughts, opinions, feelings, maintained for weeks, months, years, and predictable for the weeks, months, years ahead. We see the time of endurance, and respond to it.

In denuding herself or himself before our eyes and in our arms, she or he takes off the uniform, the categories, the endurance, and exposes the body substance in the pure chance of its shape and color. Of course, in the gym-built musculature we see another kind of clothing, body armor, uniform, a body reshaped to fit a model. But in the slight sag of the full breasts, in the smooth expanse of the belly, in the contour of the buttocks, in the bare expanse of the inside of the upper thighs, we see flesh without memory and without initiatives, without tasks or commitments, flesh meaningless and idle.

In the bodies denuded, sexual excitement surges in a meltdown of built-up structures. The posture collapses, the manipulative diagrams of the limbs soften, legs and thighs roll about, fingers and hands move in aimless, unendingly repetitive caresses, allowing themselves to be stroked and crushed. The psychic structures with which we screen, filter out, and channel the superabundance of outside stimuli that flood our senses at all times are shattered and the stimuli flood us pell-mell. The structures by which we fix an inner ego identity and censor out a whole underworld of unconscious drives and cravings buckle and crack; in sexual excitement the gates of the lower dungeons are opened and feral drives and cravings bound up and overwhelm our conscious intentions and purposes.

Every breakup of equilibrium, Freud noted, has something orgasmic about it. A child's cry lapses into voluptuous abandon when it is rocked on the knees of its father or thrown into the air. You get a hard-on during the solemnity of Christmas high Mass and during a funeral. In Leonard Cohen's novel *Beautiful Losers*, two men are driving in the country, speeding; suddenly the driver swerves off the road and hurtles the car through a wall (which turns out to be painted on a billboard); on the other side he turns to his friend and says, "Did you come?" A year or so back, there was a hurricane roaring up the Atlantic Coast, heading for Boston. A few days later, a student came to tell me why she had missed the previous class. She had heard the news, and suddenly remembered her mother, the manager of a five-star hotel in the heart of Boston, someone my student normally did her best not to think of. She had grabbed her boyfriend and raced to Boston, where her mother, surprised to see her, let them have a room on the top floor for the night. There, naked against the glass walls of the room, they waited for the eye of the hurricane.

When we see the devastated banks and police stations in the wake of a tornado, as when we witness a revolution that overturns the entire hierarchy of a society, we feel an exultant wildness. It is not simply the justice that may arise from this leveling; it is a kinship with tempestuous and torrential nature that fires us; we come to understand that revolutionaries are not driven by utopian sentimentality.

Anguish is not without exhilaration when we suffer revolutions, lightning strikes, floods, shiftings of continental plates, earthquakes, and volcanic eruptions within ourselves. It is for this that we take off, leaving everything behind, heading alone to other continents where we know nobody and speak none of the languages. Doctors and nurses report that few people go into life-threatening operations feeling nothing but panic. They feel resignation, but they also feel a heightened intensity of the mind, a curiosity, and an undercurrent of exhilaration. We feel this kind of exhilaration and attraction even when we sense that the looming disaster will plunge us into pain and possibly extinction.

A spring morning when the ground underfoot, made of all that has died on the rock core of the planet, blooms with gentle flowers and the crawlers turn into butterflies; a high noon in the rapturous depths of tropical oceans, late afternoon on ice-covered mountaintops made of minute prisms projecting rainbows back into the blue sky—such epiphanies deliver us from our demand to be protected and gratified, from making ourselves useful in the relentless world of work. On the uninhabitable continent of Antarctica we see an enormous chunk of the ice shelf break loose and with the sound of a cannon shot slip into the frazzled water as a hobbling iceberg sending a tidal wave far out into the ocean.

Far from the world of work and reason, we are nothing but a euphoria in the limitless bliss of the earth, sky, and ocean. And this elation produces in us the brutal strength to face the agony of a universe not made for our contentment and indemnification. From inhuman distances, with the fearsome farsightedness of birds of prey we see that sinister spectacle of stupidities and deceits, pillage and tortures that is the history of our species. With soaring raptor eyes we see ourselves devouring plants, birds, fish, and fellow mammals, our earthbound organisms trampling exquisite microecosystems with each step. With fierce eyes, we see the lethal tides of summer and winter which exact agony from all living things. In the remote distances we see the skies emptied but for the stars burning themselves out as fast as they can.

Is there not something catastrophic in the very nature of thought? Thought is driven by an excessive compulsion, and is itself an excess over and beyond perception. Thinking is looking for what exceeds the powers of sight, what is unbearable to look at, what exceeds the possibilities of thought.

From the most ancient times, sages and scientists found in the stars and planets in their fixed positions and regular orbits the immutable order against which the transitions and processes on this planet and the future and past of our fields of work could be located and measured. But the factor of unity in the universe, which makes us speak of all the stars, radiations, and black holes as belonging to one universe, is only the oneness of the original explosion. The speed of the explosion was at first too great to allow any organization to form among the elements; there were only radiations of energy. As the force of the explosion dispersed through empty space, stars formed, and galaxies. Molar and molecular organizations appeared. Our solar system took form, and on Earth the patterns of strata, continental plates, climate, and very soon, the first living organisms. As the eons passed, more and more complex living organisms formed, with their development from spores, seeds, or eggs programmed from the start. Long before humans recorded history, they conceived of the growth and reproduction of organisms and recognized the movements of inorganic nature to be regular, governed throughout by detectable and calculable laws.

Yet sudden, uncontrollable events—collisions, explosions that abruptly destroy organizations, patterns, and systems—continually occur. There are shiftings of continental plates, earthquakes, volcanic eruptions, tidal waves, avalanches, floods, and lightning strikes that spread fire across savanna and forest. There are solar storms; there are asteroids that have struck Earth, causing massive extinctions of most species of its life, and others may strike again. Earth itself wobbles on its axis and in its orbit, resulting in ice ages and extinctions of species of life. In outer space there are collisions of heavenly bodies. There are stars that burn out.

The astrophysicists Fred Adams and Greg Laughlin have constructed the hitherto most complete scientific analysis of the fate of the universe.[1] The received astrophysical wisdom today is that there is not quite enough gravitational force exerted by all the matter in the universe to cause it to recollapse in a Big Crunch after sixty or a hundred billion years. Adams and Laughlin have projected the future of the universe to the next two hundred cosmological decades—a cosmological decade being one-followed-by-two-hundred-zeros years. The current era, the Stelliferous Era, dominated by stars, began with the Big Bang ten billion years ago. We are currently midway through this era. It will come to an end when all the stars burn out. Our sun, four and a half billion years old, is halfway to burning itself out. It will eventually puff up into a red giant and then collapse into a white dwarf no bigger than Earth. In the process the sun will broil away Earth's oceans, leaving an uninhabitable cinder, which will perhaps spiral into the sun.

The next era the astrophysicists name the Degenerate Era. The mass of the cosmos will be locked up in the dim, dense hulks of failed, dead, exploded, and collapsed stars—white dwarfs, brown dwarfs, neutron stars, and black holes. Galaxies will begin to fall apart. As the degenerate hulks collide or sweep close to each other, some will move out beyond the fringes and go careening through intergalactic space, while others will fall toward the galactic centers, perhaps to be eaten by lurking black holes. White dwarfs will capture "dark matter" particles known as WIMPs (Weakly Interacting Massive Particles), which some theorists believe constitute 90 percent of the mass of the universe.

Toward the end of this epoch, about one hundred trillion trillion trillion years from now, the protons in the heart of every atom will begin to decay. The remaining white dwarfs and neutron stars will dissipate, converting a large fraction of the ordinary mass in the cosmos to radiation and ending the Degenerate Era. The final, Dark Era will consist in a diffuse sea of electrons, positrons, neutrinos, and radiation spread tenuously across an enormously larger region than exists today.

The effect of extending our thought this far is an irremediable desolation. Yet something in us impels us to hurl our thought that far. The thought that follows the cosmic desolation is intoxicated, polluted, infected by that desolation. The cosmic history extends before it with no possible effect on our thought, on us, except this intoxication.

1998

Trust

On a walk in the rain forest we come upon an orchid; it spreads the trembling contours of its petals before us and unreservedly fills our eyes with the tones and glow of its colors. However completely the orchid had been described to us, the moment we see it with our own eyes there is shock, astonishment, and discovery. We station ourselves on Antarctic cliffs to watch the penguins scramble up the rookery and each locate its own baby, we descend into the oceans to watch the fish that dwell in different niches in the coral reefs and different depths of the waters. That the great whales sing like birds has been only recently discovered by biologists, for their songs do not pass out of the water into the air. Modern recording technology has transferred these songs to phonograph disks so that we can hear them with our ears across the air of our living rooms. But when we descend into the ocean with the whales we find ourselves immersed in song; our whole bodies, themselves mostly composed of water, reverberate with melodies in the substance of water. All there is to know about the ancient cities now in ruins, about gods long forgotten whose temples are now protected and even meticulously restored, we get from the words and images of books and videotapes. But we go to linger among the stones and there make contact with what, though long past, is still there and sacred. We go for the shock, astonishment, and discovery.

In the great rookeries the penguins locate their own babies from among thousands by their distinctive voiceprint. In the forests we learn to identify unseen birds by their songs. But when we go to different places inhabited by members of our own species, what our eyes see of them and of the places they inhabit is blurred by the language that fills those places and that we do not understand—and even if we do. Is it not because what they say is but babble to us that what our eyes see of them, their facial contours, complexions, and garb, look exotic to us? And when someone there is standing before us, speaking directly to us, we have been cautioned that he is not speaking with his own voice but speaking the language of his gender, his family, his class, his education, his culture, his economic and political interests, his unconscious drives, indeed his state of physical health and alertness. The effort to know him gets detoured into efforts, ever more evidently fragmentary and superficial, to know all these layers. Today the professionals who study these things write books exposing how superficial and deluded have been the efforts of the experts: exposing the imperialist, Christian, Victorian, romantic, or orientalist fables written by those people who left their homelands and fell in love in some remote place, married, and never returned; the positivist, Freudian, or Marxist fables of the past generation of cultural anthropologists; the rationalist, structuralist, or post-modern fables of the current generation.

How often am I aware that others are only dealing with some role I occupy in a society, some pantomime I am performing, some set of clothes and haircut I am wearing! They see and address the American, the professor, or the decently dressed restaurant client, while *I* am thinking for myself and acting on my own, behind that image they see!

Yet it does happen that someone exterior to me approaches and makes contact with *me*—the real me, the core me, whatever I can take to be *me*. It happens every day that I feel a force that breaks out of the passing forms and takes hold of me: "Hey you!" "Hey Al!" Isn't it astounding—really our theories do not account for it—that I feel these words coming straight at me, hitting me, clamping on to *me*? An appeal is being addressed to *me*, a demand put on *me*. The words have penetrated right through the role, the social identity, the visible and interpretable form, to the very core that is *me*. Each time I do answer on my own, I have acknowledged that that is what has happened.

Every day we deal with people who occupy posts in the established social system where behaviors are socially defined and sanctioned. We rely on the bus driver following the scheduled route, we count on the bank teller giving us proper credit for our mortgage payment. Our confidence in the actions of these people is based on our knowledge of how the transportation or commercial system works. But to *trust you* is to go beyond what I know and to hold on to the real individual that is you. In listening to the several surgeons I consult about my condition, I become confident that the one or the other speaks as a representative of the state of the art of surgical methods and techniques. But the trust I extend to the one I choose to do the surgery is a bond with the real individual she is, whose insights and motives I do not see and in whom there is the possibility of ignorance and incompetence, mendacity and malevolence. When we leave our home and community to dwell awhile in some remote place, it happens every day that we trust a stranger, someone with whom we have no kinship bonds, no common loyalty to a community or creed, no contractual obligations. We have no idea what he said, what are his family, clan, and village coordinates, the categories with which he represents for himself society, nature, and the cosmos. We attach to someone whose words or whose movements we do not understand, whose reasons or motives we do not see. Our trust short-circuits across the space where we represent socially defined behaviors and makes contact with the real individual agent there—with *you*.

Once one determines to trust someone, there is not simply a calm that enters into one's soul; there is excitement and exhilaration. Trust is the most joyous kind of bond with another living being. But isn't it true that whenever we enjoy being with someone, there is a factor of risk there, and also a factor of trust, which gives our enjoyment an edge of rapture?

Fear contains a recognition of the dangerous and destructive force of something or someone approaching or possibly lurking ahead. Fear deepens as our imagination multiplies representations of the danger. We seek to dissipate the fear by representing the danger as unreal and by representing our knowledge, implements, and skill to deal with what is ahead as effective and assured. But it happens that the ideas one has fashioned about death, representing it as remote or as unreal, a sleep or a transition, break up, and one is faced with death itself.

What does one see when one faces death? Death will wipe away all there is to see in the landscape about one, in the irreversible extinction of one's individual existence. One sees the indeterminate and interminable abyss, nothingness itself. One feels it ready to gape open under every path that looks unstable, under every tool in one's hand that one senses may malfunction or break up. What feels this imminence of the abyss is the anxiety that throbs in the very core of what one is. Yet as death closes in, courage can arise from some unknown depth of oneself. Courage is a force that can hold one resolute and lucid as death itself approaches.

Courage and trust have this in common: they are not attitudes with regard to images and representations. Courage is a force that can arise and hold steadfast as one's projections, expectations, and hopes dissipate. Courage rises up and takes hold and builds on itself. Trust is a force that can arise and hold on to someone whose motivations are as unknown as those of death. It takes courage to trust someone you do not know. There is an exhilaration in trusting that builds on itself. One really cannot separate in this exhilaration the force of trust and the force of courage.

Laughter and sexual attraction are also forces that break through images and representations. Laughter is released by the outbreak of incoherence in discourse, the breakup of meaning, by awkward, bungling efforts, and by goals that collapse when one has laboriously reached them. The peals of laughter hold on to the moment when the past that gave drive and skill to movements breaks off, when the future that gave sense and purpose to words and actions disconnects. There is just left the present, the naked and meaningless things, the thrashings of bodies—and the excess energies of the one who laughs. The energies ricocheting off the raw things fuel the peals of laughter.

At the same time laughter is contagious, a force that passes through the boundaries of individual identities. The anthropologist, who has worked out in a fitness club for a year in preparation for the rigors of the field, advances with bold steps over the log fallen over the river; halfway across he slips, tries to grab the log as he holds on to his video camera, and lurches into the water and muck below. Still holding high his camera draining muddy water, he looks up and sees laughter spreading in waves across the natives he had come to ingratiate and study. He feels the immediacy and the reality of their presence in the force of the shared laughter. He laughs with them, with their hilarity.

Erotic impulses are excited by all the artifices of adornment and masquerade. Sensuality is aroused by the intense colors of sumptuous garments and by jewelry whose metal and crystal glitter across naked flesh; it is ensnared by the suggestive shiftings of someone's eyes, his or her pirouetting fingers, provocative poses, and gamy words. But the fascination with these seductive appearances and accoutrements unleashes lustful drives that crave to break through the images to take hold of and penetrate the anonymous animal body behind them. The sexual craving that torments us shuts us off to the projects and solicitations of the common and practicable world, but it is also anonymous and spreads by contagion, making us transparent to one another. In Salvador in Brazil during *carnaval* a couple are dancing clad in the tuxedo and the white wedding gown in which they were married, in this street during *carnaval* thirty years ago. As they dance they embrace and disrobe one another, revealing under the tuxedo the naked body of a woman, under the wedding gown the naked body of a man. Our eyes are held on them and fevered and feel a current of complicity with the crowd about us, men and women, white and black, adolescent and aged.

In the way that laughter and sexual craving break through the images and representations and labeling of things and make contact with the singular reality, they have a kinship with courage and with trust. Indeed, just as there is courage in trust, so there is pleasure, exhilaration in trust: trust laughs at dangers. And sexual attraction is so like trust: it careens toward sexual surrender to another as into an unconditional trust. Conversely, there is something erotic in trust, for trust is not a bare thrust of will holding on to the unintelligible core of another; it holds on to the sensibility and forces of another. There is something erotic in the trust that a skydiver extends to his buddy plummeting after him bringing him his parachute, as there is in the trust that an individual lost in the jungle extends to a native youth. Trust is courageous, giddy, and lustful.

2004

War and Splendor

The first time I went to Rio de Janeiro I arrived with a toothache and sought out a dentist. I asked him if he had ever danced in an *escola de samba* (samba club) in *carnaval.* "Oh yes," he said. "You have to, at least once in your life. There is nothing else you can do that compares with it."

The *escolas de samba* are located in the favelas and, the dentist told me, the poorest people put aside a *real* a week for years sometimes, in order to be able to afford a *fantasia* (costume) and dance in the Sambódromo. *Carnaval* is the people dancing, with anyone, with everyone, in the streets with the neighborhood bands, in costume and with floats of an *escola de samba* in the Avenida Rio Branco, in the Sambódromo. The young, old, transsexual, infirm, the poorest are transfigured with a glamour more extravagant than that of yesterday's aristocrats or today's celebrities, casting their *alegria* (joy) into the crowds where it spreads and gains momentum. I looked out over the plumes springing over tens of thousands of dancers in the Sambódromo, thinking this has got to represent the total ostrich plume production of Africa, the total peacock plume production of India. The people, a miscegenation of native American, European, and African, bare their physical splendor; even the most elaborate costume is splayed as a shrine about the bared chest, breasts, and dancing buttocks and legs of the reveler. In the great parades the *escolas de samba* present theatrically with dances and with elaborate floats the Rio Amazonas and Rio Tocantins, the spectacled bears, the golden lion tamarins, and the toucans, the Indians of the Amazon and the outposts of the Inca, the queens of Africa, the *bandeirantes* (slave hunters and prospectors), the *quilombolas* (escaped slaves), the travelers of outer space. Everything—plants, insects, birds, beasts, heroes, knaves—becomes beauty, samba, and *alegria.* The splendor of individuals, groups, and floats, this glorified humanity that is not graded into rich and poor, powerful and impotent, Carioca or foreigner, dazzles the eyes and stuns the mind, and the *alegria* that surges is a gratuitous and superabundant outpouring of energies that drowns out quotidian needs and concerns for the morrow.

I arrived the week of the outbreak of the First Gulf War, in which thirty-four advanced countries united in no higher cause than to secure for themselves the sources of cheap petroleum. At the Rio *carnaval*, I thought this is the important event on the planet. Its cause, its experience, its effects being as important as, or more important than, military alliances, political campaigns, rises in the interest rates, or downturns in the stock market.

Carnaval in Rio begins in 1845. The Guerra dos Farrapos, the bloodiest civil war of Brazil's history, had ended with victory of the imperial forces. The soldiers celebrated riotously their return, shooting their guns in the streets of the capital, setting bonfires, overturning carriages, and smashing windows. Don Pedro I had been forced to abdicate and ten years later fifteen-year-old Don Pedro II crowned emperor, in violation of the constitution; further, the Republican uprising had sympathies among the people. The following year the government feared the anniversary would be the occasion for another such popular antigovernment demonstration, and decreed that the occasion would be marked instead with masked balls, like those that in France had marked the anniversaries of the Restoration of the Bourbon dynasty. But while the ruling elite danced in their elegant ballrooms, the streets again broke out in riotous revelry, with many common people donning makeshift costumes and dancing in the streets. Candomblé priestesses from Salvador de Bahia happened to be in the city and whirled in trance in their long white dresses; they were subsequently to be a part of the celebration. But over the years this political aspect of the street assemblages and this religious significance of the dancing processions were lost, and *carnaval* became all about beauty and *alegria*. High government officials do not attend, and the now rapidly growing Evangelical churches condemn *carnaval* for its sensuality and the licentiousness that is unleashed in the commingling crowds. *Carnaval* is a locus of conscious ethical conflict—between the ethos of collective joy and the ethics of national development—Rio and São Paulo. As they say in São Paulo, there is nothing in Rio except the beach and samba. As they say in Rio, there is nothing in São Paulo but work and money.

In 1964, in Papua New Guinea, some Australian colonial administrators, remembering the Highland festivals in Scotland their immigrant fathers told of, organized the first Mount Hagen Show. The Papuans, they thought, love body adornment and spectacle; it would be a joy to behold and a joy, for them, to celebrate their beauty: a carnival in the Pacific answering the *carnaval* in Brazil on the opposite side of the planet. They summoned the tribes of the Western Highlands, who they perceived to be living in suspicion and hostility with one another, to come in ceremonial dress and parade together under Mount Hagen. The men came in triumphal war dress and with their weapons. But the Australians organized the Show as a celebration of the end of tribal hostility, a festival of the new Pax Australiana.

Before the Second World War, the Australian colonial administration was very thinly staffed, and no effort had been made to extend control over or even explore the mountainous tropical island. Then the European war extended to the Pacific, and Australians, Americans, and Japanese fought in New Guinea. The Australians enlisted Papuans in their war, and some fifty thousand of them were killed. After the end of the war, as the Australians returned to their colony, they seriously set out to pacify the country. Not to put down armed opposition to them; from their first arrival their guns had quickly showed the Papuans the futility of that. Pacification meant that conflict among the Papuans was not to be settled with weapons, but by recourse to Australian administrators and courts. The million-strong Highlands Papuans, discovered so late, only in 1930, had been a journalistic sensation, where the Papuans were called Stone Age people and savages. When it was discovered that each high valley had its own language—eventually 867 languages were identified—and the societies so individualistic that defense of one's land was up to the individual and his kinsmen and clansmen, it was easy to imagine them as in a constant state of war. The Australian colonial administration did so depict them and made pacification its overriding priority.

In fact Highlands men sought their wives from the neighboring tribe; this exogamy maintained contact and negotiations between the big men of adjacent tribes. When battles did break out, they were so constrained by rules and fought with weapons so ineffective—the arrows that are without fletching are really inaccurate—that it would be rare that anyone was actually killed. If someone were killed, the big men immediately demanded and negotiated compensation. If compensation—in the form of pigs, foodstuffs, and shells—were refused, then the fighting would resume until someone of the opposing side was killed and balance restored. Although sickness that resulted in death was attributed to ancestral ghosts, spirits, or sorcery, most often material compensation was arranged if sorcery was recognized to be the cause.

For the Australians, these last, as for the first white imperialists, Cortés and Pizarro, the colony was seen as a source of gold. Later, of silver, copper, oil, and natural gas. The problem was that the prospectors and miners depended on large trains of native bearers to carry their equipment and supplies, and they found that again and again the bearers would not cross boundary lines into the territory of the next tribe. The boundaries were protected not so much by arrayed enemy warriors as by sorcery. To break down the tribal boundaries, the Australians, as they advanced into areas where gold panning or dredging was promising, decreed that all tribal conflicts be referred to the administrators and the courts they instituted and sent military patrols to punish tribes where conflicts were being settled in the traditional ways.

The Mount Hagen Show was organized to demonstrate, to the United Nations Trusteeship Council and the home government, that pacification had been achieved. And to extend the forced pacification into Highlands societies, since the clans and tribes of the Highlands would be assembled where they could meet and communicate with their respective enemies. It was also organized to bring in tourists, for by now tourism had become a major industry around the world. An airstrip was laid out, several hotels were built, and 850 mostly Australian tourists were flown in.

The Australian organizers had announced prizes for the best costumes, the best drummers, the best marchers, the best dancers. However, as soon as the prizes were awarded, fights broke out between the losers and the winners; the prizes were subsequently suppressed. The Show was to occur every other year, but it proved difficult to get the big men of enough clans and tribes to agree for a date, so that it was difficult for tourists to plan to get there.

Now the government of independent Papua New Guinea, whose army and police are effective only to protect the mines of multinational corporations, supports the Mount Hagen Show to affirm the national identity of the Papuan clans and tribes and to display to the outside world their cultural diversity. This year (2007) there are only some two hundred tourists, most of them flown in for just the two days of the Show by tour companies. After thirty years of independence, Papua New Guinea is judged by foreign chanceries and tour companies alike to be a primitive and violent place; indeed, tribal war was raging across most of the Highlands and in the capital, Port Moresby, all the bus companies and even taxis had been immobilized for the past two months by the conflict.

A local man I had come to know points out a member of Parliament. I remark that there do not seem to be many government dignitaries here. My companion tells me that this man is the representative from this district. He introduces me to the parliamentarian; I congratulate him on the splendor of the Show. He looks down. "It is getting hard to get young people interested in it," he says. I had noted that some participants in the Show were wearing fake kina shells of painted cardboard. The government-sponsored Show was beginning to produce its kitsch offspring. Later I think the parliamentarian was thinking of the situation in Port Moresby and the coastal towns. I remembered that in Lae the arriving tourist is rushed by airport police into a van with steel plates bolted over its body and heavy steel mesh over its windows; three armed soldiers are seated in the van as it speeds through stop signs to the tourist hotel. A government report had found that fully 50 percent of the inhabitants of Port Moresby live by theft.

Before the Second World War, the Australian colonial authority had refused to grant permits for missionaries in most of the territory; its military patrols were too few to protect anything but the places where mining companies were prospecting and dredging. After the war, when Australia set out to regain control of its vast colony, the missionaries were seen as effective and permanent agents of pacification. Catholic, Lutheran, Baptist, Seventh-day Adventist, and other fundamentalist missionaries quickly spread across the whole island, building churches and schools and clinics. They are the principal source of cash wages for most villages. Everywhere the missionaries enjoined their parishioners to demolish the men's house, and husbands and wives to live together as nuclear families. They ridiculed the taboos that had prohibited sex for five years until a child was weaned, and that limited most women to two children in their lives. The missionaries staffed clinics and inculcated hygiene; the population quickly doubled. Occupancy of the narrow fertile valleys in the mountainous Highlands had always been the principal motive for conflict; now all the valleys are over-populated. The export prices for what agricultural products and coffee are raised continue to fall. Young men go down to Port Moresby, the coastal towns of Madang and Lae, where the great majority do not find work. The foreign gold, copper, silver mining companies, the U.S. InterOil refinery, and the Australian Gas Light Company laying a pipeline to bring natural gas from the Highlands across the Torres Strait to Australia are state-of-the-art high-tech projects that employ very few local people. With the abolition of the institution of the men's house, these young men have not been acculturated with the loyalties, rituals, and duties and obligations of their tribe, and the village and clan elders have lost their authority over them. In the Highlands communities men who lie in wait for travelers and kill them were feared rather than admired; they did not become respected leaders, organizers of exchanges, and orators, did not become big men, but "bad men." Now the term is "raskals." Those who return to the Highlands do so to plant marijuana, coca, and poppies for the smugglers in the coastal towns. Some of these earn enough money to buy guns. The tribal wars that break out now result in far more deaths and the tribal big men are less able to negotiate compensations.

At the Mount Hagen Show the marching groups bearing the now obsolete and purely ceremonial weapons, the presence of representatives of the government, and the large contingent of police and army affirm that henceforth violence is the monopoly of the state. However, the Westminster-style parliamentary government set in place by the Australians does not succeed in establishing political parties with national or provincial programs for development or even, malaria researcher Dr. Ivo Müller explained to me, for public health. The 109 parliamentarians are in effect tribal big men, working to divert some of the national budget to enrich themselves and their tribesmen. Corruption is rampant in the ill-trained and ill-paid army and police, who readily sell their guns to fellow tribesmen in times of conflict and allege that their outposts had been raided. During the last elections (2002), there were known cases of politicians arming their supporters; six of the nine Highlands electorates were invalidated by the High Court because of violence and intimidation. Once again individuals and clans take responsibility for exacting compensation for or avenging aggressions done to them.

With the dwindling number of tourists in attendance, the entrance fee for tourists has been increased from thirty dollars to one hundred dollars. Coca-Cola advertised itself as a sponsor this year, meaning, I suppose, that it contributed some money. The participating tribes are given five kina—about five dollars—per performer to help in transportation costs. But some groups have come from the coastal towns of Madang and Lae, and even some from the outlying Bismarck Archipelago. So they do not come for the money, but for the experience. I greet a doctor I had met in Madang; he had long practiced here and retired to New Zealand upon independence. He tells me he had attended the first Mount Hagen Shows in the '60s. I ask him how this one compares with the first ones. "Oh, it's much bigger now," he says.

Despite what the parliamentarian said, there are indeed young men marching in the Show; the majority of the men are young. You watch them, holding on to archaic but fearful weapons, chanting war chants the length of the day, and you think that this Show, far from demonstrating the pacification of the Highlands, celebrates a warrior culture, which continues in new dimensions in independent Papua New Guinea. In these marching groups of men without leaders zigzagging across other groups in the field, you see what warfare was to the Highlands peoples, where battles were fought without leaders or strategies, each warrior darting and shooting his arrows where he could, exposed to volleys of arrows and spears, exposed not only to cunning and hostile humans but also to supernatural powers and the weapons of sorcery. Battles where no territory was taken, nor women captured or wealth plundered. You are, despite all your ethics and your civilization, enthralled by the vision. You feel in your throbbing legs and arms the vulnerability and audacity of their bare legs and ballistic arms, not protected by camouflage and body armor but adorned with the most ostentatious plumage. The exultation of their battle cries and chants echoing across the mountains invades you and escalates in you. To the rages and triumphs of today are joined hopes and despairs, terrors and audacities, rages and triumphs from across thousands of years past. They are transfigured with a splendor that closes in upon itself and expands with its own logic.

These extravagant headdresses of plumes, these shell necklaces, these boars' tusks and wigs were not only arrayed for war; they were donned for all the decisive events in the lives of individuals and community—for births, for initiations, for deaths, for the great pig feasts to which surrounding tribes, even enemy tribes, were invited. Traditionally, Highlands young men did not have obligations to share in the work of building houses or work in the fields until they are married and set up their own household. Before marriage, young men have few interests in gardening, pig raising, payments, or exchange; they spent their time in group festivities and displays.[1] All-night singing and courting parties were frequent; young women dress in their finery and invite young men who come unrecognizable in the extravagance of their facial painting and body decorations, singing long-rehearsed songs in the falsetto voices of birds. The Huli young men, wearing their red wigs decorated with flowers, their faces painted red and yellow, wearing the iridescent blue breast shield of the superb bird of paradise over their bodies painted red, spent a year parading across the whole territory. They long to be like birds, fleet, brilliant, untamed. Today too one cannot wander in the Highlands without coming upon groups gathering in splendor for such events.

In the Mount Hagen Show the Highlands tribes assemble with all their different languages and cultures and conflicts and also with their past ordeals, combats, and triumphs and face the present and the uncertain and menacing future before them:

> Anyone who manages to experience the history of humanity as a whole as *his own history* will experience in an enormously generalized way all the grief of an invalid who thinks of health, of an old man who thinks of the dreams of his youth, of a lover deprived of his beloved, of the martyr whose ideal is perishing, of the hero on the evening after a battle that has decided nothing

but brought him wounds and the loss of his friend. But if one endured, if one *could* endure this immense sum of grief of all kinds while yet being the hero who, as the second day of battle breaks, welcomes the dawn and his fortune, being a person whose horizon encompasses thousands of years past and future, being the heir of all the nobility of all past spirit—an heir with a sense of obligation, the most aristocratic of old nobles and at the same time the first of a new nobility—the like of which no age has yet seen or dreamed of; if one could burden one's soul with all of this—the oldest, the newest, losses, hopes, conquests, and the victories of humanity; if one could finally contain all this in one soul and crowd it into a single feeling—this would surely have to result in a happiness that humanity has not known so far: the happiness of a god full of power and love, full of tears and laughter, a happiness that, like the sun in the evening, continually bestows its inexhaustible riches, pouring them into the sea, feeling richest, as the sun does, when the poorest fisherman is rowing with golden oars! This godlike feeling would then be called—being human.[2]

This historical sense that Friedrich Nietzsche here invokes is not produced by an intellectual operation of constructing linguistic representations of the forms and meanings of past social structures, inventions, and conflicts; instead it is produced by a return of the passions that created them—the grief over suffering and mutilation and killing, over lost causes and defeats, over ideals one has betrayed, the courage that has endured all these, the hope that opens long-range horizons, the sense of honor that despises self-interest and cynicism. It is not the individual that willfully constructs these feelings in himself; the ancient passions themselves return.[3]

Nietzsche's oldest and most fundamental source of his doctrine of the Eternal Return was his conviction that our emotions are not simply excited by the stimuli and cultural symbols at hand in our environment; they are transhistorical and animal in us and the most archaic emotions can return in the socialized modern man. It was the conviction that governed his first book: the conviction that he, and not the academic literary critics, understood the Greek tragedies because the passions of Aeschylus and Sophocles pounded in his heart. In the late nineteenth century of scientific, industrial, and mercantile Europe, he saw men and women in whom the instincts and passions of hunters and gatherers, of warriors, of sixth-century-BCE sages, and of Dark Ages saints return.

Nietzsche thinks that these ancient passions return in their full force when the representations a people now make of themselves no longer elicit them. Sigmund Freud found that when anxieties and cravings that date from some trauma or from infancy are brought to the light of consciousness, fixed in conscious representations, they lose their force to drive the individual. When those conscious representations fade out, or are lost in another traumatic event, then the old anxieties and cravings return. In Nietzsche's conception, when a people represents itself as wholly civilized, when its economy, political system, and ethics present only occasions for civilized behavior, here and there the old instincts of hunters and of warriors return; when it represents its future as that of consumers in the global mercantilist economy that, here and there, the instincts of sages and of saints return. More profoundly, the instincts and emotions of our animality return. Behind instincts and emotions that are generated by culture Nietzsche found the wolf, cave bear, camel in us; Zarathustra's overman has the instincts of lion, serpent, and dove crowded in his soul.

Nietzsche sees in the specific historical sense acquired in collective performances the production of creativity. In the crowded favelas of Rio full of immigrants from the Mato Grosso and from the Amazon, former slaves from Africa and wanderers from the old Inca provinces, invalids, old women, desperate lovers, martyrs of vanquished causes, defeated guerrillas, but also men and women who descend to the heart of the *cidade maravilhiosa* (marvelous city) and make it theirs, dressed in the garb of the old emperors and aristocrats but still more glamorous, pouring their *alegria* over the city and upon strangers from far-off lands—what is produced is splendor. The return of so many nonintegrated and conflicting passions, crowded together such that each intensifies the others, produces the discharge of excess forces, which are not channeled into economic or political projects but discharged without recompense, released gratuitously. It is this collective situation that is creative of splendor, for splendor is excessive and gratuitous.

The men and women marching, dancing, filling the air with cries and chants under Mount Hagen, are splendid with the nacreous shells of mollusks, the skeletons and fangs of serpents, the tusks of boars, the teeth of flying foxes, the plumes of birds. It is not humans who invented splendor. Since our brother apes do not sing, and indeed virtually no mammals sing, some anthropologists have speculated that we must have picked up song from birds. Contemplating the spectacular plumage and six-month-long dances of the Malay Great Argus pheasant, Charles Darwin conceded that he could not find any functional meaning in these excesses of splendor.[4] Everywhere humans have observed the dances of antelope, sea lions, emperor penguins, ostriches, pheasants, butterflies, crabs, understood them in their own bodies, and taken them up—dancing crane dances, impala dances, oryx dances. "'O Zarathustra,' the animals said, 'to those who think as we do, all things themselves are dancing: they come and offer their hands and laugh and flee—and come back.'"[5]

We shall not define with one concept the splendor that glitters and resounds under Mount Hagen, in the liturgical processions in Byzantium and the high Mass of medieval cathedrals, in the Negara, the theater-state of old Bali, in *carnaval* in Rio de Janeiro—in the plumage and dance of the Great Argus pheasant, in the sun's gold spread over the blue oceans, in the fisherman rowing with golden oars. But is not the drive creative of splendor Nature in our nature? We are mesmerized by beauty as birds of paradise are mesmerized by their glittering plumes in their courtship dances; we create beauty as in the primordial ocean mollusks create the iridescent colors and intricate designs of their shells.

You are seated on one side of a baseball field, behind a chain-link fence. There are dozens of armed soldiers among you. On the three sides of the field there are banks of earth, on which thousands of local people are seated. The drums pound, and you see a phalanx of men entering from the far corner, marching with high steps and chanting warrior songs and cries. They are marching ten abreast, linked together with adjacent men each holding on to the ten-foot-long lance, spear, bow and arrows, or battle axe between them. They are wearing multicolored woven aprons in front; behind, bunches of long cordyline leaves, green, yellow, and cherry red, like the tails of great birds. On their bare chests they have hung gold-lipped pearl kina shells cut in the shape of half-moons. Their torsos and limbs gleam with oil; their eyes are flashing in their faces that they have painted in primary colors, red, yellow, blue, black; boar tusks have been inserted in their nostrils, flying-fox teeth hooked around the rims of their ears; some wear shell disks hung from their nostrils, covering their lips. They wear woven caps tight on their heads, in which they have affixed rows of flowers and small shells and bands of gleaming green beetles. On top, over a band of filmy cassowary and bright-colored parrot feathers, they have spread crowns of golden plumes of the Cendrawasih, the Raggiana bird of paradise, the multibanded two-foot-long plumes that decorate the heads of the King of Saxony bird of paradise, the three-foot-long black or white plumes of the Sicklebill, Stephanie's, or Ribbon-tailed Astrapia birds of paradise. Then the women enter the field. These are not the young women exhibiting their beauty and sensuality who parade in festivals, carnivals, and fairs in Europe, North America, the Caribbean, and Latin America. They are the matriarchs of families and clans, their bare breasts covered with dozens of elaborate shell necklaces of all sizes, colors, and shapes, necklaces of the foot-long bailer shells, twenty, thirty pounds of them—their bridal wealth. They advance in swaying dance steps, their yellow crinkled grass skirts swirling to the tinkling sounds of the bells they have fastened about their ankles. They too wear headdresses of cuscus fur, eagle feathers, and bird of paradise plumes often much higher and far outspread than those of the men. The tourist cannot help thinking of the immense slaughter of birds of paradise, but in fact the headdresses are heirlooms carefully wrapped up and stored from year to year, even from generation to generation, as are the tons of seashell necklaces that are the bridal wealth of the matriarchs. The women pound the narrow drums they carry and chant songs extolling the proud history of their clans, their migrations and victories in battle. Another phalanx of warriors enters the field, marching with high steps. Then another. More flanks of women dancers.

The Huli wear huge wigs grown from their own hair, overhanging domes decorated with red and yellow flowers; the men march with high steps and then face one another very close up and dance in leaping ever-faster steps. The Asaro have covered their bodies with white clay and wear large globes with grotesque faces over their heads. A group of young men wearing only grass skirts and bearing no weapons from Admiralty Islands dance in the center of a circle of drummers. Here there are youths painted black with the white lines of skeletons. Some groups are performing charades: someone dressed in whiteskin's clothes cracking a whip over men laying railroad ties. There are small groups doing comedy acts.

The men march, the women dance all day in the thin air of the mountain sky; at the end of the day they withdraw to makeshift huts to take off their adornments, eat, and sleep. Behind, over the gloomy mists of Mount Hagen, a rainbow suspends its luminous colors.

The following day you arrive at sunrise to watch them don their adornments again; when they are finished they bunch into groups chanting and dancing with leaping steps while waiting their turn to enter the field. Your eyes swim in the swirling grass skirts and the glints of sunlight flashing off the shimmering multicolored plumes, your heart and muscles pound with the stamping feet and drumbeats. Their chants echo across the landscape, throbbing on the flanks of Mount Hagen, that second-highest volcano in the country, pounding too in your chest; you feel your blood hot and surging with the exultation of two thousand men and women, of 125 tribes, zigzagging back and forth like slow-motion bolts of lightning across the crowded field under the magnesium-white sun.

2011

Notes

Editor's Introduction

1 Jonas Skačkauskas, "Interview with Alphonso Lingis," in Bobby George and Tom Sparrow, eds., *Itinerant Philosophy: On Alphonso Lingis* (Brooklyn: punctum books, 2015), 164.

2 When I visited his home outside Baltimore for two days in the summer of 2016, the only attraction that Lingis insisted on having me visit was the American Visionary Art Museum.

3 Alphonso Lingis, "The Unlived Life Is Not Worth Examining," in James R. Watson, ed., *Portraits of American Continental Philosophers* (Bloomington: Indiana University Press, 1999), 121.

4 See Richard I. Sugarman, "The Importance of Alphonso Lingis in Introducing Emmanuel Levinas to America," in Randolph C. Wheeler, ed., *Passion in Philosophy: Essays in Honor of Alphonso Lingis* (Lanham, Md.: Lexington Books, 2017).

5 Alexander E. Hooke and Wolfgang W. Fuchs, "Reflections since *Dangerous Emotions*: Interview with Alphonso Lingis," in Alexander E. Hooke and Wolfgang W. Fuchs, eds., *Encounters with Alphonso Lingis* (Lanham, Md.: Lexington Books, 2003), 36.

6 Randolph C. Wheeler, "Alterity after Infinity: Interview with Alphonso Lingis," in Wheeler, *Passion in Philosophy,* 103.

7 Skačkauskas, "Interview with Alphonso Lingis," 151.

8 Alphonso Lingis, "Aconcagua," in Wheeler, *Passion in Philosophy,* 3–15.

9 Lingis, "The Unlived Life Is Not Worth Examining," 122.

10 Lingis, "Aconcagua," 6.

11 Bobby George and Tom Sparrow, "Interview with Alphonso Lingis," in George and Sparrow, *Itinerant Philosophy,* 7.

12 Mary Zournazi, "Foreign Bodies: Interview with Alphonso Lingis," in Hooke and Fuchs, *Encounters with Alphonso Lingis,* 88.

13 George and Sparrow, "Interview with Alphonso Lingis," 13.

14 Alphonso Lingis, *Body Transformations: Evolutions and Atavisms of Culture* (New York: Routledge, 2005), page unmarked.

15 Lingis, "The Unlived Life Is Not Worth Examining," 122.

16 See Alphonso Lingis, *The Imperative* (Bloomington: Indiana University Press, 1998).

17 Lingis, "The Unlived Life Is Not Worth Examining," 121.

18 Lingis, *Body Transformations,* page unmarked.

Sensation and Sentiment

1 Jean-Paul Sartre, *Situations,* vol. 1 (Paris: Gallimard, 1947), 33.

2 Martin Heidegger, *Kant and the Problem of Metaphysics,* trans. J. S. Churchill (Bloomington: Indiana University Press, 1962), §41.

3 Martin Heidegger, *Being and Time,* trans. J. Macquarrie and E. Robinson (New York: Harper & Row, 1962), 340.

4 Martin Heidegger, *Vorträge und Aufsätze* (Pfullingin: G. Neske, 1954), 108.

5 Michel Henry, *L'essence de la manifestation,* 2 vols. (Paris: Presses universitaires de France, 1963).

6 Jean-Paul Sartre, *Being and Nothingness,* trans. Hazel Barnes (New York: Philosophical Library, 1956), 331.

7 Emmanuel Levinas, "Le temps et l'autre," *Le choix, le monde, l'existence* (Grenoble: Arthaud, 1947).

8 Heidegger, *Kant and the Problem of Metaphysics,* 5.

9 Heidegger, *Being and Time,* 173.

10 Henry, *L'essence de la manifestation,* 828.

The Sensuality and the Sensitivity

1 Martin Heidegger, *Being and Time,* trans. John Macquarrie and Edward Robinson (New York: Harper & Row, 1962), 177. Subsequent references are given in the text.

2 Emmanuel Levinas, *Totality and Infinity,* trans. Alphonso Lingis (The Hague: Martinus Nijhoff, 1979), 110–12.

3 Ibid., 110–21, 127–30.

4 Emmanuel Levinas, *Otherwise Than Being, or Beyond Essence,* trans. Alphonso Lingis (The Hague: Martinus Nijhoff, 1981), 75–81.

5 Martin Heidegger, *An Introduction to Metaphysics,* trans. Ralph Manheim (Garden City, N.Y.: Doubleday, 1961).

6 Heidegger, *Being and Time,* 319–21.

7 Levinas, *Totality and Infinity,* 197–201.

8 Levinas, *Otherwise Than Being, or Beyond Essence,* 81–89.

A Phenomenology of Substances

1 This account is found in the second chapter of Genesis. The first chapter, from the Priestly tradition, depicts creation as emanation from language; it invokes a magical conception of words.

2 Jean Baudrillard, *L'échange symbolique et la mort* (Paris: Gallimard, 1976), 78–81.

3 Friedrich Nietzsche, *Thus Spoke Zarathustra*, in *The Portable Nietzsche*, trans. Walter Kaufmann (New York: Viking, 1971), 3:30, 2.

4 "Things present themselves as solids with contours clearly delimited. Along with tables, chairs, envelopes, notebooks, pens—fabricated things—stones, grains of salt, clumps of earth, icicles, apples are things. One thing is distinct from another because an interval separates them. But a part of a thing is in its turn a thing: the back, the leg of the chair, for example. But also any fragment of the leg is a thing, even if it does not constitute one of its articulations— everything one can detach and remove from it. The contours of the thing mark the possibility of detaching it, moving it without the others, taking it away" (Emmanuel Levinas, *Totality and Infinity*, trans. Alphonso Lingis [The Hague: Martinus Nijhoff, 1969], 160–61).

5 Henri Wallon, *Les origines de la pensée chez l'enfant* (Paris: Presses Universitaires de France, 1945), 2:382–402.

6 See Emmanuel Levinas, *Existence and Existents*, trans. Alphonso Lingis (The Hague: Martinus Nijhoff, 1978), 38.

7 "The access to values, usage, manipulation and manufacture rest on possession, on the hand that takes, that acquires, that brings back home" (Levinas, *Totality and Infinity*, 162).

8 Ibid., 161.

9 Ibid., 167.

10 J. M. G. Le Clézio, *L'Extase matérielle* (Paris: Gallimard, 1967).

The Elements

1 Emmanuel Levinas, *Totality and Infinity*, trans. Alphonso Lingis (The Hague: Martinus Nijhoff, 1979), 109–42.

2 Maurice Blanchot, *The Space of Literature* (Lincoln: University of Nebraska Press, 1982), 264–68.

3 Levinas, *Totality and Infinity*, 109–51.

4 Maurice Merleau-Ponty, *Phenomenology of Perception*, trans. Colin Smith (London: Routledge & Kegan Paul, 1979), 137–42.

The Levels

1 Modern epistemology, whose categories go back to the matter-form physics of Aristotle, separated, in the sensible perception of the environment, the sensory content of the sensation—taken as what is by excluding other matter from its here and now—from the structure or organization—taken to be transposable

upon other content. The perceptible structure or organization was, consequently, to be explained by an agency external to the matter of sensation; it was taken to be imposed on that matter by the categorizing and relating initiatives of thought. The sensory quale was defined as a positum, a positive fact, a punctual plenum, for which to be is to occupy exclusively and exclusionarily a here and now position. Thought then would be an activity spontaneously moving across spatiotemporal points to relate them. Continental phenomenology had introduced the concept of transcendence or ex-istence to characterize mental or intentional events as opposed to the being of external, or transcendent, facts; a mental event was said to ex-ist by projecting itself beyond the here and now where it is toward a there and a future before it. A mental or intentional event projecting itself beyond the here and now of what is posited before it projects itself beyond its own here and now. This kind of self-transcending ex-istence was identified by existential phenomenology as the inner diagram in all the conscious forces in us, which makes them not just reactions to the impact of mundane forces but comprehensive and comprehending powers. The concept of ex-istence or transcendence was introduced to differentiate decisively mental events from facts, revealing powers from intramundane events, the sensing from the sensible. Merleau-Ponty takes this very concept of ex-istence or transcendence and uses it to characterize the way the sensible is and is given. The sensible is what it is by projecting itself into an elsewhere, by approaching and passing (Maurice Merleau-Ponty, *Eye and Mind,* trans. Carleton Dallery, in James M. Edie, ed., *The Primacy of Perception* [Evanston, Ill.: Northwestern University Press, 1964], 166, 178–88; Maucie Merleau-Ponty, *The Visible and the Invisible,* trans. Alphonso Lingis [Evanston, Ill.: Northwestern University Press, 1968], 113, 115, 195, 218, 237).

2 Merleau-Ponty, *The Visible and the Invisible,* 103; Alphonso Lingis, *Phenomenological Explanations* (The Hague: Martinus Nijhoff, 1986), 41–57.

3 Merleau-Ponty, *Eye and Mind,* 182.

4 Kurt Goldstein and Otto Rosenthal, "Zum Problem der Wirkung der Farben auf den Organismus," *Schweizer Archiv für Neurologie und Psychiatrie* (1930): 3–9.

5 G. M. Stratton, "Some Preliminary Experiments on Vision without Inversion of the Retinal Image," *Psychological Review* 3 (1896): 611–17; G. M. Stratton, "Vision without Inversion of the Retinal Image," *Psychological Review* 4 (1897): 341–60, 463–81.

6 Irvin Rock argues that the persistence of the up–down axis when one lies prone indicates the persistence of a memory trace in the nervous substrate (Irvin Rock, *The Nature of Perceptual Adaptation* [New York: Basic Books, 1966], 26, 32–34, 34–39). But what has privileged this axis in the memory trace? It is not the statistically most frequent position, but the position at which one is practically most effective.

7 The Wertheimer effect: sky and earth will be seen as environmentally
up and down wherever their images fall on the retina (Max Wertheimer,
"Experimentelle Studien über das Sehen von Bewegung," *Zeitschrift für
Psychologie* [1912]: 161–265).

8 Maurice Merleau-Ponty, *Phenomenology of Perception*, trans. Colin Smith
(London: Routledge & Kegan Paul, 1979), 328.

9 "I have known patients almost totally immobilized by Parkinsonism, dys-
tonias, contortions, etc., capable of riding a horse with ease—with ease and
grace and intuitive control, forming with the horse a mutually influencing
and natural unity; indeed, the mere *sight* of riding, running, walking, swimming, of any natural movement whatever—as a purely visual experience
on a television screen—can call forth by sympathy, or suggestion, an equal
naturalness of movement in Parkinsonian patients. The art of 'handling'
Parkinsonian patients, learned by sensitive nurses and friends—assisting
them by the merest intimation or touch, or by a wordless, touchless moving-
together, in an intuitive kinetic sympathy of attunement—this is a genuine
art, which can be exercised by a man or a horse or a dog, but which can *never*
be simulated by any mechanical feedback; for it is only an ever-changing,
melodic, and *living* play of forces which can recall living beings into their own
living being…. Thus while severely affected Parkinsonians are particularly
dangerous at the controls of motorcars and motorboats (which tend to amplify all their pathological tendencies), they may be able to handle a sailing boat
with ease and skill, with an intuitive accuracy and 'feel.' Here, in effect, man-
boat-wind-wave come together in a natural, dynamic union or unison; the
man feels at one, at home, with the forces of Nature; his own natural melody
is evoked by, attuned to, the harmony of Nature…." (Oliver Sacks, *Awakenings*
[London: Picador, 1991], 348–49).

10 Merleau-Ponty, *The Visible and the Invisible*, 133.

The Pageantry of Things

1 "The most lucid writer finds himself in the world bewitched by its images. He
speaks in enigmas, by allusions, by suggestion, in equivocations, as though he
moved in a world of shadows, as though he lacked the force to arouse realities,
as though he could not go to them without wavering, as though, bloodless
and awkward, he always committed himself further than he had decided
to do, as though he is spilling half the water he is bringing us" (Emmanuel
Levinas, *Collected Philosophical Papers*, trans. Alphonso Lingis [Dordrecht, The
Netherlands: Martinus Nijhoff, 1987], 13.

The Weight of Reality

1 Henri Wallon, *Les origines de la pensée chez l'enfant*, vol. 2, *Les tâches intellectu- elles* (Paris: Presses Universitaires de France, 1945), 382–402.

2 Martin Heidegger, *Poetry, Language, Thought*, trans. Albert Hofstadter (New York: Harper, 1971), 143–82.

3 Emmanuel Levinas, *Totality and Infinity*, trans. Alphonso Lingis (The Hague: Martinus Nijhoff, 1979), 130–34.

Metaphysical Habitats

1 Hans Prinzhorn, *Artistry of the Mentally Ill: A Contribution to the Psychology and Psychopathology of Configuration*, trans. Eric von Brockdorff (Wien, N.Y.: Springer-Verlag, 1995). Second German edition, *Bildnerei der Geisteskranken*, ed. James L. Foy (Wien, N.Y.: Springer-Verlag, 1995).

2 Four years after publishing his book on asylum art, Prinzhorn published a volume on the art of prisoners: *Bildnerei der Gefangenen* (Berlin: Axel Juncker, 1926).

3 Jean Dubuffet, "Art brut in Preference to the Cultural Arts," *Art & Text* 27 (1988): 33.

4 Jean Dubuffet, "Conversation with Jean Dubuffet, August 1976," 24, cited in John M. MacGregor, *The Discovery of the Art of the Insane* (Princeton, N.J.: Princeton University Press, 1989), 303.

5 Paul Éluard, "Le génie sans miroir," in *Œuvres complètes*, vol. 2 (Paris: Gallimard, Bibliothèque de la Pléiade, 1968), 786.

6 Ananda K. Coomeraswamy, *The Transformation of Nature in Art* (New York: Dover, 1956).

7 Salvador Dalí, *The Secret Life of Salvador Dalí* (London: Vision Press, 1968), 349.

8 John M. MacGregor, "Marginal Outsiders: On the Edge of the Edge," in Simon Carr, Betsey Wells Farber, Allen S. Weiss, eds., *Portraits from the Outside: Figurative Expression in Outsider Art* (New York: Groegfeax, 1990), 12–13.

9 Roger Cardinal, "Figures and Faces in Outsider Art," in Carr, Farber, and Weiss, *Portraits from the Outside*, 26.

10 Quoted in Colin Rhodes, *Outsider Art: Spontaneous Alternatives* (London: Thames & Hudson, 2000), 60.

11 MacGregor, "Marginal Outsiders," 12.

12 Quoted in Marcus Field, "McTribal: How the Chapman Brothers Carve Up Culture," *ArtReview* 52 (February 2003): 43.

Intentionality and Corporeity

1 "Every perceiving consciousness has this peculiarity, that it is the conscious- ness of *the embodied (leibhaftigen) self-presence of an individual object*" (Edmund Husserl, *Ideas*, trans. W. R. Boyce Gibson [New York: Allen and Unwin, 1931], 114).

2 Ibid., 149.

3 Edmund Husserl, *Ideen zu einer Reinen Phänomenologie und Phänomenologischen Philosophie*, vol. 2 (The Hague: Martinus Nijhoff, 1952), 120–25, 154–57.

4 Ibid., 236–47.

5 Husserl, *Ideas*, 150.

6 Husserl, *Ideen*, 2:216.

7 Ibid., 167–69; Edmund Husserl, *Cartesian Meditations*, trans. Dorion Cairns (The Hague: Martinus Nijhoff, 1965), §§50, 51.

8 Husserl, *Ideen*, 2:56–58.

9 Ibid., 38–41, 158–59.

10 Ibid., 57–58.

11 Cf. Emmanuel Levinas, *En découvrant l'existence avec Husserl et Heidegger*, 2d ed. (Paris: Vrin, 1967), 158.

12 Ibid.

13 Husserl, *Ideen*, 2:63–64.

14 Maurice Merleau-Ponty, *The Visible and the Invisible*, trans. A. F. Lingis (Evanston, Ill.: Northwestern University Press, 1968), 7.

15 Husserl, *Ideen*, 2:65–75.

16 Ibid., 146.

17 Husserl, *Ideas*, 16.

18 Husserl, *Ideen*, 2:145.

19 Husserl, *Ideas*, 227.

20 Ibid., 264, 109.

21 Ibid., 19.

22 "It is the 'logitudinal intentionality' which makes possible the object-constitutive intentionality" (Edmund Husserl, *The Phenomenology of Internal Time-Consciousness*, trans. James S. Churchill [Bloomington and London: Indiana University Press, 1964], 107).

23 Ibid., 92.

24 Edmund Husserl, "Am Anfang ist die Tat," in *Die Krisis der Europäischen Wissenschaften und die transzendentale Phänomenologie* (The Hague: Martinus Nijhoff, 1954), 158.

25 "An impression … is to be grasped as primary consciousness which has no further consciousness behind it in which we are aware of it" (Husserl, *The Phenomenology of Internal Time-Consciousness*, 117).

26 Ibid., 131.

27 Ibid., 115.

28 "The flesh is not matter, in the sense of corpuscles of being which would add up or continue on one another to form beings. Nor is the visible (the things as well as my own body) some 'psychic' material that would be—God knows how—brought into being by the things factually existing and acting on my

factual body. In general, it is not a fact or a sum of facts 'material' or 'spiritual.' Nor is it a representation for a mind: a mind could not be captured by its own representations; it would rebel against this insertion into the visible which is essential to the seer. The flesh is not matter, is not mind, is not substance.... What we are calling flesh, this interiorly worked-over mass, has no name in any philosophy" (Merleau-Ponty, *The Visible and the Invisible*, 139, 147).

29 Maurice Merleau-Ponty, *The Structure of Behavior,* trans. Alden L. Fisher (Boston: Beacon Press, 1963), and *Phenomenology of Perception*, trans. Colin Smith (New York: Routledge, 1962).

30 "Thus all sensations are kinesthetic" (Husserl, *Ideen,* 2:153).

31 "The starting point—the critique of the usual conception of the thing and its properties → critique of the logical notion of the subject, and of logical inherence → critique of the positive signification (differences between signi-fications), signification as a separation *(écart)*, theory of predication—founded on this diacritical conception" (ibid., 224).

32 Ibid., 130.

33 Ibid., 131–33.

34 "Sensoriality: for example, a color, yellow; it surpasses itself of itself: as soon as it becomes the color of the illumination, the dominant color of the field, it ceases to be such or such a color, it has therefore of itself an ontological function, it becomes apt to represent all things (like engravings. Dioptrics, Discourse IV). With one sole movement it imposes itself as particular and ceases to be visible as particular" (ibid., 217–18).

35 Ibid., 115.

36 Ibid., 213.

37 Maurice Merleau-Ponty, *Signs,* trans. Richard C. McCleary (Evanston, Ill.: Northwestern University Press, 1964), 42.

38 Merleau-Ponty, *The Visible and the Invisible,* 241–42, 218.

39 Merleau-Ponty, *Phenomenology of Perception,* 208–12; Merleau-Ponty, *The Visible and the Invisible,* 134–35.

40 "Between the exploration and what it will teach me, between my movements and what I touch, there must exist some relationship by principle, some kinship, according to which they are not only, like the pseudopods of the amoeba, vague and ephemeral deformations of the corporeal space, but the initiation to and the opening upon a tactile world. This can happen only if my hand, while it is felt from within, is also accessible from without, itself tangible, for my other hand, for example, if it takes its place among the things it touches, is in a sense one of them, opens finally upon a tangible being of which it is also a part" (Merleau-Ponty, *The Visible and the Invisible,* 133).

41 "It is that the thickness of flesh between the seer and the thing is constitutive for the thing of its visibility as for the seer of his corporeity; it is not an obsta-cle between them, it is their means of communication" (ibid., 135).

42 Ibid., 259–60.

43 Ibid., 217.

44 Ibid., 135.

45 Ibid., 244.

46 Merleau-Ponty, *Phenomenology of Perception*, 322–27.

47 Merleau-Ponty, *The Visible and the Invisible*, 139.

48 "The meaning of being is to be disclosed: it is a question of showing that the ontic, the '*Erlebnisse*' 'sensations', 'judgments'—(the objects, the 'represented', in short all idealizations of the Psyche and of Nature) all the bric-à-brac of those positive psychic so-called 'realities' (and which are lacunar, 'insular', without *Weltlichkeit* of their own) is in reality abstractly carved out from the ontological tissue, from the 'mind's body'—Being is the 'place' where the 'modes of consciousness' are inscribed as structurations of Being and where the structurations of Being are modes of consciousness" (ibid., 253).

49 Husserl, *Ideas*, 226.

I Am a . . .

1 Friedrich Nietzsche, *On the Genealogy of Morals*, trans. Walter Kaufmann and R. J. Hollingdale (New York: Vintage, 1969), 2:2.

2 Leslie Farber, *Lying, Despair, Jealousy, Envy, Sex, Suicide, Drugs and the Good Life* (New York: Basic Books, 1976), 7.

3 Belinda Thompson, ed., *Gauguin by Himself* (Boston: Little, Brown and Company, 1993), 270.

4 Friedrich Nietzsche, *Beyond Good and Evil*, trans. Walter Kaufmann (New York: Vintage, 1966), ¶140.

5 David Abram, personal communication.

6 Jon Elster, *Sour Grapes: Studies in the Subversion of Rationality* (Cambridge: Cambridge University Press, 1987), 153.

Orchids and Muscles

1 André Leroi-Gourhan, *Le geste et la parole, Technique et langage* (Paris: A. Michel, 1964), parts I and II.

2 Franz Kafka, "Josephine the Singer, or the Mouse Folk," in *The Complete Stories*, trans. Nahum N. Glatzer (New York: Schocken, 1976).

3 Michel Foucault, *Discipline and Punish*, trans. Alan Sheridan (New York: Viking, 1979), 135ff.

4 Tamotsu Yato, *Young Samurai, Bodybuilders of Japan*, introduction by Yukio Mishima, trans. M. Weatherby and Paul T. Konya (New York: Grove Press, 1967).

5 Ernest Hemingway, *Death in the Afternoon* (New York: Scribner, 1932).

6 Leroi-Gourhan, *Le geste et la parole*, chapter 11.

7 Adolf Portman, *Animal Forms and Patterns*, trans. Hella Czech (New York: Schocken, 1967).

8 Yukio Mishima, *Sun and Steel,* trans. John Bester (Tokyo and Palo Alto: Kondasha International, 1970), 23.

Cause, Choice, Chance

1 Bernard Williams, *Moral Luck* (Cambridge: Cambridge University Press, 1981).
2 Emily Underwood-Lee, "Titillation," in *Dangerous Currents: Risk and Regulation at the Interface of Medicine and the Arts* (Newcastle-upon-Tyne: Cambridge Scholars Publishing, 2017), 93–97.
3 *Online Etymology Dictionary,* www.etymonline.com/index.php?term=happy.
4 Sam Bleakley, *Surfing Brilliant Corners* (Cornwall: Alison Hodge, 2010), 33.
5 Ibid., 6.
6 Henry David Thoreau, *Journal,* vol. 1 (Princeton, N.J.: Princeton University Press, 1981), 12.
7 Bleakley, *Surfing Brilliant Corners,* 21.
8 Cf. Kevin Krein, "Nature and Risk in Adventure Sports," in Mike MacNamee, ed., *Philosophy, Risk, and Adventure Sports* (New York: Routledge, 2007), 84–86. "There is a perverse delight in putting oneself in a potentially dangerous situation, knowing that your experience and skill makes you quite safe. To stand with a friend in eerie moonlight at the foot of a vast mountain wall and be certain that you can safely reach the top—that is a wonderful feeling of self-confidence. It might seem an absurdly pointless thing to do, but to have the nerve to go and try it, just to see if you can, is an affirmation of everything noble in humanity. The task has been rationalized, and carefully weighed, and now you must act and do it right; it is a suspended moment. As you step up onto the first hold or drive the first axe blow you step into a new perspective, a world that is absolutely and cruelly real. The power of it is indescribable, as vital on the first step as it is on the last, at the base or on the summit, and the intensity only gradually fades on your return to the valley" (Joe Simpson, *This Game of Ghosts* [London: Viking, 1994], 118–19).
9 Bleakley, *Surfing Brilliant Corners,* 138.
10 Ibid., 10.
11 Ibid., 140.

Return of the First Person Singular

1 "The Western conception of the person as a bounded, unique, more or less integrated motivational and cognitive universe, a dynamic center of awareness, emotion, judgment and action, organized into a distinctive whole and set contrastively against other such wholes and against a social and natural background is, however incorrigible it may seem to us, a rather peculiar idea within the context of the world's cultures" (Clifford Geertz, *Local Knowledge: Further Essays in Interpretive Anthropology* [New York: Basic Books, 1983], 59).
2 Ibid., 362.

3 Ibid., 362–63.

4 Clifford Geertz, *The Interpretation of Culture* (New York: Basic Books, 1973), 362.

5 Ibid., 81.

6 Ellen Fox Keller, "Whole Bodies, Whole Persons?" in João Biehl, Byron Good, and Arthur Kleinman, eds., *Subjectivity: Ethnographic Investigations* (Berkeley: University of California Press, 2007), 353.

7 Clifford Geertz, *Works and Lives* (Stanford, Calif.: Stanford University Press, 1988), 2–5.

8 Kenneth E. Read, *The High Valley* (New York: Columbia University Press, 1980); James Clifford, "On Ethnographic Authority," *Representations* 2 (1983): 118–43; James Clifford and George E. Marcus, eds., *Writing Culture* (Berkeley: University of California Press, 1986); Geertz, *Works and Lives*; Michael Taussig, *Shamanism, Colonialism, and the Wild Man* (Chicago: University of Chicago Press, 1991); Kathleen Stewart, *A Space on the Side of the Road* (Princeton, N.J.: Princeton University Press, 1996); Michael Taussig, *Law in a Lawless Land* (Chicago: University of Chicago Press, 2005).

9 João Biehl, "Other Life: AIDS, Biopolitics and Subjectivity in Brazil's Zones of Social Abandonment," PhD dissertation, University of California, Berkeley, 1999; Arthur Kleinman, *Writing at the Margins: Discourse between Anthropology and Medicine* (Berkeley: University of California Press, 1995); Paul Komesaroff, *Experiments in Love and Death: Postmodernism, Microethics and the Body* (Melbourne: Melbourne University Press, 2008); Cheryl Mattingly, *Healing Dramas and Clinical Plots: The Narrative Structure of Experience* (Cambridge: Cambridge University Press, 1998); Nancy Scheper-Hughes and Margaret Lock, "The Mindful Body: A Prolegomenon to Future Work in Medical Anthropology," *Medical Anthropology Quarterly* 1:11 (March 1967): 6–41; Howard Spiro, Lee Palmer Wandel, and Mary G. McCrea Curnen, eds., *Facing Death: Where Culture, Religion, and Medicine Meet* (New Haven: Yale University Press, 1998).

10 Robert J. Barrett, "The Schizophrenic and the Liminal Persona in Modern Society," *Culture Medicine and Psychiatry* 22 (1998): 465–94; Ellen Corin, "Facts and Meaning in Psychiatry: An Anthropological Approach to the Lived Worlds of Schizophrenics," *Culture, Medicine, and Psychiatry* 14 (1990): 153–88; Ellen Corin, "The Thickness of Being: Intentional Worlds, Strategies of Identity, and Experience among Schizophrenics," *Psychiatry* 55:3 (1998): 266–78; Ellen Corin, "The 'Other' of Culture in Psychosis: The Ex-Centricity of the Subject," in João Biehl, Byron Good, and Arthur Kleinman, eds., *Subjectivity: Ethnographic Investigations* (Berkeley: University of California Press, 2007), 273–314; Michael Goddard, "What Makes Hari Run? The Social Construction of Madness in a Highland Papua New Guinea Society," *Critique of Anthropology* 18 (1998): 61–82; Theodore Schwartz, Geoffrey M. White,

and Catherine A. Lutz, eds., *New Directions in Psychological Anthropology* (Cambridge: Cambridge University Press, 1992), 181–205; Janis Hunter Jenkins and Robert John Barrett, eds., *Schizophrenia, Culture and Subjectivity: The Edge of Experience* (Cambridge: Cambridge University Press), 110–45; Muriel Hammer, Kurt Salzinger, and Samuel Sutton, eds., *Psychopathology: Contributions from the Social, Behavioral and Biological Sciences* (New York: John Wiley and Sons, 1973); Ronald C. Simons and Charles C. Hughes, eds., *Culture-Bound Syndromes: Folk Illnesses of Psychiatric and Anthropological Interest* (Dordrecht: D. Reidel, 1985).

Mortality

1 The god of healing medicine.

2 Martin Heidegger, *What Is Metaphysics?* in Martin Heidegger, *Basic Writings*, trans. David Krell (New York: Harper & Row, 1977), 102–3; Martin Heidegger, *Being and Time*, trans. John Macquarrie and Edward Robinson (New York: Harper & Row, 1962), 227–35.

3 Heidegger, *Being and Time*, 231–34; Heidegger, *What Is Metaphysics?* 103–6.

4 Heidegger, *Being and Time*, 372–79. Subsequent references are given in the text.

5 Max Weber, *The Sociology of Religion*, trans. Ephraim Fischoff (Boston: Beacon Press, 1956), 6.

Lust

1 Charles Baudelaire, *Œuvres complètes*, ed. Claude Pichois (Paris: Gallimard, 1961), 1256.

2 Jacques Lacan, *Écrits*, trans. Alan Sheridan (New York: W. W. Norton, 1977), 72–77.

3 Gilles Deleuze and Félix Guattari, *Anti-Oedipus*, trans. Robert Hurley, Mark Seem, and Helen R. Lane (New York: Viking, 1977), 338.

4 J. G. Ballard, *Crash* (New York: Vintage, 1985).

5 Jean-François Lyotard, *Libidinal Economy*, trans. Iain Hamilton Grant (Bloomington: Indiana University Press, 1993).

6 Michel Tournier, *Friday*, trans. Norman Denny (New York: Pantheon, 1969), 192–94.

7 Gabriel García Márquez, *In Evil Hour*, trans. Gregory Rabassa (New York: Harper & Row, 1979).

8 Shirley Lindenbaum, "Variations on a Sociosexual Theme in Melanesia," in Gilbert H. Herdt, ed., *Ritualized Homosexuality in Melanesia* (Berkeley: University of California Press, 1984), 337–61.

9 Jean Baudrillard, *Seduction*, trans. Brian Singer (New York: St. Martin's Press, 1979), 96–97.

10 Daniel Wit, *Thailand—Another Vietnam?* (New York: Charles Scribner's Sons, 1968), 62.

Fluid Economy

1   Shirley Lindenbaum, "Variations on a Sociosexual Theme in Melanesia," in Gilbert Herdt, ed., *Ritualized Homosexuality in Melanesia* (Berkeley: University of California Press, 1984), 337–61.

2   Ibid., 344.

3   Ibid., 349.

4   Gilbert H. Herdt, *Guardians of the Flutes: Idioms of Masculinity* (New York: McGraw-Hill, 1981); Gilbert H. Herdt, ed., *Rituals of Manhood* (Berkeley: University of California Press, 1982); Herdt, *Ritualized Homosexuality in Melanesia.*

5   Gilbert H. Herdt, "Fetish and Fantasy in Sambia Initiation," in Herdt, *Rituals of Manhood,* 17–27, 52–53.

6   Herdt uses the term "transformation," "that is, changing semen into something else, as medieval alchemists were thought to change lead into gold" ("Semen Transactions in Sambia Culture," in *Ritualized Homosexuality in Melanesia,* 175).

7   Herdt, *Guardians of the Flutes,* 188, 289.

8   Ibid., 165n10. They also do not practice anal intercourse (ibid., 3n2). Subsequent references are given in the text.

9   Herdt, "Semen Transactions in Sambia Culture," 193. Subsequent references are given in the text.

10 Michel Foucault, *The History of Sexuality, Volume I: An Introduciton,* trans. Robert Hurley (New York: Vintage, 1990), 86.

11 Herdt, "Editor's Preface," in *Ritualized Homosexuality in Melanesia,* xv.

12 Herdt, *Guardians of the Flutes,* 65, 262–63, 273, 275, 277–78, 284–85, 333.

13 Roger M. Keesing, "Introduction," in Herdt, *Rituals of Manhood,* 36–37.

14 Ibid., 27.

15 Terence E. Hays and Patricia H. Hays, "Opposition and Complementarity of the Sexes in Ndumba Initiation," in Herdt, *Rituals of Manhood,* 236, 237.

16 Bruno Bettleheim, *Symbolic Wounds* (Glencoe, Ill.: Free Press, 1954).

17 Robert J. Stoller, *Sexual Excitement* (New York: Pantheon, 1979), 236–37.

18 Herdt, *Guardians of the Flutes,* 303, 18.

19 Kenneth E. Read, "The Nama Cult Recalled," in Herdt, *Ritualized Homosexuality in Melanesia,* 233.

20 Herdt, *Guardians of the Flutes,* 18, 48, 52, 321.

21 Georges Bataille, *L'Histoire de l'érotisme : Œuvres complètes,* vol. 8 (Paris: Gallimard, 1976), trans. Mary Dalwood, in *Death and Sensuality* (San Francisco: City Lights, 1986).

22 Stoller, *Sexual Excitement,* 236–37.

23 Robert J. Stoller, *Sex and Gender: On the Development of Masculinity and Femininity* (New York: Science House, 1968), 232.

24 John Money and Anke A. Ehrhardt, *Man & Woman Boy & Girl* (Baltimore: Johns Hopkins University Press, 1972), 176–79.

25 Herdt, *Guardians of the Flutes*, 305.

26 Fitz John Porter Poole, "The Ritual Forging of Identity," in Herdt, *Rituals of Manhood*, 139.

27 J. Layard, "Homoeroticism in a Primitive Society as a Function of the Self," *Journal of Analytical Psychology* (1959) 4: 101–15.

28 Herdt, "Semen Transactions in Sambia Culture," 210n7.

29 Herdt, "Fetish and Fantasy in Sambia Initiation," 74–76, 84–90; Herdt, *Guardians of the Flutes*, 283–84, 255–94.

30 Herdt, "Editor's Preface," xii.

31 Herdt, *Guardians of the Flutes*, 325.

32 Jean Cocteau, *Le livre blanc* (Paris: Éditions de Messine, 1983), translated as *The White Paper* (New York: Macaulay, 1958).

33 R. V. Burton and J. W. M. Whiting, "The Absent Father and Cross-Sex Identity," *Merrill-Palmer Quarterly of Behavior and Development* 7 (1961): 87.

34 Clifford Geertz, *Local Knowledge* (New York: Basic Books, 1983), 59.

35 Herdt, *Guardians of the Flutes*, 208n7.

36 Ibid., 92.

37 Gilles Deleuze and Félix Guattari, *Anti-Oedipus*, trans. Robert Hurley, Mark Seem, and Helen R. Lane (New York: Viking, 1977).

38 Keesing, "Introduction," 37.

39 Jean-François Lyotard, *Économie libidinale* (Paris: Minuit, 1974).

40 Lindenbaum, "Variations on a Sociosexual Theme in Melanesia," 340.

41 Keesing, "Introduction," 16.

The Navel of the World

1 "The mind in apprehending also experiences sensations which, properly speaking, are qualities of the mind alone," as Whitehead put it. "These sensations are projected by the mind so as to clothe appropriate bodies in external nature. Thus the bodies are perceived as with qualities which in reality do not belong to them, qualities which in fact are purely the offspring of the mind. Thus nature gets credit which should in truth be reserved for ourselves: the rose for its scent: the nightingale for his song: and the sun for his radiance. The poets are entirely mistaken. They should address their lyrics to themselves, and should turn them into odes of self-congratulation on the excellence of the human mind. Nature is a dull affair, soundless, scentless, colourless: merely the hurrying of material, endlessly, meaninglessly" (Alfred North Whitehead, *Science and the Modern World* [New York: Free Press, 1967], 54).

Rings

1 Claude Lévi-Strauss, "Introduction à l'œuvre de Marcel Mauss," in Marcel Mauss, *Sociologie et anthropologie* (Paris: Presses Universitaires de France, 1960), xlvii–xlviii.

affairs of everyday life, when we find ourselves offended or harmed, this does arouse impulses to strike back, to harm the offender. But we also find these very impulses a misery; they occupy our minds obsessively, and at some level we feel we are being invaded and obsessed by the base behavior of the one who offended us. We struggle to free ourselves of this misery, to turn to and absorb ourselves in positive undertakings and innocent friends.

12   Linton, *Reconciliation in Cambodia,* 207.

13   Laura McGrew, "Truth, Justice, Reconciliation and Peace in Cambodia: 20 Years after the Khmer Rouge," unpublished paper reporting research from December 1999 to February 2000, funded by the Canadian Embassy, Phnom Penh, March 2000, 30. Cited in Linton, *Reconciliation in Cambodia,* 207.

14   Linton, *Reconciliation in Cambodia,* 206. I reflected that in our culture remorse is demanded in the courts, and religions maintain the concept of remorse in everyday discourse. Yet our thinkers such as Nietzsche and Freud have long regarded remorse as a sickness in the soul that has to be healed. In the small matters of everyday wrongs and offenses, we may well want some sign from the offender that he or she will not do that again, but we do not want to deal with remorse. We do not know how to deal with someone who in all his dealings with us expresses remorse, acts out of remorse.

Catastrophic Time

1   Fred Adams and Greg Laughlin, *The Five Ages of the Universe: Inside the Physics of Eternity* (New York: Free Press, 1999).

War and Splendor

1   Paula Brown, *Highland Peoples of New Guinea* (Cambridge: Cambridge University Press, 1978), 156.

2   Friedrich Nietzsche, *The Gay Science,* trans. Walter Kaufmann (New York: Vintage, 1974), §337.

3   Kenneth Read recounts the ritual he attended among the Gahuku in the New Guinea Highlands: "The house was packed to its capacity, but in the blackness I was unable to discover so much as a single feature of the man who sat beside me. Almost immediately, enveloped in disembodied voices, I felt the first stirrings of a curious panic, a fear that if I relaxed my objectivity for so much as a moment I would lose my identity. At the same time the possibility that this could happen seemed immensely attractive. The air was thick with pungent odors, with the smell of unwashed bodies and stranger aromatic overtones that pricked my nostrils and my eyes. But it was the singing, reverberating in the confined space and pounding incessantly against my ears that rose to cloud my mind with the fumes of a collective motion almost too powerful for my independent will. Momentarily the night vanished, and my purpose, even the circumstances of my presence in the village were no longer important. I

stood poised at a threshold promising a release from the doubts and anxieties that separate us from one another, offering, if one took the step demanded, a surety, a comforting acceptance such as those who share an ultimate commitment may experience. Even though the words were unintelligible, the massed voices were like a hand held toward me, a proffered embrace.

"It was this thought, or, rather, this intuition, for it was hardly a conscious reaction, that held in check my feeling of suffocation. The songs followed one another without a perceptible break, a single shrill and keening voice lifting now and then to point the way to a new set. As the others joined in strongly, I felt close to the very things that eluded me in my day-to-day investigations, brought into physical confrontation with the intangible realm of hopes and shared ideas for which words and actions, though they are all we have, are quite inadequate expressions. In analytic language, the situation could be accommodated under the rubric of a rite of separation—an event by which a young girl in her father's house, surrounded by her kinsmen, was brought to the morning of the day on which she must assume a new status and be transferred to her husband's people, but its quality could not be conveyed in any professional terms. While the voices swelled inside the house, mounting to a climax, the barriers of my alien life dissolved. The sound engulfed me, bearing me with it beyond the house and into the empty spaces of the revolving universe. Thus sustained, I was one of the innumerable companies of men who, back to the shrouded entrance of the human race, have sat at night by fires and filled the forest clearings and the wilderness with recitals of their own uniqueness" (*The High Valley* [New York: Scribner's, 1965], 251–52).

4 Ornithologists have experimentally verified that female peafowl, sage grouse, and birds of paradise select for their sexual favors males that display with the most elaborate dances the most spectacular plumage, even though their ostentatious colors and entranced dances make them easy prey for predators, and the males of these species contribute nothing to the nest building and guarding and nurturing tasks that ensure the reproduction of the species.

5 Friedrich Nietzsche, *Thus Spoke Zarathustra*, trans. Walter Kaufmann, in *The Portable Nietzsche* (New York: Viking, 1968), book 3, "The Convalescent," 2.

Publication History

"Araouane" was originally published in *Antioch Review* 60:1 (2002): 87–93.

"Breakout" was originally published in *Trust* (Minneapolis: University of Minnesota Press, 2004), 179–91.

"Catastrophic Time" was originally published in *Cultural Values* 2:2–3 (1998): 174–89.

"Cause, Choice, Chance" has been published in *Irrevocable* (Chicago: University of Chicago Press, 2018).

"Contact" was originally published in *The First Person Singular* (Evanston, Ill.: Northwestern University Press, 2007), 70–71.

"Dignity" was originally published in *The Humanistic Psychologist* 38:3 (2010): 267–68. Copyright 2010 American Psychological Association. Reprinted with permission.

"The Elemental That Faces" was originally published in *The Community of Those Who Have Nothing in Common* (Bloomington: Indiana University Press, 1994), 107–34. Reprinted by permission of Indiana University Press.

"The Elements" was originally published in *The Imperative* (Bloomington: Indiana University Press, 1998), 13–24. Reprinted by permission of Indiana University Press.

"Faces, Idols, Fetishes" was originally published in *The Community of Those Who Have Nothing in Common* (Bloomington: Indiana University Press, 1994), 39–68. Reprinted by permission of Indiana University Press.

"Fluid Economy" was originally published in *Foreign Bodies* (New York: Routledge, 1994), 133–58.

"I Am a ..." was originally published in *The First Person Singular* (Evanston, Ill.: Northwestern University Press, 2007), 37–46.

"Intentionality and Corporeity" was originally published in *Analecta Husserliana 1*, ed. Anna-Teresa Tymieniecka (Dordrecht, The Netherlands: D. Reidel Publishing Company, 1970), 75–90. All rights reserved. Copyright 1970 by

D. Reidel Publishing Company, Dordrecht-Holland. Reprinted by permission from Springer Nature.

"Irrevocable Loss" was originally published in *Inter Views in Performance Philosophy*, ed. Anna Street, Magnolia Pauker, and Julien Alliot (London: Palgrave Macmillan, 2017), 279–99. Reprinted with permission of Palgrave Macmillan.

"The Levels" was originally published in *The Imperative* (Bloomington: Indiana University Press, 1998), 25–40. Reprinted by permission of Indiana University Press.

"Love Junkies" was originally published as "Armed Assault" in *Aesthetic Subjects*, ed. Pamela R. Matthews and David McWhirter (Minneapolis: University of Minnesota Press, 2003), 28–43. It was also published in *Trust* (Minneapolis: University of Minnesota Press, 2004), 109–24.

"Lust" was originally published in *Abuses* (Berkeley and Los Angeles: University of California Press, 1994), 105–30.

"Metaphysical Habitats" was originally published in *Violence and Splendor* (Evanston, Ill.: Northwestern University Press, 2011), 21–38.

"Mortality" has been published in *Irrevocable* (Chicago: University of Chicago Press, 2018).

"The Murmur of the World" was originally published in *The Community of Those Who Have Nothing in Common* (Bloomington: Indiana University Press, 1994), 69–106. Reprinted by permission of Indiana University Press.

"The Navel of the World" was originally published in *Dangerous Emotions* (Berkeley and Los Angeles: University of California Press, 2000), 1–24.

"Orchids and Muscles" was originally published in *Journal of the Philosophy of Sport* 13:1 (1986): 15–28.

"Our Uncertain Compassion" was originally published in *Janus Head* 9:1 (2006): 25–32. Copyright 2006 by Trivium Publications, Amherst, New York. All rights reserved.

"The Pageantry of Things" was originally published in *The Imperative* (Bloomington: Indiana University Press, 1998), 99–104. Reprinted by permission of Indiana University Press.

"Phantom Equator" was originally published in *The Imperative* (Bloomington: Indiana University Press, 1998), 105–18. Reprinted by permission of Indiana University Press.

"A Phenomenology of Substances" was originally published in *American Catholic Philosophical Quarterly* 71:4 (1998); copyright 1998.

"Return of the First Person Singular" was originally published in *Journal of Speculative Philosophy* 26:2 (2012): 163–74.

"Rings" was originally published in *Trust* (Minneapolis: University of Minnesota Press, 2004), 39–50.

"Sacrilege" was originally published in *Philosophy Today* 56:2 (2012): 135–40.

"Sensation and Sentiment: On the Meaning of Immanence" was originally published in *Proceedings of the American Catholic Philosophical Association* 41 (1967): 69–75.

"The Sensuality and the Sensitivity" was originally published in *Face to Face with Levinas*, ed. Richard A. Cohen (Albany: State University of New York Press, 1986), 219–30.

"Trust" was originally published as Preface to *Trust* (Minneapolis: University of Minnesota Press, 2004), vii–xii.

"Truth in Reconciliation" was originally published in *Journal of Bioethical Inquiry* 8:3 (2011): 239. Reprinted by permission from Springer Nature.

"Typhoons" was originally published in *Trust* (Minneapolis: University of Minnesota Press, 2004), 59–69.

"Unknowable Intelligence" was originally published in *Trust* (Minneapolis: University of Minnesota Press, 2004), 31–36.

"The Unlived Life Is Not Worth Examining" was originally published in *Portraits of American Continental Philosophers*, ed. James R. Watson (Bloomington: Indiana University Press, 1999), 119–25.

"Violations" was originally published in *Dangerous Emotions* (Berkeley and Los Angeles: University of California Press, 2000), 85–102.

"War and Splendor" was originally published in *Violence and Splendor* (Evanston: Northwestern University Press, 2011), 139–50.

"The Weight of Reality" was originally published in *Mosaic* 45:4 (2012): 37–49.

"Wounds and Words" was originally published in *The First Person Singular* (Evanston: Northwestern University Press, 2007), 58–66.

ALPHONSO LINGIS is the author of more than a dozen books, including *The Community of Those Who Have Nothing in Common, Dangerous Emotions, Abuses, Foreign Bodies,* and *Trust* (Minnesota, 2004), and the translator of several works of French philosophy. He is professor emeritus of philosophy at Pennsylvania State University.

TOM SPARROW is assistant professor of philosophy at Slippery Rock University. He is author of *Plastic Bodies, The End of Phenomenology,* and *Levinas Unhinged,* and coeditor of *True Detective and Philosophy, Itinerant Philosophy: On Alphonso Lingis,* and *A History of Habit.*